SOURCES OF WORLD CIVILIZATION

VOLUME I: To 1500

Edited by Oliver A. Johnson
University of California, Riverside

Prentice Hall
Englewood Cliffs, New Jersey 07632

Library of Congress Cataloging-in-Publication Data

Sources of world civilization / edited by Oliver A. Johnson.
   p. cm.
   Contents: v. 1. To 1500—v. 2. Since 1500.
   ISBN 0–13–962457–0 (v. 1)
   1. Civilization—History—Sources.
CB69.S68   1994
080—dc20   93-11660
                                 CIP

Acquisitions editor: Steve Dalphin
Editorial assistant: Caffie Risher
Editorial/production supervision and
   interior design: P. M. Gordon Associates
Copy editor: Durrae Johanek
Cover design: Carol Ceraldi
Production coordinator: Peter Havens

© 1994 by Prentice-Hall, Inc.
A Paramount Communications Company
Englewood Cliffs, New Jersey 07632

Printed in the United States of America
10 9 8 7 6 5 4 3 2 1

ISBN 0-13-962457-0

Prentice-Hall International (UK) Limited, *London*
Prentice-Hall of Australia Pty. Limited, *Sydney*
Prentice-Hall Canada Inc., *Toronto*
Prentice-Hall Hispanoamericana, S.A., *Mexico*
Prentice-Hall of India Private Limited, *New Delhi*
Prentice-Hall of Japan, Inc., *Tokyo*
Simon & Schuster Asia Pte. Ltd., *Singapore*
Editora Prentice-Hall do Brasil, Ltda., *Rio de Janeiro*

CONTENTS

THE CLASSICAL WORLD 63

PREFACE

When my late colleague, John Beatty, and I first published *Heritage of Western Civilization* thirty-five years ago we both believed that students should have some acquaintance with the historical forces and ideas that had shaped the world in which they lived. I still believe this. It remains important to understand the Western tradition because it remains the most pervasive influence on our lives. But such understanding is no longer sufficient. It is necessary to widen our horizons, and gain some appreciation of other civilizations that have a history of their own, largely independent of that of the West. *Sources of World Civilization* is an attempt to acquaint students with all major civilizations, Western and non-Western alike.

The selections included here generally have been arranged in chronological order, beginning in the third millennium B.C. and ending in the mid-twentieth century. On occasion, however, I have departed from strict chronology in the order, sacrificing it to gain greater continuity and coherence in the text. Because many of the documents included exemplify the history of Western civilization, they replicate selections that appear in *Heritage*. This is true, as well, of their editorial introductions. However, the introductions to the major epochs of history, because they encompass the world, depart from those in that book.

Oliver A. Johnson

GENERAL
INTRODUCTION

The purpose of this book is to introduce students to the history of world civilization through the documents that have formed and shaped that civilization. One word in the title of the book needs explanation. My use of the singular "civilization," rather than "civilizations," is not meant to be question-begging. I am not implying by its use that world history is the story of a single civilization, or even that the myriad of societies that have occupied various parts of the world during the past five thousand years have much more in common than the shared humanity of their people. My intent, rather, is the much more modest one of simply indicating that the book is concerned with the history of people who have lived together in organized and stable societies.

An attempt might be made to give the term "civilization" in the history of the world some substantive, positive content by selecting a central theme that would serve as an overarching principle capable of uniting the various historical societies into a single world civilization. Such a theme could be used as an organizing device for these documents, which would give this book a coherence and continuity that it may seem to lack. But any such principle, whether it be chosen from politics, religion, economics, philosophy, or another field, would distort history by reducing the variety and complexity of historical societies into an artificial and unreal unity. Although there are continuities in history and similarities among cultures that need to be recognized, there are also discontinuities and diversities as well. However convenient it might be for us to try to do so, we cannot fit world history into a straitjacket.

Although I have not found a central thread from which to hang the selections in this book, I have not chosen them arbitrarily. Instead, I have adopted three general criteria to guide my selection of documents: (1) That the document be of major significance, shaping the history of an important society or succession of societies through time; (2) that the document give us substantial insights into the nature of the society from which it sprang, either at a given period of its history or over a long period of time; and (3) that the document be intrinsically interesting. Almost all of the selections in this book satisfy one or both of my first two criteria; those that satisfy the third may appear (at least to students) to be fewer in number.

Even with the help of my criteria, the process of selecting the documents to include in this book has been difficult. It would be unrealistic to assume that *all* (or even much) of the significant literature of the societies of the world throughout history can be encapsulated within less than a hundred documents. Of necessity, innumerable items, some arguably as worthy of inclusion as those selected, have not been chosen. Readers of this book will, on occasion, undoubtedly question some of the decisions I have made, preferring other selections to those contained here. It is my hope, however, that readers will recognize that none of these decisions was made arbitrarily but all with consideration and with careful weighing of the alternative possibilities.

One way in which I might have eased the task of selection would have been through the inclusion of a much larger number of selections in the book. But, because of constraints on the length of the book, any increase in the number of selections would have necessitated a decrease in their average length. In deciding against this procedure I have been guided by educational principles. I am convinced that to gain the fullest possible understanding of history through the reading of original source materials students must have these materials presented to them at length and in detail. Short extracts excerpted from the original sources too often fail to provide a reader with anything more than a superficial and fragmented acquaintance with the society under study. If a document chosen for inclusion satisfies my criteria for selection, it should yield an understanding of the society from which it sprang that justifies its being reproduced in its entirety or, where that is not possible, at sufficient length so that its contribution to the history of that society is rendered clear.

As its title indicates, this is a sourcebook on world civilization. Yet, as its table of contents reveals, it does not give equal treatment to all civilizations. Instead, more than half of its contents is devoted to Western civilization, or that of Europe and America. This imbalance, which is deliberate, is not motivated by elitism or parochialism; it does not imply that our particular civilization is more important than any others. Rather, it rests on the belief that such a pattern of selection will yield the greatest possible benefit for the education of students. Although it is imperative that the new generation and those yet to come learn about the history of civilizations throughout the world, their first need is to become acquainted with the historical forces and ideas that have shaped the social context in which they find themselves directly immersed and which, to a large extent, make them what they are. Unless they have some comprehension of this context it is doubtful that they will be able to understand, let alone appreciate, other cultures, particularly when these are quite different from their own. (Were this sourcebook being published, say, in China for the education of students in Chinese universities its contents would justifiably be substantially different from what they now are.)

Although its various introductions contain a considerable amount of historical information, this book is not designed to be a history of world civilization. The function of the historical materials is, rather, to provide a background framework in which to exhibit the source documents themselves. Or, to reverse the metaphor, the book can be viewed as a gallery filled with documents that illuminate the societies of which they are a product. To anyone who wishes to gain a full understanding of the course of world civilization, I recommend that the study of the documents included in this book be supplemented by a reading of a standard work on the history of civilization. Many of these are available.

ANCIENT CIVILIZATIONS

When did civilization begin? We have strong evidence that human, or closely similar, beings have lived on the earth for millions of years but no one suggests that any civilization approaches that extreme age. To cope with our initial question we need to address a prior one: What constitutes civilization? Although no simple answer can be given to this question, sufficient consensus exists among archaeologists and historians that we can identify the earliest of the ancient civilizations and the approximate times of their beginnings. Civilization requires a society, or a group of people living together over a period of time in the same place. Accepting these conditions of civilized life we can conclude that a precondition of the existence of a civilization is the development of agriculture, for people who must hunt for their food cannot lead a settled, communal life. Agriculture, in its turn, leads to the domestication of animals, the tillage of fields, the acquisition of property, trade and commerce, and eventually to the growth of towns and cities. With all of these we have a fully developed civilization. For our purpose, which is to present a history of civilization, one other requirement needs mention—the written word. Although not essential (for some civilizations have existed for long periods with their past preserved in oral traditions), written records furnish the solid foundations on which the story of humankind rests.

Even if we accept these constituents of civilization, we cannot place a definite date on the first civilizations, for archaeologists continue to unearth early remains in widely scattered locations. At the present time they can point to towns they have excavated in the Near East that flourished as early as the eighth millennium B.C. Since we cannot review the entire list of ancient civilizations here we shall concentrate on those that, because of their importance or their continuity, have made significant contributions to later history.

We begin with the great river civilizations, of which three are outstanding. That complex and stable societies should have grown up first in river valleys is understandable; here the land was level and the soil rich and deep and water was available, ideal conditions for the development of agriculture. Archaeologists generally agree that the earliest of these civilizations began in the Tigris and Euphrates valleys of Mesopotamia, in what is now Iraq. Apparently the first permanent settlers in the valleys were called Subarians but they were conquered by the Sumerians, who had a well-established and flourishing society before the end of the fourth millennium B.C. They founded a number of cities, such as Lagash, Ur, and Uruk, the walled city of Gilgamesh. Their agriculture, with its intricate irrigation systems, as well as their cities, in which trade flourished, required political organization and the development of legal systems. The latter are summarized in the famous Code of Hammurabi, which dates from about 1700 B.C. but is a codification of laws of earlier origin. We know much about the early history of Mesopotamia because the inhabitants of the valleys developed a form of writing on clay tablets, called cuneiform. Since the nineteenth century thousands of these tablets have been discovered and translated.

Much of the early history of Mesopotamia is a record of turmoil as city-states strove with each other to dominate the rich land. But with the passage of time powerful leaders arose who created empires. During the course of about two thousand years four major empires came to power and passed away. First was the Akkadian empire under Sargon I, with its capital city at Assur on the upper Tigris. This was followed by the Babylonian empire, founded by Hammurabi the lawgiver, its capital city being Babylon on the Euphrates. After a considerable lapse of time a third empire, the Assyrian, arose with its capital at Ninevah, also on the upper Tigris. The final empire—one of the greatest in the history of the world—was the Persian, founded by Cyrus the Great around 550 B.C. This empire, which was centered to the east of Mesopotamia in what is now Iran, rapidly expanded until it covered most of the Near East, extending as far east as India. Under Darius I and later under Xerxes I the Persians moved westward, crossing the Hellespont and invading the Greek city-states. There the stage was set for one of the crucial military confrontations in history, whose outcome shaped the future course of civilization in the Western world.

The second ancient river civilization arose along the banks of the Nile, which has its source deep in Africa, to flow northward into the southeast corner of the Mediterranean Sea. This is Egypt, whose civilization rivals that of Mesopotamia in antiquity. Farms, and farming communities, developed on the banks of the long river in the fourth millennium B.C. and toward its end two kingdoms, Upper and Lower Egypt, had come into existence. According to tradition, about 3100 B.C. Menes, a strong leader, united the two kingdoms and inaugurated the dynastic age, whose pharaohs were to rule Egypt for millennia. The history of ancient Egypt, unlike that of Mesopotamia, was quite tranquil. The Nile overflowed its banks each year, enriching the soil, and the farmers reaped their crops, just as they continue to do. Although the land suffered a few invasions and the Egyptians as a result came under foreign domination, for the most part they remained free from conquest. The explanation of this is largely geographical. Egypt is separated from the Near East by the Red

Sea and the Nile valley protected on both sides by forbidding deserts, more than sufficient to give a potential invader pause.

We know much about both the history and the daily life of the ancient Egyptians from extensive records that survive, written in hieroglyphics, a form of picture-writing dating from the fourth millennium. Another major source of our knowledge results from the Egyptian faith in immortality. Believing in a life after death much like that on earth, the Egyptians filled the tombs of their dead with everything necessary for a prosperous, happy afterlife. Preserved intact through the ages in the dry desert air, ancient tombs like that of the pharaoh Tutankhamen, who reigned in the fourteenth century B.C., have yielded magnificent works of art and dazzling treasures to modern archaeologists.

Before leaving the Near East note should be taken of one other ancient civilization, which was neither large, powerful, nor based on a river but to which subsequent civilization, particularly in the West, owes a great debt. Located on a narrow coastal strip of the eastern Mediterranean it is now called Israel. Here a group of wandering tribes, who presumably originated in lower Mesopotamia, finally, after many vicissitudes, found their "promised land." Although often overrun by more powerful neighbors and sold into captivity the Jews persisted in their adopted land, as they do today.

The third great river civilization arose in the Far East, first in the floodplain of the lower Yellow River and later in that of the Yangtze River of China. In the rich soils of these river valleys a form of intensive farming, highly dependent on human labor, which continues to this day, developed. Although the origins of Chinese river civilization are shrouded in mythology, archaeologists believe that it developed at a somewhat later date than the previous two, probably around the middle of the third millennium B.C. The earliest royal dynasty, known as the Hsia, is said to have reigned over China (actually a relatively small area between the Yellow and Yangtze rivers) throughout the first half of the second millennium; however, we have no firm records to verify traditional accounts of these rulers. The first dynasty of which we can speak with assurance was the Shang, which governed China from 1523 to 1028 B.C. The last capital of this dynasty, Anyang (located just north of the Yellow River), was discovered and excavated early in the twentieth century; it has yielded much information about early Chinese civilization. The art of writing had been perfected, in the form of pictographs, by the time of the Shangs. We have evidence, too, that the practice of ancestor worship dates at least from their time. Coupled with it is a concentration on the family (extended to include ancestors) as the focal point of the individual person's life.

The Shang dynasty was followed by the Chou, which ruled China for nearly a thousand years (until 256 B.C.). The rule of this dynasty was divided into two periods, the first, or Western Chou, when the capital was located at Sion on the Wei River (a tributary of the Yellow), and the Eastern Chou after 769 B.C., when the capital was shifted eastward to the city of Loyang. During the Chou dynasty the borders of imperial China were greatly expanded; however, imperial rule over all but the heartland became increasingly dependent on the goodwill of often unruly local chieftains. By the end of the dynasty China had literally disintegrated into a large number of independent principalities. Traditional Chinese historians refer to the last two centuries of the Chou as the "period of warring states."

The ancient world contained another major river civilization, which has not been mentioned. The reason for its omission is simple; it was completely destroyed around 1500 B.C. and disappeared from historical memory until its remains were discovered and excavated early in the twentieth century. This civilization, which is thought to have developed around the middle of the third millennium B.C., occupied the valleys of the Indus River and its tributaries in the northwest corner of the Indian subcontinent in what is present-day Pakistan. Although we have scant evidence on which to base our speculations (the written language has not been deciphered), archaeological remains indicate that this was an advanced civilization comparable to Mesopotamia and Egypt. Two large cities have been excavated. They contain the remains of substantial buildings, built of brick and laid out on a grid system of streets. They even had a municipal sewer system. Numerous art objects of high quality have been found and evidence indicates that trade was carried on with the Sumerians in Mesopotamia.

What happened to the Indus valley civilization? The best hypothesis is that it was overrun and obliterated by groups of warrior-tribesmen who moved into the valleys from the northwest, or what is now Afghanistan. These invaders, who are known as the Aryans, had been gradually moving east from Iran and central Asia and later continued their migrations beyond the Indus valley, pushing into the Ganges basin of northern India, where they subdued the local inhabitants, who still lived in a state of precivilization, turning these natives into their slaves. From these beginnings the caste system, which was to become a permanent feature of Indian society, was later to emerge.

Undoubtedly advanced civilizations developed elsewhere in the world at an early time but we lack information about them. Mention should, however, be made of civilizations in the Western Hemisphere, because archaeological and other evidence indicates that they were comparable to those we have already described. Two centers were particularly important: Central America and Mexico, where the Mayan civilization flourished, and the Andean region of South America, where several pre-Inca centers of civilization developed. Our knowledge of these civilizations is limited, but, from the evidence that remains, it is clear that both achieved a high level of culture.

The Epic of Gilgamesh

The epic of Gilgamesh is one of the oldest stories of which we have a written record. Presumably recited orally for generations before it was inscribed on clay tablets in cuneiform script, it tells of the life and exploits of a young nobleman and king, who ruled the city of Uruk in ancient Sumer, probably between 2700 and 2600 B.C. Sumer, generally recognized to be the earliest human civilization, was centered in the lower valley between the Tigris and Euphrates rivers in what is contemporary Iraq, and Uruk was not far from the present capital city of Baghdad.

On the surface the epic is an adventure story, telling of the mighty deeds of two young comrades, Gilgamesh and Engidu. As such it is perennially fresh, capable of appealing to the imagination of readers thousands of years later. But, as the following selection makes clear, it is much more than that. Behind the screen created by the activities of the pantheon of ancient Sumerian deities, it is a disquisition on the human condition. Specifically, the issue that Gilgamesh confronts and cannot resolve is his own mortality. Although in part divine by birth, Gilgamesh is nevertheless essentially human so must, like his companion Engidu, face the inevitability of his own death. Despite his desperate attempts to avoid his fate he comes finally to the realization that he must content himself with leaving behind him the record of his life in the stones of Uruk. The epic contains an extraordinary subplot, of special interest to the student of ancient mythology. This is the story, near the end of the epic, of Utnapishtim, the far one, and the great flood.

It is almost fortuitous that we have the epic in written form today. In the seventh century B.C. (two thousand years after the time of Gilgamesh) the Assyrian king Assurbanipal, who ruled over the territory including what had been the ancient Sumerian civilization, built a great library in his capital city of Ninevah. Included among its holdings was a copy of the epic. But in 612 B.C. an invading army of Medes and Babylonians overran Ninevah, destroying the city and burying it (with its library) beneath the desert sands. There all remained lost and virtually forgotten for over two millennia until, in 1839, a young English archaeologist stumbled on this magnificent treasure. Over several decades the tablets containing the epic (as well as many other ancient writings) were unearthed and deciphered. Later other copies were discovered elsewhere. The epic, as we now have it, is a collation pieced together from these various cuneiform tablets. Although the epic is sufficiently complete to tell its story, some portions are missing and have been reconstructed by the translator.

Gilgamesh

All things he saw, even to the ends of the
    earth,
He underwent all, learned to know all,
He peered through all secrets,
Through wisdom's mantle that veileth
    all.
What was hidden he saw,
What was covered he undid;
Of times before the stormflood he
    brought report.
He went on a long far way,
Giving himself toil and distress;
Wrote then on a stone-tablet the whole
    of his labour.
He built the walls of ramparted Uruk,
He laid the foundations, steadfast as
    bronze,
Of holy Eanna, the pure temple . . .

Two thirds of him is god,
One third of him is man,
There's none can match the form of his
    body . . .

[*The inhabitants of Uruk call upon the gods
for help:*]

"Gilgamesh keeps the son from the
    father,
Building the walls through the day,
    through the night.

He is herdsman of ramparted Uruk,
He is herdsman and lord of his folk,
Strong and splendid, knowing wisdom.
Gilgamesh keeps the lover from the
    maiden,
The daughter of a hero,
The chosen of a noble!"
The great gods heard their outcries.
The gods of heaven called the lord Anu:
"Was he not of thy making, this almighty
    wild bull,
This hero Gilgamesh?
He hath not his like in the whole
    land . . .
Gilgamesh keeps the son from the
    father,
Building the walls through the day,
    through the night.
He is herdsman of ramparted Uruk,
He is herdsman and lord of his folk,
Strong and splendid,
Knowing wisdom.
Gilgamesh keeps the lover from the
    maiden,
The daughter of a hero,
The chosen of a noble!"

The great god Anu lent ear to their cries.
Aruru was summoned, she the great
    goddess:
"Thou, Aruru, madest Gilgamesh;
Now make another like unto him.

So long as he pleases
Let him come at Gilgamesh.
Let them contend together,
That Uruk may have peace."

As Aruru this heard,
She shaped in her heart a warrior of
Anu.
Aruru washed her hands,
She pinched up some clay and spat on it.
She moulded Engidu,
Fashioned a hero, a glorious scion,
A fighter of Ninurta's.
His whole body was shaggy with hair,
Hair he bore on his head like a woman,
The plenty of his hair sprouted like
grain.
He knew naught of land and people,
He was clothed like the god of the herds.
With the gazelles he eats the plants,
With the wild beasts he drinks at the
watering-place,
With the throng at the water he makes
glad his heart.

He walked to the watering-place
Toward a hunter, a stalker of wild beasts;
On one day, on a second, and a third,
Toward the hunter he walked to the
watering-place.
The hunter saw him, the hunter's face
grew troubled.
Without his quarry he turned back to his
house.
He was down-cast, troubled; he shrieked.
His heart was afraid and his face was
dark.
Grief made way into his heart,
And he looked like a wanderer of far
ways.

• • •

[The hunter] started on the way, he
entered into Uruk.
He goes to Gilgamesh, and to him he
says:
"A man that came from the hills
Hath become strong indeed in the land.
Mighty in power like a fighter of Anu's.
Ever he goeth along on the hills,
He is ever beside the wild beasts,
Ever are his feet at the watering-place.
I am afraid, I cannot go near to him.

He hath filled my pits which I dug;
My traps which I laid
He hath destroyed.
So from my hands he let my quarry get
away,
The throngs of the fields;
No catch he allows me."

Gilgamesh says to him, to the hunter:
"Go, my hunter, and get thee a priestess.
When the wild beasts come to the
watering-place,
Then let her cast her garment off,
That he may take his fill of her.
When he sees her, he will draw near;
Then will he become a stranger to his
wild beasts,
Who on his own steppes grew up with
him."

The hunter went yonder and got him a
priestess.
They made themselves ready, went forth
straight on.
On the third day they came to their goal:
The hunter and the priestess sat
themselves down.
One day, a second day, they sat by the
watering-place.
The wild beasts come along and drink at
the watering-place.
Glad is the throng of the flood.
So too comes he, Engidu . . .
With the gazelles he eats the plants,
With the beasts he drinks at the
watering-place,
His heart is happy with the throng of the
flood.
Then the priestess saw him, the great
strong one,
The wild fellow, the man of the steppes:
"There he is, woman!
Loosen thy buckle,
Unveil thy delight,
That he may take his fill of thee!
Hang not back, take up his lust!
When he sees thee, he will draw near.
Open thy robe that he rest upon thee!
Arouse in him rapture, the work of
woman.
Then will he become a stranger to his
wild beasts,

Who on his own steppes grew up with
him.
His bosom will press against thee."
Then the priestess loosened her buckle,
Unveiled her delight,
For him to take his fill of her.
She hung not back, she took up his lust,
She opened her robe that he rest upon
her.
She aroused in him rapture, the work of
woman.
His bosom pressed against her.
Engidu forgot where he was born.
For six days and seven nights
Was Engidu given over to love with the
priestess.
When he had sated himself with the fill
of her,
He raised up his face to his wild ones:
At sight of Engidu, the gazelles flee away,
The wild of the fields shrink back before
him.
Then Engidu marvelled,
His body stood as in a spell,
His knees quivered, because his wild ran
off . . .
The speed of his onset is not what it was.
He hearkens and opens his ear:
He turns about and sits down at the feet
of the priestess.
He looks the priestess in the face,
And to what the priestess now speaks
His ears give heed.

The priestess says to him, to Engidu:
"Engidu, how beautiful thou, how like a
god!
Why must thou rush with animals over
the steppes?
Come, I will lead thee into ramparted
Uruk,
To a pure house, the dwelling of Anu
and Ishtar,
Where Gilgamesh lives, matchless in
might,
And like a wild bull lords it over the
folk" . . .
She talks to him, till he likes her words.
Knowing his own heart, he seeketh a
friend.
Engidu says to her, to the priestess:

"Woman, go to! Lead me to the pure,
the holy house,
The dwelling of Anu and Ishtar,
Where Gilgamesh lives, matchless in
might,
And like a wild bull lords it over the folk.
I will challenge him to a fight.
I will call the strong one.
I will call out in Uruk:
'I too am a strong one!'
I alone can alter fate,
I, born on the steppes, matchless in
might.
O Gilgamesh, may I behold thy face!
Well I know what the outcome will be."

•   •   •

Engidu goes along the market-street
Of ramparted Uruk.
Marvelling he looks at the mighty work;
He bars the way of the warriors of Uruk;
Then the folk of Uruk crowd against
him,
The land is assembled . . .
But in fear the folk turn away.
They fall down . . . like a weak child . . .
The couch had been spread for goddess
Ishtar . . .
At the gates of her house
Engidu barred the going-to,
Allowed not Gilgamesh that he enter in.
They grappled each other at the gates of
her house.
They fought in the street . . .
That the doorposts quaked and the wall
swayed . . .
Gilgamesh crumpled his leg to the
ground,
His anger softened, he checked his
onset.
When he had checked his onset,
Says Engidu to him, to Gilgamesh:
"Thee, as one matchless, thy mother
bore,
The wild cow of the fold, the goddess
Ninsun.
Over all men is thy head lifted up,
Ellil to thee hath allotted
The kingdom over mankind!"

•   •   •

[After their wrestling match Gilgamesh
and Engidu become good friends. To-

gether they trek into a far-distant cedar forest where they slay the monster, Khumbaba. But Gilgamesh later spurns the goddess, Ishtar, who then persuades her father, Anu, to sent the bull of heaven to kill Gilgamesh.—*Ed.]*

Anu lent ear to [Ishtar's] words,
Let a bull-of-heaven descend
And come unto Uruk . . .
At his first snort he kills
Three hundred warriors.
And Engidu grasped the bull-of-heaven
By his horns.
At his second snort
Two hundred warriors he knocks over.
At his third snort
Engidu stalks up to him,
Leaps on his back,
And grasps him by the thick of the tail . . .
Then Engidu opened his mouth and
  speaks,
Says to Gilgamesh:
"My friend,
We have made our name glorious" . . .
And Gilgamesh, like a huntsman,
Thrusts his sword between nape and
  horns.
When they had laid low the bull-of-
  heaven,
Their heart had peace . . .
And in front of Shamash they sat down
  to their rest,
Both of the brothers.

Then Ishtar mounted the walls of
  ramparted Uruk,
Sprang on the battlements and shrieked
  down:
"Woe unto Gilgamesh who affronted me,
Who killed the bull-of-heaven."
As Engidu heard these words of Ishtar,
He tore loose a thigh-bone from the
  bull-of-heaven,
And flung it into her face:
"Could I but get hold of thee,
I would do unto thee as unto him!
Round thy neck would I hang his
  entrails!"
Then Ishtar assembled the damsels of
  the temple,

The harlots and the priestesses;
Over the thigh-bone of the bull-of-
  heaven
They wailed a chant . . .
Gilgamesh called the masters, the hand-
  workers all.
The masters praise the thickness of the
  horns;
Thirty pounds of lapislazuli was the
  weight of each.
Two fingers thick was their shell.
Six measures of oil (as much as both
  horns held)
Did he pour, as oil of anointing,
To his god, Lugalmaradda;
Brought the horns to his god's temple,
And fastened them on his throne.
Then they washed their hands in the
  Euphrates,
Start off and wander along
On the market-street of Uruk.
The people of Uruk stand assembled
And gaze upon them.

Gilgamesh speaks thus
To the maid-servants of his palace:
"Who is the most beautiful among the
  heroes?
Who is the mightiest among men?"

"Gilgamesh is the most beautiful among
  the heroes!
Gilgamesh is the mightiest among
  men!" . . .
Then Gilgamesh makes in his palace
A feast of rejoicing.

The warriors rest in their beds of night.
Also Engidu rests, beholding dreams.
Then Engidu rose up,
Tells the dreams, and speaks to his
  friend: ● ● ●

"Gilgamesh, my friend,
I beheld dreams this last night:
The heavens called, the earth answered.
In the dark night am I standing there
  alone,
I see a man with forbidding face . . .
He is hideous to look on,
His nails are eagle-talons . . .

He made my arms into wings like a
    bird's:
'Descend, descend, I say, into the house
    of darkness,
To the dwelling of Irkalla,
To the house
Which none leave again who have
    betrodden it,
To a way whose road turneth not,
To the house whose inhabitants do
    without light,
Where dust is their nourishment and
    clay their food.
They are as birds clothed with wings,
They see not the light,
They dwell in the darkness.'
In the house of dust which I entered . . .
Are kings' crowns bowed down.
There do dwell the mighty ones
Who from the days of old ruled the
    land . . .
In the house of dust which I entered
Dwell priest-prince and wailing-priests,
Dwell the conjurers and the rapt seers,
Dwell the high-priests of the great
    gods . . .
Dwells the queen of the earth, Eresh-
    Kigal.
Belit-Seri, she the scribe of the earth,
Standeth bowed before her . . .
And readeth to her aloud.
Then she raised her head and saw me,
She stretched out her hand and took me
    to herself" . . .

[*Then Gilgamesh moaned and said:*]

"My friend,
Who with me hast ranged through all
    hardships . . .
My friend, the dream comes true!" . . .

On the day when he saw the dream
His fate was fulfilled.
Engidu lies stricken,
For one day,
For a second day,
Engidu suffers pain in his bed.
For a third day, and a fourth,
Engidu lies stricken.
For a fifth, a sixth, and a seventh,
For an eighth, a ninth, and a tenth day.

Engidu's pain grows great.
For an eleventh and a twelfth day,
Engidu lies in his bed . . .
He calls Gilgamesh and speaks:
"A god hath cursed me, my friend.
Not like one wounded in battle
Is it mine to die.
I once feared the fight . . .
But, my friend,
He who falls in the fight is happy.
As to me, I must die in my bed. . . ."

       ● ● ●

[*And Gilgamesh returns to Engidu's bed and
    speaks:*]

"Engidu, my young friend,
Thou panther of the steppes,
Who couldst do all things,
So that we climbed the mountain,
Overthrew Khumbaba,
Who housed in the cedar-forest,
So that we seized and slew the bull-of-
    heaven,
What kind of sleep is this
That hath now seized upon thee?
Dark is thy look,
And thine ears take not my voice!"
But he lifts up his eyes no more.
Gilgamesh touched him on the heart,
But the heart beats no more.
Then he covered up his friend like a
    bride.

Like as a lion, Gilgamesh raised his voice,
Like as a lioness, he roared out.
He turns round to his friend,
He tears his hair and strews it forth . . .
Soon as beamed the first shimmer of
    morning,
Gilgamesh raised a new cry:
"I made thee to rest on a bed well-
    prepared,
I made thee to dwell in a quiet dwelling-
    place . . .
I made princes of the earth kiss thy feet.
Now will I make the people of ramparted
    Uruk
Beweep thee and sorrow for thee;
Much people will I make to serve thee,
And I will myself put on mourning for
    thee,
Will clothe myself in a lion's skin,

And haste away over the steppes." . . .

Gilgamesh weeps bitterly
For his friend Engidu,
And hastes away over the steppes:

• • •

[After many wanderings over steppes and mountains Gilgamesh reaches the sea.—Ed.]

Siduri, she the divine cup-bearer,
Sits there by the rim of the sea.
Sits there and looks afar off . . .
She is wrapped in a shawl . . .
Gilgamesh ran thither and drew nigh unto her.
He is clad in skins,
His shape is awesome,
His body godlike,
Woe is in his heart.
He is like a wanderer of far ways.
The face of her, the cup-bearer, looks afar off,
She talks to herself and says the word,
Takes counsel in her heart:
"Is he yonder one who deviseth ill?
Whither is he going in the wrath of his heart?"
As Siduri saw him, she locked her gate,
Locked her portal, locked her chamber . . .

Gilgamesh says to her, to the cup-bearer:
"Cup-bearer, what ails thee,
That thou lockest thy gate,
Lockest thy portal,
Lockest thy chamber?
I will crash the door, I will break the lock." . . .
The cup-bearer says to him, to Gilgamesh:
"Why are thy cheeks so wasted,
Thy visage so sunken,
Thy heart so sad,
Thy shape so undone?
Why is woe in thy heart?
Why art thou like a wanderer of far ways?
Why is thy countenance
So destroyed with grief and pain?
Why hast thou from wide-away
Made haste over the steppes?"

Gilgamesh says to her, to the cup-bearer:
"Why should my cheeks not be so wasted,
My visage so sunken,
My heart so sad,
My shape so undone?
How should woe not be in my heart?
Why should I not be like
A wanderer of far ways?
Why should not my countenance
Be destroyed with grief and pain?
Why should I not to the far-away
Make haste over the steppes?
My belovèd friend, the panther of the steppes,
Engidu, my belovèd friend,
The panther of the steppes who could do all things,
So that we climbed the mountain,
Overthrew Khumbaba,
Who housed in the cedar-forest,
So that we seized and slew the bull-of-heaven,
So that we laid lions low
In the ravines of the mountain,
My friend,
Who with me ranged through all hardships,
Engidu, my friend, who killed lions with me,
Who with me ranged through all hardships,
Him hath the fate of mankind overtaken.
Six days and six nights have I wept over him,
Until the seventh day
Would I not have him buried.
Then I began to be afraid . . .
Fear of death seized upon me.
Therefore I make away over the steppes.
The fate of my friend weighs me down.
Therefore I make haste
On a far way over the steppes.
The fate of Engidu, my friend,
Weigheth me down.
Therefore I make haste on a long road over the steppes.
Why should I be silent thereon?
Why should I not cry it forth?
My friend, whom I love,
Hath turned into earth.

Must not I too, as he,
Lay me down
And rise not up again
For ever and for ever?—
Ever since he is gone, I cannot find Life,
And rove, like a hunter, round over the
    fields.
Cup-bearer, now I behold thy face;
But Death, whom I fear, I would not
    behold."

The cup-bearer, she says to him, to
    Gilgamesh:
"Gilgamesh, whither runnest thou?
Life, which thou seekest, thou wilt not
    find.
When the gods created mankind,
They allotted to mankind Death,
But Life they withheld in their hands.
So, Gilgamesh, fill thy body,
Make merry by day and night,
Keep each day a feast of rejoicing!
Day and night leap and have thy delight!
Put on clean raiment,
Wash thy head and bathe thee in water,
Look cheerily at the child who holdeth
    thy hand,
And may thy wife have joy in thy arms!"

Gilgamesh says again to her, to the cup-
    bearer:
"Go to, cup-bearer!
Where is the way to Utnapishtim?
What is his sign? Give it to me!
If it can be done,
I will pass over the sea;
If it cannot be done,
I will make away over the steppes."
The cup-bearer she says to him, to
    Gilgamesh:
"Never, Gilgamesh, was there a place of
    crossing,
And no one who came since the days of
    old
Could pass over that sea.
Only Shamash, the hero,
Hath passed over that sea,
But who except Shamash can pass over
    it?
There is no getting to the place of
    crossing,

Toilsome the way thereunto,
The waters of death are deep
That lie there to thwart thee.
Where wilt thou, Gilgamesh, pass over
    that sea?
When thou comest to the waters of
    death,
What, then, wilt thou do?
Gilgamesh, Ur-Shanabi is there,
The shipman of Utnapishtim,
Who hath with him coffers of stone.
He picks plants in the forest.
Him do thou seek out.
If it can be done, fare across with him;
If it cannot be done, turn again back."

• • •

*[Gilgamesh seeks for Ur-Shanabi, but finds at
first only his stone coffers, which he breaks
to pieces in his anger. The suddenly he be-
holds Ur-Shanabi.]*

Ur-Shanabi says to him, to Gilgamesh:
"What is thy name? Say forth!
I am Ur-Shanabi,
Man-servant of Utnapishtim, the far
    one."

Gilgamesh speaks to him, to Ur-Shanabi:
"My name is Gilgamesh,
I have come from long away . . .
At last, Ur-Shanabi, I behold thy face.
Let me look on Utnapishtim, the far
    one."

And Gilgamesh says again to him,
To Ur-Shanabi, the shipman:
"Come, Ur-Shanabi, where is the way to
    Utnapishtim?
What is his sign? Give it to me!
Give me, give me his sign!
If it can be done,
I will pass over the sea;
If it cannot be done,
I will make away over the steppes."

Ur-Shanabi says to him, to Gilgamesh:
"Thy hands, O Gilgamesh,
Have hindered a landing,
Thou brakest to pieces the coffers of
    stone,
The coffers of stone are to-broken;

And so I cannot ferry thee over.
Gilgamesh, take the axe in thy arm,
Go down to the forest,
Cut poles of length sixty ells,
Smear them with pitch and bear them to
  me.''

As Gilgamesh this heard,
He took the axe in his arm,
Drew the sword from his girdle,
Went down to the forest,
And cut poles of length sixty ells,
Smeared them with pitch . . .
And brought them to Ur-Shanabi.

Gilgamesh and Ur-Shanabi boarded the
  ship,
They headed the ship into the flood,
And sailed forth,
A way of one month and fifteen days.
As he took his bearings on the third day,
Ur-Shanabi had reached the waters of
  death.
Ur-Shanabi says to him, to Gilgamesh:
"Quick, Gilgamesh, take a pole!
For thy hands must not touch
The waters of death.
A second, a third, a fourth pole,
Take, Gilgamesh!
A fifth, a sixth, a seventh pole,
Take, Gilgamesh!
An eighth, a ninth, a tenth pole,
Take, Gilgamesh!
An eleventh, a twelfth pole,
Take, Gilgamesh!''

At a hundred and twenty
Gilgamesh had used up the poles.
Now he made his hips free . . .
Gilgamesh stripped off his garment,
And with his hands made high the mast.
Utnapishtim descrieth his face afar;
Talks to himself and saith the word,
Takes counsel in his heart:
"Why are the stone-coffers
Of the ship all to-broken?
And one who belongs not to me
Sails in the ship!
He who comes yonder, he cannot be
  man! . . .
I gaze thither, but I understand it not.

I gaze thither, but I grasp it not.'' . . .

Utnapishtim says to him, to Gilgamesh:
"What is thy name? Say forth!
I am Utnapishtim who hath found Life.''

• • •

Gilgamesh says to him, to Utnapishtim:
"Methought, I will go and see
Utnapishtim, of whom men tell.
So I betook me through all lands to and
  fro,
So I betook me over the mountains
That are hard to cross over,
So I fared over all seas.
With good have I not been glutted . . .
I filled my body with pain;
Ere ever I got to Siduri, the cup-bearer,
Was my clothing gone . . .
I had to hunt all the wild of the fields,
Lions and panthers,
Hyenas, and deer, and ibex.
Their flesh do I eat,
With their skins do I clothe me.''

• • •

"I look upon thee, Utnapishtim:
Thy form is not unlike;
Even as I, so too art thou;
Yes, thou art not unlike;
Even as I, so too art thou.
Yet I was born unto this:
To fight and to do battle.
But thou art idle and liest on thy back.
How camest thou, then, into the
  assembly
Of the gods and foundest Life?''

Utnapishtim says to him, to Gilgamesh:
"I will lay open before thee, Gilgamesh,
Knowledge deep-hidden,
And a secret of the gods will I tell thee:
Shurippak is a city (thou thyself knowest
  her),
Which lieth on Euphrates' banks.
She is an ancient city,
And the gods are kind to her.
Once the great gods conceived a plan
To make a stormflood.
There foregathered Anu, their father,
Their overlord, the hero Ellil,
Their herald Ninurta, their prince
  Ennugi.

The bright-eyed Ea had sat with them at
    counsel.
He told their discussion to a reed-hut:[1]
'Reed-hut, reed-hut! Hut-wall, hut-wall!
Reed-hut, listen! Wall, take it in!
Thou man from Shurippak, son of
    Ubara-Tutu,[2]
Tear down thy house, build a ship!
Let riches go, seek Life,
Despise possessions, save thy life!
Bring living things of all kinds into the
    ship!
The ship that thou art to build,
Be its measurements strictly laid out,
For its length and its breadth to match—
On the holy lake set it at anchor!'
I understood, and I say to Ea, my lord:
'I perceive, my lord, what thou sayest;
I hold it dear, and will carry it out.'

● ● ●

Before sunset the ship was finished . . .
All that I had I laded upon it,
All that I had of silver I laded upon it,
I laded upon it all that I had of gold,
I laded upon it all that I had
Of living things of all kinds.
I made my whole family and kin
To go aboard the ship;
Cattle of the field, animals of the field,
All handworkers I made go aboard.
Shamash had given me the appointed
    time:
'Of an evening will the Sender of
    darkness
Let a cloudburst stream from on high.
Then enter the ship and close thy door.'
This appointed time came on.
The Sender of darkness
Of an evening let a cloudburst come
    down.
I observed the look of the tempest,
I was afraid to gaze on the tempest,
I went within the ship and shut my gate.

● ● ●

---

[1]In which Utnapishtim lives.

[2]That is, Utnapishtim himself, who is
revealing the "knowledge deep-hidden"
to Gilgamesh.

Six days and six nights swirls the
    stormflood,
And the southstorm is a weight on the
    land.
As the seventh day came on,
The southstorm gave up the fight,
Which it had fought like an army.
The sea grew quiet, and gathered up its
    waters.
The stormflood ceased.
I looked for the tempest, all had become
    still.
The whole race of man was turned to
    earth.
Like a flat roof were the plains.
Then I opened a hatch,
And light streamed into my face.
I sat me down weeping,
And my tears ran over my face.
I gazed about for solid earth
In the dominions of the sea.
After twelve hours an island emerged.
The ship drove for Mount Nissir.
Mount Nissir holds the ship fast
And keeps it from rocking.
One day, a second day, Mount Nissir
Holds the ship fast and keeps it from
    rocking.
A third and fourth day Mount Nissir
Holds the ship fast and keeps it from
    rocking.
A fifth, a sixth day Mount Nissir
Holds the ship fast and keeps it from
    rocking.

"As the seventh day came on,
I held a dove outside and set it free;
The dove flew forth and came back.
She found no resting-place, so she
    turned home.
I held a swallow outside and set it free;
The swallow flew forth and came back.
She found no resting-place, so she
    turned home.
I held a raven outside and set it free;
The raven flew forth, saw the water run
    dry,
He feeds, scrapes, croaks, and turned
    not home.

"Then I let all out unto the four winds,
And offered a sacrifice,

Set up a burnt-offering
On the top of the mountain.

* * *

Gilgamesh and Ur-Shanabi boarded the
ship,
They headed the ship into the flood,
And sailed away.
Then said his wife to him,
To Utnapishtim, the far one:
"Gilgamesh hath set forth;
He hath worn himself out, and suffered
torments.
What wilt thou give him,
That with it he may reach his
homeland?"

And Gilgamesh has already lifted the
pole,
And brings the ship again near the
shore:
Utnapishtim says to him, to Gilgamesh:
"Gilgamesh, thou hast set forth;
Thou hast worn thyself out, and suffered
torments.
What shall I give thee
That with it thou reachest thy
homeland?
I will lay open before thee
Knowledge deep-hidden;
About a plant of life will I tell thee.
The plant looks like the prick-thorn . . .
Its thorn like the thorn of the rose
Can prick the hand hard.
When thou gettest this plant in thy
hands,
Eat thereof and thou wilt live."

When Gilgamesh learned of this . . .
He bound heavy stones on his feet;

These drew him down deep in the sea.
He himself took the plant,
And it pricked his hand hard.
He cut off the heavy stones . . .
And laid the plant beside him.
Gilgamesh says to him,
To Ur-Shanabi, the shipman:
"Ur-Shanabi, this plant
Is a plant-of-promise,
Whereby a man obtains his desire.
I will bring it to ramparted Uruk;
I will make the warriors eat thereof . . .
Its name is: 'The-old-man-becomes-
young-again.'
I myself will eat thereof,
And return back to my youth."
After twenty miles they took a little food,
After thirty miles they rested for the
night.
Then Gilgamesh saw a pit with cool
water;
He stepped into it and bathed in the
water.
Then a serpent savoured the smell of the
plant;
She crept along and took the plant . . .
When he returned, he shrieked out a
curse.
Gilgamesh sat himself down and weeps,
His tears run over his face.
He speaks and says to Ur-Shanabi, the
shipman:
"For whom, Ur-Shanabi,
Have my arms worn themselves out?
For whom hath been spent the blood of
my heart?
I worked good not for myself—
For the worm of the earth have I
wrought good. . . ."

Egyptian Religion

It requires little imagination to appreciate the religious nature of the two selections that follow. One can easily picture congregations of Egyptian worshipers singing their praises to the Nile and to the sun. Both of these natural objects were vital to Egyptian life, as they remain to this day. As anywhere else, the sun caused the crops to mature, but the river played a special role in Egyptian agriculture. Its annual flooding inundated the valley, thus enriching the soil and producing a much greater yield than would otherwise have occurred. As the ancient Greek historian Herodotus so aptly put it, "Egypt is the gift of the Nile."

In their worship of the Nile and the sun the ancient Egyptians were exemplifying a form of religious belief common among early civilizations—*animism*, or the deification of objects of nature. Nevertheless, a close reading of the two hymns reveals differences between them. It is clear from the first that the Nile is being worshiped as only one of many gods, so the religion is not only animistic but also polytheistic. In the second, however, the worshiper makes it plain, as he says, that the sun is the "sole god." Thus, we have in this hymn an expression of monotheism. Indeed, it is generally considered to be among the earliest statements of a monotheistic theology in history. Also, and more subtly, there are indications in the hymn that the object of worship is not the physical sun itself but some power more fundamental and pervasive than any single natural object. So we find in it the beginnings of a departure from simple animism.

The date of the "Hymn to the Nile" is not known but scholars believe that it was sung during an annual festival held at Thebes (in upper Egypt), celebrating the inundation of the land by the river. It has, unfortunately, not survived intact but still is sufficiently complete so that its content is clear. The "Hymn to the Sun" is known to be the work of the Pharaoh Ikhnaton, who reigned in the early part of the fourteenth century B.C. Ikhnaton attempted to reform Egyptian religion; his attempt, however, proved to be unsuccessful for after his death the Egyptians returned to their old beliefs.

Hymn to the Nile

Praise to thee, O Nile, that issueth from the earth, and cometh to nourish Egypt. Of hidden nature, a darkness in the daytime. . . .

That watereth the meadows, he that Rē[1] hath created to nourish all cattle. That giveth drink to the desert places, which are far from water; it is his dew that falleth from heaven.

Beloved of Kēb,[2] director of the corn-god; that maketh to flourish every workshop of Ptah.[3]

Lord of fish, that maketh the water-fowl to go upstream. . . .

That maketh barley and createth wheat, so that he may cause the temples to keep festivals.

If he be sluggish,[4] the nostrils are stopped up,[5] and all men are impoverished; the victuals of the gods are diminished, and millions of men perish.

If he be niggardly the whole land is in terror and great and small lament. . . . Khnum[6] hath fashioned him. When he riseth, the land is in exultation and every body is in joy.

All jaws begin to laugh and every tooth is revealed.

He that bringeth victuals and is rich in food, that createth all that is good. The revered, sweet-smelling . . . . That createth herbage for the cattle, and giveth sacrifice to every god, be he in the underworld, in heaven, or upon earth. . . . That filleth the storehouses, and maketh wide the granaries, that giveth things to the poor.

He that maketh trees to grow according to every wish, and men have no lack thereof; the ship is built by his power, for there is no joinery with stones. . . .

. . . thy young folk and thy children shout for joy over thee, and men hail thee as king. Unchanging of laws, when he cometh forth in the presence of Upper and Lower Egypt. Men drink the water. . . .

He that was in sorrow is become glad, and every heart is joyful. Sobk,[7] the child of Neith, laugheth, and the divine Ennead, that is in thee, is glorious.

Thou that vomitest forth, giving the fields to drink and making strong the people. He that maketh the one rich and loveth the other. He maketh no distinctions, and boundaries are not made for him.

Thou light, that cometh from the

---

[1] The sun-god.

[2] The earth-god.

[3] Ptah, the craftsman, who fashions everything, could effect nothing without the Nile.

[4] On the occasion of a deficient inundation.

[5] Men no longer breathe and live.

[6] The ram-headed god, who fashions all that is.

[7] Sobk has the form of a crocodile and will originally have been a water-god, who rejoices in the inundation.

Trans. A. M. Blackman.

darkness! Thou fat for his cattle. He is a strong one, that createth. . . .

. . . one beholdeth the wealthy as him that is full of care, one beholdeth each one with his implements . . . . None that (otherwise) goeth clad, is clad,[8] and the children of notables are unadorned. . . .

He that establisheth right, whom men love. . . . It would be but lies to compare thee with the sea, that bringeth no corn. . . . no bird descendeth in the desert. . . .

Men begin to play to thee on the harp, and men sing to thee with the hand.[9] Thy young folk and thy children shout for joy over thee, and deputations to thee are appointed.

He that cometh with splendid things and adorneth the earth! That causeth the ship to prosper before men; that quickeneth the hearts in them that are with child; that would fain have there be a multitude of all kinds of cattle.

When thou art risen in the city of the sovereign, then men are satisfied with a goodly list.[10] "I would like lotus flowers," saith the little one, "and all manner of things," saith the . . . commander, "and all manner of herbs," say the children. Eating bringeth forgetfulness of him.[11] Good things are scattered over the dwelling. . . .

When the Nile floodeth, offering is made to thee, cattle are slaughtered for thee, a great oblation is made for thee. Birds are fattened for thee, antelopes are hunted for thee in the desert. Good is recompensed unto thee.

Offering is also made to every other god, even as is done for the Nile, with incense, oxen, cattle, and birds (upon) the flame. The Nile hath made him his cave in Thebes, and his name shall be known no more in the underworld. . . .

All ye men, extol the Nine Gods, and stand in awe of the might which his son, the Lord of All, hath displayed, even he that maketh green the Two River-banks. Thou art verdant, O Nile, thou art verdant. He that maketh man to live on his cattle, and his cattle on the meadow! Thou art verdant, thou art verdant: O Nile, thou art verdant.

---

[8]For hard work, clothes are taken off.

[9]It is an old custom to beat time with the hand while singing.

[10]*I.e.*, a multitude of good things.

---

[11]The Nile.

Hymn to the Sun

Thy dawning is beautiful in the horizon
of heaven,
O living Aton,[1] Beginning of life!
When thou risest in the eastern horizon
of heaven,
Thou fillest every land with thy beauty;
For thou art beautiful, great, glittering,
high over the earth;
Thy rays, they encompass the lands, even
all thou hast made.
Thou are Rē, and thou has carried them
all away captive;
Thou bindest them by thy love.
Though thou art afar, thy rays are on
earth;
Though thou art on high, thy footprints
are the day.

When thou settest in the western hori-
zon of heaven,
The world is in darkness like the dead.
They sleep in their chambers,
Their heads are wrapt up,
Their nostrils stopped, and none seeth
the other.
Stolen are all their things, that are under
their heads,
While they know it not.
Every lion cometh forth from his den,
All serpents, they sting.
Darkness reigns,
The world is in silence,
He that made them has gone to rest in
his horizon.

Bright is the earth,
When thou risest in the horizon,
When thou shinest as Aton by day.
The darkness is banished,
When thou sendest forth thy rays,

The Two Lands[2] are in daily festivity,
Awake and standing upon their feet,
For thou hast raised them up.
Their limbs bathed, they take their
clothing;
Their arms uplifted in adoration to thy
dawning.
Then in all the world, they do their
work.

All cattle rest upon their herbage,
All trees and plants flourish,
The birds flutter in their marshes.
Their wings uplifted in adoration to
thee.
All the sheep dance upon their feet,
All winged things fly,
They live when thou has shone upon
them.

The barques sail up-stream and down-
stream alike.
Every highway is open because thou hast
dawned.
The fish in the river leap up before thee,
And thy rays are in the midst of the great
sea.

Thou art he who creates the man-child
in woman,
Who makest seed in man,
Who giveth life to the son in the body of
his mother,
Who soothest him that he may not weep,
A nurse even in the womb.
Who giveth breath to animate every one
that he maketh.
When he cometh forth from the body
. . . on the day of his birth,
Thou openest his mouth in speech.
Thou suppliest his necessities.
When the chicklet crieth in the eggshell,

---

[1][One of the names given to the sun
god—*Ed.*]

[2][Upper and Lower Egypt—*Ed.*]

Trans. James H. Breasted.

19

Thou givest him breath therein, to
preserve him alive.
When thou has perfected him
That he may pierce the egg,
He cometh forth from the egg,
To chirp with all his might;
He runneth about upon his two feet,
When he hath come forth therefrom.
How manifold are thy works!
They are hidden from before us,
O thou sole god, whose powers no other
possesseth.
Thou didst create the earth according to
thy desire.
While thou wast alone:
Men, all cattle large and small,
All that are upon the earth,
That go about upon their feet;
All that are on high,
That fly with their wings.
The countries of Syria and Nubia,
The land of Egypt;
Thou settest every man in his place,
Thou suppliest their necessities.
Every one has his possessions,
And his days are reckoned.
Their tongues are divers in speech,
Their forms likewise and their skins,
For thou divider, hast divided the peoples.

Thou makest the Nile in the Nether
World,
Thou bringest it at thy desire, to
preserve the people alive.
O lord of them all, when feebleness is in
them,
O lord of every house, who risest for them,
O son of day, the fear of every distant
land,
Thou makest also their life.
Thou has set a Nile in heaven,
That is may fall for them,
Making floods upon the mountains, like
the great sea;
And watering their fields among their
towns.
How excellent are thy designs, O lord of
eternity!
The Nile in heaven is for the strangers,
And for the cattle of every land, that go
upon their feet;

But the Nile, it cometh from the Nether
World for Egypt.

Thus thy rays nourish every garden,
When thou risest they live, and grow by
thee.
Thou makest the seasons, in order to
create all thy works:
Winter bringing them coolness,
And the heat of summer likewise.
Thou has made the distant heaven to
rise therein,
In order to behold all that thou didst
make,
While thou wast alone,
Rising in thy form as living Aton,
Dawning, shining afar off and returning.
Thou makest the beauty of form,
through thyself alone.
Cities, towns and settlements,
On highway or on river,
All eyes see thee before them.
For thou art Aton of the day over the
earth.

Thou art in my heart,
There is no other that knoweth thee,
Save thy son Ikhnaton.
Thou hast made him wise in thy de-
signs
And in thy might.
The world is in thy hand,
Even as thou hast made them.
When thou hast risen, they live:
When thou settest, they die.
For thou art duration, beyond thy mere
limbs,
By thee man liveth,
And their eyes look upon thy beauty.
Until thou settest.
All labour is laid aside,
When thou settest in the west;
When thou risest, they are made to grow
. . . for the king.

Since thou didst establish the earth,
Thou hast raised them up for thy son,
Who came forth from thy limbs,
The king, living in truth,
The lord of the Two Lands Nefer-khe-
pru-Rĕ, Wan-Rĕ,

The son of Rĕ, living in truth, lord of
   diadems,
Ikhnaton, whose life is long;
And for the great royal wife, his beloved,

Mistress of the Two Lands, Nefer
   nefru aton, Nofretete,
Living and flourishing for ever and ever.

The Code of Hammurabi

At the beginning of the twentieth century a French archaeological expedition unearthed one of the most magnificent finds of our times—a stele, or tablet, on which was inscribed the entire Code of Hammurabi. Found at Susa in western Persia, where it had been taken by an Elamite king as war booty in the twelfth century B.C., the stele is of stone, about eight feet tall, and contains approximately thirty-six hundred lines of writing. Although the stone has been damaged slightly, most of the writing, in cuneiform script, is legible. At the top of the stele is a well-executed carving showing Hammurabi receiving the laws from Marduk, the sun god of Babylonia. After its discovery the stele was taken to Paris and placed in the Louvre, where it can still be seen.

Hammurabi (whose tribe, the Amorites, had occupied the middle Euphrates valley), established himself in power and founded the city of Babylon along the lower river, then reigned as king of Babylonia from 1728 to 1686 B.C. Although he was responsible for formulating and publishing the Code, he did not originate the laws it contains. Rather, the Code is a compilation and revision of older laws of the Sumerians and Akkadians (tribes occupying the same general region). These deal with almost every facet of life in the ancient Near East, including marriage and the family, relationships among social classes, regulations concerning land and business, labor relations, military service, religion, and crime. They are important not only for the light they shed on the quite complex society of that time but also for the influence they had on later Near Eastern law codes. In this regard it is instructive to compare the Code with the Mosaic law as it appears in the Old Testament. Both reveal, particularly in their sanction of the *lex talionis*, something of the cruelty and violence that was endemic throughout the ancient world.

The selection that follows includes the most important legal provisions of the Code; regulations of lesser significance have been omitted.

The Code of Hammurabi

1. If a man has accused another of laying a death spell upon him, but has not proved it, he shall be put to death.

2. If a man has accused another of laying a spell upon him, but has not proved it, the accused shall go to the sacred river, he shall plunge into the sacred river, and if the sacred river shall conquer him, he that accused him shall take possession of his house. If the sacred river shall show his innocence and he is saved, his accuser shall be put to death. He that plunged into the sacred river shall appropriate the house of him that accused him.

3. If a man has borne false witness in a trial, or has not established the statement that he has made, if that case be a capital trial, that man shall be put to death.

4. If he has borne false witness in a civil law case, he shall pay the damages in that suit.

5. If a judge has given a verdict, rendered a decision, granted a written judgment, and afterward has altered his judgment, that judge shall be prosecuted for altering the judgment he gave and shall pay twelvefold the penalty laid down in that judgment. Further, he shall be publicly expelled from his judgment-seat and shall not return nor take his seat with the judges at a trial.

6. If a man has stolen goods from a temple, or house, he shall be put to death; and he that has received the stolen property from him shall be put to death.

• • •

14. If a man has stolen a child, he shall be put to death.

15. If a man has induced either a male or female slave from the house of a patrician, or plebeian, to leave the city, he shall be put to death.

16. If a man has harbored in his house a male or female slave from a patrician's or plebeian's house, and has not caused the fugitive to leave on the demand of the officer over the slaves condemned to public forced labor, that householder shall be put to death.

• • •

22. If a man has committed highway robbery and has been caught, that man shall be put to death.

23. If the highwayman has not been caught, the man that has been robbed shall state on oath what he has lost and the city or district governor in whose territory or district the robbery took place shall restore to him what he has lost.

• • •

25. If a fire has broken out in a man's house and one who has come to put it out has coveted the property of the householder and appropriated any of it, that man shall be cast into the self-same fire.

26. If a levy-master, or warrant-officer, who has been detailed on the king's service, has not gone, or has hired a substitute in his place, that levy-master, or warrant-officer, shall be put to death and the hired substitute shall take his office.

27. If a levy-master, or warrant-officer, has been assigned to garrison

Trans. C. H. W. Johns.

duty, and in his absence his field and garden have been given to another who has carried on his duty, when the absentee has returned and regained his city, his field and garden shall be given back to him and he shall resume his duty.

28. If a levy-master, or warrant-officer, has been assigned to garrison duty, and has a son able to carry on his official duty, the field and garden shall be given to him and he shall carry on his father's duty.

29. If the son be a child and is not able to carry on his father's duty, one-third of the field and garden shall be given to his mother to educate him.

• • •

34. If either a governor, or a prefect, has appropriated the property of a levy-master, has hired him out, has robbed him by high-handedness at a trial, has taken the salary which the king gave to him, that governor, or prefect, shall be put to death.

35. If a man has bought from a levy-master the sheep, or oxen, which the king gave him, he shall lose his money.

36. The field, garden, or house, of a levy-master, warrant-officer, or tributary shall not be sold.

• • •

42. If a man has hired a field to cultivate and has caused no corn to grow on the field, he shall be held responsible for not doing the work on the field and shall pay an average rent.

• • •

45. If a man has let his field to a farmer and has received his rent for the field but afterward the field has been flooded by rain, or a storm has carried off the crop, the loss shall be the farmer's.

46. If he has not received the rent of his field, whether he let it for a half, or for a third, of the crop, the farmer and the owner of the field shall share the corn that is left in the field, according to their agreement.

• • •

53, 54. If a man has neglected to strengthen his dike and has not kept his dike strong, and a breach has broken out in his dike, and the waters have flooded the meadow, the man in whose dike the breach has broken out shall restore the corn he has caused to be lost. [54]. If he be not able to restore the corn, he and his goods shall be sold, and the owners of the meadow whose corn the water has carried away shall share the money.

• • •

100. [If an agent has received money of a merchant, he shall write down the amount] and [what is to be] the interest of the money, and when his time is up, he shall settle with his merchant.

101. If he has not had success on his travels, he shall return double what he received to the merchant.

102, 103. If the merchant has given money, as a speculation, to the agent, who during his travels has met with misfortune, he shall return the full sum to the merchant. [103]. If, on his travels, an enemy has forced him to give up some of the goods he was carrying, the agent shall specify the amount on oath and shall be acquitted.

• • •

106. If an agent has taken money of a merchant, and his principal suspects him, that principal shall prosecute his agent, put him on oath before the elders, as to the money taken; the agent shall pay to the merchant threefold what he misappropriated.

107. If the principal has overcharged the agent and the agent has [really] returned to his principal whatever his principal gave him, and if the principal has disputed what the agent has given him, that agent shall put his principal on oath before the elders, and the merchant, because he has defrauded the agent, shall pay to the agent sixfold what he misappropriated.

108. If the mistress of a beer-shop has not received corn as the price of beer or has demanded silver on an excessive scale, and has made the measure of beer less than the measure of corn, that beer-seller shall be prosecuted and drowned.

109. If the mistress of a beer-shop has assembled seditious slanderers in her house and those seditious persons have not been captured and have not been haled to the palace, that beer-seller shall be put to death.

110. If a votary, who is not living in the convent, open a beer-shop, or enter a beer-shop for drink, that woman shall be put to death.

• • •

120. If a man has deposited his corn for safe keeping in another's house and it has suffered damage in the granary, or if the owner of the house has opened the store and taken the corn, or has disputed the amount of the corn that was stored in his house, the owner of the corn shall declare on oath the amount of his corn, and the owner of the house shall return him double.

• • •

122. If a man has given another gold, silver, or any goods whatever, on deposit, all that he gives shall he show to witnesses, and take a bond and so give on deposit.

123. If he has given on deposit without witnesses and bonds, and has been defrauded where he made his deposit, he has no claim to prosecute.

124. If a man has given on deposit to another, before witnesses, gold, silver, or any goods whatever, and his claim has been contested, he shall prosecute that man, and [the man] shall return double what he disputed.

125. If a man has given anything whatever on deposit, and, where he has made his deposit, something of his has been lost together with something belonging to the owner of the house, either by house-breaking or a rebellion, the owner of the house who is in default shall make good all that has been given him on deposit, which he has lost, and shall return it to the owner of the goods. The owner of the house shall look after what he has lost and recover it from the thief.

126. If a man has said that something of his is lost, which is not lost, or has alleged a depreciation, though nothing of his is lost, he shall estimate the depreciation on oath, and he shall pay double whatever he has claimed.

• • •

128. If a man has taken a wife and has not executed a marriage-contract, that woman is not a wife.

129. If a man's wife be caught lying with another, they shall be strangled and cast into the water. If the wife's husband would save his wife, the king can save his servant.

130. If a man has ravished another's betrothed wife, who is a virgin, while still living in her father's house, and has been caught in the act, that man shall be put to death; the woman shall go free.

131. If a man's wife has been accused by her husband, and has not

been caught lying with another, she shall swear her innocence, and return to her house.

132. If a man's wife has the finger pointed at her on account of another, but has not been caught lying with him, for her husband's sake she shall plunge into the sacred river.

• • •

138. If a man has divorced his wife, who has not borne him children, he shall pay over to her as much money as was given for her bride-price and the marriage-portion which she brought from her father's house, and so shall divorce her.

139. If there was no bride-price, he shall give her one mina of silver, as a price of divorce.

140. If he be a plebeian, he shall give her one-third of a mina of silver.

141. If a man's wife, living in her husband's house, has persisted in going out, has acted the fool, has wasted her house, has belittled her husband, he shall prosecute her. If her husband has said, "I divorce her," she shall go her way; he shall give her nothing as her price of divorce. If her husband has said, "I will not divorce her," he may take another woman to wife; the wife shall live as a slave in her husband's house.

142. If a woman has hated her husband and has said, "You shall not possess me," her past shall be inquired into, as to what she lacks. If she has been discreet, and has no vice, and her husband has gone out, and has greatly belittled her, that woman has no blame, she shall take her marriage-portion and go off to her father's house.

143. If she has not been discreet, has gone out, ruined her house, belittled her husband, she shall be drowned.

• • •

150. If a man has presented field, garden, house, or goods to his wife, has granted her a deed of gift, her children, after her husband's death, shall not dispute her right; the mother shall leave it after her death to that one of her children whom she loves best. She shall not leave it to her kindred.

151. If a woman, who is living in a man's house, has persuaded her husband to bind himself, and grant her a deed to the effect that she shall not be held for debt by a creditor of her husband's; if that man had a debt upon him before he married that woman, his creditor shall not take his wife for it. Also, if that woman had a debt upon her before she entered that man's house, her creditor shall not take her husband for it.

152. From the time that that woman entered into the man's house they together shall be liable for all debts subsequently incurred.

153. If a man's wife, for the sake of another, has caused her husband to be killed, that woman shall be impaled.

154. If a man has committed incest with his daughter, that man shall be banished from the city.

155. If a man has betrothed a maiden to his son and his son has known her, and afterward the man has lain in her bosom, and been caught, that man shall be strangled and she shall be cast into the water.

156. If a man has betrothed a maiden to his son, and his son has not known her, and that man has lain in her bosom, he shall pay her half a mina of silver, and shall pay over to her whatever she brought from her father's house, and the husband of her choice shall marry her.

157. If a man, after his father's

death, has lain in the bosom of his mother, they shall both of them be burnt together.

• • •

159. If a man, who has presented a gift to the house of his prospective father-in-law and has given the bride-price, has afterward looked upon another woman and has said to his father-in-law, "I will not marry your daughter"; the father of the girl shall keep whatever he has brought as a present.

160. If a man has presented a gift to the house of his prospective father-in-law, and has given the bride-price, but the father of the girl has said, "I will not give you my daughter," the father shall return double all that was presented him.

• • •

162. If a man has married a wife, and she has borne him children, and that woman has gone to her fate, her father shall lay no claim to her marriage-portion. Her marriage-portion is her children's only.

163. If a man has married a wife, and she has not borne him children, and that woman has gone to her fate; if his father-in-law has returned to him the bride-price, which that man brought into the house of his father-in-law, her husband shall have no claim on the marriage-portion of that woman. Her marriage-portion indeed belongs to her father's house.

• • •

168. If a man has determined to disinherit his son and has declared before the judge, "I cut off my son," the judge shall inquire into the son's past, and, if the son has not committed a grave misdemeanor such as should cut him off from sonship, the father shall not disinherit his son.

169. If he has committed a grave crime against his father, which cuts off from sonship, for the first offence he shall pardon him. If he has committed a grave crime a second time, the father shall cut off his son from sonship.

170. If a man has had children borne to him by his wife, and also by a maid, if the father in his lifetime has said, "My sons," to the children whom his maid bore him, and has reckoned them with the sons of his wife; then after the father has gone to his fate, the children of the wife and of the maid shall share equally. The children of the wife shall apportion the shares and make their own selections.

171. And if the father, in his lifetime, has not said, "My sons," to the children whom the maid bore him, after the father has gone to his fate, the children of the maid shall not share with the children of the wife in the goods of their father's house. The maid and her children, however, shall obtain their freedom. The children of the wife have no claim for service on the children of the maid.

The wife shall take her marriage-portion, and any gift that her husband has given her and for which he has written a deed of gift and she shall dwell in her husband's house; as long as she lives, she shall enjoy it, she shall not sell it. After her death it is indeed her children's.

• • •

175. If either a slave of a patrician, or of a plebeian, has married the daughter of a free man, and she has borne children, the owner of the slave shall have no claim for service on the children of a free woman. And if a slave, either of a patrician or of a plebeian, has married a free woman and when he married her she

entered the slave's house with a marriage-portion from her father's estate, be he slave of a patrician or of a plebeian, and from the time that they started to keep house, they have acquired property; after the slave, whether of a patrician or of a plebeian, has gone to his fate, the free woman shall take her marriage-portion, and whatever her husband and she acquired, since they started house-keeping. She shall divide it into two portions. The master of the slave shall take one half, the other half the free woman shall take for her children.

176. If the free woman had no marriage-portion, whatever her husband and she acquired since they started house-keeping he shall divide into two portions. The owner of the slave shall take one half, the other half the free woman shall take for her children.

177. If a widow, whose children are young, has determined to marry again, she shall not marry without consent of the judge. When she is allowed to remarry, the judge shall inquire as to what remains of the property of her former husband, and shall intrust the property of her former husband to that woman and her second husband. He shall give them an inventory. They shall watch over the property, and bring up the children. Not a utensil shall they sell. A buyer of any utensil belonging to the widow's children shall lose his money and shall return the article to its owners.

• • •

181. If a father has vowed his daughter to a god, as a temple maid, or a virgin, and has given her no portion; after the father has gone to his fate, she shall share in the property of her father's estate, taking one-third of a child's share. She shall enjoy her share, as long as she lives. After her, it belongs to her brothers.

• • •

185. If a man has taken a young child, a natural son of his, to be his son, and has brought him up, no one shall make a claim against that foster child.

186. If a man has taken a young child to be his son, and after he has taken him, the child discover his own parents, he shall return to his father's house.

• • •

188, 189. If a craftsman has taken a child to bring up and has taught him his handicraft, he shall not be reclaimed. If he has not taught him his handicraft that foster child shall return to his father's house.

• • •

195. If a son has struck his father, his hands shall be cut off.

196. If a man has knocked out the eye of a patrician, his eye shall be knocked out.

197. If he has broken the limb of a patrician, his limb shall be broken.

198. If he has knocked out the eye of a plebeian or has broken the limb of a plebeian, he shall pay one mina of silver.

199. If he has knocked out the eye of a patrician's servant, or broken the limb of a patrician's servant, he shall pay half his value.

200. If a patrician has knocked out the tooth of a man that is his equal, his tooth shall be knocked out.

201. If he has knocked out the tooth of a plebeian, he shall pay one-third of a mina of silver.

202. If a man has smitten the privates of a man, higher in rank than

he, he shall be scourged with sixty blows of an ox-hide scourge, in the assembly.

• • •

209. If a man has struck a free woman with child, and has caused her to miscarry, he shall pay ten shekels for her miscarriage.

210. If that woman die, his daughter shall be killed.

• • •

215. If a surgeon has operated with the bronze lancet on a patrician for a serious injury, and has cured him, or has removed with a bronze lancet a cataract for a patrician, and has cured his eye, he shall take ten shekels of silver.

• • •

218. If a surgeon has operated with the bronze lancet on a patrician for a serious injury, and has caused his death, or has removed a cataract for a patrician, with the bronze lancet, and has made him lose his eye, his hands shall be cut off.

• • •

224. If a veterinary surgeon has treated an ox, or an ass, for a severe injury, and cured it, the owner of the ox, or the ass, shall pay the surgeon one-sixth of a shekel of silver, as his fee.

225. If he has treated an ox, or an ass, for a severe injury, and caused it to die, he shall pay one-quarter of its value to the owner of the ox, or the ass.

226. If a brander has cut out a mark on a slave, without the consent of his owner, that brander shall have his hands cut off.

• • •

229. If a builder has built a house for a man, and has not made his work sound, and the house he built has fallen, and caused the death of its owner, that builder shall be put to death.

230. If it is the owner's son that is killed, the builder's son shall be put to death.

231. If it is the slave of the owner that is killed, the builder shall give slave for slave to the owner of the house.

• • •

236. If a man has let his boat to a boatman, and the boatman has been careless and the boat has been sunk or lost, the boatman shall restore a boat to the owner.

237. If a man has hired a boat and boatman, and loaded it with corn, wool, oil, or dates, or whatever it be, and the boatman has been careless, and sunk the boat, or lost what is in it, the boatman shall restore the boat which he sank, and whatever he lost that was in it.

• • •

244. If a man has hired an ox, or an ass, and a lion has killed it in the open field, the loss falls on its owner.

245. If a man has hired an ox and has caused its death, by carelessness, or blows, he shall restore ox for ox, to the owner of the ox.

• • •

249. If a man has hired an ox, and God has struck it, and it has died, the man that hired the ox shall make affidavit and go free.

250. If a bull has gone wild and gored a man, and caused his death, there can be no suit against the owner.

251. If a man's ox be a gorer, and has revealed its evil propensity as a gorer, and he has not blunted its horn, or shut up the ox, and then that ox has gored a free man, and caused his death, the owner shall pay half a mina of silver.

• • •

265. If a herdsman, to whom oxen or sheep have been given, has defaulted, has altered the price, or sold them, he shall be prosecuted, and shall restore oxen, or sheep, tenfold, to their owner.

266. If lightning has struck a fold, or a lion has made a slaughter, the herdsman shall purge himself by oath, and the owner of the fold shall bear the loss of the fold.

267. If the herdsman has been careless, and a loss has occurred in the fold, the herdsman shall make good the loss in the fold; he shall repay the oxen, or sheep, to their owner.

• • •

278. If a man has bought a male or female slave and the slave has not fulfilled his month, but the *bennu* disease has fallen upon him, he shall return the slave to the seller and the buyer shall take back the money he paid.

279. If a man has bought a male or female slave and a claim has been raised, the seller shall answer the claim.

280. If a man, in a foreign land, has bought a male, or female, slave of another, and if when he has come home the owner of the male or female slave has recognized his slave, and if the slave be a native of the land, he shall grant him his liberty without money.

281. If the slave was a native of another country, the buyer shall declare on oath the amount of money he paid, and the owner of the slave shall repay the merchant what he paid and keep his slave.

282. If a slave has said to his master, "You are not my master," he shall be brought to account as his slave, and his master shall cut off his ear.

The Old Testament

The Old Testament, one of the greatest creations of the human mind, was the product of a weak, relatively insignificant nation that was regularly exploited and overrun by its more powerful Near-Eastern neighbors. Although we usually think of it as a religious document, it is much more than that, for in its pages is recorded, in infinite variety and rich detail, the full range of the historical experience of the ancient Jewish people.

Rather than attempting the impossible task of encompassing the wealth of the Old Testament in the selection that follows, I have chosen just two of its main themes for illustration—the belief in one God (monotheism) and the idea of God as a moral being standing in personal relationships to humanity. That the Old Testament books present views on these two subjects that are sometimes inconsistent with one another should be neither surprising nor disconcerting, for these books reveal the gradually developing moral and religious consciousness of their authors.

It is instructive to compare one of the most mature expressions of moral consciousness in the ancient world as it appears in the selection from Ezekial with the doctrine of original sin as first stated by St. Paul in his Epistle to the Romans and later developed by the Christian theologians St. Augustine and John Calvin. The source for this Christian doctrine of original sin is found in the book of Genesis, with its account of God's creation of the universe, his creation of Adam and Eve in his own image, his placing them in the idyllic Garden of Eden, and their sin of disobedience against him. Another kind of problem is expressed in the encounter between God and Abraham on the mountain, also taken from Genesis. Should God have tempted Abraham's faith in the way he did? Should Abraham have had such faith? A final moral problem of the most profound significance is found in the Book of Job. The issue concerns the question of divine justice. Although Job accepts God's answer to the question he raises, is it an answer that we should be willing to accept?

The following selections have been taken from the King James Version of the Bible; however, their form has been altered slightly to make them more readable.

Genesis

In the beginning God created the heaven and the earth. And the earth was without form, and void; and darkness was upon the face of the deep. And the Spirit of God moved upon the face of the waters. And God said, "Let there be light": and there was light. And God saw the light, that it was good and God divided the light from the darkness. And God called the light Day, and the darkness he called Night. And the evening and the morning were the first day.

And God said, "Let there be a firmament in the midst of the waters, and let it divide the waters from the waters." And God made the firmament, and divided the waters which were under the firmament from the waters which were above the firmament; and it was so. And God called the firmament Heaven. And the evening and the morning were the second day.

And God said, "Let the waters under the heaven be gathered together unto one place, and let the dry land appear": and it was so. And God called the dry land Earth; and the gathering together of the waters called he Seas; and God saw that it was good. And God said, "Let the earth bring forth grass, the herb yielding seed, and the fruit tree yielding fruit after his kind, whose seed is in itself, upon the earth": and it was so. And the earth brought forth grass, and herb yielding seed after his kind, and the tree yielding fruit, whose seed was in itself, after his kind: and God saw that it was good.

And the evening and the morning were the third day.

And God said, "Let there be lights in the firmament of the heaven to divide the day from the night; and let them be for signs, and for seasons, and for days, and years: and let them be for lights in the firmament of the heaven to give light upon the earth": and it was so. And God made two great lights; the greater light to rule the day, and the lesser light to rule the night: he made the stars also. And God set them in the firmament of the heaven to give light upon the earth. And to rule over the day and over the night, and to divide the light from darkness: and God saw that it was good. And the evening and the morning were the fourth day.

And God said, "Let the waters bring forth abundantly the moving creature that hath life, and fowl that may fly above the earth in the open firmament of heaven." And God created great whales, and every living creature that moveth, which the waters brought forth abundantly, after their kind, and every winged fowl after his kind: and God saw that it was good. And God blessed them, saying, "Be fruitful, and multiply, and fill the water in the seas, and let fowl multiply in the earth." And the evening and the morning were the fifth day.

And God said, "Let the earth bring forth the living creature after his kind, cattle, and creeping thing, and beast of the earth after his kind": and it was so. And God made the beast of the earth after his kind,

Chapters 1, 2, 3, 22:1–13.

and cattle after their kind, and every thing that creepeth upon the earth after his kind: and God saw that it was good.

And God said, "Let us make man in our image, after our likeness: and let them have dominion over the fish of the sea, and over the fowl of the air, and over the cattle, and over all the earth, and over every creeping thing that creepeth upon the earth." So God created man in his own image, in the image of God created he him: male and female created he them. And God blessed them and God said unto them, "Be fruitful, and multiply, and replenish the earth, and subdue it: and have dominion over the fish of the sea, and over the fowl of the air, and over every living thing that moveth upon the earth."

And God said, "Behold, I have given you every herb bearing seed, which is upon the face of all the earth, and every tree, in the which is the fruit of a tree yielding seed; to you it shall be for meat. And to every beast of the earth, and to every fowl of the air, and to every thing that creepeth upon the earth, wherein there is life, I have given every green herb for meat": and it was so. And God saw every thing that he had made, and, behold, it was very good. And the evening and the morning were the sixth day.

Thus the heavens and the earth were finished, and all the host of them. And on the seventh day God ended his work which he had made; and he rested on the seventh day from all his work which he had made. And God blessed the seventh day, and sanctified it: because that in it he had rested from all his work which God created and made.

These are the generations of the heavens and of the earth when they were created, in the day that the LORD God made the earth and the heavens. And every plant of the field before it was in the earth, and every herb of the field before it grew: for the LORD God had not caused it to rain upon the earth, and there was not a man to till the ground. But there went up a mist from the earth, and watered the whole face of the ground. And the LORD God formed man of the dust of the ground, and breathed into his nostrils the breath of life; and man became a living soul.

And the LORD God planted a garden eastward in Eden; and there he put the man whom he had formed. And out of the ground made the LORD God to grow every tree that is pleasant to the sight, and good for food; the tree of life also in the midst of the garden, and the tree of knowledge of good and evil. And a river went out of Eden to water a garden; and from thence it was parted, and became into four heads. The name of the first is Pison: that is it which compasseth the whole land of Havilah, where there is gold; and the gold of that land is good: there is bdellium and the onyx stone. And the name of the second river is Gihon: the same is it that compasseth the whole land of Ethiopia. And the name of the third river is Hiddekel: that is it which goeth toward the east of Assyria. And the fourth river is Euphrates. And the LORD God took the man, and put him into the garden of Eden to dress it and to keep it. And the LORD God commanded the man, saying, "Of every tree of the garden thou mayest freely eat: But of the tree of the knowledge of good and evil, thou shalt not eat of it: for in the day that thou eatest thereof thou shalt surely die."

And the LORD God said, "It is not good that the man should be alone; I will make an help meet for him." And out of the ground the LORD God formed every beast of the field, and every fowl of the air; and brought them unto Adam to see what he would call them: and whatsoever Adam called every living creature, that was the name thereof. And Adam gave names to all cattle, and to the fowl of the air, and to every beast of the field; but for Adam there was not found an help meet for him. And the LORD God caused a deep sleep to fall upon Adam, and he slept: and he took one of his ribs, and closed up the flesh instead thereof. And the rib, which the LORD God had taken from man, made he a woman, and brought her unto the man. And Adam said, "This is now bone of my bones, and flesh of my flesh: she shall be called Woman, because she was taken out of Man. Therefore shall a man leave his father and his mother, and shall cleave unto his wife: and they shall be one flesh." And they were both naked, the man and his wife, and were not ashamed.

Now the serpent was more subtle than any beast of the field which the LORD God had made. And he said unto the woman, "Yea, hath God said, 'Ye shall not eat of every tree of the garden'?" And the woman said unto the serpent, "We may eat of the fruit of the trees of the garden: But of the fruit of the tree which is in the midst of the garden God hath said, 'Ye shall not eat of it, neither shall ye touch it, lest ye die.'" And the serpent said unto the woman, "Ye shall not surely die: For God doth know that in the day ye eat thereof, then your eyes shall be opened, and ye shall be as gods, knowing good and evil." And when the woman saw that the tree was good for food, and that it was pleasant to the eyes, and a tree to be desired to make one wise, she took of the fruit thereof, and did eat, and gave also unto her husband with her and he did eat. And the eyes of them both were opened, and they knew that they were naked; and they sewed fig leaves together, and made themselves aprons.

And they heard the voice of the LORD God walking in the garden in the cool of the day: and Adam and his wife hid themselves from the presence of the LORD God amongst the trees of the garden. And the LORD God called unto Adam, and said unto him, "Where art thou?" And he said, "I heard thy voice in the garden, and I was afraid, because I was naked; and I hid myself." And he said, "Who told thee that thou wast naked? Hast thou eaten of the tree, whereof I commanded thee that thou shouldest not eat?" And the man said, "The woman whom thou gavest to be with me, she gave me of the tree, and I did eat." And the LORD God said unto the woman, "What is this that thou hast done?" And the woman said, "The serpent beguiled me, and I did eat." And the LORD God said unto the serpent, "Because thou hast done this, thou art cursed above all cattle, and above every beast of the field; upon thy belly shalt thou go, and dust shalt thou eat all the days of thy life: And I will put enmity between thee and the woman, and between thy seed and her seed; it shall bruise thy head, and thou shalt bruise his heel." Unto the woman he said, "I will greatly multiply thy sorrow and thy conception; in sorrow thou shalt bring forth children; and thy desire shall be to thy husband, and he shall rule over thee." And unto Adam he said, "Because thou hast harkened unto the voice of thy wife, and hast eaten of the tree, of which I commanded thee, saying 'Thou shalt not eat of it': cursed is the ground for thy sake; in sorrow shalt thou eat of it all the days of thy life; thorns also and thistles shall it bring forth to thee; and thou shalt eat the herb of the field; in the sweat of thy face shalt thou eat bread, till thou return unto the ground; for out of it wast thou taken: for dust thou art and unto dust shalt thou return." And Adam called his wife's name Eve; because she was the mother of all living. Unto Adam also and to his wife did the LORD God make coats of skins, and clothed them.

And the LORD God said, "Behold, the man is become as one of us, to know good and evil: and now, lest he put forth his hand, and take also of the tree of life, and eat, and live for ever": Therefore the LORD God sent him forth from the garden of Eden, to till the ground from whence he was taken. So he drove out the man; and he placed at the east of the garden of Eden Cherubim and a flaming sword which turned every way, to keep the way of the tree of life.

• • •

And it came to pass after these things, that God did tempt Abraham, and said unto him, Abraham; and he said, Behold, here I am. And he said, Take now thy son, thine only son Isaac, whom thou lovest, and get thee into the land of Moriah; and offer him there for a burnt offering upon one of the mountains which I will tell thee of.

And Abraham rose up early in the morning, and saddled his ass, and took two of his young men with him, and Isaac his son, and clave the wood for the burnt offering, and rose up, and went unto the place of which God had told him. Then on the third day Abraham lifted up his eyes, and saw the place afar off. And Abraham said unto his young men, Abide ye here with the ass; and I and the lad will go yonder and worship, and come again to you.

And Abraham took the wood of the burnt offering, and laid it upon Isaac his son; and he took the fire in his hand, and a knife; and they went both of them together. And Isaac spake unto Abraham his father, and said, My father; and he said, Here am I, my son. And he said, Behold the fire and the wood; but where is the lamb for a burnt offering? And Abraham said, My son, God will provide himself a lamb for a burnt offering; so they went both of them together. And they came to a place which God had told him of; and Abraham built an altar there, and laid the wood in order, and bound Isaac his son, and laid him on the altar upon the wood. And Abraham stretched forth his hand, and took the knife to slay his son.

And the angel of the Lord called unto him out of heaven, and said, Abraham, Abraham; and he said, Here am I. And he said, Lay not thine hand upon the lad, neither do thou any thing unto him; for now I know that thou fearest God, seeing thou hast not withheld thy son, thine only son from me. And Abraham lifted up his eyes, and looked, and behold behind him a ram caught in a thicket by his horns; and Abraham went and took the ram, and offered him up for a burnt offering in the stead of his son.

Exodus

In the third month, when the children of Israel were gone forth out of the land of Egypt, the same day came they into the wilderness of Sinai. For they were departed from Rephidim, and were come to the desert of Sinai, and had pitched in the wilderness; and there Israel camped before the mount. And Moses went up unto God, and the LORD called unto him out of the mountain, saying, "Thus shalt thou say to the house of Jacob, and tell the children of Israel; 'Ye have seen what I did unto the Egyptians, and how I bare you on eagles' wings, and brought you unto myself. Now, therefore, if ye will obey my voice indeed, and keep my covenant, then ye shall be a peculiar treasure unto me above all people: for all the earth is mine: And ye be unto me a kingdom of priests, and an holy nation.' These are the words which thou shalt speak unto the children of Israel."

And Moses came and called for the elders of the people, and laid before their faces all these words which the LORD commanded him. And all the people answered together, and said, "All that the LORD hath spoken we will do." And Moses returned the words of the people unto the LORD. And the LORD said unto Moses, "Lo, I come unto thee in a thick cloud, that the people may hear when I speak with thee, and believe thee for ever." And Moses told the words of the people unto the LORD.

And the LORD said unto Moses, "Go unto the people, and sanctify them to day and to morrow, and let them wash their clothes. And be ready against the third day: for the third day the LORD will come down in the sight of all the people upon mount Sinai. And thou shalt set bounds unto the people round about, saying 'Take heed to yourselves, that ye go not up into the mount, or touch the border of it: whoseoever toucheth the mount shall be surely put to death: There shall not an hand touch it, but he shall surely be stoned, or shot through; whether it be beast or man, it shall not live': when the trumpet soundeth long, they shall come up to the mount."

And Moses went down from the mount unto the people, and sanctified the people; and they washed their clothes. And he said unto the people, "Be ready against the third day: come not at your wives."

And it came to pass on the third day in the morning, that there were thunders and lightnings, and a thick cloud upon the mount, and the voice of the trumpet exceeding loud; so that all the people that was in the camp trembled. And Moses brought forth the people out of the camp to meet with God; and they stood at the nether part of the mount. And mount Sinai was altogether on a smoke, because the LORD descended upon it in fire: and the smoke thereof ascended as the smoke of a furnace, and the whole mount quaked greatly. And when the voice of the trumpet sounded long, and waxed louder and louder, Moses spake and God an-

Chapters 19; 20:1 –17; 21:1–25.

swered him by a voice. And the LORD came down upon the mount Sinai, on the top of the mount: and the LORD called Moses up to the top of the mount; and Moses went up. And the LORD said unto Moses, "Go down, charge the people, lest they break through unto the LORD to gaze, and many of them perish. Let the priests also, which come near to the LORD, sanctify themselves, lest the LORD break forth upon them." And Moses said unto the LORD. "The people cannot come up to mount Sinai: for thou chargest us, saying, 'Set bounds about the mount, and sanctify it.' " And the LORD said unto him, "Away, get thee down, and thou shalt come up, thou, and Aaron with thee: but let not the priests and the people break through to come up unto the LORD, lest he break forth upon them." So Moses went down unto the people, and spake unto them.

And God spake all these words, saying, "I am the LORD thy God, which have brought thee out of the land of Egypt, out of the house of bondage. Thou shalt have no other gods before me. Thou shall not make unto thee any graven image, or any likeness of any thing that is in heaven above, or that is in the earth beneath, or that is in the water under the earth. Thou shalt not bow down thyself to them, nor serve them: for I the LORD thy God am a jealous God, visiting the iniquity of the fathers upon the children unto the third and fourth generation of them that hate me: And shewing mercy unto thousands of them that love me, and keep my commandments. Thou shalt not take the name of the LORD thy God in vain; for the LORD will not hold him guiltless that taketh his name in vain. Remember the sab-

bath day, to keep it holy. Six days shalt thou labour, and do all thy work: But the seventh day is the sabbath of the LORD thy God; in it thou shalt not do any work, thou, nor thy son, nor thy daughter, thy manservant, nor thy maidservant, nor thy cattle, nor the stranger that is within thy gates. For in six days the LORD made heaven and earth, the sea, and all that in them is, and rested the seventh day: wherefore the LORD blessed the sabbath day, and hallowed it. Honour thy father and thy mother: that thy days may be long upon the land which the LORD thy God giveth thee. Thou shalt not kill. Thou shalt not commit adultery. Thou shalt not steal. Thou shalt not bear false witness against thy neighbour. Thou shalt not covet thy neighbour's house, thou shalt not covet thy neighbour's wife, nor his manservant, nor his maidservant, nor his ox, nor his ass, nor any thing that is thy neighbour's.

• • •

"Now these are the judgments which thou shalt set before them.

"If thou buy an Hebrew servant, six years he shall serve: and in the seventh he shall go out free for nothing. If he came in by himself, he shall go out by himself: if he were married, then his wife shall go out with him. If his master have given him a wife, and she have borne him sons or daughters; the wife and her children shall be her master's, and he shall go out by himself. And if the servant shall plainly say, 'I love my master, my wife, and my children; I will not go out free': Then his master shall bring him unto the judges; he shall also bring him to the door, or unto the door post; and his master shall bore his ear through with an awl; and he shall serve him for ever.

"And if a man sell his daughter to be a maidservant, she shall not go out as the menservants do. If she please not her master, who hath betrothed her to himself, then shall he let her be redeemed: to sell her unto a strange nation he shall have no power, seeing he hath dealt deceitfully with her. And if he have betrothed her unto his son, he shall deal with her after the manner of daughters. If he take him another wife; her food, her raiment, and her duty of marriage, shall he not diminish. And if he do not these three unto her, then shall she go out free without money.

"He that smiteth a man so that he die, shall be surely put to death. And if a man lie not in wait, but God deliver him into his hand; then I will appoint thee a place whither he shall flee. But if a man come presumptuously upon his neighbour to slay him with guile; thou shalt take him from mine altar, and he may die.

"And he that smiteth his father, or his mother, shall be surely put to death.

"And he that stealeth a man, and selleth him, or if he be found in his hand, he shall surely be put to death.

"And he that curseth his father, or his mother, shall surely be put to death.

"And if men strive together, and one smite another with a stone, or with his fist, and he die not, but keepeth his bed: If he rise again, and walk abroad upon his staff, then shall he that smote him be quit: only he shall pay for the loss of his time, and shall cause him to be thoroughly healed.

"And if a man smite his servant, or his maid, with a rod, and he die under his hand; he shall be surely punished. Notwithstanding, if he continue a day or two, he shall not be punished: for he is his money.

"If men strive, and hurt a woman with child, so that her fruit depart from her, and yet no mischief follow: he shall be surely punished, according as the woman's husband will lay upon him; and he shall pay as the judges determine. And if any mischief follow, then thou shalt give life for life. Eye for eye, tooth for tooth, hand for hand, foot for foot. Burning for burning, wound for wound, stripe for stripe."

The First Book of Kings

And it came to pass after many days, that the word of the LORD came to Elijah in the third year, saying, "Go shew thyself unto Ahab; and I will send rain upon the earth." And Elijah went to shew himself unto Ahab. And there was a sore famine in Samaria. And Ahab called Obadiah, which was the governor of his house. (Now Obadiah feared the LORD greatly: For it was so, when Jezebel cut off the prophets of the LORD, that Obadiah took an hundred prophets, and hid them by fifty in a cave, and fed them with bread and water.) And Ahab said unto Oba-

Chapter 18:1–45.

diah, "Go into the land, unto all fountains of water, and unto all brooks: peradventure we may find grass to save the horses and mules alive, and we lose not all the beasts." So they divided the land between them to pass throughout it: Ahab went one way by himself, and Obadiah went another way by himself.

And as Obadiah was on the way, behold, Elijah met him: and he knew him, and fell on his face, and said, "Art thou that my lord Elijah?" And he answered him, "I am: go, tell thy lord, 'Behold, Elijah is here.'" And he said, "What have I sinned, that thou wouldest deliver thy servant into the hand of Ahab, to slay me? As the LORD thy God liveth, there is no nation or kingdom, whither my lord hath not sent to seek thee: and when they said, 'He is not there'; he took an oath of the kingdom and nation, that they found thee not. And now thou sayest, 'Go, tell thy lord, "Behold, Elijah is here." 'And it shall come to pass, as soon as I am gone from thee, that the spirit of the LORD shall carry thee whither I know not; and so when I come and tell Ahab, and he cannot find thee, he shall slay me: but I thy servant fear the LORD from my youth. Was it not told my lord what I did when Jezebel slew the prophets of the LORD, how I hid an hundred men of the LORD's prophets by fifty in a cave, and fed them with bread and water? And now thou sayest, 'Go, tell thy lord, "Behold, Elijah is here" '; and he shall slay me."

And Elijah said, "As the LORD of hosts liveth, before whom I stand, I will surely shew myself unto him to day." So Obadiah went to meet Ahab, and told him: and Ahab went to meet Elijah.

And it came to pass, when Ahab saw Elijah, that Ahab said unto him, "Art thou he that troubleth Israel?" And he answered, "I have not troubled Israel; but thou, and thy father's house, in that ye have forsaken the commandments of the LORD, and thou hast followed Baalim. Now therefore send, and gather to me all Israel unto mount Carmel, and the prophets of Baal four hundred and fifty, and the prophets of the groves four hundred, which eat at Jezebel's table."

So Ahab sent unto all the children of Israel, and gathered the prophets together unto mount Carmel. And Elijah came unto all the people, and said, "How long halt ye between two opinions? If the LORD be God, follow him: but if Baal, then follow him." And the people answered him not a word. Then said Elijah unto the people, "I, even I only, remain a prophet of the LORD; but Baal's prophets are four hundred and fifty men. Let them therefore give us two bullocks; and let them choose one bullock for themselves, and cut it in pieces, and lay it on wood, and put no fire under: and I will dress the other bullock, and lay it on wood, and put no fire under: And call ye on the name of your gods, and I will call on the name of the LORD: and the God that answereth by fire, let him be God." And all the people answered and said, "It is well spoken."

And Elijah said unto the prophets of Baal, "Choose you one bullock for yourselves, and dress it first; for ye are many; and call on the name of your gods, but put no fire under." And they took the bullock which was given them, and they dressed it, and called on the name of Baal from morning even until noon, saying, "O Baal, hear us." But there was no voice, nor any that answered. And they leaped upon the alter which was made. And it came to pass at noon, that Elijah mocked them, and said, "Cry aloud: for he is a god; either he is talking, or he is pursuing, or he is in a journey, or peradventure he sleepeth, and must be awaked." And they cried aloud, and cut themselves after their manner with knives and lancets, till the blood gushed out upon them. And it came to pass, when midday was past, and they prophesied until the time of the offering of the evening sacrifice, that there was neither voice, nor any to answer, nor any that regarded.

And Elijah said unto all the people, "Come near unto me." And all the people came near unto him. And he repaired the altar of the LORD that was broken down. And Elijah took twelve stones, according to the number of the tribes of the sons of Jacob, unto whom the word of the LORD came, saying, "Israel shall be thy name": And with the stones he built an altar in the name of the LORD: and he made a trench about the altar, as great as would contain two measures of seed. And he put the wood in order, and cut the bullock in pieces, and laid him on the wood, and said, "Fill four barrels with water, and pour it on the burnt sacrifice, and on the wood." And he said, "Do it the second time." And they did it the second time. And he said, "Do it the third time." And they did it the third time. And the water ran round about the altar; and he filled the trench also with water. And it came to pass at the time of the offering of the evening sacrifice, that Elijah the prophet came near, and said, "LORD God of Abraham, Isaac, and of Israel, let it be known this day that thou art God in Israel, and that I am thy servant, and that I have done all these things at thy word. Hear me, O LORD, hear me, that this people may know that thou art the LORD God, and that thou hast turned their heart back again."

Then the fire of the LORD fell, and consumed the burnt sacrifice, and the wood, and the stones, and the dust, and licked up the water that was in the trench. And when all the people saw it, they fell on their faces: and they said, "The LORD, he is the God; the LORD, he is the God." And Elijah said unto them, "Take the prophets of Baal; let not one of them escape." And they took them: and Elijah brought them down to the brook Kishon, and slew them there.

And Elijah said unto Ahab, "Get thee up, eat and drink; for there is a sound of abundance of rain." So Ahab went up to eat and to drink. And Elijah went up to the top of Carmel: and he cast himself down upon the earth, and put his face between his knees. And said to his servant, "Go up now, look toward the sea." And he went up and looked, and said, "There is nothing." And he said, "Go again and seven more times." And it came to pass at the seventh time, that he said, "Behold there ariseth a little cloud, out of the sea, like a man's hand." And he said, "Go up, say unto Ahab, 'Prepare thy chariot, and get thee down, that the rain stop thee not.' " And it came to pass in the mean while, that the heaven was black with clouds and wind, and there was a great rain.

Isaiah

"Yet now hear, O Jacob my servant; and Israel, whom I have chosen: Thus saith the LORD that made thee, and formed thee from the womb, which will help thee; 'Fear not, O Jacob, my servant; and thou, Jesurun, whom I have chosen. For I will pour water upon him that is thirsty, and floods upon the dry ground: I will pour my spirit upon thy seed, and my blessing upon thine offspring: And they shall spring up as among the grass, as willows by the water courses. One shall say, "I am the LORD's"; and another shall call himself by the name of Jacob; and another shall subscribe with his hand unto the LORD, and surname himself by the name of Israel.' Thus saith the LORD the King of Israel, and his redeemer the LORD of hosts; 'I am the first, and I am the last; and beside me there is no God. And who, as I, shall call, and shall declare it, and set it in order to me, since I appointed the ancient people? And the things that are coming, and shall come, let them shew unto them. Fear ye not, neither be afraid: have not I told thee from that time, and have declared it? Ye are even my witnesses. Is there a God beside me? Yea, there is no God; I know not any.

'They that make a graven image are all of them vanity; and their delectable things shall not profit; and they are their own witnesses; they see not, nor know; that they may be ashamed. Who hath formed a god, or molten a graven image that is profitable for nothing? Behold, all his fellows shall be ashamed: and the workmen, they are of men: let them all be gathered together, let them stand up; yet they shall fear, and they shall be ashamed together. The smith with the tongs both worketh in the coals, and fashioneth it with hammers, and worketh it with the strength of his arms: yea, he is hungry, and his strength faileth: he drinketh no water, and is faint. The carpenter stretcheth out his rule; he marketh it out with a line; he fitteth it with planes, and he marketh it out with the compass, and maketh it after the figure of a man, according to the beauty of a man; that it may remain in the house. He heweth him down cedars, and taketh the cypress and the oak, which he strengtheneth for himself among the trees of the forest: he planteth an ash, and the rain doth nourish it. Then shall it be for a man to burn: for he will take thereof, and warm himself; yea, he kindleth it and baketh bread; yea, he maketh a god, and worshippeth it; he make it a graven image, and falleth down thereto. He burneth part thereof in the fire; with part thereof he eateth flesh; he roasteth roast, and is satisfied: yea, he warmeth himself, and saith, "Aha, I am warm, I have seen the fire." And the residue thereof he maketh a god, even his graven image: he falleth down unto it, and worshippeth it, and prayeth unto it, and saith, "Deliver me; for thou art my god." They have not known or understood: for he hath shut their eyes, that they cannot see;

Chapters 44:1–19; 45:5–25

and their hearts, that they cannot understand. And none considereth in his heart, neither is there knowledge nor understanding to say, "I have burned part of it in the fire; yea, also I have baked bread upon the coals thereof; I have roasted flesh, and eaten it: and shall I make the residue thereof an abomination? shall I fall down to the stock of a tree?"

• • •

'I am the LORD, and there is none else, there is no God beside me: I girded thee, though thou hast not known me: That they may know from the rising of the sun, and from the west, that there is none beside me. I am the LORD, and there is none else. I form the light, and create darkness: I make peace, and create evil: I the LORD do all these things. Drop down, ye heavens, from above, and let the skies pour down righteousness: let the earth open, and let them bring forth salvation, and let righteousness spring up together: I the LORD have created it. Woe unto him that striveth with his Maker! Let the potsherd strive with the potsherds of the earth. Shall the clay say to him that fashioneth it, "What makest thou?" or thy work, "He hath no hands?" Woe unto him that saith unto his father, "What begettest thou?" or to the woman, "What hast thou brought forth?"

"Thus saith the LORD, the Holy One of Israel, and his Maker, 'Ask me of things to come concerning my sons, and concerning the work of my hands command ye me. I have made the earth, and created man upon it: I, even my hands, have stretched out the heavens, and all their host have I commanded. I have raised him up in righteousness, and I will direct all his ways: he shall build my city, and he shall let go my captives, not for price

nor reward,' saith the LORD of hosts.

"Thus saith the LORD, 'The labour of Egypt, and merchandise of Ethiopia and of the Sabeans, men of stature, shall come over unto thee, and they shall be thine: they shall come after thee; in chains they shall come over, and they shall fall down unto thee, they shall make supplication unto thee, saying, "Surely God is in thee; and there is none else, there is no God. Verily thou art a God that hidest thyself, O God of Israel, the Saviour." They shall be ashamed, and also confounded, all of them they shall go to confusion together that are makers of idols. But Israel shall be saved in the LORD with an everlasting salvation: ye shall not be ashamed nor confounded world without end.' For thus saith the LORD that created the heavens; God himself that formed the earth and made it; he hath established it, he created it not in vain, he formed it to be inhabited: 'I am the LORD: and there is none else. I have not spoken in secret, in a dark place of the earth: I said not unto the seed of Jacob, "Seek ye me in vain": I the LORD speak righteousness, I declare things that are right.

'Assemble yourselves and come; draw near together, ye that are escaped of the nations: they have no knowledge that set up the wood of their graven image, and pray unto a god that cannot save. Tell ye, and bring them near; yea, let them take counsel together; who hath declared this from ancient time? Who hath told it from that time? Have not I the LORD? And there is no God else beside me; a just God and a Saviour; there is none beside me. Look unto me, and be ye saved, all the ends of the earth: for I am God, and there is none else. I have sworn by myself, the word is gone out of my mouth in righteousness, and shall not return, that unto me every knee shall bow, every tongue shall swear, "Surely," shall one say, "in the LORD have I righteousness and strength": even to him shall men come; and all that are incensed against him shall be ashamed. In the LORD shall all the seed of Israel be justified, and shall glory.'

Ezekiel

The word of the LORD came unto me again, saying, "What mean ye, that ye use this proverb concerning the land of Israel, saying, 'The fathers have eaten sour grapes, and the children's teeth are set on edge'?"

"As I live," saith the LORD God, "ye shall not have occasion any more to use this proverb in Israel. Behold, all souls are mine; as the soul of the father, so also the soul of the son is mine: the soul that sinneth, it shall die. But if a man be just, and do that which is lawful and right, and hath not eaten upon the mountains, neither hath lifted up his eyes to the idols of the house of Israel, neither hath defiled his neighbour's wife, neither hath come near to a menstruous woman, and hath not oppressed any, but hath restored to the debtor his pledge, hath spoiled none by violence, hath given his bread to the hungry, and hath covered the naked with a garment; he that hath not given forth upon usury, neither hath taken any increase, that hath withdrawn his hand from iniquity, hath executed true judgment between man and man, hath walked in my statutes, and hath kept my judgments, to deal truly; he is just, he shall surely live," saith the LORD God.

"If he beget a son that is a robber, a shedder of blood, and that doeth the like to any one of these things, and that doeth not any of those duties, but even hath eaten upon the mountains and defiled his neighbour's wife, hath oppressed the poor and needy, hath spoiled by violence, hath not restored the pledge, and hath lifted up his eyes to the idols, hath committed abomination, hath given forth upon usury, and hath taken increase; shall he then live? He shall not live: he hath done all these abominations; he shall surely die; his blood shall be upon him.

"Now, lo, if he beget a son, that seeth all his father's sins which he hath done, and considereth, and doeth not such like, that hath not eaten upon the mountains, neither hath lifted up his eyes to the idols of the house of Israel, hath not defiled his neighbour's wife, neither hath oppressed any, hath not withholden the pledge, neither hath spoiled by violence, but hath given his bread to the hungry, and hath covered the naked with a garment, that hath taken off his hand from the poor, that hath not received usury nor increase, hath executed my judgments, hath walked in my statutes; he shall not die for the iniquity of his father, he shall surely

Chapter 18:1–22.

live. As for his father, because he cruelly oppressed, spoiled his brother by violence, and did that which is not good among his people, lo, even he shall die in his iniquity.

"Yet ye say, 'Why? doth not the son bear the iniquity of the father?' When the son hath done that which is lawful and right, and hath kept all my statutes, and hath done them, he shall surely live. The soul that sinneth, it shall die. The son shall not bear the iniquity of the father, neither shall the father bear the iniquity of the son: the righteousness of the righteous shall be upon him, and the wickedness of the wicked shall be upon him. But if the wicked will turn from all his sins that he hath committed, and keep all my statutes, and do that which is lawful and right he shall surely live, he shall not die. All his transgressions that he hath committed, they shall not be mentioned unto him: in his righteousness that he hath done he shall live.

The Book of Job

There was a man in the land of Uz, whose name was Job; and that man was perfect and upright, and one that feared God, and eschewed evil. And there were born unto him seven sons and three daughters. His substance also was seven thousand sheep, and three thousand camels, and five hundred yoke of oxen, and five hundred she asses, and a very great household; so that this man was the greatest of all the men of the east. And his sons went and feasted in their houses, every one his day; and sent and called for their three sisters to eat and to drink with them. And it was so, when the days of their feasting were gone about, that Job sent and sanctified them, and rose up early in the morning, and offered burnt offerings according to the number of them all: for Job said, "It may be that my sons have sinned, and cursed God in their hearts." Thus did Job continually.

Now there was a day when the sons of God came to present themselves before the LORD, and Satan came also among them. And the LORD said unto Satan, "Whence comest thou?" Then Satan answered the LORD, and said, "From going to and fro in the earth, and from walking up and down in it." And the LORD said unto Satan, "Hast thou considered my servant Job, that there is none like him in the earth, a perfect and an upright man, one that feareth God, and escheweth evil?" Then Satan answered the LORD, and said, "Doth Job fear God for nought? Hast not thou made an hedge about him, and about his house, and about all that he hath on every side? Thou hast blessed the work of his hands, and his substance is increased in the land. But put forth thine hand now, and touch all that he hath and he will curse thee to thy face." And the LORD said unto Satan, "Behold, all that he hath is in thy power; only upon himself put not forth thine hand." So Satan went forth from the presence of the LORD.

Chapter 1; 2:1–10; 10; 21:7–15; 23:2–12; 38; 40:1–14; 42:1–6, 10–17.

And there was a day when his sons and his daughters were eating and drinking wine in their eldest brother's house. And there came a messenger unto Job, and said, "The oxen are plowing, and the asses feeding beside them: And the Sabeans fell upon them, and took them away; yea, they have slain the servants with the edge of the sword; and I only am escaped alone to tell thee." While he was yet speaking there came also another, and said, "The fire of God is fallen from heaven, and hath burned up the sheep, and the servants, and consumed them; and I only escaped alone to tell thee." While he was yet speaking, there came also another, and said, "The Chaldeans made out three bands, and fell upon the camels, and have carried them away; yea, and slain the servants with the edge of the sword; and I only am escaped alone to tell thee." While he was yet speaking, there came also another, and said, "Thy sons and thy daughters were eating and drinking wine in their eldest brother's house: And, behold, there came a great wind from the wilderness, and smote the four corners of the house, and it fell upon the young men, and they are dead; and I only am escaped alone to tell thee." Then Job arose, and rent his mantle, and shaved his head, and fell down upon the ground, and worshipped. And said, "Naked came I out of my mother's womb, and naked shall I return thither: the LORD gave, and the LORD hath taken away; blessed be the name of the LORD." In all this Job sinned not, nor charged God foolishly.

Again there was a day when the sons of God came to present themselves before the LORD, and Satan came also among them to present himself before the LORD. And the LORD said unto Satan, "From whence comest thou?" And Satan answered the LORD, and said, "From going to and fro in the earth, and from walking up and down in it." And the LORD said unto Satan, "Hath thou considered my servant Job, that there is none like him in the earth, a perfect and an upright man, one that feareth God, and escheweth evil? And still he holdeth fast his integrity, although thou movedst me against him, to destroy him without cause." And Satan answered the LORD, and said, "Skin for skin, yea, all that a man hath will he give for his life. But put forth thine hand now, and touch his bone and his flesh, and he will curse thee to thy face." And the LORD said unto Satan, "Behold, he is in thine hand; but save his life."

So went Satan forth from the presence of the LORD, and smote Job with sore boils from the sole of his foot unto his crown. And he took him a potsherd to scrape himself withal; and he sat down among the ashes.

Then said his wife unto him, "Dost thou still retain thine integrity? Curse God, and die." But he said unto her. "Thou speakest as one of the foolish women speaketh. What? shall we receive good at the hand of God, and shall we not receive evil?" In all this did not Job sin with his lips.

• • •

[*And Job spake, and said*] "My soul is weary of my life; I will leave my complaint upon myself; I will speak in the bitterness of my soul, I will say unto God, 'Do not condemn me; shew me wherefore thou contendest with me. Is it good unto thee that thou shouldest oppress, that thou shouldest despise the work of thine hands, and shine upon the counsel of the wicked? Hast thou eyes of flesh? or seest thou as man seeth? Are thy days as the days of man? Are thy years as man's days, that thou enquirest after mine iniquity, and searchest after my sin? Thou knowest that I am not wicked; and there is none that can deliver out of thine hand. Thine hands have made me and fashioned me together round about; yet thou dost destroy me. Remember, I beseech thee, that thou hast made me as the clay; and wilt thou bring me into dust again? Hast thou not poured me out as milk, and curdled me like cheese? Thou hast clothed me with skin and flesh, and hast fenced me with bones and sinews. Thou hast granted me life and favour, and thy visitation hath preserved my spirit. And these things hast thou hid in thine heart; I know that this is with thee.

'If I sin, then thou markest me, and thou wilt not acquit me from mine iniquity. If I be wicked, woe unto me; and if I be righteous, yet will I not lift up my head. I am full of confusion; therefore see thou mine affliction; for it increaseth. Thou huntest me as a fierce lion: and again thou shewest thyself marvellous upon me. Thou renewest thy witnesses against me, and increasest thine indignation upon me; changes and war are against me. Wherefore then hast thou brought me forth out of the womb? Oh that I had given up the ghost, and no eye had seen me! I should have been as though I had not been; I should have been carried from the womb to the grave. Are not my days few? Cease then, and let me alone, that I may take comfort a little, before I go whence I shall not return, even to the land of darkness and the shadow of death; a land of darkness, as darkness itself; and of the shadow of death, without any order, and where the light is as darkness.'

• • •

"Wherefore do the wicked live, become old, yea, are mighty in power? Their seed is established in their sight with them, and their offspring before their eyes. Their houses are safe from fear, neither is the rod of God upon them. Their bull gendereth, and faileth not; their cow calveth, and casteth not her calf. They send forth their little ones like a flock, and their children dance. They take the timbrel and harp, and rejoice at the sound of the organ. They spend their days in wealth, and in a moment go down to the grave. Therefore they say unto God, 'Depart from us; for we desire not the knowledge of thy ways. What is the Almighty, that we should serve him? And what profit should we have, if we pray unto him?'

• • •

"Even to day is my complaint bitter: my stroke is heavier than my groaning. Oh that I knew where I might find him! that I might come even unto his seat! I would order my cause before him, and fill my mouth with arguments. I would know the words which he would answer me, and understand what he would say unto me. Will he plead against me with his great power? No, but he would put strength in me. There the righteous might dispute with him; so should I be delivered for ever from my judge. Behold, I go forward, but he is not there; and backward, but I cannot perceive him: On the left hand, where he doth work, but I cannot behold him: he hideth himself on the right hand, that I cannot see him. But he knoweth the way that I take: when he hath tried me, I shall come forth as gold. My foot hath held his steps, his way have I kept, and not declined. Neither have I gone back from the commandment of his lips; I have esteemed the words of his mouth more than my necessary food."

• • •

Then the LORD answered Job out of the whirlwind, and said "Who is this that darkeneth counsel by words without knowledge? Gird up now thy loins like a man; for I will demand of thee, and answer thou me. Where wast thou when I laid the foundations of the earth? Declare, if thou hast understanding. Who hath laid the measures thereof, if thou knowest? Or who hath stretched the line upon it? Whereupon are the foundations thereof fastened? Or who laid the corner stone thereof; when the morning stars sang together, and all the sons of God shouted for joy? Or who shut up the sea with doors, when it brake forth, as if it had issued out of the womb? When I made the cloud the garment thereof, and thick darkness a swaddling band for it, and brake up for it my decreed place, and set bars and doors, and said, 'Hitherto shalt thou come, but no further: and here shall thy proud waves be stayed'? Hast thou commanded the morning since thy days; and caused the dayspring to know his place; that it might take hold of the end of the earth, that the wicked might be shaken out of it? It is turned as clay to the seal; and they stand as a garment. And from the wicked their light is withholden, and the high arm shall be broken. Hast thou entered into the springs of the sea? Or hast thou walked in the search of the depth? Have the gates of death been opened unto thee? Or hast thou seen the doors of the shadow of death? Hast thou perceived the breadth of the earth? Declare if thou knowest it all.

"Where is the way where light dwelleth? And as for darkness, where is the place thereof, that thou shouldest take it to the bound thereof, and that thou shouldest know the paths to the house thereof? Knowest thou it, because thou wast then born? Or because the number of thy days is great? Hast thou entered into the treasures of the snow? Or hast thou seen the treasures of the hail, which I have reserved against the time of trouble, against the day of battle and war? By what way is the light parted, which scattereth the east wind upon the earth? Who hath divided a watercourse for the overflowing of waters, or a way for the lightning or thunder; to cause it to rain on the earth, where no man is; on the Wilderness, wherein there is no man; to satisfy the desolate and waste ground; and to cause the bud of the tender herb to spring forth? Hath the rain a father? Or who hath begotten the drops of dew? Out of whose womb came the ice? And the hoary frost of heaven, who hath gendered it? The waters are hid as with a stone, and the face of the deep is frozen.

"Canst thou bind the sweet influences of Pleiades, or loose the bonds of Orion? Canst thou bring forth Massaroth in his season? Or canst thou guide Arcturus with his sons? Knowest thou the ordinances of heaven? Canst thou set the dominion thereof in the earth? Canst thou lift up thy voice to the clouds, that abundance of waters may cover thee? Canst thou send lightnings that they may go, and say unto thee, 'Here we are'? Who hath put wisdom in the inward parts? Or who hath given understanding to the heart? Who can number the clouds in wisdom? Or who can stay the bottles of heaven, when the dust groweth into hardness, and the clods cleave fast together? Wilt thou hunt the prey for the lion? Or fill the appetite of the young lions, when they couch in their dens, and abide in the covert to lie in wait? Who provideth for the raven his food? When his young ones cry unto God, they wander for lack of meat."

• • •

Moreover, the LORD answered Job, and said, "Shall he that contendeth with the Almighty instruct him? He that reproveth God, let him answer it."

Then Job answered the LORD, and said, "Behold, I am vile; what shall I answer thee? I will lay mine hand upon my mouth. Once have I spoken; but I will not answer: yea, twice, but I will proceed no further."

Then answered the LORD unto Job out of the whirlwind, and said, "Gird up thy loins now like a man: I will demand of thee, and declare thou unto me. Wilt thou also disannul my judgment? Wilt thou condemn me, that thou mayest be righteous? Hast thou an arm like God? Or canst thou thunder with a voice like him? Deck thyself now with majesty and excellency; and array thyself with glory and beauty. Cast abroad the rage of thy wrath: and behold every one that is proud, and abase him. Look on every one that is proud, and bring him low; and tread down the wicked in their place. Hide them in the dust together; and bind their faces in secret. Then will I also confess unto thee that thine own right hand can save thee."

• • •

Then Job answered the LORD, and said, "I know that thou canst do every thing, and that no thought can be witholden from thee. Who is he that hideth counsel without knowledge? Therefore have I uttered that I understood not; things too wonderful for me, which I knew not. Hear, I beseech thee, and I will speak: I will demand of thee, and declare thou unto me. I have heard of thee by the hearing of the ear: but now mine eye seeth thee. Wherefore I abhor myself, and repent in dust and ashes."

• • •

And the LORD turned the captivity of Job, when he prayed for his friends: also the LORD gave Job twice as much as he had before. Then came there unto him all his brethren, and all his sisters, and all they that had been of his acquaintance before, and did eat bread with him in his house: and they bemoaned him, and comforted him over all the evil that the LORD had brought upon him: every man also gave him a piece of money, and every one an earring of gold. So the LORD blessed the latter end of Job more than his beginning: for he had fourteen thousand sheep, and six thousand camels, and a thousand yoke of oxen, and a thousand she asses. He had also seven sons and three daughters. And he called the name of the first, Jemima; and the name of the second, Kezia; and the name of the third, Kerenhappuch. And in all the land were no women found so fair as the daughters of Job: and their father gave them inheritance among their brethren. After this lived Job an hundred and forty years, and saw his sons, and his son's sons, even four generations. So Job died, being old and full of days.

Rig Veda

Most religions, whether they have their origin in the Far East, the Middle East, or in the Western Hemisphere, contain creation "myths." The term, "myth," however, can be misleading. It should not be taken to imply that these accounts are simply "fairy stories," lacking any kind of rational foundation. On the contrary, they represent the attempts made by their originators to give answers to some of the most profound questions that we can ask, such as, How did the universe come into being? and How and when were human beings created? Such questions are still pertinent today; even though science has made great strides in providing explanations of them, the answers to the most fundamental of them still remain shrouded in mystery.

This book contains a number of creation myths, taken from various cultures throughout the world. Most of them are quite detailed and elaborate. An exception is the short poem that follows. It is taken from the *Rig Veda*, a large collection of religious poems sacred to the early period of Indian Hinduism. Because the poem was handed down by oral tradition long before being written, the time of its original composition is not known. However, it is believed to date from around 1000 to 900 B.C. The poem has been included in this book for a special reason. Although it offers what is a variation on a standard theme of creation myths, even in its short length it contains lines that set it apart from all of the others, giving it a level of intellectual sophistication that is impressive by any standards.

Song of Creation

• • •

Then there was neither being nor
   not-being.
The atmosphere was not, nor sky above
   it.

What covered all? and where? by what
   protected?
Was there the fathomless abyss of
   waters?

Trans. A. Kaegi and R. Arrowsmith. Hymn X:129. The title has been added.

Then neither death nor deathlessness
    existed;
Of day and night there was yet no dis-
    tinction.
Alone that One breathed calmly, self-
    supported,
Other than It was none, nor aught above
    It.

Darkness there was at first in darkness
    hidden;
This universe was undistinguished water.
That which in void and emptiness lay
    hidden
Alone by power of fervor was developed.

Then for the first time there arose de-
    sire,
Which was the primal germ of mind,
    within it.
And sages, searching in their heart, dis-
    covered
In Nothing the connecting bond of Be-
    ing.

And straight across their cord was then
    extended:
What then was there above? or what be-
    neath it?
Life giving principles and powers ex-
    isted;
Below the origin,— the striving upward.

Who is it knows? Who here can tell us
    surely
From what and how this universe has
    risen?
And whether not till after it the gods
    lived?
Who then can know from what it has
    arisen?

The source from which this universe has
    risen
And whether it was made, or uncreated,
He only knows, who from the highest
    heaven
Rules, the all-seeing lord.—or does not
    He know?

The Hindu Caste System

The differences between systems of social classes, which are necessary components of all complex societies, and a caste system, as a feature of Indian civilization, are a matter of degree, but the degree is great. Four characteristics distinguish the Indian caste system. First, it has the sanction of divine law; second, the castes are sharply separated from each other and movement from one to another is extremely difficult; third, the castes are hierarchically organized, with a social abyss separating the highest from the lowest; and, fourth, castes are hereditary—one is born into the caste in which he must spend his life.

The beginnings of the caste system are shrouded in the remote past, but it seems to have developed following the Aryan invasion of India in the second millennium B.C. Although references to it can be found in much early literature, its formal elaboration appears in *The Laws of Manu*, a large compendium of Hindu regulations from which the following selection is taken. These laws were, according to Hindu doctrine, established by the demigod Manu, himself a manifestation of Brahma, so represent divine commands. They divide society into four castes—the priests and scholars (Brahmanas), the nobles and warriors (Kshatriyas), the merchants and farmers (Vaisyas), and the common laborers and servants (Sudras). Although the Brahmanas (who wrote the laws that separated society into castes) were preeminent in prestige and honor, all of the first three castes shared the attribute of being "twice-born." Besides their original human first birth, they experienced a "second birth" consisting of their initiation into the mysteries of the Hindu religion. The Sudras were excluded from the "second birth" so could aspire to no higher rank than that of servants to the privileged castes. It should be added that the castes as here described offer an idealized oversimplification of the system, as it has actually existed in India. In fact, there are literally thousands of subcastes, based on such things as different occupations, area of the country, and so on.

Hindus found a religio-moral justification for the caste system. According to the divine law of Karma, an individual in each of his reincarnations is born into a rank and level of society that results from the quality of the life he had lived in his previous incarnation. Thus a member of the Sudra caste has earned that status; his position as a servant is just what he deserves. Furthermore, any attempt to change one's status or to modify the caste system itself would be immoral, as well as a breach of divine law.

Two further points should be added. Closely associated with the caste system is a set of regulations governing marriage, the status of women, and family relationships in general. Also, it should be mentioned that a substantial portion of the population of India does not fit into any of the four castes. These are the outcasts or "untouchables" who rank far below the Sudras—indeed, are often treated with less respect than animals. These are people literally "beyond the pale."

In the selection that follows from *The Laws of Manu* an attempt has been made to offer some insight into the extraordinary complexities of the caste system. To do this illustrative "laws" have been chosen and reorganized from the original to enhance their coherence; also section headings have been added.

The Laws of Manu

MANU THE LAWGIVER

The great sages approached Manu,* who was seated with a collected mind, and, having duly worshipped him, spoke as follows:

"Deign, divine one, to declare to us precisely and in due order the sacred laws of each of the four chief castes and of the intermediate ones.

"For thou, O Lord, alone knowest the purport, the rites, and the knowledge of the soul, taught in this whole ordinance of the Self-existent, which is unknowable and unfathomable."

He, whose power is measureless, being thus asked by the high-minded

---

*Manu in Hindu mythology is a being who is both divine and human.

great sages, duly honored them, and answered, "Listen!"

THE FOUR CASTES

For the sake of the prosperity of the worlds, he caused the Brahmana, the Kshatriya, the Vaisya, and the Sudra to proceed from his mouth, his arms, his thighs, and his feet.

The Brahmana, the Kshatriya, and the Vaisya castes are the twice-born ones, but the fourth, the Sudra, has one birth only; there is no fifth caste.

To Brahmanas he assigned teaching and studying the Veda, sacrificing for their own benefit and for others, giving and accepting of alms. The Kshatriya he commanded to protect the people, to bestow gifts, to

Trans. G. Bühler. Some minor modifications have been made in the text.

offer sacrifices, to study the Veda, and to abstain from attaching himself to sensual pleasures; the Vaisya to tend cattle, to bestow gifts, to offer sacrifices, to study the Veda, to trade, to lend money, and to cultivate land. One occupation only the lord prescribed to the Sudra, to serve meekly even these other three castes.

The seniority of Brahmanas is from sacred knowledge, that of Kshatriyas from valor, that of Vaisyas from wealth in grain and other goods, but that of Sudras from age alone.

A twice-born man who knowingly eats mushrooms, a village pig, garlic, a village cock, onions or leeks, will become an outcast.

Some wealthy Brahmana shall compassionately support both a Kshatriya and a Vaisya if they are distressed for a livelihood, employing them on work which is suitable for their castes. But a Brahmana who, because he is powerful, out of greed makes initiated men of the twice-born castes against their will do the work of slaves shall be fined by the king. But a Sudra, whether bought or unbought, he may compel to do servile work; for he was created by the Self-existent to be the slave of a Brahmana. A Sudra, though emancipated by his master, is not released from servitude; since that is innate in him, who can set him free from it?

With whatever limb a man of a low caste does hurt to a man of the three highest castes, even that limb shall be cut off; that is the teaching of Manu. He who raises his hand or a stick shall have his hand cut off; he who in anger kicks with his foot shall have his foot cut off.

A low-caste man who tries to place himself on the same seat with a man of a high caste shall be branded on his hip and be banished, or the king shall cause his buttock to be gashed. If out of arrogance he spits on a superior the king shall cause both his lips to be cut off; if he urines on him, the penis; if he breaks wind against him, the anus.

A man of low caste who through covetousness lives by the occupations of a higher one the king shall deprive of his property and banish.

Abstention from injuring creatures, veracity, abstention from unlawfully appropriating the goods of others, purity, and control of the organs, Manu has declared to be the summary of the law for the four castes.

THE BRAHMANA

Of created beings the most excellent are said to be those which are animated; of the animated, those which subsist by intelligence; of the intelligent, mankind; and of men, the Brahmanas. Of Brahmanas, those learned in the Veda; of the learned, those who recognize the necessity and the manner of performing the prescribed duties; of those who possess this knowledge, those who perform them; of the performers, those who know the Brahman.

The very birth of a Brahmana is an eternal incarnation of the sacred law; for he is born to fulfil the sacred law, and becomes one with Brahman. A Brahmana, coming into existence, is born as the highest on earth, the lord of all created beings, for the protection of the treasury of the law.

Whatever exists in the world is the property of the Brahmana; on account of the excellence of his origin the Brahmana is, indeed, entitled to it all. The Brahmana eats but his own food, wears but his own apparel, bestows but his own in alms; other mortals subsist through the benevolence of the Brahmana.

In order to clearly settle his duties and those of the other castes according to their order wise Manu, sprung from the Self-existent, composed these Institutes of the sacred law. A learned Brahmana must carefully study them and he must duly instruct his pupils in them, but nobody else shall do it. A Brahmana who studies these Institutes and faithfully fulfils the duties prescribed therein is never tainted by sins, arising from thoughts, words, or deeds. He sanctifies any company which he may enter, seven ancestors and seven descendents, and he alone deserves to possess this whole earth.

To study this work is the best means of securing welfare; it increases understanding, it procures fame and long life, it leads to supreme bliss. In this work the sacred law has been fully stated as well as the good and bad qualities of human actions and the immemorial rule of conduct to be followed by all the four castes. The rule of conduct is transcendent law, whether it be taught in the revealed texts or in the sacred tradition; hence a twice-born man who possesses regard for himself should be always careful to follow it. A Brahmana who departs from the rule of conduct does not reap the fruit of the Veda, but he who duly follows it will obtain the full reward.

Man is stated to be purer above the navel than below; hence the Self-existent has declared the purest part of him to be his mouth. As the Brahmana sprang from Brahman's mouth, as he was the first-born, and as he possesses the Veda, he is by right the lord of this whole creation.

A Brahmana must seek a means of subsistence which either causes no, or at least little pain to others and live by that except in times of distress. For the purpose of gaining bare subsistence let him accumulate property by following those irreproachable occupations which are prescribed for his caste, without unduly fatiguing his body. He may either possess enough to fill a granary, or a store filling a grain-jar; or he may collect what suffices for three days, or make no provision for the morrow. Let him never, for the sake of subsistence, follow the ways of the world; let him live the pure, straightforward, honest life of a Brahmana.

A Brahmana who knows the law need not bring any offence to the notice of the king; by his own power alone he can punish those men who injure him. His own power is greater than the power of the king; the Brahmana, therefore, may punish his foes by his own power alone.

A Brahmana shall never beg from a Sudra property for a sacrifice; for a sacrificer, having begged it from such a man, after death is born again as a Kandala ["the lowest of men"].

Let him not entertain at a Sraddha [sacrificial meal] one who wears his hair in braids (a student), one who has not studied the Veda, one afflicted with a skin disease, a gambler, nor those who sacrifice for a multitude of others.

Physicians, temple-priests, sellers of meat, and those who subsist by shop-keeping must be avoided at sacrifices offered to the gods and to the manes [spirits]; a paid servant of a village or of a king, a man with deformed nails or black teeth, one who opposes his teacher, one who has forsaken the sacred fire, and a usurer; one suffering from consumption, one who subsists by tending cattle, a younger brother who marries or kindles the sacred fire before the elder, one who neglects the five great sacrifices, an enemy of the Brahmana race, an elder brother who marries or kindles the sacred fire after the younger, and one who belongs to a company or corporation; an actor or singer, one who has broken the vows of studentship, one whose only or first wife is a Sudra female, the son of a remarried woman, a one-eyed man, and he in whose house a paramour of his wife resides; he who teaches for a stipulated fee and he who is taught on that condition, he who instructs Sudra pupils and he whose teacher is a Sudra, he who speaks rudely, the son of an adulteress, and the son of a widow; he who forsakes his mother, his father, or a teacher without a sufficient reason, he who has contracted an alliance with outcasts either through the Veda or through a marriage; an incendiary, a prisoner, he who eats the food given by the son of an adulteress, a seller of Soma, he who undertakes voyages by sea, a bard, an oil-man, a suborner to perjury; he who wrangles or goes to law with his father, the keeper of a gambling-house, a drunkard, he who is afflicted with a disease in punishment of former crimes, he who is accused of a mortal sin, a hypocrite, a seller of substances used for flavoring food; a maker of bows and of arrows, he who lasciviously dallies with a brother's widow, the betrayer of a friend, one who subsists by gambling, he who learns the Veda from his son; an epileptic man, one who suffers from scrofulous swellings of the glands, one afflicted with white leprosy, an informer, a madman, a blind man, and he who cavils at the Veda must all be avoided.

A trainer of elephants, oxen, horses, or camels, he who subsists by astrology, a bird-fancier, and he who teaches the use of arms; he who diverts water-courses, and he who delights in obstructing them, an architect, a messenger, and he who plants trees for money; a breeder of sporting-dogs, a falconer, one who defiles maidens, he who delights in injuring living creatures, he who gains his subsistence from Sudras, and he who offers sacrifices to the Ganas; he who does not follow the rule of conduct, a man destitute of energy like a eunuch, one who constantly asks for favors, he who lives by agriculture, a club-footed man, and he who is censured by virtuous men; a shepherd, a keeper of buffaloes, the husband of a remarried woman, and a carrier of dead bodies, all these must be carefully avoided.

A Brahmana who knows the sacred law should shun at sacrifices both to the gods and to the manes these lowest of twice-born men, whose conduct is reprehensible, and who are unworthy to sit in the company at a repast.

Let the king, after rising early in the morning, worship Brahmanas who are well versed in the threefold sacred science and learned in polity, and follow their advice. Let him daily worship aged Brahmanas who know the Veda and are pure. Let him honor those Brahmanas who have returned from their teacher's house after studying the Veda; for that money which is given to Brahmanas is declared to be an imperishable treasure for kings. Not to turn back in battle, to protect the people, to honor the Brahmanas, is the best means for a king to secure happiness.

The slayer of a Brahmana enters

the womb of a dog, a pig, an ass, a camel, a cow, a goat, a sheep, a deer, a bird, a Kandala, and a Pukkasa.

THE KSHATRIYA

Kings and Kshatriyas, the domestic priests of kings, and those who delight in the warfare of disputations constitute the middling rank of the states caused by Activity.

As the Earth supports all created beings equally, thus a king who supports all his subjects takes upon himself the office of the Earth. Employing these and other means, the king shall, ever untired, restrain thieves both in his own dominions and in those of others.

Let him not, though fallen into the deepest distress, provoke Brahmanas to anger for they, when angered, could instantly destroy him together with his army and his vehicles. Who could escape destruction, when he provokes to anger those men by whom the fire was made to consume all things, by whom the water of the ocean was made undrinkable, and by whom the moon was made to wane and to increase again? Who could prosper, while he injures those men who, provoked to anger, could create other worlds and other guardians of the world, and deprive the gods of their divine station? What man, desirous of life, would injure them to whose support the three worlds and the gods ever owe their existence, and whose wealth is the Veda?

A Brahmana, be he ignorant or learned, is a great divinity, just as the fire, whether carried forth for the performance of a burnt-oblation or not carried forth, is a great divinity. The brilliant fire is not contaminated even in burial-places, and when presented with oblations of butter at sacrifices, it again increases mightily. Thus, though Brahmanas employ themselves in all sorts of mean occupations, they must be honored in every way for each of them is a very great deity.

When the Kshatriyas become in any way overbearing towards the Brahmanas, the Brahmanas themselves shall duly restrain them, for the Kshatriyas sprang from the Brahmanas. Fire sprang from water, Kshatriyas from Brahmanas, iron from stone; the all-penetrating force of those three has no effect on that whence they were produced. Kshatriyas prosper not without Brahmanas, Brahmanas prosper not without Kshatriyas. Brahmanas and Kshatriyas, being closely united, prosper in this world and in the next. But a king who feels his end drawing nigh shall bestow all his wealth accumulated from fines on Brahmanas, make over his kingdom to his son, and then seek death in battle.

Know that a Brahmana of ten years and a Kshatriya of a hundred years stand to each other in the relation of father and son; but between those two the Brahmana is the father.

THE VAISYA

Know that the following rules apply in due order to the duties of Vaisyas:

After a Vaisya has received the sacraments and has taken a wife, he shall be always attentive to the business whereby he may subsist and to that of tending cattle. For when the Lord of creatures created cattle he made them over to the Vaisya; to the Brahmana and to the king he entrusted all created beings. A Vaisya must never conceive this wish, "I will not keep cattle," and if a Vaisya is willing to keep them they must never be kept by men of other castes.

A Vaisya must know the respective value of gems, of pearls, of coral, of metals, of cloth made of thread, of perfumes, and of condiments. He must be acquainted with the manner of sowing of seeds and of the good and bad qualities of fields and he must perfectly know all measures and weights; moreover, the excellence and defects of commodities, the advantages and disadvantages of different countries, the probable profit and loss on merchandise, and the means of properly rearing cattle.

He must be acquainted with the proper wages of servants, with the various languages of men, with the manner of keeping goods, and the rules of purchase and sale. Let him exert himself to the utmost in order to increase his property in a righteous manner, and let him zealously give food to all created beings.

The king should order a Vaisya to trade, to lend money, to cultivate the land, or to tend cattle.

There are seven lawful modes of acquiring property: Inheritance, finding or friendly donation, purchase, conquest, lending at interest, the performance of work, and the acceptance of gifts from virtuous men.

Learning, mechanical arts, work for wages, service, rearing cattle, traffic, agriculture, contentment with little, alms, and receiving interest on money are the ten modes of subsistence permitted to all men in times of distress. Neither a Brahmana nor a Kshatriya must lend money at interest but at his pleasure either of them may, in times of distress when he requires money for sacred purposes,

lend to a very sinful man at a small interest.

A king (Kshatriya) who, in times of distress, takes even the fourth part of the crops is free from guilt, if he protects his subjects to the best of his ability. His peculiar duty is conquest and he must not turn back in danger; having protected the Vaisyas by his weapons, he may cause the legal tax to be collected—from the Vaisyas one-eighth as the tax on grain, one-twentieth on the profits on gold and cattle.

THE SUDRA

That kingdom where Sudras are very numerous, which is infested by atheists and destitute of twice-born inhabitants, soon entirely perishes, afflicted by famine and disease.

A Brahmana may confidently seize the goods of his Sudra for, as that slave can have no property, his master may take his possessions.

A Brahmana who takes a Sudra wife to his bed will after death sink into hell; if he begets a child of her he will lose the rank of a Brahmana. The son whom a Brahmana begets through lust on a Sudra female is, though alive, a corpse and hence called a living corpse.

A Sudra who has intercourse with a woman of a twice-born caste, guarded or unguarded, shall be punished in the following manner: If she was unguarded he loses the offending part and all his property; if she was guarded, everything, even his life.

The foolish man who, after having eaten a dinner, gives the leavings to a Sudra falls headlong into hell.

A Sudra who is pure, the servant of his betters, gentle in his speech, and free from pride, and always seeks refuge with Brahmanas attains in his next life a higher caste.

THE DASYUS

All those tribes in this world which are excluded from the community of those born from the mouth, the arms, the thighs, and the feet of Brahman are called Dasyus, whether they speak the language of the barbarians or that of the Aryans.

The dwellings of Kandalas and Svapakas [low-order Dasyus] shall be outside the village and their wealth shall be dogs and donkeys. Their dress shall be the garments of the dead, they shall eat their food from broken dishes, black iron shall be their ornaments, and they must always wander from place to place.

A man who fulfils a religious duty shall not seek intercourse with them; their transactions shall be among themselves and their marriages with their equals.

Their food shall be given to them by others than an Aryan giver in a broken dish; at night they shall not walk about in villages and in towns. By day they may go about for the purpose of their work, distinguished by marks at the king's command, and they shall carry out the corpses of persons who have no relatives; that is a settled rule.

By the king's order they shall always execute the criminals, in accordance with the law, and they shall take for themselves the clothes, the beds, and the ornaments of such criminals.

A Kandala, a village pig, a cock, a dog, a menstruating woman, and a eunuch must not look at the Brahmanas while they eat.

Let a Brahmana gently place on the ground some food for dogs, outcasts, Kandalas, those afflicted with diseases that are punishments of former sins, crows, and insects.

MARRIAGE AND FAMILY

A twice-born man shall marry a wife of equal caste who is endowed with auspicious bodily marks. A damsel who is neither a Sapinda on the mother's side, nor belongs to the same family on the father's side, is recommended to twice-born men for wedlock and conjugal union. In connecting himself with a wife, let him carefully avoid the ten following families, be they ever so great or rich in kine, horses, sheep, grain, or other property: One which neglects the sacred rites, one in which no male children are born, one in which the Veda is not studied, one the members of which have thick hair on the body, those which are subject to hemorrhoids, phthisis, weakness of digestion, epilepsy, or white and black leprosy.

Let him not marry a maiden with reddish hair, nor one who has a redundant member, nor one who is sickly, nor one either with no hair on the body or too much, nor one who is garrulous or has red eyes, nor one named after a constellation, a tree, or a river, nor one bearing the name of a low caste, or of a mountain, nor one named after a bird, a snake, or a slave, nor one whose name inspires terror. Let him wed a female free from bodily defects, who has an agreeable name, the graceful gait of a Hamsa or of an elephant, a moderate quantity of hair on the body and on the head, small teeth, and soft limbs.

A man aged thirty years shall marry a maiden of twelve who pleases him or a man of twenty-four a girl eight years of age; if the performance of his duties would otherwise be impeded he must marry sooner.

The husband receives his wife from the gods, he does not wed her according to his own will; doing what is agreeable to the gods he must always support her while she is faithful.

He only is a perfect man who consists of three persons united—his wife, himself, and his offspring; thus says the Veda and learned Brahmanas propound this maxim likewise, "The husband is declared to be one with the wife."

Women must be honored and adorned by their fathers, brothers, husbands, and brothers-in-law, who desire their own welfare. Where women are honored there the gods are pleased but where they are not honored no sacred rite yields rewards. Where the female relations live in grief the family soon wholly perishes but that family where they are not unhappy ever prospers. The houses on which female relations, not being duly honored, pronounce a curse perish completely, as if destroyed by magic. Hence men who seek their own welfare should always honor women on holidays and festivals with gifts of ornaments, clothes, and dainty food.

"Let mutual fidelity continue until death"—this may be considered as the summary of the highest law for husband and wife.

A virtuous wife who after the death of her husband constantly remains chaste reaches heaven, though she have no son, just like those chaste men. But a woman who from a desire to have offspring violates her duty towards her deceased husband brings on herself disgrace in this world and loses her place with her husband in heaven.

Offspring begotten by another man is here not considered lawful nor does offspring begotten on another man's wife belong to the be-getter nor is a second husband anywhere prescribed for virtuous women.

She who cohabits with a man of higher caste, forsaking her own husband who belongs to a lower one, will become contemptible in this world, and is called a remarried woman. By violating her duty towards her husband a wife is disgraced in this world; after death she enters the womb of a jackal and is tormented by diseases, the punishment of her sin.

She who, controlling her thoughts, words, and deeds, never slights her lord resides after death with her husband in heaven and is called a virtuous wife. In reward of such conduct a female who controls her thoughts, speech, and actions gains in this life highest renown and in the next world a place near her husband.

Between wives who are destined to bear children, who are worthy of worship and irradiate their dwellings, and between the goddesses of fortune who reside in the houses of men there is no difference whatsoever.

The production of children, the nurture of those born, and the daily life of men, of these matters woman is visibly the cause. Offspring, the due performance of religious rites, faithful service, highest conjugal happiness and heavenly bliss for the ancestors and oneself depend on one's wife alone.

Though destitute of virtue, or seeking pleasure elsewhere, or devoid of good qualities, yet a husband must be constantly worshipped as a god by a faithful wife. No sacrifice, no vow, no fast must be performed by women apart from their husbands; if a wife obeys her husband she will for that reason alone be exalted in heaven.

A faithful wife who desires to dwell after death with her husband must never do anything that might displease him who took her hand, whether he be alive or dead. At her pleasure let her emaciate her body by living on pure flowers, roots, and fruit but she must never even mention the name of another man after her husband has died.

When the purpose of the appointment to cohabit with the widow has been attained in accordance with the law those two shall behave towards each other like a father and a daughter-in-law. If those two being thus appointed deviate from the rule and act from carnal desire they will both become outcasts, as men who defile the bed of a daughter-in-law or of a Guru.

By twice-born men a widow must not be appointed to cohabit with any other than her husband for they who appoint her to another man will violate the eternal law. In the sacred texts which refer to marriage the appointment of widows is nowhere mentioned, nor is the re-marriage of widows prescribed in the rules concerning marriage. This practice is reprehended by the learned of the twice-born castes as fit for cattle.

A wife, a son, and a slave, these three are declared to have no property; the wealth which they earn is acquired for him to whom they belong.

A wife, a son, a slave, a pupil, and a younger brother of the full blood who have committed faults may be beaten with a rope or a split bamboo.

But on the back part of the body only, never on a noble part.

To a distinguished, handsome suitor of equal caste should a father give his daughter in accordance with the prescribed rule, though she have not attained the proper age. But the maiden, though marriageable, should rather stop in the father's house until death than that he should ever give her to a man destitute of good qualities.

For the first marriage of twice-born men wives of equal caste are recommended but for those who through desire proceed to marry again the following females, chosen according to the direct order of the castes, are most approved: It is declared that a Sudra woman alone can be the wife of a Sudra; she and one of his own caste the wives of a Vaisya; those two and one of his own caste the wives of a Kshatriya; those three and one of his own caste the wives of a Brahmana. A Sudra woman is not mentioned even in any ancient story as the first wife of a Brahmana or of a Kshatriya, though they lived in the greatest distress. Twice-born men who, in their folly, wed wives of the low Sudra caste soon degrade their families and their children to the state of Sudras.

In all castes those children only which are begotten in the direct order on wedded wives, equal in caste and married as virgins, are to be considered as belonging to the same caste as their father. Sons, begotten by twice-born men on wives of the next lower castes, they declare to be similar to their fathers but blamed on account of the fault inherent in their mothers. Such is the eternal law concerning children born of wives one degree lower than their husbands.

WOMEN

Women do not care for beauty, nor is their attention fixed on age; thinking, "It is enough that he is a man," they give themselves to the handsome and to the ugly. Through their passion for men, through their mutable temper, through their natural heartlessness, they become disloyal towards their husbands, however carefully they may be guarded in this world.

Knowing their disposition, which the Lord of creatures laid in them at the creation, to be such every man should most strenuously exert himself to guard them. When creating them Manu allotted to women a love of their bed, of their seat and of ornament, impure desires, wrath, dishonesty, malice, and bad conduct.

It is the nature of women to seduce men in this world; for that reason the wise are never unguarded in the company of females. For women are able to lead astray in this world not only a fool but even a learned man and to make him a slave of desire and anger.

Day and night women must be kept in dependence by the males of their families and, if they attach themselves to sensual enjoyments, they must be kept under one's control. Her father protects her in childhood, her husband protects her in youth, and her sons protect her in old age; a woman is never fit for independence.

Reprehensible is the father who gives not his daughter in marriage at the proper time, reprehensible is the husband who approaches not his wife in due season, and reprehensible is the son who does not protect his mother after her husband has died.

A female must not seek to separate herself from her father, husband, or sons; by leaving them she would make both her own and her husband's families contemptible. She must always be cheerful, clever in the management of her household affairs, careful in cleaning her utensils, and economical in expenditure. Him to whom her father may give her, or her brother with the father's permission, she shall obey as long as he lives and when he is dead she must not insult his memory.

Drinking spirituous liquor, associating with wicked people, separation from the husband, rambling abroad, sleeping at unseasonable hours, and dwelling in other men's houses are the six causes of the ruin of women.

THE CLASSICAL WORLD

Dividing a history of the world into periods or epochs almost inevitably forces one to make arbitrary decisions, because any division that is appropriate to some country or area will almost surely be irrelevant to others. Still, some turning points of history are of such wide and lasting significance that they demand recognition. A clear example is the series of events that occurred in Greece at the beginning of the fifth century B.C. when the Greek armies and navies met and repulsed the invading forces of the mighty Persian empire, thus inaugurating the classical world. Mainly because of the subsequent history of Greece and then of Rome, the course that civilization in the Western world would take to the present day was set. We can hardly speculate on what that course might have been had Persia prevailed; suffice it to say that it would undoubtedly have been quite different from Western history as we know it.

The contributions made by Greece and Rome to the West are considerably different. Following their victories at Marathon and Salamis the Greeks, especially Athens, entered a golden age that, though little longer than a century, was to leave an indelible mark on the future. Although their contribution was primarily intellectual and aesthetic, it was also political. The Greeks were the founders of theoretical science. Although many significant scientific discoveries had been made prior to their time, by civilizations as disparate as the Egyptian and Mayan, these were for the most part practical—scientific knowledge gained to control the environment to secure specific results. With·the Greeks we find a different approach to science—the search for generality. They wanted to understand how the universe works, not just to put it to work for themselves, but rather simply to understand. The Greeks did not confine their theoretical approach to the study of nature but generalized even beyond the scientific world. Plato, in his great work *The Republic*, reached the metaphysical conclusion that ultimate Reality consists of the Form of the Good. This idea, so important to all later Western thought, is the fundamental expression of classical Greek rationalism and optimism.

But in more prosaic areas as well the Greeks sought to generalize. Thucydides, in the preface to his *History*, made it clear that he was interested not only in describing the events of the Peloponnesian War but of war in general. And the most famous statement in Aristotle's *Politics* —"Man is a political animal"—is a generalization about human nature. But Aristotle meant more by his statement. The sentence as he wrote it actually reads, "Man is by nature an animal intended to live in a polis." Thus Aristotle implied that the form of political organization developed in classical Greece—the polis (whence our word "politics")—was ideally suited for human life. Greece was divided into scores of these poleis, or small city-states, each independent and many with quite different forms of government. Athens, the most important, was, during the Golden Age of the fifth century, a democracy. But, whatever its form, the polis was the center of each individual's life and the object of his pride and devotion. Pericles, in his Funeral Oration eulogizing the dead after the first year of the Peloponnesian War, said of them that "they were worthy of Athens"; no greater praise could he have accorded them.

But the Greek poleis represented an anomaly. Whereas they generalized in their theories the Greeks failed to do so in their practical politics. The separate poleis were often at odds with each other; their bickerings culminated in the disastrous Peloponnesian War in the late fifth century B.C., which so weakened them, defeated Athens in particular, that they fell easy prey to the organized Macedonian hosts who moved on them from the north.

As these events were occurring in the eastern Mediterranean, another city-state halfway across the sea to the west was pursuing its destiny—Rome. According to tradition Rome was founded in 753 B.C. Ruled at first by kings it became a republic, much as described by Polybius in his *Histories*, in 509 B.C. Not long afterward it began a process of expansion that, before it ended, had transformed this tiny city-state into one of the most powerful empires the world has ever known. Unlike the Greeks, with their theories and generalizations, the Romans were an intensely practical people. Where the former pursued mathematics for its rational elegance, for example, the latter put it to use in engineering, to build highways and aqueducts.

To conquer the Western world required the Romans to develop their military might. This they did through recruiting citizen-soldiers who were highly trained, disciplined, and dedicated to their legion. To maintain their empire, however, involved them in much more complex functions. They had to develop a code of laws that could be applied to a wide variety of places and political traditions, administrators capable of governing the far-flung outposts of empire, and systems of communication and transportation to link them all together. This the Romans accomplished with remarkable efficiency and success.

The history of Rome is divided almost equally in half. In the early period, until the first century B.C., the government was republican, with a tri-partite division of political power among Consuls, the Senate, and the people. Then, after several decades of turmoil, Rome emerged an empire—meaning by this term that power rested in the hands of a supreme ruler. Imperial rule continued until the disintegration of Roman power in the fifth century A.D., under the onslaught of invasions by tribal warriors from the north and east. Although several of the emperors were outstanding leaders, one example being Marcus Aurelius (121–180), who was an important Stoic philosopher as well, too many, particularly in the latter stages of imperial Rome, were corrupt and debauched. Rome seemed not able to sustain its great power and finally fell of its own weight, but only after a thousand years of might and glory.

One event, almost unnoticed at the time, occurred early in the imperial period, during the reign of Caesar Augustus. This was the birth, in a remote province of the empire, of the child Jesus. It is not necessary to comment here on the influence his life and teachings have had on the subsequent history of civilization.

At about the same time that Rome was expanding and consolidating its empire the Chinese empire was in the process of disintegration, as the centralized government of the Chou dynasty more and more lost control over the provinces. To conclude from this that Chinese civilization was in decline, however, would be a mistake. Quite the opposite, for the later centuries of the Chou are often referred to as China's golden age. The preeminent figure of this age was Confucius, who flourished early in the fifth century B.C. Confucius is often called a philosopher but he would be better described as a teacher, his pupils being the people of China for over the next two thousand years. The teachings of Confucius were essentially conservative. He believed in the importance of tradition and the following of traditional ways, urging his students and also those who held political power to devote their efforts to the preservation of an orderly and stable society. This attitude, with its respect for the past, was to become a controlling influence on Chinese civilization through much of its history.

At the same time that Confucius was teaching his social gospel a quite different movement was stirring in China, which was to rival Confucianism both at the time and throughout succeeding millennia. This was Taoism, a mystical form of religion said to have been founded by a man named Lao-Tzu. The Taoists, unlike the Confucianists, who instilled in their followers a strong sense of duty to society and the state, were individualists. Instead of conforming to society, they believed one should conform to nature. For them the best life was one in which a person separated himself from the social scene to commune in isolation with nature.

The political disintegration of the later Chou was brought to an end by the Ch'in dynasty, which, although it held power for only a few years (221–206 B.C.), succeeded in uniting China under its iron rule. Its head, Shi Huang Ti, took the title Emperor of Ch'in [China], a title that was held by succeeding monarchs until the revolution of 1912. Another accomplishment of the Ch'in was the construction of the Great Wall, to protect the country from invaders from the north. It came finally to stretch along China's border for fifteen hundred miles and remains today a sight for tourists' eyes.

The Ch'in dynasty, which did not long outlive its founder, was followed by the Han, which ruled China for more than four hundred years (until A.D. 220), a period of general peace and prosperity. Once again, however, disintegration finally set in and China experienced a period of fluctuating political fortunes. Two developments of the Han period are worthy of note. With Chinese leadership the "silk road" was constructed, linking China by a long and arduous route to the Mediterranean Sea, thus promoting both trade and greater contact between East and West. Also, Buddhism was introduced into China from India, the first major step leading to its spread throughout the Far East.

The other great civilization of the classical world was India. Here the Aryan invaders moved east from their original foothold in the Indus valley, gradually expanding their power and subjugating the local population. By around 600 B.C. they controlled most of the Ganges plain. Unlike China, which developed a largely secular society, Indian life from early times was dominated by religion. Hinduism, the predominant religion of India, developed out of an amalgamation of aboriginal cults with those of the invading Aryans. The priests, or Brahmins, who developed the religion and compiled its scriptures, gave themselves a preeminent status in the social structure, organizing the society into four occupational groups that later hardened into the unique caste system of India, described in the *Laws of Manu.*

At the beginning of the fifth century B.C. two new religions were born in India. The first was Jainism, which taught an extreme form of asceticism. Although it still has a following in India, it never spread beyond that country. The second was Buddhism. Founded by a young Indian prince, Siddhartha Gautama (who was an almost exact contemporary of Confucius), Buddhism later spread throughout Asia.

Political consolidation of India dates from the Mauryan dynasty whose first king, Chandragupta, conquered most of northern India at the end of the fourth century B.C. More important, however, was his grandson, Asoka (273–232 B.C .), the most famous of Indian kings, who conquered all but the southern tip of the peninsula. A convert to Buddhism, Asoka sent out missionaries to spread the religion to other parts of the world. Shortly after the death of Asoka the Maurya empire disintegrated. After a period of Greek influence, India experienced a long interim of divided rule. But in the fourth century A.D. a new dynasty, the Guptas, again began to consolidate much of the land. The Gupta empire was brought to an end after two hundred years, by invading Huns from the north, in the sixth century A.D.

Herodotus

When the Persians under their emperor Darius invaded Greece in 490
B.C. their attack was as much defen-
sive as aggressive. They were intent
on securing the flank of their empire
along the Ionian coast of Asia Minor
from attack from the west. But the defeat they suffered at the hands of the
Athenians at the battle of Marathon
that year convinced them that they
could not tolerate the independent
existence of this thorn in their side.
(When the Greek Philippides ran
twenty-six miles from Marathon to
Athens with news of the great victory
over the Persians he little knew that
his feat would be actively commemorated twenty-five hundred years
later.) So ten years afterward, under
Darius's successor Xerxes, the Persians attacked again, moving their
army across the narrows of the Hellespont on a bridge of boats and then
descending on the Greeks from the
north.

The year 480 witnessed two crucial encounters. The first, at the pass
of Thermopylae, where a small band
of Spartans and their allies under
Leonidas held the entire Persian army
at bay for three days, is a story of
heroism and treachery. The second
was a naval encounter that took
place off the island of Salamis, very
near Athens. There, in one of the
most decisive sea battles in Western
history, the combined Greek fleet,
led by the Athenians, routed their
Persian adversaries, as Xerxes looked
on from the shore in impotent rage.

The selection that follows recounts
the stirring events of the fateful year
480. It was written by Herodotus
(484–c.424 B.C.), the first of the great
Greek historians. Herodotus, though
a Greek, was born in Halicarnassus,
on the Ionian coast across the
Aegean Sea from the Peloponnesian
peninsula. He wrote his history, as he
says, "in the hope thereby of preserving from decay the remembrance of
what men have done. . . ."

The History of Herodotus

THE FIRST BOOK ENTITLED
"CLIO"

These are the researches of Herodotus of Halicarnassus, which he publishes, in the hope of thereby preserving from decay the remembrance of what men have done, and of preventing the great and wonderful actions of the Greeks and the Barbarians from losing their due meed of glory; and withal to put on record what were their grounds of feud.

• • •

THE SEVENTH BOOK, ENTITLED
"POLYMNIA"

**[THE BATTLE OF
THERMOPYLAE]**

• • •

The Greek forces at Thermopylae, when the Persian army drew near to the entrance of the pass, were seized with fear; and a council was held to consider about a retreat. It was the wish of the Peloponnesians generally that the army should fall back upon the Peloponnese, and there guard the Isthmus. But Leonidas, who saw with what indignation the Phocians and Locrians heard of this plan, gave his voice for remaining where they were, while they sent envoys to the several cities to ask for help, since they were too few to make a stand against an army like that of the Medes.

While this debate was going on, Xerxes sent a mounted spy to observe the Greeks, and note how many they were, and see what they were

Trans. G. Rawlinson.

doing. He had heard, before he came out of Thessaly, that a few men were assembled at this place, and that at their head were certain Lacedaemonians, under Leonidas, a descendant of Hercules. The horseman rode up to the camp, and looked about him, but did not see the whole army; for such as were on the further side of the wall (which had been rebuilt and was now carefully guarded) it was not possible for him to behold; but he observed those on the outside, who were encamped in front of the rampart. It chanced that at this time the Lacedaemonians held the outer guard, and were seen by the spy, some of them engaged in gymnastics exercises, others combing their long hair. At this the spy greatly marvelled, but he counted their number, and when he had taken accurate note of everything, he rode back quietly; for no one pursued after him, nor paid any heed to his visit. So he returned and told Xerxes all that he had seen.

Upon this, Xerxes, who had no means of surmising the truth—namely, that the Spartans were pre-paring to do or die manfully—but thought it laughable that they should be engaged in such employments, sent and called to his presence Demaratus the son of Ariston, who still remained with the army. When he appeared Xerxes told him all that he had heard, and questioned him concerning the news, since he was anxious to understand the meaning of such behaviour on the part of the Spartans. Then Demaratus said—

"I spake to thee, O king! concerning these men long since, when we had but just begun our march upon Greece; thou, however, didst only laugh at my words, when I told thee of all this, which I saw would come to pass. Earnestly do I struggle at all times to speak truth to thee, sire; and now listen to it once more. These men have come to dispute the pass with us; and it is for this that they are now making ready. 'Tis their custom, when they are about to hazard their lives, to adorn their heads with care. Be assured, however, that if thou canst subdue the men who are here and the Lacedaemonians who remain in Sparta, there is no other nation in all the world which will venture to lift a hand in their defence. Thou hast now to deal with the first kingdom and town in Greece, and with the bravest men."

Then Xerxes, to whom what Demaratus said seemed altogether to surpass belief, asked further how it was possible for so small an army to contend with his.

"O king!" Demaratus answered, "let me be treated as a liar, if matters fall not out as I say."

But Xerxes was not persuaded any the more. Four whole days he suffered to go by, expecting that the Greeks would run away. When, however, he found on the fifth that they were not gone, thinking that their firm stand was merely impudence and recklessness, he grew wroth, and sent against them the Medes and Cissians, with orders to take them alive and bring them into his presence. Then the Medes rushed forward and charged the Greeks, but fell in vast numbers: others, however took the places of the slain, and would not be beaten off, though they suffered terrible losses. In this way it became

clear to all, and especially to the king, that though he had plenty of combatants, he had but very few warriors. The struggle, however, continued during the whole day.

Then the Medes, having met so rough a reception, withdrew from the fight; and their place was taken by the band of Persians under Hydarnes, whom the king called his "Immortals": they, it was thought would soon finish the business. But when they joined battle with the Greeks, 'twas with no better success than the Median detachment— things went much as before—the two armies fighting in a narrow space, and the barbarians using shorter spears than the Greeks, and having no advantage from their numbers. The Lacedaemonians fought in a way worthy of note, and showed themselves far more skilful in fight than their adversaries, often turning their backs, and making as though they were all flying away, on which the barbarians would rush after them with much noise and shouting, when the Spartans at their approach would wheel round and face their pursuers, in this way destroying vast numbers of the enemy. Some Spartans likewise fell in these encounters, but only a very few. At last the Persians, finding that all their efforts to gain the pass availed nothing, and that, whether they attacked by divisions or in any other way, it was to no purpose, withdrew to their own quarters.

During these assaults, it is said that Xerxes, who was watching the battle, thrice leaped from the throne on which he sat, in terror for his army.

Next day the combat was renewed, but with no better success on the part of the barbarians. The Greeks were so few that the barbarians hoped to find them disabled, by reason of their wounds, from offering any further resistance; and so they once more attacked them. But the Greeks were drawn up in detachments according to their cities, and bore the brunt of the battle in turns,—all except the Phocians, who had been stationed on the mountain to guard the pathway. So, when the Persians found no difference between that day and the preceding, they again retired to their quarters.

Now, as the king was in a great strait, and knew not how he should deal with the emergency, Ephialtes, the son of Eurydemus, a man of Malis, came to him and was admitted to a conference. Stirred up by hope of receiving a rich reward at the king's hands, he had come to tell him of the pathway which led across the mountain to Thermopylae; by which disclosure he brought destruction on the band of Greeks who had there withstood the barbarians.

• • •

Great was the joy of Xerxes on this occasion; and as he approved highly of the enterprise which Ephialtes undertook to accomplish, he forthwith sent upon the errand Hydarnes, and the Persians under him. The troops left the camp about the time of the lighting of the lamps. The pathway along which they went was first discovered by the Malians of these parts, who soon afterwards led the Thessalians by it to attack the Phocians, at the time when the Phocians fortified the pass with a wall, and so put themselves under cover from danger. And ever since, the path has always been put to an ill use by the Malians.

The course which it takes is the following:—Beginning at the Asopus, where that stream flows through the cleft in the hills, it runs along the ridge of the mountain, which is called, like the pathway over it, Anopaea, and ends at the city of Alpenus—the first Locrian town as you come from Malis—by the stone called Melampygus and the seats of the Cercopians. Here it is as narrow as at any other point.

The Persians took this path, and, crossing the Asopus, continued their march through the whole of the night, having the mountains of Ceta on their right hand, and on their left those of Trachis. At dawn of day they found themselves close to the summit. Now the hill was guarded, as I have already said, by a thousand Phocian men-at-arms, who were placed there to defend the pathway, and at the same time to secure their own country. They had been given the guard of the mountain path, while the other Greeks defended the pass below, because they had volunteered for the service, and had pledged themselves to Leonidas to maintain the post.

The ascent of the Persians became known to the Phocians in the following manner:—During all the time that they were making their way up, the Greeks remained unconscious of it, inasmuch as the whole mountain was covered with groves of oak; but it happened that the air was very still, and the leaves which the Persians stirred with their feet made, as it was likely they would, a loud rustling, whereupon the Phocians jumped up and flew to seize their arms. In a moment the barbarians came in sight, and, perceiving men arming themselves, were greatly amazed; for they had fallen in with an enemy when they expected no opposition. Hydarnes, alarmed at the sight, and fearing lest the Phocians might be Lacedaemonians, inquired of Ephialtes to what nation these troops belonged. Ephialtes told him the exact truth, whereupon he arrayed his Persians for battle. The Phocians, galled by the showers of arrows to which they were exposed, and imagining themselves the special object of the Persian attack, fled hastily to the crest of the mountain, and there made ready to meet death; but while their mistake continued, the Persians, with Ephialtes and Hydarnes, not thinking it worth their while to delay on account of Phocians, passed on and descended the mountain with all possible speed.

The Greeks at Thermopylae received the first warning of the destruction which the dawn would bring on them from the seer Megistias, who read their fate in the victims as he was sacrificing. After this deserters came in, and brought the news that the Persians were marching round by the hills: it was still night when these men arrived. Last of all, the scouts came running down from the heights, and brought in the same accounts, when the day was just beginning to break. Then the Greeks held a council to consider what they should do, and here opinions were divided: some were strong against quitting their post, while others contended to the contrary. So when the council had broken up, part of the troops departed and went their ways homeward to their several states; part however resolved to remain, and to stand by Leonidas to the last.

• • •

At sunrise Xerxes made libations, after which he waited until the time when the forum is wont to fill, and then began his advance. Ephialtes had instructed him thus, as the descent of the mountain is much quicker, and the distance much shorter, than the way round the hills,

and the ascent. So the barbarians under Xerxes began to draw nigh; and the Greeks under Leonidas, as they now went forth determined to die, advanced much further than on previous days, until they reached the more open portion of the pass. Hitherto they had held their station within the wall, and from this had gone forth to fight at the point where the pass was the narrowest. Now they joined battle beyond the defile, and carried slaughter among the barbarians, who fell in heaps. Behind them the captains of the squadrons, armed with whips, urged their men forward with continual blows. Many were thrust into the sea, and there perished; a still greater number were trampled to death by their own soldiers; no one heeded the dying. For the Greeks, reckless of their own safety and desperate, since they knew that, as the mountain had been crossed, their destruction was nigh at hand, exerted themselves with the most furious valour against the barbarians.

By this time the spears of the greater number were all shivered, and with their swords they hewed down the ranks of the Persians; and here, as they strove, Leonidas fell fighting bravely, together with many other famous Spartans, whose names I have taken care to learn on account of their great worthiness, as indeed I have those of all the three hundred. There fell too at the same time very many famous Persians: among them, two sons of Darius, Abrocomes and Hyperanthes, his children by Phratagune, the daughter of Artanes. Artanes was brother of King Darius, being a son of Hystaspes, the son of Arsames; and when he gave his daughter to the king, he made him heir likewise of all his substance; for she was his only child.

Thus two brothers of Xerxes here fought and fell. And now there arose a fierce struggle between the Persians and the Lacedaemonians over the body of Leonidas, in which the Greeks four times drove back the enemy, and at last by their great bravery succeeded in bearing off the body. This combat was scarcely ended when the Persians with Ephialtes approached; and the Greeks, informed that they drew nigh, made a change in the manner of their fighting. Drawing back into the narrowest part of the pass, and retreating even behind the cross wall, they posted themselves upon a hillock, where they stood all drawn up together in one close body except only the Thebans. The hillock whereof I speak is at the entrance of the straits, where the stone lion stands which was set up in honour of Leonidas. Here they defended themselves to the last, such as still had swords using them, and the others resisting with their hands and teeth; till the barbarians, who in part had pulled down the wall and attacked them in front, in part had gone round and now encircled them upon every side, overwhelmed and buried the remnant which was left beneath showers of missile weapons.

THE EIGHTH BOOK, ENTITLED "URANIA"

[THE BATTLE OF SALAMIS]

• • •

Meanwhile, at Salamis,[1] the Greeks no sooner heard what had befallen

---

[1][Several days after the battle of Thermopylae and immediately following the sacking of Athens by the Persians—*Ed.*]

the Athenian citadel, than they fell into such alarm that some of the captains did not even wait for the council to come to a vote, but embarked hastily on board their vessels, and hoisted sail as though they would take to flight immediately. The rest, who stayed at the council board, came to a vote that the fleet should give battle at the Isthmus. Night now drew on, and the captains, dispersing from the meeting, proceeded on board their receptive ships.

Themistocles, as he entered his own vessel, was met by Mnesiphilus, an Athenian, who asked him what the council had resolved to do. On learning that the resolve was to stand away from the Isthmus, and there give battle on behalf of the Peloponnese, Mnesiphilus exclaimed:—

If these men shall sail way from Salamis, thou wilt have no fight at all for the one fatherland; for they will scatter themselves to their own homes; and neither Eurybiades nor any one else will be able to hinder them, or to stop the breaking up of the armament. Thus will Greece be brought to ruin through evil counsels. But haste thee now; and, if there be any possible way, seek to unsettle these resolves—mayhap thou mightest persuade Eurybiades to change his mind, and continue here.

The suggestion greatly pleased Themistocles; and without answering a word, he went straight to the vessel of Eurybiades. Arrived there, he let him know that he wanted to speak with him on a matter touching the public service. So Eurybiades bade him come on board, and say whatever he wished. Then Themistocles, seating himself at his side, went over all the arguments which he had heard from Mnesiphilus, pretending as if they were his own, and added to them many new ones besides; until at last he persuaded Eurybiades, by his importunity, to quit his ship and again collect the captains to council.

As soon as they were come, and before Eurybiades had opened to them his purpose in assembling them together, Themistocles, as men are wont to do when they are very anxious, spoke much to divers of them; whereupon the Corinthian captain, Adeimantus, the son of Ocytus, observed—"Themistocles, at the games they who start too soon are scourged." "True," rejoined the other in his excuse, "but they who wait too late are not crowned."

Thus he gave the Corinthian at this time a mild answer; and towards Eurybiades himself he did not use any of those arguments which he had urged before, or say aught of the allies betaking themselves to flight if once they broke up from Salamis; it would have been ungraceful for him, when the confederates were present, to make accusation against any; but he had recourse to quite a new sort of reasoning, and addressed him as follows:—

With thee it rests, O! Eurybiades, to save Greece, if thou wilt only hearken unto me, and give the enemy battle here, rather than yield to the advice of those among us, who would have the fleet withdrawn to the Isthmus. Hear now, I beseech thee, and judge between the two courses. At the Isthmus thou wilt fight in an open sea, which is greatly to our disadvantage, since our ships are heavier and fewer in number than the enemy's; and further, thou wilt in any case lose Salamis, Megara, and Egina, and even if all the rest goes well with us. The land and sea force of the Persians will advance together; and thy retreat will but draw them towards the Peloponnese, and so bring all Greece into peril. If, on the other hand, thou doest as I advise, these are the advantages which thou wilt so secure: in the first place, as we shall fight in a narrow sea with few ships against many, if the war follows the common course, we shall gain a great victory: for to fight in a narrow space is favorable to us—in an open sea, to them. Again, Salamis will in this case be preserved, where we have placed our wives and children. Nay, that very point by which ye set most store, is secured as much by the other: for whether we fight here or at the Isthmus, we shall equally give battle in defense of the Peloponnese. Assuredly ye will not do wisely to draw the Persians upon that region. For if things turn out as I anticipate, and we beat them by sea, then we shall have kept your Isthmus free from the barbarians, and they will have advanced no further than Attica, but from thence have fled back in disorder; and we shall, moreover, have saved Megara, Egina, and Salamis itself, where an oracle has said that we are to overcome our enemies. When men counsel reasonably, reasonable success ensues; but when in their counsels they reject reason, God does not choose to follow the wonderings of human fancies.

When Themistocles had thus spoken, Adeimantus the Corinthian again attacked him, and bade him be silent, since he was a man without a city; at the same time, he called on Eurybiades not to put the question at the instance of one who had no country, and urged that Themistocles should show of what state he was envoy, before he gave his voice with the rest. This reproach he made, because the city of Athens had been taken, and was in the hands of the barbarians. Hereupon Themistocles spake many bitter things against Adeimantus and the Corinthians generally; and for proof that he had a country, reminded the captains, that with two hundred ships at his command all fully manned for battle, he had both city and territory as good as theirs; since there was no Grecian state which could resist his men if they were to make a descent.

After this declaration, he turned to Eurybiades, and addressing him with greater warmth and earnestness—"If thou wilt stay here," he said, "and behave like a brave man, all will be well—if not, thou will bring Greece to ruin. For the whole fortune of the war depends on our ships. Be thou persuaded by my words. If not, we will take our families on board, and go, just as we are, to Siris in Italy, which is ours from of old, and which the prophecies declare we are to colonise some day or other. You then, when you have lost allies like us, will hereafter call to mind what I have now said."

At these words of Themistocles, Eurybiades changed his determination; principally, as I believe, because he feared that if he withdrew the fleet to the Isthmus, the Athenians would sail away, and knew that without the Athenians, the rest of their ships could be no match for the fleet of the enemy. He therefore decided to remain, and give battle at Salamis. And now, the different chiefs, notwithstanding their skirmish of words, on learning the decision of Eurybiades, at once made ready for the fight.

• • •

The men belonging to the fleet of Xerxes, after they had seen the Spartan dead at Thermopylae, and crossed the channel from Trachis to Histiaca, waited there by the space of three days, and then sailing down through the Euripus, in three more came to Phalêrum. In my judgment, the Persian forces both by land and sea when they invaded Attica, were not less numerous than they had been on their arrival at Sêpias and Thermopylae. For against the Persian loss in the storm and at Thermopylae, and again in the sea-fights off Artemisium, I set the various nations which had since joined the king—as the Malians, the Dorians, the Locrians, and the Boeotians— each serving full force in his army except the last, who did not number in their ranks either the Thespians or the Plataeans; and together with these, the Carystians, the Andrians, the Tenians, and the other people of the islands, who all fought on this side, except the five states already mentioned. For as the Persians penetrated further into Greece, they were joined continually by fresh nations.

Reinforced by the contingents of all these various states, except Paros, the barbarians reached Athens. As for the Parians, they tarried at Cythnus, waiting to see how the war would go. The rest of the sea forces came safe to Phalêrum, where they were visited by Xerxes, who had conceived a desire to go aboard and learn the wishes of the fleet. So he came and sate in a seat of honour; and the sovereigns of the nations, and the captains of the ships, were sent for to appear before him, and as they arrived took their seats according to the rank assigned them by the king. In the first seat sate the king of Sidon; after him, the king of Tyre; then the rest in their order. When the whole had taken their places, one after another, and were set down in orderly array, Xerxes, to try them, sent Mardonius and questioned each, whether a sea-fight should be risked or no.

Mardonius accordingly went round the entire assemblage, beginning with the Sidonian monarch, and asked this question; to which all gave the same answer, advising to engage the Greeks, except only Artemisia, who spake as follows: —

Say to the king, Mardonius, that these are my words to him: I was not the least brave of those who fought at Euboea, nor were my achievements there among the meanest; it is my right, therefore, O my lord, to tell thee plainly, what I think to be most for thy advantage now. This then is my advice. Spare thy ships, and do not risk a battle; for these people are as much superior to thy people in seamanship, as men to women. What so great need is there for thee to incur hazard at sea? Art thou not master of Athens, for which thou didst undertake thy expedition? Is not Greece subject to thee? Not a soul now resists thy advance. They who once resisted, were handled even as they deserved. Now learn how I expect that affairs will go with thy adversaries. If thou art not overhasty to engage with them by sea, but wilt keep thy fleet near the land, then whether thou abidest as thou art, or marchest forward towards the Peloponnese, thou wilt easily accomplish all for which thou art come hither. The Greeks cannot hold out against thee very long; thou wilt soon part them asunder, and scatter them to their several homes. In the island where they lie, I hear they have no food in store; nor is it likely, if thy land force begins its march towards the Peloponnese, that they will remain quietly where they are—at least such as come from that region. Of a surety they will not greatly trouble themselves to give battle on behalf of the Athenians. On the other hand, if thou art hasty to fight, I tremble last the defeat of thy sea force bring harm likewise to thy land army. This, too, thou shouldst remember, O king; good masters are apt to have bad servants; and bad masters good ones. Now, as thou art the best of men, thy servants must needs be a sorry set. These Egyptians, Cyprians, Cilicians, and Pamphylians, who are counted in the number of thy subject-allies, of how little service are they to thee!

As Artemisia spake, they who wished her well were greatly troubled concerning her words, thinking that she would suffer some hurt at the king's hands, because she exhorted him not to risk a battle; they, on the other hand, who disliked and envied her, favoured as she was by the king above all the rest of the allies, rejoiced at her declaration, expecting that her life would be the forfeit. But Xerxes, when the words of the several speakers were reported to him, was pleased beyond all others with the reply of Artemisia; and whereas, even before this, he had always esteemed her much, he now praised her more than ever. Nevertheless, he gave orders that the advice of the greater number should be followed; for he thought that at Euboea the fleet had not done its best, because he himself was not there to see— whereas this time he resolved that he would be an eye-witness of the combat.

Orders were now given to stand out to sea; and the ships proceeded towards Salamis, and took up the stations to which they were directed, without let or hindrance from the enemy. The day, however, was too far spent for them to begin the battle, since night already approached: so they prepared to engage upon the morrow. The Greeks, meanwhile, were in great distress and alarm, more especially those of the Peloponnese; who were troubled that they had been kept at Salamis to fight on behalf of the Athenian territory; and feared that, if they should suffer defeat, they would be pent up and besieged in an island, while their own country was left unprotected.

• • •

At first they conversed together in low tones, each man with his fellow, secretly, and marvelled at the folly shown by Eurybiades; but presently the smothered feeling broke out, and another assembly was held; whereat the old subjects provoked much talk from the speakers, one side maintaining that it was best to sail to the Peloponnese and risk battle for that, instead of abiding at Salamis and fighting for a land already taken by the enemy; while the other, which consisted of the Athenians, Eginetans, and Megarians, was urgent to remain and have the battle fought where they were.

Then Themistocles, when he saw that the Peloponnesians would carry the vote against him, went out secretly from the council, and instructing a certain man what he should say, sent him on board a merchant ship to the fleet of the Medes. The man's name was Sicinnus; he was one of Themistocles' household slaves, and acted as tutor to his sons; in after times, when the Thespians were admitting persons to citizenship. Themistocles made him a Thespian, and a rich man to boot. The ship brought Sicinnus to the Persian fleet, and there he delivered his message to the leaders in these words:—

The Athenian commander has sent me to you privily, without the knowledge of the other Greeks. He is a well-wisher to the king's cause, and would rather success attend on you than on your countrymen; wherefore he bids me tell you, that fear has seized the Greeks and they are meditating a hasty flight. Now then it is open to you to achieve the best work that ever ye wrought, if only ye will hinder their escaping. They no longer agree among themselves, so that they will not now make any resistance—nay, 'tis likely ye may see a fight already begun between such as favour and such as oppose your cause.

The Messenger, when he had thus expressed himself, departed and was seen no more.

Then the captains, believing all that the messenger had said, proceeded to land a large body of Persian troops on the islet of Psyttaleia, which lies between Salamis and the mainland; after which, about the hour of midnight, they advanced their western wing towards Salamis, so as to inclose the Greeks. At the same time the force stationed about Ceos and Cynosura moved forward, and filled the whole strait as far as Munychias with their ships. This advance was made to prevent the Greeks from escaping by flight, and to block them up in Salamis, where it was thought that vengeance might be taken upon them for the battles fought near Artemisium. The Persian troops were landed on the islet of Psyttaleia, because, as soon as the battle began, the men and wrecks were likely to be drifted thither, as the isle lay in the very path of the coming fight—and they would thus be able to save their own men and destroy those of the enemy. All these movements were made in silence, that the Greeks might have no knowledge of them; and they occupied the whole night, so that the men had no time to get their sleep.

I cannot say that there is no truth in prophecies, or feel inclined to call in question those which speak with clearness, when I think of the following:—

When they shall bridge with their ships to the sacred strand of Diana, Girt with the golden falchion, and eke to marine Cynasura, Mad hope swelling their hearts at the downfall of beautiful Athens— Then shall godlike Right extinguish haughty Presumption, Insult's furious offspring, who thinketh to overthrow all things. Brass with brass shall mingle, and Mars with blood shall purple Ocean's waves. Then—then shall the day of Grecia's freedom Come from Victory fair, and Saturn's son all-seeing.

When I look to this, and perceive how clearly Bacis spoke, I neither venture myself to say anything against prophecies, nor do I approve of others impugning them.

Meanwhile, among the captains at Salamis, the strife of words grew fierce. As yet they did not know that they were encompassed, but imagined that the barbarians remained in the same places where they had seen them the day before.

In the midst of their contention, Aristides, the son of Lysimachus, who had crossed from Egina, arrived in Salamis. He was an Athenian, and had been ostracised by the commonality, yet I believe, from what I have heard concerning his character, that there was not in all Athens a man so worthy or so just as he. He now came to the council, and standing outside, called for Themistocles. Now Themistocles was not his friend, but his most determined enemy. However, under the pressure of the great dangers impending, Aristides forgot their feud, and called Themistocles out of the council, since he wished to confer with him. He had heard before his arrival of the impatience of the Peloponnesians to withdraw the fleet to the Isthmus. As soon therefore as Themistocles came forth, Aristides addressed him in these words:—

Our rivalry at all times, and especially at the present season, ought to be a struggle, which of us shall most advantage our country. Let me then say to thee, that so far as regards the departure of the Peloponnesians from this place, much talk

and little will be found precisely alike. I have seen with my own eyes that which I now report; that, however, much the Corinthians or Eurybiades himself may wish it, they cannot now retreat; for we are enclosed on every side by the enemy. Go in to them, and make this known.

"Thy advice is excellent," answered the other, "and thy tidings are also good. That which I earnestly desired to happen, thine eyes have beheld accomplished. Know that what the Medes have now done was at my instance; for it was necessary, as our men would not fight here at their own free will, to make them fight whether they would or no. But come now, as thou hast brought the good news, go in and tell it. For if I speak to them, they will think it a feigned tale, and will not believe that the barbarians have inclosed us around. Therefore do thou go to them, and inform them how matters stand. If they believe thee, 'twill be for the best; but if otherwise, it will not harm. For it is impossible that they should now flee away, if we are indeed shut in on all sides, as thou sayest."

Then Aristides entered the assembly, and spoke to the captains: he had come, he told them, from Egina, and had but barely escaped the blockading vessels—the Greek fleet was entirely inclosed by the ships of Xerxes—and he advised them to get themselves in readiness to resist the foe. Having said so much, he withdrew. And now another contest arose, for the greater part of the captains would not believe the tidings.

But while they still doubted, a Tenian trireme, commanded by Paneatius the son of Sôsimenes, deserted from the Persians and joined the Greeks, bringing full intelligence. For this reason the Tenians were inscribed upon the tripod at Delphi among those who overthrew the barbarians. With this ship, which deserted to their side at Salamis, and the Lemnian vessel which came over before at Artemisium, the Greek fleet was brought to the full number of 380 ships; otherwise it fell short by two of that amount.

The Greeks now, not doubting what the Tenians told them, made ready for the coming fight. At dawn of day, all the men-at-arms were assembled together, and speeches were made to them, of which the best was that of Themistocles; who throughout contrasted what was noble with what was base, and bade them, in all that came within the range of man's nature and constitution, *always* to make choice of the nobler part. Having thus wound up his discourse, he told them to go at once on board their ships, which they accordingly did; and about this time the trireme, that had been sent to Egina for the Æacidae, returned; whereupon the Greeks put to sea with all their fleet.

The fleet had scarce left the land when they were attacked by the barbarians. At once most of the Greeks began to back water, and were about touching the shore, when Ameinias of Pallené, one of the Athenian captains, darted forth in front of the line, and charged a ship of the enemy. The two vessels became entangled, and could not separate, whereupon the rest of the fleet came up to help Ameinias, and engaged with the Persians. Such is the account which the Athenians give of the way in which the battle began; but the Eginetans maintain that the vessel which had been to Egina for the Æacidae, was the one that brought on the fight. It

is also reported, that a phantom in the form of a woman appeared to the Greeks, and, in a voice that was heard from end to end of the fleet, cheered them on to the fight; first, however, rebuking them, and saying—"Strange men, how long are ye going to back water?"

Against the Athenians, who held the western extremity of the line towards Eleusis, were placed the Phoenicians; against the Lacedaemonians, whose station was eastward towards the Piraeus, the Ionians. Of these last a few only followed the advice of Themistocles, to fight backwardly; the greater number did far otherwise. I could mention here the names of many trierarchs who took vessels from the Greeks, but I shall pass over all excepting Theomêstor the son of Androdamas, and Phylacus the son of Histiacus, both Samians. I show this preference to them, inasmuch as for this service Theomêstor was made tyrant of Samos by the Persians, while Phylacus was enrolled among the king's benefactors, and presented with a large estate in land. In the Persian tongue the king's benefactors are called Orosangs.

Far the greater number of the Persian ships engaged in this battle were disabled—either by the Athenians or by the Eginetans. For as the Greeks fought in order and kept their line, while the barbarians were in confusion and had no plan in anything that they did, the issue of the battle could scarce be other than it was. Yet the Persians fought far more bravely here than at Euboea, and indeed surpassed themselves; each did his utmost through fear of Xerxes, for each thought that the king's eye was upon himself.

What part the several nations, whether Greek or barbarian, took in the combat, I am not able to say for certain; Artemisia, however, I know, distinguished herself in such a way as raised her even higher than she stood before in the esteem of the king. For after confusion had spread throughout the whole of the king's fleet, and her ship was closely pursued by an Athenian trireme, she, having no way to fly, since in front of her were a number of friendly vessels, and she was nearest of all the Persians to the enemy, resolved on a measure which in fact proved her safety. Pressed by the Athenian pursuer, she bore straight against one of the ships of her own party, a Calyndian, which had Damasithymus, the Calyndian king, himself on board. I cannot say whether she had had any quarrel with the man while the fleet was at the Hellespont, or not—neither can I decide whether she of set purpose attacked his vessel, or whether it merely chanced that the Calyndian ship came in her way—but certain it is that she bore down upon his vessel and sank it, and that thereby she had the good fortune to procure herself a double advantage. For the commander of the Athenian trireme, when he saw her bear down on one of the enemy's fleet, thought immediately that her vessel was a Greek, or else had deserted from the Persians, and was now fighting on the Greek side; he therefore gave up the chase, and turned away to attack others.

Thus in the first place she saved her life by the action, and was enabled to get clear off from the battle; while further, it fell out that in the very act of doing the king an injury she raised herself to a greater height than ever in his esteem. For as Xerxes beheld the fight, he remarked (it is said) the destruction of the vessel, whereupon the bystanders observed to him— "Seest thou, master, how well Artemisia fights, and how she has just sunk a ship of the enemy?" Then Xerxes asked if it were really Artemisia's doing; and they answered, "Certainly," for they knew her ensign: while all made sure that the sunken vessel belonged to the opposite side. Everything, it is said, conspired to prosper the queen—it was especially fortunate for her, that not one of those on board the Calyndian ship survived to become her accuser. Xerxes, they say, in reply to the remarks made to him, observed—"My men have behaved like women, and my women like men!"

There fell in this combat Ariabignes, one of the chief commanders of the fleet, who was son of Darius and brother of Xerxes, and with him perished a vast number of men of high repute, Persians, Medes, and allies. Of the Greeks there died only a few; for as they were able to swim, all those that were not slain outright by the enemy escaped from the sinking vessels and swam across to Salamis. But on the side of the barbarians more perished by drowning than in any other way, since they did not know how to swim. The great destruction took place when the ships which had been first engaged began to fly; for they who were stationed in the rear, anxious to display their valour before the eyes of the king, made every effort to force their way to the front, and thus became entangled with such of their own vessels as were retreating.

In this confusion the following event occurred: certain Phoenicians belonging to ships which had thus perished made their appearance before the king, and laid the blame of their loss on the Ionians, declaring that they were traitors, and had willfully destroyed the vessels. But the upshot of this complaint was, that the Ionian captains escaped the death which threatened them, while their Phoenician accusers received death as their reward. For it happened that, exactly as they spoke, a Samothracian vessel bore down on an Athenian and sank it, but was attacked and crippled immediately by one of the Eginetan squadron. Now the Samothracians were expert with the javelin, and aimed their weapons so well, that they cleared the deck of the vessel which had disabled their own, after which they sprang on board, and took it. This saved the Ionians. Xerxes, when he saw the exploit, turned fiercely on the Phoenicians—(he was ready, in his extreme vexation, to find fault with any one)—and ordered their heads to be cut off, to prevent them, he said, from casting the blame of their own misconduct upon braver men. During the whole time of the battle Xerxes sate at the base of the hill called Ægaleôs, over against Salamis; and whenever he saw any of his own captains perform any worthy exploit he inquired concerning him; and the man's name was taken down by his scribes, together with the names of his father and his city. Ariarammes too, a Persian, who was a friend of the Ionians, and present at the time whereof I speak, had a share in bringing about the punishment of the Phoenicians.

When the rout of the barbarians began, and they sought to make their escape to Phalêrum, the Eginetans, awaiting them in the channel, performed exploits worthy to be recorded. Through the whole of the confused struggle the Athenians employed themselves in destroying such ships as either made resistance or fled to shore, while the Eginetans dealt with those which endeavoured to escape down the straits; so that the Persian vessels were no sooner clear of the Athenians than straightway they fell into the hands of the Eginetan squadron.

It chanced here that there was a meeting between the ship of Themistocles, which was hasting in pursuit of the enemy, and that of Polycritus, son of Crius the Eginetan, which had just charged a Sidonian trireme. The Sidonian vessel was the same that captured the Eginetan guardship off Sciathus, which had Pytheas, the son of Ischenous, on board—that Pytheas, I mean, who fell covered with wounds, and whom the Sidonians kept on board their ship, from admiration of his gallantry. This man afterwards returned in safety to Egina, for when the Sidonian vessel with its Persian crew fell into the hands of the Greeks, he was still found on board. Polycritus no sooner saw the Athenian trireme than knowing at once whose vessel it was, as he observed that it bore the ensign of the admiral, he shouted to Themistocles jeeringly, and asked him, in a tone of reproach, if the Eginetans did not show themselves rare friends to the Medes. At the same time, while he thus reproached Themistocles, Polycritus bore straight down on the Sidonian. Such of the barbarian vessels as escaped from the battle fled to Phalêrum, and there sheltered themselves under the protection of the land army.

The Greeks who gained the greatest glory of all in the sea-fight of Salamis were the Eginetans, and after them the Athenians. The individuals of most distinction were Polycritus and Eginetan, and two Athenians,

Eumenes of Anayrus, and Aminias of Pallené; the latter of whom had pressed Artemisia so hard. And assuredly, if he had known that the vessel carried Artemisia on board, he would never have given over the chase till he had either succeeded in taking her, or else been taken himself. For the Athenian captains had received special orders touching the queen, and moreover a reward of ten thousand drachmas had been proclaimed for any one who should make her prisoner; since there was great indignation felt that a woman should appear in arms against Athens. However, as I said before, she escaped; and so did some others whose ships survived the engagement; and these were all now assembled at the port of Phalêrum.

•   •   •

As soon as the sea-fight was ended, the Greeks drew together to Salamis all the wrecks that were to be found in that quarter, and prepared themselves for another engagement, supposing that the king would renew the fight with the vessels still remained to him. Many of the wrecks had been carried away by a westerly wind to the coast of Attica, where they were thrown upon the strip of shore called Côlias. Thus not only were the prophecies of Bacis and Musaeus concerning this battle fulfilled completely, but likewise, by the place to which the wrecks were drifted, the prediction of Lysistratus, an Athenian soothsayer, uttered many years before these events, and quite forgotten at the time by all the Greeks, was fully accomplished. The words were:—

Then shall the sight of the oars fill Colian dames with amazement.

Sophocles

The life of Sophocles, the tragic poet, spanned the fifth century. Born in 496 B.C., he was just old enough to remember the battle of Marathon, and in 480 he led a chorus of Athenian youths in the ceremonial celebration of the naval victory at Salamis. He reached the height of his creative powers in the Age of Pericles. His *Antigone* was produced in 441, three years before the completion of the Parthenon, and his *King Oedipus* was produced around 430, the year before the death of Pericles. Sophocles lived to witness the end of the Golden Age, dying in 406 at the age of ninety, two years before the Athenian defeat in the Peloponnesian War.

To understand the tragic drama *Antigone*, we must realize that, according to Greek religion, the body of a deceased person had to be buried before the soul could enter Hades. Thus, Antigone had a sacred duty to bury her brother, a duty that she believed took precedence over all others, even obedience to the decrees of the state. Creon, on the other hand, viewed Polyneices as an enemy, to be treated as such. The tragedy, therefore, can be interpreted as a clash between divine law, championed by Antigone, and human or political law, championed by Creon. Such an interpretation, however, does not exhaust the meaning of the play, which may also be viewed as a dramatic portrayal of human character. The tragedy that destroys both Antigone and Creon becomes the inevitable result of a clash between two strong-willed individuals, each dedicated to an ideal in itself good, but neither willing to compromise that ideal.

Antigone

ANTIGONE: Ismene, my sister, mine own dear sister, knowest thou what ill there is, of all bequeathed by Oedipus, that Zeus fulfils not for us twain while we live? Nothing painful is there, nothing fraught with ruin, no shame, no dishonour, that I have not seen in thy woes and mine.

And now what new edict is this of which they tell, that our Captain hath just published to all Thebes? Knowest thou aught? Hast thou heard? Or is it hidden from thee that our friends are threatened with the doom of our foes?

ISMENE: No word of friends, Antigone, gladsome or painful, hath come to me, since we two sisters were bereft of brothers twain, killed in one day by a twofold blow; and since in this last night the Argive host hath fled, I know no more, whether my fortune be brighter, or more grievous.

AN: I knew it well, and therefore sought to bring thee beyond the gates of the court, that thou mightest hear alone.

IS: What is it? 'Tis plain that thou art brooding on some dark tidings.

AN: What, hath not Creon destined our brothers, the one to honoured burial, the other to unburied shame? Eteocles, they say, with due observance of right and custom, he hath laid in the earth, for his honour among the dead below. But the hapless corpse of Polyneices—as rumour saith, it hath been published to the town that none shall entomb him or mourn, but leave unwept, unsepulchred, a welcome store for the birds, as they espy him, to feast on at will.

Such, 'tis said, is the edict that the good Creon hath set forth for thee and for me,—yes, for *me*,—and is coming hither to proclaim it clearly to those who know it not; nor counts the matter light, but, whoso disobeys in aught, his doom is death by stoning before all the folk. Thou knowest it now; and thou wilt soon show whether thou art nobly bred, or the base daughter of a noble line.

IS: Poor sister,—and if things stand thus, what could I help to do or undo?

AN: Consider if thou wilt share the toil and the deed.

IS: In what venture? What can be thy meaning?

AN: Wilt thou aid this hand to lift the dead?

IS: Thou wouldst bury him,—when 'tis forbidden to Thebes?

AN: I will do my part,—and thine, if thou wilt not,—to a brother. False to him will I never be found.

IS: Ah, over-bold! when Creon hath forbidden?

AN: Nay, he hath no right to keep me from mine own.

IS: Ah me! think, sister, how our father perished, amid hate and scorn, when sins bared by his own search had moved him to strike both eyes with self-blinding hand; then the mother wife, two names in one, with twisted noose did despite unto her life; and last, our two brothers in one day,—each shedding, hapless one, a kinsman's blood,—wrought

Trans: R.C. Jebb.

out with mutual hands their common doom. And now *we* in turn—we two left all alone—think how we shall perish, more miserably than all the rest, if, in defiance of the law, we brave a king's decree or his powers. Nay, we must remember, first, that we were born women, as who should not strive with men; next, that we are ruled of the stronger, so that we must obey in these things, and in things yet sorer. I, therefore, asking the Spirits Infernal to pardon, seeing that force is put on me herein, will hearken to our rulers; for 'tis witless to be over-busy.

AN: I will not urge thee,—no, nor, if thou yet shouldst have the mind, wouldst thou be welcome as a worker with *me*. Nay, be what thou wilt; but I will bury him: well for me to die in doing that. I shall rest, a loved one with him whom I have loved, sinless in my crime; for I owe a longer allegiance to the dead than to the living: in that world I shall abide for ever. But if *thou* wilt, be guilty of dishonouring laws which the gods have established in honour.

IS: I do them no dishonour; but to defy the State,—I have no strength for that.

AN: Such be thy plea:—I, then, will go to heap the earth above the brother whom I love.

IS: Alas, unhappy one! How I fear for thee!

AN: Fear not for me: guide thine own fate aright.

IS: At least, then, disclose this plan to none, but hide it closely,—and so, too, will I.

IS: Oh, denounce it! Thou wilt be far more hateful for thy silence, if thou proclaim not these things to all.

IS: Thou hast a hot heart for chilling deeds.

AN: I know that I please where I am most bound to please.

IS: Aye, if thou canst; but thou wouldst what thou canst not.

AN: Why, then, when my strength fails, I shall have done.

IS: A hopeless quest should not be made at all.

AN: If thus thou speakest, thou wilt have hatred from me, and wilt justly be subject to the lasting hatred of the dead. But leave me, and the folly that is mine alone, to suffer this dread thing; for I shall not suffer aught so dreadful as an ignoble death.

IS: Go, then, if thou must; and of this be sure,—that, though thine errand is foolish, to thy dear ones thou art truly dear.

[*Exit* ANTIGONE *on the spectators' left.* ISMENE *retires into the palace by one of the two side-doors.*]

CHORUS: Beam of the sun, fairest light that ever dawned on Thebè of the seven gates, thou hast shone forth at last, eye of golden day, arisen above Dircè's streams! The warrior of the white shield, who came from Argos in his panoply, hath been stirred by thee to headlong flight, in swifter career; who set forth against our land by reason of the vexed claims of Polyneices; and, like shrill-screaming eagle, he flew over into our land, in snow-white pinion sheathed, with an armed throng, and with plumage of helms.

He paused above our dwellings; he ravened around our sevenfold portals with spears athirst for blood; but he went hence, or ever his jaws were glutted with our gore, or the Fire-god's pine-fed flame had seized our crown of towers. So fierce was the noise of battle raised behind him, a thing too hard for him to conquer, as he wrestled with his dragon foe.

For Zeus utterly abhors the boasts of a proud tongue; and when he beheld them coming on in a great stream, in the haughty pride of clanging gold, he smote with brandished fire one who was now hasting to shout victory at his goal upon our ramparts.

Swung down, he fell on the earth with a crash, torch in hand, he who so lately, in the frenzy of the mad onset, was raging against us with the blasts of his tempestuous hate. But those threats fared not as he hoped; and to other foes the mighty Wargod dispensed their several dooms, dealing havoc around, a mighty helper at our need.

For seven captains at seven gates, matched against seven, left the tribute of their panoplies to Zeus who turns the battle; save those two of cruel fate, who, born of one sire and one mother, set against each other their twain conquering spears, and are sharers in a common death.

But since Victory of glorious name hath come to us, with joy responsive to the joy of Thebè whose chariots are many, let us enjoy forgetfulness after the late wars, and visit all the temples of the gods with night-long dance and song; and may Bacchus be our leader, whose dancing shakes the land of Thebè.

But lo, the king of the land comes yonder, Creon, son of Menoeceus, our new ruler by the new fortunes that the gods have given; what counsel is he pondering, that he hath proposed this special conference of elders, summoned by his general mandate?

[*Enter* CREON, *from the central doors of the palace, in the garb of king; with two attendants.*]

CR: Sirs, the vessel of our State, after being tossed on wild waves, hath once more been safely steadied by the gods: and ye, out of all the folk, have been called apart by my summons, because I knew, first of all, how true and constant was your reverence for the royal power of Laïus; how, again, when Oedipus was ruler of our land, and when he had perished, your steadfast loyalty still upheld their children. Since, then, his sons have fallen in one day by a twofold doom,—each smitten by the other, each stained with a brother's blood,—I now possess the throne and all its powers, by nearness of kinship to the dead.

No man can be fully known, in soul and spirit and mind, until he hath been seen versed in rule and law-giving. For if any, being supreme guide of the State, cleaves not to the best counsels, but, through some fear, keeps his lips locked, I hold, and have ever held, him most base; and if any makes a friend of more account than his fatherland, that man hath no place in my regard. For I—be Zeus my witness, who sees all things always—would not be silent if I saw ruin, instead of safety, coming to the citizens; nor would I ever deem the country's foe a friend to myself; remembering this, that our country is the ship that bears us safe, and that only while she prospers in our voyage can we make true friends.

Such are the rules by which I guard this city's greatness. And in accord with them is the edict which I have now published to the folk touching the sons of Oedipus;—that Eteocles, who hath fallen fighting for our city, in all renown of arms, shall be entombed, and crowned with every rite that follows the noblest dead to their rest. But for his brother, Polyneices,—who came back from exile, and sought to consume utterly with fire the city of his fathers and the shrines of his fathers' gods,—sought to taste of kindred blood, and to lead the remnant into slavery;—touching this man, it hath been proclaimed to our people that none shall grace him with sepulture or lament, but leave him unburied, a corpse for birds and dogs to eat, a ghastly sight of shame.

Such the spirit of my dealing; and never, by deed of mine, shall the wicked stand in honour before the just; but whoso hath good will to Thebes, he shall be honoured of me, in his life and in his death.

CH: Such is thy pleasure, Creon, son of Menoeceus, touching this city's foe, and its friend; and thou hast power, I ween, to take what order thou wilt, both for the dead, and for all us who live.

CR: See, then, that ye be guardians of the mandate.

CH: Lay the burden of this task on some younger man.

CR: Nay, watchers of the corpse have been found.

CH: What, then, is this further charge that thou wouldst give?

CR: That ye side not with the breakers of these commands.

CH: No man is so foolish that he is enamoured of death.

CR: In sooth, that is the meed; yet lucre hath oft ruined men through their hopes.

[*Enter* GUARD.]

My liege, I will not say that I come breathless from speed, or that I have plied a nimble foot; for often did my thoughts make me pause, and wheel round in my path, to return. My mind was holding large discourse with me; 'Fool, why goest thou to thy certain doom?' 'Wretch, tarrying again? And if Creon hears this from another, must not thou smart for it?' So debating, I went on my way with lagging steps, and thus a short road was made long. At last, however, it carried the day that I should come hither—to thee; and, though my tale be nought, yet will I tell it; for I come with a good grip on one hope,—that I can suffer nothing but what is my fate.

CR: And what is it that disquiets thee thus?

GU: I wish to tell thee first about myself—I did not do the deed—I did not see the doer—it were not right that I should come to any harm.

CR: Thou hast a shrewd eye for thy mark; well dost thou fence thyself round against the blame:—clearly thou hast some strange thing to tell.

GU: Aye, truly; dread news makes one pause long.

CR: Then tell it, wilt thou, and so get thee gone?

GU: Well, this is it.—The corpse— some one hath just given it burial, and gone away,—after sprinkling thirsty dust on the flesh, with such other rites as piety enjoins.

CR: What sayest thou? What living man hath dared this deed?

GU: I know not; no stroke of pick-axe was seen there, no earth thrown up by mattock; the ground was hard and dry, unbroken, without track of wheels; the doer was one who had left no trace. And when the first day-watchman showed it to us, sore wonder fell on all. The dead man was veiled from us; not shut within a tomb, but lightly strewn with dust, as by the hand of one who shunned a curse.

And no sign met the eye as though any beast of prey or any dog had come nigh to him, or torn him.

Then evil words flew fast and loud among us, guard accusing guard; and it would e'en have come to blows at last, nor was there any to hinder. Every man was the culprit, and no one was convicted, but all disclaimed knowledge of the deed. And we were ready to take red-hot iron in our hands;—to walk through fire;—to make oath by the gods that we had not done the deed,—that we were not privy to the planning or the doing.

At last, when all our searching was fruitless, one spake, who made us all bend our faces on the earth in fear; for we saw not how we could gainsay him, or escape mischance if we obeyed. His counsel was that this deed must be reported to thee, and not hidden. And this seemed best; and the lot doomed my hapless self to win this prize. So here I stand,—as unwelcome as unwilling, well I wot; for no man delights in the bearer of bad news.

CH: O King, my thoughts have long been whispering, can this deed, perchance, be e'en the work of gods?

CR: Cease, ere thy words fill me utterly with wrath, lest thou be found at once an old man and foolish. For thou sayest what is not to be borne, in saying that the gods have care for this corpse. Was it for high reward of trusty service that they sought to hide his nakedness, who came to burn their pillared shrines and sacred treasures, to burn their land, and scatter its laws to the winds? Or dost thou behold the gods honouring the wicked? It cannot be. No! From the first there were certain in the town that muttered against me, chafing at this edict, wagging their heads in secret; and kept not their necks duly under the yoke, like men contented with my sway.

'Tis by them, well I know, that these have been beguiled and bribed to do this deed. Nothing so evil as money ever grew to be current among men. This lays cities low, this drives men from their homes, this trains and warps honest souls till they set themselves to works of shame; this still teaches folk to practise villanies, and to know every godless deed.

But all the men who wrought this thing for hire have made it sure that, soon or late, they shall pay the price. Now, as Zeus still hath my reverence, know this—I tell it thee on my oath:—If ye find not the very author of this burial, and produce him before mine eyes, death alone shall not be enough for you, till first, hung up alive, ye have revealed this outrage,—that henceforth ye may thieve with better knowledge whence lucre should be won, and learn that it is not well to love gain from every source. For thou wilt find that ill-gotten pelf brings more men to ruin than to weal.

GU: May I speak? Or shall I just turn and go?

CR: Knowest thou not that even now thy voice offends?

GU: Is thy smart in the ears, or in the soul?

CR: And why wouldst thou define the seat of my pain?

GU: The doer vexes thy mind, but I, thine ears.

CR: Ah, thou art a born babbler, 'tis well seen.

GU: May be, but never the doer of this deed.

CR: Yea, and more,—the seller of thy life for silver.

GU: Alas! 'Tis sad, truly, that he who judges should misjudge.

CR: Let thy fancy play with 'judgment' as it will;—but, if ye show me not the doers of these things, ye shall avow that dastardly gains work sorrows.

[Exit.]

GU: Well, may he be found! so 'twere best. But, be he caught or be he not—fortune must settle that— truly thou wilt not see me here again. Saved, even now, beyond hope and thought, I owe the gods great thanks.

[Exit.]

CHORUS: Wonders are many, and none is more wonderful than man; the power that crosses the white sea, driven by the stormy south-wind, making a path under surges that threaten to engulf him; and Earth, the eldest of the gods, the immortal, the unwearied, doth he wear, turning the soil with the offspring of horses, as the ploughs go to and fro from year to year.

And the light-hearted race of birds, and the tribes of savage beasts, and the sea-brood of the deep, he snares in the meshes of his woven toils, he leads captive, man excellent in wit. And he masters by his arts the beast whose lair is in the wilds, who roams the hills; he tames the horse of shaggy mane, he puts the yoke upon its neck, he tames the tireless mountain bull.

And speech, and wind-swift thought, and all the moods that mould a state, hath he taught himself; and how to flee the arrows of the frost, when 'tis hard lodging under the clear sky, and the arrows of the rushing rain; yea, he hath resource for all; without resource he meets nothing that must come: only against Death shall he call for aid in vain; but from baffling maladies he hath devised escapes.

Cunning beyond fancy's dream is the fertile skill which brings him, now to evil, now to good. When he honours the laws of the land, and that justice which he hath sworn by the gods to uphold, proudly stands his city: no city hath he who, for his rashness, dwells with sin. Never may he share my hearth, never think my thoughts, who doth these things!

Enter GUARD, *on the spectators' left, leading in* ANTIGONE

What portent from the gods is this?—my soul is amazed. I know her—how can I deny that yon maiden is Antigone?

O hapless, and child of hapless sire,—of Oedipus! What means this? Thou brought a prisoner?—thou, disloyal to the King's laws, and taken in folly?

GU: Here she is, the doer of the deed:—we caught this girl burying him:—but where is Creon?

CH: Lo, he comes forth again from the house, at our need.

CR: What is it? What hath chanced, that makes my coming timely?

GU: O King, against nothing should men pledge their word; for the after-thought belies the first intent. I could have vowed that I should not soon be here again,—scared by thy threats, with which I had just been lashed: but,—since the joy that surprises and transcends our hopes is like in fulness to no other pleasure,—I have come, though 'tis in breach of my sworn oath, bringing this maid; who was taken showing grace to the dead. This time there was no casting of lots; no, this luck hath fallen to me, and to none else. And now, Sire, take her thyself, question her, examine her, as thou wilt; but I have a right to free and final quittance of this trouble.

CR: And thy prisoner here—how and whence hast thou taken her?

GU: She was burying the man; thou knowest all.

CR: Dost thou mean what thou sayest? Dost thou speak aright?

GU: I saw her burying the corpse that thou hadst forbidden to bury. Is that plain and clear?

CR: And how was she seen? how taken in the act?

GU: It befell on this wise. When we had come to the place,—with those dread menaces of thine upon us,—we swept away all the dust that covered the corpse, and bared the dank body well; and then sat us down on the brow of the hill, to windward, heedful that the smell from him should not strike us; every man was wide awake, and kept his neighbour alert with torrents of threats, if any one should be careless of this task.

So went it, until the sun's bright orb stood in mid heaven, and the heat began to burn: and then suddenly a whirlwind lifted from the earth a storm of dust, a trouble in the sky, and filled the plain, marring all the leafage of its woods; and the wide air was choked therewith: we closed our eyes, and bore the plague from the gods.

And when, after a long while, this storm had passed, the maid was seen; and she cried aloud with the sharp cry of a bird in its bitterness,—even as when, within the empty nest, it sees the bed stripped of its nestlings. So she also, when she saw the corpse bare, lifted up a voice of wailing, and called down curses on the doers of that deed. And straightway she brought thirsty dust in her hands; and from a shapely ewer of bronze, held high, with thrice-poured drink-offering she crowned the dead.

We rushed forward when we saw it, and at once closed upon our quarry, who was in no wise dismayed. Then we taxed her with her past and present doings; and she stood not on denial of aught,—at once to my joy and to my pain. To have escaped from ills one's self is a great joy; but 'tis painful to bring friends to ill. Howbeit, all such things are of less account to me than mine own safety.

CR: Thou—thou whose face is bent to earth—dost thou avow, or disavow, this deed?

AN: I avow it; I make no denial.

CR: (To GUARD.) Thou canst betake thee whither thou wilt, free and clear of a grave charge.

[*Exit* GUARD.]

(*To* ANTIGONE): Now, tell me thou—not in many words, but briefly—knewest thou that an edict had forbidden this?

AN: I knew it: could I help it? It was public.

CR: And thou didst indeed dare to transgress that law?

AN: Yes; for it was not Zeus that had published me that edict; not such are the laws set among men by the Justice who dwells with the gods below; nor deemed I that thy decrees were of such force, that a mortal could override the unwritten and unfailing statutes of heaven. For their life is not of today or yesterday, but from all time, and no man knows when they were first put forth.

Not through dread of any human pride could I answer to the gods for breaking *these*. Die I must,—I knew that well (how should I not?)—even without thy edicts. But if I am to die before my time, I count that a gain: for when any one lives, as I do, compassed about with evils, can such an one find aught but gain in death?

So for me to meet this doom is trifling grief; but if I had suffered my mother's son to lie in death an unburied corpse, that would have grieved me; for this, I am not grieved. And if my present deeds are foolish in thy sight, it may be that a foolish judge arraigns my folly.

CH: The maid shows herself passionate child of passionate sire, and knows not how to bend before troubles.

CR: Yet I would have thee know that o'er-stubborn spirits are most often humbled; 'tis the stiffest iron, baked to hardness in the fire, that thou shalt oftenest see snapped and shivered; and I have known horses that show temper brought to order by a little curb; there is no room for pride, when thou art thy neighbour's slave.—This girl was already versed in insolence when she transgressed the laws that had been set forth; and, that done, lo, a second insult,—to vaunt of this, and exult in her deed.

Now verily I am no man, she is the man, if this victory shall rest with her, and bring no penalty. No! be she sister's child, or nearer to me in blood than any that worships Zeus at the altar of our house,—she and her kinsfolk shall not avoid a doom most dire; for indeed I charge that other with a like share in the plotting of this burial.

And summon her—for I saw her e'en now within,—raving, and not mistress of her wits. So oft, before the deed, the mind stands self-convicted in its treason, when folks are plotting mischief in the dark. But verily this, too, is hateful,—when one who hath been caught in wickedness then seeks to make the crime a glory.

AN: Wouldst thou do more than take and slay me?

CR: No more, indeed; having that, I have all.

AN: Why then dost thou delay? In thy discourse there is nought that pleases me,—never may there be!—and so my words must needs be unpleasing to thee. And yet, for glory—whence could I have won a nobler, than by giving burial to mine own brother? All here would own that they thought it well, were not their lips sealed by fear. But royalty, blest in so much besides, hath the power to do and say what it will.

CR: Thou differest from all these Thebans in that view.

AN: These also share it; but they curb their tongues for thee.

CR: And art thou not ashamed to act apart from them?

AN: No; there is nothing shameful in piety to a brother.

CR: Was it not a brother, too, that died in the opposite cause?

AN: Brother by the same mother and the same sire.

CR: Why, then, dost thou render a grace that is impious in his sight?

AN: The dead man will not say that he so deems it.

CR: Yea, if thou makest him but equal in honour with the wicked.

AN: It was his brother, not his slave, that perished.

CR: Wasting this land; while *he* fell as its champion.

AN: Nevertheless, Hades desires these rites.

CR: But the good desires not a like portion with the evil.

AN: Who knows but this seems blameless in the world below?

CR: A foe is never a friend—not even in death.

AN: 'Tis not my nature to join in hating, but in loving.

CR: Pass, then, to the world of the dead, and, if thou must needs love, love them. While I live, no woman shall rule me.

[*Enter* ISMENE *from the house, led in by two attendants.*]

CH: Lo, yonder Ismene comes forth, shedding such tears as fond sisters weep; a cloud upon her brow casts its shadow over her darkly-flushing face, and breaks in rain on her fair cheek.

CR: And thou, who, lurking like a viper in my house, wast secretly draining my life-blood, while I knew not that I was nurturing two pests, to rise against my throne—come, tell me now, wilt thou also confess thy part in this burial, or wilt thou forswear all knowledge of it?

IS: I have done the deed,—if she allows my claim,—and share the burden of the charge.

AN: Nay, justice will not suffer thee to do that: thou didst not consent to the deed, nor did I give thee part in it.

IS: But, now that ills beset thee, I am not ashamed to sail the sea of trouble at thy side.

AN: Whose was the deed, Hades and the dead are witnesses: a friend in words is not the friend that I love.

IS: Nay, sister, reject me not, but let me die with thee, and duly honour the dead.

AN: Share not thou my death, nor claim deeds to which thou hast not put thy hand: my death will suffice.

IS: And what life is dear to me, bereft of thee?

AN: Ask Creon; all thy care is for him.

IS: Why vex me thus, when it avails thee nought?

AN: Indeed, if I mock, 'tis with pain that I mock thee.

IS: Tell me,—how can I serve thee, even now?

AN: Save thyself: I grudge not thy escape.

IS: Ah, woe is me! And shall I have no share in thy fate?

AN: Thy choice was to live; mine, to die.

IS: At least thy choice was not made without my protest.

AN: One world approved thy wisdom; another, mine.

IS: Howbeit, the offence is the same for both of us.

AN: Be of good cheer; thou livest; but my life hath long been given to death, that so I might serve the dead.

CR: Lo, one of these maidens hath newly shown herself foolish, as the other hath been since her life began.

IS: Yea, O King, such reason as nature may have given abides not with the unfortunate, but goes astray.

CR: Thine did, when thou chosest vile deeds with the vile.

IS: What life could I endure, without her presence?

CR: Nay, speak not of her 'presence'; she lives no more.

IS: But wilt thou slay the betrothed of thine own son?

CR: Nay, there are other fields for him to plough.

IS: But there can never be such love as bound him to her.

CR: I like not an evil wife for my son.

AN: Haemon, beloved! How thy father wrongs thee!

CR: Enough, enough of thee and of thy marriage!

CH: Wilt thou indeed rob thy son of this maiden?

CR: 'Tis Death that shall stay these bridals for me.

CH: 'Tis determined, it seems, that she shall die.

CR: Determined, yes, for thee and for me.—(*To the two Attendants.*) No more delay—servants, take them within! Henceforth they must be women, and not range at large; for verily even the bold seek to fly, when they see Death now closing on their life.

[*Exeunt Attendants, guarding*
ANTIGONE *and* ISMENE—CREON
remains.]

CH: Blest are they whose days have not tasted of evil. For when a house hath once been shaken from heaven, there the curse fails nevermore, passing from life to life of the race; even as, when the surge is driven over the darkness of the deep by the fierce breath of Thracian sea-winds, it rolls up the black sand from the depths, and there is a sullen roar from wind-vexed headlands that front the blows of the storm.

I see that from olden time the sorrows in the house of the Labdacidae are heaped upon the sorrows of the dead; and generation is not freed by generation, but some god strikes them down, and the race hath no deliverance.

For now that hope of which the light had been spread above the last root of the house of Oedipus—that hope, in turn, is brought low—by the blood-stained dust due to the gods infernal, and by folly in speech, and frenzy at the heart.

Thy power, O Zeus, what human trespass can limit? That power which neither Sleep, the all-ensnaring, nor the untiring months of the gods can master; but thou, a ruler to whom time brings not old age, dwellest in the dazzling splendour of Olympus.

And through the future, near and far, as through the past, shall this law hold good: Nothing that is vast enters into the life of mortals without a curse.

For that hope whose wanderings are so wide is to many men a comfort, but to many a false lure of giddy desires; and the disappointment comes on one who knoweth nought till he burn his foot against the hot fire.

For with wisdom hath some one given forth the famous saying, that evil seems good, soon or late, to him whose mind the god draws to mischief; and but for the briefest space doth he fare free of woe.

But lo, Haemon, the last of thy sons;—comes he grieving for the doom of his promised bride, Antigone, and bitter for the baffled hope of his marriage?

[*Enter* HAEMON.]

CR: We shall know soon, better than seers could tell us.—My son, hearing the fixed doom of thy betrothed, art thou come in rage against thy father? Or have I thy good will, act how I may?

HAE: Father, I am thine; and thou, in thy wisdom, tracest for me rules which I shall follow. No marriage shall be deemed by me a greater gain than thy good guidance.

CR: Yea, this, my son, should be thy heart's fixed law,—in all things to obey thy father's will. 'Tis for this that men pray to see dutiful children grow up around them in their homes,—that such may requite their father's foe with evil, and honour, as their father doth, his friend. But he who begets unprofitable children— what shall we say that he hath sown, but troubles for himself, and much triumph for his foes? Then do not thou, my son, at pleasure's beck, dethrone thy reason for a woman's sake; knowing that this is a joy that soon grows cold in clasping arms,— an evil woman to share thy bed and thy home. For what wound could strike deeper than a false friend? Nay, with loathing, and as if she were thine enemy, let this girl go to find a husband in the house of Hades. For since I have taken her, alone of all the city, in open disobedience, I will not make myself a liar to my people—I will slay her.

So let her appeal as she will to the majesty of kindred blood. If I am to nurture mine own kindred in naughtiness, needs must I bear with it in aliens. He who does his duty in his own household will be found righteous in the State also. But if any one transgresses, and does violence to the laws, or thinks to dictate to his rulers, such an one can win no praise from me. No, whomsoever the city may appoint, that man must be obeyed, in little things and great, in just things and unjust; and I should feel sure that one who thus obeys would be a good ruler no less than a good subject, and in the storm of spears would stand his ground where he was set, loyal and dauntless at his comrade's side.

But disobedience is the worst of evils. This it is that ruins cities; this makes homes desolate; by this, the ranks of allies are broken into headlong rout: but, of the lives whose course is fair, the greater part owes safety to obedience. Therefore we must support the cause of order, and in no wise suffer a woman to worst us. Better to fall from power, if we must, by a man's hand; then we should not be called weaker than a woman.

CH: To us, unless our years have stolen our wit thou seemest to say wisely what thou sayest.

HAE: Father, the gods implant reason in men, the highest of all things that we call our own. Not mine the skill—far from me be the quest!—to say wherein thou speakest not aright; and yet another man, too, might have some useful thought. At least, it is my natural office to watch, on thy behalf, all that men say, or do, or find to blame. For the dread of thy frown forbids the citizen to speak such words as would offend thine ear; but I can hear these murmurs in the dark, these moanings of the city for this maiden; 'no woman,' they say, 'ever merited her doom less,— none ever was to die so shamefully for deeds so glorious as hers; who, when her own brother had fallen in bloody strife, would not leave him unburied, to be devoured by carrion dogs, or by any bird:—deserves not *she* the meed of golden honour?'

Such is the darkling rumour that spreads in secret. For me, my father, no treasure is so precious as thy welfare. What, indeed, is a nobler ornament for children than a prospering sire's fair fame, or for sire than son's?

Wear not, then, one mood only in thyself; think not that thy word, and thine alone, must be right. For if any man thinks that he alone is wise,—that in speech, or in mind, he hath no peer,—such a soul, when laid open, is ever found empty.

No, though a man be wise, 'tis no shame for him to learn many things, and to bend in season. Seest thou, beside the wintry torrent's course, how the trees that yield to it save every twig, while the stiff-necked perish root and branch? And even thus he who keeps the sheet of his sail taut, and never slackens it, upsets his boat, and finishes his voyage with keel uppermost.

Nay, forego thy wrath; permit thyself to change. For if I, a younger man, may offer my thought, it were far best, I ween, that men should be all-wise by nature; but, otherwise—and oft the scale inclines not so—'tis good also to learn from those who speak aright.

CH: Sire, 'tis meet that thou shouldest profit by his words, if he speaks aught in season, and thou, Haemon, by thy father's; for on both parts there hath been wise speech.

CR: Men of my age—are we indeed to be schooled, then, by men of his?

HAE: In nothing that is not right; but if I am young, thou shouldest look to my merits, not to my years.

CR: Is it a merit to honour the unruly?

HAE: I could wish no one to show respect for evil-doers.

CR: Then is not she tainted with that malady?

HAE: Our Theban folk, with one voice, denies it.

CR: Shall Thebes prescribe to me how I must rule?

HAE: See, there thou hast spoken like a youth indeed.

CR: Am I to rule this land by other judgment than mine own?

HAE: That is no city, which belongs to one man.

CR: Is not the city held to be the ruler's?

HAE: Thou wouldst make a good monarch of a desert.

CR: This boy, it seems, is the woman's champion.

HAE: If thou art a woman; indeed, my care is for thee.

CR: Shameless, at open feud with thy father!

HAE: Nay, I see thee offending against justice.

CR: Do I offend, when I respect mine own prerogatives?

HAE: Thou dost not respect them, when thou tramplest on the gods' honours.

CR: O dastard nature, yielding place to a woman!

HAE: Thou wilt never find me yield to baseness.

CR: All thy words, at least, plead for that girl.

HAE: And for thee, and for me, and for the gods below.

CR: Thou canst never marry her, on this side the grave.

HAE: Then she must die, and in death destroy another.

CR: How! doth thy boldness run to open threats?

HAE: What threat is it, to combat vain resolves?

CR: Thou shalt rue thy witless teaching of wisdom.

HAE: Wert thou not my father, I would have called thee unwise.

CR: Thou woman's slave, use not wheedling speech with me.

HAE: Thou wouldest speak, and then hear no reply?

CR: Sayest thou so? Now, by the heaven above us—be sure of it—thou shalt smart for taunting me in this opprobrious strain. Bring forth that hated thing, that she may die forthwith in his presence—before his eyes—at her bridegroom's side!

HAE: No, not at my side—never think it—shall she perish; nor shalt thou ever set eyes more upon my face:—rave, then, with such friends as can endure thee.

[*Exit* HAEMON.]

CH: The man is gone, O King, in angry haste; a youthful mind, when stung, is fierce.

CR: Let him do, or dream, more than man—good speed to him!—But he shall not save these two girls from their doom.

CH: Dost thou indeed purpose to slay both?

CR: Not her whose hands are pure: thou sayest well.

CH: And by what doom mean'st thou to slay the other?

CR: I will take her where the path is loneliest, and hide her, living, in a rocky vault, with so much food set forth as piety prescribes, that the city may avoid a public stain. And there, praying to Hades, the only god whom she worships, perchance she will obtain release from death; or else will learn, at last, though late, that it is lost labour to revere the dead.

[*Exit* CREON.]

CH: Love, unconquered in the fight, Love, who makest havoc of wealth, who keepest thy vigil on the soft cheek of a maiden; thou roamest over the sea, and among the homes of dwellers in the wilds; no immortal can escape thee, nor any among men whose life is for a day; and he to whom thou hast come is mad.

The just themselves have their minds warped by thee to wrong, for their ruin: 'tis thou that hast stirred up this present strife of kinsmen; victorious is the love-kindling light from the eyes of the fair bride; it is a power enthroned in sway beside the eternal laws; for there the goddess Aphrodite is working her unconquerable will.

But now I also am carried beyond the bounds of loyalty, and can no more keep back the streaming tears, when I see Antigone thus passing to the bridal chamber where all are laid to rest.

AN: See me, citizens of my fatherland, setting forth on my last way, looking my last on the sunlight that is for me no more; no, Hades who gives sleep to all leads me living to Acheron's shore; who have had no portion in the chant that brings the bride, nor hath any song been mine for the crowning of bridals; whom the lord of the Dark Lake shall wed.

CH: Glorious, therefore, and with praise, thou departest to that deep place of the dead: wasting sickness hath not smitten thee; thou hast not found the wages of the sword; no, mistress of thine own fate, and still alive, thou shalt pass to Hades, as no other of mortal kind hath passed.

AN: I have heard in other days how dread a doom befell our Phrygian guest, the daughter of Tantalus, on the Sipylian heights; how, like clinging ivy, the growth of stone subdued her; and the rains fail not, as men tell, from her wasting form, nor fails the snow, while beneath her weeping lids the tears bedew her bosom; and most like to hers is the fate that brings me to my rest.

CH: Yet she was a goddess, thou knowest, and born of gods; we are mortals, and of mortal race. But 'tis great renown for a woman who hath perished that she should have shared the doom of the godlike, in her life, and afterward in death.

AN: Ah, I am mocked! In the name of our fathers' gods, can ye not wait till I am gone,—must ye taunt me to my face, O my city, and ye, her wealthy sons? Ah, fount of Dircè, and thou holy ground of Thebè whose chariots are many; ye, at least, will bear me witness, in what sort, unwept of friends, and by what laws I pass to the rock-closed prison of my strange tomb, ah me unhappy! who have no home on the earth or in the shades, no home with the living or with the dead.

CH: Thou hast rushed forward to the utmost verge of daring; and against that throne where Justice sits on high thou hast fallen, my daughter, with a grievous fall. But in this ordeal thou art paying, haply, for thy father's sin.

AN: Thou hast touched on my bitterest thought,—awaking the ever-new lament for my sire and for all the doom given to us, the famed house of Labdacus. Alas for the horrors of the mother's bed! alas for the wretched mother's slumber at the side of her own son,—and my sire! From what manner of parents did I take my miserable being! And to them I go thus, accursed, unwed, to share their home. Alas, my brother, ill-starred in thy marriage, in thy death thou hast undone my life!

CH: Reverent action claims a certain praise for reverence; but an offence against power cannot be brooked by him who hath power in his keeping. Thy self-willed temper hath wrought thy ruin.

AN: Unwept, unfriended, without marriage-song, I am led forth in my sorrow on this journey that can be delayed no more. No longer, hapless one, may I behold you day-star's sacred eye; but for my fate no tear is shed, no friend makes moan.

CR: Know ye not that songs and wailings before death would never cease, if it profited to utter them? Away with her—away! And when ye have enclosed her, according to my word, in her vaulted grave, leave her alone, forlorn—whether she wishes to die, or to live a buried life in such a home. Our hands are clean as touching this maiden. But this is certain—she shall be deprived of her sojourn in the light.

AN: Tomb, bridal-chamber, eternal prison in the caverned rock, whither I go to find mine own, those many who have perished, and whom Persephone hath received among the dead! Last of all shall I pass thither, and far most miserably of all, before the term of my life is spent. But I cherish good hope that my coming will be welcome to my father, and pleasant to thee, my mother, and welcome, brother, to thee; for, when ye died, with mine own hands I washed and dressed you, and poured drink-offerings at your graves; and now, Polyneices, 'tis for tending thy corpse that I win such recompense as this.

And yet I honoured thee, as the wise will deem, rightly. Never, had I been a mother of children, or if a husband had been mouldering in death, would I have taken this task upon me in the city's despite. What law, ye ask, is my warrant for that word? The husband lost, another might have been found, and child from another, to replace the first-born; but, father and mother hidden with Hades, no brother's life could ever bloom for me again. Such was the law whereby I held thee first in honour; but Creon deemed me guilty of error therein, and of outrage, ah brother mine! And now he leads me thus, a captive in his hands; no bridal bed, no bridal song hath been mine, no joy of marriage, no portion in the nurture of children; but thus, forlorn of friends, unhappy one, I go living to the vaults of death.

And what law of heaven have I transgressed? Why, hapless one, should I look to the gods any more,— what ally should I invoke,— when by piety I have earned the name of impious? Nay, then, if these things are pleasing to the gods, when I have suffered my doom, I shall come to know my sin; but if the sin is with my judges, I could wish them no fuller measure of evil than they, on their part, mete wrongfully to me.

CH: Still the same tempest of the soul vexes this maiden with the same fierce gusts.

CR: Then for this shall her guards have cause to rue their slowness.

AN: Ah me! that word hath come very near to death.

CR: I can cheer thee with no hope that this doom is not thus to be fulfilled.

AN: O city of my fathers in the land of Thebè! O ye gods, eldest of our race!—they lead me hence— now, now—they tarry not! Behold me, princes of Thebes, the last daughter of the house of your kings,—see what I suffer, and from whom, because I feared to cast away the fear of Heaven!

[ANTIGONE *is led away by the guards.*]

CH: Even thus endured Danaë in her beauty to change the light of day for brass-bound walls; and in that chamber, secret as the grave, she was held close prisoner; yet was she of a proud lineage, O my daughter, and charged with the keeping of the seed of Zeus, that fell in the golden rain.

But dreadful is the mysterious power of fate; there is no deliverance from it by wealth or by war, by fenced city, or dark, sea-beaten ships.

And bonds tamed the son of Dryas, swift to wrath, that king of the Edonians; so paid he for his frenzied taunts, when, by the will of Dionysus, he was pent in a rocky prison. There the fierce exuberance of his madness slowly passed away. That man learned to know the god, whom in his frenzy he had provoked with mockeries; for he had sought to quell the god-possessed women, and the Bacchanalian fire; and he angered the Muses that love the flute.

And by the waters of the Dark Rocks, the waters of the twofold sea, are the shores of Bosporus, and Thracian Salmydessus; where Ares, neighbour to the city, saw the accurst, blinding wound dealt to the two sons of Phineus by his fierce wife,—the wound that brought darkness to those vengeance-craving orbs, smitten with her bloody hands, smitten with her shuttle for a dagger.

Pining in their misery, they bewailed their cruel doom, those sons of a mother hapless in her marriage; but she traced her descent from the ancient line of the Erechtheidae; and in far-distant caves she was nursed amid her father's storms, that child of Boreas, swift as a steed over the steep hills, a daughter of gods; yet upon her also the grey Fates bore hard, my daughter.

[*Enter* TEIRESIAS, *led by a boy, on the spectators' right.*]

TE: Princes of Thebes, we have come with linked steps, both served by the eyes of one; for thus, by a guide's help, the blind must walk.

CR: And what, aged Teiresias, are thy tidings?

TE: I will tell thee; and do thou hearken to the seer.

CR: Indeed, it has not been my wont to slight thy counsel.

TE: Therefore didst thou steer our city's course aright.

CR: I have felt, and can attest, thy benefits.

TE: Mark that now, once more, thou standest on fate's fine edge.

CR: What means this? How I shudder at thy message!

TE: Thou wilt learn, when thou hearest the warnings of mine art. As I took my place on mine old seat of augury, where all birds have been wont to gather within my ken, I heard a strange voice among them; they were screaming with dire, feverish rage, that drowned their language in a jargon; and I knew that they were rending each other with their talons, murderously; the whirr of wings told no doubtful tale.

Forthwith, in fear, I essayed burnt-sacrifice on a duly kindled altar: but from my offerings the Fire-god showed no flame; a dank moisture, oozing from the thigh-flesh, trickled forth upon the embers, and smoked, and sputtered; the gall was scattered to the air; and the streaming thighs lay bared of the fat that had been wrapped round them.

Such was the failure of the rites by which I vainly asked a sign, as from this boy I learned; for he is my guide, as I am guide to others. And 'tis thy counsel that hath brought this sickness on our state. For the altars of our city and of our hearths have been tainted, one and all, by birds and dogs, with carrion from the hapless corpse, the son of Oedipus: and therefore the gods no more accept prayer and sacrifice at our hands, or the flame of meat-offering; nor doth any bird give a clear sign by its shrill cry, for they have tasted the fatness of a slain man's blood.

Think, then, on these things, my son. All men are liable to err; but when an error hath been made, that man is no longer witless or unblest who heals the ill into which he hath fallen, and remains not stubborn. Self-will, we know, incurs the charge of folly. Nay, allow the claim of the dead; stab not the fallen; what prowess is it to slay the slain anew? I have sought thy good, and for thy good I speak: and never is it sweeter to learn from a good counsellor than when he counsels for thine own gain.

CR: Old man, ye all shoot your shafts at me, as archers at the butts;—ye must needs practise on me with seer-craft also;—aye, the seer-tribe hath long trafficked in me, and made me their merchandise. Gain your gains, drive your trade, if ye list, in the silver-gold of Sardis and the gold of India; but ye shall not hide that man in the grave,—no, though the eagles of Zeus should bear the carrion morsels to their Master's throne—no, not for dread of that defilement will I suffer his burial:—for well I know that no mortal can defile the gods.—But, aged Teiresias, the wisest fall with a shameful fall, when they clothe shameful thoughts in fair words, for lucre's sake.

TE: Alas! Doth any man know, doth any consider . . .

CR: Whereof? What general truth dost thou announce?

TE: How precious, above all wealth, is good counsel.

CR: As folly, I think, is the worst mischief.

TE: Yet thou art tainted with that distemper.

CR: I would not answer the seer with a taunt.

TE: But thou dost, in saying that I prophesy falsely.

CR: Well, the prophet-tribe was ever fond of money.

TE: And the race bred of tyrants loves base gain.

CR: Knowest thou that thy speech is spoken of thy King?

TE: I know it; for through me thou hast saved Thebes.

CR: Thou art a wise seer; but thou lovest evil deeds.

TE: Thou wilt rouse me to utter the dread secret in my soul.

CR: Out with it!—Only speak it not for gain.

TE: Indeed, methinks, I shall not,—as touching thee.

CR: Know that thou shalt not trade on my resolve.

TE: Then know thou—aye, know it well—that thou shalt not live through many more courses of the sun's swift chariot, ere one begotten of thine own loins shall have been given by thee, a corpse for corpses; because thou hast thrust children of the sunlight to the shades, and ruthlessly lodged a living soul in the grave; but keepest in this world one who belongs to the gods infernal, a corpse unburied, unhonoured, all unhallowed. In such thou hast no part, nor have the gods above, but this is a violence done to them by thee. Therefore the avenging destroyers lie in wait for thee, the Furies of Hades and of the gods, that thou mayest be taken in these same ills.

And mark well if I speak these things as a hireling. A time not long to be delayed shall awaken the wailing of men and of women in thy house. And a tumult of hatred against thee stirs all the cities whose mangled sons had the burial-rite from dogs, or from wild beasts, or from some winged bird that bore a polluting breath to each city that contains the hearths of the dead.

Such arrows for thy heart—since thou provokest me—have I launched at thee, archer-like, in my anger,— sure arrows, of which thou shalt not escape the smart.—Boy, lead me home, that he may spend his rage on younger men, and learn to keep a tongue more temperate, and to bear within his breast a better mind than now he bears.

[*Exit* TEIRESIAS.]

CH: The man hath gone, O King, with dread prophecies. And, since the hair on this head, once dark, hath been white, I know that he hath never been a false prophet to our city.

CR: I, too, know it well, and am troubled in soul. 'Tis dire to yield; but, by resistance, to smite my pride with ruin—this, too, is a dire choice.

CH: Son of Menoeceus, it behoves thee to take wise counsel.

CR: What should I do, then? Speak, and I will obey.

CH: Go thou, and free the maiden from her rocky chamber, and make a tomb for the unburied dead.

CR: And this is thy counsel? Thou wouldst have me yield?

CH: Yea, King, and with all speed; for swift harms from the gods cut short the folly of men.

CR: Ah me, 'tis hard, but I resign my cherished resolve,—I obey. We must not wage a vain war with destiny.

CH: Go, thou, and do these things; leave them not to others.

CR: Even as I am I'll go:—on, on, my servants, each and all of you,—take axes in your hands, and hasten to the ground that ye see yonder! Since our judgment hath taken this turn, I will be present to unloose her, as I myself bound her. My heart misgives me, 'tis best to keep the established laws, even to life's end.

CH: O thou of many names, glory of the Cadmeian bride, offspring of loud-thundering Zeus! thou who watchest over famed Italia, and reignest, where all guests are welcomed, in the sheltered plain of Eleusinian Deô! O Bacchus, dweller in Thebè, mother-city of Bacchants, by the softly-gliding stream of Ismenus, on the soil where the fierce dragon's teeth were sown!

Thou hast been seen where torch-flames glare through smoke, above the crests of the twin peaks, where move the Corycian nymphs, thy votaries, hard by Castalia's stream.

Thou comest from the ivy-mantled slopes of Nysa's hills, and from the shore green with many-clustered vines, while thy name is lifted up on strains of more than mortal power, as thou visitest the ways of Thebè:

Thebè, of all cities, thou holdest first in honour, thou, and thy mother whom the lightning smote; and now, when all our people is captive to a violent plague, come thou with healing feet over the Parnassian height, or over the moaning strait!

O thou with whom the stars rejoice as they move, the stars whose breath is fire; O master of the voices of the night; son begotten of Zeus; appear, O king, with thine attendant Thyiads, who in night-long frenzy dance before thee, the giver of good gifts, Iacchus!

[*Enter* MESSENGER, *on the spectators' left hand.*]

ME: Dwellers by the house of Cadmus and of Amphion, there is no estate of mortal life that I would ever praise or blame as settled. Fortune raises and Fortune humbles the lucky or unlucky from day to day, and no one can prophesy to men concerning those things which are established. For Creon was blest once, as I count bliss; he had saved this land of Cadmus from its foes; he was clothed with sole dominion in the land; he reigned, the glorious sire of princely children. And now all hath been lost. For when a man hath forfeited his pleasures, I count him not as living,—I hold him but a breathing corpse. Heap up riches in thy house, if thou wilt; live in kingly state; yet, if there be no gladness therewith, I would not give the shadow of a vapour for all the rest, compared with joy.

CH: And what is this new grief that thou hast to tell for our princes?

ME: Death; and the living are guilty for the dead.

CH: And who is the slayer? Who the stricken? Speak.

ME: Haemon hath perished; his blood hath been shed by no stranger.

CH: By his father's hand, or by his own?

ME: By his own, in wrath with his sire for the murder.

CH: O prophet, how true, then, hast thou proved thy word!

ME: These things stand thus; ye must consider of the rest.

CH: Lo, I see the hapless Eurydicè, Creon's wife, approaching; she comes from the house by chance, haply,—or because she knows the tidings of her son.

[*Enter* EURYDICÈ]

EU: People of Thebes, I heard your words as I was going forth, to salute the goddess Pallas with my prayers. Even as I was loosing the fastenings of the gate, to open it, the message of a household woe smote on mine ear: I sank back, terror-stricken, into the arms of my hand-maids, and my senses fled. But say again what the tidings were; I shall hear them as one who is no stranger to sorrow.

ME: Dear lady, I will witness of what I saw, and will leave no word of the truth untold. Why, indeed, should I soothe thee with words in which I must presently be found false? Truth is ever best. —I attended thy lord as his guide to the furthest part of the plain, where the body of Polyneices, torn by dogs, still lay un-pitied. We prayed the goddess of the roads, and Pluto, in mercy to restrain their wrath; we washed the dead with holy washing; and with freshly-plucked boughs we solemnly burned such relics as there were. We raised a high mound of his native earth; and then we turned away to enter the maiden's nuptial chamber with rocky couch, the caverned mansion of the bride of Death. And, from afar off, one of us heard a voice of loud wail-ing at that bride's unhallowed bower; and came to tell our master Creon.

And as the King drew nearer, doubtful sounds of a bitter cry floated around him; he groaned, and said in accents of anguish, 'Wretched that I am, can my foreboding be true? Am I going on the wofullest way that ever I went? My son's voice greets me.—Go, my servants,—haste ye nearer, and when ye have reached the tomb, pass through the gap, where the stones have been wrenched away, to the cell's very mouth,—and look, and see if 'tis Haemon's voice that I know, or if mine ear is cheated by the gods.'

This search, at our despairing master's word, we went to make; and in the furthest part of the tomb we descried *her* hanging by the neck, slung by a threadwrought halter of fine linen; while *he* was embracing her with arms thrown around her waist,—bewailing the loss of his bride who is with the dead, and his father's deeds, and his own ill-starred love.

But his father, when he saw him, cried aloud with a dread cry, and went in, and called to him with a voice of wailing:—'Unhappy, what a deed hast thou done! What thought hath come to thee? What manner of mischance hath marred thy reason? Come forth, my child! I pray thee—I implore!' But the boy glared at him with fierce eyes, spat in his face, and, without a word of answer, drew his cross-hilted sword:—as his father rushed forth in flight, he missed his aim;—then, hapless one, wroth with himself, he straightway leaned with all his weight against his sword, and drove it, half its length, into his side; and, while sense lingered, he clasped the maiden to his faint embrace, and, as he gasped, sent forth on her pale cheek the swift stream of the oozing blood.

Corpse enfolding corpse he lies; he hath won his nuptial rites, poor youth, not here, yet in the halls of Death; and he hath witnessed to mankind that, of all curses which cleave to man, ill counsel is the sover-eign curse.

[EURYDICÈ *retires into the house.*]

CH: What wouldst thou augur from this? The lady hath turned back, and is gone, without a word, good or evil.

ME: I, too, am startled; yet I nourish the hope that, at these sore tidings of her son, she cannot deign to give her sorrow public vent, but in the privacy of the house will set her handmaids to mourn the household grief. For she is not untaught of discretion, that she should err.

CH: I know not; but to me, at least, a strained silence seems to portend peril, no less than vain abundance of lament.

ME: Well, I will enter the house, and learn whether indeed she is not hiding some repressed purpose in the depths of a passionate heart. Yea, thou sayest well: excess of silence, too, may have a perilous meaning.

[*Exit* MESSENGER.]

[*Enter* CREON, *on the spectator's left, with attendants, carrying the shrouded body of* HAEMON *on a bier.*]

CH: Lo, yonder the King himself draws near, bearing that which tells too clear a tale,—the work of no stranger's madness,—if we may say it,—but of his own misdeeds.

CR: Woe for the sins of a darkened soul, stubborn sins, fraught with death! Ah, ye behold us, the sire who hath slain, the son who hath perished! Woe is me, for the wretched blindness of my counsels! Alas, my son, thou hast died in thy youth, by a timeless doom, woe is me!—thy spirit hath fled,—not by thy folly, but by mine own!

CH: Ah me, how all too late thou seemest to see the right!

CR: Ah me, I have learned the bitter lesson! But then, methinks, oh then, some god smote me from above with crushing weight, and hurled me into ways of cruelty, woe is me,—over-throwing and trampling on my joy! Woe, woe, for the troublous toils of men!

[*Enter* MESSENGER *from the house.*]

ME: Sire, thou hast come, methinks, as one whose hands are not empty, but who hath store laid up besides; thou bearest yonder burden with thee; and thou art soon to look upon the woes within thy house.

CR: And what worse ill is yet to follow upon ills?

ME: Thy queen hath died, true mother of yon corpse—ah, hapless lady!—by blows newly dealt.

CR: Oh Hades, all-receiving, whom no sacrifice can appease! Hast thou, then, no mercy for me? O thou herald of evil, bitter tidings, what word dost thou utter? Alas, I was already as dead, and thou hast smitten me anew! What sayest thou, my son? What is this new message that thou bringest—woe, woe is me!—of a wife's doom,—of slaughter heaped on slaughter?

CH: Thou canst behold: 'tis no longer hidden within.

[*The doors of the palace are opened, and the corpse of* EURYDICÈ *is disclosed.*]

CR: Ah me,—yonder I behold a new, a second woe! What destiny, ah what, can yet await me? I have but now raised my son in my arms,—and there, again, I see a corpse before me! Alas, alas, unhappy mother! Alas, my child!

ME: There, at the altar, self-stabbed with a keen knife, she suffered her darkening eyes to close, when she had wailed for the noble fate of Megareus who died before, and then for his fate who lies there,—and when, with her last breath, she had invoked evil fortunes upon thee, the slayer of thy sons.

CR: Woe, woe! I thrill with dread. Is there none to strike me to the heart with two-edged sword?—O miserable that I am, and steeped in miserable anguish!

ME: Yea, both this son's doom, and that other's, were laid to thy charge by her whose corpse thou seest.

CR: And what was the manner of the violent deed by which she passed away?

ME: Her own hand struck her to the heart, when she had learned her son's sorely lamented fate.

CR: Ah me, this guilt can never be fixed on any other of mortal kind, for my acquittal! I, even I, was thy slayer, wretched that I am—I own the truth. Lead me away, O my servants, lead me hence with all speed, whose life is but as death!

CH: Thy counsels are good, if there can be good with ills; briefest is best, when trouble is in our path.

CR: Oh, let it come, let it appear, that fairest of fates for me, that brings my last day,—aye, best fate of all! Oh, let it come, that I may never look upon to-morrow's light!

CH: These things are in the future; present tasks claim our care: the ordering of the future rests where it should rest.

CR: All my desires, at least, were summed in that prayer.

CH: Pray thou no more; for mortals have no escape from destined woe.

CR: Lead me away, I pray you; a rash, foolish man; who have slain thee, ah my son, unwittingly, and thee, too, my wife—unhappy that I am! I know not which way I should bend my gaze, or where I should seek support; for all is amiss with that which is in my hands,—and yonder, again, a crushing fate hath leapt upon my head.

[*As* CREON *is being conducted into the house, the Coryphaeus speaks the closing verses.*]

CH: Wisdom is the supreme part of happiness; and reverence towards the gods must be inviolate. Great words of prideful men are ever punished with great blows, and, in old age, teach the chastened to be wise.

Thucydides

The period of Athenian greatness, to which the world owes so much, did not last long. Only about seventy-five years lay between the time of Athens's victory over the Persians and their defeat by the Spartans and their allies in the Peloponnesian War. The two wars were causally connected together through a link that was both political and economic in nature. Even after their repulsion of the Persians, the Greeks were fearful of a return of the invaders so Athens and other city-states of the Aegean Sea and the Ionian coast formed the Delian League, for mutual self-defense. The League began as a voluntary and equitable association, but, largely under the leadership of the great statesman, Pericles, Athens came to dominate the League, exacting heavy taxes from the other members (much of the money being used to beautify Athens) and refusing to allow any city-state to withdraw from the association. Thus the Delian League was transformed into an Athenian Empire. As a consequence Sparta (as well as other Greek city-states) became alarmed and set out to stem the growing power of Athens.

The result was the Peloponnesian War, which raged intermittently during much of the latter part of the fifth century B.C.

Our great source of information about this war comes from the historian, Thucydides, who was born sometime around 470 and probably died soon after 400. Thucydides, a descendant of Miltiades—the victor of the battle of Marathon—was himself a soldier, but not a successful one. Early in the war he failed in his defense of a city against a Spartan force; for this failure he was stripped of his command and sent into exile from Athens for twenty years.

If not an outstanding military leader, Thucydides was a great historian—in the opinion of some scholars the greatest who ever lived. The qualities of his writing that they generally cite in support of this judgment are such attributes as his objectivity, his accuracy, his penetrating analyses of character, his appreciation of the demoralizing effects of warfare on society, and his recognition of the logical connections between events. Finally, he considered history to have a moral value, believing that events like wars, not being chance things but the results of causes, would recur in the future if similar conditions arose. From this one can infer that, if we are acquainted with history, and aware of the mistakes that our predecessors made, we can profit from our knowledge and avoid repeating the past. As Thucydides put it, "My history is an everlasting possession, not a prize composition which is heard and forgotten."

History of the Peloponnesian War

BOOK I

1. Thucydides, an Athenian, wrote the history of the war in which the Peloponnesians and the Athenians fought against one another. He began to write when they first took up arms, believing that it would be great and memorable above any previous war.[1] For he argued that both states were then at the full height of their military power, and he saw the rest of the Hellenes either siding or intending to side with one or the other of them. No movement ever stirred Hellas more deeply than this; it was shared by many of the Barbarians, and might be said even to affect the world at large.

• • •

22. As to the speeches which were made either before or during the war, it was hard for me, and for others who reported them to me, to recollect the exact words. I have therefore put into the mouth of each speaker the sentiments proper to the occasion, expressed as I thought he would be likely to express them, while at the same time I endeavored, as nearly as I could, to give the general purport of what was actually said. Of the events of the war I have not ventured to speak from any chance information, nor according to any notion of my own; I have described nothing but what I either saw myself, or learned from others of whom I made the most careful and particular inquiry. The task was a laborious one, because eye-witnesses of the same occurrences gave different accounts of them, as they remembered or were interested in the actions of one side or the other. And very likely the strictly historical character of my narrative may be disappointing to the ear. But if he who desires to have before his eyes a true picture of the events which have happened, and of the like events which may be expected to happen hereafter in the order of human things, shall pronounce what I have written to be useful, then I shall be satisfied. My history is an everlasting possession, not a prize composition which is heard and forgotten.

• • •

----

[1] [Thucydides is here referring to himself in the third person.—*Ed.*]

Trans. B. Jowett, 2nd ed.

BOOK II

• • •

34. During the same winter,[2] in accordance with an old national custom, the funeral of those who first fell in this war was celebrated by the Athenians at the public charge. The ceremony is as follows: Three days before the celebration they erect a tent in which the bones of the dead are laid out, and every one brings to his own dead any offering which he pleases. At the time of the funeral the bones are placed in chests of cypress wood, which are conveyed on hearses; there is one chest for each tribe. They also carry a single empty litter decked with a pall for all whose bodies are missing, and cannot be recovered after the battle. The procession is accompanied by any one who chooses, whether citizen or stranger, and the female relatives of the deceased are present at the place of interment and make lamentation. The public sepulchre is situated in the most beautiful spot outside the walls; there they always bury those who fall in war; only after the battle of Marathon the dead, in recognition of their preeminent valor, were interred on the field. When the remains have been laid in the earth, some man of known ability and high reputation, chosen by the city, delivers a suitable oration over them; after which the people depart. Such is the manner of interment; and the ceremony was repeated from time to time throughout the war. Over those who were the first buried Pericles was chosen to speak. At the fitting moment he advanced from the sepulchre to a lofty stage, which had been erected in order that he might be heard as far as possible by the multitude, and spoke as follows:—

Funeral Speech

35. "Most of those who have spoken here before me have commended the law-giver who added this oration to our other funeral customs; it seemed to them a worthy thing that such an honor should be given at their burial to the dead who have fallen on the field of battle. But I should have preferred that, when men's deeds have been brave, they should be honored in deed only, and with such an honor as this public funeral, which you are now witnessing. Then the reputation of many would not have been imperilled on the eloquence or want of eloquence of one and their virtues believed or not as he spoke well or ill. For it is difficult to say neither too little nor too much; and even moderation is apt not to give the impression of truthfulness. The friend of the dead who knows the facts is likely to think that the words of the speaker fall short of his knowledge and of his wishes; another who is not so well informed, when he hears of anything which surpasses his own powers, will be envious and will suspect exaggeration. Mankind are tolerant of the praises of others so long as each hearer thinks that he can do as well or nearly as well himself, but, when the speaker rises above him, jealousy is aroused and he begins to be incredulous. However, since our ancestors have set the seal of their approval upon the practice, I must obey, and to the utmost of my power shall endeavor to satisfy the wishes and beliefs of all who hear me.

---

[2][At the end of the first year of the Peloponnesian War, 431 B.C.—*Ed.*]

36. "I will speak first of our ances-tors, for it is right and becoming that now, when we are lamenting the dead, a tribute should be paid to their memory. There has never been a time when they did not inhabit this land, which by their valor they have handed down from generation to generation, and we have received from them a free state. But if they were worthy of praise, still more were our fathers, who added to their in-heritance, and after many a struggle transmitted to us their sons this great empire. And we ourselves assembled here today, who are still most of us in the vigor of life, have chiefly done the work of improvement, and have richly endowed our city with all things, so that she is sufficient for herself both in peace and war. Of the military exploits by which our various possessions were acquired, or of the energy with which we or our fathers drove back the tide of war, Hellenic or Barbarian, I will not speak; for the tale would be long and is familiar to you. But before I praise the dead, I should like to point out by what principles of action we rose to power, and under what institutions and through what manner of life our empire became great. For I conceive that such thoughts are not unsuited to the occasion, and that this num-erous assembly of citizens and stran-gers may profitably listen to them.

37. "Our form of government does not enter into rivalry with the institutions of others. We do not copy our neighbors, but are an ex-ample to them. It is true that we are called a democracy, for the adminis-tration is in the hands of the many and not of the few. But while the law secures equal justice to all alike in their private disputes, the claim of excellence is also recognized; and when a citizen is in any way distin-guished, he is preferred to the public service, not as a matter of privilege, but as the reward of merit. Neither is poverty a bar, but a man may benefit his country whatever be the obscurity of his condition. There is no exclu-siveness in our public life, and in our private intercourse we are not suspi-cious of one another, nor angry with our neighbor if he does what he likes; we do not put on sour looks at him which, though harmless, are not pleasant. While we are thus uncon-strained in our private intercourse, a spirit of reverence pervades our pub-lic acts; we are prevented from doing wrong by respect for authority and for the laws, having an especial re-gard to those which are ordained for the protection of the injured as well as those unwritten laws which bring upon the transgressor of them the reprobation of the general senti-ment.

38. "And we have not forgotten to provide for our weary spirits many re-laxations from toil; we have regular games and sacrifices throughout the year; at home the style of our life is refined; and the delight which we daily feel in all these things helps to banish melancholy. Because of the greatness of our city the fruits of the whole earth flow in upon us; so that we enjoy the goods of other coun-tries as freely as of our own.

39. "Then, again, our military training is in many respects, superior to that of our adversaries. Our city is thrown open to the world, and we never expel a foreigner or prevent him from seeing or learning any-thing of which the secret if revealed to an enemy might profit him. We rely not upon management or trick-ery, but upon our own hearts and hands. And in the matter of educa-

tion, whereas they from early youth are always undergoing laborious exercises which are to make them brave, we live at ease, and yet are equally ready to face the perils which they face. And here is the proof. The Lacedaemonians come into Attica not by themselves, but with their whole confederacy following; we go alone into a neighbor's country; and although our opponents are fighting for their homes and we on a foreign soil, we have seldom any difficulty in overcoming them. Our enemies have never yet felt our united strength; the care of a navy divides our attention, and on land we are obliged to send our own citizens everywhere. But they, if they meet and defeat a part of our army, are as proud as if they had routed us all, and when defeated they pretend to have been vanquished by us all.

40. "If then we prefer to meet danger with a light heart but without laborious training, and with a courage which is gained by habit and not enforced by law, are we not greatly the gainers? Since we do not anticipate the pain, although, when the hour comes, we can be as brave as those who never allow themselves to rest; and thus too our city is equally admirable in peace and in war. For we are lovers of the beautiful, yet simple in our tastes, and we cultivate the mind without a loss of manliness. Wealth we employ, not for talk and ostentation, but when there is a real use for it. To avow poverty with us is no disgrace: the true disgrace is in doing nothing to avoid it. An Athenian citizen does not neglect the state because he takes care of his own household; and even those of us who are engaged in business have a very fair idea of politics. We alone regard a man who

takes no interest in public affairs, not as a harmless, but as a useless character; and if few of us are originators, we are all sound judges of a policy. The great impediment to action is, in our opinion, not discussion, but the want of that knowledge which is gained by discussion preparatory to action. For we have a peculiar power of thinking before we act and of acting too, whereas other men are courageous from ignorance but hesitate upon reflection. And they are surely to be esteemed the bravest spirits who, having the clearest sense both of the pains and pleasures of life, do not on that account shrink from danger. In doing good, again, we are unlike others; we make our friends by conferring, not by receiving favors. Now, he who confers a favor is the firmer friend, because he would fain by kindness keep alive the memory of an obligation; but the recipient is colder in his feelings, because he knows that in requiting another's generosity he will not be winning gratitude, but only paying a debt. We alone do good to our neighbors not upon a calculation of interest, but in the confidence of freedom and in a frank and fearless spirit.

41. "To sum up: I say that Athens is the school of Hellas, and that the individual Athenian in his own person seems to have the power of adapting himself to the most varied forms of action with the utmost versatility and grace. This is no passing and idle word, but truth and fact; and the assertion is verified by the position to which these qualities have raised the state. For in the hour of trial Athens alone among her contemporaries is superior to the report of her. No enemy who comes against her is indignant at the reverses which

he sustains at the hands of such a city; no subject complains that his masters are unworthy of him. And we shall assuredly not be without witnesses; there are mighty monuments of our power which will make us the wonder of this and of succeeding ages; we shall not need the praises of Homer or of any other panegyrist whose poetry may please for the moment, although his representation of the facts will not bear the light of day. For we have compelled every land and every sea to open a path for our valor, and have everywhere planted eternal memorials of our friendship and of our enmity. Such is the city for whose sake these men nobly fought and died; they could not bear the thought that she might be taken from them; and every one of us who survive should gladly toil on her behalf.

42. "I have dwelt upon the greatness of Athens because I want to show you that we are contending for a higher prize than those who enjoy none of these privileges, and to establish by manifest proof the merit of these men whom I am now commemorating. Their loftiest praise has been already spoken. For in magnifying the city I have magnified them, and men like them whose virtues made her glorious. And of how few Hellenes can it be said as of them, that their deeds when weighted in the balance have been found equal to their fame! Methinks that a death such as theirs has been gives the true measure of a man's worth; it may be the first revelation of his virtues, but is at any rate their final seal. For even those who come short in other ways may justly plead the valor with which they have fought for their country; they have blotted out the evil with the good, and have benefited the state more by their public services

than they have injured her by their private actions. None of these men were enervated by wealth or hesitated to resign the pleasures of life; none of them put off the evil day in the hope, natural to poverty, that a man, though poor, may one day become rich. But, deeming that the punishment of their enemies was sweeter than any of these things, and that they could fall in no nobler cause, they determined at the hazard of their lives to be honorably avenged, and to leave the rest. They resigned to hope their unknown chance of happiness; but in the face of death they resolved to rely upon themselves alone. And when the moment came they were minded to resist and suffer, rather than to fly and save their lives; they ran away from the word of dishonor, but on the battle-field their feet stood fast, and in an instant, at the height of their fortune, they passed away from the scene, not of their fear, but of their glory.

43. "Such was the end of these men; they were worthy of Athens, and the living need not desire to have a more heroic spirit, although they may pray for a less fatal issue. The value of such a spirit is not to be expressed in words. Any one can discourse to you forever about the advantage of a brave defence which you know already. But instead of listening to him I would have you day by day fix your eyes upon the greatness of Athens, until you become filled with the love of her; and when you are impressed by the spectacle of her glory, reflect that this empire has been acquired by men who knew their duty and had the courage to do it, who in the hour of conflict had the fear of dishonor always present to them, and who, if ever they failed in an enterprise, would not allow

their virtues to be lost to their country, but freely gave their lives to her as the fairest offering which they could present at her feast. The sacrifice which they collectively made was individually repaid to them; for they received again each one for himself a praise which grows not old, and the noblest of all sepulchres—I speak not of that in which their remains are laid, but of that in which their glory survives, and is proclaimed always and on every fitting occasion both in word and deed. For the whole earth is the sepulchre of famous men; not only are they commemorated by columns and inscriptions in their own country, but in foreign lands there dwells also an unwritten memorial of them, graven not on stone but in the hearts of men. Make them your examples, and esteeming courage to be freedom and freedom to be happiness, do not weigh too nicely the perils of war. The unfortunate who has no hope of a change for the better has less reason to throw away his life than the prosperous who, if he survives, is always liable to a change for the worse, and to whom any accidental fall makes the most serious difference. To a man of spirit, cowardice and disaster coming together are far more bitter than death, striking him unperceived at a time when he is full of courage and animated by the general hope.

44. "Wherefore I do not now commiserate the parents of the dead who stand here; I would rather comfort them. You know that your life has been passed amid manifold vicissitudes; and that they may be deemed fortunate who have gained most honor, whether an honorable death like theirs, or an honorable sorrow like yours, and whose days have been so ordered that the term of their happiness is likewise the term of their life. I know how hard it is to make you feel this, when the good fortune of others will too often remind you of the gladness which once lightened your hearts. And sorrow is felt at the want of those blessings, not which a man never knew, but which were a part of his life before they were taken from him. Some of you are of an age at which they may hope to have other children, and they ought to bear their sorrow better; not only will the children who may hereafter be born make them forget their own lost ones, but the city will be doubly a gainer. She will not be left desolate, and she will be safer. For a man's counsel cannot have equal weight or worth, when he alone has no children to risk in the general danger. To those of you who have passed their prime, I say; 'Congratulate yourselves that you have been happy during the greater part of your days; remember that your life of sorrow will not last long, and be comforted by the glory of those who are gone. For the love of honor alone is ever young, and not riches, as some say, but honor is the delight of men when they are old and useless.'

45. "To you who are the sons and brothers of the departed, I see that the struggle to emulate them will be an arduous one. For all men praise the dead, and, however preeminent your virtue may be, hardly will you be thought, I do not say to equal, but even to approach them. The living have their rivals and detractors, but when a man is out of the way, the honor and goodwill which he receives is unalloyed. And, if I am to speak of womanly virtues to those of you who will henceforth be widows, let me sum them up in one short ad-

monition: To a woman not to show more weakness than is natural to her sex is a great glory, and not to be talked about for good or for evil among men.

46. "I have paid the required tribute, in obedience to the law, making use of such fitting words as I had. The tribute of deeds has been paid in part; for the dead have been honorably interred, and it remains only that their children should be maintained at the public charge until they are grown up; this is the solid prize with which, as with a garland, Athens crowns her sons living and dead, after a struggle like theirs. For where the rewards of virtue are greatest, there the noblest citizens are enlisted in the service of the state. And now, when you have duly lamented, every one his own dead, you may depart."

• • •

BOOK III

• • •

82. For not long afterwards[5] nearly the whole Hellenic world was in commotion; in every city the chiefs of the democracy and of the oligarchy were struggling, the one to bring in the Athenians, the other the Lacedaemonians. Now, in time of peace, men would have had no excuse for introducing either, and no desire to do so, but when they were at war and both sides could easily obtain allies to the hurt of their enemies and the advantage of themselves, the dissatisfied party were only too ready to invoke foreign aid. And revolution brought upon the cities of Hellas many terrible calamities, such as

---

[5][In 427 B.C., or four years after Pericles' Funeral Oration.—Ed.]

have been and always will be while human nature remains the same, but which are more or less aggravated and differ in character with every new combination of circumstances. In peace and prosperity both states and individuals are actuated by high motives, because they do not fall under the dominion of imperious necessities; but war which takes away the comfortable provision of daily life is a hard master, and tends to assimilate men's characters to their conditions.

When troubles had once begun in the cities, those who followed carried the revolutionary spirit further and further, and determined to outdo the report of all who had preceded them by the ingenuity of their enterprises and the atrocity of their revenges. The meaning of words had no longer the same relation to things, but was changed by them as they thought proper. Reckless daring was held to be loyal courage; prudent delay was the excuse of a coward; moderation was the disguise of unmanly weakness; to know everything was to do nothing. Frantic energy was the true quality of man. A conspirator who wanted to be safe was a recreant in disguise. The lover of violence was always trusted, and his opponent suspected. He who succeeded in a plot was deemed knowing, but a still greater master in craft was he who detected one. On the other hand, he who plotted from the first to have nothing to do with plots was a breaker up of parties and a poltroon who was afraid of the enemy. In a word, he who could outstrip another in a bad action was applauded, and so was he who encouraged to evil one who had no idea of it. The tie of party was stronger than the tie of blood, because a partisan was more ready to dare without asking why. (For party associations are not based upon established law, nor do they seek the public good; they are formed in defiance of the laws and from self-interest.) The seal of good faith was not divine law, but fellowship in crime. If any enemy when he was in the ascendant offered fair words, the opposite party received them, not in a generous spirit, but by a jealous watchfulness of his actions. Revenge was dearer than self-preservation. Any agreements sworn to by either party, when they could do nothing else, were binding as long as both were powerless. But he who on a favorable opportunity first took courage and struck at his enemy when he saw him off his guard, had greater pleasure in a perfidious than he would have had in an open act of revenge; he congratulated himself that he had taken the safer course, and also that he had over-reached his enemy and gained the prize of superior ability. In general, the dishonest more easily gain credit for cleverness than the simple for goodness; men take a pride in the one, but are ashamed of the other.

The cause of all these evils was the love of power originating in avarice and ambition, and the party-spirit which is engendered by them when men were fairly embarked in a contest. For the leaders on either side used specious names, the one party professing to uphold the constitutional equality of the many, the other the wisdom of an aristocracy, while they made the public interests, to which in name they were devoted, in reality their prize. Striving in every way to overcome each other, they committed the most monstrous crimes; yet even these were surpassed by the magnitude of their revenges which they pursued to the very utmost, neither party observing any definite limits either of justice or public expediency, but both alike making the caprice of the moment their law. Either by the help of an unrighteous sentence, or grasping power with the strong hand, they were eager to satiate the impatience of party-spirit. Neither faction cared for religion; but any fair pretence which succeeded in effecting some odious purpose was greatly lauded. And the citizens who were of neither party fell a prey to both; either they were disliked because they held aloof, or men were jealous of their surviving.

83. Thus revolution gave birth to every form of wickedness in Hellas. The simplicity which is so large an element in a noble nature was laughed to scorn and disappeared. An attitude of perfidious antagonism everywhere prevailed; for there was no word binding enough, nor oath terrible enough to reconcile enemies. Each man was strong only in the conviction that nothing was secure; he must look to his own safety, and could not afford to trust others.

• • •

BOOK V
• • •

84. In the ensuing summer, Alcibiades sailed to Argos with twenty ships, and seized any of the Argives who were still suspected to be of the Lacedaemonian faction, three hundred in number; and the Athenians deposited them in the subject islands near at hand. The Athenians next made an expedition against the island of Melos[4] with thirty ships of

---

[4] [In 416 B.C.—*Ed.*]

their own, six Chian, and two Lesbian, twelve hundred hoplites and three hundred archers besides twenty mounted archers of their own, and about fifteen hundred hoplites furnished by their allies in the islands. The Melians are colonists of the Lacedaemonians who would not submit to Athens like the other islanders. At first they were neutral and took no part. But when the Athenians tried to coerce them by ravaging their lands they were driven into open hostilities. The generals, Cleomedes the son of Lycomedes and Tisias the son of Tisimachus, encamped with the Athenian forces on the island. But before they did the country any harm they sent envoys to negotiate with the Melians. Instead of bringing these envoys before the people, the Melians desired them to explain their errand to the magistrates and to the chief men. They spoke as follows—

85. "Since we are not allowed to speak to the people, lest, forsooth, they should be deceived by seductive and unanswerable arguments which they would hear set forth in a single uninterrupted oration (for we are perfectly aware that this is what you mean in bringing us before a select few), you who are sitting here may as well make assurance yet surer. Let us have no set speeches at all, but do you reply to each several statement of which you disapprove, and criticise it at once. Say first of all how you like this mode of proceeding."

86. The Melian representatives answered:—"The quiet interchange of explanations is a reasonable thing, and we do not object to that. But your warlike movements, which are present not only to our fears but to our eyes, seem to belie your words. We see that, although you may reason with us, you mean to be our judges; and that at the end of the discussion if the justice of our cause prevail and we therefore refuse to yield, we may expect war; if we are convinced by you, slavery."

87. ATHENIAN: Nay, but if you are only going to argue from fancies about the future, or if you meet us with any other purpose than that of looking your circumstances in the face and saving your city, we have done; but if this is your intention we will proceed.

88. MELIAN: It is an excusable and natural thing that men in our position should have much to say and should indulge in many fancies. But we admit that this conference has met to consider the question of our preservation; and therefore let the argument proceed in the manner which you propose.

89. ATHENIAN: Well, then, we Athenians will use no fine words; we will not go out of our way to prove at length that we have a right to rule, because we overthrew the Persians; or that we attack you now because we are suffering any injury at your hands. We should not convince you if we did; nor must you expect to convince us by arguing that, although a colony of the Lacedaemonians, you have taken no part in their expeditions, or that you have never done us any wrong. But you and we should say what we really think, and aim only at what is possible, for we both alike know that into the discussion of human affairs, the question of justice only enters where the pressure of necessity is equal, and that the powerful exact what they can, and the weak grant what they must.

90. MELIAN: Well, then, since you set aside justice and invite us to speak of expediency, in our judgment it is

certainly expedient that you should respect a principle which is for the common good; and that to every man when in peril a reasonable claim should be accounted a claim of right, and any plea which he is disposed to urge, even if failing of the point a little, should help his cause. Your interest in this principle is quite as great as ours, inasmuch as you, if you fall, will incur the heaviest vengeance, and will be the most terrible example to mankind.

91. ATHENIAN: The fall of our empire, if it should fall, is not an event to which we look forward with dismay; for ruling states such as Lacedaemon are not cruel to their vanquished enemies. And we are fighting not so much against the Lacedaemonians as against our own subjects who may some day rise up and overcome their former masters. But this is a danger which you may leave to us. And we will now endeavor to show that we have come in the interests of our empire, and that in what we are about to say we are only seeking the preservation of your city. For we want to make you ours with the least trouble to ourselves, and it is for the interests of us both that you should not be destroyed.

92. MELIAN: It may be your interest to be our masters, but how can it be ours to be your slaves?

93. ATHENIAN: To you the gain will be that by submission you will avert the worst; and we shall be all the richer for your preservation.

94. MELIAN: But must we be your enemies? Will you not receive us as friends if we are neutral and remain at peace with you?

95. ATHENIAN: No, your enmity is not half so mischievous to us as your friendship; for the one is in the eyes of our subjects an argument of our power, the other of our weakness.

96. MELIAN: But are your subjects really unable to distinguish between states in which you have no concern, and those which are chiefly your own colonies, and in some cases have revolted and been subdued by you?

97. ATHENIAN: Why, they do not doubt that both of them have a good deal to say for themselves on the score of justice, but they think that states like yours are left free because they are able to defend themselves, and that we do not attack them because we dare not. So that your subjection will give us an increase of security, as well as an extension of empire. For we are masters of the sea, and you who are islanders, and insignificant islanders too, must not be allowed to escape us.

98. MELIAN : But do you not recognise another danger? For once more, since you drive us from the plea of justice and press upon us your doctrine of expediency, we must show you what is for our interest, and, if it be for yours also, may hope to convince you:—Will you not be making enemies of all who are now neutrals? When they see how you are treating us they will expect you some day to turn against them; and if so, are you not strengthening the enemies whom you already have, and bringing upon you others who, if they could help, would never dream of being your enemies at all?

99. ATHENIAN: We do not consider our really dangerous enemies to be any of the peoples inhabiting the mainland who, secure in their freedom, may defer indefinitely any measures of precaution which they take against us, but islanders who, like you, happen to be under no control,

and all who may be already irritated by the necessity of submission to our empire—these are our real enemies, for they are the most reckless and most likely to bring themselves as well as us into a danger which they cannot but foresee.

100. MELIAN: Surely then, if you and your subjects will brave all this risk, you to preserve your empire and they to be quit of it, how base and cowardly it would be in us, who retain our freedom, not to do and suffer anything rather than be your slaves.

101. ATHENIAN: Not so, if you calmly reflect: for you are not fighting against equals to whom you cannot yield without disgrace, but you are taking counsel whether or not you shall resist an overwhelming force. The question is not one of honor but of prudence.

102. MELIAN: But we know that the fortune of war is sometimes impartial, and not always on the side of numbers. If we yield now all is over; but if we fight there is yet a hope that we may stand upright.

103. ATHENIAN: Hope is a good comforter in the hour of danger, and when men have something else to depend upon, although hurtful, she is not ruinous. But when her spendthrift nature has induced them to stake their all, they see her as she is in the moment of their fall, and not till then. While the knowledge of her might enable them to beware of her, she never fails. You are weak and a single turn of the scale might be your ruin. Do not you be thus deluded; avoid the error of which so many are guilty, who, although they might still be saved if they would take the natural means, when visible grounds of confidence forsake them, have re-course to the invisible, to prophecies and oracles and the like, which ruin men by the hopes which they inspire in them.

104. MELIAN: We know only too well how hard the struggle must be against your power, and against fortune, if she does not mean to be impartial. Nevertheless we do not despair of fortune, for we hope to stand as high as you in the favor of heaven, because we are righteous, and you against whom we contend are unrighteous; and we are satisfied that our deficiency in power will be compensated by the aid of our allies the Lacedaemonians; they cannot refuse to help us, if only because we are their kinsmen, and for the sake of their own honor. And therefore our confidence is not so utterly blind as you suppose.

105. ATHENIAN: As for the Gods, we expect to have quite as much of their favor as you: for we are not doing or claiming anything which goes beyond common opinion about divine or men's desires about human things. For of the Gods we believe, and of men we know, that by a law of their nature wherever they can rule they will. This law was not made by us, and we are not the first who have acted upon it; we did but inherit it, and shall bequeath it to all time, and we know that you and all mankind, if you were as strong as we are, would do as we do. So much for the Gods; we have told you why we expect to stand as high in their good opinion as you. And then as to the Lacedaemonians—when you imagine that out of very shame they will assist you, we admire the simplicity of your idea, but we do not envy you the folly of it. The Lacedaemonians are exceedingly virtuous among them-

selves, and according to their national standard of morality. But in respect of their dealings with others, although many things might be said, a word is enough to describe them— of all men whom we know they are the most notorious for identifying what is pleasant with what is honorable, and what is expedient with what is just. But how inconsistent is such a character with your present blind hope of deliverance!

106. MELIAN: That is the very reason why we trust them; they will look to their interest, and therefore will not be willing to betray the Melians, who are their own colonists, lest they should be distrusted by their friends in Hellas and play into the hands of their enemies.

107. ATHENIAN: But do you not see the path of expediency is safe, whereas justice and honor involve danger in practice, and such dangers the Lacedaemonians seldom care to face?

108. MELIAN: On the other hand we think that whatever perils there may be, they will be ready to face them for our sakes, and will consider danger less dangerous where we are concerned. For if they need our aid we are close at hand, and they can better trust our loyal feeling because we are their kinsmen.

109. ATHENIAN: Yes, but what encourages men who are invited to join in a conflict is clearly not the goodwill of those who summon them to their side, but a decided superiority in real power. To this no men look more keenly than the Lacedaemonians; so little confidence have they in their own resources that they only attack their neighbors when they have numerous allies, and therefore they are not likely to find their way by themselves to an island, when we are masters of the sea.

110. MELIAN: But they may send their allies; the Cretan sea is a large place; and the masters of the sea will have more difficulty in overtaking vessels which want to escape than the pursued in escaping. If the attempt should fail, they may invade Attica itself, and find their way to allies of yours whom Brasidas did not reach; and then you will have to fight, not for the conquest of a land in which you have no concern, but nearer home, for the preservation of your confederacy and of your own territory.

111. ATHENIAN: Help may come from Lacedaemon to you as it has come to others, and should you ever have actual experience of it, then you will know that never once have the Athenians retired from a siege through fear of a foe elsewhere. You told us that the safety of your city would be your first care, but we remark that, in this long discussion, not a word has been uttered by you which would give a reasonable man expectation of deliverance. Your strongest grounds are hopes deferred, and what power you have is not to be compared with that which is already arrayed against you. Unless after we have withdrawn you mean to come, as even now you may, to a wiser conclusion, you are showing a great want of sense. For surely you cannot dream of flying to that false sense of honor which has been the ruin of so many when danger and dishonor were staring them in the face. Many men with their eyes still open to the consequences have found the word "honor" too much for them, and have suffered a mere name to lure them on, until it has

drawn down upon them real and irretrievable calamities; through their own folly they have incurred a worse dishonor than fortune would have inflicted upon them. If you are wise you will not run this risk; you ought to see that there can be no disgrace in yielding to a great city which invites you to become her ally on reasonable terms, keeping your own land, and merely paying tribute, and that you will certainly gain no honor if, having to choose between two alternatives, safety and war, you obstinately prefer the worse. To maintain our rights against equals, to be politic with superiors, and to be moderate towards inferiors is the path of safety. Reflect once more when we have withdrawn, and say to yourselves over and over again that you are deliberating about your one and only country, which may be saved or may be destroyed by a single decision.

112. The Athenians left the conference: the Melians, after consulting among themselves, resolved to persevere in their refusal, and made answer as follows:—"Men of Athens, our resolution is unchanged; and we will not in a moment surrender that liberty which our city, founded seven hundred years ago, still enjoys; we will trust to the good-fortune which by the favor of the Gods has hitherto preserved us, and for human help to the Lacedaemonians, and endeavor to save ourselves. We are ready however to be your friends, and the enemies neither of you nor of the Lacedaemonians, and we ask you to leave our country when you have made such a peace as may appear to be in the interest of both parties."

113. Such was the answer of the Melians; the Athenians, as they quitted the conference, spoke as follows:—"Well, we must say, judging from the decision at which you have arrived, that you are the only men who deem the future to be more certain than the present, and regard things unseen as already realized in your fond anticipation, and that the more you cast yourselves upon the Lacedaemonians and fortune, and hope, and trust them, the more complete will be your ruin."

114. The Athenian envoys returned to the army, and the generals, when they found that the Melians would not yield, immediately commenced hostilities. They surrounded the town of Melos with a wall, dividing the work among the several contingents. They then left troops of their own and of the allies to keep guard both by land and by sea, and retired with the greater part of their army; the remainder carried on the blockade.

116. . . . The place was now closely invested, and there was treachery among the citizens themselves. So the Melians were induced to surrender at discretion. The Athenians thereupon put to death all who were of military age, and made slaves of the women and children. They then colonised the island, sending thither five hundred settlers of their own.

The Trial and Death of Socrates

Although Socrates (c. 470–399 B.C.) was an influential philosopher and teacher, he wrote nothing. So we must rely on secondary accounts for information about his life and beliefs. Such accounts, particularly the writings of his most famous disciple, Plato, make it possible to reconstruct the broad outlines of his career. Socrates was born in Athens, the son of a stonecutter. Instead of following his father's trade, he began early in life to frequent the Athenian agora (marketplace), where he listened to the intellectuals of the city argue questions of politics, art, morality, and philosophy.

Before long, he had acquired a reputation for wisdom and had gathered about himself a group of young disciples, who were intrigued by the unusual manner in which he taught. Unlike the sophists ("wise men"), the professional teachers of the day who were willing to teach anyone anything for a suitable fee, Socrates professed himself to be ignorant. Instead of attempting to teach, he wandered about Athens seeking wisdom by asking questions of everyone he met, including the city's leading politicians,

generals, artists, and philosophers. As might be expected, under Socrates' questioning many of the self-styled sages proved to be without wisdom. Although Socrates' unflinching quest for wisdom and truth won him many loyal followers, it inevitably aroused the enmity of those whose ignorance he unmasked. Through their influence in Athens, his enemies succeeded in having him brought to trial and condemned to death. But they were unable to silence him, for his words live on in the dialogues of Plato.

Although he professed no wisdom of his own, Socrates did have a positive philosophy. The basic premise of this philosophy was the doctrine that *virtue is knowledge,* or that the good life is the life of wisdom. To gain knowledge and hence virtue, he believed, education is necessary. But knowledge is not something that can be poured into an individual from the outside. Rather, it lies deep within each person and needs only to be drawn out. Socrates' method for bringing this inborn knowledge to the surface was to ask a series of questions, a technique known as the *dialectic method.*

The selections that follow are an account of the last days of Socrates written by Plato some time after the events described. Socrates had been hauled into court by a group of accusers, a sort of "un-Athenian activities committee," who charged him with being an atheist and a corrupter of youth. In Plato's *Apology*, Socrates is represented as replying to the charges with a general defense of his way of life. In the *Crito*, Plato pictures Socrates waiting in prison for his execution and arguing with a friend (who has arranged for his escape) about whether he would be justified in running away, even though he has been unjustly convicted. The extract from the *Phaedo* records Socrates' death. These selections give us a fresh and living portrait of Socrates the man, a fairly comprehensive account of his philosophy, and a glimpse of the social and legal structure of the Athens of his day.

The Apology

SCENE: The Court of Justice

I cannot tell what impression my accusers have made upon you, Athenians: for my own part, I know that they nearly made me forget who I was, so plausible were they; and yet they have scarcely uttered one single word of truth. But of all their many falsehoods, the one which astonished me most, was when they said that I was a clever speaker, and that you must be careful not to let me mislead you. I thought that it was most impudent of them not to be ashamed to talk in that way; for as soon as I opened my mouth the lie will be exposed, and I shall prove that I am not a clever speaker in any way at all: unless, indeed, by a clever speaker they mean a man who speaks the truth. If that is their meaning, I agree with them that I am a much greater orator than they. My accusers, then I repeat, have said little or nothing that is true: but from me you shall hear the whole truth. Certainly you will not hear an elaborate speech, Athenians, drest up, like theirs, with words and phrases. I will say to you what I have to say, without preparation, and in the words which come first, for I believe that my cause is just; so let none of you expect anything else. Indeed, my friends, it would hardly be seemly for me, at my age, to come before you like a young man with his specious falsehoods. But there is one thing, Athenians, which I do most earnestly beg and entreat of you. Do not be surprised and do not interrupt, if in my defence I speak in the same way that I am accustomed to speak in the market-place, at the tables of the money-changers, where many of you have heard me, and elsewhere. The truth is this: I am more than seventy years old, and this is the first time that I have ever come before a Court of

Trans. F. J. Church.

Law; so your manner of speech here is quite strange to me. If I had been really a stranger, you would have forgiven me for speaking in the language and the fashion of my native country: and so now I ask you to grant me what I think I have a right to claim. Never mind the style of my speech—it may be better or it may be worse—give your whole attention to the question, Is what I say just, or is it not? That is what makes a good judge, as speaking the truth makes a good advocate.

I have to defend myself, Athenians, first against the old false charges of my old accusers, and then against the later ones of my present accusers. For many men have been accusing me to you, and for very many years, who have not uttered a word of truth: and I fear them more than I fear Anytus and his companions, formidable as they are. But, my friends, those others are still more formidable; for they got hold of most of you when you were children, and they have been more persistent in accusing me with lies, and in trying to persuade you that there is one Socrates, a wise man, who speculates about the heavens, and who examines into all things that are beneath the earth, and who can "make the worse appear the better reason." These men, Athenians, who spread abroad this report, are the accusers whom I fear; for their hearers think that persons who pursue such inquiries never believe in the gods. And then they are many, and their attacks have been going on for a long time; and they spoke to you when you were at the age most readily to believe them: for you were all young, and many of you were children: and there was no one to answer them when they attacked me. And the most unreasonable

thing of all is that commonly I do not even know their names: I cannot tell you who they are, except in the case of the comic poets. But all the rest who have been trying to prejudice you against me, from motives of spite and jealousy, and sometimes, it may be, from conviction, are the enemies whom it is hardest to meet. For I cannot call any one of them forward in Court, to cross-examine him: I have, as it were, simply to fight with shadows in my defense, and to put questions which there is no one to answer. I ask you, therefore, to believe that, as I say, I have been attacked by two classes of accusers —first by Meletus and his friends, and then by those older ones of whom I have spoken. And, with your leave, I will defend myself first against my old enemies; for you heard their accusations first, and they were much more persistent than my present accusers are.

Well, I must make my defence, Athenians, and try in the short time allowed me to remove the prejudice which you have had against me for a long time. I hope that I may manage to do this, if it be good for you and for me, and that my defence may be successful, but I am quite aware of the nature of my task, and I know that it is a difficult one. Be the issue, however, as God wills, I must obey the law, and make my defence.

Let us begin again, then, and see what is the charge which has given rise to the prejudice against me, which was what Meletus relied on when he drew his indictment. What is the calumny which my enemies have been spreading about me? I must assume that they are formally accusing me, and read their indictment. It would run somewhat in this fashion: "Socrates is an evil-doer, who meddles with inquiries into things beneath the earth, and in heaven, and who 'makes the worse appear the better reason,' and who teaches others these same things." That is what they say: and in the Comedy of Aristophanes you yourselves saw a man called Socrates swinging round in a basket, and saying that he walked the air, and talking a great deal of nonsense about matters of which I understand nothing, either more or less. I do not mean to disparage that kind of knowledge, if there is any man who possesses it. I trust Meletus may never be able to prosecute me for that. But, the truth is, Athenians, I have nothing to do with these matters, and almost all of you are yourselves my witnesses of this. I beg all of you who have heard me converse, and they are many, to inform your neighbors and tell them if any of you ever heard me conversing about such matters, either more or less. That will show you that the other common stories about me are as false as this one.

But, the fact is, that not one of these stories is true; and if you have heard that I undertake to educate men, and exact money from them for so doing, that is not true either; though I think that it would be a fine thing to be able to educate men, as Gorgias of Leontini, and Prodicus of Ceos, and Hippias of Elis do. For each of them, my friends, can go into any city, and persuade the young men to leave the society of their fellow-citizens, with any of whom they might associate for nothing, and to be only too glad to be allowed to pay money for the privilege of associating with themselves. And I believe that there is another wise man from Paros residing in Athens at this mo-

ment. I happened to meet Callias, the son of Hipponicus, a man who has spent more money on the Sophists than every one else put together. So I said to him—he has two sons—"Callias, if your two sons had been foals, or calves, we could have hired a trainer for them who would have made them perfect in the excellence which belongs to their nature. He would have been either a groom or a farmer. But whom do you intend to take to train them, seeing that they are men? Who understands the excellence which belongs to men and to citizens? I suppose that you must have thought of this, because of your sons. Is there such a person," said I, "or not?" "Certainly there is," he replied. "Who is he," said I, "and where does he come from, and what is his fee?" "His name is Evenus, Socrates," he replied. "He comes from Paros, and his fee is five minae." Then I thought that Evenus was a fortunate person if he really understood this art and could teach so cleverly. If I had possessed knowledge of that kind, I should have given myself airs and prided myself on it. But, Athenians, the truth is that I do not possess it.

Perhaps some of you may reply: "But, Socrates, what is this pursuit of yours? Whence come these calumnies against you? You must have become engaged in some pursuit out of the common. All these stories and reports of you would never have gone about, if you had not been in some way different from other men. So tell us what your pursuits are, that we may not give our verdict in the dark." I think that that is a fair question, and I will try to explain to you what it is that has raised these calumnies against me, and given me this name. Listen, then: some of you perhaps will think that I am jesting, but I assure you that I will tell you the whole truth. I have gained this name, Athenians, simply by reason of a certain wisdom. But by what kind of wisdom? It is by just that wisdom which is, I believe, possible to men. In that, it may be, I am really wise. But the men of whom I was speaking just now must be wise in a wisdom which is greater than human wisdom, or in some way which I cannot describe, for certainly I know nothing of it myself, and if any man says that I do, he lies and wants to slander me. Do not interrupt me, Athenians, even if you think that I am speaking arrogantly. What I am going to say is not my own: I will tell you who says it, and he is worthy of your credit. I will bring the god of Delphi to be the witness of the fact of my wisdom and of its nature. You remember Chaerephon. From youth upwards he was my comrade; and he went into exile with the people,[1] and with the people he returned. And you remember, too, Chaerephon's character; how vehement he was in carrying through whatever he took in hand. Once he went to Delphi and ventured to put this question to the oracle,—I entreat you again, my friends, not to cry out,—he asked if there was any man who was wiser than I: and the priestess answered that there was no man. Chaerephon himself is dead, but his brother here will confirm what I say.

Now see why I tell you this. I am going to explain to you the origin of my unpopularity. When I heard of the oracle I began to reflect: What can God mean by this dark saying? I know very well that I am not wise,

even in the smallest degree. Then what can he mean by saying that I am the wisest of men? It cannot be that he is speaking falsely, for he is a god and cannot lie. And for a long time I was at a loss to understand his meaning: then, very reluctantly, I turned to seek for it in this manner. I went to a man who was reputed to be wise, thinking that there, if anywhere, I should prove the answer wrong, and meaning to point out to the oracle its mistake, and to say, "You said that I was the wisest of men, but this man is wiser than I am." So I examined the man—I need not tell you his name, he was a politician—but this was the result, Athenians. When I conversed with him I came to see that, though a great many persons, and most of all he himself, thought that he was wise, yet he was not wise. And then I tried to prove to him that he was not wise, though he fancied that he was: and by so doing I made him, and many of the bystanders, my enemies. So when I went away, I thought to myself, "I am wiser than this man: neither of us probably knows anything that is really good, but he thinks he has knowledge, when he has not, while I, having no knowledge, do not think that I have. I seem at any rate, to be a little wiser than he is on this point: I do not think that I know what I do not know." Next I went to another man who was reputed to be still wiser than the last, with exactly the same result. And there again I made him, and many other men, my enemies. Then I went on to one man after another, seeing that I was making enemies every day, which caused me much unhappiness and anxiety: still I thought that I must set God's command above everything. So I had to go to every man who seemed to possess any knowledge, and search for

---

[1][At the time of the oligarchy of the Thirty, 404 B.C.— *Trans.*]

the meaning of the oracle: and, Athenians, I must tell you the truth; verily, by the dog of Egypt, this was the result of the search which I made at God's bidding. I found that the men, whose reputation for wisdom stood highest, were nearly the most lacking in it; while others, who were looked down on as common people, were much better fitted to learn. Now, I must describe to you the wanderings which I undertook, like a series of Heraclean labours, to make full proof of the oracle. After the politicians, I went to the poets, tragic, dithyrambic, and others, thinking that there I should find myself manifestly more ignorant than they. So I took up the poems on which I thought that they had spent most pains, and asked them what they meant, hoping at the same time to learn something from them. I am ashamed to tell you the truth, my friends, but I must say it. Almost any one of the bystanders could have talked about the works of these poets better than the poets themselves. So I soon found that it is not by wisdom that the poets create their works, but by a certain natural power and by inspiration, like soothsayers and prophets, who say many fine things, but who understand nothing of what they say. The poets seemed to me to be in a similar case. And at the same time I perceived that, because of their poetry, they thought that they were the wisest of men in other matters too, which they were not. So I went away again, thinking that I had the same advantage over the poets that I had over the politicians.

Finally, I went to the artizans, for I knew very well that I possessed no knowledge at all, worth speaking of, and I was sure that I should find that they knew many fine things. And in that I was not mistaken. They knew what I did not know, and so far they were wiser than I. But, Athenians, it seemed to me that the skilled artizans made the same mistake as the poets. Each of them believed himself to be extremely wise in matters of the greatest importance, because he was skilful in his own art: and this mistake of theirs threw their real wisdom into the shade. So I asked myself, on behalf of the oracle, whether I would choose to remain as I was, without either their wisdom or their ignorance, or to possess both, as they did. And I made answer to myself and to the oracle that it was better for me to remain as I was.

By reason of this examination, Athenians, I have made many enemies of a very fierce and bitter kind, who have spread abroad a great number of calumnies about me, and people say that I am "a wise man." For the bystanders always think that I am wise myself in any matter wherein I convict another man of ignorance. But, my friends, I believe that only God is really wise: and that by this oracle he meant that men's wisdom is worth little or nothing. I do not think that he meant that Socrates was wise. He only made use of my name, and took me as an example, as though he would say to men, "He among you is the wisest, who, like Socrates, knows that in very truth his wisdom is worth nothing at all." And therefore I still go about testing and examining every man whom I think wise, whether he be a citizen or a stranger, as God has commanded me; and whenever I find that he is not wise, I point out to him on the part of God that he is not wise. And I am so busy in this pursuit that I have never had leisure to take any part worth mentioning in public matters, or to look after my private affairs. I am in very great poverty by reason of my service to God.

And besides this, the young men who follow me about, who are the sons of wealthy persons and have a great deal of spare time, take a natural pleasure in hearing men cross-examined: and they often imitate me among themselves: then they try their hands at cross-examining other people. And I imagine, they find a great abundance of men who think that they know a great deal, when in fact they know little or nothing. And then the persons who are cross-examined get angry with me instead of with themselves, and say that Socrates is an abominable fellow who corrupts young men. And when they are asked, "Why, what does he do? what does he teach?" they do not know what to say; but, not to seem at a loss, they repeat the stock charges against all philosophers, and allege that he investigates things in the air and under the earth, and that he teaches people to disbelieve in the gods, and "to make the worse appear the better reason." For, I fancy, they would not like to confess the truth, which is that they are shown up as ignorant pretenders to knowledge that they do not possess. And so they have been filling your ears with their bitter calumnies for a long time, for they are zealous and numerous and bitter against me; and they are well disciplined and plausible in speech. On these grounds Meletus and Anytus and Lycon have attacked me. Meletus is indignant with me on the part of the poets, and Anytus on the part of the artizans and politicians, and Lycon on the part of the orators. And so, as I said at the beginning, I shall be surprised if I am able, in the short time allowed me for my defence, to remove from

your minds this prejudice which has grown so strong. What I have told you, Athenians, is the truth: I neither conceal, nor do I suppress anything, small or great. And yet I know that it is just this plainness of speech which makes me enemies. But that is only a proof that my words are true, and that the prejudice against me, and the causes of it, are what I have said. And whether you look for them now or hereafter, you will find that they are so.

[Socrates then cross-examines and discredits his chief accuser.—*Ed.*]

• • •

Perhaps some one will say: "Are you not ashamed, Socrates, of following pursuits which are very likely now to cause your death?" I should answer him with justice, and say: My friend, if you think that a man of any worth at all ought to reckon the chances of life and death when he acts, or that he ought to think of anything but whether he is acting rightly or wrongly, and as a good or a bad man would act, you are grievously mistaken. According to you, the demigods who died at Troy would be men of no great worth, and among them the son of Thetis, who thought nothing of danger when the alternative was disgrace. For when his mother, a goddess, addressed him, as he was burning to slay Hector, I suppose in this fashion, "My son, if thou avengest the death of thy comrade Patroclus, and slayest Hector, thou wilt die thyself, for 'fate awaits thee straightway after Hector's death' "; he heard what she said, but he scorned danger and death; he feared much more to live a coward, and not to avenge his friend. "Let me punish the evil-doer and straightway die," he said, "that I may not remain here by the beaked ships, a scorn of men, encumbering the earth." Do you suppose that he thought of danger or of death? For this, Athenians, I believe to be the truth. Wherever a man's post is, whether he has chosen it of his own will, or whether he has been placed at it by his commander, there it is his duty to remain and face the danger, without thinking of death, or of any other thing, except dishonour.

When the generals whom you chose to command me, Athenians, placed me at my post at Potidaea, and at Amphipholis, and at Delium, I remained where they placed me, and ran the risk of death, like other men: and it would be very strange conduct on my part if I were to desert my post now from fear of death or of any other thing, when God has commanded me, as I am persuaded that he has done, to spend my life searching for wisdom, and in examining myself and others. That would indeed be a very strange thing: and then certainly I might with justice be brought to trial for not believing in the gods: for I should be disobeying the oracle, and fearing death, and thinking myself wise, when I was not wise. For to fear death, my friends, is only to think ourselves wise, without being wise: for it is to think that we know what we do not know. For anything that men can tell, death may be the greatest good that can happen to them: but they fear it as if they knew quite well that it was the greatest of evils. And what is this but that shameful ignorance of thinking that we know what we do not know? In this manner too, my friends, perhaps I am different from the mass of mankind: and if I were to claim to be at all wiser than others, it would be because I do not think that I have

any clear knowledge about the other world, when, in fact, I have none. But I do know very well that it is evil and base to do wrong, and to disobey my superior, whether he be man or god. And I will never do what I know to be evil, and shrink in fear from what, for all that I can tell, may be a good. And so, even if you acquit me now, and do not listen to Anytus' argument that, if I am to be acquitted, I ought never to have been brought to trial at all; and that, as it is, you are bound to put me to death, because, as he said, if I escape, all your children will forthwith be utterly corrupted by practising what Socrates teaches; if you were therefore to say to me, "Socrates, this time we will not listen to Anytus: we will let you go; but on this condition, that you cease from carrying on this search of yours, and from philosophy; if you are found following those pursuits again, you shall die": I say, if you offered to let me go on these terms, I should reply:—"Athenians, I hold you in the highest regard and love; but I will obey God rather than you: and as long as I have breath and strength I will not cease from philosophy, and from exhorting you, and declaring the truth to everyone of you whom I meet, saying, as I am wont, 'My excellent friend, you are a citizen of Athens, a city which is very great and very famous for wisdom and power of mind; are you not ashamed of caring so much for the making of money, and for reputation, and for honour? Will you not think or care about wisdom, and truth, and the perfection of your soul?' " And if he disputes my words, and says that he does care about these things, I shall not forthwith release him and go away: I shall question him and cross-examine him and test him: and if I think that he has not virtue, though he says that he has, I shall reproach him for setting the lower value on the most important things, and a higher value on those that are of less account. This I shall do to every one whom I meet, young or old, citizen or stranger: but more especially to the citizens, for they are more nearly akin to me. For, know well, God has commanded me to do so. And I think that no better piece of fortune has ever befallen you in Athens than my service to God. For I spend my whole life in going about and persuading you all to give your first and chiefest care to the perfection of your souls, and not till you have done that to think of your bodies, or your wealth; and telling you that virtue does not come from wealth, but that wealth, and every other good thing which men have, whether in public, or in private, comes from virtue. If then I corrupt the youth by this teaching, the mischief is great: but if any man says that I teach anything else, he speaks falsely. And therefore, Athenians, I say, either listen to Anytus, or do not listen to him: either acquit me, or do not acquit me: but be sure that I shall not alter my way of life; no, not if I have to die for it many times.

Do not interrupt me, Athenians. Remember the request which I made to you, and listen to my words. I think that it will profit you to hear them. I am going to say something more to you, at which you may be inclined to cry out: but do not do that. Be sure that if you put me to death, who am what I have told you that I am, you will do yourselves more harm than me. Meletus and Anytus can do me no harm: that is impossible: for I am sure that God will not allow a good man to be injured by a bad one. They may indeed kill me, or drive me into exile, or deprive me of my civil rights; and perhaps Meletus and others think those things great evils. But I do not think so: I think that it is a much greater evil to do what he is doing now, and to try to put a man to death unjustly. And now, Athenians, I am not arguing in my own defence at all, as you might expect me to do: I am trying to persuade you not to sin against God, by condemning me, and rejecting his gift to you. For if you put me to death, you will not easily find another man to fill my place. God has sent me to attack the city, as if it were a great and noble horse, to use a quaint simile, which was rather sluggish from its size, and which needed to be aroused by a gadfly: and I think that I am the gadfly that God has sent to the city to attack it; for I never cease from settling upon you, as it were, at every point, and rousing, and exhorting, and reproaching each man of you all day long. You will not easily find any one else, my friends, to fill my place: and if you take my advice, you will spare my life. You are vexed, as drowsy persons are, when they are awakened, and of course, if you listen to Anytus, you could easily kill me with a single blow, and then sleep on undisturbed for the rest of your lives, unless God were to care for you enough to send another man to arouse you. And you may easily see that it is God who has given me to your city: a mere human impulse would never have led me to neglect all my own interests, or to endure seeing my private affairs neglected now for so many years, while it made me busy myself unceasingly in your interests, and go to each man of you by himself, like a father, or an elder brother, trying to persuade him to care for virtue. There would have been a reason for it, if I had gained any advantage by this conduct, or if I had been paid for my exhortations; but you see yourselves that my accusers, though they accuse me of everything else without blushing, have not had the effrontery to say that I ever either extracted or demanded payment. They could bring no evidence of that. And I think that I have sufficient evidence of the truth of what I say in my poverty.

Perhaps it may seem strange to you that, though I am so busy in going about in private with my counsel, yet I do not venture to come forward in the assembly, and take part in the public councils. You have often heard me speak of my reason for this, and in many places: it is that I have a certain divine sign from God, which is the divinity that Meletus has caricatured in his indictment. I have had it from childhood: it is a kind of voice, which whenever I hear it, always turns me back from something which I was going to do, but never urges me to act. It is this which forbids me to take part in politics. And I think that it does well to forbid me. For, Athenians, it is quite certain that if I had attempted to take part in politics, I should have perished at once and long ago, without doing any good either to you or to myself. And do not be vexed with me for telling the truth. There is no man who will preserve his life for long, either in Athens or elsewhere, if he firmly opposes the wishes of the people, and tries to prevent the commission of much injustice and illegality in the State. He who would really fight for justice, must do so as a private man, not in public, if he means to preserve his life, even for a short time.

I will prove to you that this is so by very strong evidence, not by mere words, but by what you value highly, actions. Listen then to what has happened to me, that you may know that there is no man who could make me consent to do wrong from the fear of death; but that I would perish at once rather than give way. What I am going to tell you may be a commonplace in the Courts of Law; nevertheless it is true. The only office that I ever held in the State, Athenians, was that of Senator. When you wished to try the ten generals, who did not rescue their men after the battle of Arginusae, in a body, which was illegal, as you all came to think afterwards, the tribe Antiochis, to which I belong, held the presidency. On that occasion I alone of all the presidents opposed your illegal action, and gave my vote against you. The speakers were ready to suspend me and arrest me; and you were clamouring against me, and crying out to me to submit. But I thought that I ought to face the danger out in the cause of law and justice, rather than join with you in your unjust proposal, from fear of imprisonment or death. That was before the destruction of the democracy. When the oligarchy came, the Thirty sent for me, with four others, to the Council-Chamber and ordered us to bring over Leon the Salaminian from Salamis, that they might put him to death. They were in the habit of frequently giving similar orders to many others, wishing to implicate as many men as possible in their crimes. But then I again proved, not by mere words, but by my actions, that, if I may use a vulgar expression, I do not care a straw for death; but that I do care very much indeed about not doing anything against the laws of God or man. That government with all its power did not terrify me into doing anything wrong, but when we left the Council-Chamber, the other four went over to Salamis, and brought Leon across to Athens; and I went away home: and if the rule of the Thirty had not been destroyed soon afterwards, I should very likely have been put to death for what I did then. Many of you will be my witnesses in this matter.

Now do you think that I should have remained alive all these years, if I had taken part in public affairs, and had always maintained the cause of justice like an honest man, and had held it a paramount duty, as it is, to do so? Certainly not, Athenians, nor any other man either. But throughout my whole life, both in private, and in public, whenever I have had to take part in public affairs, you will find that I have never yielded a single point in a question of right and wrong to any man; no, not to those whom my enemies falsely assert to have been my pupils. But I was never any man's teacher. I have never withheld myself from any one, young or old, who was anxious to hear me converse while I was about my mission; neither do I converse for payment, and refuse to converse without payment: I am ready to ask questions of rich and poor alike, and if any man wishes to answer me, and then listen to what I have to say, he may. And I cannot justly be charged with causing these men to turn out good or bad citizens: for I never either taught, or professed to teach any of them any knowledge whatever. And if any man asserts that he ever learnt or heard any thing from me in private, which every one else did not hear as well as he, be sure that he does not speak the truth.

Why is it, then, that people delight in spending so much time in my company? You have heard why, Athenians. I told you the whole truth when I said that they delight in hearing me examine persons who think that they are wise when they are not wise. It is certainly very amusing to listen to that. And, I say, God has commanded me to examine men in oracles, and in dreams, and in every way in which the divine will was ever declared to man. This is the truth, Athenians, and if it were not the truth, it would be easily refuted. For if it were really the case that I have already corrupted some of the young men, and I am now corrupting others, surely some of them, finding as they grew older that I had given them evil counsel in their youth, would have come forward to-day to accuse me and take their revenge. Or if they were unwilling to do so themselves, surely their kinsmen, their fathers, or brothers, or other relatives, would, if I had done them any harm, have remembered it, and taken their revenge. Certainly I see many of them in Court. Here is Crito, of my own deme and of my own age, the father of Critobulus; here is Lysanias of Sphettus, the father of Aeschinus: here is also Antiphon of Cephisus, the father of Epigenes. Then here are others, whose brothers have spent their time in my company; Nicostratus, the son of Theozotides, and brother of Theodotus—and Theodotus is dead, so he at least cannot entreat his brother to be silent: here is Paralus, the son of Demodocus, and the brother of Theages: here is Adeimantus, the son of Ariston, whose brother is Plato here: and Aeantodorus, whose brother is Aristodorus. And I can name many others to you, some of whom Meletus ought to have called as witnesses in the course of his own speech: but if he forgot to call them then, let him call them now—I will stand aside while he does so—and tell us if he has any such evidence. No, on the contrary, my friends, you will find all these men ready to support me, the corrupter, the injurer of their kindred, as Meletus and Anytus call me. Those of them who have been already corrupted might perhaps have some reason for supporting me: but what reason can their relatives, who are grown up, and who are uncorrupted, have, except the reason of truth and justice, that they know very well that Meletus is a liar, and that I am speaking the truth?

Well, my friends, this, together it may be with other things of the same nature, is pretty much what I have to say in my defence. There may be some one among you who will be vexed when he remembers how, even in a less important trial than this, he prayed and entreated the judges to acquit him with many tears, and brought forward his children and many of his friends and relatives in Court, in order to appeal to your feelings; and then finds that I shall do none of these things, though I am in what he would think the supreme danger. Perhaps he will harden himself against me when he notices this: it may make him angry, and he may give his vote in anger. If it is so with any of you—I do not suppose that it is, but in case it should be so—I think that I should answer him reasonably if I said: "My friend, I have kinsmen too, for in the words of Homer, 'I am not born of sticks and stones,' but of woman"; and so, Athenians, I have kinsmen, and I have three sons, one of them a lad, and the other two still children. Yet I will not bring any of them forward before you, and implore you to acquit me. And why will I do none of these things? It is not from arrogance, Athenians, nor because I hold you cheap: whether or not I can face death bravely is another question: but for my own credit, and for your credit, and for the credit of our city, I do not think it well, at my age, and with my name, to do anything of that kind. Rightly or wrongly, men have made up their minds that in some way Socrates is different from the mass of mankind. And it will be a shameful thing if those of you who are thought to excell in wisdom, or in bravery, or in any other virtue, are going to act in this fashion. I have often seen men with a reputation behaving in a strange way at their trial, as if they thought it a terrible fate to be killed, and as though they expected to live for ever, if you did not put them to death. Such men seem to me to bring discredit on the city: for any stranger would suppose that the best and most eminent Athenians, who are selected by their fellow-citizens to hold office, and for other honours, are no better than women. Those of you, Athenians, who have any reputation at all, ought not to do these things: and you ought not to allow us to do them: you should show that you will be much more merciless to men who make the city ridiculous by these pitiful pieces of acting, than to men who remain quiet.

But apart from the question of credit, my friends, I do not think that it is right to entreat the judge to acquit us, or to escape condemnation in that way. It is our duty to convince his mind by reason. He does not sit to give away justice to his friends, but to pronounce judgment: and he has sworn not to favour any man whom he would like to favour, but to decide questions according to law. And therefore we ought not teach you to forswear yourselves; and you ought not to allow yourselves to be taught, for then neither you nor we would be acting righteously. Therefore, Athenians, do not require me to do these things, for I believe them to be neither good nor just nor holy; and, more especially do not ask me to do them today, when Meletus is prosecuting me for impiety. For were I to be successful, and to prevail on you by my prayers to break your oaths, I should be clearly teaching you to believe that there are no gods; and I should be simply accusing myself by my defence of not believing in them. But, Athenians, that is very far from the truth. I do believe in the gods as no one of my accusers believes in them: and to you and to God I commit my cause to be decided as is best for you and for me.

[He is found guilty by 281 votes to 220, and in a second vote is condemned to death.—*Ed.*]

• • •

You have not gained very much time, Athenians, and, as the price of it, you will have an evil name from all who wish to revile the city, and they will cast in your teeth that you put Socrates, a wise man, to death. For they will certainly call me wise, whether I am wise or not, when they want to reproach you. If you would have waited for a little while, your wishes would have been fulfilled in the course of nature; for you see that I am an old man, far advanced in years, and near to death. I am speaking not to all of you, only to those who have voted for my death. And now I am speaking to them still. Perhaps, my friends, you think that I have been defeated because I was

wanting in the arguments by which I could have persuaded you to acquit me, if, that is, I had thought it right to do or to say anything to escape punishment. It is not so. I have been defeated because I was wanting, not in arguments, but in overboldness and effrontery: because I would not plead before you as you would have liked to hear me plead, or appeal to you with weeping and wailing, or say and do many other things, which I maintain are unworthy of me, but which you have been accustomed to from other men. But when I was defending myself, I thought that I ought not to do anything unmanly because of the danger which I ran, and I have not changed my mind now. I would very much rather defend myself as I did, and die, than as you would have had me do, and live. Both in a law suit, and in war, there are some things which neither I nor any other man may do in order to escape from death. In battle a man often sees that he may at least escape from death by throwing down his arms and falling on his knees before the pursuer to beg for his life. And there are many other ways of avoiding death in every danger, if a man will not scruple to say and to do anything. But, my friends, I think that it is a much harder thing to escape from wickedness than from death; for wickedness is swifter than death. And now I, who am old and slow, have been overtaken by the slower pursuer: and my accusers, who are clever and swift, have been overtaken by the swifter pursuer, which is wickedness. And now I shall go hence, sentenced by you to death; and they will go hence, sentenced by truth to receive the penalty of wickedness and evil. And I abide by this award as well as they. Perhaps it was right for these things to be so: and I think that they are fairly measured.

And now I wish to prophesy to you, Athenians who have condemned me. For I am going to die, and that is the time when men have most prophetic power. And I prophesy to you who have sentenced me to death, that a far severer punishment than you have inflicted on me, will surely overtake you as soon as I am dead. You have done this thing, thinking that you will be relieved from having to give an account of your lives. But I say that the result will be very different from that. There will be more men who will call you to account, whom I have held back, and whom you did not see. And they will be harder masters to you than I have been, for they will be younger, and you will be more angry with them. For if you think that you will restrain men from reproaching you for your evil lives by putting them to death, you are very much mistaken. That way of escape is hardly possible, and it is not a good one. It is much better, and much easier, not to silence reproaches, but to make yourselves as perfect as you can. This is my parting prophecy to you who have condemned me.

With you who have acquitted me I should like to converse touching this thing that has come to pass, while the authorities are busy, and before I go to the place where I have to die. So, I pray you, remain with me until I go hence: there is no reason why we should not converse with each other while it is possible. I wish to explain to you, as my friends, the meaning of what has befallen me. A wonderful thing has happened to me, judges— for you I am right in calling judges.

The prophetic sign, which I am wont to receive from the divine voice, has been constantly with me all through my life till now, opposing me in quite small matters if I were not going to act rightly. And now you yourselves see what has happened to me; a thing which might be thought, and which is sometimes actually reckoned, the supreme evil. But the sign of God did not withstand me when I was leaving my house in the morning, nor when I was coming up hither to the Court, nor at any point in my speech, when I was going to say anything: though at other times it has often stopped me in the very act of speaking. But now, in this matter, it has never once withstood me, either in my words or my actions. I will tell you what I believe to be the reason of that. This thing that has come upon me must be a good: and those of us who think that death is an evil must needs be mistaken. I have a clear proof that that is so; for my accustomed sign would certainly have opposed me, if I had not been going to fare well.

And if we reflect in another way we shall see that we may well hope that death is a good. For the state of death is one of two things: either the dead man wholly ceases to be, and loses all sensation; or, according to the common belief, it is a change and migration of the soul unto another place. And if death is the absence of all sensation, and like the sleep of one whose slumbers are unbroken by any dreams, it will be a wonderful gain. For if a man had to select that night in which he slept so soundly that he did not even see any dreams, and had to compare with it all the other nights and days of his life, and then had to say how many days and nights in his life he had spent better and more pleasantly than this night, I think that a private person, nay, even the great King himself, would find them easy to count, compared with the others. If that is the nature of death, I for one count it a gain. For then it appears that eternity is nothing more than a single night. But if death is a journey to another place, and the common belief be true, that there are all who have died, what good could be greater than this, my judges? Would a journey not be worth taking, at the end of which, in the other world, we should be released from the self-styled judges who are here, and should find the true judges, who are said to sit in judgment below, such as Minos, and Rhadamanthus, and Aeacus, and Triptolemus, and the other demigods who were just in their lives? Or what would you not give to converse with Orpheus and Musaeus and Hesiod and Homer? I am willing to die many times, if this be true. And for my own part I should have a wonderful interest in meeting there Palamedes, and Ajax the son of Telamon, and the other men of old who have died through an unjust judgment, and in comparing my experiences with theirs. That I think would be no small pleasure. And, above all, I could spend my time in examining those who are there, as I examine men here, and in finding out which of them is wise, and which of them thinks himself wise, when he is not wise. What would we not give, my judges, to be able to examine the leader of the great expedition against Troy, or Odysseus, or Sisyphus, or countless other men and women whom we could name? It would be an

infinite happiness to converse with them, and to live with them, and to examine them. Assuredly there they do not put men to death for doing that. For besides the other ways in which they are happier than we are, they are immortal, at least if the common belief be true.

And you too, judges, must face death with a good courage, and believe this as a truth, that no evil can happen to a good man, either in life, or after death. His fortunes are not neglected by the gods; and what has come to me today has not come by chance. I am persuaded that it was better for me to die now, and to be released from trouble: and that was the reason why the sign never turned me back. And so I am hardly angry with my accusers, or with those who have condemned me to die. Yet it was not with this mind that they accused me and condemned me, but meaning to do me an injury. So far I may find fault with them.

Yet I have one request to make of them. When my sons grow up, visit them with punishment, my friends, and vex them in the same way that I have vexed you, if they seem to you to care for riches, or for any other thing, before virtue: and if they think that they are something, when they are nothing at all, reproach them, as I have reproached you, for not caring for what they should, and for thinking that they are great men when in fact they are worthless. And if you will do this, I myself and my sons will have received our deserts at your hands.

But now the time has come, and we must go hence; I to die, and you to live. Whether life or death is better is known to God, and to God only.

Crito

SCENE: The Prison of Socrates

SOCRATES: Why have you come at this hour, Crito? Is it not still early?

CRITO: Yes, very early.

SOCRATES: About what time is it?

CRITO: It is just day-break.

SOCRATES: I wonder that the jailor was willing to let you in.

CRITO: He knows me now, Socrates, I come here so often; and besides, I have done him a service.

SOCRATES: Have you been here long?

CRITO: Yes; some time.

SOCRATES: Then why did you sit down without speaking? Why did you not wake me at once?

CRITO: Indeed, Socrates, I wish that I myself were not so sleepless and sorrowful. But I have been wondering to see how sweetly you sleep. And I purposely did not wake you, for I was anxious not to disturb your repose. Often before, all through your life, I have thought that your temper was a happy one; and I think so more than ever now, when I see how easily and calmly you bear the calamity that has come to you.

SOCRATES: Nay Crito, it would be absurd if at my age I were angry at having to die.

CRITO: Other men as old are overtaken by similar calamities, Socrates; but their age does not save them from being angry with their fate.

SOCRATES: That is so: but tell me, why are you here so early?

CRITO: I am the bearer of bitter news, Socrates: not bitter, it seems, to you; but to me, and to all your friends, both bitter and grievous: and to none of them, I think, is it more grievous than to me.

SOCRATES: What is it? Has the ship come from Delos, at the arrival of which I am to die?

CRITO: No, it has not actually arrived: but I think that it will be here to-day, from the news which certain persons have brought from Sunium, who left it there. It is clear from their news that it will be here to-day; and then, Socrates, to-morrow your life will have to end.

SOCRATES: Well, Crito, may it end fortunately. Be it so, if so the gods will. But I do not think that the ship will be here to-day.

CRITO: Why do you suppose not?

SOCRATES: I will tell you. I am to die on the day after the ship arrives, am I not?

CRITO: That is what the authorities say.

SOCRATES: Then I do not think that it will come to-day, but tomorrow. I judge from a certain dream which I saw a little while ago in the night: so it seems to be fortunate that you did not wake me.

CRITO: And what was this dream?

SOCRATES: A fair and comely woman, clad in white garments, seemed to come to me, and call me and say, "O Socrates—

The third day hence shall thou fair Phthia reach."

CRITO: What a strange dream, Socrates!

SOCRATES: But its meaning is clear; at least to me, Crito.

Trans. F. J. Church.

CRITO: Yes, too clear, it seems. But, O my good Socrates, I beseech you for the last time to listen to me and save yourself. For to me your death will be more than a single disaster: not only shall I lose a friend the like of whom I shall never find again, but many persons, who do not know you and me well, will think that I might have saved you if I had been willing to spend money, but that I neglected to do so. And what character could be more disgraceful than the character of caring more for money than for one's friends? The world will never believe that we were anxious to save you, but that you yourself refused to escape.

SOCRATES: But, my excellent Crito, why should we care so much about the opinion of the world? The best men, of whose opinion it is worth our while to think, will believe that we acted as we really did.

CRITO: But you see, Socrates, that it is necessary to care about the opinion of the world too. This very thing that has happened to you proves that the multitude can do a man not the least, but almost the greatest harm, if he be falsely accused to them.

SOCRATES: I wish that the multitude were able to do a man the greatest harm, Crito, for then they would be able to do him the greatest good too. That would have been well. But, as it is, they can do neither. They cannot make a man either wise or foolish: they act wholly at random.

CRITO: Well, be it so. But tell me this, Socrates. You surely are not anxious about me and your other friends, and afraid lest, if you escape, the informers should say that we stole you away, and get us into trouble, and involve us in a great deal of expense, or perhaps in the loss of all of our property, and, it may be, bring

some other punishment upon us besides? If you have any fear of that kind, dismiss it. For of course we are bound to run those risks, and still greater risks than those if necessary, in saving you. So do not, I beseech you, refuse to listen to me.

SOCRATES: I am anxious about that, Crito, and about much besides.

CRITO: Then have no fear on that score. There are men who, for no very large sum, are ready to bring you out of prison into safety. And then, you know, these informers are cheaply bought, and there would be no need to spend much upon them. My fortune is at your service, and I think that it is sufficient: and if you have any feeling about making use of my money, there are strangers in Athens, whom you know, ready to use theirs, and one of them, Simmias of Thebes, has actually brought enough for this very purpose. And Cebes and many others are ready too. And therefore, I repeat, do not shrink from saving yourself on that ground. And do not let what you said in the Court, that if you went into exile you would not know what to do with yourself, stand in your way; for there are many places for you to go to, where you will be welcomed. If you choose to go to Thessaly, I have friends there who will make much of you, and shelter you from any annoyance from the people of Thessaly.

And besides, Socrates, I think that you will be doing what is wrong, if you abandon your life when you might preserve it. You are simply playing the game of your enemies; it is exactly the game of those who wanted to destroy you. And what is more, to me you seem to be abandoning your children too: you will leave them to take their chance in life, as far as you are concerned, when you might bring them up and educate them. Most likely their fate will be the usual fate of children who are left orphans. But you ought not to beget children unless you mean to take the trouble of bringing them up and educating them. It seems to me that you are choosing the easy way, and not the way of a good and brave man, as you ought, when you have been talking all your life long of the value that you set upon virtue. For my part, I feel ashamed both for you, and for us who are your friends. Men will think that the whole of this thing which has happened to you—your appearance in court to take your trial, when you need not have appeared at all; the very way in which the trial was conducted; and then lastly this, for the crowning absurdity of the whole affair, is due to our cowardice. It will look as if we had shirked the danger out of miserable cowardice; for we did not save you, and you did not save yourself, when it was quite possible to do so, if we had been good for anything at all. Take care, Socrates, lest these things be not evil only, but also dishonourable to you and to us. Consider then; or rather the time for consideration is past; we must resolve; and there is only one plan possible. Everything must be done to-night. If we delay any longer, we are lost. O Socrates, I implore you not to refuse to listen to me.

SOCRATES: My dear Crito, if your anxiety to save me be right, it is most valuable: but if it be not right, its greatness makes it all the more dangerous. We must consider then whether we are to do as you say, or not; for I am still what I always have been, a man who will listen to no voice but the voice of the reasoning which on consideration I find to be truest. I cannot cast aside my former arguments because this misfortune has come to me. They seem to me to be as true as ever they were, and I hold exactly the same ones in honour and esteem as I used to: and if we have no better reasoning to substitute for them, I certainly shall not agree to your proposal, not even though the power of the multitude should scare us with fresh terrors, as children are scared with hobgoblins, and inflict upon us new fines, and imprisonments, and deaths. How then shall we most fitly examine the question? Shall we go back first to what you say about the opinions of men, and ask if we used to be right in thinking that we ought to pay attention to some opinions, and not to others? Used we to be right in saying so before I was condemned to die, and has it now become apparent that we were talking at random, and arguing for the sake of argument, and that it was really nothing but play and nonsense? I am anxious, Crito, to examine our former reasoning with your help, and to see whether my present position will appear to me to have affected its truth in any way, or not; and whether we are to set it aside, or to yield assent to it. Those of us who thought at all seriously, used always to say, I think, exactly what I said just now, namely, that we ought to esteem some of the opinions which men form highly, and not others. Tell me, Crito, if you please, do you not think that they were right? For you, humanly speaking, will not have to die tomorrow, and your judgment will not be biased by that circumstance. Consider then: do you not think it reasonable to say that we should not esteem all the opinions of men, but only some, nor the opinions of all men, but only of some men? What do you think? Is not this true?

CRITO: It is.

SOCRATES: And we should esteem the good opinions, and not the worthless ones?

CRITO: Yes.

SOCRATES: But the good opinions are those of the wise, and the worthless ones those of the foolish?

CRITO: Of course.

SOCRATES: And what used we to say about this? Does a man who is in training, and who is in earnest about it, attend to the praise and blame and opinion of all men, or of the one man only who is a doctor or a trainer?

CRITO: He attends only to the opinion of the one man.

SOCRATES: Then he ought to fear the blame and welcome the praise of this one man, not of the many?

CRITO: Clearly.

SOCRATES: Then he must act and exercise, and eat and drink in whatever way the one man who is his master, and who understands the matter, bids him; not as others bid him?

CRITO: That is so.

SOCRATES: Good. But if he disobeys this one man, and disregards his opinion and his praise, and esteems instead what the many, who understand nothing of the matter, say, will he not suffer for it?

CRITO: Of course he will.

SOCRATES: And how will he suffer? In what direction, and in what part of himself?

CRITO: Of course in his body. That is disabled.

SOCRATES: You are right. And, Crito, to be brief, is it not the same, in everything? And, therefore, in questions of right and wrong, and of the base and the honourable, and of good and evil, which we are now consider-ing, ought we to follow the opinion of the many and fear that, or the opinion of the one man who understands these matters (if we can find him), and feel more shame and fear before him than before all other men? For if we do not follow him, we shall cripple and maim that part of us which, we used to say, is improved by right and disabled by wrong. Or is this not so?

CRITO: No, Socrates, I agree with you.

SOCRATES: Now, if, by listening to the opinions of those who do not understand, we disable that part of us which is improved by health and crippled by disease, is our life worth living, when it is crippled? It is the body, is it not?

CRITO: Yes.

SOCRATES: Is life worth living with the body crippled and in a bad state?

CRITO: No, certainly not.

SOCRATES: Then is life worth living when that part of us which is maimed by wrong and benefited by right is crippled? Or do we consider that part of us, whatever it is, which has to do with right and wrong to be of less consequence than our body?

CRITO: No, certainly not.

SOCRATES: But more valuable?

CRITO: Yes, much more so.

SOCRATES: Then, my excellent friend, we must not think so much of what the many will say of us; we must think of what the one man, who understands right and wrong, and of what Truth herself will say of us. And so you are mistaken to begin with, when you invite us to regard the opinion of the multitude concerning the right and the honourable and the good, and their opposites. But, it may be said, the multitude can put us to death?

CRITO: Yes, that is evident. That may be said, Socrates.

SOCRATES: True. But, my excellent friend, to me it appears that the conclusion which we have just reached, is the same as our conclusion of former times. Now consider whether we still hold to the belief, that we should set the highest value, not on living, but on living well?

CRITO: Yes, we do.

SOCRATES: And living well and honourably and rightly mean the same thing: do we hold to that or not?

CRITO: We do.

SOCRATES: Then, starting from these premises, we have to consider whether it is right or not right for me to try to escape from prison, without the consent of the Athenians. If we find that it is right, we will try: if not, we will let it alone. I am afraid that considerations of expense, and of reputation, and of bringing up my children, of which you talk, Crito, are only the reflections of our friends, the many, who lightly put men to death, and who would, if they could, as lightly bring them to life again, without a thought. But reason, which is our guide, shows us that we can have nothing to consider but the question which I asked just now: namely, shall we be doing right if we give money and thanks to the men who are to aid me in escaping, and if we ourselves take our respective parts in my escape? Or shall we in truth be doing wrong, if we do all this? And if we find that we should be doing wrong, then we must not take any account either of death, or of any other evil that may be the consequence of remaining quietly here, but only of doing wrong.

CRITO: I think that you are right, Socrates. But what are we to do?

SOCRATES: Let us consider that together, my good sir, and if you can contradict anything that I say, do so,

and I will be convinced: but if you cannot, do not go on repeating to me any longer, my dear friend, that I should escape without the consent of the Athenians. I am very anxious to act with your approval: I do not want you to think me mistaken. But now tell me if you agree with the doctrine from which I start, and try to answer my questions as you think best.

CRITO: I will try.

SOCRATES: Ought we never to do wrong intentionally at all; or may we do wrong in some ways, and not in others? Or, as we have often agreed in former times, is it never either good or honourable to do wrong? Have all our former conclusions been forgotten in these few days? Old men as we were, Crito, did we not see, in days gone by, when we were gravely conversing with each other, that we were no better than children? Or is not what we used to say most assuredly the truth, whether the world agrees with us or not? Is not wrong-doing an evil and a shame to the wrong-doer in every case, whether we incur a heavier or a lighter punishment than death as the consequence of doing right? Do we believe that?

CRITO: We do.

SOCRATES: Then we ought never to do wrong at all?

CRITO: Certainly not.

SOCRATES: Neither, if we ought never to do wrong at all, ought we to repay wrong with wrong, as the world thinks we may?

CRITO: Clearly not.

SOCRATES: Well then, Crito, ought we to do evil to any one?

CRITO: Certainly I think not, Socrates.

SOCRATES: And is it right to repay evil with evil, as the world thinks, or not right?

CRITO: Certainly it is not right.

SOCRATES: For there is no difference, is there, between doing evil to a man, and wronging him?

CRITO: True.

SOCRATES: Then we ought not to repay wrong with wrong or do harm to any man, no matter what we may have suffered from him. And in conceding this, Crito, be careful that you do not concede more than you mean. For I know that only a few men hold, or ever will hold this opinion. And so those who hold it, and those who do not, have no common ground of argument; they can of necessity only look with contempt on each other's belief. Do you therefore consider very carefully whether you agree with me and share my opinion. Are we to start in our inquiry from the doctrine that it is never right either to do wrong, or to repay wrong with wrong, or to avenge ourselves on any man who harms us, by harming him in return? Or do you disagree with me and dissent from my principle? I myself have believed in it for a long time, and I believe in it still. But if you differ in any way, explain to me how. If you still hold to our former opinion, listen to my next point.

CRITO: Yes, I hold to it, and I agree with you. Go on.

SOCRATES: Then, my next point, or rather my next question, is this: Ought a man to perform his just agreements, or may he shuffle out of them?

CRITO: He ought to perform them.

SOCRATES: Then consider. If I escape without the State's consent, shall I be injuring those whom I ought least to injure, or not? Shall I be abiding by my just agreements or not?

CRITO: I cannot answer your question, Socrates. I do not understand it.

SOCRATES: Consider it in this way. Suppose the laws and the commonwealth were to come and appear to me as I was preparing to run away (if that is the right phrase to describe my escape) and were to ask, "Tell us, Socrates, what have you in your mind to do? What do you mean by trying to escape, but to destroy us, the laws, and the whole city, so far as in you lies? Do you think that a state can exist and not be overthrown, in which the decisions of law are of no force, and are disregarded and set at nought by private individuals?" How shall we answer questions like that, Crito? Much might be said, especially by an orator, in defence of the law which makes judicial decisions supreme. Shall I reply, "But the state has injured me: it has decided my cause wrongly." Shall we say that?

CRITO: Certainly we will, Socrates.

SOCRATES: And suppose the laws were to reply, "Was that our agreement? or was it that you would submit to whatever judgments the state should pronounce?" And if we were to wonder at their words, perhaps they would say, "Socrates, wonder not at our words, but answer us; you yourself are accustomed to ask questions and to answer them. What complaint have you against us and the city, that you are trying to destroy us? Are we not, first, your parents? Through us your father took your mother and begat you. Tell us, have you any fault to find with those of us that are the laws of marriage?" "I have none," I should reply. "Or have you any fault to find with those of us that regulate the nurture and education of the child, which you, like others, received? Did not we do well in bidding your father educate you in music and gymnastic?" "You did," I should say. "Well then, since you were brought into the world and nurtured and educated by us, how, in the first place, can you deny that you are our child and our slave, as your fathers were before you? And if this be so, do you think that your rights are on a level with ours? Do you think that you have a right to retaliate upon us if we should try to do anything to you? You had not the same rights that your father had, or that your master would have had, if you had been a slave. You had no right to retaliate upon them if they ill-treated you, or to answer them if they reviled you, or to strike them back if they struck you, or to repay them evil with evil in any way. And do you think that you may retaliate on your country and its laws? If we try to destroy you, because we think it right, will you in return do all that you can to destroy us, the laws, and your country, and say that in so doing you are doing right, you, the man, who in truth thinks so much of virtue? Or are you too wise to see that your country is worthier, and more august, and more sacred, and holier and held in higher honour both by the gods and by all men of understanding, than your father and your mother and all your other ancestors; and that it is your bounden duty to reverence it, and to submit to it, and to approach it more humbly than you would approach your father, when it is angry with you; and either to do whatever it bids you to do or to persuade it to excuse you; and to obey in silence if it orders you to endure stripes or imprisonment, or if it send you to battle to be wounded or to die? That is what is your duty. You must not give way, nor

retreat, nor desert your post. In war, and in the court of justice, and everywhere, you must do whatever your city and your country bid you do, or you must convince them that their commands are unjust. But it is against the law of God to use violence to your father or to your mother; and much more so is it against the law of God to use violence to your country." What answer shall we make, Crito? Shall we say that the laws speak truly, or not?

CRITO: I think that they do.

SOCRATES: "Then consider, Socrates," perhaps they would say, "if we are right in saying that by attempting to escape you are attempting to injure us. We brought you into the world, we nurtured you, we educated you, we gave you and every other citizen a share of all the good things we could. Yet we proclaim that if any man of the Athenians is dissatisfied with us, he may take his goods and go away whithersoever he pleases: we give that permission to every man who chooses to avail himself of it, so soon as he has reached man's estate, and sees us, the laws, and the administration of our city. No one of us stands in his way or forbids him to take his goods and go wherever he likes, whether it be to an Athenian colony, or to any foreign country, if he is dissatisfied with us and with the city. But we say that every man of you who remains here, seeing how we administer justice, and how we govern the city in other matters, has agreed, by the very fact of remaining here, to do whatsoever we bid him. And, we say, he who disobeys us, does a threefold wrong: he disobeys us who are his parents, and he disobeys us who fostered him, and he disobeys us after he has agreed to obey us, without persuading us that we are wrong. Yet we did not bid him sternly to do whatever we told him. We offered him an alternative; we gave him his choice, either to obey us, or to convince us that we were wrong: but he does neither.

"These are the charges, Socrates, to which we say that you will expose yourself, if you do what you intend; and that not less, but more than other Athenians." And if I were to ask, "And why?" they might retort with justice that I have bound myself by the agreement with them more than other Athenians. They would say, "Socrates, we have very strong evidence that you were satisfied with us and with the city. You would not have been content to stay at home in it more than other Athenians, unless you had been satisfied with it more than they. You never went away from Athens to the festivals, save once to the Isthmian games, nor elsewhere except on military service; you never made other journeys like other men; you had no desire to see other cities or other laws; you were contented with us and our city. So strongly did you prefer us, and agree to be governed by us: and what is more, you begat children in this city, you found it so pleasant. And besides, if you had wished, you might at your trial have offered to go into exile. At that time you could have done with the State's consent, what you are trying now to do without it. But then you gloried in being willing to die. You said that you preferred death to exile. And now you are not ashamed of those words; you do not respect us the laws, for you are trying to destroy us: and you are acting just as a miserable slave would act, trying to run away, and breaking the covenant and agreement which you made to submit to our government. First, therefore, answer this question. Are we right, or are we wrong, in saying that you have agreed not in mere words, but in reality to live under our government?" What are we to say, Crito? Must we not admit that it is true?

CRITO: We must, Socrates.

SOCRATES: Then they would say, "Are you not breaking your covenants and agreements with us? And you were not led to make them by force or by fraud: you had not to make up your mind in a hurry. You had seventy years in which you might have gone away, if you had been dissatisfied with us, or if the agreement had seemed to you unjust. But you preferred neither Lacedaemon nor Crete, though you are fond of saying that they are well governed, nor any other state, either of the Hellenes, or the Barbarians. You went away from Athens less than the lame and the blind and the cripple. Clearly you, far more than other Athenians, were satisfied with the city, and also with us who are its laws: for who would be satisfied with a city which had no laws? And now will not you abide by your agreement? If you take our advice, you will, Socrates: then you will not make yourself ridiculous by going away from Athens.

"For consider: what good will you do yourself or your friends by thus transgressing, and breaking your agreement? It is tolerably certain that they, on their part, will at least run the risk of exile, and of losing their civil rights, or of forfeiting their property. For yourself, you might go to one of the neighbouring cities, to Thebes or to Megara for instance—for both of them are well governed—but, Socrates, you will come as an enemy to these commonwealths; and all who care for their city will look askance at you, and think that you are a subverter of law. And you will confirm the judges in their opinion, and make it seem that their verdict was a just one. For a man who is a subverter of law, may well be supposed to be a corrupter of the young and thoughtless. Then will you avoid well-governed states and civilised men? Will life be worth having, if you do? Or will you consort with such men, and converse without shame—about what, Socrates? About the things which you talk of here? Will you tell them that virtue, and justice, and institutions, and law are the most precious things that men can have? And do you not think that will be a shameful thing in Socrates? You ought to think so. But you will leave these places; you will go to the friends of Crito in Thessaly: for there is most disorder and license: and very likely, they will be delighted to hear of the ludicrous way in which you escaped from prison, dressed up in peasant's clothes, or in some other disguise which people put on when they are running away, and with your appearance altered. But will no one say how you, an old man, with probably only a few more years to live, clung so greedily to life that you dared to transgress the highest laws? Perhaps not, if you do not displease them. But if you do, Socrates, you will hear much that will make you blush. You will pass your life as the flatterer and the slave of all men; and what will you be doing but feasting in Thessaly? It will be as if you had made a journey to Thessaly for an entertainment. And where will be all our old sayings about justice and virtue then? But you wish to live for the sake of your children? You want to bring them up and educate them? What? Will you take them with you to Thessaly, and bring them up and ed-

ucate them there? Will you make them strangers to their own country, that you may bestow this benefit on them too? Or supposing that you leave them in Athens, will they be brought up and educated better if you are alive, though you are not with them? Yes; your friends will take care of them. Will your friends take care of them if you make a journey to Thessaly, and not if you make a journey to Hades? You ought not to think that, at least if those who call themselves your friends are good for anything at all.

"No, Socrates, be advised by us who have fostered you. Think neither of children, nor of life, nor of any other thing before justice, that when you come to the other world you may be able to make your defence before the rulers who sit in judgment there. It is clear that neither you nor any of your friends will be happier, or juster, or holier in this life, if you do this thing, nor will you be happier after you are dead. Now you will go away wronged, not by us, the laws, but by men. But if you repay evil with evil, and wrong with wrong, in this shameful way, and break your agreements and covenants with us, and injure those whom you should least injure, yourself, and your friends, and your country, and us, and so escape, then we shall be angry with you while you live, and when you die our brethren, the laws in Hades, will not receive you kindly; for they will know that on earth you did all that you could to destroy us. Listen then to us, and let not Crito persuade you to do as he says."

Know well, my dear friend Crito, that this is what I seem to hear, as the worshippers of Cybele seem, in their frenzy, to hear the music of flutes: and the sound of these words rings loudly in my ears, and drowns all other words. And I feel sure that if you try to change my mind you will speak in vain; nevertheless, if you think that you will succeed, say on.

CRITO: I can say no more, Socrates.

SOCRATES: Then let it be, Crito and let us do as I say, seeing that God so directs us.

Phaedo

SCENE: The Prison of Socrates

• • •

When he had finished speaking Crito said, "Be it so, Socrates. But have you any commands for your friends or for me about your children, or about other things? How shall we serve you best?"

"Simply by doing what I always tell you, Crito. Take care of your own selves, and you will serve me and mine and yourselves in all that you do, even though you make no promises now. But if you are careless of your own selves, and will not follow the path of life which we have pointed out in our discussions both today and at other times, all your promises now, however profuse and earnest they are, will be of no avail."

"We will do our best," said Crito. "But how shall we bury you?"

"As you please," he answered; "only you must catch me first, and not let me escape you." And then he looked at us with a smile and said, "My friends, I cannot convince Crito that I am the Socrates who has been conversing with you, and arranging his arguments in order. He thinks that I am the body which he will presently see a corpse, and he asks how he is to bury me. All the arguments which I have used to prove that I shall not remain with you after

I have drunk the poison, but that I shall go away to the happiness of the blessed, with which I tried to comfort you and myself, have been thrown away on him. Do you therefore be my sureties to him, as he was my surety at the trial, but in a different way. He was surety for me then that I would remain; but you must be my sureties to him that I shall go away when I am dead, and not remain with you: then he will feel my death less; and when he sees my body being burnt or buried, he will not be grieved because he thinks that I am suffering dreadful things: and at my funeral he will not say that it is Socrates whom he is laying out, or bearing to the grave, or burying." "For, dear Crito," he continued, "you must know that to use words wrongly is not only a fault in itself; it also creates evil in the soul. You must be of good cheer, and say that you are burying my body: and you must bury it as you please, and as you think right."

With these words he rose and went into another room to bathe himself: Crito went with him and told us to wait. So we waited, talking of the argument, and discussing it, and then again dwelling on the greatness of the calamity which had fallen upon us: it seemed as if we

Trans. F. J. Church.

were going to lose a father, and to be orphans for the rest of our life. When he had bathed, and his children had been brought to him,—he had two sons quite little, and one grown up,—and the women of his family were come, he spoke with them in Crito's presence, and gave them his last commands; then he sent the women and children away, and returned to us. By that time it was near the hour of sunset, for he had been a long while within. When he came back to us from the bath he sat down, but not much was said after that. Presently the servant of the Eleven came and stood before him and said, "I know that I shall not find you unreasonable like other men, Socrates. They are angry with me and curse me when I bid them drink the poison because the authorities make me do it. But I have found you all along the noblest and gentlest and best man that has ever come here; and now I am sure that you will not be angry with me, but with those who you know are to blame. And so farewell, and try to bear what must be as lightly as you can; you know why I have come." With that he turned away weeping, and went out.

Socrates looked up at him, and replied, "Farewell: I will do as you say." Then he turned to us and said, "How courteous the man is! And the whole time that I have been here, he has constantly come in to see me, and sometimes he has talked to me, and has been the best of men; and now, how generously he weeps for me! Come, Crito, let us obey him: let the poison be brought if it is ready; and if it is not ready, let it be prepared."

Crito replied, "Nay, Socrates, I think that the sun is still upon the hills; it has not set. Besides, I know that other men take the poison quite late, and eat and drink heartily, and even enjoy the company of their chosen friends, after the announcement has been made. So do not hurry; there is still time."

Socrates replied, "And those whom you speak of, Crito, naturally do so; for they think that they will be gainers by so doing. And I naturally shall not do so; for I think that I should gain nothing by drinking the poison a little later, but my own contempt for so greedily saving up a life which is already spent. So do not refuse to do as I say."

Then Crito made a sign to his slave who was standing by; and the slave went out, and after some delay returned with the man who was to give the poison, carrying it prepared in a cup. When Socrates saw him, he asked, "You understand these things, my good sir, what have I to do?"

"You have only to drink this," he replied, "and to walk about until your legs feel heavy, and then lie down; and it will act of itself." With that he handed the cup to Socrates, who took it quite cheerfully, without trembling, and without any change of colour or of feature, and looked up at the man with that fixed glance of his, and asked, "What say you to making a libation from this draught? May I, or not?" "We only prepare so much as we think sufficient, Socrates," he answered. "I understand," said Socrates. "But I suppose that I may, and must, pray to the gods that my journey hence may be prosperous: that is my prayer; be it so." With these words he put the cup to his lips and drank the poison quite calmly and cheerfully. Till then most of us had been able to control our grief fairly well; but when we saw him drinking, and then the poison finished, we could do so no longer: my tears came fast in spite of myself, and I covered my face and wept for myself: it was not for him, but at my own misfortune at losing such a friend. Even before that Crito had been unable to restrain his tears, and had gone away; and Apollodorus, who had never once ceased weeping the whole time, burst into a loud cry, and made us one and all break down by his sobbing and grief, except only Socrates himself. "What are you doing, my friends?" he exclaimed. "I sent away the women chiefly in order that they might not offend in this way; for I have heard that a man should die in silence. So calm yourselves and bear up." When we heard that we were ashamed, and we ceased from weeping. But he walked about, until he said that his legs were getting heavy, and then he lay down on his back, as he was told. And the man who gave the poison began to examine his feet and legs, from time to time: then he pressed his foot hard, and asked if there was any feeling in it; and Socrates said, "No": and then his legs, and so higher and higher, and showed us that he was cold and stiff. And Socrates felt himself, and said that when it came to his heart, he should be gone. He was already growing cold about the groin, when he uncovered his face, which had been covered, and spoke for the last time. "Crito," he said, "I owe a cock to Asclepius: do not forget to repay it." "It shall be done," replied Crito. "Is there anything else that you wish?" He made no answer to this question; but after a short interval there was a movement, and the man uncovered him, and his eyes were fixed. Then Crito closed his mouth and his eyes.

Such was the end of our friend, a man, I think, who was the wisest and justest, and the best man that I have ever known.

Plato

Among the host of handsome and brilliant young men who dogged the footsteps of Socrates about Athens, one youth, Plato, stood out from the rest. The son of a wealthy and noble family —on his mother's side he was descended from the great law-giver, Solon—Plato (427–347 B.C.) was preparing for a career in politics when the trial and execution of Socrates changed the course of his life. He abandoned his political career and turned to philosophy, opening a school on the outskirts of Athens dedicated to the Socratic search for wisdom. Plato's school, known as the Academy, was the first university in the history of the West. It continued operating for over nine hundred years, from 387 B.C. until it was closed by an edict of the Roman emperor Justinian in A.D. 529.

Unlike Socrates, Plato was a writer as well as a teacher. His writings are in the form of dialogues, with Socrates as the principal speaker. In the selection that follows, the Allegory of the Cave (perhaps the most famous passage in all his works), Plato describes symbolically the predicament in which human beings find them-

selves and proposes a way of salvation. In addition, the allegory presents, in brief form, most of Plato's main philosophical theories: his belief that the world revealed by our senses is not the real world but only a poor copy of it, and that the real world can be apprehended only intellectually; his idea that knowledge cannot be transferred from teacher to student, but rather that education consists in directing students' minds toward what is real and important and allowing them to apprehend it for themselves; his faith that the universe ultimately is good; his conviction that enlightened individuals have an obligation to the rest of society, and that a good society must be one in which the truly wise are the rulers. Woven into these themes is a defense of the life of Socrates and a condemnation of Athenian society for having executed him.

The allegory is from Book VII of Plato's best-known work, *The Republic*, which represents a conversation between Socrates and some friends on the nature of justice, and which includes Plato's plan for an ideal state ruled by philosophers.

The Republic

[THE ALLEGORY OF THE CAVE]

Next, said I [Socrates], here is a parable to illustrate the degrees in which our nature may be enlightened or unenlightened. Imagine the condition of men living in a sort of cavernous chamber underground, with an entrance open to the light and a long passage all down the cave. Here they have been from childhood, chained by the leg and also by the neck, so that they cannot move and can see only what is in front of them, because the chains will not let them turn their heads. At some distance higher up is the light of a fire burning behind them; and between the prisoners and the fire is a track with a parapet built along it, like the screen at a puppet-show, which hides the performers while they show their puppets over the top.

I see, said he [Glaucon].[1]

Now behind this parapet imagine persons carrying along various artificial objects, including figures of men and animals in wood or stone or other materials, which project above the parapet. Naturally, some of these persons will be talking, others silent.[2]

It is a strange picture, he said, and a strange sort of prisoners.

Like ourselves, I replied; for in the first place prisoners so confined would have seen nothing of themselves or of one another, except the shadows thrown by the fire-light on the wall of the Cave facing them, would they?

Not if all their lives they had been prevented from moving their heads.

And they would have seen as little of the objects carried past.

Of course.

Now, if they could talk to one another, would they not suppose that their words referred only to those passing shadows which they saw?

Necessarily.

And suppose their prison had an echo from the wall facing them? When one of the people crossing behind them spoke, they could only suppose that the sound came from the shadow passing before their eyes?

No doubt.

In every way, then, such prisoners would recognize as reality nothing but the shadows of those artificial objects.

Inevitably.

---

[1] [A brother of Plato.—*Ed.*]

[2] [A modern Plato would compare his Cave to an underground cinema, where the audience watch the play of shadows thrown by the film passing before a light at their backs. The film itself is only an image of "real" things and events in the world outside the cinema. For the film Plato has to substitute the clumsier apparatus of a procession of artificial objects carried on their heads by persons who are merely part of the machinery, providing for the movement of the objects and the sounds whose echo the prisoners hear. The parapet prevents these persons' shadows from being cast on the wall of the Cave.— *Trans.*]

The Republic of Plato, trans. F. M. Cornford (Oxford: The Clarendon Press, 1941). Reprinted by permission of Oxford University Press.

Now consider what would happen if their release from the chains and the healing of their unwisdom should come about in this way. Suppose one of them set free and forced suddenly to stand up, turn his head, and walk with eyes lifted to the light; all these movements would be painful, and he would be too dazzled to make out the objects whose shadows he had been used to see. What do you think he would say, if someone told him that what he had formerly seen was meaningless illusion, but now, being somewhat nearer to reality and turned towards more real objects, he was getting a truer view? Suppose further that he were shown the various objects being carried by and were made to say, in reply to questions, what each of them was. Would he not be perplexed and believe the objects now shown him to be not so real as what he formerly saw?

Yes, not nearly so real.

And if he were forced to look at the fire-light itself, would not his eyes ache, so that he would try to escape and turn back to the things which he could see distinctly, convinced that they really were clearer than these other objects now being shown to him?

Yes.

And suppose someone were to drag him away forcibly up the steep and rugged ascent and not let him go until he had hauled him out into the sunlight, would he not suffer pain and vexation at such treatment, and, when he had come out into the light, find his eyes so full of its radiance that he could not see a single one of the things that he was now told were real?

Certainly he would not see them all at once.

He would need, then, to grow ac-customed before he could see things in that upper world. At first it would be easiest to make out shadows, and then the images of men and things reflected in water, and later on the things themselves. After that, it would be easier to watch the heavenly bodies and the sky itself by night, looking at the light of the moon and stars rather than the Sun and the Sun's light in the day-time.

Yes, surely.

Last of all, he would be able to look at the Sun and contemplate its nature, not as it appears when reflected in water or any alien medium, but as it is in itself in its own domain.

No doubt.

And now he would begin to draw the conclusion that it is the Sun that produces the seasons and the course of the year and controls everything in the visible world, and moreover is in a way the cause of all that he and his companions used to see.

Clearly he would come at last to that conclusion.

Then if he called to mind his fellow prisoners and what passed for wisdom in his former dwelling-place, he would surely think himself happy in the change and be sorry for them. They may have had a practice of honouring and commending one another, with prizes for the man who had the keenest eye for the passing shadows and the best memory for the order in which they followed or accompanied one another, so that he could make a good guess as to which was going to come next. Would our released prisoner be likely to covet those prizes or to envy the men exalted to honour and power in the Cave? Would he not feel like Homer's Achilles, that he would far sooner "be on earth as a hired servant in the house of a landless man" or endure anything rather than go back to his old beliefs and live in the old way?

Yes, he would prefer any fate to such a life.

Now imagine what would happen if he went down again to take his former seat in the Cave. Coming suddenly out of the sunlight, his eyes would be filled with darkness. He might be required once more to deliver his opinion on those shadows, in competition with the prisoners who had never been released, while his eyesight was still dim and unsteady; and it might take some time to become used to the darkness. They would laugh at him and say that he had gone up only to come back with his sight ruined; it was worth no one's while even to attempt the ascent. If they could lay hands on the man who was trying to set them free and lead them up, they would kill him.[3]

Yes, they would.

Every feature in this parable, my dear Glaucon, is meant to fit our earlier analysis. The prison dwelling corresponds to the region revealed to us through the sense of sight, and the fire-light within it to the power of the Sun. The ascent to see the things in the upper world you may take as standing for the upward journey of the soul into the region of the intelligible; then you will be in possession of what I surmise, since that is what you wish to be told. Heaven knows whether it is true; but this, at any rate, is how it appears to me. In the world of knowledge, the last thing to be perceived and only with great difficulty is the essential Form of Good-

ness. Once it is perceived, the conclusion must follow that, for all things, this is the cause of whatever is right and good; in the visible world it gives birth to light and to the lord of light, while it is itself sovereign in the intelligible world and the parent of intelligence and truth. Without having had a vision of this Form no one can act with wisdom, either in his own life or in matters of state.

So far as I can understand, I share your belief.

Then you may also agree that it is no wonder if those who have reached this height are reluctant to manage the affairs of men. Their souls long to spend all their time in that upper world—naturally enough, if here once more our parable holds true. Nor, again, is it at all strange that one who comes from the contemplation of divine things to the miseries of human life should appear awkward and ridiculous when, with eyes still dazed and not yet accustomed to the darkness, he is compelled, in a law-court or elsewhere, to dispute about the shadows of justice or the images that cast those shadows, and to wrangle over the notions of what is right in the minds of men who have never beheld Justice itself.

It is not at all strange.

No; a sensible man will remember that the eyes may be confused in two ways—by a change from light to darkness or from darkness to light; and he will recognize that the same thing happens to the soul. When he sees it troubled and unable to discern anything clearly, instead of laughing thoughtlessly, he will ask whether, coming from a brighter existence, its unaccustomed vision is obscured by the darkness, in which case he will think its condition enviable and its life a happy one; or

---

[3][An allusion to the fate of Socrates.—*Trans.*]

whether, emerging from the depths of ignorance, it is dazzled by excess of light. If so, he will rather feel sorry for it; or, if he were inclined to laugh, that would be less ridiculous than to laugh at the soul which has come down from the light.

That is a fair statement.

If this is true, then, we must conclude that education is not what it is said to be by some, who profess to put knowledge into a soul which does not possess it, as if they could put sight into blind eyes. On the contrary, our own account signifies that the soul of every man does possess the power of learning the truth and the organ to see with; and that, just as one might have to turn the whole body round in order that the eye should see light instead of darkness, so that entire soul must be turned away from this changing world, until its eye can bear to contemplate reality and that supreme splendour which we have called the Good. Hence there may well be an art whose aim would be to effect this very thing, the conversion of the soul, in the readiest way; not to put the power of sight into the soul's eye, which already has it, but to ensure that, instead of looking in the wrong direction, it is turned the way it ought to be.

Yes, it may well be so.

It looks, then, as though wisdom were different from those ordinary virtues, as they are called, which are not far removed from bodily qualities, in that they can be produced by habituation and exercise in a soul which has not possessed them from the first. Wisdom, it seems, is certainly the virtue of some diviner faculty, which never loses its power, though its use for good or harm depends on the direction towards

which it is turned. You must have noticed in dishonest men with a reputation for sagacity the shrewd glance of a narrow intelligence piercing the objects to which it is directed. There is nothing wrong with their power of vision, but it has been forced into the service of evil, so that the keener its sight, the more harm it works.

Quite true.

And yet if the growth of a nature like this had been pruned from earliest childhood, cleared of those clinging overgrowths which come of gluttony and all luxurious pleasure and, like leaden weights charged with affinity to this mortal world, hang upon the soul, bending its vision downwards; if, freed from these, the soul were turned round towards true reality, then this same power in these very men would see the truth as keenly as the objects it is turned to now.

Yes, very likely.

Is it not also likely, or indeed certain after what has been said, that a state can never be properly governed either by the uneducated who know nothing of truth or by men who are allowed to spend all their days in the pursuit of culture? The ignorant have no single mark before their eyes at which they must aim in all the conduct of their own lives and of affairs of state; and the others will not engage in action if they can help it, dreaming that, while still alive, they have been translated to the Islands of the Blest.

Quite true.

It is for us, then, as founders of a commonwealth, to bring compulsion to bear on the noblest natures. They must be made to climb the ascent to the vision of Goodness, which we called the highest object of knowledge; and, when they have looked upon it long enough, they must not be allowed, as they now are, to remain on the heights, refusing to come down again to the prisoners or to take any part in their labours and rewards, however much or little these may be worth.

Shall we not be doing them an injustice, if we force on them a worse life than they might have?

You have forgotten again, my friend, that the law is not concerned to make any one class specially happy, but to ensure the welfare of the commonwealth as a whole. By persuasion or constraint it will unite the citizens in harmony, making them share whatever benefits each class can contribute to the common good; and its purpose in forming men of that spirit was not that each should be left to go his own way, but that they should be instrumental in binding the community into one.

True, I had forgotten.

You will see, then, Glaucon, that there will be no real injustice in compelling our philosophers to watch over and care for the other citizens. We can fairly tell them that their compeers in other states may quite reasonably refuse to collaborate: there they have sprung up, like a self-sown plant, in despite of their country's institutions; no one has fostered their growth, and they cannot be expected to show gratitude for a care they have never received. "But," we shall say, "it is not so with you. We have brought you into existence for your country's sake as well as for your own, to be like leaders and king-bees in a hive; you have been better and more thoroughly educated than those others and hence you are more capable of playing your part both as men of thought and as men of action. You

must go down, then, each in his turn, to live with the rest and let your eyes grow accustomed to the darkness. You will then see a thousand times better than those who live there always; you will recognize every image for what it is and know what it represents, because you have seen justice, beauty, and goodness in their reality; and so you and we shall find life in our commonwealth no mere dream, as it is in most existing states, where men live fighting one another about shadows and quarrelling for power, as if that were a great prize; whereas in truth government can be at its best and free from dissension only where the destined rulers are least desirous of holding office."

Quite true.

Then will our pupils refuse to listen and to take their turns at sharing in the work of the community, though they may live together for most of their time in a purer air?

No; it is a fair demand, and they are fair-minded men. No doubt, unlike any ruler of the present day, they will think of holding power as an unavoidable necessity.

Yes, my friend; for the truth is that you can have a well-governed society only if you can discover for your future rulers a better way of life than being in office; then only will power be in the hands of men who are rich, not in gold, but in wealth that brings happiness, a good and wise life. All goes wrong when, starved for lack of anything good in their own lives, men turn to public affairs hoping to snatch from thence the happiness they hunger for. They set about fighting for power, and this internecine conflict ruins them and their country. The life of true philosophy is the only one that looks down upon offices of state; and access to power must be confined to men who are not in love with it; otherwise rivals will start fighting. So whom else can you compel to undertake the guardianship of the commonwealth, if not those who, besides understanding best the principles of government, enjoy a nobler life than the politician's and look for rewards of a different kind?

There is indeed no other choice.

Aristotle

Aristotle (384–322 B.C.) was a native of Macedonia. At the age of eighteen he journeyed to Athens and enrolled as a student in the Academy, where he remained for twenty years until the death of Plato. He then moved to Asia Minor to become political adviser to the ruler of a small kingdom. There he married the king's niece. It is said that he spent his honeymoon gathering seashells for use in scientific studies. From Asia Minor he was called back to his native Macedonia to serve as tutor to Alexander (later "the Great"), who was then a boy of twelve. When Alexander set out to conquer the world, Aristotle returned to Athens and established a school of his own, the Lyceum, as a rival to the Academy. For the next eleven years he divided his time among teaching, public lecturing, and writing. His philosophical system is known as the *peripatetic* (or "walking") philosophy, a title derived from his habit of pacing back and forth as he lectured. At the death of Alexander in 323 B. C., Aristotle, because of his former association with the conqueror, found himself unpopular in Athens. Fearing the anger of the mob and re-membering the fate of Socrates, he fled the city, not wishing, as he put it, "to give the Athenians a second chance of sinning against philosophy." He died in exile the following year.

Aristotle was a remarkably productive and versatile thinker. His extant works include major treatises on physics, astronomy, zoology, biology, botany, psychology, logic, ethics, metaphysics, political theory, constitutional history, rhetoric, and the theory of art. His influence on intellectual history has been comparable to that of Plato. Wherever his works have been studied, there has been intellectual ferment, activity, and development. Partly as a result of Aristotle's influence, the Muslims of the Near East enjoyed an intellectual golden age while Europe was still deep in the Dark Ages. The redis-covery of Aristotle by Europeans, through their contacts with the Muslims, contributed directly to the cultural awakening in Europe that culminated in the High Middle Ages of the thirteenth century. Although the philosophy of Aristotle has come under increasingly sharp attack since the rise of modern science, many of his main concepts and theories still remain alive and vigorous.

The following selection is from one of Aristotle's major works, *The Politics*. His views in *The Politics* on the social nature of humanity, the purpose of government, and the most desirable kind of society have formed the basis, along with Plato's *Republic*, for almost all subsequent political theory in the West.

The Politics

BOOK I

Every state is a community of some kind, and every community is established with a view to some good; for mankind always act in order to obtain that which they think good. But, if all communities aim at some good, the state or political community, which is the highest of all, and which embraces all the rest, aims, and in a greater degree than any other, at the highest good.

Now there is an erroneous opinion that a statesman, king, householder, and master are the same, and that they differ, not in kind, but only in the number of their subjects. For example, the ruler over a few is called a master; over more, the manager of a household; over a still larger number, a statesman or king, as if there were no difference between a great household and a small state. The distinction which is made between the king and the statesman is as follows: When the government is personal, the ruler is a king; when, according to the principles of the political science, the citizens rule and are ruled in turn, then he is called a statesman.

But all this is a mistake; for governments differ in kind, as will be evident to any one who considers the matter according to the method which has hitherto guided us. As in other departments of science, so in politics, the compound should always be resolved into the simple elements or least parts of the whole. We must therefore look at the elements of which the state is composed, in order that we may see in what they differ from one another, and whether any scientific distinction can be drawn between the different kinds of rule.

He who thus considers things in their first growth and origin, whether a state or anything else, will obtain the clearest view of them. In the first place (1) there must be a union of those who cannot exist without each other; for example, of male and female, that the race may continue; and this is a union which is formed, not of deliberate purpose, but because, in common with other animals and with plants, mankind have a natural desire to leave behind them an image of themselves. And (2) there must be a union of natural ruler and subject, that both may be preserved. For he who can foresee

Trans. B. Jowett.

with his mind is by nature intended to be lord and master, and he who can work with his body is a subject, and by nature a slave; hence master and slave have the same interest. Nature, however, has distinguished between the female and the slave. For she is not niggardly, like the smith who fashions the Delphian knife for many uses; she makes each thing for a single use, and every instrument is best made when intended for one and not for many uses. But among barbarians no distinction is made between women and slaves, because there is no natural ruler among them: they are a community of slaves, male and female. Wherefore the poets say—

"It is meet that Hellenes should rule over barbarians;"

as if they thought that the barbarian and the slave were by nature one.

Out of these two relationships between man and woman, master and slave, the family first arises, and Hesiod is right when he says—

"First house and wife and an ox for the plough,"

for the ox is the poor man's slave. The family is the association established by nature for the supply of men's every day wants, and the members of it are called by Charondas "companions of the cupboard," and by Epimenides the Cretan, "companions of the manger." But when several families are united, and the association aims at something more than the supply of daily needs, then comes into existence the village. And the most natural form of the village appears to be that of a colony from the family, composed of the children and grandchildren, who are said to be "suckled with the same milk." And this is the reason why Hellenic states were originally governed by kings; because the Hellenes were under royal rule before they came together, as the barbarians still are. Every family is ruled by the eldest, and therefore in the colonies of the family the kingly form of government prevailed because they were of the same blood. As Homer says [of the Cyclopes]:—

"Each one gives law to his children and to his wives."

For they lived dispersedly, as was the manner in ancient times. Wherefore men say that the Gods have a king, because they themselves either are or were in ancient times under the rule of a king. For they imagine, not only the forms of the Gods, but their ways of life to be like their own.

When several villages are united in a single community, perfect and large enough to be nearly or quite self-sufficing, the state comes into existence, originating in the bare needs of life, and continuing in existence for the sake of a good life. And therefore, if the earlier forms of society are natural, so is the state, for it is the end of them, and the completed nature is the end. For what each thing is when fully developed, we call its nature, whether we are speaking of a man, a horse, or a family. Besides, the final cause and end of a thing is the best, and to be self-sufficing is the end and the best.

Hence it is evident that the state is a creation of nature, and that man is by nature a political animal. And he who by nature and not by mere accident is without a state, is either above humanity, or below it; he is the

"Tribeless, lawless, heartless one,"

whom Homer denounces—the outcast who is a lover of war; he may be compared to a bird which flies alone.

Now the reason why man is more of a political animal than bees or any other gregarious animals is evident. Nature, as we often say, makes nothing in vain, and man is the only animal whom she has endowed with the gift of speech. And whereas mere sound is but an indication of pleasure or pain, and is therefore found in other animals (for their nature attains to the perception of pleasure and pain and the intimation of them to one another, and no further), the power of speech is intended to set forth the expedient and inexpedient, and likewise the just and the unjust. And it is a characteristic of man that he alone has any sense of good and evil, of just and unjust, and the association of living beings who have this sense makes a family and a state.

Thus the state is by nature clearly prior to the family and to the individual, since the whole is of necessity prior to the part; for example, if the whole body be destroyed, there will be no foot or hand, except in an equivocal sense, as we might speak of a stone hand; for when destroyed the hand will be no better. But things are defined by their working and power; and we ought not to say that they are the same when they are no longer the same, but only that they have the same name. The proof that the state is a creation of nature and prior to the individual is that the individual, when isolated, is not self-sufficing;

and therefore he is like a part in relation to the whole. But he who is unable to live in society, or who has no need because he is sufficient for himself, must be either a beast or a god: he is no part of a state. A social instinct is implanted in all men by nature, and yet he who first founded the state was the greatest of benefactors. For man, when perfected, is the best of animals, but, when separated from law and justice, he is the worst of all; since armed injustice is the more dangerous, and he is equipped at birth with the arms of intelligence and with moral qualities which he may use for the worst ends. Wherefore, if he have not virtue, he is the most unholy and the most savage of animals, and the most full of lust and gluttony. But justice is the bond of men in states, and the administration of justice, which is the determination of what is just, is the principle of order in political society.

•   •   •

BOOK III
•   •   •

Having determined these questions, we have next to consider whether there is only one form of government or many, and if many, what they are, and how many, and what are the differences between them.

A constitution is the arrangement of magistracies in a State, especially of the highest of all. The government is everywhere sovereign in the State, and the constitution is in fact the government. For example, in democracies the people are supreme, but in oligarchies, the few; and, therefore, we say that these two forms of government are different: and so in other cases.

First, let us consider what is the

purpose of a State, and how many forms of government there are by which human society is regulated. We have already said, in the former part of this treatise, when drawing a distinction between household management and the rule of a master, that man is by nature a political animal. And therefore, men, even when they do not require one another's help, desire to live together all the same, and are in fact brought together by their common interests in proportion as they severally attain to any measure of well-being. This is certainly the chief end, both of individuals and of States. And also for the sake of mere life (in which there is possibly some noble element) mankind meet together and maintain the political community, so long as the evils of existence do not greatly overbalance the good. And we all see that men cling to life even in the midst of misfortune, seeming to find in it a natural sweetness and happiness.

There is no difficulty in distinguishing the various kinds of authority; they have been often defined already in popular works. The rule of a master, although the slave by nature and the master by nature have in reality the same interests, is nevertheless exercised primarily with a view to the interest of the master, but accidentally considers the slave, since, if the slave perish, the rule of the master perishes with him. On the other hand, the government of a wife and children and of a household, which we have called household management, is exercised in the first instance for the good of the governed or for the common good of both parties, but essentially for the good of the governed, as we see to be the case in medicine, gymnastic, and

the arts in general, which are only accidentally concerned with the good of the artists themselves. (For there is no reason why the trainer may not sometimes practise gymnastics, and the pilot is always one of the crew.) The trainer or the pilot considers the good of those committed to his care. But, when he is one of the persons taken care of, he accidentally participates in the advantage, for the pilot is also a sailor, and the trainer becomes one of those in training. And so in politics: when the State is framed upon the principle of equality and likeness, the citizens think that they ought to hold office by turns. In the order of nature everyone would take his turn of service; and then again, somebody else would look after his interest, just as he, while in office, had looked after theirs. But nowadays, for the sake of the advantage which is to be gained from the public revenues and from office, men want to be always in office. One might imagine that the rulers, being sickly, were only kept in health while they continued in office; in that case we may be sure that they would be hunting after places. The conclusion is evident: that governments, which have a regard to the common interest, are constituted in accordance with strict principles of justice, and are therefore true forms; but those which regard only the interest of the rulers are all defective and perverted forms, for they are despotic, whereas a State is a community of freemen.

Having determined these points, we have next to consider how many forms of government there are, and what they are; and in the first place what are the true forms, for when they are determined the perversions of them will at once be apparent.

The words "constitution" and "government" have the same meaning, and the government, which is the supreme authority in States, must be in the hands of one, or of a few, or of many. The true forms of government, therefore, are those in which the one, or the few, or the many, govern with a view to the common interest; but governments which rule with a view to the private interest, whether of the one, or of the few, or of the many, are perversions. For citizens, if they are truly citizens, ought to participate in the advantages of a State. Of forms of government in which one rules, we call that which regards the common interests, kingship or royalty; that in which more than one, but not many, rule, aristocracy [the rule of the best]; and it is so called, either because the rulers are the best men, or because they have at heart the best interests of the State and of the citizens. But when the citizens at large administer the State for the common interest, the government is called by the generic name—a constitution. And there is a reason for this use of language. One man or a few may excel in virtue; but of virtue there are many kinds: and as the number increases it becomes more difficult for them to attain perfection in very kind, though they may in military virtue, for this is found in the masses. Hence, in a constitutional government the fighting-men have the supreme power, and those who possess arms are the citizens.

Of the above-mentioned forms, the perversions are as follows:— of royalty, tyranny; of aristocracy, oligarchy; of constitutional government, democracy. For tyranny is a kind of monarchy which has in view the interest of the monarch only; oligarchy has in view the interest of the wealthy; democracy, of the needy: none of them the common good of all.

But there are difficulties about these forms of government, and it will therefore be necessary to state a little more at length the nature of each of them. For he who would make a philosophical study of the various sciences, and does not regard practice only, ought not to overlook or omit anything, but to set forth the truth in every particular. Tyranny, as I was saying, is monarchy exercising the rule of a master over political society; oligarchy is when men of property have the government in their hands; democracy, the opposite, when the indigent, and not the men of property, are the rulers.

• • •

But a State exists for the sake of a good life, and not for the sake of life only: if life only were the object, slaves and brute animals might form a State, but they cannot, for they have no share in happiness or in a life of free choice. Nor does a State exist for the sake of alliance and security from injustice, nor yet for the sake of exchange and mutual intercourse; for then the Tyrrhenians and the Carthaginians, and all who have commercial treaties with one another, would be the citizens of one State. True, they have agreements about imports, and engagements that they will do no wrong to one another, and written articles of alliance. But there are no magistracies common to the contracting parties who will enforce their engagements; different States have each their own magistracies. Nor does one State take care that the citizens of the other are such as they ought to be, nor see that those who come under the terms of the treaty do no wrong or wickedness at all, but only that they do no injustice to one another. Whereas, those who care for good government take into consideration [the larger question of] virtue and vice in States. Whence it may be further inferred that virtue must be the serious care of a State which truly deserves the name: for [without this ethical end] the community becomes a mere alliance which differs only in place from alliances of which the members live apart; and law is only a convention, "a surety to one another of justice," as the sophist Lycophron says, and has no real power to make the citizens good and just.

This is obvious; for suppose distinct places, such as Corinth and Megara, to be united by a wall, still they would not be one city, not even if the citizens had the right to intermarry, which is one of the rights peculiarly characteristic of States. Again, if men dwelt at a distance from one another, but not so far off as to have no intercourse, and there were laws among them that they should not wrong each other in their exchanges, neither would this be a State. Let us suppose that one man is a carpenter, another a husbandman, another a shoemaker, and so on, and that their number is ten thousand: nevertheless, if they have nothing in common but exchange, alliance, and the like, that would not constitute a State. Why is this? Surely not because they are at a distance from one another: for even supposing that such a community were to meet in one place, and that each man had a house of his own, which was in a manner his State, and that they made alliance with one another, but only against evil-doers; still an accurate thinker would not deem this to be a State, if their intercourse with one another was of the same character after as before their union. It is clear then that a State is not a mere society, having a common place, established for the prevention of crime and for the sake of exchange. These are conditions without which a State cannot exist; but all of them together do not constitute a State, which is a community of well-being in families and aggregations of families, for the sake of a perfect and self-sufficing life. Such a community can only be established among those who live in the same place and intermarry. Hence arise in cities family connections, brotherhoods, common sacrifices, amusements which draw men together. They are created by friendship, for friendship is the motive of society. The end is the good life, and these are the means towards it. And the State is the union of families and villages having for an end a perfect and self-sufficing life, by which we mean a happy and honorable life.

Our conclusion, then, is that political society exists for the sake of noble actions, and not of mere companionship. And they who contribute most to such a society have a greater share in it than those who have the same or a greater freedom or nobility of birth but are inferior to them in political virtue; or than those who exceed them in wealth but are surpassed by them in virtue.

From what has been said it will be clearly seen that all the partisans of different forms of government speak of a part of justice only.

There is also a doubt as to what is to be the supreme power in the State:—Is it the multitude? Or the wealthy? Or the good? Or the one best man? Or a tyrant? Any of these alternatives seems to involve disagreeable consequences. If the poor, for example, because they are more in number, divide among themselves the property of the rich—is not this unjust? No, by heaven (will be the reply), for the lawful authority [*i.e.* the people] willed it. But if this is not injustice, pray what is? Again, when [in the first division] all has been taken, and the majority divide anew the property of the minority, is it not evident, if this goes on, that they will ruin the State? Yet surely, virtue is not the ruin of those who possess her, nor is justice destructive of a State; and therefore this law of confiscation clearly cannot be just. If it were, all the acts of a tyrant must of necessity be just; for he only coerces other men by superior power, just as the multitude coerce the rich. But is it just then that the few and the wealthy should be the rulers? And what if they, in like manner, rob and plunder the people—is this just? If so, the other case [*i.e.*, the case of the majority plundering the minority] will likewise be just. But there can be no doubt that all these things are wrong and unjust.

Then ought the good to rule and have supreme power? But in that case everybody else, being excluded from power, will be dishonored. For the offices of a State are posts of honor; and if one set of men always hold them, the rest must be deprived of them. Then will it be well that the one best man should rule? Nay, that is still more oligarchical, for the number of those who are dishonored is thereby increased. Some one may say that it is bad for a man, subject as he is to all the accidents of human passion, to have the supreme power, rather than the law. But what if the law itself be democratical or oligarchical, how will that help us out of our difficulties? Not at all; the same consequences will follow.

Most of these questions may be reserved for another occasion. The principle that the multitude ought to be supreme rather than the few best is capable of a satisfactory explanation, and, though not free from difficulty, yet seems to contain an element of truth. For the many, of whom each individual is but an ordinary person, when they meet together may very likely be better than the few good, if regarded not individually but collectively, just as a feast to which many contribute is better than a dinner provided out of a single purse. For each individual among the many has a share of virtue and prudence, and when they meet together they become in a manner one man, who has many feet, and hands, and senses; that is a figure of their mind and disposition. Hence the many are better judges than a single man of music and poetry; for some understand one part, and some another, and among them, they understand the whole. There is a similar combination of qualities in good men, who differ from any individual of the many, as the beautiful are said to differ from those who are not beautiful, and works of art from realities, because in them the scattered elements are combined, although, if taken separately, the eye of one person or some other feature in another person would be fairer than in the picture.

• • •

In all sciences and arts the end is a good, and especially and above all in the highest of all—this is the political science of which the good is justice, in other words, the common interest. All men think justice to be a sort of equality; and to a certain extent they agree in the philosophical distinctions which have been laid down by us about ethics. For they admit that justice is a thing having relation to persons, and that equals ought to have equality. But there still remains a question; equality or inequality of what? here is a difficulty which the political philosopher has to resolve. For very likely some persons will say that offices of State ought to be unequally distributed according to superior excellence, in whatever respect, of the citizen, although there is no other difference between him and the rest of the community; for that those who differ in any one respect have different rights and claims. But, surely, if this is true, the complexion or height of a man, or any other advantage, will be a reason for his obtaining a greater share of political rights. The error here lies upon the surface, and may be illustrated from the other arts and sciences. When a number of flute-players are equal in their art, there is no reason why those of them who are better born should have better flutes given to them; for they will not play any better on the flute, and the superior instrument should be reserved for him who is the superior artist. If what I am saying is still obscure, it will be made clearer as we proceed. For if there were a superior flute-player who was far inferior in birth and beauty, although either of these may be a greater good than the art of flute-playing, and persons gifted with these qualities may excel the flute-player in a greater ratio than he excels them in his art, still he ought to have the best flutes given to him, unless the advantages of wealth and birth contribute to excellence in flute-playing, which they do not. Moreover upon this principle any good may be compared with any other. For if a given height, then height in general may be measured either against height or against freedom. Thus if A excels in height more than B in virtue, and height in general is more excellent than virtue, all things will be commensurable [which is absurd]; for if a certain magnitude is greater than some other, it is clear that some other will be equal. But since no such comparison can be made, it is evident that there is good reason why in politics men do not ground their claim to office on every sort of inequality any more than in the arts. For if some be slow, and others swift, that is no reason why the one should have little and the others much; it is in gymnastic contests that such excellence is rewarded. Whereas the rival claims of candidates for office can only be based on the possession of elements which enter into the composition of a State [such as wealth, virtue, etc.]. And therefore the noble, or free-born, or rich, may with good reason claim office; for holders of offices must be freemen and taxpayers: a State can be no more composed entirely of poor men than entirely of slaves. But if wealth and freedom are necessary elements, justice and valor are equally so; for without the former a State cannot exist at all, without the latter not well.

If the existence of the State is alone to be considered, then it would seem that all, or some at least, of these claims are just; but, if we take into account a good life, as I have already said, education and virtue have superior claims. As, however, those who are equal in one thing ought not to be equal in all, nor those who are unequal in one thing to be unequal in all, it is certain that all forms of government which rest on either of these principles are perversions. All men have a claim in a certain sense, as I have already admitted, but they have not an absolute claim. The rich claim because they have a greater share in the land, and land is the common element of the State; also they are generally more trustworthy in contracts. The free claim under the same title as the noble; for they are nearly akin. And the noble are citizens in a truer sense than the ignoble, since good birth is always valued in a man's own home and country. Another reason is, that those who are sprung from better ancestors are likely to be better men, for nobility is excellence of race. Virtue, too, may be truly said to have a claim, for justice has been acknowledged by us to be a social virtue, and it implies all others. Again, the many urge their claim against the few; for, when taken collectively, and compared with the few, they are stronger and richer and better. But, what if the good, the rich, the noble, and the other classes who make up a State, are all living together in the same city, will there, or will there not, be any doubt who shall rule?— No doubt at all in determining who ought to rule in each of the above-mentioned forms of government. For States are characterized by differences in their governing bodies— one of them has a government of the rich, another of the virtuous, and so on. But a difficulty arises when all these elements coexist. How are we to decide? Suppose the virtuous to be very few in number; may we consider their numbers in relation to their duties, and ask whether they are enough to administer a State, or

must they be so many as will make up a State? Objections may be urged against all the aspirants to political power. For those who found their claims on wealth or family have no basis of justice; on this principle, if any one person were richer than all the rest, it is clear that he ought to be the ruler of them. In like manner he who is very distinguished by his birth ought to have the superiority over all those who claim on the ground that they are freeborn. In an aristocracy, or government of the best, a like difficulty occurs about virtue; for if one citizen be better than the other members of the government, however good they may be, he too, upon the same principle of justice, should rule over them. And if the people are to be supreme because they are stronger than the few, then if one man, or more than one, but not a majority, is stronger than the many, they ought to rule, and not the many.

All these considerations appear to show that none of the principles on which men claim to rule, and hold all other men in subjection to them, are strictly right. To those who claim to be masters of the State on the ground of their virtue or their wealth, the many might fairly answer that they themselves are often better and richer than the few—I do not say individually, but collectively. And another ingenious objection which is sometimes put forward may be met in a similar manner. Some persons doubt whether the legislator who desires to make the justest laws ought to legislate with a view to the good of the higher classes or of the many, when the case which we have mentioned occurs [*i.e.*, when all the elements coexist]. Now what is just or right is to be interpreted in the sense of "what is equal"; and that which is right in the sense of being equal is to be considered with reference to the advantage of the State, and the common good of the citizens. And a citizen is one who shares in governing and being governed. He differs under different forms of government, but in the best State he is one who is able and willing to be governed and to govern with a view to the life of virtue.

• • •

BOOK IV

• • •

We have now to inquire what is the best constitution for most States, and the best life for most men, neither assuming a standard of virtue which is above ordinary persons, nor an education which is exceptionally favored by nature and circumstances, nor yet an ideal State which is an aspiration only, but having regard to the life in which the majority are able to share, and to the form of government which States in general can attain. As to those aristocracies, as they are called, of which we were just now speaking, they either lie beyond the possibilities of the greater number of States, or they approximate to the so-called constitutional government, and therefore need no separate discussion. And in fact the conclusion at which we arrive respecting all these forms rests upon the same grounds. For if it has been truly said in the "Ethics" that the happy life is the life according to unimpeded virtue, and that virtue is a mean, then the life which is in a mean, and in a mean attainable by everyone, must be the best.* And the same prin-

---

*[Following a middle path between excess and deficiency.—*Ed.*]

ciples of virtue and vice are characteristic of cities and of constitutions; for the constitution is in a figure the life of a city.

Now in all States there are three elements; one class is very rich, another very poor, and a third in a mean. It is admitted that moderation and the mean are best, and therefore it will clearly be best to possess the gifts of fortune in moderation; for in that condition of life men are most ready to listen to reason. But he who greatly excels in beauty, strength, birth or wealth, or on the other hand who is very poor, or very weak, or very much disgraced, finds it difficult to follow reason. Of these two the one sort grow into violent and great criminals, the others into rogues and petty rascals. And two sorts of offences correspond to them, the one committed from violence, the other from roguery. The petty rogues are disinclined to hold office, whether military or civil, and their aversion to these two duties is as great an injury to the State as their tendency to crime. Again, those who have too much of the goods of fortune, strength, wealth, friends, and the like, are neither willing nor able to submit to authority. The evil begins at home: for when they are boys, by reason of the luxury in which they are brought up, they never learn, even at school, the habit of obedience. On the other hand, the very poor, who are in the opposite extreme, are too degraded. So that the one class cannot obey, and can only rule despotically; the other knows not how to command and must be ruled like slaves. Thus arises a city, not of freemen, but of masters and slaves, the one despising, the other envying; and nothing can be more fatal to friendship and good-fellowship in States than this: for good-fellowship tends to friendship; when men are at enmity with one another, they would rather not even share the same path. But a city ought to be composed, as far as possible, of equals and similars; and these are generally the middle classes. Wherefore the city which is composed of middle-class citizens is necessarily best governed; they are, as we say, the natural elements of a State. And this is the class of citizens which is most secure in a State, for they do not, like the poor, covet their neighbors' goods; nor do others covet theirs, as the poor covet the goods of the rich; and as they neither plot against others, nor are themselves plotted against, they pass through life safely. Wisely then did Phocylides pray, "Many things are best in the mean; I desire to be of a middle condition in my city."

Plutarch

Plutarch (c. 40–120) is known for one work, his *Parallel Lives*, a book in which he paired the biography of a famous Greek with that of an equally famous Roman. His life of Alexander (who was actually a Macedonian), from which the selection that follows is taken, is paired, for obvious reasons, with that of Julius Caesar. As an account of the life of its subject it leaves something to be desired, mainly because Plutarch is as prolix in character analysis as he is niggardly about factual information. Nevertheless, he paints a colorful picture of his extraordinary subject.

Alexander the Great (356–323 B.C.) is a figure who has captured the imagination of subsequent generations in a way that few others have done. Even today parents regularly choose his name for their sons. Yet his meteoric military career was quite brief. As a conqueror he quickly defeated the Persians in Asia Minor, moved south to occupy Egypt, there founding the famous city of Alexandria (one of many he named after himself), then returned to defeat the Persians again and to destroy their magnificent capital city of Persepolis. From there he turned eastward, marching into and occupying a portion of India. But his career was cut short by his sudden death at the age of thirty-two.

If one accepts Plutarch's account, Alexander owed his military success mainly to his personal courage and audacity. But, if one looks behind surface appearances it is hard not to conclude that his victories must equally have been the result of his genius as a military leader, as well as the superb training and discipline of his troops.

Although the empire he created by his conquests did not long survive Alexander's death, his incursion with his army into the Middle East had significant effects, particularly in the blending of diverse cultures. Western ideas and practices followed Alexander and his army, as Greeks settled in the various cities he founded in the conquered lands. But the cultural influence also worked in the opposite direction, as these settlers assimilated the ways of thought and life of the East.

We have little information about the life of Plutarch, the biographer of Alexander. A Greek, he apparently traveled quite widely, spending time in Egypt as well as in Rome. His *Parallel Lives* has remained popular, being widely read particularly in the early modern period. Shakespeare, for example, drew heavily on it for material for such plays as *Julius Caesar* and *Antony and Cleopatra.*

Alexander

It being my purpose to write the lives of Alexander the king, and of Caesar, by whom Pompey was destroyed, the multitude of their great actions affords so large a field that I were to blame if I should not by way of apology forewarn my reader that I have chosen rather to epitomize the most celebrated parts of their story, than to insist at large on every particular circumstance of it. It must be borne in mind that my design is not to write histories, but lives. And the most glorious exploits do not always furnish us with the clearest discoveries of virtue or vice in men; sometimes a matter of less moment, an expression or a jest, informs us better of their characters and inclinations, than the most famous sieges, the greatest armaments, or the bloodiest battles whatsoever. Therefore as portrait-painters are more exact in the lines and features of the face, in which the character is seen, than in the other parts of the body, so I must be allowed to give my more particular attention to the marks and indications of the souls of men, and while I endeavor by these to portray their lives, may be free to leave more weighty matters and great battles to be treated of by others.

• • •

Alexander was born the sixth of Hecatombaeon, which month the Macedonians call Lous, the same day that the temple of Diana at Ephesus was burnt; which Hegesias of Magnesia makes the occasion of a conceit, frigid enough to have stopped the conflagration. The temple, he says, took fire and was burnt while its mistress was absent, assisting at the birth of Alexander. And all the Eastern soothsayers who happened to be then at Ephesus, looking upon the ruin of this temple to be the forerunner of some other calamity, ran about the town, beating their faces, and crying, that this day had brought forth something that would prove fatal and destructive to all Asia.

Just after Philip had taken Potidaea, he received these three messages at one time, that Parmenio had overthrown the Illyrians in a great battle, that his race-horse had won the course at the Olympic games, and that his wife had given birth to Alexander; with which being naturally well pleased, as an addition to his satisfaction, he was assured by the diviners that a son, whose birth was accompanied with three successes, could not fail of being invincible.

The statues that gave the best representation of Alexander's person,

Trans. John Dryden.

were those of Lysippus (by whom alone he would suffer his image to be made), those peculiarities which many of his successors afterwards and his friends used to affect to imitate, the inclination of his head a little on one side towards his left shoulder, and his melting eye, having been expressed by this artist with great exactness. But Apelles, who drew him with thunderbolts in his hand, made his complexion browner and darker than it was naturally; for he was fair and of light color, passing into ruddiness in his face and upon his breast. Aristoxenus in his Memoirs tells us that a most agreeable odor exhaled from his skin, and that his breath and body all over was so fragrant as to perfume the clothes which he wore next him; the cause of which might probably be the hot and adust temperament of his body. For sweet smells, Theophrastus conceives, are produced by the concoction of moist humours by heat, which is the reason that those parts of the world which are driest and most burnt up, afford spices of the best kind, and in the greatest quantity; for the heat of the sun exhausts all the superfluous moisture which lies in the surface of bodies, ready to generate putrefaction. And this hot constitution, it may be, rendered Alexander so addicted to drinking, and so choleric. His temperance, as to the pleasures of the body, was apparent in him in his very childhood, as he was with much difficulty incited to them, and always used them with great moderation; though in other things he was extremely eager and vehement, and in his love of glory, and the pursuit of it, he showed a solidity of high spirit and magnanimity far above his age. For he neither sought nor valued it upon every occasion, as his father Philip did (who affected to show his eloquence almost to a degree of pedantry, and took care to have the victories of his racing chariots at the Olympic games engraven on his coin), but when he was asked by some about him, whether he would run a race in the Olympic games, as he was very swift-footed, he answered, he would, if he might have kings to run with him. Indeed, he seems in general to have looked with indifference, if not with dislike, upon the professed athletes. He often appointed prizes, for which not only tragedians and musicians, pipers and harpers, but rhapsodists also, strove to outvie one another; and delighted in all manner of hunting and cudgel-playing, but never gave any encouragement to contests either of boxing or of the pancratium.[1]

While he was yet very young, he entertained the ambassadors from the king of Persia, in the absence of his father, and entering much into conversation with them, gained so much upon them by his affability, and the questions he asked them, which were far from being childish or trifling (for he inquired of them the length of the ways, the nature of the road into inner Asia, the character of their king, how he carried himself to his enemies, and what forces he was able to bring into the field), that they were struck with admiration of him, and looked upon the ability so much famed of Philip, to be nothing in comparison with the forwardness and high purpose that appeared thus early to his son. Whenever he heard Philip had taken any town of

---

[1] [A combination of boxing and wrestling. —*Ed.*]

importance, or won any signal victory, instead of rejoicing at it altogether, he would tell his companions that his father would anticipate everything, and leave him and them no opportunities of performing great and illustrious actions. For being more bent upon action and glory than either upon pleasure or riches, he esteemed all that he should receive from his father as a diminution and prevention of his own future achievements; and would have chosen rather to succeed to a kingdom involved in troubles and wars, which would have afforded him frequent exercise of his courage, and a large field of honor, than to one already flourishing and settled, where his inheritance would be an inactive life, and the mere enjoyment of wealth and luxury.

The care of his education, as it might be presumed, was committed to a great many attendants, preceptors, and teachers, over the whole of whom Leonidas, a near kinsman of Olympias, a man of an austere temper, presided, who did not indeed himself decline the name of what in reality is a noble and honorable office, but in general his dignity, and his near relationship, obtained him from other people the title of Alexander's foster father and governor. But he who took upon him the actual place and style of his pedagogue, was Lysimachus the Acarnanian, who, though he had nothing specially to recommend him, but his lucky fancy of calling himself Phoenix, Alexander Achilles, and Philip Peleus, was therefore well enough esteemed, and ranged in the next degree after Leonidas.

Philonicus the Thessalian brought the horse Bucephalas to Philip, offering to sell him for thirteen talents; but when they went into the field to try him, they found him so very vicious and unmanageable, that he reared up when they endeavored to mount him, and would not so much as endure the voice of any of Philip's attendants. Upon which, as they were leading him away as wholly useless and untractable, Alexander, who stood by, said, "What an excellent horse do they lose, for want of address and boldness to manage him!" Philip at first took no notice of what he said; but when he heard him repeat the same thing several times, and saw that he was much vexed to see the horse sent away, "Do you reproach," said he to him, "those who are older than yourself, as if you knew more, and were better able to manage him than they?" "I could manage this horse," replied he, "better than others do." "And if you do not," said Philip, "what will you forfeit for your rashness?" "I will pay," answered Alexander, "the whole price of the horse." At this the whole company fell a laughing; and as soon as the wager was settled amongst them, he immediately ran to the horse, and taking hold of the bridle, turned him directly towards the sun, having, it seems, observed that he was disturbed at and afraid of the motion of his own shadow; then letting him go forward a little, still keeping the reins in his hand, and stroking him gently when he found him begin to grow eager and fiery, he let fall his upper garment softly, and with one nimble leap securely mounted him, and when he was seated, by little and little drew in the bridle, and curbed him without either striking or spurring him. Presently, when he found him free from all rebelliousness, and only impatient for the course, he let him go at full speed, inciting him now with a commanding voice, and urging him also with his heel. Philip and his friends looked on at first in silence and anxiety for the result, till seeing him turn at the end of his career, and come back rejoicing and triumphing for what he had performed, they all burst out into acclamations of applause; and his father, shedding tears, it is said, for joy, kissed him as he came down from his horse, and in his transport, said, "O my son, look thee out a kingdom equal to and worthy of thyself, for Macedonia is too little for thee."

After this, considering him to be of a temper easy to be led to his duty by reason, but by no means to be compelled, he always endeavored to persuade rather than to command or force him to any thing; and now looking upon the instruction and tuition of his youth to be of greater difficulty and importance, than to be wholly trusted to the ordinary masters in music and poetry, and the common school subjects, and to require, as Sophocles says,

The bridle and the rudder too,

he sent for Aristotle, the most learned and most celebrated philosopher of his time, and rewarded him with a munificence proportionable to and becoming the care he took to instruct his son. For he repeopled his native city Stagira, which he had caused to be demolished a little before, and restored all the citizens who were in exile or slavery, to their habitations. As a place for the pursuit of their studies and exercises, he assigned the temple of the Nymphs, near Mieza, where, to this very day, they show you Aristotle's stone seats, and the shady walks which he was wont to frequent. It would appear that Alexander received from him not only his doctrines of Morals, and of Politics, but also something of those more abstruse and profound theories which these philosophers, by the very names they gave them, professed to reserve for oral communication to the initiated, and did not allow many to become acquainted with. For when he was in Asia, and heard Aristotle had published some treatises of that kind, he wrote to him, using very plain language to him in behalf of philosophy, the following letter:

Alexander to Aristotle greeting. You have not done well to publish your books of oral doctrine; for what is there now that we excel others in, if those things which we have been particularly instructed in be laid open to all? For my part, I assure you, I had rather excel others in the knowledge of what is excellent, than in the extent of my power and dominion. Farewell.

And Aristotle, soothing this passion for preeminence, speaks, in his excuse for himself, of these doctrines, as in fact both published and not published; as indeed, to say the truth, his books on metaphysics are written in a style which makes them useless for ordinary teaching, and instructive only, in the way of memoranda, for those who have been already conversant in that sort of learning.

Doubtless also it was to Aristotle, that he owed the inclination he had, not to the theory only, but likewise to the practice of the art of medicine. For when any of his friends were sick, he would often prescribe them their course of diet, and medicines proper to their disease, as we may find in his epistles. He was naturally a great lover of all kinds of learning and reading; and Onesicritus informs us, that he constantly laid Homer's *Iliad,* according to the copy corrected by Aristotle, called the casket copy, with his dagger under his pillow, declaring that he esteemed it a perfect portable treasure of all military virtue and knowledge. When he was in the upper Asia, being destitute of other books, he ordered Harpalus to send him some; who furnished him with Philistus's History, a great many of the plays of Euripides, Sophocles, and Aeschylus, and some dithyrambic odes, composed by Telestes and Philoxenus. For a while he loved and cherished Aristotle no less, as he was wont to say himself, than if he had been his father, giving this reason for it, that as he had received life from the one, so the other had taught him to live well. But afterwards, upon some mistrust of him, yet not so great as to make him do him any hurt, his familiarity and friendly kindness to him abated so much of its former force and affectionateness, as to make it evident he was alienated from him. However, his violent thirst after and passion for learning, which were once implanted, still grew up with him, and never decayed; as appears by his veneration of Anaxarchus, by the present of fifty talents which he sent to Xeonocrates, and his particular care and esteem of Dandamis and Calanus.

• • •

[Some years later,] the Grecians, being assembled at the Isthmus, declared their resolution of joining with Alexander in the war against the Persians, and proclaimed him their general. While he stayed here, many public ministers and philosophers came from all parts to visit him, and congratulated him on his election, but contrary to his expectation, Diogenes of Sinope,[2] who then was living at Corinth, thought so little of him, that instead of coming to compliment him, he never so much as stirred out of the suburb called the Cranium, where Alexander found him lying alone in the sun. When he saw so much company near him, he raised himself a little, and vouchsafed to look upon Alexander; and when he kindly asked him whether he wanted any thing, "Yes," said he, "I would have you stand from between me and the sun." Alexander was so struck at this answer, and surprised at the greatness of the man, who had taken so little notice of him, that as he went away, he told his followers who were laughing at the moroseness of the philosopher, that if he were not Alexander, he would choose to be Diogenes.

Then he went to Delphi, to consult Apollo concerning the success of the war he had undertaken, and happening to come on one of the forbidden days, when it was esteemed improper to give any answers from the oracle, he sent messengers to desire the priestess to do her office; and when she refused, on the plea of a law to the contrary, he went up himself, and began to draw her by force into the temple, until tired and overcome with his importunity, "My son," said she, "thou art invincible." Alexander taking hold of what she spoke, declared he had received such an answer as he wished for, and that it was needless to consult the god any further. Among other prodi-

---

[2][A famous Greek philosopher, who lived in a tub and went about carrying a lighted lantern, "in search of an honest man."—*Ed.*]

gies that attended the departure of
his army, the image of Orpheus at Li-
bethra, made by cypresswood, was
seen to sweat in great abundance, to
the discouragement of many. But
Aristander told him, that far from
presaging any ill to him, it signified
he should perform acts so important
and glorious as would make the poets and musicians of future ages labor and sweat to describe and
celebrate them.

His army, by their computation
who make the smallest amount, consisted of thirty thousand foot, and
four thousand horse; and those who
make the most of it, speak but of
forty-three thousand foot, and three
thousand horse. Aristobulus says, he
had not a fund of above seventy talents for their pay, nor had he more
than thirty days' provision, if we may
believe Duris; Onesicritus tells us, he
was two hundred talents in debt.
However narrow and disporportion-
able the beginnings of so vast an undertaking might seem to be, yet he
would not embark his army until he
had informed himself particularly
what means his friends had to enable
them to follow him, and supplied
what they wanted, by giving good
farms to some, a village to one, and
the revenue of some hamlet or har-
bor town to another. So that at last
he had portioned out or engaged almost all the royal property; which
giving Perdiccas an occasion to ask
him what he would leave himself, he
replied, his hopes. "Your soldiers,"
replied Perdiccas, "will be your partners in those," and refused to accept
of the estate he had assigned him.
Some others of his friends did the
like, but to those who willingly received, or desired assistance of him,
he liberally granted it, as far as his
patrimony in Macedonia would

reach, the most part of which was
spent in these donations.

With such vigorous resolutions,
and his mind thus disposed, he
passed the Hellespont, and at Troy
sacrificed to Minerva, and honored
the memory of the heroes who were
buried there, with solemn libations;
especially Achilles, whose gravestone
he anointed, and with his friends, as
the ancient custom is, ran naked
about his sepulchre, and crowned it
with garlands, declaring how happy
he esteemed him, in having while he
lived so faithful a friend, and when
he was dead, so famous a poet to proclaim his actions. While he was view-
ing the rest of the antiquities and
curiosities of the place, being told he
might see Paris's harp, if he pleased,
he said, he thought it not worth looking on, but he should be glad to see
that of Achilles, to which he used to
sing the glories and great actions of
brave men.

In the mean time Darius's captains having collected large forces,
were encamped on the further bank
of the river Granicus, and it was necessary to fight, as it were, in the gate
of Asia for an entrance into it. The
depth of the river, with the unevenness and difficult ascent of the opposite bank, which was to be gained by
main force, was apprehended by
most, and some pronounced it an
improper time to engage, because it
was unusual for the kings of Macedonia to march with their forces in the
month called Daesius. But Alexander
broke through these scruples, telling
them they should call it a second
Artemisium. And when Parmenio advised him not to attempt any thing
that day, because it was late, he told
him that he should disgrace the
Hellespont, should he fear the
Granicus. And so without more say-

ing, he immediately took the river with thirteen troops of horse, and advanced against whole showers of darts thrown from the steep opposite side, which was covered with armed multitudes of the enemy's horse and foot, notwithstanding the disadvantage of the ground and the rapidity of the stream; so that the action seemed to have more of frenzy and desperation in it, than of prudent conduct. However, he persisted obstinately to gain the passage, and at last with much ado making his way up the banks, which were extremely muddy and slippery, he had instantly to join in a mere confused hand-to-hand combat with the enemy, before he could draw up his men, who were still passing over, into any order. For the enemy pressed upon him with loud and warlike outcries; and charging horse against horse, with their lances, after they had broken and spent these, they fell to it with their swords. And Alexander, being easily known by his buckler, and a large plume of white feathers on each side of his helmet, was attacked on all sides, yet escaped wounding, though his cuirass was pierced by a javelin in one of the joinings. And Rhoesaces and Spithridates, two Persian commanders, falling upon him at once, he avoided one of them, and struck at Rhoesaces, who had a good cuirass on, with such force, that his spear breaking in his hand, he was glad to betake himself to his dagger. While they were thus engaged, Spithridates came up on one side of him, and raising himself upon his horse, gave him such a blow with his battle-axe on the helmet, that he cut off the crest of it, with one of his plumes, and the helmet was only just so far strong enough to save him, that the edge of the weapon touched the hair

of his head. But as he was about to repeat his stroke, Clitus, called the black Clitus, prevented him, by running him through the body with his spear. At the same time Alexander despatched Rhoesaces with his sword. While the horses were thus dangerously engaged, the Macedonian phalanx passed the river, and the foot on each side advanced to fight. But the enemy hardly sustained the first onset, soon gave ground and fled, all but the mercenary Greeks, who, making a stand upon a rising ground, desired quarter, which Alexander, guided rather by passion than judgment, refused to grant, and charging them himself first, had his horse (not Bucephalas, but another) killed under him. And this obstinacy of his to cut off these experienced desperate men, cost him the lives of more of his own soldiers than all the battle before, besides those who were wounded. The Persians lost in this battle twenty thousand foot, and two thousand five hundred horse. On Alexander's side, Aristobulus says there were not wanting above four and thirty, of whom nine were foot-soldiers; and in memory of them he caused so many statues of brass, of Lysippus's making, to be erected. And that the Grecians might participate in the honor of his victory, he sent a portion of the spoils home to them, particularly to the Athenians three hundred bucklers, and upon all the rest he ordered this inscription to be set: "Alexander the son of Philip, and the Grecians, except the Lacedaemonians, won these from the barbarians who inhabit Asia." All the plate and purple garments, and other things of the same kind that he took from the Persians, except a very small quantity which he reserved for himself, he sent as a present to his mother.

This battle presently made a great change of affairs to Alexander's advantage. For Sardis itself, the chief seat of the barbarian's power in the maritime provinces, and many other considerable places were surrendered to him; only Halicarnassus and Miletus stood out, which he took by force, together with the territory about them. After which he was a little unsettled in his opinion how to proceed. Sometimes he thought it best to find out Darius as soon as he could, and put all to the hazard of a battle; another while he looked upon it as a more prudent course to make an entire reduction of the seacoast, and not to seek the enemy till he had first exercised his power here and made himself secure of the resources of these provinces. While he was thus deliberating what to do, it happened that a spring of water near the city of Xanthus in Lycia, of its own accord swelled over its banks, and threw up a copper plate upon the margin, in which was engraven in ancient characters, that the time would come, when the Persian empire should be destroyed by the Grecians. Encouraged by this accident, he proceeded to reduce the maritime parts of Cilicia and Phoenicia, and passed his army along the seacoasts of Pamphylia with such expedition that many historians have described and extolled it with that height of admiration, as if it were no less than a miracle, and an extraordinary effect of divine favor, that the waves which usually come rolling in violently from the main, and hardly ever leave so much as a narrow beach under the steep, broken cliffs at any time uncovered, should on a sudden retire to afford him passage. Menander, in one of his comedies, alludes to this marvel when he says:

Was Alexander ever favored more?
Each man I wish for meets me at my door,
And should I ask for passage through the sea,
The sea I doubt not would retire for me.

But Alexander himself in his epistles mentioned nothing unusual in this at all, but says he went from Phaselis, and passed through what they call the Ladders. At Phaselis he stayed some time, and finding the statue of Theodectes, who was a native of this town and was now dead, erected in the marketplace, after he had supped, having drunk pretty plentifully, he went and danced about it, and crowned it with garlands, honoring not ungracefully in his sport, the memory of a philosopher whose conversation he had formerly enjoyed, when he was Aristotle's scholar.

• • •

Darius was by this time upon his march from Susa, very confident, not only in the number of his men, which amounted to six hundred thousand, but likewise in a dream, which the Persian soothsayers interpreted rather in flattery to him, than according to the natural probability. He dreamed that he saw the Macedonian phalanx all on fire, and Alexander waiting on him, clad in the same dress which he himself had been used to wear when he was courier to the late king; after which, going into the temple of Belus, he vanished out of his sight. The dream would appear to have supernaturally signified to him the illustrious actions the Macedonians were to perform, and that as he from a courier's place had risen to the throne, so Alexander should come to be master of Asia, and not long surviving his conquests, conclude his life with glory. Darius's confidence increased the more, because Alexander spent so much time in Cilicia, which he imputed to his cowardice. But it was sickness that detained him there, which some say he contracted from his fatigues, others from bathing in the river Cydnus, whose waters were exceedingly cold. However it happened, none of his physicians would venture to give him any remedies, they thought his case so desperate, and were so afraid of the suspicions and ill-will of the Macedonians if they should fail in the cure; till Philip, the Acarnanian, seeing how critical his case was, but relying on his own well-known friendship for him, resolved to try the last efforts of his art, and rather hazard his own credit and life, than suffer him to perish for want of physic, which he confidently administered to him, encouraging him to take it boldly, if he desired a speedy recovery, in order to prosecute the war. At this very time, Parmenio wrote to Alexander from the camp, bidding him have a care of Philip, as one who was bribed by Darius to kill him, with great sums of money, and a promise of his daughter in marriage. When he had perused the letter, he put it under his pillow, without showing it so much as to any of his most intimate friends, and when Philip came in with the potion, he took it with great cheerfulness and assurance, giving him meantime the letter to read. This was a spectacle well worth being present at, to see Alexander take the draught, and Philip read the letter at the same time, and then turn and look upon one another, but with different sentiments; for Alexander's looks were cheerful and open, to show his kindness to and confidence in his physician, while the other was full of surprise and alarm at the accusation, appealing to the gods to witness his innocence, sometimes lifting up his hands to heaven, and then throwing himself down by the bedside, and beseeching Alexander to lay aside all fear, and follow his directions without apprehension. For the medicine at first worked so strongly as to drive, so to say, the vital forces into the interior, he lost his speech, and falling into a swoon, had scarce any sense of pulse left. However, in no long time, by Philip's means, his health and strength returned, and he showed himself in public to the Macedonians, who were in continual fear and dejection until they saw him abroad again.

• • •

In his diet, also, he was most temperate, as appears, omitting many other circumstances, by what he said to Ada, whom he adopted, with the title of mother, and afterwards created queen of Caria. For when she out of kindness sent him every day many curious dishes, and sweetmeats, and would have furnished him with some cooks and pastrymen, who were thought to have great skill, he told her he wanted none of them, his preceptor, Leonidas, having already given him the best, which were a night march to prepare for breakfast, and a moderate breakfast to create an appetite for supper. Leonidas also, he added, used to open and search the furniture of his chamber, and his wardrobe, to see if his mother had left him any thing that was delicate or superfluous. He was much less addicted to wine than was generally believed; that which gave people occasion to think so of him was, that when he had nothing else to do, he loved to sit long and talk, rather than drink, and over every cup hold a long conversation. For when his affairs called upon him, he would not be detained, as other generals often were, either by wine, or sleep, nuptial solemnities, spectacles, or any other diversion whatsoever; a convincing argument of which is, that in the short time he lived, he accomplished so many and so great actions. When he was free from employment, after he was up, and had sacrificed to the gods, he used to sit down to breakfast, and then spend the rest of the day in hunting, or writing memoirs, giving decisions on some military questions, or reading. In marches that required no great haste, he would practise shooting as he went along, or to mount a chariot, and alight from it in full speed. Sometimes, for sport's sake, as his journals tell us, he would hunt foxes and go fowling. When he came in for the evening, after he had bathed and was anointed, he would call for his bakers and chief cooks, to know if they had his dinner ready. He never cared to dine till it was pretty late and beginning to be dark, and was wonderfully circumspect at meals that every one who sat with him should be served alike and with proper attention; and his love of talking, as was said before, made him delight to sit long at his wine. And then, though otherwise no prince's conversation was ever so agreeable, he would fall into a temper of ostentation and soldierly boasting, which gave his flatterers a great advantage to ride him, and made his better friends very uneasy. For though they thought it too base to strive who should flatter him most, yet they found it hazardous not to do it; so that between the shame and the danger, they were in great strait how to behave themselves. After such an entertainment, he was wont to bathe, and then perhaps he would sleep till noon, and sometimes all day long. He was so very temperate in his eating, that when any rare fish or fruits were sent him, he would distribute them among his friends, and often reserve nothing for himself. His table, however, was always magnificent, the expense of it still increasing with his good fortune, till it amounted to ten thousand drachmas a day, to which sum he limited it, and beyond this he would suffer none to lay out in any entertainment where he himself was the guest.

• • •

After he had reduced all Asia on this side of the Euphrates, he advanced towards Darius, who was coming down against him with a million of men. In his march, a very ridiculous passage happened. The servants who followed the camp, for sport's sake divided themselves into two parties, and named the commander of one of them Alexander, and of the other Darius. At first they only pelted one another with clods of earth, but presently took to their fists, and at last, heated with the contention, they fought in good earnest with stones and clubs, so that they had much ado to part them; till Alexander, upon hearing of it, ordered the two captains to decide the quarrel by single combat, and armed him who bore his name himself, while Philotas did the same to him who represented Darius. The whole army were spectators of this encounter, willing from the event of it to derive an omen of their own future success. After they had fought stoutly a pretty long while, at last he who was called Alexander had the better, and for a reward of his prowess, had twelve villages given him, with leave to wear the Persian dress. So we are told by Eratosthenes.

But the great battle of all that was fought with Darius, was not, as most writers tells us, at Arbela, but at Gaugamela. . . . The oldest of his commanders, and chiefly Parmenio, when they beheld all the plain between Niphates and the Gordyaean mountains shining with the lights and fires which were made by the barbarians, and heard the uncertain and confused sound of voices out of their camp, like the distant roaring of a vast ocean, were so amazed at the thoughts of such a multitude, that after some conference among themselves, they concluded it an enterprise too difficult and hazardous for them to engage so numerous an enemy in the day, and therefore meeting the king as he came from sacrificing, besought him to attack Darius by night, that the darkness might conceal the danger of the ensuing battle. To this he gave them the celebrated answer, "I will not steal a victory," which though some at the time thought a boyish and inconsiderate speech, as if he played with danger, others, however, regarded as an evidence that he confided in his present condition, and acted on a true judgment of the future, not wishing to leave Darius, in case he were worsted, the pretext of trying his fortune again, which he might suppose himself to have, if he could impute his overthrow to the disadvantage of the night, as he did before to the mountains, the narrow passages, and the sea. For while he had such numerous forces and large dominions still remaining, it was not any want of men or arms that could induce him to give up the war, but

only the loss of all courage and hope upon the conviction of an undeniable and manifest defeat.

After they were gone from him with this answer, he laid himself down in his tent and slept the rest of the night more soundly than was usual with him, to the astonishment of the commanders, who came to him early in the morning, and were fain themselves to give order that the soldiers should breakfast. But at last, time not giving them leave to wait any longer, Parmenio went to his bedside, and called him twice or thrice by his name, till he waked him, and then asked him how it was possible, when he was to fight the most important battle of all, he could sleep as soundly as if he were already victorious. "And are we not so, indeed," replied Alexander smiling, "since we are at last relieved from the trouble of wandering in pursuit of Darius through a wide and wasted country, hoping in vain that he would fight us?" And not only before the battle, but in the height of the danger, he showed himself great, and manifested the self-possession of a just foresight and confidence. For the battle for some time fluctuated and was dubious. The left wing, where Parmenio commanded, was so impetuously charged by the Bactrian horse that it was disordered and forced to give ground, at the same time that Mazaeus had sent a detachment round about to fall upon those who guarded the baggage, which so disturbed Parmenio, that he sent messengers to acquaint Alexander that the camp and baggage would be all lost unless he immediately relieved the rear by a considerable reinforcement drawn out of the front. This message being brought him just as he was giving the signal to those about him for the onset, he bade them tell Parmenio that he must have surely lost the use of his reason, and had forgotten, in his alarm, that soldiers, if victorious, become masters of their enemies' baggage; and if defeated, instead of taking care of their wealth or their slaves, have nothing more to do but to fight gallantly and die with honor. When he had said this, he put on his helmet, having the rest of his arms on before he came out of his tent, which were a coat of the Sicilian make, girt close about him, and over that a breastpiece of thickly quilted linen, which was taken among other booty at the battle of Issus. The helmet, which was made by Theophilus, though of iron, was so well wrought and polished, that it was as bright as the most refined silver. To this was fitted a gorget of the same metal, set with precious stones. His sword, which was the weapon he most used in fight, was given him by the king of the Citieans, and was of an admirable temper and lightness. The belt which he also wore in all engagements, was of much richer workmanship than the rest of his armor. It was a work of the ancient Helicon, and had been presented to him by the Rhodians, as a mark of their respect to him. So long as he was engaged in drawing up his men, or riding about to give orders or directions, or to view them, he spared Bucephalas, who was now growing old, and made use of another horse; but when he was actually to fight, he sent for him again, and as soon as he was mounted, commenced the attack.

He made the longest address that day to the Thessalians and other Greeks, who answered him with loud shouts, desiring him to lead them on against the barbarians, upon which he shifted his javelin into his left hand, and with his right lifted up towards heaven, besought the gods, as Callisthenes tells us, that if he was of a truth the son of Jupiter, they would be pleased to assist and strengthen the Grecians. At the same time the augur Aristander, who had a white mantle about him, and a crown of gold on his head, rode by and showed them an eagle that soared just over Alexander, and directed his flight towards the enemy; which so animated the beholders, that after mutual encouragements and exhortations, the horses charged at full speed, and were followed in a mass by the whole phalanx of the foot. But before they could well come to blows with the first ranks, the barbarians shrunk back, and were hotly pursued by Alexander, who drove those that fled before him into the middle of the battle, where Darius himself was in person, whom he saw from a distance over the foremost ranks, conspicuous in the midst of his lifeguard, a tall and fine-looking man, drawn in a lofty chariot, defended by an abundance of the best horse, who stood close in order about it, ready to receive the enemy. But Alexander's approach was so terrible, forcing those who gave back upon those who yet maintained their ground, that he beat down and dispersed them almost all. Only a few of the bravest and valiantest opposed the pursuit, who were slain in their king's presence, falling in heaps upon one another, and in the very pangs of death striving to catch hold of the horses. Darius now seeing all was lost, that those who were placed in front to defend him were broken and beat back upon him, that he could not turn or disengage his chariot without great difficulty, the wheels being clogged and entangled among the dead bodies, which lay in such heaps as not only stopped, but almost covered the horses, and made them rear and grow so unruly, that the frighted charioteer could govern them no longer, in this extremity was glad to quit his chariot and his arms, and mounting, it is said, upon a mare that had been taken from her foal, betook himself to flight. But he had not escaped so either, if Parmenio had not sent fresh messengers to Alexander, to desire him to return and assist him against a considerable body of the enemy which yet stood together, and would not give ground. For, indeed, Parmenio is on all hands accused of having been sluggish and unserviceable in this battle, whether age had impaired his courage, or that, as Callisthenes says, he secretly disliked and envied Alexander's growing greatness. Alexander, though he was not a little vexed to be so recalled and hindered from pursuing his victory, yet concealed the true reason from his men, and causing a retreat to be sounded, as if it were too late to continue the execution any longer, marched back towards the place of danger and by the way met with the news of the enemy's total overthrow and flight.

This battle being thus over, seemed to put a period to the Persian empire, and Alexander, who was now proclaimed king of Asia, returned thanks to the gods in magnificent sacrifices, and rewarded his friends and followers with great sums of money, and palaces, and governments of provinces. And eager to gain honor with the Grecians, he wrote to them that he would have all tyrannies abolished, that they might live free according to their own laws, and specially to the Plataeans, that their city should be rebuilt, because their ancestors had permitted their countrymen of old to make their territory the seat of the war, when they fought with the barbarians for their common liberty. He sent also part of the spoils into Italy, to the Crotoniats, to honor the zeal and courage of their citizen Phayllus, the wrestler, who, in the Median war, when the other Grecian colonies in Italy disowned Greece, that he might have a share in the danger, joined the fleet at Salamis, with a vessel set forth at his own charge. So affectionate was Alexander to all kind of virtue, and so desirous to preserve the memory of laudable actions.

• • •

At the taking of Susa, Alexander found in the palace forty thousand talents in money already coined, besides an unspeakable quantity of other furniture and treasure; amongst which was five thousand talents' worth of Hermionian purple, that had been laid up there an hundred and ninety years, and yet kept its color as fresh and lively as at first. The reason of which, they say, is that in dyeing the purple they made use of honey, and of white oil in the white tincture, both which after the like space of time preserve the clearness and brightness of their lustre. Dinon also relates that the Persian kings had water fetched from the Nile and the Danube, which they laid up in their treasuries as a sort of testimony of the greatness of their power and universal empire.

The entrance into Persia was through a most difficult country, and was guarded by the noblest of the Persians, Darius himself having escaped further. Alexander, however, chanced to find a guide in exact correspondence with what the Pythia had foretold when he was a child, that a lycus should conduct him into Persia. For by such an one, whose father was a Lycian, and his mother a Persian, and who spoke both languages, he was now led into the country, by a way something about, yet without fetching any considerable compass. Here a great many of the prisoners were put to the sword, of which himself gives this account, that he commanded them to be killed in the belief that it would be for his advantage. Nor was the money found here less, he says, than at Susa, besides other movables and treasure, as much as ten thousand pair of mules and five thousand camels could well carry away. Amongst other things he happened to observe a large statue of Xerxes thrown carelessly down to the ground in the confusion made by the multitude of soldiers pressing into the palace. He stood still, and accosting it as if it had been alive, "Shall we," said he, "neglectfully pass thee by, now thou are prostrate on the ground, because thou once invadedst Greece, or shall we erect thee again in consideration of the greatness of thy mind and thy other virtues?" But at last, after he had paused some time, and silently considered with himself, he went on without taking any further notice of it. In this place he took up his winter quarters, and stayed four months to refresh his soldiers. It is related that the first time he sat on the royal throne of Persia, under the canopy of gold, Demaratus, the Corinthian, who was much attached to him and had been one of his father's friends, wept, in an old man's manner, and deplored the misfortune of those Greeks whom death had deprived of

the satisfaction of seeing Alexander seated on the throne of Darius.

From hence designing to march against Darius, before he set out, he diverted himself with his officers at an entertainment of drinking and other pastimes, and indulged so far as to let every one's mistress sit by and drink with them. The most celebrated of them was Thais, an Athenian, mistress of Ptolemy, who was afterwards king of Egypt. She, partly as a sort of well-turned compliment to Alexander, partly out of sport, as the drinking went on, at last was carried so far as to utter a saying, not misbecoming her native country's character, though somewhat too loftily for her own condition. She said it was indeed some recompense for the toils she had undergone in following the camp all over Asia, that she was that day treated in, and could insult over, the stately palace of the Persian monarchs. But, she added, it would please her much better, if while the king looked on, she might in sport, with her own hands, set fire to the court of that Xerxes who reduced the city of Athens to ashes, that it might be recorded to posterity, that the women who followed Alexander had taken a severer revenge on the Persians for the sufferings and affronts of Greece, than all the famed commanders had been able to do by sea or land. What she said was received with such universal liking and murmurs of applause, and so seconded by the encouragement and eagerness of the company, that the king himself, persuaded to be of the party, started from his seat, and with a chaplet of flowers on his head, and a lighted torch in his hand, led them the way, while they went after him in a riotous manner, dancing and making loud cries about the place; which when the rest of the Macedonians perceived, they also in great delight ran thither with torches; for they hoped the burning and destruction of the royal palace was an argument that he looked homeward, and had no design to reside among the barbarians. Thus some writers give their account of this action, while others say it was done deliberately; however, all agree that he soon repented of it, and gave order to put out the fire.

Alexander, now intent upon his expedition into India, took notice that his soldiers were so charged with booty that it hindered their marching. Therefore, at break of day, as soon as the baggage wagons were laden, first he set fire to his own, and to those of his friends, and then commanded those to be burnt which belonged to the rest of the army. An act which in the deliberation of it had seemed more dangerous and difficult than it proved in the execution, with which few were dissatisfied; for most of the soldiers, as if they had been inspired, uttering loud outcries and warlike shoutings, supplied one another with what was absolutely necessary, and burnt and destroyed all that was superfluous, the sight of which redoubled Alexander's zeal and eagerness for his design. And, indeed, he was now grown very severe and inexorable in punishing those who committed any fault. For he put Menander, one of his friends, to death, for deserting a fortress where he had placed him in garrison, and shot Orsodates, one of the barbarians who revolted from him, with his own hand.

At this time a sheep happened to yean a lamb, with the perfect shape and color of a tiara upon the head, and testicles on each side; which por-

tent Alexander regarded with such dislike that he immediately caused his Babylonian priests, whom he usually carried about with him for such purposes, to purify him, and told his friends he was not so much concerned for his own sake as for theirs, out of an apprehension that after his death the divine power might suffer his empire to fall into the hands of some degenerate, impotent person. But this fear was soon removed by a wonderful thing that happened not long after, and was thought to presage better. For Proxenus, a Macedonian, who was the chief of those who looked to the king's furniture, as he was breaking up the ground near the river Oxus, to set up the royal pavilion, discovered a spring of a fat, oily liquor, which after the top was taken off, ran pure, clear oil, without any difference either of taste or smell, having exactly the same smoothness and brightness, and that, too, in a country where no olives grew. The water, indeed, of the river Oxus is said to be the smoothest to the feeling of all waters and to leave a gloss on the skins of those who bathe themselves in it. Whatever might be the cause, certain it is that Alexander was wonderully pleased with it, as appears by his letters to Antipater, where he speaks of it as one of the most remarkable presages that God had ever favored him with. The diviners told him it signified his expedition would be glorious in the event, but very painful, and attended with many difficulties; for oil, they said, was bestowed on mankind by God as a refreshment of their labors.

Nor did they judge amiss for he exposed himself to many hazards in the battles which he fought, and received very severe wounds, but the greatest loss in his army was occasioned through the unwholesomeness of the air and the want of necessary provisions. But he still applied himself to overcome fortune and whatever opposed him, by resolution and virtue, and thought nothing impossible to true intrepidity, and on the other hand nothing secure or strong for cowardice. It is told of him that when he besieged Sisimithres, who held an inaccessible, impregnable rock against him, and his soldiers began to despair of taking it, he asked Oxyartes whether Sisimithres was a man of courage, who assuring him he was the greatest coward alive, "Then you tell me," said he, "that the place may easily be taken, since what is in command of it is weak." And in a little time he so terrified Sisimithres that he took it without any difficulty. At an attack which he made upon such another precipitous place with some of his Macedonian soldiers he called to one whose name was Alexander and told him he at any rate must fight bravely, if it were but for his name's sake. The youth fought gallantly and was killed in the action, at which he was sensibly afflicted. Another time, seeing his men march slowly and unwillingly to the siege of the place called Nysa, because of a deep river between them and the town, he advanced before them and standing upon the bank, "What a miserable man," said he, "am I, that I have not learned to swim!" and then was hardly dissuaded from endeavoring to pass it upon his shield. Here, after the assault was over, the ambassadors, who from several towns which he had blocked up came to submit to him and make their peace, were surprised to find him still in his armor, without any one in waiting or attendance upon him, and when at last

some one brought him a cushion, he made the eldest of them, named Acuphis, take it and sit down upon it. The old man, marvelling at his magnanimity and courtesy, asked him what his countrymen should do to merit his friendship. "I would have them," said Alexander, "choose you to govern them, and send one hundred of the most worthy men among them to remain with me as hostages." Acuphis laughed and answered, "I shall govern them with more ease, Sir, if I send you so many of the worst, rather than the best of my subjects."

The extent of king Taxiles's dominions in India was thought to be as large as Egypt, abounding in good pastures and producing beautiful fruits. The king himself had the reputation of a wise man and at his first interview with Alexander he spoke to him in these terms: "To what purpose," said he, "should we make war upon one another, if the design of your coming into these parts be not to rob us of our water or our necessary food, which are the only things that wise men are indispensably obliged to fight for? As for other riches and possessions, as they are accounted in the eye of the world, if I am better provided of them than you, I am ready to let you share with me, but if fortune has been more liberal to you than me, I have no objection to be obliged to you." This discourse pleased Alexander so much that, embracing him, "Do you think," said he to him, "your kind words and courteous behavior will bring you off in this interview without a contest? No, you shall not escape so. I shall contend and do battle with you so far that, how obliging soever you are, shall not have the better of me." Then receiving some presents from him, he returned him others of greater value, and to complete his bounty gave him in money ready-coined one thousand talents, at which his old friends were much displeased, but it gained him the hearts of many of the barbarians. But the best soldiers of the Indians now entering into the pay of several of the cities undertook to defend them, and did it so bravely that they put Alexander to a great deal of trouble, till at last, after a capitulation, upon the surrender of the place he fell upon them as they were marching away and put them all to the sword. This one breach of his word remains as a blemish upon his achievements in war, which he otherwise had performed throughout with that justice and honor that became a king.

• • •

Alexander was now eager to see the ocean [the Arabian Sea]. To which purpose he caused a great many row-boats and rafts to be built, in which he fell gently down the rivers at his leisure, yet so that his navigation was neither unprofitable nor inactive. For by several descents upon the banks he made himself master of the fortified towns and consequently of the country on both sides. But at a siege of a town of the Mallians, who have the repute of being the bravest people of India, he ran in great danger of his life. For having beaten off the defendants with showers of arrows, he was the first man that mounted the wall by scaling ladder, which, as soon as he was up, broke and left him almost alone, exposed to the darts which the barbarians threw at him in great numbers from below. In this distress, turning himself as well as he could, he leaped down in the midst of his enemies and had the good fortune to light upon his feet. The brightness

and clattering of his armor when he came to the ground made the barbarians think they saw rays of light, or some bright phantom playing before his body, which frightened them so at first that they ran away and dispersed. Till seeing him seconded but by two of his guards they fell upon him hand to hand and some, while he bravely defended himself, tried to wound him through his armor with their swords and spears. And one who stood further off drew a bow with such just strength that the arrow finding its way through his cuirass stuck in his ribs under the breast. This stroke was so violent that it made him give back and set one knee to the ground, upon which the man ran up with his drawn scimitar, thinking to dispatch him and had done it, if Peucestes and Limnaeus had not interposed, who were both wounded, Limnaeus mortally, but Peucestes stood his ground, while Alexander killed the barbarian. But this did not free him from danger for besides many other wounds at last he received so weighty a stroke of a club upon his neck that he was forced to lean his body against the wall, still, however, facing the enemy. At this extremity the Macedonians made their way in and gathered round him. They took him up, just as he was fainting away, having lost all sense of what was done near him, and conveyed him to his tent, upon which it was presently reported all over the camp that he was dead. But when they had with great difficulty and pains sawed off the shaft of the arrow, which was of wood, and so with much trouble got off his cuirass, they came to cut out the head of it, which was three fingers broad and four long, and stuck fast in the bone. During the operation he was taken with almost mortal swoonings but when it was out he came to himself again. Yet though all danger was past he continued very weak and confined himself a great while to a regular diet and the method of his cure, til one day hearing the Macedonians clamoring outside in their eagerness to see him he took his cloak and went out. And having sacrificed to the gods, without more delay he went on board again and, as he coasted along, subdued a great deal of the country on both sides, and several considerable towns.

• • •

When he came into Persia, he distributed money among the women, as their own kings had been wont to do, who as often as they came thither, gave every one of them a piece of gold; on account of which custom, some of them, it is said, had come but seldom, and Ochus was so sordidly covetous, that to avoid this expense, he never visited his native country once in all his reign. Then finding Cyrus's sepulchre opened and rifled, he put Polymachus, who did it, to death, though he was a man of some distinction, a born Macedonian of Pella. And after he had read the inscription, he caused it to be cut again below the old one in Greek characters; the words being these: "O man, whosoever thou art, and from whencesoever thou comest (for I know thou wilt come), I am Cyrus, the founder of the Persian empire; do not grudge me this little earth which covers my body." The reading of this sensibly touched Alexander, filling him with the thought of the uncertainty and mutability of human affairs. . . .

At Susa, he married Darius' daughter Statira, and celebrated also the nuptials of his friends, bestowing the noblest of the Persian ladies upon the worthiest of them, at the same time making it an entertainment in honor of the other Macedonians whose marriages had already taken place. At this magnificent festival, it is reported, there were no less than nine thousand guests, to each of whom he gave a golden cup for the libations.

• • •

When once Alexander had given way to fears of supernatural influence, his mind grew so disturbed and so easily alarmed, that if the least unusual or extraordinary thing happened, he thought it a prodigy or a presage, and his court was thronged with diviners and priests whose business was to sacrifice and purify and foretell the future. So miserable a thing is incredulity and contempt of divine power on the one hand, and so miserable, also, superstition on the other, which like water, where the level has been lowered, flowing in and never stopping, fills the mind with slavish fears and follies, as now in Alexander's case. But upon some answers which were brought him from the oracle concerning Hephaestion, he laid aside his sorrow, and fell again to sacrificing and drinking, and having given Nearchus a splendid entertainment, after he had bathed, as was his custom, just as he was going to bed, at Medius's request he went to supper with him. Here he drank all the next day, and was attacked with a fever, which seized him, not as some write, after he had drunk of the bowl of Hercules; nor was he taken with any sudden pain in his back, as if he had been struck with a lance, for these are the inventions of some authors who thought it their duty to make the last scene of so great an action as tragical and moving as they could. Aristobulus tells us, that in the rage of his fever and a violent thirst, he took a draught of wine upon which he fell into delirium, and died on the thirtieth day of the month Daesius.

But the journals give the following record. On the eighteenth of the month, he slept in the bathing-room on account of his fever. The next day he bathed and removed into his chamber, and spent his time in playing at dice with Medius. In the evening he bathed and sacrificed, and ate freely, and had the fever on him through the night. On the twentieth, after the usual sacrifices and bathing, he lay in the bathing-room and heard Nearchus's narrative of his voyage, and the observations he had made in the great sea. The twenty-first he passed in the same manner, his fever still increasing, and suffered much during the night. The next day the fever was very violent, and he had himself removed and his bed set by the great bath, and discoursed with his principal officers about finding fit men to fill up the vacant places in the army. On the twenty-fourth he was much worse, and was carried out of his bed to assist at the sacrifices, and gave order that the general officers should wait within the court, while the inferior officers kept watch without doors. On the twenty-fifth he was removed to his palace on the other side of the river, where he slept a little, but his fever did not abate, and when the generals came into his chamber, he was speechless, and continued so the following day. The Macedonians, therefore, supposing he was dead, came with great clamors to the gates, and menaced his friends so that they were forced to admit them, and let them pass through unarmed along by his bedside. The same day Python and Seleucus were despatched to the temple of Serapis to inquire if they should bring Alexander thither, and were answered by the god, that they should not remove him. On the twenty-eighth, in the evening, he died. This account is most of it word for word as it is written in the diary.

Polybius

It is easy to misunderstand what Polybius meant when he wrote that he was going to interrupt his history of Rome to enter on a disquisition "on the Roman constitution." We may immediately think that he will go on to describe some document comparable to our own Constitution, but this is far from his intent. What Polybius meant by "constitution" is the organization of the Roman people themselves, and particularly of their political powers and relationships. His ultimate aim was to explain the success of the Roman social and political system, and, especially, to account for Rome's quick and phenomenal rise to domination of "nearly the whole world." To do this he chose as his crucial date the very time of one of Rome's greatest military defeats, at the hands of the Carthaginians in 216 B.C.

The social and political structure that Polybius is describing in the following selection is, of course, that of the Roman republic, as it existed more than a century before the revolutions and power struggles that eventuated in a quite different system—that of imperial Rome. Behind the details that he discusses there emerges the picture of an arrangement that bears a curious resemblance to our own; namely, the balance of powers. That the balance, between the Consuls, the Senate, and the people, was a success is amply verified by the longevity and stability of republican Rome. But its very success was a major contributor to its ultimate downfall. Rome became powerful, rich, and increasingly corrupt—so eventually fell prey to adventurers and despots.

Although his exact dates are not known, Polybius was probably born around 200 B.C. He was a Greek from the Peloponnesus. How such a person should come to write the history of Rome is of special interest. As a young man Polybius became a political leader of the Achaean League in southern Greece. Their Roman masters, convinced that the Greeks were plotting to throw off Roman rule, in 168 B.C. arrested one thousand members of the League, including Polybius, and transported them to Italy as hostages. There Polybius remained in exile for the next sixteen years. With his career destroyed and far from his homeland Polybius devoted his time to study. Fortunately, he was sent to Rome where he had ready access to records and documents, so he took that government as the subject of his scholarship. The result was the *Histories*. Polybius was finally set free in 151 B.C. and returned to Greece, where he again became active in political and diplomatic affairs.

Histories

BOOK VI

1. I am aware that some will be at a loss to account for my interrupting the course of my narrative for the sake of entering upon the following disquisition on the Roman constitution. But I think that I have already in many passages made it fully evident that this particular branch of my work was one of the necessities imposed on me by the nature of my original design; and I pointed this out with special clearness in the preface which explained the scope of my history. I there stated that the feature of my work which was at once the best in itself, and the most instructive to the students of it, was that it would enable them to know and fully realise in what manner, and under what kind of constitution, it came about that nearly the whole world fell under the power of Rome in somewhat less than fifty-three years—an event certainly without precedent. This being my settled purpose, I could see no more fitting period than the present for making a pause, and examining the truth of the remarks about to be made on this constitution. In private life if you wish to satisfy yourself as to the badness or goodness of particular persons, you would not, if you wish to get a genuine test, examine their conduct at a time of uneventful repose, but in the hour of brilliant success or conspicuous reverse. For the true test of a perfect man is the power of bearing with spirit and dignity violent changes of fortune. An examination of a constitution should be conducted in the same way: and therefore being unable to find in our day a more rapid or more signal change than that which has happened to Rome, I reserve my disquisition on its constitution for this place. . . .

What is really educational and beneficial to students of history is the clear view of the causes of events, and the consequent power of choosing the better policy in a particular case. Now in every practical undertaking by a state we must regard as the most powerful agent for success or failure the form of its constitution; for from this as from a fountainhead all conceptions and plans of action not only proceed, but attain their consummation.

• • •

11. . . . I will now endeavour to describe [the constitution] of Rome at the period of their disastrous defeat at Cannae [in 216 B.C.]. . . .

Trans. Evelyn S. Shuckburgh.

As for the Roman constitution, it had three elements, each of them possessing sovereign powers: and their respective share of power in the whole state had been regulated with such a scrupulous regard to equality and equilibrium, that no one could say for certain, not even a native, whether the constitution as a whole were an aristocracy or democracy or despotism. And no wonder: for if we confine our observation to the power of the Consuls we should be inclined to regard it as despotic; if on that of the Senate, as aristocratic; and if finally one looks at the power possessed by the people it would seem a clear case of democracy. What the exact powers of these several parts were, and still, with slight modifications, are, I will now state.

12. The Consuls, before leading out the legions, remain in Rome and are supreme masters of the administration. All other magistrates, except the Tribunes, are under them and take their orders. They introduce foreign ambassadors to the Senate; bring matters requiring deliberation before it; and see to the execution of its decrees. If, again, there are any matters of state which require the authorisation of the people, it is their business to see to them, to summon the popular meetings, to bring the proposals before them, and to carry out the decrees of the majority. In the preparations for war, also, and in a word in the entire administration of a campaign, they have all but absolute power. It is competent to them to impose on the allies such levies as they think good, to appoint the Military Tribunes, to make up the roll for soldiers and select those that are suitable. Besides they have absolute power of inflicting punish-ment on all who are under their command while on active service: and they have authority to expend as much of the public money as they choose, being accompanied by a quaestor who is entirely at their orders. A survey of these powers would in fact justify our describing the constitution as despotic,—a clear case of royal government. Nor will it affect the truth of my description, if any of the institutions I have described are changed in our time, or in that of our posterity: and the same remarks apply to what follows.

13. The Senate has first of all the control of the treasury, and regulates the receipts and disbursements alike. For the Quaestors cannot issue any public money for the various departments of the state without a decree of the Senate, except for the service of the Consuls. The Senate controls also what is by far the largest and most important expenditure, that, namely, which is made by the censors every lustrum for the repair or construction of public buildings; this money cannot be obtained by the censors except by the grant of the Senate. Similarly all crimes committed in Italy requiring a public investigation, such as treason, conspiracy, poisoning, or wilful murder, are in the hands of the Senate. Besides, if any individual or state among the Italian allies requires a controversy to be settled, a penalty to be assessed, help or protection to be afforded,— all this is the province of the Senate. Or again, outside Italy, if it is necessary to send an embassy to reconcile warring communities, or to remind them of their duty, or sometimes to impose requisitions upon them, or to receive their submission, or finally to proclaim war against them,—this too

is the business of the Senate. In like manner the reception to be given foreign ambassadors in Rome, and the answers to be returned to them, are decided by the Senate. With such business the people have nothing to do. Consequently, if one were staying at Rome when the Consuls were not in town, one would imagine the constitution to be a complete aristocracy: and this has been the idea entertained by many Greeks, and by many kings as well, from the fact that nearly all the business they had to do with Rome was settled by the Senate.

14. After this one would naturally be inclined to ask what part is left for the people in the constitution, when the Senate has these various functions, especially the control of the receipts and expenditure of the exchequer; and when the Consuls, again, have absolute power over the details of military preparation, and an absolute authority in the field? There is, however, a part left the people, and it is a most important one. For the people is the sole fountain of honour and of punishment; and it is by these two things and these alone that dynasties and constitutions and, in a word, human society are held together: for where the distinction between them is not sharply drawn both in theory and practice, there no undertaking can be properly administered,—as indeed we might expect when good and bad are held in exactly the same honour. The people then is the only court to decide matters of life and death; and even in cases where the penalty is money, if the sum to be assessed is sufficiently serious, and especially when the accused have held the higher magistracies. And in regard to this arrangement there is one point de-

serving especial commendation and record. Men who are on trial for their lives at Rome, while sentence is in process of being voted,—if even only one of the tribes whose votes are needed to ratify the sentence has not voted,—have the privilege at Rome of openly departing and condemning themselves to a voluntary exile. Such men are safe at Naples or Praeneste or at Tibur, and at other towns with which this arrangement has been duly ratified on oath.

Again, it is the people who bestow offices on the deserving, which are the most honourable rewards of virtue. It has also the absolute power of passing or repealing laws; and, most important of all, it is the people who deliberate on the question of peace and war. And when provisional terms are made for alliance, suspension of hostilities, or treaties, it is the people who ratify them or the reverse.

These considerations again would lead one to say that the chief power in the state was the people's, and that the constitution was a democracy.

15. Such, then, is the distribution of power between the several parts of the state. I must now show how each of these several parts can, when they choose, oppose or support each other.

The Consul, then, when he has started on an expedition with the powers I have described, is to all appearance absolute in the administration of the business in hand; still he has need of the support both of people and Senate, and, without them, is quite unable to bring the matter to a successful conclusion. For it is plain that he must have supplies sent to his legions from time to time; but without a decree of the Senate they can be supplied neither with corn, nor clothes, nor pay, so that all the plans of a commander must be futile, if the Senate is resolved either to shrink from danger or hamper his plans. And again, whether a Consul shall bring any undertaking to a conclusion or no depends entirely on the Senate: for it has absolute authority at the end of a year to send another Consul to supersede him, or to continue the existing one in his command. Again, even to the successes of the generals, the Senate has the power to add distinction and glory, and on the other hand to obscure their merits and lower their credit. For these high achievements are brought in tangible form before the eyes of the citizens by what are called "triumphs." But in these triumphs the commanders cannot celebrate with proper pomp, or in some cases celebrate at all, unless the Senate concurs and grants the necessary money. As for the people, the Consuls are pre-eminently obliged to court their favour, however distant from home may be the field of their operations; for it is the people, as I have said before, that ratifies, or refuses to ratify, terms of peace and treaties; but most of all because when laying down their office they have to give account of their administration before it. Therefore in no case is it safe for the Consuls to neglect either the Senate or the goodwill of the people.

16. As for the Senate, which possesses the immense power I have described, in the first place it is obliged in public affairs to take the multitude into account, and respect the wishes of the people; and it cannot put into execution the penalty for offences against the republic, which are punishable with death, unless the people first ratifies its decrees. Similarly even in matters which directly affect the senators,—for instance, in the case of a law depriving senators of certain dignities and offices, or even actually cutting down their property,—even in such cases the people has the sole power of passing or rejecting the law. But most important of all is the fact that, if the Tribunes interpose their veto, the Senate not only is unable to pass a decree, but cannot even hold a meeting at all, whether formal or informal. Now, the Tribunes are always bound to carry out the decree of the people, and above all things to have regard for their wishes: therefore, for all these reasons the Senate stands in awe of the multitude, and cannot neglect the feelings of the people.

17. In like manner the people on its part is far from being independent of the Senate, and is bound to take its wishes into account both collectively and individually. For contracts, too numerous to count, are given out by the censors in all parts of Italy, for the repairs or construction of public buildings; there is also the collection of revenue, from many rivers, harbours, gardens, mines, and land—every thing, in a word, that comes under the control of the Roman government: and in all these the people at large are engaged; so that there is scarcely a man, so to speak, who is not interested either as a contractor or as being employed in the works. For some purchase the contracts from the censors for themselves; and others go partners with them; while others again go security for these contractors, or actually pledge their property to the treasury for them. Now over all these transactions the Senate has absolute con-

trol. It can grant an extension of time; and in case of unforeseen accident can relieve the contractors from a portion of their obligation, or release them from it altogether, if they are absolutely unable to fill it. And there are many details in which the Senate can inflict great hardships, or, on the other hand, grant great indulgences to the contractors: for in every case the appeal is to it. But the most important point of all is that the judges are taken from its members in the majority of trials, whether public or private, in which the charges are heavy. Consequently, all citizens are much at its mercy; and being alarmed at the uncertainty as to when they may need its aid, are cautious about resisting or actively opposing its will. And for a similar reason men do not rashly resist the wishes of the Consuls, because one and all may become subject to their absolute authority on a campaign.

18. The result of this power of the several estates for mutual help or harm is a union sufficiently firm for all emergencies, and a constitution than which it is impossible to find a better. For whenever any danger from without compels them to unite and work together, the strength which is developed by the State is so extraordinary, that everything required is unfailingly carried out by the eager rivalry shown by all classes to devote their whole minds to the needs of the hour, and to secure that any determination come to should not fail for want of promptitude; while each individual works, privately and publicly alike, for the accomplishment of the business in hand. Accordingly, the peculiar constitution of the State makes it irresistible, and certain of obtaining whatever it determines to attempt. Nay, even

when these external alarms are past, and the people are enjoying their good fortune and the fruits of their victories, and, as usually happens, growing corrupted by flattery and idleness, show a tendency to violence and arrogance,—it is in these circumstances, more than ever, that the constitution is seen to possess within itself the power of correcting abuses. For when any one of the three classes becomes puffed up, and manifests an inclination to be contentious and unduly encroaching, the mutual interdependency of all the three, and the possibility of the pretentions of any one being checked and thwarted by the others, must plainly check this tendency: and so the proper equilibrium is maintained by the impulsiveness of the one part being checked by its fear of the other.

The Roman Republic Compared with Others

51. Now the Carthaginian constitution seems to me originally to have been well contrived in these most distinctively important particulars. For they had kings, and the Gerusia had the powers of an aristocracy, and the multitude were supreme in such things as affected them; and on the whole the adjustment of its several parts was very like that of Rome and Sparta. But about the period of its entering on the Hannibalian war the political state of Carthage was on the decline, that of Rome improving. For whereas there is in every body, or polity, or business a natural stage of growth, zenith, and decay; and whereas everything in them is best at the zenith; we may thereby judge of the difference between these two constitutions as they existed at that period. For exactly so far as the

strength and prosperity of Carthage preceded that of Rome in point of time, by so much was Carthage then past its prime, while Rome was exactly at its zenith, as far as its political constitution was concerned. In Carthage therefore the influence of the people in the policy of the state had already risen to be supreme, while at Rome the Senate was at the height of its power: and so, as in the one measures were deliberated upon by the many, in the other by the best men, the policy of the Romans in all public undertakings proved the stronger; on which account, though they met with capital disasters, by force of prudent counsels they finally conquered the Carthaginians in the war.

52. If we look however at separate details, for instance at the provisions for carrying on a war, we shall find that whereas for a naval expedition the Carthaginians are the better trained and prepared,—as it is only natural with a people with whom it has been hereditary for many generations to practise this craft, and to follow the seaman's trade above all nations in the world,—yet, in regard to military service on land, the Romans train themselves to a much higher pitch than the Carthaginians. The former bestow their whole attention upon this department: whereas the Carthaginians wholly neglect their infantry, though they do take some slight interest in the cavalry. The reason of this is that they employ foreign mercenaries, the Romans native and citizen levies. It is in this point that the latter policy is preferable to the former. They have their hopes of freedom ever resting on the courage of mercenary troops: the Romans on the valour of their own citizens and the aid of their al-

lies. The result is that even if the Romans have suffered a defeat at first, they renew the war with undiminished forces, which the Carthaginians cannot do. For, as the Romans are fighting for country and children, it is impossible for them to relax the fury of their struggle; but they persist with obstinate resolution until they have overcome their enemies. What has happened in regard to their navy is an instance in point. In skill the Romans are much behind the Carthaginians, as I have already said; yet the upshot of the whole naval war has been a decided triumph for the Romans, owing to the valour of their men. For although nautical science contributes largely to success in sea-fights, still it is the courage of the marines that turns the scale most decisively in favour of victory. The fact is that Italians as a nation are by nature superior to Phoenicians and Libyans both in physical strength and courage; but still their habits also do much to inspire the youth with enthusiasm for such exploits. One example will be sufficient of the pains taken by the Roman state to turn out men ready to endure anything to win a reputation in their country for valour.

53. Whenever one of their illustrious men dies, in the course of his funeral, the body with all its paraphernalia is carried into the forum to the Rostra, as a raised platform there is called, and sometimes is propped upright upon it so as to be conspicuous, or, more rarely, is laid upon it. Then with all the people standing round, his son, if he has left one of full age and he is there, or, failing him, one of his relations, mounts the Rostra and delivers a speech concerning the virtues of the deceased, and the successful exploits

performed by him in his lifetime. By these means the people are reminded of what has been done, and made to see it with their own eyes,—not only such as were engaged in the actual transactions but those also who were not;—and their sympathies are so deeply moved, that the loss appears not to be confined to the actual mourners, but to be a public one affecting the whole people. After the burial and all the usual ceremonies have been performed, they place the likeness of the deceased in the most conspicuous spot in his house, surmounted by a wooden canopy or shrine. This likeness consists of a mask made to represent the deceased with extraordinary fidelity both in shape and colour. These likenesses they display at public sacrifices adorned with much care. And when any illustrious member of the family dies, they carry these masks to the funeral, putting them on men whom they thought as like the originals as possible in height and other personal peculiarities. And these substitutes assume clothes according to the rank of the person represented; if he was a consul or praetor, a toga with purple stripes; if a censor, whole purple; if he had also celebrated a triumph or performed any exploit of that kind, a toga embroidered with gold. These representatives also ride themselves in chariots, while the fasces and axes, and all the other customary insignia of the particular offices, lead the way, according to the dignity of the rank in the state enjoyed by the deceased in his lifetime; and on arriving at the Rostra they all take their seats on ivory chairs in their order. There could not easily be a more inspiring spectacle than this for a young man of noble ambitions and virtuous aspirations.

For can we conceive any one to be unmoved at the sight of all the likenesses collected together of the men who have earned glory, all as if were living and breathing? Or what could be a more glorious spectacle?

54. Besides, the speaker over the body about to be buried, after having finished the panegyric of this particular person, starts upon the others whose representatives are present, beginning with the most ancient, and recounts the successes and achievements of each. By this means the glorious memory of brave men is continually renewed; the fame of those who have performed any noble deed is never allowed to die; and the renown of those who have done good service to their country becomes a matter of common knowledge to the multitude, and part of the heritage of posterity. But the chief benefit of the ceremony is that it inspires young men to shrink from no exertion for the general welfare, in the hope of obtaining the glory which awaits the brave. And what I say is confirmed by this fact. Many Romans have volunteered to decide a whole battle by single combat; not a few have deliberately accepted certain death, some in time of war to secure the safety of the rest, some in time of peace to preserve the safety of the commonwealth. There have also been instances of men in office putting their own sons to death, in defiance of every custom and law, because they rated the interests of their country higher than those of natural ties even with their nearest and dearest. There are many stories of this kind, related of many men in Roman history; but one will be enough for our present purpose; and I will give the name as an instance to prove the truth of my words.

55. The story goes that Horatius Cocles, while fighting with two enemies at the head of the bridge over the Tiber, which is the entrance to the city on the north, seeing a large body of men advancing to support his enemies, and fearing that they would force their way into the city, turned round, and shouted to those behind him to hasten back to the other side and break down the bridge. They obeyed him: and whilst they were breaking the bridge, he remained at his post receiving numerous wounds, and checked the progress of the enemy: his opponents being panic stricken, not so much by his strength as by the audacity with which he held his ground. When the bridge had been broken down, the attack of the enemy was stopped; and Cocles then threw himself into the river with his armour on and deliberately sacrificed his life, because he valued the safety of his country and his own future reputation more highly than his present life, and the years of existence that remained to him. Such is the enthusiasm and emulation for noble deeds that are engendered among the Romans by their customs.

56. Again the Roman customs and principles regarding money transactions are better than those of the Carthaginians. In the view of the latter nothing is disgraceful that makes for gain; with the former nothing is more disgraceful than to receive bribes and to make profit by improper means. For they regard wealth obtained from unlawful transactions to be as much a subject of reproach, as a fair profit from the most unquestioned source is of commendation. A proof of the fact is this. The Carthaginians obtain office by open bribery, but among the Romans the penalty for it is death. With such a radical difference, therefore, between the rewards offered to virtue among the two people, it is natural that the ways adopted for obtaining them should be different also.

But the most important difference for the better which the Roman commonwealth appears to me to display is in their religious beliefs. For I conceive that what in other nations is looked upon as a reproach, I mean a scrupulous fear of the gods, is the very thing which keeps the Roman Commonwealth together. To such an extraordinary height is this carried among them, both in private and public business, that nothing could exceed it. Many people might think this unaccountable; but in my opinion their object is to use it as a check upon the common people. If it were possible to form a state wholly of philosophers, such a custom would perhaps be unnecessary. But seeing that every multitude is fickle, and full of lawless desires, unreasoning anger, and violent passion, the only resource is to keep them in check by mysterious terrors and scenic effects of this sort. Wherefore, to my mind, the ancients were not acting without purpose or at random, when they brought in among the vulgar those opinions about the gods, and the belief in the punishments in Hades: much rather do I think that men nowadays are acting rashly and foolishly in rejecting them. This is the reason why, apart from anything else, Greek statesmen, if entrusted with a single talent, though protected by ten checking-clerks, as many seals, and twice as many witnesses, yet cannot be induced to keep faith: whereas among the Romans, in their magistracies and embassies, men have the handling of a great amount of money, and yet from pure respect to their oath keep their faith intact. And, again, in other nations it is a rare thing to find a man who keeps his hands out of the public purse, and is entirely pure in such matters: but among the Romans it is a rare thing to detect a man in the act of committing such a crime.

Suetonius

Julius Caesar is generally acknowledged to be one of the great figures in Western history. But is this reputation justified? In what did his greatness lie? One thing certainly can be said. He was one of the most successful military men of all times. More than that, he was an extraordinarily popular political leader. As a conqueror he dramatically expanded the Roman Empire and in doing so brought the benefits of Roman civilization to large areas, particularly of Western Europe, that were then culturally primitive. As a statesman he enacted a series of laws that substantially benefited the soldiers and ordinary citizens but he did so often at the expense of the liberties the people had enjoyed under the republic. In any event, Caesar held power for only two years after his return to Rome after his military adventures in Western Europe and the Near East, before being assassinated by his political enemies. So the question remains, unanswered: Had he lived, what further might Caesar have accomplished?

We know a good deal about the life and character of Caesar, thanks mainly to the writings of two gifted biographers—Plutarch and Suetonius—both of whom lived about a hundred years after the death of their subject. Little is known about Suetonius, from whom the following selection is taken, except that he was at one time secretary to the emperor Hadrian. The biography, which is part of a larger work, *Lives of the Caesars*, is by no means adulatory; indeed, the author often seems intent on destroying the reputation of Caesar. On the other hand he is generous in his estimate of Caesar's strengths. Above all the entire piece gives a vivid picture of the political intrigues, turbulence, and violence of the years of the decline and collapse of republican Rome.

The Lives of the Caesars

BOOK I

The Deified Julius

• • •

Backed by his father-in-law and son-in-law, out of all the numerous provinces [Caesar] made the Gauls his choice, as the most likely to enrich him and furnish suitable material for triumphs. At first, it is true, by the bill of Vatinius he received only Cisalpine Gaul* with the addition of Illyricum; but presently he was assigned Gallia Comata as well by the senate, since the members feared that even if they should refuse it, the people would give him this also. Transported with joy at this success, he could not keep from boasting a few days later before a crowded house, that having gained his heart's desire to the grief and lamentation of his opponents, he would therefore from that time mount on their heads; and when someone insultingly remarked that that would be no easy matter for any woman, he replied in the same vein that Semiramis too had been queen in Syria and the Amazons in days of old had held sway over a great part of Asia.

When at the close of his consulship the praetors Gaius Memmius and Lucius Domitius moved an inquiry into his conduct the previous year, Caesar laid the matter before the senate; and when they failed to take it up, and three days had been wasted in fruitless wrangling, went off to his province. Whereupon his quaestor was at once arraigned on several counts, as a preliminary to his own impeachment. Presently he himself too was prosecuted by Lucius Antistius, tribune of the commons, and it was only by appealing to the whole college that he contrived not to be brought to trial, on the ground that he was absent on public service. Then to secure himself for the future, he took great pains always to put the magistrates for the year under personal obligation, and not to aid any candidates or suffer any to be elected, save as guaranteed to defend him in his absence. And he did not hesitate in some cases to exact an oath to keep this pledge or even a written contract.

When however Lucius Domitius, candidate for the consulship, openly threatened to effect as consul what he had been unable to do as praetor, and to take his armies from him, Caesar compelled Pompeius and Crassus to come to Luca, a city in his province, where he prevailed on them to stand for a second consulship, to defeat Domitius; and he also succeeded through their influence in having his term as governor of Gaul made five years longer. Encouraged by this, he added to the legions which he had received from the state others at his own cost, one actually composed of men of Transalpine Gaul and bearing a Gallic name too (for it was called Alauda), which he trained in the Roman tactics and equipped with Roman arms; and

---

*[Roughly Northern Italy.—*Ed.*]

Trans. J. C. Rolfe.

195

later on he gave every man of it citizenship. After that he did not let slip any pretext for war, however unjust and dangerous it might be, picking quarrels as well with allied as with hostile and barbarous nations; so that once the senate decreed that a commission be sent to inquire into the condition of the Gallic provinces, and some even recommended that Caesar be handed over to the enemy. But as his enterprises prospered, thanksgivings were appointed in his honour oftener and for longer periods than for anyone before his time.

During the nine years of his command this is in substance what he did. All that part of Gaul which is bounded by the Pyrenees, the Alps and the Cevennes, and by the Rhine and Rhone rivers, a circuit of some thirty-two hundred miles, with the exception of some allied states which had rendered him good service, he reduced to the form of a province; and imposed upon it a yearly tribute of forty million sesterces. He was the first Roman to build a bridge and attack the Germans beyond the Rhine, and he inflicted heavy losses upon them. He invaded the Britons too, a people unknown before, vanquished them, and exacted moneys and hostages. Amid all these successes he met with adverse fortune but three times in all: in Britain, where his fleet narrowly escaped destruction in a violent storm; in Gaul, when one of his legions was routed at Gergovia; and on the borders of Germany, when his lieutenants Titurius and Aurunculeius were ambushed and slain.

Within this same space of time he lost first his mother, then his daughter, and soon afterwards his grandchild. Meanwhile, as the community was aghast at the murder of Publius

Clodius, the senate had voted that only one consul should be chosen, and expressly named Gnaeus Pompeius. When the tribunes planned to make him Pompey's colleague, Caesar urged them rather to propose to the people that he be permitted to stand for a second consulship without coming to Rome, when the term of his governorship drew near its end, to prevent his being forced for the sake of the office to leave his province prematurely and without finishing the war. On the granting of this, aiming still higher and flushed with hope, he neglected nothing in the way of lavish expenditure or of favours to anyone, either in his public capacity or privately. He began a forum with the proceeds of his spoils, the ground for which cost more than a hundred million sesterces. He announced a combat of gladiators and a feast for the people in memory of his daughter, a thing quite without precedent. To raise the expectation of these events to the highest possible pitch, he had the material for the banquet prepared in part by his own household, although he had let contracts to the markets as well. He gave orders too that whenever famous gladiators fought without winning the favour of the people, they should be rescued by force and kept for him. He had the novices trained, not in a gladiatorial school by professionals, but in private houses by Roman knights and even by senators who were skilled in arms, earnestly beseeching them, as is shown by his own letters, to give the recruits individual attention and personally direct their exercises. He doubled the pay of the legions for all time. Whenever grain was plentiful, he distributed it to them without stint or measure, and now and then gave each man a slave from among the captives.

Moreover, to retain his relationship and friendship with Pompey, Caesar offered him his sister's granddaughter Octavia in marriage, although she was already the wife of Gaius Marcellus, and asked for the hand of Pompey's daughter, who was promised to Faustus Sulla. When he had put all Pompey's friends under obligation, as well as the great part of the senate, through loans made without interest or at a low rate, he lavished gifts on men of all other classes, both those whom he invited to accept his bounty and those who applied to him unasked, including even freedmen and slaves who were special favourites of their masters or patrons. In short, he was the sole and ever ready help of all who were in legal difficulties or in debt and of young spendthrifts, excepting only those whose burden of guilt or of poverty was so heavy, or who were so given up to riotous living, that even he could not save them; and to these he declared in the plainest terms that what they needed was a civil war.

He took no less pains to win the devotion of princes and provinces all over the world, offering prisoners to some by the thousand as a gift, and sending auxiliary troops to the aid of others whenever they wished, and as often as they wished, without the sanction of the senate or people, besides adorning the principal cities of Asia and Greece with magnificent public works, as well as those of Italy and the provinces of Gaul and Spain. At last, when all were thunderstruck at his actions and wondered what their purpose could be, the consul Marcus Claudius Marcellus, after first

making proclamation that he purposed to bring before the senate a matter of the highest public moment, proposed that a successor to Caesar be appointed before the end of his term, on the ground that the war was ended, peace was established, and the victorious army ought to be disbanded; also that no account be taken of Caesar at the elections, unless he were present, since Pompey's subsequent action had not annulled the decree of the people. And it was true that when Pompey proposed a bill touching the privileges of officials, in the clause where he debarred absentees from candidacy for office he forgot to make a special exception in Caesar's case, and did not correct the oversight until the law had been inscribed on a tablet of bronze and deposited in the treasury. Not content with depriving Caesar of his provinces and his privilege, Marcellus also moved that the colonists whom Caesar had settled in Novum Comum by the bill of Vatinius should lose their citizenship, on the ground that it had been given from political motives and was not authorized by the law.

Greatly troubled by these measures, and thinking, as they say he was often heard to remark, that now that he was the leading man of the state, it was harder to push him down from the first place to the second than it would be from the second to the lowest, Caesar stoutly resisted Marcellus, partly through vetoes of the tribunes and partly through the other consul, Servius Sulpicius. When next year Gaius Marcellus, who had succeeded his cousin Marcus as consul, tried the same thing, Caesar by a heavy bribe secured the support of the other consul, Aemilius Paulus, and of Gaius Curio, the most reckless of the tribunes. But seeing that everything was being pushed most persistently, and that even the consuls-elect were among the opposition, he sent a written appeal to the senate, not to take from him the privilege which the people had granted, or else to compel the others in command of armies to resign also; feeling sure, it was thought, that he could more readily muster his veterans as soon as he wished, than Pompey his newly levied troops. He further proposed a compromise to his opponents, that after giving up eight legions and Transalpine Gaul, he be allowed to keep two legions and Cisalpine Gaul, or at least one legion and Illyricum, until he was elected consul.

But when the senate declined to interfere, and his opponents declared that they would accept no compromise in a matter affecting the public welfare, he crossed to Hither Gaul, and after holding all the assizes, halted at Ravenna, intending to resort to war if the senate took any drastic action against the tribunes of the commons who interposed vetoes in his behalf. Now this was his excuse for the civil war, but it is believed that he had other motives. Gnaeus Pompeius used to declare that since Caesar's own means were not sufficient to complete the works which he had planned, nor to do all that he had led the people to expect on his return, he desired a state of general unrest and turmoil. Others say that he dreaded the necessity of rendering an account for what he had done in his first consulship contrary to the auspices and the laws, and regardless of vetoes; for Marcus Cato often declared, and took oath too, that he would impeach Caesar the moment

he had disbanded his army. It was openly said too that if he was out of office on his return, he would be obliged, like Milo, to make his defence in a court hedged about by armed men. The latter opinion is the more credible one in view of the assertion of Asinius Pollio, that when Caesar at the battle of Pharsalus saw his enemies slain or in flight, he said, word for word: "They would have it so. Even I, Gaius Caesar, after so many great deeds, should have been found guilty, if I had not turned to my army for help." Some think that habit had given him a love of power, and that weighing the strength of his adversaries against his own, he grasped the opportunity of usurping the depotism which had been his heart's desire from early youth. Cicero too was seemingly of this opinion, when he wrote in the third book of his *De Officiis* that Caesar ever had upon his lips these lines of Euripides, of which Cicero himself adds a version:—

If wrong may e'er be right, for a
  throne's sake
Were wrong most right:—be God in all
  else feared.

Accordingly, when word came that the veto of the tribunes had been set aside and they themselves had left the city, he at once sent on a few cohorts with all secrecy, and then, to disarm suspicion, concealed his purpose by appearing at a public show, inspecting the plans of a gladiatorial school which he intended building, and joining as usual in a banquet with a large company. It was not until after sunset that he set out very privily with a small company, taking the mules from a bakeshop hard by and harnessing them to a carriage; and when his lights went out and he lost his way, he was astray for some time, but at last found a guide at dawn and got back to the road on foot by narrow by-paths. Then, overtaking his cohorts at the river Rubicon, which was the boundary of his province, he paused for a while, and realising what a step he was taking, he turned to those about him and said: "Even yet we may draw back; but once cross yon little bridge, and the whole issue is with the sword."

As he stood in doubt, this sign was given him. On a sudden there appeared hard by a being of wondrous stature and beauty, who sat and played upon a reed; and when not only the shepherds flocked to hear him, but many of the soldiers left their posts, and among them some of the trumpeters, the apparition snatched a trumpet from one of them, rushed to the river, and sounding the war-note with mighty blast, strode to the opposite bank. Then Caesar cried: "Take we the course which the signs of the gods and the false dealing of our foes point out. The die is cast," said he.

Accordingly, crossing with his army, and welcoming the tribunes of the commons, who had come to him after being driven from Rome, he harangued the soldiers with tears, and rending his robe from his breast besought their faithful service. It is even thought that he promised every man a knight's estate, but that came of a misunderstanding; for since he often pointed to the finger of his left hand as he addressed them and urged them on, declaring that to satisfy all those who helped him to defend his honor he would gladly tear his very ring from his hand, those on the edge of the assembly, who could see him better than they could hear his words, assumed that he said what his gesture seemed to mean; and so the report went about that he had promised them the right of the ring and four hundred thousand sesterces as well.

The sum total of his movements after that is, in their order, as follows: He overran Umbria, Picenum, and Etruria, took prisoner Lucius Domitius, who had been irregularly named his successor, and was holding Corfinium with a garrison, let him go free, and then proceeded along the Adriatic to Brundisium, where Pompey and the consuls had taken refuge, intending to cross the sea as soon as might be. After vainly trying by every kind of hindrance to prevent their sailing, he marched off to Rome, and after calling the senate together to discuss public business, went to attack Pompey's strongest forces, which were in Spain under command of three of his lieutenants—Marcus Petreius, Lucius Afranius, and Marcus Varro—saying to his friends before he left, "I go to meet an army without a leader, and I shall return to meet a leader without an army." And in fact, though his advance was delayed by the siege of Massilia, which had shut its gates against him, and by extreme scarcity of supplies, he nevertheless quickly gained a complete victory.

Returning thence to Rome, he crossed into Macedonia, and after blockading Pompey for almost four months behind mighty ramparts, finally routed him in the battle at Pharsalus, followed him in his flight to Alexandria, and when he learned that his rival had been slain, made war on King Ptolemy, whom he perceived to be plotting against his own safety as well; a war in truth of great difficulty, convenient neither in time nor place, but carried on during the winter season, within the walls of a well-provisioned and crafty foeman, while Caesar himself was without supplies of any kind and ill-prepared. Victor in spite of all, he turned over the rule of Egypt to Cleopatra and her young brother, fearing that if he made a province of it, it might one day under a headstrong governor be a source of revolution. From Alexandria he crossed to Syria, and from there went to Pontus, spurred on by the news that Pharnaces, son of Mithridates the Great, had taken advantage of the situation to make war, and was already flushed with numerous successes; but Caesar vanquished him in a single battle within five days after his arrival and four hours after getting sight of him, often remarking on Pompey's good luck in gaining his principal fame as a general by victories over such feeble foemen. Then he overcame Scipio and Juba, who were patching up the remnants of their party in Africa, and the sons of Pompey in Spain.

In all the civil wars he suffered not a single disaster except through his lieutenants, of whom Gaius Curio perished in Africa, Gaius Antonius fell into the hands of the enemy in Illyricum, Publius Dolabella lost a fleet also off Illyricum, and Gnaeus Domitius Calvinus an army in Pontus. Personally he always fought with the utmost success, and the issue was never even in doubt save twice: once at Dyrrachium, where he was put to flight, and said of Pompey, who failed to follow up his success, that he did not know how to use a victory; again in Spain, in the final struggle, when, believing the battle lost, he actually thought of suicide.

Having ended the wars, he celebrated five triumphs, four in a single month, but at intervals of a few days, after vanquishing Scipio; and another on defeating Pompey's sons. The first and most splendid was the Gallic triumph, the next the Alexandrian, then the Pontic, after that the African, and finally the Spanish, each differing from the rest in its equipment and display of spoils. As he rode through the Velabrum on the day of his Gallic triumph, the axle of his chariot broke, and he was all but thrown out; and he mounted the Capitol by torchlight, with forty elephants bearing lamps on his right and his left. In his Pontic triumph he displayed among the show-pieces of the procession an inscription of but three words, "I came, I saw, I conquered," not indicating the events of the war, as the others did, but the speed with which it was finished.

To each and every foot-soldier of his veteran legions he gave twenty-four thousand sesterces by way of booty, over and above the two thousand apiece which he had paid them at the beginning of the civil strife. He also assigned them lands, but not side by side, to avoid dispossessing any of the former owners. To every man of the people, besides ten pecks of grain and the same number of pounds of oil, he distributed the three hundred sesterces which he had promised at first, and one hundred apiece to boot because of the delay. He also remitted a year's rent in Rome to tenants who paid two thousand sesterces or less, and in Italy up to five hundred sesterces. He added a banquet and a dole of meat, and after his Spanish victory two dinners; for deeming that the former of these had not been served with a liberality creditable to his generosity, he gave another five days later on a most lavish scale.

He gave entertainments of divers kinds: a combat of gladiators and also stage-plays in every ward all over the city, performed too by actors of all languages, as well as races in the circus, athletic contests, and a sham sea-fight. In the gladiatorial contest in the Forum Furius Leptinus, a man of praetorian stock, and Quintus Calpenus, a former senator and pleader at the bar, fought to a finish. A Pyrrhic dance was performed by the sons of the princes of Asia and Bithynia. During the plays Decimus Laberius, a Roman Knight, acted a farce of his own composition, and having been presented with five hundred thousand sesterces and a gold ring, passed from the stage through the orchestra and took his place in the fourteen rows. For the races the circus was lengthened at either end and a broad canal was dug all about it; then young men of the highest rank drove four-horse and two-horse chariots and rode pairs of horses, vaulting from one to the other. The game called Troy was performed by two troops, of younger and of older boys. Combats with wild beasts were presented on five successive days, and last of all there was a battle between two opposing armies, in which five hundred foot-soldiers, twenty elephants, and thirty horsemen engaged on each side. To make room for this, the goals were taken down and in their place two camps were pitched over against each other. The athletic competitions lasted for three days in a temporary stadium built for the purpose in the region of the Campus Martius. For the naval battle a pool was dug in the lesser Codeta

and there was a contest of ships of two, three, and four banks of oars, belonging to the Tyrian and Egyptian fleets, manned by a large force of fighting men. Such a throng flocked to all these shows from every quarter, that many strangers had to lodge in tents pitched in the streets or along the roads, and the press was often such that many were crushed to death, including two senators.

Then turning his attention to the reorganisation of the state, he reformed the calendar, which the negligence of the pontiffs had long since so disordered, through their privilege of adding months or days at pleasure, that the harvest festivals did not come in summer nor those of the vintage in the autumn; and he adjusted the year to the sun's course by making it consist of three hundred and sixty-five days, abolishing the intercalary month, and adding one day every fourth year. Furthermore, that the correct reckoning of seasons might begin with the next Kalends of January, he inserted two other months between those of November and December; hence the year in which these arrangements were made was one of fifteen months, including the intercalary month, which belonged to that year according to the former custom.

He filled the vacancies in the senate, enrolled additional patricians, and increased the number of praetors, aediles, and quaestors, as well as of the minor officials; he reinstated those who had been degraded by official action of the censors or found guilty of bribery by verdict of the jurors. He shared the elections with the people on this basis: that except in the case of the consulship, half of the magistrates should be appointed by the people's choice, while the rest should be those whom he had personally nominated. And these he announced in brief notes like the following, circulated in each tribe: "Caesar the Dictator to this or that tribe. I commend to you so and so, to hold their positions by your votes." He admitted to office even the sons of those who had been proscribed. He limited the right of serving as jurors to two classes, the equestrian and senatorial orders, disqualifying the third class, the tribunes of the treasury.

He made the enumeration of the people neither in the usual manner nor place, but from street to street aided by the owners of blocks of houses, and reduced the number of those who received grain at public expense from three hundred and twenty thousand to one hundred and fifty thousand. And to prevent the calling of additional meetings at any future time for purposes of enrollment, he provided that the places of such as died should be filled each year by the praetors from those who were not on the list.

Moreover, to keep up the population of the city, depleted as it was by the assignment of eighty thousand citizens to colonies across the sea, he made a law that no citizen older than twenty or younger than forty, who was not detained by service in the army, should be absent from Italy for more than three successive years; that no senator's son should go abroad except as the companion of a magistrate or on his staff; and that those who made a business of grazing should have among their herdsmen at least one-third who were men of free birth. He conferred citizenship on all who practised medicine at Rome, and on all teachers of the liberal arts, to make them more desirous of living in the city and to induce others to resort to it.

As to debts, he disappointed those who looked for their cancellation, which was often agitated, but finally decreed that the debtors should satisfy their creditors according to a valuation of their possessions at the price which they had paid for them before the civil war, deducting from the principal whatever interest had been paid in cash or pledged through bankers; an arrangement which wiped out about a fourth part of their indebtedness. He dissolved all guilds, except those of ancient foundation. He increased the penalties for crimes; and inasmuch as the rich involved themselves in guilt with less hesitation because they merely suffered exile, without any loss of property, he punished murderers of freemen by the confiscation of all their goods, as Cicero writes, and others by the loss of one-half.

He administered justice with the utmost conscientiousness and strictness. Those convicted of extortion he even dismissed from the senatorial order. He annulled the marriage of an ex-praetor, who had married a woman the very day after her divorce, although there was no suspicion of adultery. He imposed duties on foreign wares. He denied the use of litters and the wearing of scarlet robes or pearls to all except to those of a designated position and age, and on set days. In particular he enforced the law against extravagance, setting watchmen in various parts of the market, to seize and bring to him dainties which were exposed for sale in violation of the law; and sometimes he sent his lictors and soldiers to take from a dining-room any articles which had escaped the vigilance of his watchmen, even after they had been served.

In particular, for the adornment and convenience of the city, also for the protection and extension of the Empire, he formed more projects and more extensive ones every day: first of all, to rear a temple to Mars, greater than any in existence, filling up and levelling the pool in which he had exhibited the sea-fight, and to build a theatre of vast size, sloping down from the Tarpeian rock; to reduce the civil code to fixed limits, and of the vast and prolix mass of statutes to include only the best and most essential in a limited number of volumes; to open to the public the greatest possible libraries of Greek and Latin books, assigning to Marcus Varro the charge of procuring and classifying them; to drain the Pomptine marshes; to let out the water from Lake Fucinus; to make a highway from the Adriatic across the summit of the Apennines as far as the Tiber; to cut a canal through the Isthmus; to check the Dacians, who had poured into Pontus and Thrace; then to make war on the Parthians by way of Lesser Armenia, but not to risk a battle with them until he had first tested their mettle.

All these enterprises and plans were cut short by his death. But before I speak of that, it will not be amiss to describe briefly his personal appearance, his dress, his mode of life, and his character, as well as his conduct in civil and military life.

He is said to have been tall of stature, with a fair complexion, shapely limbs, a somewhat full face, and keen black eyes; sound of health, except that towards the end he was subject to sudden fainting fits and to nightmare as well. He was twice attacked by the falling sickness during his campaigns. He was somewhat over-nice in the care of his person, being not only carefully trimmed and shaved, but even having superfluous hair plucked out, as some have charged; while his baldness was a disfigurement which troubled him greatly, since he found that it was often the subject of the gibes of his detractors. Because of it he used to comb forward his scanty locks from the crown of his head, and of all the honours voted him by the senate people there was none which he received or made use of more gladly than the privilege of wearing a laurel wreath at all times. They say, too, that he was remarkable in his dress; that he wore a senator's tunic with fringed sleeves reaching to the wrist, and always had a girdle over it, though rather a loose one; and this, they say, was the occasion of Sulla's *mot*, when he often warned the nobles to keep an eye on the ill-girt boy.

He lived at first in the Subura in a modest house, but after he became pontifex maximus, in the official residence of the Sacred Way. Many have written that he was very fond of elegance and luxury; that having laid the foundations of a country-house on his estate at Nemi and finished it at great cost, he tore it all down because it did not suit him in every particular, although at the time he was still poor and heavily in debt; and that he carried tessellated and mosaic floors about with him on his campaigns.

They say that he was led to invade Britain by the hope of getting pearls, and that in comparing their size he sometimes weighed them with his own hand; that he was always a most enthusiastic collector of gems, carvings, statues, and pictures by early artists; also of slaves of exceptional figure and training at enormous prices, of which he himself was so ashamed that he forbade their entry in his accounts.

It is further reported that in the provinces he gave banquets constantly in two dining-halls, in one of which his officers or Greek companions, in the other Roman civilians and the more distinguished of the provincials reclined at table. He was so punctilious and strict in the management of his household, in small matters as well as in those of greater importance, that he put his baker in irons for serving him with one kind of bread and his guests with another; and he inflicted capital punishment on a favorite freedman for adultery with the wife of a Roman knight, although no complaint was made against him.

There was no stain on his reputation for chastity except his intimacy with King Nicomedes, but that was a deep and lasting reproach, which laid him open to insults from every quarter. I say nothing of the notorious lines of Licinius Calvus:

Whate'er Bithynia had, and Caesar's
   paramour.

I pass over, too, the invectives of Dolabella and the elder Curio, in which Dolabella calls him "the queen's rival, the inner partner of the royal couch," and Curio, "the brothel of Nicomedes and the stew of Bithynia." I take no account of the edicts of Bibulus, in which he posted his colleague as "the queen of Bithynia," saying that "of yore he was enamoured of a king, but now of a king's estate." At this same time, so Marcus Brutus declares, one Octavius, a man whose disordered mind made him somewhat free with his tongue, after

saluting Pompey as "king" in a crowded assembly, greeted Caesar as "queen." But Gaius Memmius makes the direct charge that he acted as cup-bearer to Nicomedes with the rest of his wantons at a large dinner party, and that among the guests were some merchants from Rome, whose names Memmius gives. Cicero, indeed, is not content with having written in sundry letters that Caesar was led by the king's attendants to the royal apartments, that he lay on a golden couch arrayed in purple, and that the virginity of this son of Venus was lost in Bithynia; but when Caesar was once addressing the senate in defence of Nysa, daughter of Nicomedes, and was enumerating his obligations to the king, Cicero cried: "No more of that, pray, for it is well known what he gave you, and what you gave him in turn." Finally, in his Gallic triumph his soldiers, among the bantering songs which are usually sung by those who follow the chariot, shouted these lines, which became a by-word:—

All the Gauls did Caesar vanquish,
   Nicomedes vanquished him:
Lo! now Caesar rides in triumph,
   victor over all the Gauls,
Nicomedes does not triumph, who
   subdued the conqueror.

That he was unbridled and extravagant in his intrigues is the general opinion, and that he seduced many illustrious women, among them Postumia, wife of Servius Sulpicius, Lollia, wife of Aulus Gabinius, Tertulla, wife of Marcus Crassus, and even Gnaeus Pompey's wife Mucia. At all events there is no doubt that Pompey was taken to task by the elder and the younger Curio, as well as by many others, because through a desire for power he had afterwards married the daughter of a man on whose account he divorced a wife who had borne him three children, and whom he had often referred to with a groan as an Aegisthus. But beyond all others Caesar loved Servilla, the mother of Marcus Brutus, for whom in his first consulship he bought a pearl costing six million sesterces. During the civil war, too, besides other presents, he knocked down some fine estates to her in a public auction at a nominal price, and when some expressed their surprise at the low figure, Cicero wittily remarked: "It's a better bargain than you think, for there is a third off." And in fact it was thought that Servilla was prostituting her own daughter Tertia to Caesar.

That he did not refrain from intrigues in the provinces is shown in particular by this couplet, which was also shouted by the soldiers in his Gallic triumph:—

Men of Rome, keep close your
   consorts, here's a bald adulterer.
Gold in Gaul you spent in dalliance,
   which you borrowed here in Rome

He had love affairs with queens too, including Eunoe that Moor, wife of Bogudes, on whom, as well as on her husband, he bestowed many splendid presents, as Naso writes; but above all with Cleopatra, with whom he often feasted until daybreak, and he would have gone through Egypt with her in her statebarge almost to Aethiopia, had not his soldiers refused to follow him. Finally he called her to Rome and did not let her leave until he had ladened her with high honours and rich gifts, and he allowed her to give his name to the child which she bore. In fact, according to certain Greek writers, this child was very like Caesar in looks

and carriage. Mark Anthony declared to the senate that Caesar had really acknowledged the boy, and that Gaius Matius, Gaius Oppius, and other friends of Caesar knew this. Of these Gaius Oppius, as if admitting that the situation required apology and defence, published a book, to prove that the child whom Cleopatra fathered on Caesar was not his. Helvius Cinna, tribune of the commons, admitted to several that he had a bill drawn up in due form, which Caesar had ordered him to propose to the people in his absence, making it lawful for Caesar to marry what wives he wished, "for the purpose of begetting children." But to remove all doubt that he had an evil reputation for shameless vice and for adultery, I have only to add that the elder Curio in one of his speeches calls him "every woman's man and every man's woman."

That he drank very little wine not even his enemies denied. There is a saying of Marcus Cato that Caesar was the only man who undertook to overthrow the state when sober. Even in the matter of food Gaius Oppius tells us that he was so indifferent, that once when his host served stale oil instead of fresh, and the other guests would have none of it, Caesar partook even more plentifully than usual, not to seem to charge his host with carelessness or lack of manners.

Neither when in command of armies nor as a magistrate at Rome did he show a scrupulous integrity; for as certain men have declared in their memoirs, when he was proconsul in Spain, he not only begged money from the allies, to help pay his debts, but also attacked and sacked some towns of the Lusitanians although they did not refuse his terms and opened their gates to him on his arrival. In Gaul he pillaged shrines and temples of the gods filled with offerings, and oftener sacked towns for the sake of plunder than for any fault. In consequence he had more gold than he knew what to do with, and offered it for sale throughout Italy and the provinces at the rate of three thousand sesterces the pound. In his first consulship he stole three thousand pounds of gold from the Capitol, replacing it with the same weight of gilded bronze. He made alliances and thrones a matter of barter, for he extorted from Ptolemy alone in his own name and that of Pompey nearly six thousand talents, while later on he met the heavy expenses of the civil wars and of his triumphs and entertainments by the most barefaced pillage and sacrilege.

In eloquence and in the art of war he either equalled or surpassed the fame of their most eminent representatives. After his accusation of Dolabella, he was without question numbered with the leading advocates. At all events when Cicero reviews the orators in his *Brutus*, he says that he does not see to whom Caesar ought to yield the palm, declaring that his style is elegant as well as transparent, even grand and in a sense noble. Again in a letter to Cornelius Nepos he writes thus of Caesar: "Come now, what orator would you rank above him of those who have devoted themselves to nothing else? Who has cleverer or more frequent epigrams? Who is either more picturesque or more choice in diction?" He appears, at least in his youth, to have imitated the manner of Caesar Strabo, from whose speech entitled "For the Sardinians" he actually transferred some passages word for word to a trial address of his own. He is said to have delivered himself in a high-pitched voice with impassioned action and gestures, which were not without grace. He left several speeches, including some which are attributed to him on insufficient evidence. Augustus had good reason to think that the speech "For Quintus Metellus" was rather taken down by shorthand writers who could not keep pace with his delivery, than published by Caesar himself; for in some copies I find that even the title is not "For Metellus," but, "Which He Wrote for Metellus," although the discourse purports to be from Caesar's lips, defending Metellus and himself against the charges of their common detractors. Augustus also questions the authenticity of the address "To His Soldiers in Spain," although there are two sections of it, one purporting to have been spoken at the first battle, the other at the second, when Asinius Pollio writes that because of the sudden onslaught of the enemy he actually did not have time to make an harangue.

He left memoirs too of his deeds in the Gallic war and in the civil strife with Pompey; for the author of the Alexandrian, African, and Spanish Wars is unknown; some think it was Oppius, others Hirtius, who also supplied the final book of the Gallic War, which Caesar left unwritten. With regard to Caesar's memoirs Cicero, also in the *Brutus* speaks in the following terms: "He wrote memoirs which deserve the highest praise; they are naked in their simplicity, straightforward yet graceful, stripped of all rhetorical adornment, as of a garment; but while his purpose was to supply material to others, on which those who wished to write history might draw, he haply gratified silly folk, who will try to use the curling-irons on his narrative, but he has kept men of any sense from touching the subject." Of these same memoirs Hirtius uses this emphatic language: "They are so highly rated in the judgment of all men, that he seems to have deprived writers of an opportunity, rather than given them one; yet our admiration for this feat is greater than that of others; for they know how well and faultlessly he wrote, while we know besides how easily and rapidly he finished his task." Asinius Pollio thinks that they were put together somewhat carelessly and without strict regard for truth; since in many cases Caesar was too ready to believe the accounts which others gave of their actions, and gave a perverted account of his own, either designedly or perhaps from forgetfulness; and he thinks that he intended to rewrite and revise them. He left besides a work in two volumes "On Analogy," the same number of "Speeches Criticising Cato," in addition to a poem, entitled "The Journey." He wrote the first of these works while crossing the Alps and returning to his army from Hither Gaul, where he had held the assizes; the second about the time of the battle of Munda, and the third in the course of a twenty-four days' journey from Rome to Farther Spain. Some letters of his to the senate are also preserved, and he seems to have been the first to reduce such documents to pages and the form of a notebook, whereas previously consuls and generals sent their reports written right across the sheet. There are also letters of his to Cicero, as well as to his intimates on private affairs, and in the latter, if he had anything confidential to say, he wrote it in cipher, that is, by so changing the order of the letters of the alphabet,

that not a word could be made out. If anyone wishes to decipher these, and get at their meaning, he must substitute the fourth letter of the alphabet, namely D, for A, and so with the others. We also have mention of certain writings of his boyhood and early youth, such as the "Praises of Hercules," a tragedy "Oedipus," and a "Collection of Apophthegms"; but Augustus forbade the publication of all these minor works in a very brief and frank letter sent to Pompeius Macer, whom he had selected to set his libraries in order.

He was highly skilled in arms and horsemanship, and of incredible powers of endurance. On the march he headed his army, sometimes on horseback, but oftener on foot, bareheaded both in the heat of the sun and in the rain. He covered great distances with incredible speed, making a hundred miles a day in a hired carriage and with little baggage, swimming the rivers which barred his path or crossing them on inflated skins, and very often arriving before the messengers sent to announce his coming.

In the conduct of his campaigns it is a question whether he was more cautious or more daring, for he never led his army where ambuscades were possible without carefully reconnoitering the country, and he did not cross to Britain without making personal inquiries about the harbours, the course, and the approach to the island. But on the other hand, when news came that his camp in Germany was beleaguered, he made his way to his men through the enemies' pickets, disguised as a Gaul. He crossed from Brundisium to Dyrrachium in winter time, running the blockade of the enemy's fleets; and when the troops which he had ordered to follow him delayed to do so, and he had sent to fetch them many times in vain, at last in secret and alone he boarded a small boat at night with his head muffled up; and he did not reveal who he was, or suffer the helmsman to give way to the gale blowing in their teeth, until he was all but overwhelmed by the waves.

No regard for religion ever turned him from any undertaking, or even delayed him. Though the victim escaped as he was offering sacrifice, he did not put off his expedition against Scipio and Juba. Even when he had a fall as he disembarked, he gave the omen a favourable turn by crying: "I hold thee fast, Africa." Furthermore, to make the prophecies ridiculous which declared that the stock of the Scipios was fated to be fortunate and invincible in that province, he kept with him in camp a contemptible fellow belonging to the Cornelian family, to whom the nickname Salvito had been given as a reproach for his manner of life.

He joined battle, not only after planning his movements in advance but on a sudden opportunity, often immediately at the end of a march, and sometimes in the foulest weather, when one would least expect him to make a move. It was not until his later years that he became slower to engage, through a conviction that the oftener he had been victor, the less he ought to tempt fate, and that he could not possibly gain as much by success as he might lose by a defeat. He never put his enemy to flight without also driving him from his camp, thus giving him no respite in his panic. When the issue was doubtful, he used to send away the horses, and his own among the first, to impose upon his troops the greater necessity of standing their ground by taking away that aid to flight.

He rode a remarkable horse, too, with feet that were almost human; for its hoofs were cloven in such a way as to look like toes. This horse was foaled on his own place, and since the soothsayer had declared that it foretold the rule of the world for its master, he reared it with the greatest care, and was the first to mount it, for it would endure no other rider. Afterwards, too, he dedicated a statute of it before the temple of Venus Genetrix.

Juvenal

The typical present-day picture of ancient Rome is one of awesome grandeur. Although the monuments—like the Colosseum, the Forum, and the triumphal arches—have been damaged by the ravages of time, they still convey a sense of the Imperial City. But Rome, as it really existed, was much more than these monuments; it was the great urban metropolis of the Western world. And it is about Rome, the metropolis, that Juvenal writes in his "Third Satire." From his description of life in urban Rome during the early empire it is abundantly clear that Juvenal envied his friend, Umbricius, who decided to abandon the city to settle in a quiet village in the country.

Was Rome actually as dirty and debauched as Juvenal describes it? Certainly his was not the only negative voice; other contemporary writers (like Tacitus) have given us similar critical appraisals. But two points can help us to keep a proper perspective. First, Juvenal was a satirist. Not only is it apparent from "The Third Satire" that he detested Rome but also that he found joy in depicting its shortcomings in picturesque and lurid detail. So we must use some judgment in evaluating the accuracy of his description. Second, Rome was a big city and anyone who has lived in a modern big city can recognize that many of the things Juvenal talks about could, if translated into contemporary terms, be said about any of our great metropolitan centers. But that does not mean that they lack all redeeming qualities. So, too, of ancient Rome.

Little is known of the life of Juvenal. He was born Decimus Junius Juvenalis, probably around A.D. 55. He obviously knew the city of Rome very well and presumably lived in or near it most of his life. There is a story, which cannot be verified, that he was exiled, perhaps by the emperor Domitian, and spent a number of years in Egypt. He may also have served in the Roman army. He probably died sometime around the year 140 but the exact date is unknown.

Altogether we have sixteen satires that Juvenal wrote, on a wide range of topics, including a long one titled "Against Women." Although the translation of "The Third Satire," as given in the following selection, is somewhat free, it conveys very well the flavor of Juvenal's verse.

The Third Satire

AGAINST THE CITY OF ROME

Troubled because my old friend is
   going, I still must commend him
For his decision to settle down in the
   ghost town of Cumae,
Giving the Sibyl one citizen more.
   That's the gateway to Baiae
There, a pleasant shore, a delightful
   retreat. I'd prefer
Even a barren rock in that bay to the
   brawl of Subura.
Where have we ever seen a place so
   dismal and lonely
We'd not be better off there, than
   afraid, as we are here, of fires,
Roofs caving in, and the thousand
   risks of this terrible city
Where the poets recite all through
   the dog days of August?

While they are loading his goods on
   one little four-wheeled wagon,
Here he waits, by the old archways
   which the aqueducts moisten.
This is where Numa, by night, came to
   visit his goddess.
That once holy grove, its sacred
   spring, and its temple,
Now are let out to the Jews, if they
   have some straw and a basket.
Every tree, these days, has to pay rent
   to the people.
Kick the Muses out; the forest is
   swarming with beggars.
So we go down to Egeria's vale, with
   its modern improvements.
How much more close the presence
   would be, were there lawns by the
   water.
Turf to the curve of the pool, not this
   unnatural marble!
Umbricius has much on his mind.
   "Since there's no place in the city,"

He says, "For an honest man, and no
   reward for his labors,
Since I have less today than yesterday,
   since by tomorrow
That will have dwindled still more, I
   have made my decision. I'm going
To the place where, I've heard,
   Daedalus put off his wings,
While my white hair is still new, my old
   age in the prime of its straightness,
While my fate spinner still has yarn on
   her spool, while I'm able
Still to support myself on two good
   legs, without crutches.
Rome, good-bye! Let the rest stay in
   the town if they want to,
Fellows like A, B, and C, who make
   black white at their pleasure,
Finding it easy to grab contracts for
   rivers and harbors,
Putting up temples, or cleaning out
   sewers, or hauling off corpses,
Or, if it comes to that, auctioning
   slaves in the market.
Once they used to be hornblowers,
   working the carneys;
Every wide place in the road knew
   their puffed-out cheeks and their
   squealing.
Now they give shows of their own.
   Thumbs up! Thumbs down! And
   the killers
Spare or slay, and then go back to
   concessions for private privies.
Nothing they won't take on. Why
   not?—since the kindness of Fortune
(Fortune is out for laughs) has exalted
   them out of the gutter.
"What should I do in Rome? I am no
   good at lying.
If a book's bad, I can't praise it, or go
   around ordering copies.
I don't know the stars; I can't hire out
   as assassin

The Satires of Juvenal, trans. Rolfe Humphries (Bloomington: Indiana University Press, 1958). Courtesy of Indiana University Press.

When some young man wants his
father knocked off for a price; I
have never
Studied the guts of frogs, and plenty of
others know better
How to convey to a bride the gifts of
the first man she cheats with.
I am no lookout for thieves, so I
cannot expect a commission
On some governor's staff. I'm a useless
corpse, or a cripple.
Who has a pull these days, except your
yes men and stooges
With blackmail in their hearts, yet
smart enough to keep silent?
No honest man feels in debt to those
he admits to his secrets,
But your Verres must love the man
who can tattle on Verres
Any old time that he wants. Never let
the gold of the Tagus,
Rolling under its shade, become so
important, so precious
You have to lie awake, take bribes that
you'll have to surrender,
Tossing in gloom, a threat to your
mighty patron forever.

"Now let me speak of the race that our
rich men dote on most fondly.
These I avoid like the plague, let's
have no coyness about it.
Citizens, I can't stand a Greekized
Rome. Yet what portion
Of the dregs of our town comes from
Achaia only?
Into the Tiber pours the silt, the mud
of Orontes,
Bringing its babble and brawl, its
dissonant harps and its timbrels,
Bringing also the tarts who display
their wares at the Circus.
Here's the place, if your taste is
for hatwearing whores, brightly
colored!
What have they come to now, the
simple souls from the country
Romulus used to know? They put on
the *trechedipna*
(That might be called, in our tongue,
their running-to-dinner outfit),

Pin on their *niketeria* (medals), and
smell *ceromatic*
(Attar of wrestler). They come,
trooping from Samos and Tralles,
Adros, wherever that is, Azusa and
Cucamonga,
Bound for the Esquiline or the hill we
have named for the vineyard,
Termites, into great halls where they
hope, some day, to be tyrants.
Desperate nerve, quick wit, as ready in
speech as Isaeus,
Also a lot more long-winded. Look
over there! See that fellow?
What do you take him for? He can be
anybody he chooses,
Doctor of science or letters, a vet or a
chiropractor,
Orator, painter, masseur, palmologist,
tightrope walker.
If he is hungry enough, your little
Greek stops at nothing.
Tell him to fly to the moon, and he
runs right off for his space ship.
Who flew first? Some Moor, some
Turk, some Croat, or some Slovene?
Not on your life, but a man from the
very center of Athens.

"Should I not run away from these
purple-wearing freeloaders?
Must I wait while they sign their
names? Must their couches always be
softer?
Stowaways that's how they got here, in
the plums and figs from Damascus.
I was here long before they were: my
boyhood drank in the sky
Over the Aventine hill; I was
nourished by Sabine olives.
Agh, what lackeys they are, what
sycophants! See how they flatter
Some ignoramus's talk, or the looks of
some horrible eyesore,
Saying some Ichabod Crane's long
neck reminds them of muscles
Hercules strained when he lifted
Antaeus aloft on his shoulders,
Praising some cackling voice that really
sounds like a rooster's
When he's pecking a hen. We can
praise the same objects that they do,

Only, they are believed. Does an actor
do any better
Mimicking Thais, Alcestis, Doris
without any clothes on?
It seems that a woman speaks, not a
mask; the illusion is perfect
Down to the absence of bulge and the
little cleft under the belly.
Yet they win no praise at home, for all
of their talent.
Why?—Because Greece is a stage, and
every Greek is an actor.
Laugh, and he splits his sides; weep,
and his tears flow in torrents
Though he's not sad; if you ask for a
little more fire in the winter
He will put on his big coat; if you say
'I'm hot,' he starts sweating.
We are not equals at all; he always has
the advantage,
Able, by night or day, to assume, from
another's expression,
This or that look, prepared to throw
up his hands, to cheer loudly
If his friend gives a good loud belch
or doesn't piss crooked,
Or if a gurgle comes from his golden
cup when inverted
Straight up over his nose—a good
deep swig, and no heeltaps!

"Furthermore, nothing is safe from his
lust, neither matron nor virgin,
Nor her affianced spouse, or the boy
too young for the razor.
If he can't get at these, he would just
as soon lay his friend's grandma.
(Anything, so he'll get in to knowing
the family secrets!)
Since I'm discussing the Greeks,
let's turn to their schools and
professors,
The crimes of the hood and gown. Old
Dr. Egnatius, informant,
Brought about the death of Barea, his
friend and his pupil,
Born on that riverbank where the
pinion of Pegasus landed.
No room here, none at all, for any
respectable Roman
Where a Protogenes rules, or a Diphilus,
or a Hermarchus,

Never sharing their friends—a racial
characteristic!
Hands off! He puts a drop of his own,
or his countryside's poison
Into his patron's ear, an ear which is
only too willing
And I am kicked out of the house, and
all my years of long service
Count for nothing. Nowhere does the
loss of a client mean less.
"Let's not flatter ourselves. What's the
use of our service?
What does a poor man gain by
hurrying out in the nighttime,
All dressed up before dawn, when the
praetor nags at his troopers
Bidding them hurry along to convey
his respects to the ladies,
Barren, of course, like Albina, before
any others can get there?
Sons of men freeborn give right of
way to rich man's
Slave; a crack, once or twice, at Calvina
or Catiena
Costs an officer's pay, but if you like
the face of some floozy
You hardly have money enough to
make her climb down from her high
chair.
Put on the stand, at Rome, a man with
a record unblemished,
No more a perjurer than Numa was,
or Metellus,
What will they question? His wealth,
right away, and possibly, later,
(Only possibly, though) touch on his
reputation.
'How many slaves does he feed?
What's the extent of his acres?
How big are his platters? How many?
What of his goblets and wine bowls?'
His word is as good as his bond—if he
has enough bonds in his strongbox.
But a poor man's oath, even if sworn
on all altars
All the way from here to the farthest
Dodecanese island,
Has no standing in court. What has he
to fear from the lightnings
Of the outraged gods? He has nothing
to lose; they'll ignore him.

"If you're poor, you're a joke, on each
      and every occasion.
What a laugh, if your cloak is dirty or
      torn, if your toga
Seems a little bit soiled, if your shoe
      has a crack in the leather,
Or if more than one patch attests to
      more than one mending!
Poverty's greatest curse, much worse
      than the fact of it, is that
It makes men objects of mirth,
      ridiculed, humbled, embarrassed.
'Out of the front-row seats!' they cry
      when you're out of money,
Yield your place to the sons of some
      pimp, the spawn of some cathouse,
Some slick auctioneer's brat, or the
      louts some trainer has fathered
Or the well-groomed boys whose sire is
      a gladiator.
Such is the law of the place, decreed
      by the nitwitted Otho:
All the best seats are reserved for the classes
who have the most money.
Who can marry a girl if he has less
      money than she does?
What poor man is an heir, or can hope
      to be? Which of them ever
Rates a political job, even the meanest
      and lowest?
Long before now, all poor Roman
      descendants of Romans
Ought to have marched out of town in
      one determined migration.
Men do not easily rise whose poverty
      hinders their merit.
Here it is harder than anywhere else:
      the lodgings are hovels,
Rents out of sight; your slaves take
      plenty to fill up their bellies
While you make do with a snack.
      You're ashamed of your earthenware
      dishes—
Ah, but that wouldn't be true if you
      lived content in the country,
Wearing a dark-blue cape, and the hood
      thrown back on your shoulders.

"In a great part of this land of Italy,
      might as well face it,
No one puts on a toga unless he is
      dead. On festival days

Where the theater rises, cut from
      green turf, and with the great pomp
Old familiar plays are staged again,
      and a baby,
Safe in his mother's lap, is scared of
      the grotesque mask,
There you see all dressed alike, the
      balcony and the front rows,
Even His Honor content with a tunic
      of simple white.
Here, beyond our means, we have to
      be smart, and too often
Get our effects with too much, an
      elaborate wardrobe, on credit!
This is a common vice; we must keep
      up with the neighbors,
Poor as we are. I tell you, everything
      here costs you something.
How much to give Cossus the time of
      day, or receive from Veiento
One quick glance, with his mouth
      buttoned up for fear he might greet
      you?
One shaves his beard, another cuts off
      the locks of his boy friend,
Offerings fill the house, but these, you
      find, you will pay for.
Put this in your pipe and smoke it—we
      have to pay tribute
Giving the slaves a bribe for the
      prospect of bribing their masters.

"Who, in Praeneste's cool, or the
      wooded Volsinian uplands,
Who, on Tivoli's heights, or a small
      town like Gabii, say,
Fears the collapse of his house? But
      Rome is supported on pipestems,
Matchsticks; it's cheaper, so, for the
      landlord to shore up his ruins,
Patch up the old cracked walls, and
      notify all the tenants
They can sleep secure, though the
      beams are in ruins above them.
No, the place to live is out there,
      where no cry of *Fire*
Sounds the alarm of the night, with a
      neighbor yelling for water,
Moving his chattels and goods, and the
      whole third story is smoking.
This you'll never know: for if the
      ground floor is scared first,

You are the last to burn, up where the
  eaves of the attic
Keep off the rain, and the doves are
  brooding over their nest eggs.
Codrus owned one bed, too small for a
  midget to sleep on.
Six little jugs he had, and a tankard
  adorning his sideboard,
Under whose marble (clay), a bust or a
  statue of Chiron,
Busted, lay on its side; an old locker
  held Greek books
Whose divinest lines were gnawed by
  the mice, those vandals.
Codrus had nothing, no doubt, and
  yet he succeeded, poor fellow,
Losing that nothing, his all. And this is
  the very last straw—
No one will help him out with a meal
  or lodging or shelter.
Stripped to the bone, begging for
  crusts, he still receives nothing.

"Yet if Asturicus' mansion burns down,
  what a frenzy of sorrow!
Mothers dishevel themselves, the
  leaders dress up in black,
Courts are adjourned. We groan at the
  fall of the city, we hate
The fire, and the fire still burns, and
  while it is burning,
Somebody rushes up to replace the
  loss of the marble,
Some one chips in toward a building
  fund, another gives statues,
Naked and shining white, some
  masterpiece of Euphranor
Or Polyclitus' chef d'oeuvre; and here's
  a fellow with bronzes
Sacred to Asian gods. Books, chests, a
  bust of Minerva,
A bushel of silver coins. *To him that hath
  shall be given!*
This Persian, childless, of course, the
  richest man in the smart set,
Now has better things, and more, than
  before the disaster.
How can we help but think he started
  the fire on purpose?

"Tear yourself from the games, and
  get a place in the country!

One little Latian town, like Sora, say,
  or Frusino,
Offers a choice of homes, at a price
  you pay here, in one year,
Renting some hole in the wall. Nice
  houses, too, with a garden,
Springs bubbling up from the grass,
  no need for a windlass or bucket,
Plenty to water your flowers, if they
  need it, without any trouble.
Live there, fond of your hoe, an
  independent producer,
Willing and able to feed a hundred
  good vegetarians.
Isn't it something, to feel, wherever
  you are, how far off,
You are a monarch? At least, lord of a
  single lizard.

"Here in town the sick die from
  insomnia mostly.
Undigested food, on a stomach
  burning with ulcers,
Brings on listlessness, but who can
  sleep in a flophouse?
Who but the rich can afford sleep and
  a garden apartment?
That's the source of infection. The
  wheels creak by on the narrow
Streets of the wards, the drivers
  squabble and brawl when they're
  stopped,
More than enough to frustrate the
  drowsiest son of a sea cow.
When his business calls, the crowd
  makes way, as the rich man,
Carried high in his car, rides over
  them, reading or writing,
Even taking a snooze, perhaps, for the
  motion's composing.
Still, he gets where he wants before we
  do; for all of our hurry
Traffic gets in our way, in front,
  around and behind us.
Somebody gives me a shove with an
  elbow, or two-by-two-four scantling.
One clunks my head with a beam,
  another cracks down with a beer
  keg.
Mud is thick on my shins, I am
  trampled by somebody's big feet.

Now what?—a soldier grinds his
  hobnails into my toes.
"Don't you see the mob rushing along
  to the handout?
There are a hundred guests, each one
  with his kitchen servant.
Even Samson himself could hardly
  carry those burdens,
Pots and pans some poor little slave
  tries to keep on his head, while he
  hurries
Hoping to keep the fire alive by the
  wind of his running.
Tunics, new-darned, and ripped to
  shreds; there's the flash of a fir
  beam
Huge on some great dray, and another
  carries a pine tree,
Nodding above our heads and
  threatening death to the people.
What will be left of the mob, if that
  cart of Ligurian marble
Breaks its axle down and dumps its
  load on these swarms?
Who will identify limbs or bones? The
  poor man's cadaver,
Crushed, disappears like his breath.
  And meanwhile, at home, his household
Washes the dishes, and puffs up the
  fire, with all kinds of a clatter
Over the smeared flesh-scrapers, the
  flasks of oil, and the towels.
So the boys rush around, while their
  late master is sitting,
Newly come to the bank of the Styx,
  afraid of the filthy
Ferryman there, since he has no fare,
  not even a copper
In his dead mouth to pay for the ride
  through that muddy whirlpool.

"Look at other things, the various
  dangers of nighttime.
How high it is to the cornice that
  breaks, and a chunk beats my brains
  out,
Or some slob heaves a jar, broken or
  cracked, from a window.
Bang! It comes down with a crash and
  proves its weight on the sidewalk

You are a thoughtless fool, unmindful
  of sudden disaster,
If you don't make your will before you
  go out to have dinner.
There are as many deaths in the night
  as there are open windows
Where you pass by; if you're wise, you
  will pray, in your wretched
  devotions,
People may be content with no more
  than emptying slop jars.

"There your hell-raising drunk, who
  has had the bad luck to kill no one,
Tosses in restless rage, like Achilles
  mourning Patroclus,
Turns from his face to his back, can't
  sleep, for only a fracas
Gives him the proper sedation. But
  any of these young hoodlums,
All steamed up on wine, watches his
  step when the crimson
Cloak goes by, a lord, with a long, long
  line of attendants,
Torches and brazen lamps, warning
  him, *Keep your distance*!
Me, however, whose torch is the moon,
  or the feeblest candle
Fed by a sputtering wick, he absolutely
  despises.
Here is how it all starts, the fight, if
  you think it is fighting
When he throws all the punches, and
  all I do is absorb them.
He stops. He tells me to stop. I stop. I
  have to obey him.
What can you do when he's mad and
  bigger and stronger than you are?
'Where do you come from?' he cries,
  'you wino, you bean-bloated bastard?
Off what shoemaker's dish have you fed
  on chopped leeks and boiled lamb-lip?
What? No answer? Speak up, or take a
  swift kick in the rear.
Tell me where you hang out—in some
  praying-house with the Jew-boys?'
If you try to talk back, or sneak away
  without speaking,
All the same thing: you're assaulted,
  and then put under a bail bond
For committing assault. This is a poor
  man's freedom.

Beaten, cut up by fists, he begs and
  implores his assailant,
Please, for a chance to go home with a
  few teeth left in his mouth.
"This is not all you must fear. Shut up
  your house or your store,
Bolts and padlocks and bars will never
  keep out all the burglars,
Or a holdup man will do you in with a
  switch blade.
If the guards are strong over Pontine
  marshes and pinewoods
Near Volturno, the scum of the
  swamps and the filth of the forest
Swirl into Rome, the great sewer, their
  sanctuary, their haven.
Furnaces blast and anvils groan with
  the chains we are forging:
What other use have we for iron and
  steel? There is danger
We will have little left for hoes and
  mattocks and ploughshares.

Happy the men of old, those primitive
  generations
Under the tribunes and kings, when
  Rome had only one jailhouse!
"There is more I could say, I could
  give you more of my reasons,
But the sun slants down, my oxen
  seem to be calling,
My man with the whip is impatient, I
  must be on my way.
So long! Don't forget me. Whenever
  you come to Aquino
Seeking relief from Rome, send for
  me. I'll come over
From my bay to your hills, hiking
  along in my thick boots
Toward your chilly fields. What's
  more, I promise to listen
If your satirical verse esteems me
  worthy the honor."

Marcus Aurelius

No visitor to Rome who is interested in history and art should miss the magnificent bronze statue of Marcus Aurelius seated on a horse and gazing out over the city from the Capitoline hill.* Although portrayed in the full majesty of a Roman emperor, the figure nevertheless conveys a feeling of understanding and compassion for the human condition. For Marcus, besides being emperor of Rome, was a Stoic philosopher. According to one account, the statue has survived because during the Middle Ages it was believed to represent the emperor Constantine (who had become a Christian), so was not destroyed. About the statue Nathaniel Hawthorne has written (in *The Marble Faun*): "It is the most majestic representation of the kingly character that ever the world has seen."

The nephew and adopted son of

the emperor Antoninus Pius, Marcus (121–180) ascended to the purple on the death of Antoninus in the year 161. He is often referred to as the last of the "good emperors." Unfortunately, much of his reign was spent far from Rome on military campaigns along the borders of the empire in the Danube valley. During his campaigning on the frontier Marcus wrote his *Meditations* at night in his tent. In them he devoted his attention to the universal but personal problems of human life and fate. The *Meditations*, which contain most of the major themes of the Stoic philosophy, were probably not meant for publication but were rather simply a written soliloquy that Marcus held with himself, summing up his thoughts of each day.

The selection that follows contains a sampling of the daily thoughts of Marcus. In reading it, do not forget that the author of these meditations was the emperor of Rome, the most powerful political figure in the Western world.

---

*To preserve the statue it has recently been removed from its pedestal and placed in a nearby museum.—*Ed.*

Meditations

• • •

BOOK II

1. Say this to yourself in the morning: To-day I shall have to do with meddlers, with the ungrateful, with the insolent, with the crafty, with the envious and the selfish. All these vices have beset them, because they know not what is good and what is evil. But I have considered the nature of the good, and found it beautiful: I have beheld the nature of the bad, and found it ugly. I also understand the nature of the evil-doer, and know that he is my brother, not because he shares with me the same blood or the same seed, but because he is a partaker of the same mind and of the same portion of immortality. I therefore cannot be hurt by any of these, since none of them can involve me in any baseness. I cannot be angry with my brother, or sever myself from him, for we are made by nature for mutual assistance, like the feet, the hands, the eyelids, the upper and lower rows of teeth. It is against nature for men to oppose each other; and what else is anger and aversion?

2. All that I am is either flesh, breath, or the ruling part. Cast your books from you; distract yourself no more; for you have not the right to do so. Like one at the point of death despise this flesh, this corruptible bone and blood, this network texture of nerves, veins, and arteries. Consider, too, what breath is—mere air, and that always changing, expelled and inhaled again every moment.

The third is the ruling part. As to this, take heed, now that you are old, that it remain no longer in servitude; that it be no more dragged hither and thither like a puppet by every selfish impulse. Repine no more at what fate now sends, nor dread what may befall you hereafter.

3. Whatever the Gods ordain is full of wise forethought. The workings of chance are not apart from nature, and not without connexion and intertexture with the designs of Providence. Providence is the source of all things; and, besides, there is necessity, and the utility of the Universe, of which you are a part. For, to every part of a being, that is good which springs from the nature of the whole and tends to its preservation. Now, the order of Nature is preserved in the changes of elements, just as it is in the changes of things that are compound. Let this suffice you, and be your creed unchangeable. Put from you the thirst of books, that you may not die murmuring, but meekly, and with true and heartfelt gratitude to the Gods.

4. Think of your long procrastination, and of the many opportunities given you by the Gods, but left unused. Surely it is high time to understand the Universe of which you are a part, and the Ruler of that Universe, of whom you are an emanation; that a limit is set to your days, which, if you use them not for your enlightenment, will depart, as you yourself will, and return no more.

5. Hourly and earnestly strive, as a Roman and a man, to do what falls to

Trans. George W Chrystal

218

your hand with perfect unaffected dignity, with kindliness, freedom and justice, and free your soul from every other imagination. This you will accomplish if you perform each action as if it were your last, without wilfulness, or any passionate aversion to what reason approves; without hypocrisy or selfishness, or discontent with the decrees of Providence. You see how few things it is necessary to master in order that a man may live a smooth-flowing, God-fearing life. For of him that holds to these principles the Gods require no more.

• • •

7. Cares from without distract you: take leisure, then, to add some good thing to your knowledge; have done with vacillation, and avoid the other error. For triflers, too, are they who, by their activities, weary themselves in life, and have no settled aim to which they may direct, once and for all, their every desire and project.

8. Seldom are any found unhappy from not observing what is in the minds of others. But such as observe not well the stirrings of their own souls must of necessity be unhappy.

9. Remember always what the nature of the Universe is, what your own nature is, and how these are related—the one to the other. Remember what part your qualities are of the qualities of the whole, and that no man can prevent you from speaking and acting always in accordance with that nature of which you are a part.

• • •

11. Do every deed, speak every word, think every thought in the knowledge that you may end your days any moment. To depart from men, if there be really Gods, is nothing terrible. The Gods could bring no evil thing upon you. And if there be no Gods, or if they have no regard to human affairs, why should I desire to live in a world void of Gods and without Providence? But Gods there are, and assuredly they regard human affairs; and they have put it wholly in man's power that he should not fall into what is truly evil. And of other things, had any been bad, they would have made provision also that man should have the power to avoid them altogether. For how can that make a man's life worse which does not corrupt the man himself? Presiding Nature could not in ignorance, or in knowledge impotent, have omitted to prevent or rectify these things. She could not fail us so completely that, either from want of power or want of skill, good and evil should happen promiscuously to good men and to bad alike. Now death and life, glory and reproach, pain and pleasure, riches and poverty—all these happen equally to the good and to the bad. But, as they are neither honourable nor shameful, they are therefore neither good nor evil.

12. It is the office of our rational power to apprehend how swiftly all things vanish; how the corporeal forms are swallowed up in the material world, and the memory of them in the tide of ages. Such are all the things of sense, especially those which ensnare us with pleasure or terrify us with pain, or those things which vanity trumpets in our ears. How mean, how despicable, how sordid, how perishable, how dead are they! What are they whose opinions and whose voices bestow renown? What is it to die? Your mind can tell you that, did a man think of it alone, and, by close consideration, strip it of its ghastly trappings, he would no longer deem it anything but a work of Nature. To dread a work of Nature is a childish thing, and this is, in-

deed, not only Nature's work, but beneficial to her. Your reason tells you how man reaches God, and through what part, and what is the state of that part, when he has attained unto him.

• • •

14. Though you should live three thousand years or as many myriads, yet remember that no man loses any other life than that which he now lives, nor lives any other than that which he is now losing. The longest and the shortest lives come to one effect. The present moment is the same for all men, and their loss, therefore, is equal, for it is clear that what they lose in death is but a fleeting instant of time. No man can lose either the past or the future, for how can a man be deprived of what he has not? These two things then are to be remembered: First, that all things recur in cycles, and are the same from everlasting, and that, therefore, it matters nothing whether a man shall contemplate these same things for one hundred years, or for two hundred, or for an infinite stretch of time: and, secondly, that he who lives longest and he who dies soonest have an equal loss in death. The present moment is all of which either is deprived, since that is all he has. No man can be robbed of that which he has not.

• • •

16. Man's soul dishonours itself, firstly and chiefly when it does all it can to become an excrescence, and as it were an abscess on the Universe. To fret against any particular event is to revolt against the general law of Nature, which comprehends the order of all events whatsoever. Again it is dishonour for the soul when it has aversion to any man, and opposes him with intention to hurt him, as wrathful men do. Thirdly, it affronts

itself when conquered by pleasure or pain; fourthly, when it does or says anything hypocritically, feignedly or falsely; fifthly, when it does not direct to some proper end all its desires and actions, but exerts them inconsiderately and without understanding. For, even the smallest things should be referred to the end, and the end of rational beings is to follow the order and law of the venerable state and polity which comprehends them all.

17. The duration of man's life is but an instant; his substance is fleeting, his senses dull; the structure of his body corruptible; the soul but a vortex. We cannot reckon with fortune, or lay our account with fame. In fine, the life of the body is but a river, and the life of the soul a misty dream. Existence is a warfare, and a journey in a strange land; and the end of fame is to be forgotten. What then avails to guide us? One thing, and one alone—Philosophy.

BOOK IV

3. Men seek retirement in the country, on the sea-coast, in the mountains; and you too have frequent longings for such distractions. Yet surely this is great folly, since you may retire into yourself at any hour you please. Nowhere can a man find any retreat more quiet and more full of leisure than in his own soul; especially when there is that within it on which, if he but look, he is straightway quite at rest. And rest I hold to be naught else but perfect order in the soul. Constantly, therefore, allow yourself this retirement, and so renew yourself. Have also at hand thoughts brief and fundamental, which readily may occur; sufficing to shut out the discordant clamour of

the world, and to send you back without fretting at the task to which you return. For at what do you fret? At the wickedness of mankind. Recollect the maxim that all reasoning beings are created for one another, that to bear with them is a part of justice, and that they cannot help their sin. Remember how many of those who lived in enmity, suspicion, and hatred, at daggers drawn, have been stretched on their funeral pyres, and turned to ashes. Remember and cease from your complaints. Is it your allotted part in the world's destiny that chagrins you? Be calm, and renew your knowledge of the alternative, that "Either providence directs the world, or there is nothing but unguided atoms;" and recollect the many proofs that the Universe is as it were a state. Do the ills of the body still have power to touch you? Reflect that the mind, once withdrawn within itself, once grown conscious of its own power, has no concern with the motions, rough or smooth, of the breathing body. Remember, too, all that you have heard and assented to concerning pain and pleasure. Are you distracted by the poor thing called fame? Think how swiftly all things are forgotten. Behold the chaos of eternity which besets us on either side. Think how empty is the noisy echo of acclamation; how fickle and how scant of judgment are they who would seem to praise us, and how narrow the bounds within which their praise is confined. All the earth is but a point in the Universe; how small a corner of that little is inhabited, and even there how few are they and of how little worth who are to praise us! Remember then that there ever remains for you retirement into the little field within. And, above all, be neither distraught nor over-strained. Hold fast your freedom: consider all things as a man of courage, as a human being, as a citizen, as a mortal. Readiest among the principles to which you look let there be these two: Firstly, things external do not touch the soul, but remain powerless without; and all trouble comes from what we think of them within. Secondly, all things visible change in a moment, and are gone for ever. Recollect all the changes of which you have yourself been a witness. The world is a succession of changes: life is but thought.

4. If mind be common to us all, the reason in virtue of which we are rational is also common; so too is the power which bids us do or not do. Therefore we have all a common law; and if so, we are fellow-citizens and members of some common polity. The Universe, then, must in a manner be a state, for of what other common polity can all mankind be said to be members? Wherefore it is from this common state that we derive our intellectual power, our reason, and our law; or whence do we derive them? For that which is earthy in me is derived from earth, my moisture from some other element, my breath and what is warm or fiery from their proper sources. And therefore, as nothing can arise from nothing or return thereto, my intellectual part has also a source.

• • •

19. He who is careful and troubled about the fame which is to live after him considers not that each one of those who remember him must very soon die himself, and thereafter also the succeeding generation, until every memory of him, handed on by excited and ephemeral admirers, dies utterly away. Grant that your memory were immortal, and those

immortal who retain it; yet what is that to you? I ask not, what is that to the dead? But to the living what is the profit in praise, except it be in some convenience that it brings? And you now abandon what nature has put in your power in order to set your hopes upon the report of others.

• • •

32. Recall, for example, the age of Vespasian. It is as the spectacle of our own time. You will see men marrying, bringing up children, sick and dying, warring and feasting, trading and farming. You will see men flattering, obstinate in their own will, suspecting, plotting, wishing for the death of others, repining at fortune, courting mistresses, hoarding treasure, pursuing consulships and kingdoms. Yet all that life is spent and gone. Come down to Trajan's days. Again all is the same; and again, that life, too, is dead. Consider, likewise, the records of other times and nations, and see how, after their fit of eagerness, all quickly fell, and were resolved into the elements. But most of all, remember those whom you yourself have known, men who were distracted about vain things, men who neglected the course which suited their own nature, neither holding fast to it nor finding their contentment there. And, herein, forget not that care is to be bestowed on any enterprise only in proportion to its proper worth. For if you keep this in mind you will not be disheartened from over concern with things of less account.

• • •

43. Time is a river, a violent torrent of things coming into being. Each one, as soon as it has appeared, is swept away: it is succeeded by another which is swept away in its turn.

44. All that happens is as natural and familiar as a rose in spring, or fruit in summer. Such are disease and death, calumny and treachery, and all else which gives fools joy or sorrow.

• • •

48. Constantly consider how many physicians are dead and gone, who frequently knitted their brows over their patients; how many astrologers, who foretold the deaths of others with great ostentation of their art; how many philosophers, who wrote endlessly on death and immortality; how many warriors, who slew their thousands; and how many tyrants, who used their power of life and death with cruel wantonness, as though they had been immortal. How many whole cities, if I may so speak, are dead: Helice and Pompeii and Herculaneum, and others past counting. Tell over next all those you have known, one after the other: think how one buried his fellow, then lay dead himself, to be buried by a third. And all this within a little time. In sum, look upon human things, and behold how short-lived and how vile they are mucus yesterday, to-morrow ashes or pickled carrion. Spend, then, the fleeting remnant of your time in a spirit that accords with Nature, and depart contentedly. So the olive falls when it is grown ripe, blessing the ground from whence it sprung, and thankful to the tree that bore it.

• • •

BOOK VI

13. Keep these thoughts for meats and eatables: This that is before me is the dead carcase of a fish, a fowl, a hog. This Falernian is but a little grape juice. Think of your purple robes as sheep's wool stained in the blood of a shell-fish. Such concep-

tions, which touch reality so near, and set forth the sum and substance of these objects, are powerful indeed to display to us their despicable value. In this spirit we should act throughout life; and when things of great apparent worth present themselves, we should strip them naked, view their meanness, and cast aside the glowing description which makes them seem so glorious. Vanity is a great sophist, and most imposes on us when we believe ourselves to be busy about the noblest ends. Remember the saying of Crates about Xenocrates himself.

• • •

16. It is a small privilege to transpire like plants, or even to breathe as cattle or wild beasts do. To feel the impressions of sense, to be swayed like puppets by passion, to herd together and to live by bread; all this is no great thing. There is nothing here superior to our power of discharging our superfluous food. What, then, is of value? To be received with clapping of hands? No. Neither, therefore, is the applause of tongues more valuable, for the praises of the multitude are naught but the idle clapping of tongues. Dismiss the vanity called fame, and what remains to be prized? This, I think: in all things to act, or to restrain yourself from action, as best suits the particular structure of your nature. This is the end of all arts and studies, for every art aims at making what it produces well adapted to the work for which it was designed. The gardener, the vine-dresser, the horse-breaker, the dog-trainer all try for this; and what else is the aim of all education and teaching? Here, then, is what you may truly value: this well won, you will seek for nothing more. Will you, then, cease valuing the multitude of other things? If you do not,

you will never attain to freedom, self-sufficiency, or tranquillity. You cannot escape envying, suspecting, and striving against those who have the power to deprive you of your cherished objects, nor plotting against men who are in possession of that on which you set your heart. The man who lacks any of these things must, of necessity, be distracted, and be for ever complaining against the Gods. But reverence and respect for your own intelligence will bring you to agreement with yourself, into concord with mankind, and into harmony with the Gods, whom you will praise for all their good gifts and guidance.

• • •

30. See to it that you fall not into Caesarism: avoid that stain, for it may come to you. Guard your simplicity, your goodness, your sincerity, your dignity, your reticence, your love of justice, your piety, your kindliness, your affection for your kin, and your constancy to your duty. Endeavour earnestly to continue such as philosophy would make you. Reverence the Gods, and help mankind. Life is short, and the one fruit of it in this world is a pure mind and unselfish conduct. Be in all things the disciple of Antonine [uncle of Marcus and Roman emperor, 138–161]. Imitate his resolute constancy to rational action, his level equability, his godliness, his serenity of countenance, his sweetness of temper, his contempt of vainglory, his keen attempts to comprehend things. Remember how he never quitted any subject till he had thoroughly examined it and understood it, and how he bore with those who blamed him unjustly, without making any angry retort: how he was never in a hurry; how he discouraged calumny; how closely he scanned the

manners and actions of men; how cautious he was in reproaching any man; how free from fear, suspicion, or sophistry; how little contented him in the matter of house, furniture, dress, food, servants; how patient he was of labour, and how slow to anger. So abstemious was his life that he could hold out until evening without relieving himself, except at the usual hour. What a firm and loyal friend he was; how patient of frank opposition to his opinions; how glad if any one could set him right! How religious he was, and yet how free from superstition! Follow in his steps that your last hour may find you with a conscience as easy as his.

• • •

44. If the Gods took counsel about me and what should befall me, doubtless their counsel was good. It is difficult to imagine Gods wanting in forethought, and what could move them to do me wilful harm? What advantage would thence accrue, either to themselves or to the Universe which is their special care? If they have not taken counsel about me in particular, they certainly have done so about the common interest of the Universe, and I therefore should accept cheerfully and contentedly the fate which is the outcome of their ordinance. If, indeed, they take no counsel about anything (which it were impious to believe), then let us quit our sacrifices, our prayers, and our oaths, and all acts of devotion which we now perform as if they lived and moved amongst us. But, granting that the Gods take no thought for my affairs, I may still deliberate about myself. It is my business to consider my own interest. Now, each man's interest is that which agrees with the structure of his nature, and my nature is rational and social. As Antoninus, my city and my country is Rome; as a human being it is the world. That alone, then, which profits these two cities can profit me.

The New Testament

In the province of Judea, tucked away in a far corner of the Roman Empire, was born midway through the reign of Caesar Augustus a man whose influence on world history was far to surpass that of the *princeps*—Jesus of Nazareth. The selections that follow from the New Testament contain excerpts illustrating the teachings of Jesus and the early history and theological doctrines of his followers. From the Gospel of St. Matthew comes the Sermon on the Mount, the most complete and one of the most beautiful statements of the religious views of Jesus. The Acts, written by Luke, is a historical book detailing the activities of the founders of the Christian church in the years immediately following the crucifixion, as seen through the eyes of the early church fathers several years later. Of crucial importance to history is the transformation of Christianity from the exclusive possession of an obscure Jewish sect into a message of salvation open to Gentiles as well as to Jews. This was the first step on Christianity's long road to religious domination of the Western world. The selection from Romans contains a statement of Christian doctrine by the apostle Paul (Saul of Tarsus), one of the most influential of all Christian theologians. It was Paul who began the task of developing the teachings of Jesus into an organized and consistent body of theological doctrine.

The cornerstone of Paul's doctrine is the theory of original sin (see p. 32), with its related concepts of predestination, election, and grace. Originated by Paul, elaborated by St. Augustine in the fifth century, and reiterated by the Protestant reformer John Calvin in the sixteenth century, the doctrine of original sin is of fundamental importance in the history of Christian theology. Although of lesser significance, the notion of justification by faith, also included in the selection from Romans, has had a long history. It is associated particularly with the Protestant theology of Martin Luther. The New Testament selections have been taken from the King James Version of the Bible, with slight alterations in form.

The Gospel According to Matthew

And seeing the multitudes, he went up into a mountain: And when he was set, his disciples came unto him: And he opened his mouth, and taught them, saying, "Blessed are the poor in spirit: for theirs is the kingdom of heaven. Blessed are they that mourn: for they shall be comforted. Blessed are the meek: for they shall inherit the earth. Blessed are they which do hunger and thirst after righteousness: for they shall be filled. Blessed are the merciful: for they shall obtain mercy. Blessed are the pure in heart: for they shall see God. Blessed are the peace-makers: for they shall be called the children of God. Blessed are they which are persecuted for righteousness' sake: for theirs is the kingdom of heaven. Blessed are ye, when men shall revile you, and persecute you, and shall say all manner of evil against you falsely, for my sake. Rejoice, and be exceeding glad: for great is your reward in heaven: for so persecuted they the prophets which were before you.

"Ye are the salt of the earth: but if the salt have lost his saviour, wherewith shall it be salted? It is thenceforth good for nothing, but to be cast out, and to be trodden under foot of men. You are the light of the world. A city that is set on a hill cannot be hid. Neither do men light a candle, and put it under a bushel, but on a candlestick; and it giveth light unto all that are in the house. Let your light so shine before men, that they may see your good works, and glorify your Father which is in heaven.

"Think not that I am come to destroy the law, or the prophets: I am not come to destroy, but to fulfil. For verily I say unto you, till heaven and earth pass, one jot or one tittle shall in no wise pass from the law, till all be fulfilled. Whosoever therefore shall break one of these least commandments, and shall teach men so, he shall be called the least in the kingdom of heaven: but whosoever shall do and teach them, the same shall be called great in the kingdom of heaven. For I say unto you, that except your righteousness shall exceed the righteousness of the scribes and Pharisees, ye shall in no case enter into the kingdom of heaven.

"Ye have heard that it was said by them of old time, thou shalt not kill; and whosoever shall kill shall be in danger of the judgment. But I say unto you, That whosoever is angry with his brother without a cause shall be in danger of the judgment: and whosoever shall say to his brother, 'Ra-ca,' shall be in danger of the council: but whosoever shall say, 'Thou fool,' shall be in danger of hell fire. Therefore if thou bring thy gift to the altar, and there rememberest that thy brother hath ought against thee; leave there thy gift before the altar, and go thy way; first be reconciled to thy brother, and then come and offer thy gift. Agree with thine adversary quickly, whiles though art in the way with him; lest at any time the adversary deliver thee to the judge, and the judge deliver thee to the officer, and thou be cast

Chapters 5, 6, 7

into prison. Verily I say unto thee, Thou shalt by no means come out thence, till thou hast paid the uttermost farthing.

"Ye have heard that it was said by them of old time, Thou shalt not commit adultery. But I say unto you, That whosoever looketh on a woman to lust after her hath committed adultery with her already in his heart. And if thy right eye offend thee, pluck it out, and cast it from thee: for it is profitable for thee that one of thy members should perish, and not that thy whole body should be cast into hell. And if thy right hand offend thee: cut it off, and cast it from thee: for it is profitable for thee that one of thy members should perish, and not that thy whole body should be cast into hell. It hath been said, Whoever shall put away his wife, let him give her a writing of divorcement. But I say unto you, That whosoever shall put away his wife, saving for the cause of fornication, causeth her to commit adultery: and whosoever shall marry her that is divorced committeth adultery.

"Again, ye have heard that it hath been said by them of old time, Thou shalt not forswear thyself, but shalt perform unto the Lord thine oaths. But I say unto you, Swear not at all; neither by heaven; for it is God's throne: nor by the earth; for it is his footstool: neither by Jerusalem; for it is the city of the great King. Neither shalt thou swear by thy head, because thou canst not make one hair white or black. But let your communication be, Yea, yea; Nay, nay: for whatsoever is more than these cometh of evil.

"Ye have heard that it hath been said, An eye for an eye, and a tooth for a tooth. But I say unto you, That ye resist not evil: but whosoever shall smite thee on thy right cheek, turn to him the other also. And if any man will sue thee at the law, and take away thy coat, let him have thy cloke also. And whosoever shall compel thee to go a mile, go with him twain. Give to him that asketh thee, and from him that would borrow of thee turn not thou away.

"Ye have heard that it hath been said, Thou shalt love thy neighbor, and hate thine enemy. But I say unto you, Love your enemies, bless them that curse you, do good to them that hate you, and pray for them which despitefully use you, and persecute you; that ye may be the children of your Father which is in heaven: for he maketh his sun to rise on the evil and on the good, and sendeth rain on the just and on the unjust. For if ye love them which love you, what reward have ye? Do not even the publicans the same? And if ye salute your brethren only, what do ye more than others? Do not even the publicans so? Be ye therefore perfect, even as your Father which is in heaven is perfect.

"Take heed that ye do not your alms before men, to be seen of them: otherwise ye have no reward of your Father which is in heaven. Therefore when thou doest thine alms do not sound a trumpet before thee, as the hypocrites do in the synagogues and in the streets, that they may have glory of men. Verily I say unto you, they have their reward. But when thou doest alms, let not thy left hand know what thy right hand doeth: that thine alms may be in secret: and thy Father which seeth in secret himself shall reward thee openly.

"And when thou prayest, thou shalt not be as the hypocrites are: for they love to pray standing in the synagogues and in the corners of the street, that they may be seen of men. Verily I say unto you, They have their reward. But thou, when thou prayest, enter into thy closet, and when thou hast shut thy door, pray to thy father which is in secret: and thy Father which seeth in secret shall reward thee openly. But when ye pray, use not vain repetitions, as the heathen do: for they think that they shall be heard for their much speaking. Be not ye therefore like unto them: for your father knoweth what things ye have need of, before ye ask him. After this manner therefore pray ye: Our Father which art in heaven, hallowed be thy name. Thy kingdom come. Thy will be done in earth, as it is in heaven. Give us this day our daily bread. And forgive us our debts, as we forgive our debtors. And lead us not into temptation, but deliver us from evil: For thine is the kingdom, and the power, and the glory, for ever. A-men.

"For if ye forgive men their trespasses, your heavenly Father will also forgive you: But if ye forgive not men their trespasses, neither will your father forgive your trespasses.

"Moreover when ye fast, be not, as the hypocrites, of a sad countenance: for they disfigure their faces, that they may appear unto men to fast. Verily I say unto you, They have their reward. But thou, when thou fastest, anoint thine head, and wash thy face; that thou appear not unto men to fast, but unto thy Father which is in secret: and thy Father, which seeth in secret, shall reward thee openly.

"Lay not up for yourselves, treasures upon earth, where moth and rust doth corrupt, and where thieves break through and steal. But lay up for yourselves treasures in heaven, where neither moth nor rust doth corrupt, and where thieves do not break through nor steal: For where your treasure is, there will your heart be also. The light of the body is the eye: if therefore thine eye be single thy whole body shall be full of light. But if thine eye be evil, thy whole body shall be full of darkness. If therefore the light that is in thee be darkness, how great is that darkness!

"No man can serve two masters: for either he will hate the one, and love the other; or else he will hold to the one, and despise the other. Ye cannot serve God and mammon. Therefore I say unto you, Take no thought for your life, what ye shall eat, or what ye shall drink; nor yet for your body, what ye shall put on. Is not the life more than meat, and the body than raiment? Behold the fowls of the air: for they sow not, neither do they reap, nor gather into barns; yet your heavenly Father feedeth them. Are ye not much better than they? Which of you by taking thought can add one cubit unto his stature? And why take ye thought for raiment? Consider the lilies of the field, how they grow; they toil not, neither do they spin: And yet I say unto you, That even Solomon in all his glory was not arrayed like one of these. Wherefore, if God so clothe the grass of the field, which today is, and tomorrow is cast into the oven, shall he not much more clothe you, O ye of little faith? Therefore take no thought, saying, What shall we eat? or, What shall we drink? or Wherewithal shall we be clothed? (For after all these things do the Gentiles seek:) for your heavenly Father knoweth that ye have need of all these things. But seek ye first the kingdom of God, and his righteousness; and all these things shall be added unto you. Take therefore no thought for the morrow: for the morrow shall take thought for the things of itself. Sufficient unto the day is the evil thereof.

"Judge not, that ye be not judged. For with what judgment ye judge, ye shall be judged: and with what measure ye mete, it shall be measured to you again. And why beholdest thou the mote that is in thy brother's eye, but considerest not the beam that is in thine own eye? Or how wilt thou say to thy brother, Let me pull out the mote out of thine eye; and, behold, a beam is in thine own eye? Thou hypocrite, first cast out the beam out of thine own eye; and then shalt thou see clearly to cast out the mote out of thy brother's eye.

"Give not that which is holy unto the dogs, neither cast ye your pearls before swine, lest they trample them under their feet, and turn again and rend you.

"Ask, and it shall be given you; seek, and ye shall find; knock, and it shall be opened unto you: For every one that asketh receiveth; and he that seeketh findeth; and to him that knocketh it shall be opened. Or what man is there of you, whom if his son ask bread, will he give him a stone? Or if he ask a fish, will he give him a serpent? If ye then, being evil, know how to give good gifts unto your children, how much more shall your Father which is in heaven give good things to them that ask him? Therefore all things whatsoever ye would that men should do to you, do ye even so to them: for this is the law and the prophets.

"Enter ye in the strait gate: for wide is the gate, and broad is the way, that leadeth to destruction, and many there be which go in thereat: Because strait is the gate, and narrow is the way, which leadeth unto life, and few there be that find it.

"Beware of false prophets, which come to you in sheep's clothing, but inwardly they are ravening wolves. Ye shall know them by their fruits. Do men gather grapes of thorns, or figs of thistles? Even so every good tree bringeth forth good fruit; but a corrupt tree bringeth forth evil fruit. A good tree cannot bring forth evil fruit, neither can a corrupt tree bring forth good fruit. Every tree that bringeth not forth good fruit is hewn down, and cast into the fire. Wherefore by their fruits ye shall know them.

"Not every one that saith unto me, Lord, Lord, shall enter into the kingdom of heaven; but he that doeth the will of my Father which is in heaven. Many will say to me in that day, Lord, Lord, have we not prophesied in thy name? And in thy name have cast out devils? And in thy name done many wonderful works? And then will I profess unto them, I never knew you; depart from me, ye that work iniquity.

"Therefore whosoever heareth these sayings of mine, and doeth them I will liken him unto a wise man, which built his house upon a rock: And the rain descended, and the floods came, and the winds blew, and beat upon that house and it fell not: for it was founded upon a rock. And every one that heareth these sayings of mine, and doeth them not, shall be likened unto a foolish man, which built his house upon the sand: And the rain descended, and the floods came, and the winds blew, and beat upon that house; and it fell: and great was the fall of it." And it came to pass, when Jesus had ended these sayings, the people were astonished at his doctrine: For he taught them as one having authority, and not as the scribes.

The Acts of the Apostles

The former treatise have I made, O Theophilus, of all that Jesus began both to do and teach, until the day in which he was taken up, after that he through the Holy Ghost had given commandments unto the apostles whom he had chosen. To whom also he shewed himself alive after his passion by many infallible proofs, being seen of them forty days, and speaking of the things pertaining to the kingdom of God: And, being assembled together with them, commanded them that they should not depart from Jerusalem, but wait for the promise of the Father, which, saith he, ye have heard of me. For John truly baptized with water; but ye shall be baptized with the Holy Ghost not many days hence.

When they therefore were come together, they asked of him, saying, "Lord, wilt thou at this time restore again the kingdom to Israel?" And he said unto them, "It is not for you to know the times or the seasons, which the Father hath put in his own power. But ye shall receive power, after that the Holy Ghost is come upon you: and ye shall be witnesses unto me both in Jerusalem, and in all Judaea, and in Samaria, and unto the uttermost part of the earth." And when he had spoken these things, while they beheld, he was taken up; and a cloud received him out of their sight. And while they looked stedfastly toward heaven as he went up, behold, two men stood by them in white apparel; which also said, "Ye men of Galilee, why stand ye gazing up into heaven? This same Jesus, which is taken up from you into heaven, shall so come in like manner as ye have seen him go into heaven." Then returned they unto Jerusalem from the mount called Olivet, which is from Jerusalem a sabbath day's journey.

• • •

And when the day of Pentecost was fully come, they were all with one accord in one place. And suddenly there came a sound from heaven as of a rushing mighty wind, and it filled all the house where they were sitting. And there appeared unto them cloven tongues like as of fire, and it sat upon each of them. And they were all filled with the Holy Ghost, and began to speak with other tongues, as the Spirit gave them utterance. And there were dwelling at Jerusalem Jews, devout men, out of every nation under heaven. Now when this was noised abroad, the multitude came together, and were confounded, because that every man heard them speak in his own language. And they were all amazed and marvelled, saying one to another, "Behold are not all these which speak Galilaeans? And how hear we every man in our own tongue, wherein we were born? Parthians, and Medes, and Elamites, and the dwellers in Mesopotamia, and in Judaea, and Cappadocia, in Pontus, and Asia, Phrygia, and Pamphylia, in Egypt, and in the parts of Libya about Cyrene, and strangers of Rome, Jews and proselytes, Cretes and Arabians, we do hear them speak in our tongues the wonderful

Chapters 1:1–12; 2:1–41; 6:7–15; 7:1–2, 51–60; 8:1–3; 9:1–22; 10.

works of God." And they were all amazed, and were in doubt, saying one to another, "What meaneth this?" Others mocking said, "These men are full of new wine."

But Peter, standing up with the eleven, lifted up his voice, and said unto them, "Ye men of Judaea, and all ye that dwell at Jerusalem, be this known unto you, and hearken to my words. For these are not drunken, as ye suppose, seeing it is but the third hour of the day. But this is that which was spoken by the prophet Joel: 'And it shall come to pass in the last days,' saith God, 'I will pour out of my Spirit upon all flesh: and your sons and your daughters shall prophesy, and your young men shall see visions, and your old men shall dream dreams: And on my servants and on my handmaidens I will pour out in those days of my Spirit; and they shall prophesy. And I will shew wonders in heaven above, and signs in the earth beneath; blood, and fire, and vapour of smoke: The sun shall be turned into darkness, and the moon into blood, before the great and notable day of the Lord come. And it shall come to pass, that whosoever shall call on the name of the Lord shall be saved.' Ye men of Israel, hear these words; Jesus of Nazareth, a man approved of God among you by miracles and wonders and signs, which God did by him in the midst of you, as ye yourselves also know: Him, being delivered by the determinate counsel and foreknowledge of God, ye have taken, and by wicked hands have crucified and slain: Whom God hath raised up, having loosed the pains of death: because it was not possible that he should be holden of it. For David speaketh concerning him, 'I foresaw the Lord always before my face, for he is on my right hand, that I should not be moved. Therefore did my heart rejoice, and my tongue was glad; moreover also my flesh shall rest in hope: Because thou wilt not leave my soul in hell, neither wilt thou suffer thine Holy One to see corruption. Thou hast made known to me the ways of life; thou shalt make me full of joy with thy countenance.' Men and brethren, let me freely speak unto you of the patriarch David, that he is both dead and buried, and his sepulchre is with us unto this day. Therefore being a prophet, and knowing that God had sworn with an oath to him, that of the fruit of his loins, according to the flesh, he would raise up Christ to sit on his throne; he seeing this before spake of the resurrection of Christ, and his soul was not left in hell neither his flesh did see corruption. Thus Jesus hath God raised up, whereof we all are witnesses. Therefore being by the right hand of God exalted, and having received of the Father the promise of the Holy Ghost, he hath shed forth this, which ye now see and hear. For David is not ascended into the heavens: but he saith himself, 'The LORD said unto my Lord, "Sit thou on my right hand, until I make thy foes thy footstool." ' Therefore let all the houses of Israel know assuredly, that God hath made that same Jesus, whom ye have crucified, both Lord and Christ."

Now when they heard this, they were pricked in their heart, and said unto Peter and to the rest of the apostles, "Men and brethren, what shall we do?" Then Peter said unto them, "Repent, and be baptized every one of you in the name of Jesus Christ for the remission of sins, and ye shall receive the gift of the Holy Ghost. For the promise is unto you, and to your children, and to all that are afar off, even as many as the Lord our God shall call." And with many other words did he testify and exhort, saying, "Save yourselves from this untoward generation."

Then they that gladly received his word were baptized; and the same day there were added unto them about three thousand souls.

• • •

And the word of God increased; and the number of the disciples multiplied in Jerusalem greatly; and a great company of the priests were obedient to the faith. And Stephen, full of faith and power, did great wonders and miracles among the people.

Then there arose certain of the synagogue, which is called the synagogue of the Libertines, and Cyrenians, and Alexandrians, and of them of Cilicia and of Asia, disputing with Stephen. And they were not able to resist the wisdom and the spirit by which he spake. Then they suborned men, which said, "We have heard him speak blasphemous words against Moses, and against God." And they stirred up the people, and the elders, and the scribes, and came upon him, and caught him, and brought him to the council, and set up false witnesses, which said, "This man ceaseth not to speak blasphemous words against this holy place, and the law: For we have heard him say that his Jesus of Nazareth shall destroy this place, and shall change the customs which Moses delivered us." And all that sat in the council, looking stedfastly on him, saw his face as it had been the face of an angel.

Then said the high priest, "Are these things so?" And he said, "Men, brethren, and fathers, hearken: [*After defending himself by an appeal to the Old Testament, Stephen concludes,*] Ye stiffnecked and uncircumcised in heart and ears, ye do always resist the Holy Ghost: as your fathers did, so shall ye. Which of the prophets have not your fathers persecuted? And they have slain them which shewed before of the coming of the Just One; of whom ye have been now the betrayers and murderers: who have received the law by the disposition of angels, and have not kept it."

When they heard these things, they were cut to the heart, and they gnashed on him with their teeth. But he, being full of the Holy Ghost, looked up stedfastly into heaven, and saw the glory of God, and Jesus standing on the right hand of God, and said, "Behold, I see the heavens opened, and the Son of man standing on the right hand of God." Then they cried out with a loud voice, and stopped their ears, and ran upon him with one accord, and cast him out of the city, and stoned him: and the witnesses laid down their clothes at a young man's feet, whose name was Saul. And they stoned Stephen, calling upon God, and saying, "Lord Jesus, receive my spirit." And he kneeled down, and cried with a loud voice, "Lord, lay not this sin to their charge." And when he had said this, he fell asleep.

And Saul was consenting unto his death. And at that time there was a great persecution against the church which was at Jerusalem; and they were all scattered abroad throughout the regions of Judaea and Samaria, except the apostles. And devout men carried Stephen to his burial, and made great lamentation over him. As for Saul, he made havoc of the church, entering into every house, and haling men and women committed them to prison.

• • •

And Saul, yet breathing out threatenings and slaughter against the disciples of the Lord, went unto the high priest, and desired of him letters to Damascus to the synagogues, that if he found any of this way, whether they were men or women, he might bring them bound into Jerusalem. And as he journeyed, he came near Damascus: and suddenly there shined round about him a light from heaven. And he fell to the earth, and heard a voice saying unto him, "Saul, Saul, why persecutest thou me?" And he said, "Who art thou, Lord?" And the Lord said, "I am Jesus whom thou persecutest: it is hard for thee to kick against the pricks." And he trembling and astonished said, "Lord, what wilt thou have me to do?" And the Lord said unto him, "Arise, and go into the city, and it shall be told thee what thou must do." And the men which journeyed with him stood speechless, hearing a voice, but seeing no man. And Saul arose from the earth; and when his eyes were opened he saw no man: but they led him by the hand, and brought him into Damascus. And he was three days without sight, and neither did eat nor drink.

And there was a certain disciple at Damascus, named Ananias; and to him said the Lord in a vision, "Ananias." And he said, "Behold, I am here, Lord." And the Lord said unto him, "Arise, and go into the street which is called Straight, and enquire in the house of Judas for one called Saul, of Tarsus: for, behold, he prayeth, and hath seen in a vision, a man named Ananias coming in, and putting his hand on him, that he might receive his sight." Then Ananias answered, "Lord, I have heard by many of this man, how much evil he hath done to thy saints at Jerusalem: And here he hath authority from the chief priests to bind all that call on thy name." But the Lord said unto him, "Go thy way: for he is a chosen vessel unto me, to bear my name before the Gentiles, and kings, and the children of Israel: For I will shew him how great things he must suffer for my name's sake." And Ananias went his way and entered into the house; and putting his hands on him said, "Brother Saul, the Lord, even Jesus, that appeared unto thee in the way as thou camest, hath sent me, that thou mightest receive thy sight, and be filled with the Holy Ghost." And immediately there fell from his eyes as it had been scales: and he received sight forthwith, and arose, and was baptized. And when he had received meat, he was strengthened.

Then was Saul certain days with the disciples which were at Damascus. And straightway he preached Christ in the synagogues, that he is the Son of God. But all that heard him were amazed, and said; "Is not this he that destroyed them which called on this name in Jerusalem, and came hither for that intent, that he might bring them bound unto the chief priests?" But Saul increased the more in strength, and confounded the Jews which dwelt at Damascus, proving that this is very Christ.

• • •

There was a certain man in Caesarea called Cornelius, a centurion of the band called the Italian band. A devout man, and one that feared God with all his house, which gave much alms to the people, and prayed to God always. He saw in a vision evidently about the ninth hour of the day an angel of God coming in to him, and saying unto him, "Cornelius." And when he looked on him, he was afraid, and said, "What is it, Lord?" And he said unto him, "Thy prayers and thine alms are come up for a memorial before God. And now send men to Joppa, and call for one Simon, whose surname is Peter: He lodgeth with one Simon a tanner, whose house is by the sea side: he shall tell thee what thou oughtest to do." And when the angel which spake unto Cornelius was departed, he called two of his household servants, and a devout soldier of them that waited on him continually; and when he had declared all these things unto them, he sent them to Joppa.

On the morrow, as they went on their journey, and drew nigh into the city, Peter went up upon the housetop to pray about the sixth hour. And he became very hungry, and would have eaten: but while they made ready, he fell into a trance, and saw heaven opened, and a certain vessel descending unto him, as it had been a great sheet knit at the four corners, and let down to the earth: wherein were all manner of four-footed beasts of the earth, and wild beasts, and creeping things, and fowls of the air. And there came a voice to him, "Rise, Peter; kill, and eat." But Peter said, "Not so, Lord; for I have never eaten any thing that is common or unclean." And the voice spake unto him again the second time, "What God hath cleansed, that call not thou common." This was done thrice: and the vessel was received up again into heaven. Now while Peter doubted in himself what this vision which he had seen should mean, behold, the men which were sent from Cornelius had made enquiry for Simon's house, and stood before the gate, and called, and asked whether Simon,

which was surnamed Peter, were lodged there.

While Peter thought on the vision, the Spirit said unto him, "Behold, three men seek thee. Arise therefore, and get thee down, and go with them, doubting nothing: for I have sent them." Then Peter went down to the men which were sent unto him from Cornelius; and said, "Behold, I am he whom ye seek: what is the cause wherefore ye are come?" And they said, "Cornelius the centurion, a just man, and one that feareth God, and of good report among all the nation of the Jews, was warned from God by an holy angel to send for thee into his house, and to hear words of thee." Then called he them in, and lodged them. And on the morrow Peter went away with them, and certain brethren from Joppa accompanied him. And the morrow after they entered into Caesarea. And Cornelius waited for them, and had called together his kinsmen and near friends. And as Peter was coming in, Cornelius met him, and fell down at his feet, and worshipped him. But Peter took him up, saying, "Stand up; I myself also am a man." And as he talked with him, he went in, and found many that were come together. And he said unto them, "Ye know how that it is an unlawful thing for a man that is a Jew to keep company, or come unto one of another nation; but God hath shewed me that I should not call any man common or unclean. Therefore came I unto you without gainsaying, as soon as I was sent for: I ask therefore for what intent ye have sent for me? And Cornelius said, "Four days ago I was fasting until this hour; and at the ninth hour I prayed in my house, and, behold, a man stood before me in bright clothing. And said, 'Cornelius, thy prayer is heard, and thine alms are had in remembrance in the sight of God. Send therefore to Joppa, and call hither Simon, whose surname is Peter; he is lodged in the house of one Simon a tanner by the sea side: who, when he cometh, shall speak unto thee.' Immediately therefore I sent to thee; and thou hast well done that thou art come. Now therefore are we all here present before God, to hear all things that are commanded thee of God.''

Then Peter opened his mouth, and said, "Of a truth I perceive that God is no respecter of persons: But in every nation he that feareth him, and worketh righteousness, is accepted with him. The word which God sent unto the children of Israel, preaching peace by Jesus Christ (He is Lord of all:) The word, I say, ye know, which was published throughout all Judaea, and began from Galilee, after the baptism which John preached; how God anointed Jesus of Nazareth with the Holy Ghost and with power: who went about doing good, and healing all that were oppressed of the devil; for God was with him. And we are wit-

nesses of all things which he did both in the land of the Jews, and in Jerusalem; whom they slew and hanged on a tree: Him God raised up the third day, and shewed him openly; not to all the people, but unto witnesses chosen before of God, even to us, who did eat and drink with him after he rose from the dead. And he commanded us to preach unto the people, and to testify that it is he which was ordained of God to be the Judge of quick and dead. To him give all the prophets witness, that through his name whosoever believeth in him shall receive remission of sins.''

While Peter yet spake these words, the Holy Ghost fell on all them which heard the word. And they of the circumcision which believed were astonished, as many as came with Peter, because that on the Gentiles also was poured out the gift of the Holy Ghost. For they heard them speak with tongues, and magnify God. Then answered Peter, "Can any man forbid water, that these should not be baptized, which have received the Holy Ghost as well as we?'' And he commanded them to be baptized in the name of the Lord.

The Epistle of Paul the Apostle to the Romans

● ● ●

As it is written, There is none righteous, no, not one: There is none that understandeth, there is none that seeketh after God. They are all gone out of the way, they are together be-

come unprofitable; there is none that doeth good, no, not one. Their throat is an open sepulchre; with their tongues they have used deceit; the poison of asps is under their lips: Whose mouth is full of cursing

Chapters 3:10–31; 5; 6; 9:8–21.

and bitterness: Their feet are swift to shed blood: Destruction and misery are in their ways: And the way of peace have they not known: There is no fear of God before their eyes.

Now we know that what things soever the law saith, it saith to them who are under the law: that every mouth may be stopped, and all the world may become guilty before God. Therefore by the deeds of the law there shall no flesh be justified in his sight: for by the law is the knowledge of sin. But now the righteousness of God without the law is manifested, being witnessed by the law and the prophets; even the righteousness of God which is by faith of Jesus Christ unto all and upon all them that believe: for there is no difference. For all have sinned, and come short of the glory of God; being justified freely by his grace through the redemption that is in Christ Jesus: Whom God hath set forth to be a propitiation through faith in his blood, to declare his righteousness for the remission of sins that are past, through the forbearance of God; to declare, I say, at this time his righteousness: that he might be just, and the justifier of him which believeth in Jesus. Where is boasting then? It is excluded. By what law? or works? Nay: but by the law of faith. Therefore we conclude that a man is justified by faith without the deeds of the law. Is he the God of the Jews only? Is he not also of the Gentiles? Yes, of the Gentiles also: Seeing it is one God, which shall justify the circumcision by faith, and uncircumcision through faith. Do we then make void the law through faith? God forbid: yea, we establish the law.

• • •

Therefore being justified by faith, we have peace with God through our Lord Jesus Christ: By whom also we have access by faith into this grace wherein we stand, and rejoice in hope of the glory of God. And not only so, but we glory in tribulations also: knowing that tribulation worketh patience; and patience, experience; and experience, hope: And hope maketh not ashamed; because the love of God is shed abroad in our hearts by the Holy Ghost which is given unto us. For when we were yet without strength, in due time Christ died for the ungodly. For scarcely for a righteous man will one die: yet peradventure for a good man some would even dare to die. But God commandeth his love toward us, in that, while we were yet sinners, Christ died for us. Much more then, being now justified by his blood, we shall be saved from wrath through him. For if, when we were enemies, we were reconciled to God by the death of his Son, much more, being reconciled, we shall be saved by his life. And not only so, but we also joy in God through our Lord Jesus Christ, by whom we have now received the atonement.

Wherefore, as by one man sin entered into the world, and death by sin; and so death passed upon all men, for that all have sinned. (For until the law sin was in the world: but sin is not imputed when there is no law. Nevertheless death reigned from Adam to Moses, even over them that had not sinned after the similitude of Adam's transgression, who is the figure of him that was to come. But not as the offence, so also is the free gift. For if through the offence of one many be dead, much more the grace of God, and the gift by grace, which is by one man, Jesus Christ, hath abounded unto many. And not as it was by one that sinned, so is the gift: for the judgment was by one to condemnation, but the free gift is of many offences unto justification. For if by one man's offence death reigned by one; much more they which receive abundance of grace and of the gift of righteousness shall reign in life by one, Jesus Christ. Therefore as by the offence of one judgment came upon all men to condemnation; even so, by the righteousness of one the free gift came upon all men unto justification of life. For as by one man's disobedience many were made sinners, so by the obedience of one shall many be made righteous. Moreover the law entered, that the offence might abound. But where sin abounded, grace did much more abound: That as sin hath reigned unto death, even so might grace reign through righteousness unto eternal life by Jesus Christ our Lord.

What shall we say then? Shall we continue in sin, that grace may abound? God forbid. How shall we, that are dead to sin, live any longer therein? Know ye not, that so many of us as were baptized into Jesus Christ were baptized into his death? Therefore we are buried with him by baptism into death: that like as Christ was raised up from the dead by the glory of the Father, even so we also should walk in newness of life. For if we have been planted together in the likeness of his death, we shall be also in the likeness of his resurrection: Knowing this, that our old man is crucified with him, that the body of sin might be destroyed, that henceforth we should not serve sin. For he that is dead is freed from sin.

Now if we be dead with Christ, we believe that we shall also live with him: Knowing that Christ being raised from the dead dieth no more; death hath no more dominion over him. For in that he died, he died unto sin once: but in that he liveth, he liveth unto God. Likewise reckon ye also yourselves to be dead indeed unto sin, but alive unto God through Jesus Christ our Lord.

Let not sin therefore reign in your mortal body, that ye should obey it in the lusts thereof. Neither yield ye your members as instruments of unrighteousness unto sin: But yield yourselves unto God, as those that are alive from the dead, and your members as instruments of righteousness unto God. For sin shall not have dominion over you: for ye are not under the law, but under grace. What then? Shall we sin, because we are not under the law, but under grace? God forbid. Know ye not, that to whom ye yield yourselves servants to obey, his servants ye are to whom ye obey; whether of sin unto death, or of obedience unto righteousness? But God be thanked, that ye were the servants of sin, but ye have obeyed from the heart that form of doctrine which was delivered you. Being then made free from sin, ye became the servants of righteousness.

I speak after the manner of men because of the infirmity of your flesh: for as ye have yielded your members servants to uncleanness and to iniquity unto iniquity; even so now yield your members servants to righteousness unto holiness. For when ye were the servant of sin, ye were free from righteousness. What fruit had ye then in those things whereof ye are now ashamed? For the end of those things is death. But now being made free from sin, and become servants of God, ye have your fruit unto holiness, and the end everlasing life. For the wages of sin is death; but the gift of God is eternal life through Jesus Christ our Lord.

• • •

They which are the children of the flesh, these are not the children of God: but the children of the promise are counted for the seed. For this is the word of promise. At this time will I come, and Sarah shall have a son. And not only this; but when Rebecca also had conceived by one, even by our father Isaac; (for the children being not yet born, neither having done any good or evil, that the purpose of God according to election might stand, not of works, but of him that calleth): it was said unto her, The elder shall serve the younger. As it is written, Jacob have I loved, but Esau have I hated. What shall we say then? Is there unrighteousness with God? God forbid. For he saith to Moses, I will have mercy on whom I will have mercy, and I will have compassion on whom I will have compassion. So then it is not of him that willeth, nor of him that runneth, but of God that sheweth mercy. For the scripture saith unto Pharaoh, Even for this same purpose have I raised thee up, that I might shew my power in thee, and that my name might be declared throughout all the earth. Therefore hath he mercy on whom he will have mercy, and whom he will he hardeneth. Thou wilt say then unto me, Why doth he yet find fault? For who hath resisted his will? Nay but, O man, who are thou that repliest against God? Shall the thing formed say to him that formed it, Why hast thou made me thus? Hath not the potter power over the clay, of the same lump to make one vessel unto honour, and another into dishonour?

Confucius

To many of us the words "Confucius say" are the preamble to a witticism, but to billions of Chinese people over thousands of years the sayings of the master have been words of highest wisdom, to be received with respect, if not with reverence. As a result Confucius has molded the Chinese mind and character in a manner and to an extent that has hardly been equaled by any other single figure in the history of a major civilization.

Although it is difficult to summarize briefly the teachings of Confucius, certain of their basic features are apparent. He was an optimistic moralist; believing people to be fundamentally good, he thought that with proper education and leadership they could realize their potential and achieve the form of life which he described as that of "the superior man." A social order composed of such individuals, including particularly its political leaders, would constitute the ideal society. Although he also believed that such a society is in harmony with the will of heaven, Confucius, unlike many early social philosophers, did not found his ideal society on principles derived from theology. On the contrary, he is well described as a secular humanist.

Many of the details of the moral and social ideals of Confucius appear in his *Analects*, or "Collection" (of sayings). This collection, which is rambling, ill-arranged, and repetitious, contains twenty "Books," in which, besides the master's sayings, there can be found descriptions of contemporary Chinese society, excursions into past history, stories about various political leaders, and so on.

Confucius (551–479 B.C.) was born of a poor family that apparently had ancestors of substance. Early in life he decided to become a scholar and teacher. He soon gathered a group of disciples about him and, because he believed that society could be reformed only if those who were properly educated held the reins of government, he sought public office and encouraged his students to do so as well. During his career he held a number of government posts, some of consequence. But practical politicians were suspicious of his lofty ideals and he was finally dismissed, to spend the twilight of his career wandering about China, but still teaching. Near the end of his life he wrote the following succinct autobiography: "At fifteen, I set my heart on learning. At thirty, I was firmly established. At forty, I had no more doubts. At fifty, I knew the will of Heaven. At sixty, I was ready to listen to it. At seventy, I could follow my heart's desire without transgressing what was right."

The moral teachings of the *Analects*, which Confucius did not actually originate but which he edited and molded to reflect his own ideals, were gathered together, mainly after his death, by his admirers. The selection that follows includes some of his central sayings. These have been rearranged to give them greater coherency, and the topic headings have been added.

Analects

The Master said, "Is it not pleasant to learn with a constant perseverance and application? Is it not delightful to have friends coming from distant quarters? Is he not a man of complete virtue who feels no discomposure though men may take no note of him?

• • •

FILIAL PIETY

The Master said, "A youth, when at home, should be filial, and, abroad, respectful to his elders. He should be earnest and truthful. He should overflow in love to all, and cultivate the friendship of the good. When he has time and opportunity, after the performance of these things, he should employ them in polite studies."

Mang I asked what filial piety was. The Master said, "It is not being disobedient." Soon after, as Fan Ch'ih was driving him, the Master told him, saying, "Mang'sun asked me what filial piety was, and I answered him,— "not being disobedient." Fan Ch'ih

said, "What did you mean?" The Master replied, "That parents, when alive, should be served according to propriety; that, when dead, they should be buried according to propriety; and that they should be sacrificed to according to propriety."

The Master said, "In serving his parents, a son may remonstrate with them, but gently; when he sees that they do not incline to follow his advice, he shows an increased degree of reverence, but does not abandon his purpose; and should they punish him, he does not allow himself to murmur."

EDUCATION

The Master said, "If the scholar be not grave, he will not call forth any veneration, and his learning will not be solid."

The Master said, "If a man keeps cherishing his old knowledge, so as continually to be acquiring new, he may be a teacher of others."

Trans. James Legge.

The Master said, "The accomplished scholar is not a utensil."

The Master said, "Learning without thought is labor lost; thought without learning is perilous."

The Master said, "Yu, shall I teach you what knowledge is? When you know a thing, to hold that you know it; and when you do not know a thing, to allow that you do not know it;—this is knowledge."

The Master said, "They who know the truth are not equal to those who love it, and they who love it are not equal to those who delight in it."

The Master said, "The scholar who cherishes the love of comfort is not fit to be deemed a scholar."

When the Master went to Wei, Zan Yu acted as driver of his carriage. The Master observed, "How numerous are the people!" Yu said, "Since they are so numerous, what more shall be done for them?" "Enrich them," was the reply. "And when they have been enriched, what more shall be done?" The Master said, "Teach them."

GOVERNMENT

The Master said, "To rule a country of a thousand chariots, there must be reverent attention to business, and sincerity; economy in expenditure, and love for men; and the employment of the people at the proper seasons."

The Master said, "He who exercises government by means of his virtue may be compared to the north polar star, which keeps its place and all the stars turn towards it."

The Master said, "If the people be led by laws, and uniformity sought to be given them by punishment, they will try to avoid the punishment, but have no sense of shame. If they be led by virtue, and uniformity sought to be given them by the rules of propriety, they will have the sense of shame, and moreover will become good."

Chi K'ang asked how to cause the people to reverence their ruler, to be faithful to him, and to go on to nerve themselves to virtue. The Master said, "Let him preside over them with gravity;—then they will reverence him. Let him be filial and kind to all;—then they will be faithful to him. Let him advance the good and teach the incompetent;—then they will eagerly seek to be virtuous."

Tsze-kung asked about government. The Master said, "The requisites of government are that there be sufficiency of food, sufficiency of military equipment, and the confidence of the people in their ruler." Tsze-kung said, "If it cannot be helped, and one of these must be dispensed with, which of the three should be foregone first?" "The military equipment," said the Master. Tsze-kung again asked, "If it cannot be helped, and one of the remaining two must be dispensed with, which of them should be foregone?" The Master answered, "Part with the food. From of old, death has been the lot of all men; but if the people have no faith in their rulers, there is no standing for the State."

Chi K'ang asked Confucius about government, saying, "What do you say to killing the unprincipled for the good of the principled?" Confucius replied, "Sir, in carrying on your government, why should you use killing at all? Let your evinced desires be for what is good, and the people will be good. The relation between superiors and inferiors is like that between the wind and the grass. The grass must bend, when the wind blows across it."

The Master said, "When a prince's personal conduct is correct, the government is effective without the issuing of orders. If his personal conduct is not correct, he may issue orders, but they will not be followed."

Tsze-chang asked Confucius, saying, "In what way should a person in authority act in order that he may conduct government properly?" The Master replied, "Let him honor the five excellent, and banish away the four bad, things;—then may he conduct government properly." Tsze-chang said, "What are meant by the five excellent things?" The Master said, "When the person in authority is beneficent without great expenditure; when he lays tasks on the people without their repining; when he pursues what he desires without being covetous; when he maintains a dignified ease without being proud; when he is majestic without being fierce." . . .

Tsze-chang then asked, "What are meant by the four bad things?" The Master said, "To put the people to death without having instructed them;—this is called cruelty. To require from them, suddenly, the full tale of work, without having given them warning;— this is called oppression. To issue orders as if without urgency, at first, and, when the time comes, to insist on them with severity;—this is called injury. And, generally, in the giving pay or rewards to men, to do it in a stingy way;—this is called acting the part of a mere official."

RELIGION

The Master said, . . . "He who offends against Heaven has none to whom he can pray."

Chi Lu asked about serving the spirits of the dead. The Master said, "While you are not able to serve men, how can you serve their spirits?" Chi Lu added, "I venture to ask about death." He was answered, "While you do not know life, how can you know about death?"

The Master said, "Alas! there is no one that knows me." Tsze-kung said, "What do you mean by thus saying— that no one knows you?" The Master replied, "I do not murmur against Heaven. I do not grumble against men. My studies lie low, and my penetration rises high. But there is Heaven;—that knows me!"

The Master said, "I would prefer not speaking." Tsze-kung said, "If you, Master, do not speak, what shall we, your disciples, have to record?" The Master said, "Does Heaven speak? The four seasons pursue their courses, and all things are continually being produced, but does Heaven say anything?"

The Master said, "Without recognizing the ordinances of Heaven, it is impossible to be a superior man."

VIRTUE AND GOODNESS

The Master said, "Fine words and an insinuating appearance are seldom associated with true virtue."

The Master said, "See what a man does. Mark his motives. Examine in what things he rests. How can a man conceal his character?

The Master said, "I do not know how a man without truthfulness is to get on. How can a large carriage be made to go without the cross-bar for yoking the oxen to, or a small carriage without the arrangement for yoking the horses?"

The Master said, . . . "To see what

is right and not to do it is want of courage."

The Master said, "If the will be set on virtue, there will be no practice of wickedness."

The Master said, "Riches and honors are what men desire. If virtue cannot be obtained in the proper way, they should not be held. Poverty and meanness are what men dislike. If virtue cannot be obtained in the proper way, they should be avoided."

The Master said, "I have not seen a person who loved virtue, or one who hated what was not virtuous. He who loved virtue, would esteem nothing above it. He who hated what is not virtuous, would practice virtue in such a way that he would not allow anything that is not virtuous to approach his person. Is any one able for one day to apply his strength to virtue? I have not seen the case in which his strength would be insufficient."

The Master said, "A man should say, I am not concerned that I have no place, I am concerned how I may fit myself for one. I am not concerned that I am not known, I seek to be worthy to be known."

The Master said, "When we see men of worth, we should think of equalling them; when we see men of a contrary character, we should turn inwards and examine ourselves."

The Master said, "Virtue is not left to stand alone. He who practices it will have neighbors."

The Master said, "Let the will be set on the path of duty. Let every attainment in what is good be firmly grasped. Let perfect virtue be accorded with. Let relaxation and enjoyment be found in the polite arts."

The Master said, "With coarse rice to eat, with water to drink, and my bended arm for a pillow;—I have still joy in the midst of these things. Riches and honors acquired by unrighteousness are to me as a floating cloud."

The Master said, "Is virtue a thing remote? I wish to be virtuous, and lo! virtue is at hand."

The Master said, "Respectfulness, without the rules of propriety, becomes laborious bustle; carefulness, without the rules of propriety, becomes timidity; boldness, without the rules of propriety, becomes insubordination; straightforwardness, without the rules of propriety, becomes rudeness."

The Master said, "Can men refuse to assent to the words of strict admonition? But it is reforming the conduct because of them which is valuable. Can men refuse to be pleased with words of gentle advice? But it is unfolding their aim which is valuable. If a man be pleased with these words, but does not unfold their aim, and assents to those, but does not reform his conduct, I can really do nothing with him."

The Master said, "Hold faithfulness and sincerity as first principles. Have no friends not equal to yourself. When you have faults, do not fear to abandon them."

The Master said, "The commander of the forces of a large State may be carried off, but the will of even a common man cannot be taken from him."

The Master said, "The wise are free from perplexities; the virtuous from anxiety; and the bold from fear."

The Master said, "To go beyond is as wrong as to fall short."

Chung-kung asked about perfect virtue. The Master said, "It is, when you go abroad, to behave to every one as if you were receiving a great guest; to employ the people as if you were assisting at a great sacrifice; not to do to others as you would not wish done to yourself; to have no murmuring against you in the country, and none in the family."

Fan Ch'ih asked about benevolence. The Master said, "It is to love all men." He asked about knowledge. The Master said, "It is to know all men."

Fan Ch'ih asked about perfect virtue. The Master said, "It is, in retirement, to be sedately grave; in the management of business, to be reverently attentive; in intercourse with others, to be strictly sincere. Though a man go among rude, uncultivated tribes, these qualities may not be neglected."

Tsze-kung asked, saying, "What do you say of a man who is loved by all the people of his neighborhood?" The Master replied, "We may not for that accord our approval of him." "And what do you say of him who is hated by all the people of his neighborhood?" The Master said, "We may not for that conclude that he is bad. It is better than either of these cases that the good in the neighborhood love him, and the bad hate him."

The Master said, "He who speaks without modesty will find it difficult to make his words good."

Some one said, "What do you say concerning the principle that injury should be recompensed with kindness?" The Master said, "With what then will you recompense kindness? Recompense injury with justice, and recompense kindness with kindness."

Tsze-kung asked, saying, "Is there one word which may serve as a rule of practice for all one's life?" The Master said, "Is not RECIPROCITY such a word? What you do not want done to yourself, do not do to others."

The Master said, "Virtue is more to man than either water or fire. I have seen men die from treading on water and fire, but I have never seen a man die from treading the course of virtue."

Confucius said, "There are three friendships which are advantageous, and three which are injurious. Friendship with the upright; friendship with the sincere; and friendship with the man of much observation;—these are advantageous. Friendship with the man of specious airs; friendship with the insinuatingly soft; and friendship with the glib-tongued;—these are injurious."

Confucius said, "There are three things men find enjoyment in which are advantageous, and three things they find enjoyment in which are injurious. To find enjoyment in the discriminating study of ceremonies and music; to find enjoyment in speaking of the goodness of others; to find enjoyment in having many worthy friends;—these are advantageous. To find enjoyment in extravagant pleasures; to find enjoyment in idleness and sauntering; to find enjoyment in the pleasures of feasting;—these are injurious."

Tsze-chang asked Confucius about perfect virtue. Confucius said, "To be able to practice five things everywhere under Heaven constitutes perfect virtue." He begged to ask what they were, and was told, "Gravity, generosity of soul, sincerity, earnestness, and kindness. If you are grave, you will not be treated with disrespect. If you are generous, you will win all. If you are sincere, people will repose trust in you. If you are earnest, you will accomplish much. If you are kind, this will enable you to employ the services of others.''

THE SUPERIOR MAN

The Master said, ''The superior man, in the world, does not set his mind either for anything, or against anything; what is right he will follow.''

The Master said, ''The superior man thinks of virtue; the small man thinks of comfort. The superior man thinks of the sanctions of law; the small man thinks of favors which he may receive.''

The Master said, ''The mind of the superior man is conversant with righteousness; the mind of the mean man is conversant with gain.''

The Master said, ''The superior man is modest in his speech, but exceeds in his actions.''

The Master said, ''The superior man in everything considers righteousness to be essential. He performs it according to the rules of propriety. He brings it forth in humility. He completes it with sincerity. This is indeed a superior man.

The Master said, ''The superior man is distressed by his want of ability. He is not distressed by men's not knowing him.''

The Master said, ''The superior man dislikes the thought of his name not being mentioned after his death.''

The Master said, ''What the superior man seeks, is in himself. What the mean man seeks, is in others.''

The Master said, ''The superior man is dignified, and does not wrangle. He is sociable, but not a partisan.''

The Master said, ''The superior man does not promote a man simply on account of his words, nor does he put aside good words because of the man.''

Confucius said, ''There are three things which the superior man guards against. In youth, when the physical powers are not yet settled, he guards against lust. When he is strong, and the physical powers are full of vigor, he guards against quarrelsomeness. When he is old, and the animal powers are decayed, he guards against covetousness.''

Confucius said, ''There are three things of which the superior man stands in awe. He stands in awe of the ordinances of Heaven. He stands in awe of great men. He stands in awe of the words of sages. The mean man does not know the ordinances of Heaven, and consequently does not stand in awe of them. He is disrespectful of great men. He makes sport of the words of sages.''

Confucius said, ''The superior man has nine things which are subjects with him of thoughtful consideration. In regard to the use of his eyes, he is anxious to see clearly. In regard to the use of his ears, he is anxious to hear distinctly. In regard to his countenance, he is anxious that it should be benign. In regard to his demeanor, he is anxious that it should be respectful. In regard to his speech, he is anxious that it should be sincere. In regard to his doing of business, he is anxious that it should be reverently careful. In regard to what he doubts about, he is anxious to question others. When he is angry, he thinks of the difficulties his anger may involve him in. When he sees gain to be got, he thinks of righteousness.''

Taoism

Taoism developed in China concurrently with Confucianism, indeed as a rival to it. According to tradition, Lao-Tzu, the originator of Taoism, and Confucius actually once met. Taoism gave the Chinese people what Confucianism did not—a religion. As a result it has through the centuries always had a strong appeal to the great masses.

But the religion of Taoism, at least as it appears in the classic *Tao Te Ching* ("The Book of the Way and Its Power"), is different from most other religions, being almost devoid of a theology. Its central concept is the Tao but this is not a god, or indeed any being at all. The Tao (or the Way) is beyond all being, that from which heaven and earth have sprung. What exactly it is cannot really be said because to put a description of it into words would be to lose it. Yet the Tao can be known, in the sense that the sage can respond to it in such a way that he identifies himself with it. Essentially, thus, Taoism is a form of mysticism. Rather than being intellectual, it is emotional; rather than being articulated, it is simply felt.

When one translates the mystery of the Tao into a guide for life, the central precept becomes: Maintain yourself in harmony with nature. Since nature is an expression of the Tao the sage will conform his actions to it, accepting whatever comes as it comes and never trying to change things. Thus, in practice Taoism engenders quietism. Also, since the attempt to understand the world is ultimately self-defeating, Taoism deprecates learning in favor of ignorance. Finally, any activities of officials aimed at regulating the lives of the people are necessarily counterproductive; the least government is the best government.

Classical Taoism, which thrived on paradox, might thus be described as an otherwordly religion whose sole emphasis was on this world. Through its long history, however, it underwent many changes. In particular it acquired a theology, gathering together under its aegis a whole host of deities from early Chinese mythology. Also, its sages, in later centuries, turned increasingly to the practice of magic, one of their perennial occupations being the attempt to transmute base metals into gold.

According to tradition, the *Tao Te Ching* was written by Lao-Tzu, who lived in the sixth century B.C. But this attribution is questionable; in fact it can be questioned whether Lao-Tzu himself ever lived, or is only a figure of legend. In any case, most scholars have concluded that the *Tao Te Ching* was compiled by several authors and that, although it contains elements from a much older tradition, the form in which we now have it dates from some time after the reputed lifetime of Lao-Tzu.

Tao Te Ching

BOOK ONE

The Tao that can be spoken of is not the
    eternal Tao;
The Name that can be named is not the
    eternal Name.
The Nameless [non-being] is the origin
    of heaven and earth;
The Namable [being] is the mother of
    all things.

Therefore constantly without desire,
    There is the recognition of subtlety;
But constantly with desire,
    Only the realization of potentiality.
The two come from the same source,
    Having different names.
Both are called mysteries,
More mystical than the most mystical,
The gate of all subtleties.
When all in the world recognize beauty
    as beauty,
    it is ugliness.
When they recognize good as good,
    it is not good.

Therefore, being and non-being beget
    each other,
    hard and easy complement each other,
    long and short shape each other,
    high and low rely on each other,
    sound and voice harmonize with each
    other,
    front and back follow each other.

Therefore, the Sage administers without
    action
    and instructs without words.
He lets all things rise without dominating
    them,
    produces without attempting to
        possess,
    acts without asserting,
    achieves without taking credit.

And because he does not take credit,
    it will never leave him.
Exalt not the worthy,
    so that the people will not fight.
Prize not the rare treasure,
    so that they will not steal.
Exhibit not the desirable,
    so that their hearts will not be
        distracted.

Therefore in governing, the Sage
    empties the people's hearts and fills
        their stomachs,
    weakens their will and strengthens
        their bones.
He always keeps them void of knowledge
    and desire,
    so that those who know will not dare
        to act.
Acting through inaction, he leaves noth-
    ing ungoverned.
Tao is empty, used yet never filled.
    It is deep, like the forefather of all
        things.

Lin, Paul J., *A Translation of Lao Tzu's* Tao Te Ching *and Wang Pu's* Commentary (Ann Arbor: Center for Chinese Studies, 1977). Courtesy of Center for Chinese Studies, the University of Michigan.

It dulls sharpness,
   and sorts tangles,
Blends with the light,
   becoming one with the dust.
So serene, as if it hardly existed.
I do not know whose son it is.
It seems to have preceded God.
The man of supreme goodness resembles
   water.
Water benefits all things
   Without competing with them,
Staying in places that men despise;
Therefore, it is very close to Tao.

Dwelling in good places,
Having a heart that loves the profound,
Allying with benevolence,
Inviting trust with words,
Being righteous in governing,
Managing all things well,
Moving at the right time—
Just because he does not compete,
The man of supreme goodness frees
   himself of blame.
Thirty spokes converge in a nave;
   just because of its nothingness [void]
   the usefulness of the cart exists.
Molded clay forms a vessel;
   just because of its nothingness
     [hollowness]
   the usefulness of the utensil exists.
Doors and windows are cut into a house;
   just because of their nothingness
     [emptiness]
   the usefulness of the house exists.
Therefore, profit from that which exists
   and utilize that which is absent.
Looked at, it cannot be seen;
   it is called colorless.
Listened to, it cannot be heard;
   it is called soundless.
Grasped, it cannot be obtained;
   it is called formless.

These three cannot be investigated further,
   so they merge together to make one.
The upper part is not bright;
The lower part is not dark.
So subtle, it cannot be named,
But returns to nothingness.
This is called the shape without shape,
   the image without image.

This is called indistinct:
   confronting it, one cannot see the
     head;
   following it, one cannot see the back.
Grasp the Ancient Tao to manage
   present existence.
Thus we may know the beginning of the
   Ancient.
This is called the record of Tao.
Attain the ultimate emptiness;
   Maintain the absolute tranquility.
All things rise together.
And I observe their return . . .
The multitude of all things return each
   to their origin.
To return to the origin means repose;
It means return to their destiny.
To return to their destiny means
   eternity;
To know eternity means enlightenment.
Not knowing eternity is to do evil things
   blindly.

To know eternity means having capacity.
   Capacity leads to justice.
   Justice leads to kingship.
   Kingship leads to Heaven.
   Heaven leads to Tao.
   Tao is everlasting.
Thus the entire life will be without danger.
Banish sagacity; forsake wisdom.
The people will benefit a hundredfold.
Banish human-heartedness; forsake
   righteousness.
The people will recover filial piety and
   paternal affection.
Banish craftiness; forsake profit.
Thieves and robbers will no longer exist.
Those three are superficial and
   inadequate.
Hence the people need something to
   abide by:
   Discern plainness.
   Embrace simplicity.
   Reduce selfishness.
   Restrain desires.
Abandon learning; then one has no
   sorrow.
Between "yes" and "no," what is the
   difference?
Between good and evil, what is the
   difference?

If I should fear what the people fear,
Then where is the end of my fear?
Lustily the people seem to be enjoying a
feast
Or ascending a tower in the springtime.
I alone am unmoved, showing no
sentiment,
Like a baby who does not yet know how
to smile.
So weary, I seem not to know where to
return.
While the multitudes have plenty,
I alone seem to be left out.
My heart is like a fool's.
How chaotic! Chaotic!
While the common people are so bright,
I alone am so dull!
While the common people know how to
differentiate,
I alone cannot see the difference.
Boundless as the sea,
Aimless as the breeze,
I seem to have no stop.
All the people have their purpose,
But I alone am stubborn and despicable.
I alone differ from the others
And value getting nourishment from the
Mother.
The feature of great virtue
is to follow only Tao.
Tao is something elusive and vague!
Though vague and elusive, in it is the
image.
Though elusive and vague, in it is the
substance.
Obscure and dim, in it is the spirit.
The spirit is truly genuine; in it is
credibility.

From ancient times until now,
Its name has never disappeared.
By this the beginning of all things is
known.
How can I know the beginning of all
things?
By this.
To yield is to have the whole.
To be crooked is to be straightened.
To be hollow is to be filled.
To be worn out is to be renewed.
To have a little is to get more.
To have a lot is to be confused.

Therefore the Sage sets an example for
the world
By embracing the One.
By not insisting on his view, he may
become enlightened.
By not being self-righteous, he may
become illustrious.
By not boasting, he may receive credit.
By not being arrogant, he may last long.
And just because he does not compete,
the entire world cannot compete with
him.
The Ancients say:
"to yield is to have the whole."
Are these merely words?
Truly the whole will return to him.
To spare words is to be natural.
Therefore a whirlwind does not last all
morning,
And a sudden shower does not last all
day.
Who causes this?
Heaven and earth.
If even Heaven and earth cannot last
long,
What can man do?
Therefore one dealing with Tao will
resemble Tao.
Dealing with virtue, one will resemble
virtue.
Dealing with loss, one will resemble
loss.
If one resembles Tao, Tao is pleased to
accept him.
If one resembles virtue, virtue is pleased
to accept him.
If one resembles loss, loss is also pleased
to accept him.

By not having enough credibility,
One will not be trusted [by others].
Those who rise on tiptoe cannot stand.
Those who stride cannot walk.

Those who hold to their views
cannot be enlightened.
Those who are self-righteous
cannot shine.
Those who boast
cannot receive credit.
Those who are arrogant
cannot last long.

In the light of Tao, they are like left-over
  food
  and burdensome wens,
Even despised by all creatures.
So those with Tao do not want to stay
  with them.
There is a thing formed in chaos
Existing before Heaven and Earth.
Silent and solitary, it stands alone,
  unchanging.
It goes around without peril.
It may be the Mother of the world.
Not knowing its name, I can only style it
  Tao.
With reluctance, I would call it Great.
Great means out-going.
Out-going means far-reaching.
Far-reaching means returning.

Therefore, Tao is great.
  Heaven is great.
  Earth is great.
  The king is great.
In the universe, there are four great
  things,
  and the king is one of them.
  Man abides by earth,
  Earth abides by heaven,
  Heaven abides by Tao,
  Tao abides by nature.
Fine weapons are the tools of evil;
All things are likely to hate them.
So those with Tao do not want to deal
  with them.
The gentleman who stays at home values
  the left;
In war, he values the right.
Weapons are the tools of evil,
  not the tools of the gentleman.
When he uses them unavoidably, he is
  most calm and detached
And does not glorify his victory.

To glorify means to relish the murder of
  people,
Relishing the murder of people,
  One cannot exercise his will in the
  world.
Happy occasions prefer the left.
Sorrowful occasions prefer the right.
The lieutenant-general is placed on the
  left.

The general-in-chief is placed on the
  right.
This means observing this occasion with
  funeral rites.
Having killed many people, one should
  lament
  with sorrow and grief.
Victory in war must be observed with
  funeral rites.
The great Tao overflows,
  able to move left and right.
All things rely on it for life,
But it does not dominate them.
Completing its task without possession,
Clothing and feeding all things,
Without wanting to be their master.
Always void of desire,
  It can be called Small.
All things return to it
Without its being their master;
  It can be called Great.
Just because the Sage would never
  regard himself as great,
He is able to attain his own greatness.
Tao is always inactive.
But it leaves nothing undone.
If dukes and kings can keep it,
Then all things will be naturally
  transformed.
If transformation raises desires,
I would suppress them with nameless
  simplicity.
Nameless simplicity means being without
  desires.
Being without desires and with
  tranquility,
The world will keep peace by itself.
Those of ancient times obtained the
  One:
  Heaven obtained the One for its
    clarity;
  Earth obtained the One for its
    tranquility;
  The Spirit obtained the One for its
    divinity;
  The Valley obtained the One for its
    repletion;
  All things obtained the One for their
    lives;
  Dukes and kings obtained the One for
    the rectitude of the world.
What causes these is the One.

Without clarity,
Heaven could not avoid disrupting.
Without tranquility,
Earth could not avoid explosion.
Without divinity,
The Spirit could not avoid dissolving.
Without repletion,
The Valley could not avoid dissipating.
Without life,
All things could not avoid perishing.
Without rectitude and dignity,
Dukes and kings could not avoid
falling.

Therefore, distinction has humility as its
root;
The high regards the low as its
foundation.
Therefore dukes and kings call themselves
Orphans, widowers, and starvers.
Does this not mean regarding humility
as a base?
Doesn't it?
He who is most praise-worthy
Does not need any praise.
He prefers to be neither rare as jade,
Nor as common as rocks.
Returning is Tao's motion.
Weakness is Tao's function.
All things in the world are produced by
being.
And being is produced by non-being.
The superior man, on hearing Tao,
Practices it diligently.
The average man, on hearing Tao,
Regards it both as existing and not
existing.
The inferior man, on hearing Tao,
Laughs aloud at it.
Without his laughter, it would not be
Tao.

Therefore the established word says:
The luminous Tao seems obscure.
The advancing Tao seems retreating.
The even Tao seems rough.
The highest virtue seems empty.
Great whiteness seems blackened.
Broad virtue seems insufficient.
Established virtue seems secret.
Pure substance seems fluid.
The great square has no corners.

The great vessel is late in completing.
The great voice sounds faint.
The great image has no shape.
Tao is concealed and has no name.
Yet only Tao is good in giving and
completing.
Tao begets One.
One begets Two.
Two begets Three.
Three begets all things.
All things carry the female and embrace
the male.
And by breathing together, they live in
harmony.

What the people hate is being orphaned,
widowed, and starved.
But kings and dukes call themselves
these names.
Therefore everything can be augmented
when diminished,
and diminished when augmented.
What the people teach, I teach too.
The violent and fierce cannot die a
natural death.
I will become the father of teaching.
The world's softest thing gallops to and fro
through the world's hardest thing.
Things without substance
can penetrate things without crevices.
Thus I know the benefit of inaction.
But teaching without words and benefit-
ting without action
are understood by few in the entire
world.
Without going out-of-doors,
One can know the whole world.
Without looking out of windows,
One can see the Tao of heaven.
The farther one goes, the less one knows.
Therefore, the Sage does not go and yet
knows,
Doesn't see and yet names,
Doesn't act and yet completes.
The pursuit of learning increases daily.
The pursuit of Tao decreases daily,
Decreasing more and more
Until it reaches the point of inaction.
Inaction: then nothing cannot be done
by it,
Therefore the capture of the world
should always be done by inactivity.

As for activity, it is insufficient to capture
   the world.
If only I could have a little knowledge,
I would walk in the Great Tao,
   Being afraid only of acting on it.
The Great Tao is very smooth,
But people prefer the by-paths;
The court is very well kept;
The fields are full of weeds;
And the granaries are extremely empty.
To wear embroidered clothes,
To carry sharp weapons,
To be satiated in food and drink,
And to have excessive treasures and
   goods—
This is called robbery and extravagance.
Really, this is not Tao.
The one who knows does not speak.
The one who speaks does not know.

Block the passage.
Close the door.
Dull the sharpness.
Loosen the tangles.
Blend with light.
Become one with the dust.

This is called mystical identity.
Hence one can be neither close to it,
   nor far from it;
One can neither benefit it,
   nor harm it;
One can neither value it,
   nor despise it.
Therefore, it is valued by the world.
Rule the state with rectitude.
Direct the army with trickery.
Capture the world through inactivity.
How can I know it shall be so?
By this:
   When the world is full of taboos and
      prohibitions,
      The people will become very poor.
   When the people possess many sharp
      weapons,
      The nation will become more
         chaotic.
   When the people possess much
      craftiness,
      Trickery will flourish.
   When law and order become more
      conspicuous,

There will be more robbers and
   thieves.
Therefore the Sage says:
   I do not act and the people reform
      themselves;
   I love serenity and the people rectify
      themselves;
   I employ inactivity and the people
      become prosperous themselves;
   I have no desires and the people
      become simple by themselves.
A large state is like the low land;
   It is the focus point of the world
And the female of the world.

The female always conquers the male by
   serenity.
In serenity, she puts herself low.

Therefore, the large state puts itself
   beneath the small state,
And thereby absorbs the small state.
The small state puts itself under the
   large state,
And thereby joins with the large state.

Therefore, one either puts himself
   beneath to absorb others,
Or puts himself under to join with others.

What the large state wants is no more
   than to feed the people.
What the small state wants is no more
   than to join and serve the people.
Both have their needs satisfied.

Thus the large ought to stay low.
The Ancients who were good in
   practicing Tao
Did not teach the people with
   intelligence
But kept them in ignorance.
The people are hard to govern when
   they know too much.
Therefore, one who rules the nation
   with knowledge
   robs the nation.
One who does not rule the nation with
   knowledge
   brings good fortune to the nation.
To know these two things
   means to know the standard.

To constantly know the standard is
    called mystical virtue.
Mystical virtue goes deep and far.
It returns with all things
    to reach great harmony.
He who knows that he does not know is
    the best.
He who does not know but pretends to
    know is sick.
He who realizes the sickness is
    sickness
    Doesn't have any sickness.
The Sage is without sickness
Because he realizes the sickness is
    sickness.
Therefore, he doesn't have any
    sickness.
The people are starving
Because the man on top devours too
    much tax money.
So they are starving.

The people are hard to govern
Because the man on top is too active in
    governing.
So they are hard to govern.

The people think little of death
Because the man on top strives for a rich
    life.
So they think little of death.

Therefore it is better to do nothing for
    one's life
    Than to value it.
In life, man is supple and tender.
In death, he becomes rigid and stark.
Myriad things such as grass and trees
    are supple and frail in life,
And shrivelled and dry in death.

Therefore, the rigid and stark are disci-
    ples of death,
While the supple and weak are disciples
    of life.

Therefore the army that uses strength
    cannot win.
The tree that stands firm will break.

The strong and large are subordinate;
The soft and weak are superior.

Perhaps the Tao of heaven resembles
    the drawing of a bow.
When it is high, lower it.
When low, raise it.
When excessive, diminish it.
When deficient, replenish it.

The Tao of heaven diminishes the
    excessive
    and replenishes the deficient.
The Tao of man is not so—while
    decreasing the deficient,
    it supplies the excessive.
Who can supply the world with
    overabundance?
Only the man with Tao.

Therefore the Sage acts without exalting
    his ability.
He achieves without dwelling upon it.
He does not want to display his
    superiority.
Nothing in the world is softer and
    weaker than water.
Yet, in attacking the hard and strong,
    nothing can surpass it.

Because nothing can exchange places
    with it,
    Use weakness to overcome strength.
    Use softness to overcome hardness.
None in the world do not know this.
But none can practice it.

Therefore the Sage says:
    To suffer dishonor for the state
        is to be the lord of the community;
    To bear the calamity of the state
        is to be the king of the world.

True words seem paradoxical.
The state may be small; its people may
    be few.
Let the people have tenfold and
    one-hundredfold of utensils,
But never make use of them.

Let the people weigh death heavily
    And have no desires to move far
        away.
Though there be boats and carriages,
    No one will ride in them.

Though there be armour and weapons,
  No one will exhibit them.

Let the people return to tying knots and
  using them.
  Relish their food,
  Appreciate their clothes,
  Secure in their homes,
  Happy with their customs.

The neighboring states will be so close
  that they can see each other,
  and hear the sounds of roosters and
  dogs.
But the people will grow old and die,
  Without having visited each other.
Sincere words are not kind;
  Kind words are not sincere.

One who is good will never argue;
  One who argues is not good.
One who knows does not know all;
  One who knows all does not know at
  all.

The Sage does not store things for
  himself.
The more one does for others,
  The more he has for himself.
The more one gives to others,
  The more he keeps for himself.

The Tao of heaven is to benefit others
  without hurting them.
The Tao of the Sage is to act without
  competing.

Hinduism

The *Bhagavad Gita* ("The Song of God"), the best-known work of Indian Hinduism, dates from about the same time as the Christian gospels, or perhaps a bit earlier. Although not considered by Hindus to be a direct revelation to humans from the gods, like the earlier *Vedas*, it is accepted nevertheless as being of divine origin. In it can be found statements of most Hindu religious beliefs; these are set in the context of a poetic story of a great battle being fought between warring noble factions. Among the many cults that fall within the broad expanse of Hinduism, the *Bhagavad Gita* represents in particular that of the hero-god Krishna, who appears as one of the central characters in the drama.

While accepting the main religious beliefs of the Hindu tradition, but decrying its excessive ritualism, the *Bhagavad Gita* makes some significant shifts in emphasis from earlier texts. It modifies the idea that, since the phenomenal world and the life we live are both unreal, the individual should divorce himself from mundane matters to seek union with the supreme Reality. While recogniz-

ing the ultimate goal of human life to be escape from endless rebirth through the achievement of Nirvana, it nevertheless maintains that one should participate actively in the affairs of this world, fulfilling the duties of one's station in life. But, in doing so one must strive for selfless action, or action for its own sake, without yearning for the results to which such action will lead. At the same time the *Bhagavad Gita* accepts two other paths to salvation than that of selfless action. One is the way of knowledge, or a recognition that Reality is one and spiritual rather than material. The other is the way of devotion, or belief in a personal God with whom one can have communion and, ultimately, union.

The background to the discussion of Hinduism in the *Bhagavad Gita* is worthy of note. The setting of the poem is sometime near the beginning of the first millennium B.C. Two armies are drawn up for a decisive battle. The commander of one, Prince Arjuna, takes a ride in his chariot before the battle begins, to survey the opposing hosts. To his dismay he sights many of his kinsmen in the enemy ranks, so, reluctant to wage war against them, he asks his chariot-driver, Krishna, what he ought to do. His driver, however, is no ordinary mortal but Lord Krishna, a god who has here taken on human form. He begins by telling Arjuna that he must fight and then explains why he must do so. Then, in answer to a series of further questions that Arjuna puts to him, he elaborates the basic principles of Hinduism.

Bhagavad Gita

ARJUNA: How can I, in the battle, shoot with shafts
On Bhishma, or on Drona—O thou Chief!—
Both worshipful, both honourable men?

Better to live on beggar's bread
  With those we love alive,
Than taste their blood in rich feasts spread
  And guiltily survive!
Ah! were it worse—who knows?—to be
  Victor or vanquished here,
When those confront us angrily
  Whose death leaves living drear?
In pity lost, by doubtings tossed,
  My thoughts—distracted—turn
To Thee, the Guide I reverence most,
  That I may counsel learn:
I know not what would heal the grief
  Burned into soul and sense,
If I were earth's unchallenged chief—
  A god—and these gone thence!

SANJAYA: So spake Arjuna to the Lord of Hearts,
And sighing, "I will not fight!" held silence then.
To whom, with tender smile,
While the Prince wept despairing 'twixt those hosts,
Krishna made answer in divinest verse:

KRISHNA: Thou grievest where no grief should be! thou speak'st
Words lacking wisdom! for the wise in heart
Mourn not for those that live, nor those that die.
Nor I, nor thou, nor any one of these,
Ever was not, nor ever will not be,
For ever and for ever afterwards.
All, that doth live, lives always! To man's frame
As there come infancy and youth and age,
So come there raising-up and layings-down
Of other and of other life-abodes,
Which the wise know, and fear not. This that irks—
Thy sense-life thrilling to the elements—
Bringing thee heat and cold, sorrows and joys,
'Tis brief and mutable! Bear with it, Prince!
As the wise bear. The soul which is not moved,
The soul that with a strong and constant calm
Takes sorrow and takes joy indifferently,
Lives in the life undying! That which is
Can never cease to be; that which is not
Will not exist. To see this truth of both
Is theirs who part essence from accident,

Trans. E. Arnold

Substance from shadow. Indestructible,
Learn thou! the Life is, spreading life
    through all;
It cannot anywhere, by any means,
Be anywise diminished, stayed, or
    changed.
But for these fleeting frames which it
    informs
With spirit deathless, endless, infinite,
They perish. Let them perish, Prince!
    and fight!

• • •

Specious, but wrongful deem
The speech of those ill-taught ones who
    extol
The letter of their Vedas, saying, "This
Is all we have, or need;" being weak at
    heart
With wants, seekers of Heaven: which
    comes—they say—
As "fruit of good deeds done;"
    promising men
Much profit in new births for works of
    faith;
In various rites abounding; following
    whereon
Large merit shall accrue towards wealth
    and power;
Albeit, who wealth and power do most
    desire
Least fixity of soul have such, least hold
On heavenly meditation. Much these
    teach,
From Veds, concerning the "three
    qualities;"
But thou, be free of the "three
    qualities,"
Free of the "pairs of opposites," and
    free
From that sad righteousness which
    calculates;
Self-ruled, Arjuna! simple, satisfied!
Look! like as when a tank pours water
    forth
To suit all needs, so do these Brahmans
    draw
Texts for all wants from tank of Holy
    Writ

But thou, want not! ask not! Find full
    reward
Of doing right in right! Let right deeds
    be
Thy motive, not the fruit which comes
    from them.

• • •

ARJUNA: What is his mark who hath that
    steadfast heart,
Confirmed in holy meditation? How
Know we his speech, Kesava? Sits he,
    moves he
Like other men?

KRISHNA: When one, O Pritha's Son!—
Abandoning desires which shake the
    mind—
Finds in his soul full comfort for his soul,
He hath attained the Yog—that man is
    such!
In sorrows not dejected, and in joys
Not overjoyed; dwelling outside the
    stress
Of passion, fear, and anger; fixed in
    calms
Of lofty contemplation;—such an one
Is Muni, is the Sage, the true Recluse!
He, who to none and nowhere
    overbound
By ties of flesh, takes evil things and
    good
Neither desponding nor exulting, such
Bears wisdom's plainest mark! He who
    shall draw,
As the wise tortoise draws its four feet
    safe
Under its shield, his five frail senses back
Under the spirit's buckler from the
    world
Which else assails them, such an one, my
    Prince!
Hath wisdom's mark! Things that solicit
    sense
Hold off from the self-governed; nay, it
    comes,
The appetites of him who lives beyond
Depart,—aroused no more. Yet may it
    chance,

O Son of Kunti! that a governed mind
Shall some time feel the sense-storms
  sweep, and wrest
Strong self-control by the roots. Let him
  regain
His kingdom! let him conquer this, and
  sit
On Me intent. That man alone is wise
Who keeps the mastery of himself! If one
Ponders on objects of the sense, there
  springs
Attraction; from attraction grows desire
Desire flames to fierce passion, passion
  breeds
Recklessness; then the memory—all
  betrayed—
Lets noble purpose go, and saps the
  mind,
Till purpose, mind, and man are all
  undone.
But, if one deals with objects of the sense
Not loving and not hating, making them
Serve his free soul, which rests serenely
  lord,
Lo! such a man comes to tranquillity;
And out of that tranquillity shall rise
The end and healing of his earthly pains,
Since the will governed sets the soul at
  peace.
The soul of the ungoverned is not his,
Nor hath he knowledge of himself;
  which lacked
How grows serenity? and, wanting that,
Whence shall he hope for happiness?
                  The mind
That gives itself to follow shows of sense
Seeth its helm of wisdom rent away,
And, like a ship in waves of whirlwind,
  drives
To wreck and death. Only with him,
  great Prince!
Whose senses are not swayed by things of
  sense—
Only with him who holds his mastery,
Shows wisdom perfect. What is midnight-
  gloom
To unenlightened souls shines wakeful
  day

To his clear gaze; what seems as wakeful
  day
Is known for night, thick night of
  ignorance,
To his true-seeing eyes. Such is the Saint!

And like the ocean, day by day receiving
  Floods from all lands, which never
    overflows;
Its boundary-line not leaping, and not
  leaving,
  Fed by the rivers, but unswelled by
    those;—

So is the perfect one! to his soul's ocean
  The world of sense pours streams of
    witchery;
They leave him as they find, without
  commotion,
  Taking their tribute, but remaining sea.

Yea! whoso, shaking off the yoke of
  flesh
Lives lord, not servant, of his lusts; set
  free
From pride, from passion, from the sin
  of "Self,"
Toucheth tranquillity! O Pritha's Son!
That is the state of Brahm! There rests
  no dread
When that last step is reached! Live
  where he will,
Die when he may, such passeth from all
  'plaining,
To blest Nirvana, with the Gods,
  attaining.
             ● ● ●

ARJUNA: Yet, Krishna! at the one time
  thou dost laud
Surcease of works, and, at another time,
Service through work. Of these twain
  plainly tell
Which is the better way?

KRISHNA: To cease from works
Is well, and to do works in holiness
Is well; and both conduct to bliss
  supreme;

But of these twain the better way is his
Who working piously refraineth not.

That is the true Renouncer, firm and
    fixed,
Who—seeking nought, rejecting nought
    —dwells proof
Against the "opposites."[1] O valiant
    Prince!
In doing, such breaks lightly from all
    deed:
'Tis the new scholar talks as they were
    two,
This Sankhya and this Yoga: wise men
    know
Who husbands one plucks golden fruit
    of both!
The region of high rest which Sankhyans
    reach
Yogins attain. Who sees these twain as
    one
Sees with clear eyes! Yet such
    abstraction, Chief!
Is hard to win without much holiness.
Whoso is fixed in holiness, self-ruled,
Pure-hearted, lord of senses and of self,
Lost in the common life of all which
    lives—
A "Yogayukt"—he is a Saint who wends
Straightway to Brahm. Such an one is
    not touched
By taint of deeds. "Nought of myself I
    do!"
Thus will he think—who holds the truth
    of truths—
In seeing, hearing, touching, smelling;
    when
He eats, or goes, or breathes; slumbers
    or talks,
Holds fast or loosens, opes his eyes or
    shuts;
Always assured "This is the sense-world
    plays
With senses." He that acts in thought of
    Brahm,

Detaching end from act, with act
    content,
The world of sense can no more stain his
    soul
Than waters mar th' enamelled lotus-
    leaf.
With life, with heart, with mind,—nay,
    with the help
Of all five senses—letting selfhood go—
Yogins toil ever towards their souls'
    release.
Such votaries, renouncing fruit of deeds,
Gain endless peace: the unvowed, the
    passion-bound,
Seeking a fruit from works, are fastened
    down.
The embodied sage, withdrawn within
    his soul,
At every act sits godlike in "the town
Which hath nine gateways,"[2] neither
    doing aught
Nor causing any deed. This world's Lord
    makes
Neither the work, nor passion for the
    work,
Nor lust for fruit of work; the man's own
    self
Pushes to these!

•   •   •

The world is overcome—aye! even here!
By such as fix their faith on Unity.
The sinless Brahma dwells in Unity,
And they in Brahma. Be not over-glad
Attaining joy, and be not over-sad
Encountering grief, but, stayed on
    Brahma, still
Constant let each abide! The sage whose
    soul
Holds off from outer contacts, in himself
Finds bliss; to Brahma joined by piety,
His spirit tastes eternal peace. The joys
Springing from sense-life are but
    quickening wombs
Which breed sure griefs: those joys begin
    and end!

---

[1]That is, "joy and sorrow, success and
failure, heat and cold," & c.

[2]*i.e.*, the body.

The wise mind takes no pleasure, Kunti's
    Son!
In such as those! But if a man shall learn,
Even while he lives and bears his body's
    chain,
To master lust and anger, he is blest!
He is the *Yukta*; he hath happiness,
Contentment, light, within: his life is
    merged
In Brahma's life; he doth Nirvana touch!
Thus go the Rishis unto rest, who dwell
With sins effaced, with doubts at end,
    with hearts
Governed and calm. Glad in all good
    they live,
Nigh to the peace of God; and all those
    live
Who pass their days exempt from greed
    and wrath,
Subduing self and senses, knowing the
    Soul!

The Saint who shuts outside his placid
    soul
All touch of sense, letting no contact
    through;
Whose quiet eyes gaze straight from
    fixëd brows,
Whose outward breath and inward
    breath are drawn
Equal and slow through nostrils still and
    close;
That one—with organs, heart, and mind
    constrained,
Bent on deliverance, having put away
Passion, and fear, and rage;—hath, even
    now,
Obtained deliverance, ever and ever
    freed.
Yea! for he knows Me Who am He that
    heeds
The sacrifice and worship, God revealed;
And He who heeds not, being Lord of
    Worlds,
Lover of all that lives, God unrevealed,
Wherein who will shall find surety and
    shield!

· · ·

Sequestered should he sit,
Steadfastly meditating, solitary,
His thoughts controlled, his passions laid
    away,
Quit of belongings. In a fair, still spot
Having his fixed abode,—not too much
    raised,
Nor yet too low,—let him abide, his
    goods
A cloth, a deerskin, and the Kusa-grass.
There, setting hard his mind upon The
    One,
Restraining heart and senses, silent,
    calm,
Let him accomplish Yoga, and achieve
Pureness of soul, holding immovable
Body and neck and head, his gaze
    absorbed
Upon his nose-end, rapt from all
    around,
Tranquil in spirit, free of fear, intent
Upon his Brahmacharya vow, devout,
Musing on Me, lost in the thought of Me.
That Yojin, so devoted, so controlled,
Comes to the peace beyond,—My peace,
    the peace
Of high Nirvana!
                    But for earthly needs
Religion is not his who too much fasts
Or too much feasts, nor his who sleeps
    away
An idle mind; nor his who wears to waste
His strength in vigils. Nay, Arjuna! call
That the true piety which most removes
Earth-aches and ills, where one is
    moderate
In eating and in resting, and in sport;
Measured in wish and act; sleeping
    betimes,
Waking betimes for duty.
                        When the man,
So living, centres on his soul the thought
Straitly restrained—untouched
    internally
By stress of sense—then is he *Yukta*. See!
Steadfast a lamp burns sheltered from
    the wind;
Such is the likeness of the Yogi's mind

Shut from sense-storms and burning
bright to Heaven.
When mind broods placid, soothed with
holy wont;
When Self contemplates self, and in
itself
Hath comfort; when it knows the
nameless joy
Beyond all scope of sense, revealed to
soul—
Only to soul! and, knowing, wavers not,
True to the farther Truth; when, holding
this,
It deems no other treasure comparable,
But, harboured there, cannot be stirred
or shook
By any gravest grief, call that state
"peace,"
That happy severance Yoga; call that man
The perfect Yogin!
                 Steadfastly the will
Must toil thereto, till efforts end in ease,
And thought has passed from thinking.
Shaking off
All longings bred by dreams of fame and
gain,
Shutting the doorways of the senses close
With watchful ward; so, step by step, it
comes
To gift of peace assured and heart
assuaged,
When the mind dwells self-wrapped, and
the soul broods
Cumberless. But, as often as the heart
Breaks—wild and wavering—from
control, so oft
Let him re-curb it, let him rein it back
To the soul's governance; for perfect
bliss
Grows only in the bosom tranquillised,
The spirit passionless, purged from
offence,
Vowed to the Infinite. He who thus vows
His soul to the Supreme Soul, quitting
sin,
Passes unhindered to the endless bliss
Of unity with Brahma.

            •   •   •

ARJUNA: And what road goeth he who,
having faith,
Fails, Krishna! in the striving; falling
back
From holiness, missing the perfect rule?
Is he not lost, straying from Brahma's
light,
Like the vain cloud, which floats 'twixt
earth and heaven
When lightning splits it, and it
vanisheth?
Fain would I hear thee answer me
herein,
Since, Krishna! none save thou can clear
the doubt.

KRISHNA: He is not lost, thou Son of
Pritha! No!
Nor earth, nor heaven is forfeit, even for
him,
Because no heart that holds one right
desire
Treadeth the road of loss! He who
should fail,
Desiring righteousness, cometh at death
Unto the Region of the Just; dwells there
Measureless years, and being born anew,
Beginneth life again in some fair home
Amid the mild and happy. It may chance
He doth descend into a Yogin house
On Virtue's breast; but that is rare! Such
birth
Is hard to be obtained on this earth,
Chief!
So hath he back again what heights of
heart
He did achieve, and so he strives anew
To perfectness, with better hope, dear
Prince!
For by the old desire he is drawn on
Unwittingly; and only to desire
The purity of Yoga is to pass
Beyond the *Sabdabrahm*, the spoken Ved.
But, being Yogi, striving strong and long,
Purged from transgressions, perfected by
births
Following on births, he plants his feet at
last

Upon the farther path. Such an one
  ranks
Above ascetics, higher than the wise,
Beyond achievers of vast deeds!

KRISHNA: Learn now, dear Prince! how, if
  thy soul be set
Ever on Me—still exercising Yog,
Still making Me thy Refuge—thou shalt
  come
Most surely unto perfect hold of Me.
I will declare to thee that utmost lore,
Whole and particular, which, when thou
  knowest,
Leaveth no more to know here in this
  world.

Of many thousand mortals, one,
  perchance,
Striveth for Truth; and of those few that
  strive—
Nay, and rise high—one only—here and
  there—
Knoweth Me, as I am, the very Truth.

Earth, water, flame, air, ether, life, and
  mind,
And individuality—those eight
Make up the showing of Me, Manifest.

These be my lower Nature; learn the
  higher,
Whereby, thou Valiant One! this
  Universe
Is, by its principle of life, produced;
Whereby the worlds of visible things are
  born
As from a *Yoni*. Know! I am that womb:
I make and I unmake this Universe:
Than me there is no other Master,
  Prince!
No other Maker! All these hang on me
As hangs a row of pearls upon its string.
I am the fresh taste of the water; I
The silver of the moon, the gold o' the
  sun,
The word of worship in the Veds, the
  thrill

That passeth in the ether, and the
  strength
Of man's shed seed. I am the good sweet
  smell
Of the moistened earth, I am the fire's
  red light,
The vital air moving in all which moves,
The holiness of hallowed souls, the root
Undying, whence hath sprung whatever
  is;
The wisdom of the wise, the intellect
Of the informed, the greatness of the
  great,
The splendour of the splendid. Kunti's
  Son!
These am I, free from passion and
  desire;
Yet am I right desire in all who yearn,
Chief of the Bharatas! for all those
  moods,
Soothfast, or passionate, or ignorant,
Which Nature frames, deduce from me;
  but all
Are merged in me—not I in them!

• • •

ARJUNA : Who is that BRAHMA? What that
  Soul of Souls,
The ADHYATMAN ? What, Thou Best of
  All!
Thy work, the KARMA? Tell me what it is
Thou namest ADHIBHUTA? What again
Means ADHIDAIVA? Yea, and how it comes
Thou canst be ADHIYAJNA in thy flesh?
Slayer of Madhu! Further, make me
  know
How good men find thee in the hour of
  death?

KRISHNA: I BRAHMA am! the One Eternal
  GOD,
And ADHYATMAN is My Being's name,
The Soul of Souls! What goeth forth
  from Me,
Causing all life to live, is KARMA called:
And, Manifested in divided forms,
I am the ADHIBHUTA, Lord of Lives;
And ADHIDAIVA, Lord of all the Gods,
Because I am PURUSHA, who begets.

And ADHIYAJNA, Lord of Sacrifice,
I—speaking with thee in this body
    here—
Am, thou embodied one! (for all the
    shrines
Flame unto Me!) And, at the hour of
    death,
He that hath meditated Me alone,
In putting off his flesh, comes forth to
    Me,
Enters into My Being—doubt thou not!
But, if he meditated otherwise
At hour of death, in putting off the flesh,
He goes to what he looked for, Kunti's
    Son!
Because the Soul is fashioned to its like.

Have Me, then, in thy heart always! and
    fight!
Thou too, when heart and mind are
fixed on Me,
Shalt surely come to Me!

● ● ●

By Me the whole vast Universe of things
Is spread abroad;—by Me, the
    Unmanifest!
In Me are all existences contained;
Not I in them!

            Yet they are not contained,
Those visible things! Receive and strive
    to embrace
The mystery majestical! My Being—
Creating all, sustaining all—still dwells
Outside of all!

            See! as the shoreless airs
Move in the measureless space, but are
    not space,
[And space were space without the
    moving airs];
So all things are in Me, but are not I.

At closing of each Kalpa, Indian Prince!
All things which be back to My Being
    come:
At the beginning of each Kalpa, all
Issue new-born from Me.

            By Energy
And help of Prakriti, my outer Self,
Again, and yet again, I make go forth
The realms of visible things—without
    their will—
All of them—by the power of Prakriti.

Yet these great makings, Prince! involve
    Me not,
Enchain Me not! I sit apart from them,
Other, and Higher, and Free; nowise
    attached!

Thus doth the stuff of worlds, moulded
    by Me,
Bring forth all that which is, moving or
    still,
Living or lifeless! Thus the worlds go on!

The minds untaught mistake Me, veiled
    in form;—
Naught see they of My secret Presence,
    nought
Of My hid Nature, ruling all which lives.
Vain hopes pursuing, vain deeds doing;
    fed
On vainest knowledge, senselessly they
    seek
An evil way, the way of brutes and fiends.
But My Mahatmas, those of noble soul
Who tread the path celestial, worship Me
With hearts unwandering,—knowing Me
    the Source,
Th' Eternal Source, of Life. Unendingly
They glorify Me; seek Me; keep their
    vows
Of reverence and love, with changeless
    faith
Adoring Me. Yea, and those too adore,
Who, offering sacrifice of wakened
    hearts,
Have sense of one pervading Spirit's
    stress,
One Force in every place, though
    manifold!
I am the Sacrifice! I am the Prayer!
I am the Funeral-Cake set for the dead!
I am the healing herb! I am the ghee,

The Mantra, and the flame, and that
which burns!
I am —of all this boundless Universe—
The Father, Mother, Ancestor, and
Guard!
The end of Learning! That which
purifies
In lustral water! I am OM! I am
Rig-Veda, Sama-Veda, Yajur-Ved;
The Way, the Fosterer, the Lord, the
Judge,
The Witness; the Abode, the Refuge-
House,
The Friend, the Fountain and the Sea of
Life
Which sends, and swallows up; Treasure
of Worlds
And Treasure-Chamber! Seed and Seed-
Sower,
Whence endless harvests spring! Sun's
heat is mine;
Heaven's rain is mine to grant or to
withhold;
Death am I, and Immortal Life I am,
Arjuna!

• • •

But to those blessed ones who worship
Me,
Turning not otherwhere, with minds set
fast,
I bring assurance of full bliss beyond.

Nay, and of hearts which follow other
gods
In simple faith, their prayers arise to me,
O Kunti's Son! though they pray
wrongfully;
For I am the Receiver and the Lord
Of every sacrifice, which these know
not
Rightfully; so they fall to earth again!
Who follow gods go to their gods; who
vow
Their souls to Pitris go to Pitris; minds
To evil Bhuts given o'er sink to the
Bhuts;
And whoso loveth Me cometh to Me.

• • •

KRISHNA: So be it! Kuru Prince! I will to
thee unfold
Some portions of My Majesty, whose
powers are manifold!
I am the Spirit seated deep in every
creature's heart;
From Me they come; by Me they live; at
My word they depart!
Vishnu of the Adityas I am, those Lords
of Light;
Maritchi of the Maruts, the Kings of
Storm and Blight;
By day I gleam, the golden Sun of
burning cloudless Noon;
By Night, amid the asterisms I glide, the
dappled Moon!
Of Vedas I am Sama-Ved, of gods in
Indra's Heaven
Vasava; of the faculties to living beings
given
The mind which apprehends and thinks;
of Rudras Sankara;
Of Yakshas and of Rakshasas, Vittesh;
and Pavaka
Of Vasus, and of mountain-peaks Meru;
Vrihas-pati
Know Me 'mid planetary Powers; 'mid
Warriors heavenly
Skanda; of all the water-floods the Sea
which drinketh each,
And Bhrigu of the holy Saints, and OM
of sacred speech;
Of prayers the prayer ye whisper; of hills
Him-ala's snow,
And Aswattha, the fig-tree, of all the
trees that grow;
Of the Devarshis, Narada; and
Chitrarath of them
That sing in Heaven, and Kapila of
Munis, and the gem
Of flying steeds, Uchehaisravas, from
Amrit-wave which burst;
Of elephants Airavata; of males the Best
and First;
Of weapons Heav'n's hot thunderbolt; of
cows white Kamadhuk,
From whose great milky udder-teats all
hearts' desires are strook;

Vasuki of the serpent-tribes, round
Mandara en-twined;
And thousand-fanged Ananta, on whose
broad coils reclined
Leans Vishnu; and of water-things
Varuna; Aryam
Of Pitris, and, of those that judge, Yama
the Judge I am;
Of Daityas dread Prahlada; of what
metes days and years,
Time's self I am; of woodland-beasts—
buffaloes, deers, and bears—
The lordly-painted tiger; of birds the vast
Garud,
The whirlwind 'mid the winds; 'mid
chiefs Rama with blood imbrued,
Makar 'mid fishes of the sea, and Ganges
'mid the streams;
Yea! First, and Last, and Centre of all
which is or seems
I am, Arjuna! Wisdom Supreme of what
is wise,
Words on the uttering lips I am, and
eyesight of the eyes,
And "A" of written characters, Dwandwa
of knitted speech,
And Endless Life, and boundless Love,
whose power sustaineth each;
And bitter Death which seizes all, and
joyous sudden Birth,
Which brings to light all beings that are
to be on earth;
And of the viewless virtues, Fame,
Fortune, Song am I,
And Memory, and Patience; and Craft,
and Constancy:
Of Vedic hymns the Vrihatsam, of
metres Gayatri,
Of months the Margasirsha, of all the
seasons three
The flower-wreathed Spring; in dicer's-
play the conquering Double-Eight;
The splendour of the splendid, and the
greatness of the great,
Victory I am, and Action! and the
goodness of the good,
And Vasudev of Vrishni's race, and of
this Pandu brood

Thyself!—Yea, my Arjuna! thyself; for
thou art Mine!
Of poets Usana, of saints Vyasa, sage
divine;
The policy of conquerors, the potency of
kings,
The great unbroken silence in learning's
secret things;
The lore of all the learned, the seed of
all which springs.
Living or lifeless, still or stirred, whatever
beings be,
None of them is in all the worlds, but it
exists by Me!
Nor tongue can tell, Arjuna! nor end of
telling come
Of these My boundless glories, whereof I
teach thee some;
For wheresoe'er is wondrous work, and
majesty, and might,
From Me hath all proceeded. Receive
thou this aright!
Yet how shouldst thou receive, O Prince!
the vastness of this word?
I, who am all, and made it all, abide its
separate Lord!

• • •

ARJUNA: Lord! of the men who serve
Thee—true in heart—
As God revealed; and of the men who
serve,
Worshipping Thee Unrevealed,
Unbodied, Far,
Which take the better way of faith and
life?

KRISHNA: Whoever serve Me—as I show
Myself—
Constantly true, in full devotion fixed,
Those hold I very holy. But who serve—
Worshipping Me The One, The
Invisible,
The Unrevealed, Unnamed,
Unthinkable,
Uttermost, All-pervading, Highest,
Sure—
Who thus adore Me, mastering their
sense,

Of one set mind to all, glad in all good,
These blessed souls come unto Me.
                              Yet, hard
The travail is for such as bend their
    minds
To reach th' Unmanifest. That viewless
    path
Shall scarce be trod by man bearing the
    flesh!
But whereso any doeth all his deeds
Renouncing self for Me, full of Me, fixed
To serve only the Highest, night and day
Musing on Me—him will I swiftly lift
Forth from life's ocean of distress and
    death,
Whose soul clings fast to Me. Cling thou
    to Me!
Clasp Me with heart and mind! so shalt
    thou dwell
Surely with Me on high. But if thy
    thought
Droops from such height; if thou be'st
    weak to set
Body and soul upon Me constantly,
Despair not! give Me lower service! seek
To reach Me, worshipping with steadfast
    will;
And, if thou canst not worship
    steadfastly,
Work for Me, toil in works pleasing to
    Me!
For he that laboureth right for love of
    Me
Shall finally attain! But, if in this
Thy faint heart fails, bring Me thy
    failure! find
Refuge in Me! let fruits of labour go,
Renouncing hope for Me, with lowliest
    heart,
So shalt thou come; for, though to know
    is more
Than diligence, yet worship better is
Than knowing, and renouncing better
    still.
Near to renunciation—very near—
Dwelleth Eternal Peace!
                    Who hateth nought
Of all which lives, living himself benign,

Compassionate, from arrogance exempt,
Exempt from love of self, unchangeable
By good or ill; patient, contented, firm
In faith, mastering himself, true to his
    word,
Seeking Me, heart and soul; vowed unto
    Me,—
That man I love! Who troubleth not his
    kind,
And is not troubled by them; clear of
    wrath,
Living too high for gladness, grief, or
    fear,
That man I love! Who, dwelling quiet-
    eyed,
Stainless, serene, well-balanced,
    unperplexed,
Working with Me, yet from all works
    detached,
That man I love! Who, fixed in faith on
    Me,
Dotes upon none, scorns none; rejoices
    not,
And grieves not, letting good or evil hap
Light when it will, and when it will
    depart,
That man I love! Who, unto friend and
    foe
Keeping an equal heart, with equal mind
Bears shame and glory; with an equal
    peace
Takes heat and cold, pleasure and pain;
    abides
Quit of desires, hears praise or calumny
In passionless restraint, unmoved by
    each;
Linked by no ties to earth, steadfast in Me,
That man I love! But most of all I love
Those happy ones to whom 'tis life to
    live
In single fervid faith and love unseeing,
Drinking the blessed Amrit of my
    Being!

ARJUNA : Now would I hear, O gracious
    Kesava!
Of Life which seems, and Soul beyond,
    which sees,

And what it is we know—or think to
know.

KRISHNA: Yea! Son of Kunti! for this
flesh ye see
Is *Kshetra*, is the field where Life disports;
And that which views and knows it is the
Soul,
Kshetrajna. In all "fields," thou Indian
prince!
I am *Kshetrajna*. I am what surveys!
Only that knowledge knows which knows
the known
By the knower! What it is, that "field" of
life,
What qualities it hath, and whence it is,
And why it changeth, and the faculty
That wotteth it, the mightiness of this,
And how it wotteth—hear these things
from Me!

The elements, the conscious life, the
mind,
The unseen vital force, the nine strange
gates
Of the body, and the five domains of
sense;
Desire, dislike, pleasure and pain, and
thought
Deep-woven, and persistency of being;
These all are wrought on Matter by the
Soul!

Humbleness, truthfulness, and
harmlessness,
Patience and honour, reverence for the
wise,
Purity, constancy, control of self,
Contempt of sense-delights, self-sacrifice,
Perception of the certitude of ill
In birth, death, age, disease, suffering,
and sin;
Detachment, lightly holding unto home,
Children, and wife, and all that bindeth
men;
An ever-tranquil heart in fortunes good
And fortunes evil, with a will set firm
To worship Me—Me only! ceasing not;

Loving all solitudes, and shunning noise
Of foolish crowds; endeavours resolute
To reach perception of the Utmost Soul,
And grace to understand what gain it
were
So to attain,—this is true Wisdom,
Prince!
And what is otherwise is ignorance!

Now will I speak of knowledge best to
know—
That Truth which giveth man Amrit to
drink,
The Truth of HIM, the Para-Brahm, the
All,
The Uncreated; not *Asat*, not *Sat*,
Not Form, nor the Unformed; yet both,
and more;—
Whose hands are everywhere, and
everywhere
Planted His feet, and everywhere His
eyes
Beholding, and His ears in every place
Hearing, and all His faces everywhere
Enlightening and encompassing His
worlds.
Glorified in the senses He hath given,
Yet beyond sense He is; sustaining all,
Yet dwells He unattached: of forms and
modes
Master, yet neither form nor mode hath
He;
He is within all beings—and without—
Motionless, yet still moving; not
discerned
For subtlety of instant presence; close
To all, to each; yet measurelessly far!
Not manifold, and yet subsisting still
In all which lives; for ever to be known
As the Sustainer, yet, at the End of
Times,
He maketh all to end—and re-creates.
The Light of Lights He is, in the heart of
the Dark
Shining eternally. Wisdom He is
And Wisdom's way, and Guide of all the
wise,
Planted in every heart.

                              So have I told
Of Life's stuff, and the moulding, and
   the lore
To comprehend. Whoso, adoring Me,
Perceiveth this, shall surely come to Me!

Know thou that Nature and the Spirit
   both
Have no beginning! Know that qualities
And changes of them are by Nature
   wrought;
That Nature puts to work the acting
   frame,
But Spirit doth inform it, and so cause
Feeling of pain and pleasure. Spirit,
   linked
To moulded matter, entereth into bond
With qualities by Nature framed, and,
   thus
Married to matter, breeds the birth
   again
In good or evil *yonis.*[3]
                              Yet is this —
Yea! in its bodily prison!—Spirit pure.
Spirit supreme; surveying, governing,
Guarding, possessing; Lord and Master
   still
PURUSHA, Ultimate, One Soul with Me.

Whoso thus knows himself, and knows
   his soul
PURUSHA, working through the
   qualities
With Nature's modes, the light hath
   come for him!
Whatever flesh he bears, never again
Shall he take on its load. Some few there
   be
By meditation find the Soul in Self
Self-schooled; and some by long
   philosophy
And holy life reach thither; some by
   works:
Some, never so attaining, hear of light
From other lips, and seize, and cleave to it

Worshipping; yea! and those—to
   teaching true—
Overpass Death!

                 •   •   •

                              For in this world
Being is twofold: the Divided, one;
The Undivided, one. All things that live
Are "the Divided." That which sits apart,
"The Undivided."

                              Higher still is He,
The Highest, holding all, whose Name is
   LORD,
The Eternal, Sovereign, First! Who fills
   all worlds,
Sustaining them. And—dwelling thus
   beyond
Divided Being and Undivided—I
Am called of men and Vedas, Life
   Supreme,
The PURUSHOTTAMA.

                              Who knows Me thus,
With mind unclouded, knoweth all, dear
   Prince!
And with his whole soul ever
   worshippeth Me.

Now is the sacred, secret Mystery
Declared to thee! Who comprehendeth
   this
Hath wisdom!

KRISHNA: Fearlessness, singleness of soul,
   the will
Always to strive for wisdom; opened
   hand
And governed appetites; and piety,
And love of lonely study; humbleness,
Uprightness, heed to injure nought
   which lives,
Truthfulness, slowness unto wrath, a mind
That lightly letteth go what others prize;
And equanimity, and charity
Which spieth no man's faults; and
   tenderness
Towards all that suffer; a contended
   heart,

---

[3]Wombs.

Fluttered by no desires; a bearing mild,
Modest, and grave, with manhood nobly
    mixed,
With patience, fortitude, and purity;
An unrevengeful spirit, never given
To rate itself too high;—such be the signs,
O Indian Prince! of him whose feet are
    set
On that fair path which leads to heavenly
    birth!

Deceitfulness, and arrogance, and pride,
Quickness to anger, harsh and evil
    speech,
And ignorance, to its own darkness
    blind,—
These be the signs, My Prince! of him
    whose birth
Is fated for the regions of the vile.

The Heavenly Birth brings to
    deliverance,
So should'st thou know! The birth with
    Asuras
Brings into bondage. Be thou joyous,
    Prince!
Whose lot is set apart for heavenly Birth.

Two stamps there are marked on all
    living men,
Divine and Undivine; I spake to thee
By what marks thou shouldst know the
    Heavenly Man,
Hear from me now of the Unheavenly!

They comprehend not, the Unheavenly,
How Souls go forth from Me; nor how
    they come
Back unto Me: nor is there Truth in
    these,
Nor purity, nor rule of Life. "This world
Hath not a Law, nor Order, nor a Lord,"
So say they: "nor hath risen up by Cause
Following on Cause, in perfect
    purposing,
But is none other than a House of Lust."
And, this thing thinking, all those ruined
    ones—

Of little wit, dark-minded—give
    themselves
To evil deeds, the curses of their kind.
Surrendered to desires insatiable,
Full of deceitfulness, folly, and pride,
In blindness cleaving to their errors,
    caught
Into the sinful course, they trust this lie
As it were true—this lie which leads to
    death—
Finding in Pleasure all the good which
    is,
And crying "Here it finisheth!"

                              Ensnared
In nooses of a hundred idle hopes,
Slaves to their passion and their wrath,
    they buy
Wealth with base deeds, to glut hot
    appetites;
"Thus much, to-day," they say, "we
    gained! thereby
Such and such wish of heart shall have
    its fill;
And this is ours! and th' other shall be ours!
To-day we slew a foe, and we will slay
Our other enemy to-morrow! Look!
Are we not lords? Make we not goodly
    cheer?
Is not our fortune famous, brave, and
    great?
Rich are we, proudly born! What other
    men
Live like to us? Kill, then, for sacrifice!
Cast largesse, and be merry!" So they
    speak
Darkened by ignorance; and so they
    fall —
Tossed to and fro with projects, tricked,
    and bound
In net of black delusion, lost in lusts—
Down to foul Naraka. Conceited, fond,
Stubborn and proud, dead-drunken with
    the wine
Of wealth, and reckless, all their
    offerings
Have but a show of reverence, being not
    made

In piety of ancient faith. Thus vowed
To self-hood, force, insolence, feasting,
    wrath,
These My blasphemers, in the forms they
    wear
And in the forms they breed, my foemen
    are,
Hateful and hating; cruel, evil, vile,
Lowest and least of men, whom I cast
    down
Again, and yet again, at end of lives,
Into some devilish womb, whence—
    birth by birth—
The devilish wombs re-spawn them, all
    beguiled;
And, till they find and worship Me, sweet
    Prince!
Tread they that Nether Road.

                    The Doors of Hell
Are threefold, whereby men to ruin
    pass,—
The door of Lust, the door of Wrath, the
    door
Of Avarice. Let a man shun those three!
            • • •
  Whoso performeth—diligent, content—
The work allotted him, whate'er it be,
Lays hold of perfectness! Hear how a
    man
Findeth perfection, being so content:
He findeth it through worship—
    wrought by work—
Of HIM that is the Source of all which
    lives,
Of HIM by Whom the universe was
    stretched.

Better thine own work is, though done
    with fault,
Than doing others' work, ev'n
    excellently.
He shall not fall in sin who fronts the
    task
Set him by Nature's hand! Let no man
    leave
His natural duty, Prince! though it bear
    blame!

For every work hath blame, as every
    flame
Is wrapped in smoke! Only that man
    attains
Perfect surcease of work whose work was
    wrought
With mind unfettered, soul wholly
    subdued,
Desires for ever dead, results renounced.

Learn from me, Son of Kunti! also this,
How one, attaining perfect peace, attains
BRAHM, the supreme, the highest height
    of all!

Devoted—with a heart grown pure,
    restrained
In lordly self-control, foregoing wiles
Of song and senses, freed from love and
    hate,
Dwelling 'mid solitudes, in diet spare,
With body, speech, and will tamed to
    obey,
Ever to holy meditation vowed,
From passions liberate, quit of the Self,
Of arrogance, impatience, anger, pride;
Freed from surroundings, quiet, lacking
    nought—
Such an one grows to oneness with the
    BRAHM;
Such an one, growing one with BRAHM,
    serene,
Sorrows no more, desires no more; his
    soul,
Equally loving all that lives, loves well
Me, Who have made them, and attains to
    Me.
By this same love and worship doth he
    know
Me as I am, how high and wonderful,
And knowing, straightway enters into
    Me.
And whatsoever deeds he doeth—fixed
In Me, as in his refuge—he hath won
For ever and for ever by My grace
Th' Eternal Rest!

Buddhism

Unlike Hinduism, which developed gradually over several centuries through the fusion of the religious myths of the early, indigenous population of India with those of the Aryan invaders, Buddhism owes its origin to the career of one person—Siddhartha Gautama (563?–483? B.C.), who later came to be called the Buddha (the "Enlightened One"). Also unlike Hinduism, which has largely remained a religion of India, Buddhism spread throughout the rest of Asia, and beyond, to become one of history's great world-religions. Nevertheless, Buddhism, although it arose in part as a reaction against traditional Hinduism, shares several of the features, in a modified form, of the older religion.

Gautama, the founder of Buddhism, was born in northern India, the son of a local chieftain. Although innumerable legends have grown up about him, the facts apparently are that, as a young man, he became disillusioned with life, as he was living it, and decided to seek salvation through enlightenment. He pursued his goal (it is said for six years), first through philosophical meditation and then through asceticism and the mortification of his body. But neither method produced the result he sought. Finally, in desperation, he sat down under a fig tree (later famous as the "Bo-tree") and reviewed his past, unsuccessful endeavors. There the realization struck him that his efforts must be self-defeating because they were the result of his own desires. From this it followed that he must abandon desires altogether, if he was to gain true peace of mind and blessedness. Here was his great Enlightenment; he became the Buddha. Returning from this experience to the town of Benares, he accosted five ascetics with whom he had previously been living. In a deer park nearby he preached his first sermon to them.

Gautama spent the remainder of his life teaching, preaching, and organizing his growing band of disciples. Each initiate of the Buddhist order subscribed to the following confession: "I take refuge in the Buddha, I take refuge in the Law of Truth, I take refuge in the Order." However, about a century after Gautama's death, a schism developed within the faith, with the result that historically

Buddhism can be divided into two large branches. First is what is known as Theravada Buddhism, the more conservative branch, which has attempted to adhere as closely as possible to the fundamental doctrines of the founder. The second is Mahayana Buddhism. Its main doctrinal difference from Theravada Buddhism is the belief in a multiplicity of Buddhas (known as Bodhisattvas), both actual and potential, who delay entering Nirvana in order to help others. This change has had great practical effects because it gives assurance to the faithful that there will always be a power in the universe to ameliorate their sufferings and guarantee their salvation.

The first of the following selections is from the Buddha's Deer Park Sermon, as it was later recorded. It contains statements of three basic concepts of the Buddhist faith—the Four Noble Truths, the Noble Eightfold Path, and the Middle Way. The second, longer selection also, according to tradition, repeats the words of the Buddha himself. The title may be translated in a variety of ways; a good rendition is *The Path of Virtue*. The work itself consists mainly of a discussion of Buddhist morality; its main goal is to draw distinctions between an evil and a good way of life. More particularly, the author instructs novices in the requirements they must fulfill to become worthy Buddhist monks, wearing "the yellow gown."

The Foundation of the Kingdom of Righteousness

Reverence to the Blessed One, the Holy One, the Fully-Enlightened One.

Thus have I heard. The Blessed One was once staying at Benares, at the hermitage called Migadâya. And there the Blessed One addressed the company of the five Bhikkhus [monks], and said:

'There are two extremes, O Bhikkhus, which the man who has given up the world ought not to follow—the habitual practice, on the one hand, of those things whose attraction depends upon the passions, and especially of sensuality—a low and pagan way (of seeking satisfaction) unworthy, unprofitable, and fit only for the worldly-minded—and the habitual practice, on the other hand, of asceticism (or self-mortification), which is painful, unworthy, and unprofitable.

'There is a middle path, O Bhikkhus, avoiding these two extremes, discovered by the Tathâgata [Buddha]—a path which opens the eyes, and bestows understanding, which leads to peace of mind, to the higher wisdom, to full enlightenment, to Nirvâna.

'What is that middle path, O Bhikkhus, avoiding these two extremes, discovered by the Tathâgata—that path which opens the

Trans. T. W. Rhys Davids.

eyes, and bestows understanding, which leads to peace of mind, to the higher wisdom, to full enlightenment, to Nirvâna? Verily! it is this noble eightfold path; that is to say:

'Right views;
Right aspirations;
Right speech;
Right conduct;
Right livelihood;
Right effort;
Right mindfulness; and
Right contemplation.

'This, O Bhikkhus, is that middle path, avoiding these two extremes, discovered by the Tathâgata—that path which opens the eyes, and bestows understanding, which leads to peace of mind, to the higher wisdom, to full enlightenment, to Nirvâna!

'Now this, O Bhikkhus, is the noble truth concerning suffering.

'Birth is attended with pain, decay is painful, disease is painful, death is painful. Union with the unpleasant is painful, painful is separation from the pleasant; and any craving that is unsatisfied, that too is painful. In brief, the five aggregates which spring from attachment (the conditions of individuality and their cause) are painful.

'This then, O Bhikkhus, is the noble truth concerning suffering.

'Now this, O Bhikkhus, is the noble truth concerning the origin of suffering.

'Verily, it is that thirst (or craving), causing the renewal of existence, accompanied by sensual delight, seeking satisfaction now here, now there—that is to say, the craving for the gratification of the passions, or the craving for (a future) life, or the craving for success (in this present life).

'This then, O Bhikkhus, is the noble truth concerning the origin of suffering.

'Now this, O Bhikkhus, is the noble truth concerning the destruction of suffering.

'Verily, it is the destruction, in which no passion remains, of this very thirst; the laying aside of, the getting rid of, the being free from, the harbouring no longer of this thirst.

'This then, O Bhikkhus, is the noble truth concerning the destruction of suffering.

'Now this, O Bhikkhus, is the noble truth concerning the way which leads to the destruction of sorrow. Verily! it is this noble eightfold path.'

Dhammapada

CHAPTER I

The Twin-Verses

All that we are is the result of what we have thought: it is founded on our thoughts, it is made up of our thoughts. If a man speaks or acts with an evil

thought . . . , pain follows him, as the wheel follows the foot of the ox that draws the carriage.

All that we are is the result of what we have thought: it is founded on our thoughts, it is made up of our thoughts. If a man speaks or acts with

Trans. F. Max Müller.

a pure thought, happiness follows him, like a shadow that never leaves him.

'He abused me, he beat me, he defeated me, he robbed me,'—in those who harbour such thoughts hatred will never cease.

'He abused me, he beat me, he defeated me, he robbed me,'—in those who do not harbour such thoughts hatred will cease.

For hatred does not cease by hatred at any time: hatred ceases by love, this is an old rule.

The world does not know that we must all come to an end here;— but those who know it, their quarrels cease at once.

He who lives looking for pleasures only, his senses uncontrolled, immoderate in his food, idle, and weak, Mâra (the tempter) will certainly overthrow him, as the wind throws down a weak tree.

He who lives without looking for pleasures, his senses well controlled, moderate in his food, faithful and strong, him Mâra will certainly not overthrow, any more than the wind throws down a rocky mountain.

He who wishes to put on the yellow dress without having cleansed himself from sin, who disregards also temperance and truth, is unworthy of the yellow dress.

But he who has cleansed himself from sin, is well grounded in all virtues, and regards also temperance and truth, he is indeed worthy of the yellow dress.

They who imagine truth in untruth, and see untruth in truth, never arrive at truth, but follow vain desires.

They who know truth in truth, and untruth in untruth, arrive at truth, and follow true desires.

As rain breaks through an ill-thatched house, passion will break through an unreflecting mind.

As rain does not break through a well-thatched house, passion will not break through a well-reflecting mind.

The evil-doer mourns in this world, and he mourns in the next; he mourns in both. He mourns and suffers when he sees the evil of his own work.

The virtuous man delights in this world, and he delights in the next; he delights in both. He delights and rejoices, when he sees the purity of his own work.

The evil-doer suffers in this world, and he suffers in the next; he suffers in both. He suffers when he thinks of the evil he has done; he suffers more when going on the evil path.

The virtuous man is happy in this world, and he is happy in the next; he is happy in both. He is happy when he thinks of the good he has done; he is still more happy when going on the good path.

The thoughtless man, even if he can recite a large portion (of the law), but is not a doer of it, has no share in the priesthood, but is like a cowherd counting the cows of others.

The follower of the law, even if he can recite only a small portion (of the law), but, having forsaken passion and hatred and foolishness, possesses true knowledge and serenity of mind, he, caring for nothing in this world or that to come, has indeed a share in the priesthood.

CHAPTER III

Thought

As a fletcher makes straight his arrow, a wise man makes straight his trembling and unsteady thought, which is difficult to guard, difficult to hold back,

As a fish taken from his watery home and thrown on the dry ground, our thought trembles all over in order to escape the dominion of Mâra (the tempter).

It is good to tame the mind, which is difficult to hold in and flighty, rushing wherever it listeth; a tamed mind brings happiness.

Let the wise man guard his thoughts, for they are difficult to perceive, very artful, and they rush wherever they list: thoughts well guarded bring happiness.

Those who bridle their mind which travels far, moves about alone, is without a body, and hides in the chamber (of the heart), will be free from the bonds of Mâra (the tempter).

If a man's thoughts are unsteady, if he does not know the true law, if his peace of mind is troubled, his knowledge will never be perfect.

If a man's thoughts are not dissipated, if his mind is not perplexed, if he has ceased to think of good or evil, then there is no fear for him while he is watchful.

Knowing that this body is (fragile) like a jar, and making this thought firm like a fortress, one should attack Mâra (the tempter) with the weapon of knowledge, one should watch him when conquered, and should never rest.

Before long, alas! this body will lie on the earth, despised, without understanding, like a useless log.

Whatever a hater may do to a hater, or an enemy to an enemy, a wrongly directed mind will do us greater mischief.

Not a mother, not a father will do so much, nor any other relative; a well-directed mind will do us greater service.

CHAPTER V

The Fool

Long is the night to him who is awake; long is a mile to him who is tired; long is life to the foolish who do not know the true law.

If a traveller does not meet with one who is his better, or his equal, let him firmly keep to his solitary journey; there is no companionship with a fool.

'These sons belong to me, and this wealth belongs to me,' with such thoughts a fool is tormented. He himself does not belong to himself; how much less sons and wealth?

The fool who knows his foolishness, is wise at least so far. But a fool who thinks himself wise, he is called a fool indeed.

If a fool be associated with a wise man even all his life, he will perceive the truth as little as a spoon perceives the taste of soup.

If an intelligent man be associated for one minute only with a wise man, he will soon perceive the truth, as the tongue perceives the taste of soup.

Fools of little understanding have themselves for their greatest enemies, for they do evil deeds which must bear bitter fruits.

That deed is not well done of which a man must repent, and the reward of which he receives crying and with a tearful face.

No, that deed is well done of which a man does not repent, and the reward of which he receives gladly and cheerfully.

As long as the evil deed done does not bear fruit, the fool thinks it is like honey: but when it ripens, then the fool suffers grief.

Let a fool month after month eat his food (like an ascetic) with the tip of a blade of Kusa grass, yet is he not worth the sixteenth particle of those who have well weighed the law.

An evil deed, like newly drawn milk, does not turn (suddenly); smouldering, like fire covered by ashes, it follows the fool.

* * *

CHAPTER VI

The Wise Man

If you see an intelligent man who tells you where true treasures are to be found, who shows what is to be avoided, and administers reproofs, follow that wise man; it will be better, not worse, for those who follow him.

Let him admonish, let him teach, let him forbid what is improper!—he will be beloved of the good, by the bad he will be hated.

Do not have evil-doers for friends, do not have low people for friends: have virtuous people for friends, have for friends the best of men.

He who drinks in the law lives happily with a serene mind: the sage rejoices always in the law, as preached by the elect (Ariyas).

Well-makers lead the water (wherever they like); fletchers bend the arrow; carpenters bend a log of wood; wise people fashion themselves.

As a solid rock is not shaken by the wind, wise people falter not amidst blame and praise.

Wise people, after they have listened to the laws, become serene, like a deep, smooth, and still lake.

Good people walk on whatever befall, the good do not prattle, longing for pleasure; whether touched by happiness or sorrow wise people never appear elated or depressed.

If, whether for his own sake, or for the sake of others, a man wishes neither for a son, nor for wealth, nor for lordship, and if he does not wish for his own success by unfair means, then he is good, wise, and virtuous.

* * *

CHAPTER IX

Evil

If a man would hasten towards the good, he should keep his thought away from evil; if a man does what is good slothfully, his mind delights in evil.

If a man commits a sin, let him not do it again; let him not delight in sin: pain is the outcome of evil.

If a man does what is good, let him do it again; let him delight in it: happiness is the outcome of good.

Even an evil-doer sees happiness as long as his evil deed has not ripened; but when his evil deed has ripened, then does the evil-doer see evil.

Even a good man sees evil days, as long as his good deed has not ripened; but when his good deed has ripened, then does the good man see happy days.

Let no man think lightly of evil, saying in his heart, It will not come nigh unto me. Even by the falling of water-drops a water-pot is filled; the fool becomes full of evil, even if he gather it little by little.

Let no man think lightly of good, saying in his heart, It will not come nigh unto me. Even by the falling of water-drops a water-pot is filled; the wise man becomes full of good, even if he gather it little by little.

Let a man avoid evil deeds, as a

merchant, if he has few companions and carries much wealth, avoids a dangerous road; as a man who loves life avoids poison.

He who has no wound on his hand, may touch poison with his hand; poison does not affect one who has no wound; nor is there evil for one who does not commit evil.

If a man offend a harmless, pure, and innocent person, the evil falls back upon that fool, like light dust thrown up against the wind.

Some people are born again; evil-doers go to hell; righteous people go to heaven; those who are free from all worldly desires attain Nirvâ*n*a.

• • •

CHAPTER XIII

The World

Do not follow the evil law! Do not live on in thoughtlessness! Do not follow false doctrine! Be not a friend of the world.

Rouse thyself! do not be idle! Follow the law of virtue! The virtuous rests in bliss in this world and in the next.

Follow the law of virtue; do not follow that of sin. The virtuous rests in bliss in this world and in the next.

Look upon the world as a bubble, look upon it as a mirage: the king of death does not see him who thus looks down upon the world.

Come, look at this glittering world, like unto a royal chariot; the foolish are immersed in it, but the wise do not touch it.

He who formerly was reckless and afterwards became sober, brightens up this world, like the moon when freed from clouds.

He whose evil deeds are covered by good deeds, brightens up this world, like the moon when freed from clouds.

This world is dark, few only can see here; a few only go to heaven, like birds escaped from the net.

The swans go on the path of the sun, they go through the ether by means of their miraculous power; the wise are led out of this world, when they have conquered Mâra and his train.

If a man has transgressed one law, and speaks lies, and scoffs at another world, there is no evil he will not do.

The uncharitable do not go to the world of the gods; fools only do not praise liberality; a wise man rejoices in liberality, and through it becomes blessed in the other world.

Better than sovereignty over the earth, better than going to heaven, better than lordship over all worlds, is the reward of the first step in holiness.

CHAPTER XIV

The Buddha

He whose conquest is not conquered again, into whose conquest no one in this world enters, by what track can you lead him, the Awakened, the Omniscient, the trackless?

He whom no desire with its snares and poisons can lead astray, by what track can you lead him, the Awakened, the Omniscient, the trackless?

Even the gods envy those who are awakened and not forgetful, who are given to meditation, who are wise, and who delight in the repose of retirement (from the world).

Difficult (to obtain) is the conception of men, difficult is the life of mortals, difficult is the hearing of the True Law, difficult is the birth of the

Awakened (the attainment of Buddhahood).

Not to commit any sin, to do good, and to purify one's mind, that is the teaching of (all) the Awakened.

The Awakened call patience the highest penance, long-suffering the highest Nirvâna; for he is not an anchorite who strikes others, he is not an ascetic who insults others.

Not to blame, not to strike, to live restrained under the law, to be moderate in eating, to sleep and sit alone, and to dwell on the highest thoughts,—this is the teaching of the Awakened.

There is no satisfying lusts, even by a shower of gold pieces; he who knows that lusts have a short taste and cause pain, he is wise;

Even in heavenly pleasures he finds no satisfaction, the disciple who is fully awakened delights only in the destruction of all desires.

Men, driven by fear, go to many a refuge, to mountains and forests, to groves and sacred trees.

But that is not a safe refuge, that is not the best refuge; a man is not delivered from all pains after having gone to that refuge.

He who takes refuge with Buddha, the Law, and the Church; he who, with clear understanding, sees the four holy truths:—

Viz, pain, the origin of pain, the destruction of pain, and the eightfold holy way that leads to the quieting of pain;—

That is the safe refuge, that is the best refuge; having gone to that refuge, a man is delivered from all pain.

A supernatural person (a Buddha) is not easily found, he is not born everywhere. Wherever such a sage is born, that race prospers.

Happy is the arising of the awakened, happy is the teaching of the True Law, happy is peace in the church, happy is the devotion of those who are at peace.

He who pays homage to those who deserve homage, whether the awakened (Buddha) or their disciples, those who have overcome the host (of evils), and crossed the flood of sorrow, he who pays homage to such as have found deliverance and know no fear, his merit can never be measured by anybody.

CHAPTER XVI

Pleasure

He who gives himself to vanity, and does not give himself to meditation, forgetting the real aim (of life) and grasping at pleasure, will in time envy him who has exerted himself in meditation.

Let no man ever look for what is pleasant, or what is unpleasant. Not to see what is pleasant is pain, and it is pain to see what is unpleasant.

Let, therefore, no man love anything; loss of the beloved is evil. Those who love nothing, and hate nothing, have no fetters.

From pleasure comes grief, from pleasure comes fear; he who is free from pleasure knows neither grief nor fear.

From affection comes grief, from affection comes fear; he who is free from affection knows neither grief nor fear.

From lust comes grief, from lust comes fear; he who is free from lust knows neither grief nor fear.

From love comes grief, from love comes fear; he who is free from love knows neither grief nor fear.

From greed comes grief, from greed comes fear; he who is free from greed knows neither grief nor fear.

He who possesses virtue and intelligence, who is just, speaks the truth, and does what is his own business, him the world will hold dear.

• • •

CHAPTER XVII

Anger

Let a man leave anger, let him forsake pride, let him overcome all bondage! No sufferings befall the man who is not attached to name and form, and who calls nothing his own.

He who holds back rising anger like a rolling chariot, him I call a real driver; other people are but holding the reins.

Let a man overcome anger by love, let him overcome evil by good; let him overcome the greedy by liberality, the liar by truth!

Speak the truth, do not yield to anger; give, if thou art asked for little; by these three steps thou wilt go near the gods.

The sages who injure nobody, and who always control their body, they will go to the unchangeable place (Nirvâna), where, if they have gone, they will suffer no more.

Those who are ever watchful, who study day and night, and who strive after Nirvâna, their passions will come to an end.

This is an old saying, O Atula, this is not only of to-day: 'They blame him who sits silent, they blame him who speaks much, they also blame him who says little; there is no one on earth who is not blamed.'

There never was, there never will be, nor is there now, a man who is always blamed, or a man who is always praised.

But he whom those who discriminate praise continually day after day, as without blemish, wise, rich in knowledge and virtue, who would dare to blame him, like a coin made of gold from the Gambû river? Even the gods praise him, he is praised even by Brahman.

Beware of bodily anger, and control thy body! Leave the sins of the body, and with thy body practise virtue!

Beware of the anger of the tongue, and control thy tongue! Leave the sins of the tongue, and practise virtue with thy tongue!

Beware of the anger of the mind, and control thy mind! Leave the sins of the mind, and practise virtue with thy mind!

The wise who control their body, who control their tongue, the wise who control their mind, are indeed well controlled.

CHAPTER XVIII

Impurity

Thou art now like a sear leaf, the messengers of death have come near to thee; thou standest at the door of thy departure, and thou hast no provision for thy journey.

Make thyself an island, work hard, be wise! When thy impurities are blown away, and thou art free from guilt, thou wilt enter into the heavenly world of the elect.

Thy life has come to an end, thou art come near to death, there is no resting-place for thee on the road, and thou hast no provision for thy journey.

Make thyself an island, work hard, be wise! When thy impurities are blown away, and thou art free from guilt, thou wilt not enter again into birth and decay.

Let a wise man blow off the impurities of his self, as a smith blows off the impurities of silver, one by one, little by little, and from time to time.

As the impurity which springs from the iron, when it springs from it, destroys it; thus do a transgressor's own works lead him to the evil path.

The taint of prayers is non-repetition; the taint of houses, non-repair; the taint of the body is sloth; the taint of a watchman, thoughtlessness.

Bad conduct is the taint of woman, greediness the taint of a benefactor; tainted are all evil ways, in this world and in the next.

But there is a taint worse than all taints,—ignorance is the greatest taint. O mendicants! throw off that taint, and become taintless!

Life is easy to live for a man who is without shame, a crow hero, a mischief-maker, an insulting, bold, and wretched fellow.

But life is hard to live for a modest man, who always looks for what is pure, who is disinterested, quiet, spotless, and intelligent.

He who destroys life, who speaks untruth, who in this world takes what is not given him, who goes to another man's wife;

And the man who gives himself to drinking intoxicating liquors, he, even in this world, digs up his own root.

O man, know this, that the unrestrained are in a bad state; take care that greediness and vice do not bring thee to grief for a long time!

The world gives according to their faith or according to their pleasure: if a man frets about the food and the drink given to others, he will find no rest either by day or by night.

He in whom that feeling is destroyed, and taken out with the very root, finds rest by day and by night.

There is no fire like passion, there is no shark like hatred, there is no snare like folly, there is no torrent like greed.

The fault of others is easily perceived, but that of oneself is difficult to perceive; a man winnows his neighbour's faults like chaff, but his own fault he hides, as a cheat hides the bad die from the gambler.

• • •

CHAPTER XXII

The Downward Course

He who says what is not, goes to hell; he also who, having done a thing, says I have not done it. After death both are equal, they are men with evil deeds in the next world.

Many men whose shoulders are covered with the yellow gown are ill-conditioned and unrestrained; such evil-doers by their evil deeds go to hell.

Better it would be to swallow a heated iron ball, like flaring fire, than that a bad unrestrained fellow should live on the charity of the land.

Four things does a reckless man gain who covets his neighbour's wife,—a bad reputation, an uncomfortable bed, thirdly, punishment, and lastly, hell.

There is bad reputation, and the evil way (to hell), there is the short pleasure of the frightened in the arms of the frightened, and the king imposes heavy punishment; therefore let no man think of his neighbour's wife.

As a grass-blade, if badly grasped, cuts the arm, badly-practised asceticism leads to hell.

An act carelessly performed, a broken vow, and hesitating obedience to discipline, all this brings no great reward.

If anything is to be done, let a man do it, let him attack it vigorously! A careless pilgrim only scatters the dust of his passions more widely.

An evil deed is better left undone, for a man repents of it afterwards; a good deed is better done, for having done it, one does not repent.

Like a well-guarded frontier fort, with defences within and without, so let a man guard himself. Not a moment should escape, for they who allow the right moment to pass, suffer pain when they are in hell.

They who are ashamed of what they ought not to be ashamed of, and are not ashamed of what they ought to be ashamed of, such men, embracing false doctrines, enter the evil path.

They who fear when they ought not to fear, and fear not when they ought to fear, such men, embracing false doctrines, enter the evil path.

They who forbid when there is nothing to be forbidden, and forbid not when there is something to be forbidden, such men, embracing false doctrines, enter the evil path.

They who know what is forbidden as forbidden, and what is not forbidden as not forbidden, such men, embracing the true doctrine, enter the good path.

CHAPTER XXIV

Thirst

The thirst of a thoughtless man grows like a creeper; he runs from life to life, like a monkey seeking fruit in the forest.

Whomsoever this fierce thirst overcomes, full of poison, in this world, his sufferings increase like the abounding Bîra*na* grass.

He who overcomes this fierce thirst, difficult to be conquered in this world, sufferings fall off from him, like water-drops from a lotus leaf.

This salutary word I tell you, 'Do ye, as many as are here assembled, dig up the root of thirst, as he who wants the sweet-scented Usîra root must dig up the Bîra*na* grass, that Mâra (the tempter) may not crush you again and again, as the stream crushes the reeds.'

As a tree, even though it has been cut down, is firm so long as its root is safe, and grows again, thus, unless the feeders of thirst are destroyed, this pain (of life) will return again and again.

He whose thirst running towards pleasure is exceeding strong in the thirty-six channels, the waves will carry away that misguided man, viz, his desires which are set on passion.

The channels run everywhere, the creeper (of passion) stands sprouting; if you see the creeper springing up, cut its root by means of knowledge.

A creature's pleasures are extravagant and luxurious; sunk in lust and looking for pleasure, men undergo (again and again) birth and decay.

Men, driven on by thirst, run about like a snared hare; held in fetters and bonds, they undergo pain for a long time, again and again.

Men, driven on by thirst, run about like a snared hare; let therefore the mendicant drive out thirst, by striving after passionlessness for himself.

He who having got rid of the forest (of lust) (i.e. after having reached Nirvâna) gives himself over to forest-life (i.e. to lust), and who, when removed from the forest (i.e. from lust), runs to the forest (i.e. to lust), look at that man! though free, he runs into bondage.

Wise people do not call that a strong fetter which is made of iron, wood, or hemp; far stronger is the care for precious stones and rings, for sons and a wife.

That fetter wise people call strong which drags down, yields, but is difficult to undo; after having cut this at last, people leave the world, free from cares, and leaving desires and pleasures behind.

Those who are slaves to passions, run down with the stream (of desires), as a spider runs down the web which he has made himself; when they have cut this, at last, wise people leave the world, free from cares, leaving all affection behind.

Give up what is before, give up what is behind, give up what is in the middle, when thou goest to the other shore of existence; if thy mind is altogether free, thou wilt not again enter into birth and decay.

If a man is tossed about by doubts, full of strong passions, and yearning only for what is delightful, his thirst will grow more and more, and he will indeed make his fetters strong.

If a man delights in quieting doubts, and, always reflecting, dwells on what is not delightful (the impurity of the body, &c.), he certainly will remove, nay, he will cut the fetter of Mâra.

He who has reached the consummation, who does not tremble, who is without thirst and without sin, he has broken all the thorns of life: this will be his last body.

THE MEDIEVAL EPOCH

The medieval epoch, or the Middle Ages, is a somewhat amorphous period in world history. In the West it designates the thousand years between the decline of the Roman Empire in the fifth century and the Renaissance in the fifteenth. But even there it was far from a cohesive unit of history. The single institution that gave coherence to the period was the Christian church; for this reason the Middle Ages is often called the Age of Faith. Although this title captures much of the flavor of the era it also camouflages important historical changes that occurred during it. Historically, the medieval epoch in the West can be divided into two culturally contrasting parts, cutting it approximately in half.

The first half is called the Dark Ages, with some reason. Extending from the fifth to the eleventh centuries, this period, viewed from our present perspective, is one neither of light nor enlightenment. Although life went on, it was little enriched by any of the higher activities of the mind. Most of the population, in fact, were sunk in ignorance and superstition. Yet this negative appraisal must be qualified at one point. There was a spurt of cultural activity at the beginning of the ninth century, known in history as the Carolingian Renaissance, and centered in the court of Charlemagne (Charles the Great). Charlemagne was a Frankish king of unusual abilities and wide interests. A warrior, he succeeded in bringing much of western Europe under his dominion, having himself crowned as Holy Roman Emperor in Rome on Christmas Day, 800. Charlemagne was interested in learning and encouraged education, but after his death the cultural advances of his regime were lost for two hundred years, as Europe returned to its state of semisomnolence.

But, setting Europe aside, world civilization was far from stagnant during these centuries. Beginning early in the seventh century a robust culture began to develop in the hot desert sands of Arabia. It owed its origin to one man, Muhammad the prophet, the founder of the Muslim faith. Following Muhammad's death, the Muslims quickly expanded their power and influence so that within about three hundred years they controlled an area greater in extent than the Roman Empire. Even during the lifetime of Muhammad (570–632) they had gained control over the entire Arabian peninsula. From there they expanded in all directions, moving into Asia Minor, Persia, and Egypt by the middle of the seventh century, then pushing westward across northern Africa toward the Atlantic coast and eastward, first into Afghanistan, and then into the Indus valley of India.

The conquest of northern Africa brought the Muslims to the Strait of Gibralter, which they crossed at the beginning of the eighth century, quickly occupying most of the Iberian peninsula then crossing the Pyrenees to begin a northward probe into France. But they had finally reached the limit of their military resources. They were defeated in a crucial encounter by a Frankish force under the leadership of Charles Martel in 732 near the city of Tours and had to retreat back into Spain. There they remained in control, but against increasing pressure from local rulers, who gradually pushed them southward until finally, in 1492, they were forced from their last Spanish stronghold of Granada.

It is not easy to explain how the Muslims were able to conquer such vast areas so quickly. But two factors certainly contributed to their success. First, their armies were imbued with the enthusiasm of their religious faith, which they believed they had a mission to propagate, by arms if necessary. Second, their foes, for the most part, were ill-prepared and ill-equipped, so often offered little more than token opposition to their forces. Even less easy to explain is the flowering of Muslim culture during these centuries, for certainly the faith itself hardly favored learning and art. Nevertheless, the Muslims made important contributions in a wide variety of fields. Baghdad, on the Tigris River, became their cultural center; here they founded a university in the eleventh century. But well before that time Muslim scientists and scholars were active. Probably the greatest impetus to this activity came from their translation of the great works of the ancient Greeks into the Arabic language, which was accomplished in the ninth century. In medicine the writings of the Greek, Galen, became the foundation for the important work of people like Ibn Sina, or Avicenna (980–1037), who compiled a great medical encyclopedia. Astronomy, based on Ptolemy, was developed, with observatories at Damascus and Baghdad. Although the growth of this science was a result, in part, of the need for navigational aids, another strong force was its utility, here as in other cultures, in the "science" of astrology, or the prediction of the future. One important scientific development, not derived from Greece but from India, needs special mention—Arabic numberals, including the use of "zero." This proved a great advance over anything that Greece and Rome had done and marked a milestone in the history of mathematics. The Muslims also produced a major historian, Ibn Khaldun (1332–1406), who wrote a *Universal History*. In philosophy they were inspired by the great works of the classical Greeks but faced the problem of how to fit such speculations into the framework of their Muslim faith. Ibn Rushd, or Averroes (1126–1198) devoted much of his effort to the reconciliation of reason with faith. Al-Farabi (c.

870–950), on the other hand, was a rationalist, who was more concerned with providing a reconciliation between Plato and Aristotle.

Although the Muslim empire began to disintegrate as early as the ninth century, the cultural unity provided by the Muslim faith has continued to persist. Also, the accomplishments of the Muslim scientists and scholars were gradually to find their way into western Europe, with significant effects. Finally, monuments of their high art and architecture can still be viewed, in Spain and elsewhere.

In China these centuries were, on the whole, a time of political and social stability, punctuated by periods of turmoil. Dynasty succeeded dynasty—the Sui (589–618), the T'ang (618–907), the Sung (960–1279). But in the thirteenth century a new political force entered the Chinese scene, coming from the north and west. The Mongols under the great warrior, Genghis Khan (1162–1227), began to penetrate into northern China (as well as central Asia and even eastern Europe). Under Kublai Khan, who reigned from 1260 to 1294 in the capital city of Cambaluc (Beijing), the remainder of China came under Mongol rule. His court, his capital city, and his administration of China are vividly described in the famous account by the Venetian merchant and traveler, Marco Polo. In the following century, however, control of China by the Mongols gradually weakened until in 1368 they were driven out and a new dynasty, the Ming, came into power. This dynasty was to rule China until 1644.

Much of the stability of Chinese political life resulted from the organization of its government. Although the emperor ruled, the administration of the country was in the hands of a corps of bureaucrats, called mandarins. These, recruited mainly from the class of landed gentry, gained their appointments through passing a set of examinations based on their knowledge of the ancient Chinese classics. These famous examinations, for which aspirants had to prepare for many years, were instituted as far back as the Han dynasty and continued for two thousand years, until the early twentieth century.

China, because of her fertile river valleys, has always been a land of farmers but, because of the population density, the farms have been small. In early times only grains like millet could be grown in the northern Yellow River valley, while rice prospered farther south in the Yangtze valley. During the Sui dynasty these two valleys were linked by construction of the Grand Canal. Cheap transportation by barge traffic greatly encouraged trade and commerce, leading to economic prosperity and a steadily increasing population. Concurrently other forms of technology were developed. Prosperity led to the use of money and the manufacture of paper to that of paper money. The invention of printing in the eighth century came centuries before its introduction in the West. The same is true of gunpowder, which the Chinese were using as early as the tenth century. Before the end of the Middle Ages the Chinese were the most technologically advanced civilization in the world.

Just across the East China Sea from the Chinese coast lie the islands of

Japan. Although they had lived on the islands at least since neolithic times, the Japanese did not develop an advanced civilization until very late. The beginnings came around the first century A.D. (roughly three thousand years later than China) when warrior clans from Korea began to infiltrate the land. About the fourth century one of these clans gained ascendency over the others and its chief became the source for the imperial family which was to rule Japan thereafter. The latter half of the sixth century marked the real beginnings of Japanese civilization, as the mature culture of China began to penetrate the islands, particularly through the agency of proselytizing Chinese Buddhist monks. Although much of the later culture of Japan is, as a result, derivative from that of China, it developed its own, distinctive Japanese character.

After a centralized government based on the Chinese model with the emperor at its head proved unsuccessful, Japan, from the twelfth century, developed a feudal form of society. Although the emperor continued to reign he had little real power. Instead, effective control was in the hands of a hierarchy of warrior-knights, known as samurai, at whose head was a chief warrior, the shogun. This peculiarly Japanese system of government by feudal warriors with a puppet emperor was to remain much the same until the nineteenth century. But for several centuries during the medieval epoch, until the Tokugawa Shogunate crushed all opposition at the end of the sixteenth century, no single shogun succeeded in gaining full control of Japan. Instead there was almost constant warfare as various contenders, with their categories of warrior-knights, struggled for supremacy. One event of military significance that was to have historical effects many centuries later occurred during this time. In 1281 Kublai Khan, having brought all of China under his dominion, decided to invade Japan, so he dispatched a large fleet carrying an army across the sea. Before the Chinese could mount their invasion, however, a typhoon struck and destroyed their fleet. To this storm the Japanese gave the name "Divine Wind," or kamikaze.

In Africa the medieval epoch saw the rise of several powerful empires, generally centered in the northwestern part of the continent. The most important were the Ghana empire, which reached its height in the eleventh century; the Mali empire, which flourished in the thirteenth and fourteenth centuries and whose beginning is described in the epic *Sundiata;* and the Songhai empire of the fifteenth and sixteenth centuries.

We left Europe deep in the Dark Ages. This long period came to an end after the year 1000 with a gradual cultural awakening that was to culminate in the high Middle Ages of the thirteenth century. The reasons for this development were quite complex, involving economic, political, social, and religious causes. Yet it is hard to overlook one factor of profound significance, the introduction into western Europe of the culture of the ancient world, particularly that of classical Greece. This came in part through the medium of the Muslims in Spain, who had long since translated writers like Plato and Aristotle into Arabic. Later more direct and wider contacts with Mediterranean and Muslim civilization occurred during the Crusades. The result of this intellectual fertilization was a surge of learning. The great universities of Europe—in Italy and at Paris, Oxford, and Cambridge—were founded. Scholasticism, which combined a study of ancient thought with the attempt to reconcile pagan philosophy with Christian theology, became the dominant occupation of scholars. As the church and society both prospered, great cathedrals, in the magnificent Gothic style, soon became the pride of many a provincial town.

The feudal system with its knightly class of lords and vassals providing military protection and the bulk of the population tilling the land as serfs, continued, as it had for centuries, to provide the basic social and economic structure of the populace. But with the growth of trade, commerce, and manufacturing, towns grew both in size and importance. Also, new classes of society—entrepreneurs and artisans—who did not fit into the feudal pattern of life, began to exert their influence. European society was in the process of change. This became apparent particularly in the political arena. For centuries the church, though its realm was presumably that of the spirit, had asserted its claim to temporal supremacy, using the "two-swords" argument to support its position. But, increasingly, the kings of western Europe took exception to the church's assumption of supreme power. As their own power grew they challenged that of the pope. After long and bitter struggles, the temporal heads of state emerged victorious and the church was forced to retreat back toward the realm of the spirit.

St. Augustine

For three hundred years after the death of Jesus, the Christian churches were engaged in a continuing struggle. Confronted by scores of pagan cults in the Mediterranean world and by the persecution of the Roman government, the new religion was unable to establish its supremacy until the fourth century. Early in that century, under the emperors Galerius and Constantine (himself a convert), Christianity was recognized and tolerated; later in the century, under Theodosius, it was proclaimed the official religion of the Roman Empire.

But the problems of the churches were far from over, for a host of controversies now arose within the ranks of the Christians themselves. The most serious dispute was over questions of doctrine. Innumerable sects, each preaching its special version of Christian doctrine and combating the views of the others, were scattered throughout the empire. Clearly, if Christianity was to survive, some order had to be brought out of such theological chaos. Into this scene of confusion stepped Augustine (354–430), the most important of Christian theologians. Highly intelligent, firmly devoted to his conception of the truth, and possessed of unusual administrative abil-

ity, Augustine was admirably fitted for the task of developing a theological doctrine for the Christian religion and then making that doctrine prevail.

After having been attracted as a youth to various pagan cults, Augustine was converted to Christianity in 386 through the influence of Ambrose, bishop of Milan. Following his conversion, Augustine devoted most of the rest of his life to formulating and disseminating what he believed to be the true Christian doctrine. The main features of this doctrine are given in the following selection from *The Enchiridion* ("Manual"). The central concept, as with St. Paul, is original sin, but with Augustine the theory becomes systematically articulated. Once he had worked out his doctrine completely, Augustine was in a good position to brand opposing theories as heresies. And he devoted much of his time, thought, and energy, especially in later life, to doctrinal controversies in an effort to purge Christian theology of all heretical elements. He was singularly successful in this endeavor, and orthodox Christianity (even with the later additions made by Thomas Aquinas and others) has remained basically Augustinian.

The Enchiridion

• • •

God's judgments upon fallen men and angels. The death of the body is man's peculiar punishment.

. . . Now the evils I have mentioned are common to all who for their wickedness have been justly condemned by God, whether they be men or angels. But there is one form of punishment peculiar to man—the death of the body. God had threatened him with this punishment of death if he should sin, leaving him indeed to the freedom of his own will, but yet commanding his obedience under pain of death; and He placed him amid the happiness of Eden, as it were in a protected nook of life, with the intention that, if he preserved his righteousness, he should thence ascend to a better place.

Through Adam's sin his whole posterity were corrupted, and were born under the penalty of death, which he had incurred.

Thence, after his sin, he was driven into exile, and by his sin the whole race of which he was the root was corrupted in him, and thereby subjected to the penalty of death. And so it happens that all descended from him, and from the woman who had led him into sin, and was condemned at the same time with him,—being the offspring of carnal lust on which the same punishment of disobedience was visited,—were tainted with the original sin, and were by it drawn through divers errors and sufferings into that last and endless punishment which they suffer in common with the fallen angels, their corrupters and masters, and the partakers of their doom. And thus "by one man sin entered into the world, and death by sin; and so death passed upon all men, for that all have sinned." By "the world" the apostle,[1] of course, means in this place the whole human race.

The state of misery to which Adam's sin reduced mankind, and the restoration effected through the mercy of God.

Thus, then, matters stood. The whole mass of the human race was under condemnation, was lying steeped and wallowing in misery, and was being tossed from one form of evil to another, and, having joined the faction of the fallen angels, was paying the well-merited penalty of that impious rebellion. For whatever the wicked freely do through blind and unbridled lust, and whatever they suffer against their will in the way of open punishment, this all evidently pertains to the just wrath of God. But the goodness of the Creator never fails either to supply life and vital power to the wicked angels (without which their existence would soon come to an end); or, in the case of mankind, who spring from a condemned and corrupt stock, to impart

---

[1] [St. Paul—*Ed.*]

"The Enchiridion," in *The Works of Aurelius Augstine*, ed. M. Dods. Vol. IX.

289

form and life to their seed, to fashion their members, and through the various seasons of their life, and in the different parts of the earth, to quicken their senses, and bestow upon them the nourishment they need. For He judged it better to bring good out of evil, than not to permit any evil to exist. And if He had determined that in the case of men, as in the case of the fallen angels, there should be no restoration to happiness, would it not have been quite just, that the being who rebelled against God, who in the abuse of his freedom spurned and transgressed the command of his Creator when he could so easily have kept it, who defaced in himself the image of his Creator by stubbornly turning away from His light, who by an evil use of his free-will broke away from his wholesome bondage to the Creator's laws,—would it not have been just that such a being should have been wholly and to all eternity deserted by God, and left to suffer the everlasting punishment he had so richly earned? Certainly so God would have done, had He been only just and not also merciful, and had He not designed that His unmerited mercy should shine forth the more brightly in contrast with the unworthiness of its objects.

• • •

Men are not saved by good works, nor by the free determination of their own will, but by the grace of God through faith.

But this part of the human race to which God has promised pardon and a share in His eternal kingdom, can they be restored through the merit of their own works? God forbid. For what good work can a lost man perform, except so far as he has been delivered from perdition? Can they do anything by the free determination of their own will? Again I say, God forbid. For it was by the evil use of his free-will that man destroyed both it and himself. For, as a man who kills himself must, of course, be alive when he kills himself, but after he has killed himself ceases to live, and cannot restore himself to life; so, when man by his own free-will sinned, then sin being victorious over him, the freedom of his will was lost. "For of whom a man is overcome, of the same is he brought in bondage." This is the judgment of the Apostle Peter. And as it is certainly true, what kind of liberty, I ask, can the bond-slave possess, except when it pleases him to sin? For he is freely in bondage who does with pleasure the will of his master. Accordingly, he who is the servant of sin is free to sin. And hence he will not be free to do right, until, being freed from sin, he shall begin to be the servant of righteousness. And this is true liberty, for he has pleasure in the righteous deed; and it is at the same time a holy bondage, for he is obedient to the will of God. But whence comes this liberty to do right to the man who is in bondage and sold under sin, except he be redeemed by Him who has said, "If the Son shall make you free, ye shall be free indeed"? And before this redemption is wrought in a man, when he is not yet free to do what is right, how can he talk of the freedom of his will and his good works, except he be inflated by that foolish pride of boasting which the apostle restrains when he says, "By grace are ye saved, through faith"?

Faith itself is the gift of God; and good works will not be wanting in those who believe.

And lest men should arrogate to themselves the merit of their own faith at least, not understanding that this too is the gift of God, this same apostle, who says in another place that he had "obtained mercy of the Lord to be faithful," here also adds: "and that not of yourselves; it is the gift of God: not of works, lest any man should boast." And lest it should be thought that good works will be wanting in those who believe, he adds further: "For we are His workmanship, created in Christ Jesus unto good works, which God hath before ordained that we should walk in them." We shall be made truly free, then, when God fashions us, that is, forms and creates us anew, not as men—for He has done that already—but as good men, which His grace is now doing, that we may be a new creation in Christ Jesus, according as it is said: "Create in me a clean heart, O God." For God had already created his heart, so far as the physical structure of the human heart is concerned; but the psalmist prays for the renewal of the life which is still lingering in his heart.

The freedom of the will is also the gift of God, for God worketh in us both to will and to do.

And further, should any one be inclined to boast, not indeed of his works, but of the freedom of his will, as if that first merit belong to him, this very liberty of good action being given to him as a reward he had earned, let him listen to this same preacher of grace, when he says: "For it is God which worketh in you, both to will and to do of His own good pleasure"; and in another place: "So, then, it is not of him that willeth, nor of him that runneth, but of God that showeth mercy." Now as, undoubtedly, if a man is of the age to use his reason, he cannot believe, hope, love, unless he will to do so, nor obtain the prize of the high calling of God unless he voluntarily run for it; in what sense is it "not of him that willeth, nor of him that runneth, but of God that showeth mercy," except that, as it is written, "The preparation of the heart is from the Lord"? Otherwise, if it is said, "it is not of him that willeth nor of him that runneth, but of God that showeth mercy," because it is of both, that is, both of the will of man and of the mercy of God, so that we are to understand the saying, "It is not of him that willeth, nor of him that runneth, but of God that showeth mercy," as if it meant the will of man alone is not sufficient, if the mercy of God go not with it—then it will follow that the mercy of God alone is not sufficient, if the will of man go not with it; and therefore, if we may rightly say, "it is not of man that willeth, but of God that showeth mercy," because the will of man by itself is not enough, why may we not also rightly put it in the converse way: "It is not of God that showeth mercy, but of man that willeth," because the mercy of God by itself does not suffice? Surely, if no Christian will dare to say this, "It is not of God that showeth mercy, but of man that willeth," lest he should openly contradict the apostle, it follows that the true interpretation of the saying, "It is not of him that willeth, nor of him that runneth, but of God that showeth mercy," is that the whole work belongs to God, who both makes the will of man righteous, and thus prepares it for assistance, and assists it when it is prepared. For the man's righteousness of will precedes many of God's gifts, but not all and it must itself be included among those which it does not precede. We read in Holy Scripture, both that God's mercy "shall prevent me," and that His mercy "shall follow me." It prevents the unwilling to make him willing; it follows the willing to make his will effectual. Why are we taught to pray for our enemies, who are plainly unwilling to lead a holy life, unless that God may work willingness in them? And why are we ourselves taught to ask that we may receive, unless that He who has created in us the wish, may Himself satisfy the wish? We pray, then, for our enemies, that the mercy of God may prevent them, as it has prevented us: we pray for ourselves that His mercy may follow us.

Men, being by nature the children of wrath, needed a Mediator. In what sense God is said to be angry.

And so the human race was lying under a just condemnation, and all men were the children of wrath. Of which wrath it is written: "All our days are passed away in Thy wrath; we spend our years as a tale that is told." Of which wrath also Job says: "Man that is born of a woman is of few days, and full of trouble." Of which wrath also the Lord Jesus says: "He that believeth on the Son hath everlasting life: and he that believeth not the Son shall not see life; but the wrath of God abideth on him." He does not say it will come, but it "abideth on him." For every man is born with it; wherefore the apostle says: "We were by nature the children of wrath, even as others." Now, as men were lying under this wrath by reason of their original sin, and as this original sin was the more heavy

and deadly in proportion to the number and magnitude of the actual sins which were added to it, there was need for a Mediator, that is, for a reconciler, who, by the offering of one sacrifice, of which all the sacrifices of the law and the prophets were types, should take away this wrath. Wherefore the apostle says: "For if, when we were enemies, we were reconciled to God by the death of His Son, much more, being reconciled, we shall be saved by His life." Now when God is said to be angry, we do not attribute to Him such a disturbed feeling as exists in the mind of an angry man; but we call His just displeasure against sin by the name "anger," a word transferred by analogy from human emotions. But our being reconciled to God through a Mediator, and receiving the Holy Spirit, so that we who were enemies are made sons ("For as many as are led by the Spirit of God, they are the sons of God"): this is the grace of God through Jesus Christ our Lord.

• • •

Christ, who was Himself free from sin, was made sin for us, that we might be reconciled to God.

Begotten and conceived, then, without any indulgence of carnal lust, and therefore bringing with Him no original sin, and by the grace of God joined and united in a wonderful and unspeakable way in one person with the Word, the Only-begotten of the Father, a son by nature, not by grace, and therefore having no sin of His own; nevertheless, on account of the likeness of sinful flesh in which He came, He was called sin, that He might be sacrificed to wash away sin. For, under the Old Covenant, sacrifices for sin were called sins. And He, of whom all these sacrifices were types and shadows, was Himself truly made sin. Hence the apostle, after saying, "We pray you in Christ's stead, be ye reconciled to God," forthwith adds: "for He hath made Him to be sin for us who knew no sin; that we might be made the righteousness of God in Him." He does not say, as some incorrect copies read, "He who knew no sin did sin for us," as if Christ had Himself sinned for our sakes; but he says, "Him who knew no sin," that is, Christ, God, to whom we are to be reconciled, "hath made to be sin for us," that is, hath made Him a sacrifice for our sins, by which we might be reconciled to God. He, then being made sin, just as we are made righteousness (our righteousness being not our own, but God's, not in ourselves, but in Him); He being made sin, not His own, but ours, not in Himself, but in us, showed, by the likeness of sinful flesh in which He was crucified, that though sin was not in Him, yet that in a certain sense He died to sin, by dying in the flesh which was the likeness of sin; and that although He himself had never lived the old life of sin, yet by His resurrection He typified our new life springing up out of the old death in sin.

• • •

By the sacrifice of Christ all things are restored, and peace is made between earth and heaven.

And, of course, the holy angels, taught by god, in the eternal contemplation of whose truth their happiness consists, know how great a number of the human race are to supplement their ranks, and fill up the full tale of their citizenship. Wherefore the apostle says, that "all things are gathered together in one in Christ, both which are in heaven and which are on earth." The things which are in heaven are gathered together when what was lost therefrom in the fall of the angels is restored from among men; and the things which are on earth are gathered together, when those who are predestined to eternal life are redeemed from their old corruption. And thus, through that single sacrifice in which the Mediator was offered up, the one sacrifice of which the many victims under the law were types, heavenly things are brought into peace with earthly things, and earthly things with heavenly. Wherefore, as the same apostle says: "For it pleased the Father that in Him should all fulness dwell: and, having made peace through the blood of His cross, by Him to reconcile all things to Himself: by Him, I say, whether they be things in earth or things in heaven."

• • •

Predestination to eternal life is wholly of God's free grace.

And, moreover, who will be so foolish and blasphemous as to say that God cannot change the evil wills of men, whichever, whenever and wheresoever He chooses, and direct them to what is good? But when He does this, He does it of mercy; when He does it not, it is of justice that He does it not; for "He hath mercy on whom He will have mercy, and whom He will He hardeneth." And when the apostle said this, he was illustrating the grace of God, in connection with which he had just spoken of the twins in the womb of Rebecca, "who being not yet born, neither having done any good or evil, that the purpose of God according to election might stand, not of works, but of

Him that calleth, it was said unto her, "The elder shall serve the younger." And in reference to this matter he quotes another prophetic testimony: "Jacob have I loved, but Esau have I hated." But perceiving how what he had said might affect those who could not penetrate by their understanding the depth of this grace: "What shall we say then?" he says: "Is there unrighteousness with God? God forbid." For it seems unjust that, in the absence of any merit or demerit from good or evil works, God should love the one and hate the other. Now, if the apostle had wished us to understand that there were future good works of the one, and evil works of the other, which of course God foreknew, he would never have said, "not of works," but, "of future works," and in that way would have solved the difficulty, or rather there would then have been no difficulty to solve. As it is, however, after answering, "God forbid"; that is, God forbid that there should be unrighteousness with God; he goes on to prove that there is no unrighteousness in God's doing this, and says: "For he saith to Moses, I will have mercy on whom I will have mercy, and I will have compassion on whom I will have compassion." Now who but a fool would think that God was unrighteous, either in inflicting penal justice on those who earned it, or in extending mercy to the unworthy? Then he draws his conclusion: "So then it is not of him that willeth, nor of him that runneth, but of God that showeth mercy." Thus both the twins were born children of wrath, not on account of any works of their own, but because they were bound in the fetters of that original condemnation which came through Adam. But He who said, "I will have mercy on whom I will have mercy," loved Jacob of His undeserved grace, and hated Esau of His deserved judgment. And as this judgment was due to both, the former learnt from the case of the latter that the fact of the same punishment not falling upon himself gave him no room to glory in any merit of his own, but only in the riches of the divine grace; because "it is not of him that willeth, nor of him that runneth, but of God that showeth mercy." And indeed the whole face, and, if I may use the expression, every lineament of the countenance of Scripture conveys by a very profound analogy this wholesome warning to every one who looks carefully into it, that he who glories should glory in the Lord.

As God's mercy is free, so His judgments are just, and cannot be gainsaid.

Now after commending the mercy of God, saying, "So it is not of him that willeth, nor of him that runneth, but of God that showeth mercy," that he might commend His Justice also (for the man who does not obtain mercy finds, not iniquity, but justice, there being no iniquity with God), he immediately adds: "For the scripture saith unto Pharaoh, Even for this same purpose have I raised thee up, that I might show my power in thee, and that my name might be declared throughout all the earth." And then he draws a conclusion that applies to both, that is, both to His mercy and His justice: "Therefore hath He mercy on whom He will have mercy, and whom He will He hardeneth." "He hath mercy" of His great goodness, "He hardeneth" without any injustice; so that neither can he that is pardoned glory in any merit of his own, nor he that is condemned complain of anything but his own demerit. For it is grace alone that separates the redeemed from the lost, all having been involved in one common perdition through their common origin. Now if any one, on hearing this, should say, "Why doth He yet find fault? for who hath resisted His will?" as if a man ought not to be blamed for being bad, because God hath mercy on whom He will have mercy, and whom He will He hardeneth, God forbid that we should be ashamed to answer as we see the apostle answered: "Nay, but, O man, who are thou that repliest against God? Shall the thing formed say to Him that formed it, Why hast Thou made me thus? Hath not the potter power over the clay, of the same lump to make one vessel unto honour, and another unto dishonour?" Now some foolish people think that in this place the apostle had no answer to give; and for want of a reason to render, rebuked the presumption of his interrogator. But there is great weight in this saying: "Nay, but, O man, who art thou?" and in such a matter as this it suggests to a man in a single word the limits of his capacity, and at the same time does in reality convey an important reason. For if a man does not understand these matters, who is he that he should reply against God? And if he does understand them, he finds no further room for reply. For then he perceives that the whole human race was condemned in its rebellious head by a divine judgment so just, that if not a single member of the race had been redeemed, no one could justly have questioned the justice of God; and that it was right that those who are redeemed should be redeemed in such a way as to show, by the greater number who are unre-

deemed and left in their just condemnation, what the whole race deserved, and whither the deserved judgment of God would lead even the redeemed, did not His undeserved mercy interpose, so that every mouth might be stopped of those who wish to glory in their own merits, and that he that glorieth might glory in the Lord.

• • •

There is no ground in Scripture for the opinion of those who deny the eternity of future punishments.

It is in vain, then, that some, indeed very many, make moan over the eternal punishment, and perpetual, unintermitted torments of the lost, and say they do not believe it shall be so; not, indeed, that they directly oppose themselves to Holy Scripture, but, at the suggestion of their own feelings, they soften down everything that seems hard, and give a milder turn to statements which they think are rather designed to terrify than to be received as literally true. For "Hath God," they say, "forgotten to be gracious? hath He in anger shut up His tender mercies?" Now, they read this in one of the holy psalms. But without doubt we are to understand it as spoken of those who are elsewhere called "vessels of mercy," because even they are freed from misery not on account of any merit of their own, but solely through the pity of God. Or, if the men we speak of insist that this passage applies to all mankind, there is no reason why they should therefore suppose that there will be an end to the punishment of those of whom it is said, "These shall go away into everlasting punishment"; for this shall end in the same manner and at the same time as the happiness of those of whom it is said, "but the righteous unto life eternal." But let them suppose, if the thought gives them pleasure, that the pains of the damned are, at certain intervals, in some degree assuaged. For even in this case the wrath of God, that is, their condemnation (for it is this, and not any disturbed feeling in the mind of God that is called his wrath), abideth upon them; that is, His wrath, though it still remains, does not shut up His tender mercies; though His tender mercies are exhibited, not in putting an end to their eternal punishment, but in mitigating, or in granting them a respite from, their torments; for the psalm does not say, "to put an end to His anger," or, "when His anger is passed by," but "in His anger." Now, if this anger stood alone, or if it existed in the smallest conceivable degree, yet to be lost out of the kingdom of God, to be an exile from the city of God, to be alienated from the life of God, to have no share in that great goodness which God hath laid up for them that fear Him, and hath wrought out for them that trust in Him, would be a punishment so great, that, supposing it to be eternal, no torments that we know of, continued through as many ages as man's imagination can conceive, could be compared with it.

The death of the wicked shall be eternal in the same sense as the life of the saints.

This perpetual death of the wicked, then, that is, their alienation from the life of God, shall abide for ever, and shall be common to them all, whatever men, prompted by their human affections, may conjecture as to a variety of punishments, or as to a mitigation or intermission of their woes; just as the eternal life of the saints shall abide for ever, and shall be common to them all, whatever grades of rank and honour there may be among those who shine with an harmonious effulgence.

Muhammad

Although of more recent origin than the others, Islam is one of the great world religions; today the number of its adherents is comparable to that of Christianity. The word "Islam" itself means submission or surrender, and a Muslim, or follower of Islam, is one who surrenders or submits himself to the will of Allah (God).

Islam had its beginnings on the Arab peninsula in the seventh century A.D. Its founder, Muhammad (c. 571–632), was orphaned in early childhood and grew up in poverty. As he matured he became increasingly estranged from the polytheistic religion of his native city of Mecca, with its worship of idols and its practice of female infanticide. He began to absent himself from Mecca for protracted periods, retiring to a cave in the mountains to meditate. There, one night, he had a vision in which the angel Gabriel appeared before him, telling him he was a messenger, transmitting to him the word of God. On later occasions Gabriel reappeared with more messages, which Muhammad memorized and repeated to his disciples. These were collected together and became the Koran (or Qur'an). Opposed by the traditional religious functionaries in Mecca, Muhammad was forced to flee for his life to the city of Medina, where he consolidated his forces, finally returning in triumph to Mecca. By the time of his death in 632 Muhammad and Islam had achieved both religious and political control over Arabia.

The Koran is the sacred book of Islam; it is held by Muslims to be the infallible word of God, directly revealed to Muhammad. Although it was written in part during the prophet's lifetime it was completed and arranged in its present form shortly after his death. The Islamic creed rests on two central articles of faith. The first is "There is no god but God (Allah)." Thus Islam is a strict monotheism; as such it rejects not only the traditional Arabian polytheism that it supplanted but the trinitarianism of Christianity as well. The second article of faith is "Muhammad is the messenger, or prophet, of Allah." Islam recognizes other important prophets, like Abraham, Moses, and Jesus, and frequent references to them appear in the Koran, but it insists that Muhammad is the ultimate, authoritative prophet. Yet he is a human and not a divine being. Although Muslims believe that on one occasion Muhammad actually ascended to the throne of God and conversed with him, he lived and died as an ordinary mortal.

As an elaborated religion the Muslim faith rests on "Five Pillars," which are obligatory on its adherents: (1) Repetition of the creed "There is no god but Allah, and Muhammad is the prophet of Allah"; (2) prayer, normally done five times daily while bowing toward Mecca; (3) alms-giving, for the support of the poor and needy; (4) the fast, for a full day during the sacred month of Ramadan; and (5) the pilgrimage, to Mecca, which every Muslim is expected to make once in a lifetime.

To one outside of the Muslim community the organization of the Koran may appear baffling because it seems to lack any recognizable logical coherence. To give the Koran's message greater structure and continuity, the contents of the selection that follows have been rearranged. The numbers of the "Suras" or chapters of the Koran from which the excerpts have been taken are given in parentheses at the end of each quotation. Also, headings describing the contents of each of these have been added.

The Koran

PREAMBLE

In the Name of God, The
    Compassionate, the Merciful

Praise be to God, Lord of the worlds!
The compassionate, the merciful!
King on the day of reckoning!
Thee *only* do we worship, and to Thee do
    we cry for help.
Guide Thou us on the straight path,
The path of those to whom Thou hast been
    gracious;—with whom thou are not
angry, and who go not astray. (1)

GOD

He is God alone;
God the eternal!
He begetteth not, and He is not
    begotten;
And there is none like unto Him. (112)

Trans. J. M. Rodwell.

MUHAMMAD THE PROPHET

Muhammad is not more than an apostle; other apostles have already passed away before him. If he die, therefore, or be slain, will ye turn upon your heels? But he who turneth on his heels shall not injure God at all, and God will certainly reward the thankful! (3)

THE KORAN

This Book is without a doubt a revelation sent down from the Lord of the Worlds.

Will they say, he [Muhammad] hath forged it? Nay, it is the truth from thy Lord that thou mayest warn a people to whom no warner hath come before thee, that haply they may be guided.

God it is who hath created the heavens and the earth and all that is between them in six days, then ascended his throne. Save Him ye have no patron, and none to plead for you. Will ye not then reflect?

From the heaven to the earth He governeth all things; hereafter shall they come up to him on a day, whose length shall be a thousand of such years as ye reckon.

This is He who knoweth the unseen and the seen; the Mighty, the Merciful. Who hath made everything which he hath created most good; and began the creation of man with clay;

Then ordained his progeny from germs of life, from sorry water;

Then shaped him and breathed of His Spirit into him, and gave you hearing and seeing and hearts: What little thanks do ye return? (32)

By the star when it setteth,
Your compatriot [Muhammad] erreth
    not, nor is he led astray,
Neither speaketh he from mere impulse.
The Koran is no other than a revelation
    revealed to him.
One terrible in power [Gabriel] taught it
    him,
Endued with wisdom. With even balance
    stood he
In the highest part of the horizon;
Then came he nearer and approached,
And was at the distance of two bows, or
    even closer,—
And he revealed to his servant what he
    revealed. (53)

GOD'S CREATION AND CREATURES

Verily God causeth the grain and the date stone to put forth. He bringeth forth the living from the dead, and dead from the living! This is God!

Why, then, are ye turned aside from Him?

He causeth the dawn to appear, and hath ordained the night for rest, and the sun and the moon for computing time! The ordinance of the Mighty, the Wise!

And it is He who hath ordained the stars for you that ye may be guided thereby in the darknesses of the land and of the sea! Clear have we made our signs to men of knowledge.

And it is He who hath produced you from one man, and hath provided for you an abode and resting place! Clear have we made our signs for men of insight.

And it is He who sendeth down rain from heaven; and we bring forth by it the buds of all the plants, and from them bring we forth the green foliage, and the close growing grain, and palm trees with sheaths of clustering dates, and gardens of grapes, and the olive and the pomegranate, like and unlike. Look ye on their fruits when they fruit and ripen. Truly herein are signs unto people who believe. (6)

Now of fine clay have we created man;

Then we placed him a moist germ, in a safe abode;

Then made we the moist germ a clot of blood; then made the clotted blood into a piece of flesh; then made the piece of flesh into bones; and we clothed the bones with flesh; then brought forth man of yet another make—Blessed therefore be God, the most excellent of makers—

Then after this ye shall surely die;

Then shall ye be waked up on the day of resurrection.

And we have created over you seven heavens:—and we are not careless of the creation.

And we send down water from the heaven in its due degree, and we cause it to settle on the earth;—and we have power for its withdrawal;—

And by it we cause gardens of palm trees, and vineyards to spring forth for you, in which ye have plenteous fruits, and whereof ye eat;

And the tree that groweth up on Mount Sinai; which yieldeth oil and a juice for those who eat.

And there is a lesson for you in the cattle. We give you to drink of what is in their bellies, and many advantages do ye derive from them, and for food they serve you;

And on them and on ships are ye borne. (23)

Nay! but it (the Koran) is a warning;
(And whoso is willing beareth it in
    mind)
Written on honored pages,
Exalted, purified,
By the hands of scribes, honored,
    righteous.
Cursed be man! What hath made him
    unbelieving?
Of what thing did God create him?
Out of moist germs,
He created him and fashioned him,
Then made him an easy passage from
    the womb,
Then causeth him to die and burieth
    him;
Then, when he pleaseth, will raise him
    again to life.
Aye! but man hath not yet fulfilled the
    bidding of his Lord.
Let man look at his food;
It was We who rained down the copious
    rains,
Then cleft the earth with clefts,
And caused the upgrowth of the grain,
And grapes and healing herbs,
And the olive and the palm,
And enclosed gardens thick with trees,
And fruits and herbage,
For the service of yourselves and of your
    cattle. (80)

GOD'S PROVIDENCE

And with Him are the keys of the secret things; none knoweth them but He. He knoweth whatever is on the land and in the sea; and no leaf falleth but He knoweth it; neither is there a grain in the darknesses of the earth, nor a thing green or sere, but it is noted in a distinct writing.

It is He who taketh your souls at night, and knoweth what ye have merited in the day; then he awaketh any one of you, our messengers take his soul, and fail not.

Then are they returned to God their Lord, the True. Is not judgment His? (6)

Thus unto thee as unto those who preceded thee doth God, the Mighty, the Wise, reveal!

All that is in the heavens and all that is in the earth is His, and He is the High, the Great!

Ready are the heavens to cleave asunder from above for very awe, and the angels celebrate the praise of their Lord, and ask forgiveness for the dwellers on earth. Is not God the Indulgent, the Merciful?

But whoso take aught beside Him as lords—God watcheth them! But thou hast them not in thy charge.

It is thus moreover that we have revealed to thee an Arabic Koran, that thou mayest warn the mother city [Mecca] and all around it, and that thou mayest warn them of that day of the Gathering, of which there is no doubt—when part shall be in Paradise and part in the flame.

Had God so pleased, He had made them one people and of one creed, but He bringeth whom He will within His mercy; and as for the doers of evil, no patron, no helper shall there be for them.

Will they take other patrons than Him? But God is man's only Lord. He quickeneth the dead, and He is mighty over all things.

And whatever the subject of your disputes, with God doth its decision rest. This is God, my Lord; in Him do I put my trust, and to Him do I turn in penitence.

Creator of the heavens and of the earth! He giveth with open hand, or sparingly, to whom He will; He knoweth all things.

To you hath He prescribed the faith which He commanded unto Noah, and which we have revealed to thee, and which we commanded unto Abraham and Moses and Jesus, saying, "Observe this faith, and be not divided into sects therein." Intolerable to those who worship idols jointly with God is that faith to which thou dost call them. Whom He pleaseth will God choose for it, and whosoever shall turn to Him in penitence will He guide to it. (42)

ESCHATOLOGY

By the night when she spreads her veil;
By the day when it brightly shineth;
By Him who made male and female;
At different ends truly do ye aim!
But as to him who giveth alms and
   feareth God,
And yieldeth assent to the good,
To him will we make easy the path to
   happiness.
But as to him who is covetous and bent
   on riches,
And calleth the good a lie,
To him will we make easy the path to
   misery,
And what shall his wealth avail him when
   he goeth down?
Truly man's guidance is with Us,
And ours, the future and the past.
I warn you therefore of the flaming fire;

None shall be cast to it but the most
   wretched,—
Who hath called the truth a lie and
   turned his back.
But the God-fearing shall escape it,—
Who giveth away his substance that he
   may become pure;
And who offereth not favors to any one
   for the sake of recompense,
But only as seeking the face of his Lord
   the Most High.
And surely in the end he shall be well
   content. (92)

Of what ask they of one another?
Of the great news.
The theme of their disputes.
Nay! they shall certainly know its truth!
Again. Nay! they shall certainly know it.
Have we not made the earth a couch?
And the mountains its tent-stakes?
We have created you of two sexes,
And ordained you sleep for rest,
And ordained the night as a mantle,
And ordained the day for gaining
   livelihood.
And built above you seven solid heavens,
And placed therein a burning lamp;
And we send down water in abundance
   from the rain-clouds,
That we may bring forth by it corn and
   herbs,
And gardens thick with trees.
Lo! the day of Severance is fixed;
The day when there shall be a blast on
   the trumpet, and ye shall come in
   crowds,
And the heaven shall be opened and be
   full of portals,
And the mountains shall be set in
   motion, and melt into thin vapor.
Hell truly shall be a place of snares,
The home of transgressors,
To abide therein ages.
No coolness shall they taste therein nor
   any drink,
Save boiling water and running sores;
Meet recompense!
For they looked not forward to their
   account;
And they gave the lie to our signs,
   charging them with falsehood.
But we noted and wrote down all.

"Taste this then, and we will give you increase of nought but torment."
But for the God-fearing is a blissful abode,
Enclosed gardens and vineyards;
And damsels with swelling breasts, their peers in age,
And a full cup.
There shall they hear no vain discourse nor any falsehood;
A recompense from thy Lord—sufficing gift!—

Lord of the heavens and of the earth, and of all that between them lieth—the God of Mercy! But not a word shall they obtain from Him.

On the day whereon the Spirit and the Angels shall be ranged in order, they shall not speak; save he whom the God of Mercy shall permit, and who shall say that which is right.

This is the sure day. Whoso then will, let him take the path of return to his Lord.

Verily, we warn you of a chastisement close at hand.

The day on which a man shall see the deeds which his hands have sent before him; and when the unbeliever shall say, "Oh! would I were dust!" (78)

O children of Adam! There shall come to you apostles from among yourselves, rehearsing my signs to you; and whoso shall fear God and do good works, no fear shall be upon them, neither shall they be put to grief.

But they who charge our signs with falsehood, and turn away from them in their pride, shall be inmates of the fire; for ever shall they abide therein. And who is worse than he who deviseth a lie of God, or treateth our signs as lies? To them shall a portion here below be assigned in accordance with the Book of our decrees, until the time when our messengers, as they receive their souls, shall say, "Where are they on whom ye called beside God?" They shall say, "Gone from us." And they shall witness against themselves that they were infidels.

He shall say, "Enter ye into the Fire with the generations of Djinn and men who have preceded you. So oft as a fresh generation entereth, it shall curse its sister, until when they have all reached it, the last comers shall say to the former, "O our Lord! these are they who led us astray; assign them therefore a double torment of the fire." He will say, "Ye shall all have double." But of this are ye ignorant.

And the former of them shall say to the latter, "What advantage have ye over us? Taste ye therefore the torment for that which ye have done."

Verily, they who have charged our signs with falsehood and have turned away from them in their pride, heaven's gates shall not be opened to them, nor shall they enter Paradise, until the camel passeth through the eye of the needle. After this manner will we recompense the transgressors.

They shall make their bed in hell, and above them shall be coverings of fire! And this way will we recompense the evil doers.

But as to those who have believed and done the things which are right (we will lay on no one a burden beyond his power)—these shall be inmates of Paradise, for ever shall they abide therein.

And we will remove whatever rancor was in their bosoms; rivers shall roll at their feet, and they shall say, "Praise be to God who hath guided us hither! We had not been guided had not God guided us! Of a surety the apostles of our Lord came to us with truth." And a voice shall cry to them, "This is Paradise, of which, as the meed of your works, ye are made heirs."

And the inmates of Paradise shall cry to the inmates of the fire, "Now have we found what our Lord promised us to be true. Have ye too found what your Lord promised you to be true?" And they shall answer, "Yes." And a herald shall proclaim between them, "The curse of God be upon the evil doers."

Who turn men aside from the way of God, and seek to make it crooked, and who believe not in the life to come!"

And between them shall be a partition, and on the wall Al Araf [between heaven and hell] shall be men who will know all, by their tokens, and they shall cry to the inmates of Paradise, "Peace be on you!" but they shall not yet enter it, although they long to do so.

And when their eyes are turned towards the inmates of the fire they shall say, "O our Lord! place us not with the offending people."

And they who upon Al Araf shall cry to those whom they shall know by their tokens, "Your amassings and your pride have availed you nothing.

Are these they on whom ye sware God would not bestow mercy? Enter ye into Paradise! where no fear shall be upon you, neither shall ye be put to grief."

And the inmates of the fire shall cry to the inmates of Paradise, "Pour upon us some water, or of the refreshments God hath given you." They shall say, "Truly God hath forbidden both to unbelievers, who made their religion a sport and pastime, and whom the life of the world hath deceived." This day therefore will we forget them. . . . (71)

MORAL PRECEPTS

Kill not your children for fear of want; for them and for you will we provide. Verily, the killing them is a great wickedness.

Have nought to do with adultery; for it is a foul thing and an evil way.

Neither slay any one whom God hath forbidden you to slay, unless for a just cause; and whosoever shall be slain wrongfully, to his heir have we given powers; but let him not outstep bounds in putting the manslayer to death, for he too, in his turn, will be assisted and avenged.

And touch not the substance of the orphan, unless in an upright way, till he attain his age of strength. And perform your covenant; verily the covenant shall be inquired of.

And give full measure when you measure, and weigh with just balance. This will be better, and fairest for settlement.

And follow not that of which thou hast no knowledge; because the hearing and the sight and the heart—each of these shall be inquired of.

And walk not proudly on the earth, for thou canst not cleave the earth, neither shalt thou reach to the mountains in height. (17)

There is no piety in turning your faces toward the east or the west, but he is pious who believeth in God, and the last day, and the angels, and the scriptures, and the prophets; who for the love of God disburseth his wealth to his kindred, and to the orphans, and the needy, and the wayfarer, and those who ask, and for ransoming; who observeth prayer, and payeth the legal alms, and who is of those who are faithful to their engagements when they have engaged in them, and patient under ills and hardships, and in time of trouble. These are they who are just, and these are they who fear the Lord.

O believers! retaliation for bloodshedding is prescribed to you; the free man for the free, and the slave for the slave, and the woman for the woman. But he to whom his brother shall make any remission is to be dealt with equitably, and to him should he pay a fine with liberality.

This is a relaxation from your Lord and a mercy. For him who after this shall transgress a sore punishment!

But in this law of retaliation is your security for life, O men of understanding! to the intent that ye may fear God.

It is prescribed to you, when any one of you is at the point of death, if he leave goods, that he bequeath equitably to his parents and kindred. This is binding on those who fear God. But as for him who after he hath heard the bequest shall change it, surely the wrong of this shall be on those who change it; verily, God heareth, knoweth.

But he who feareth from the testator any mistake or wrong, and shall make a settlement between the parties—that shall be no wrong in him; verily, God is Lenient, Merciful.

O believers! a Fast is prescribed to you as it was prescribed to those before you, that ye may fear God, for certain days.

But he among you who shall be sick, or on a journey shall fast that same number of other days; and as for those who are able to keep it and yet break it, the expiation of this shall be the maintenance of a poor man. And he who of his own accord performeth a good work shall derive good from it, and good shall it be for you to fast—if ye knew it.

As to the month Ramadhan in which the Koran was sent down to be man's guidance, and an explanation of that guidance, and of that illumination, as soon as any one of you observeth the moon, let him set about the fast; but he who is sick, or upon a journey, shall fast a like number of other days. God wisheth you ease, but wisheth not your discomfort, and that you fulfil the number of days, and that you glorify God for his guidance, and that you be thankful.

And when my servants ask thee concerning me, then will I be nigh unto them. I will answer the cry of him that crieth, when he crieth unto me; but let them hearken unto me, and believe in me, that they may proceed aright.

You are allowed on the night of the fast to approach your wives; they are your garment and ye are their garment. God knoweth that ye defraud yourselves therein, so He turneth unto you and forgiveth you! Now, therefore, go in unto them with full desire for that which God hath ordained for you; and eat and drink until ye can discern a white thread from a black thread by the daybreak, then fast strictly till night, and go not in unto them, but rather pass the time in the Mosque.

• • •

The likeness of those who expend their wealth for the cause of God is that of a grain of corn which produceth seven ears, and in each ear a hundred grains; and God will multiply to whom He pleaseth. God is Liberal, Knowing!

They who expend their wealth for the cause of God, and never follow what they have laid out with reproaches or harm, shall have their reward with their Lord; no fear shall come upon them, neither shall they be put to grief.

A kind speech and forgiveness is better than alms followed by injury. God is Rich, Clement.

O ye who believe! make not your alms void by reproaches and injury, like him who spendeth his substance to be seen of men, and believeth not in God and in the latter day. The likeness of such an one is that of a rock with a thin soil upon it, on which a heavy rain falleth but leaveth it hard. No profit from their works shall they be able to gain; for God guideth not the unbelieving people.

And the likeness of those who expend their substance from a desire to please God, and for the stablishing of their souls, is as a garden on a hill, on which the heavy rain falleth, and it yieldeth its fruits twofold; and even if a heavy rain fall not on it, yet is there a dew. God beholdeth your actions.

• • •

Ye may divorce your wives twice. Keep them honorably or put them away with kindness. But it is not allowed you to appropriate to yourselves aught of what ye have given to them, unless both fear that they cannot keep within the bounds set up by God. And if ye fear that they cannot observe the ordinances of God, no blame shall attach to either of you for what the wife shall herself give for her redemption. These are the bounds of God; therefore overstep them not, for whoever oversteppeth the bounds of God, they are evildoers.

But if the husband divorce her a third time, it is not lawful for him to take her again, until she shall have married another husband; and if he also divorce her, then shall no blame attach to them if they return to each other, thinking that they can keep within the bounds fixed by God. (2)

O men! fear your Lord, who hath created you of one man (soul), and of him created his wife, and from these twain hath spread abroad so many men and women. And fear ye God, in whose name ye ask mutual favors,— and reverence the wombs that bare you. Verily is God watching over you!

And give to the orphans their property; substitute not worthless things of your own for their valuable ones, and devour not their property after adding it to your own, for this is a great crime.

And if ye are apprehensive that ye shall not deal fairly with orphans, then of other women who seem good in your eyes, marry but two, or three, or four; and if ye still fear that ye shall not act equitably, then one only; or the slaves whom ye have acquired. This will make justice on your part easier. Give women their dowry freely; but if of themselves they give up aught thereof to you, then enjoy it as convenient, and profitable.

And entrust not to the incapable the substance which God hath placed with you for their support; but maintain them therewith, and clothe them, and speak to them with kindly speech.

• • •

And if ye be desirous to exchange one wife for another, and have given one of them a talent, make no deduction from it. Would ye take it by slandering her, and with manifest wrong?

How, moreover, could ye take it, when one of you hath gone in unto the other, and they have received from you a strict bond of union?

And marry not women whom your fathers have married; for this is a shame, and hateful, and an evil way:—though what is past may be allowed.

Forbidden to you are your mothers, and your daughters, and your sisters, and your aunts, both on the father and mother's side, and your nieces on the brother and sister's side, and your foster-mothers, and your foster-sisters, and the mothers of your wives, and your step-daughters who are your wards, born of your wives to whom ye have gone in; (but if ye have not gone in unto them, it shall be no sin in you to marry them); and the wives of your sons who proceed out of your loins; and ye may not have two sisters, except where it is already done. Verily, God is Indulgent, Merciful!

Forbidden to you also are married women, except those who are in your hands as slaves. This is the law of God for you. And it is allowed you, beside this, to seek out wives by means of your wealth, with modest conduct, and without fornication. And give those with whom ye have cohabited their dowry. This is the law. But it shall be no crime in you to make agreements over and above the law.

• • •

Men are superior to women on account of the qualities with which God hath gifted the one above the other, and on account of the outlay they make from their substance for them. Virtuous women are obedient, careful, during the husband's absence, because God hath of them been careful. But chide those for whose refractoriness ye have cause to fear; remove them into beds apart, and scourge them. But if they are obedient to you, then seek not occasion against them. (4)

WARFARE

Fight for the cause of God against those who fight against you; but commit not the injustice of attacking them first. God loveth not such injustice.

And kill them wherever ye shall find them, and eject them from whatever place they have ejected you; for civil discord is worse than carnage. Yet attack them not at the sacred Mosque, unless they attack you therein; but if they attack you, slay them. Such is the reward of the infidels.

But if they desist, then verily God is Gracious, Merciful.

Fight therefore against them until there be no more civil discord, and the only worship be that of God. But if they desist, then let there be no hostility, save against the wicked. (2)

CHRISTIANS AND JEWS

We believe in God, and in what hath been sent down to us, and what hath been sent down to Abraham, and Ismael, and Isaac, and Jacob, and the tribes, and in what was given to Moses, and Jesus, and the Prophets, from their Lord. We make no difference between them. And to Him are we resigned (Muslims).

Whoso desireth any other religion than Islam, that religion shall never be accepted from him, and in the next world he shall be among the lost. (3)

Verily, they who believe (Muslims), and they who follow the Jewish religion, and the Christians, and the Sabeites—whoever of these believeth in God and the last day, and doeth that which is right, shall have their reward with their Lord. Fear shall not come upon them, neither shall they be grieved. (2)

Make war upon such of those to whom the Scriptures have been given as believe not in God, or in the last day, and who forbid not that which God and His Apostle have forbidden, and who profess not the profession of the truth, until they pay tribute out of hand, and they be humbled.

The Jews say, "Ezra is a son of God," and the Christians say, "The Messiah is a son of God." Such the sayings in their mouths! They resemble the saying of the infidels of old! God do battle with them! How are they misguided!

They take their teachers, and their monks, and the Messiah, son of Mary, for Lords beside God, though bidden to worship one God only. There is no God but He! Far from His glory be what they associate with Him! (9)

Al-Farabi

One of the most important Muslim thinkers during the Golden Age of Islam was Abu Nasr Muhammad al-Farabi (c. 870–950). Of Turkish descent al-Farabi was born in Turkestan, in the interior of southern Asia. For most of his life he lived in the city of Baghdad, where he became a student of philosophy as it was taught there by Christians steeped in the classical Greek tradition as it had been developed during the Hellenistic age and later in the school of Alexandria in Egypt. Although he was a noted philosopher in his own time, al-Farabi shunned fame and publicity, preferring to live a secluded and austere life.

The influence of classical Greek philosophy on al-Farabi, particularly of Plato, Aristotle, and the neo-Platonists, is evident throughout his writings, including his book *The Perfect State*. Although the title of this work indicates its subject to be politics, al-Farabi turns to his description of the ideal state only in chapter 15, after he has grounded his views in a full theory both of metaphysics (including theology and natural science) and psychology, employing arguments from analogy as the basis for his political conclusions. His use of this kind of philosophical generalization and integration reveals the influence of Aristotle, as does the opening paragraph of the following selection, in which he reiterates the Aristotelian view that "man is a political animal." In his description of the ideal ruler, whom al-Farabi conceives to be a philosopher-king, can be found a strong echo of the central theme of Plato's *Republic*.

But al-Farabi's thought was not just derivative from the Greeks. As a Muslim he added a further dimension to the philosopher-king concept. The ideal ruler must also be a prophet. Not only is such a ruler an individual of high intelligence but one of an intellect of "divine quality" who can look into the future and warn "of things to come." This addition raises a question: Which quality of the ideal ruler did al-Farabi consider to be of preeminent importance—his prophetic ability or his intellectual eminence? Judging from the concluding statment of the selection it seems fair to conclude: the latter. However much a religious believer he may have been, al-Farabi was first and foremost a philosopher.

The Perfect State

Chapter 15

Perfect Associations and Perfect Ruler; Faulty Associations

1. In order to preserve himself and to attain his highest perfections every human being is by his very nature in need of many things which he cannot provide all by himself; he is indeed in need of people who each supply him with some particular need of his. Everybody finds himself in the same relation to everybody in this respect. Therefore man cannot attain the perfection, for the sake of which his inborn nature has been given to him, unless many (societies of) people who co-operate come together who each supply everybody else with some particular need of his, so that as a result of the contribution of the whole community all the things are brought together which everybody needs in order to preserve himself and to attain perfection. Therefore human individuals have come to exist in great numbers, and have settled in the inhabitable (inhabited?) region of the earth, so that human societies have come to exist in it, some of which are perfect, others imperfect.

2. There are three kinds of perfect society, great, medium and small. The great one is the union of all the societies in the inhabitable world; the medium one the union of one nation in one part of the inhabitable world; the small one the union of the people of a city in the territory of any nation whatsoever. Imperfect are the union of people in a village, the union of people in a quarter, then the union in a street, eventually the union in a house, the house being the smallest union of all. Quarter and village exist both for the sake of the city, but the relation of the village to the city is one of service whereas the quarter is related to the city as a part of it; the street is a part of the quarter, the house a part of the street. The city is a part of the territory of a nation, the nation a part of all the people of the inhabitable world.

3. The most excellent good and the utmost perfection is, in the first instance, attained in a city, not in a society which is less complete than it. But since good in its real sense is such as to be attainable through choice and will and evils are also due to will and choice only, a city may be established to enable its people to co-operate in attaining some aims that are evil. Hence felicity is not attainable in every city. The city, then, in which people aim through association at co-operating for the things by which felicity in its real and true sense can be attained, is the excellent city, and the society in which there is a co-operation to acquire felicity is the excellent society; and the nation in which all of its cities co-operate for those things through which felicity is attained is the excellent nation. In the same way, the excellent universal state will arise only when all the nations in it co-operate for the purpose of reaching felicity.

Al-Farabi on the Perfect State, trans. Richard Walzer (Oxford: Clarendon Press, 1985). Reprinted by permission of Oxford University Press.

4. The excellent city resembles the perfect and healthy body, all of whose limbs co-operate to make the life of the animal perfect and to preserve it in this state. Now the limbs and organs of the body are different and their natural endowments and faculties are unequal in excellence, there being among them one ruling organ, namely the heart, and organs which are close in rank to that ruling organ, each having been given by nature a faculty by which it performs its proper function in conformity with the natural aim of that ruling organ. Other organs have by nature faculties by which they perform their functions according to the aims of those organs which have no intermediary between themselves and the ruling organ; they are in the second rank. Other organs, in turn, perform their functions according to the aim of those which are in the second rank, and so on until eventually organs are reached which only serve and do not rule at all. The same holds good in the case of the city. Its parts are different by nature, and their natural dispositions are unequal in excellence: there is in it a man who is the ruler, and there are others whose ranks are close to the ruler, each of them with a disposition and a habit through which he performs an action in conformity with the intention of that ruler; these are the holders of the first ranks. Below them are people who perform their actions in accordance with the aims of those people; they are in the second rank. Below them in turn are people who perform their actions according to the aims of the people mentioned in the second instance, and the parts of the city continue to be arranged in this way, until eventu-ally parts are reached which perform their actions according to the aims of others, while there do not exist any people who perform their actions according to their aims; these, then, are the people who serve without being served in turn, and who are hence in the lowest rank and at the bottom of the scale. But the limbs and organs of the body are natural, and the dispositions which they have are natural faculties, whereas, although the parts of the city are natural, their dispositions and habits, by which they perform their actions in the city, are not natural but voluntary—notwithstanding that the parts of the city are by nature provided with endowments unequal in excellence which enable them to do one thing and not another. But they are not parts of the city by their inborn nature alone but rather by the voluntary habits which they acquire such as the arts and their likes; to the natural faculties which exist in the organs and limbs of the body correspond the voluntary habits and dispositions in the parts of the city.

5. The ruling organ in the body is by nature the most perfect and most complete of the organs in itself and in its specific qualification, and it also has the best of everything of which another organ has a share as well; beneath it, in turn, are other organs which rule over organs inferior to them, their rule being lower in rank than the rule of the first and indeed subordinate to the rule of the first; they rule and are ruled. In the same way, the ruler of the city is the most perfect part of the city in his specific qualification and has the best of everything which anybody else shares with him; beneath him are people who are ruled by him and rule others.

The heart comes to be first and becomes then the cause of the existence of the other organs and limbs of the body, and the cause of the existence of their faculties in them and of their arrangement in the ranks proper to them, and when one of its organs is out of order, it is the heart which provides the means to remove that disorder. In the same way the ruler of this city must come to be in the first instance, and will subsequently be the cause of the rise of the city and its parts and the cause of the presence of the voluntary habits of its parts and of their arrangement in the ranks proper to them; and when one part is out of order he provides it with the means to remove its disorder.

The parts of the body close to the ruling organ perform of the natural functions, in agreement—by nature— with the aim of the ruler, the most noble ones; the organs beneath them perform those functions which are less noble, and eventually the organs are reached which perform the meanest functions. In the same way the parts of the city which are close in authority to the ruler of the city perform the most noble voluntary actions, and those below them less noble actions, until eventually the parts are reached which perform the most ignoble actions. The inferiority of such actions is sometimes due to the inferiority of their matter, although they may be extremely useful—like the action of the bladder and the action of the lower intestine in the body; sometimes it is due to their being of little use; at other times it is due to their being very easy to perform. This applies equally to the city and equally to every whole which is composed by nature of well ordered coherent parts: they have a ruler whose relation to the other parts is like the one just described.

6. This applies also to all existents. For the relation of the First Cause to the other existents is like the relation of the king of the excellent city to its other parts. For the ranks of the immaterial existents are close to the First. Beneath them are the heavenly bodies, and beneath the heavenly bodies the material bodies. All these existents act in conformity with the First Cause, follow it, take it as their guide and imitate it; but each existent does that according to its capacity, choosing its aim precisely on the strength of its established rank in the universe: that is to say the last follows the aim of that which is slightly above it in rank, equally the second existent, in turn, follows what is above itself in rank, and in the same way the third existent has an aim which is above it. Eventually existents are reached which are linked with the First Cause without any intermediary whatsoever. In accordance with this order of rank all the existents permanently follow the aim of the First Cause. Those which are from the very outset provided with all the essentials of their existence are made to imitate the First (Cause) and its aim from their very outset, and hence enjoy eternal bliss and hold the highest ranks; but those which are not provided from the outse with all the essentials of thei exis tence, are provided with a faculty by which they move towards the expected attainment of those essentials and will then be able to follow the aim of the First (Cause). The excellent city ought to be arranged in the same way: all its parts ought to imitate in their actions the aim of their first ruler according to their rank.

7. The ruler of the excellent city cannot just be any man, because rulership requires two conditions: (a) he should be predisposed for it by his inborn nature, (b) he should have acquired the attitude and habit of will for rulership which will develop in a man whose inborn nature is predisposed for it. Nor is every art suitable for rulership, most of the arts, indeed, are rather suited for service within the city, just as most men are by their very nature born to serve. Some of the arts rule certain (other) arts while serving others at the same time, whereas there are other arts which, not ruling anything at all, only serve. Therefore the art of ruling the excellent city cannot just be any chance art, nor due to any chance habit whatever. For just as the first ruler in a genus cannot be ruled by anything in that genus—for instance the ruler of the limbs cannot be ruled by any other limb, and this holds good for any ruler of any composite whole—so the art of the ruler in the excellent city of necessity cannot be a serving art at all and cannot be ruled by any other art, but his art must be an art towards the aim of which all the other arts tend, and for which they strive in all the actions of the excellent city.

8. That man is a person over whom nobody has any sovereignty whatsoever. He is a man who has reached his perfection and has become actually intellect and actually being thought (intelligized), his representative faculty having by nature reached its utmost perfection in the way stated by us; this faculty of his is predisposed by nature to receive, either in waking life or in sleep, from the Active Intellect the particulars, either as they are or by imitating them, and also the intelligibles, by imitating them. His Passive Intellect will have reached its perfection by [having apprehended] all the intelligibles, so that none of them is kept back from it, and it will have become actually intellect and actually being thought. Indeed any man whose Passive Intellect has thus been perfected by [having apprehended] all the intelligibles and has become actually intellect and actually being thought, so that the intelligible in him has become identical with that which thinks in him, acquires an actual intellect which is superior to the Passive Intellect and more perfect and more separate from matter (immaterial?) than the Passive Intellect. It is called the 'Acquired Intellect' and comes to occupy a middle position between the Passive Intellect and the Active Intellect, nothing else being between it and the Active Intellect. The Passive Intellect is thus like matter and substratum for the Acquired Intellect, and the Acquired Intellect like matter and substratum for the Active Intellect, and the rational faculty, which is a natural disposition, is a matter underlying the Passive Intellect which is actually intellect.

9. The first stage, then, through which man becomes man is the coming to be of the receptive natural disposition which is ready to become actually intellect; this disposition is common to all men. Between this disposition and the Active Intellect are two stages, the Passive Intellect which has become actually intellect, and [the rise of] the Acquired Intellect. There are thus two stages between the first stage of being a man and the Active Intellect. When the perfect Passive Intellect and the natural disposition become one thing in the way the compound of matter and form is one—and when the form of the humanity of this man is taken as identical with the Passive Intellect which has become actually intellect, there will be between this man and the Active Intellect only one stage. And when the natural disposition is made the matter of the Passive Intellect which has become actually intellect, and the Passive Intellect the matter of the Acquired Intellect, and the Acquired Intellect the matter of the Active Intellect, and when all this is taken as one and the same thing, then this man is the man on whom the Active Intellect has descended.

10. When this occurs in both parts of his rational faculty, namely the theoretical and the practical rational faculties, and also in his representative faculty, then it is this man who receives Divine Revelation, and God Almighty grants him Revelation through the mediation of the Active Intellect, so that the emanation from God Almighty to the Active Intellect is passed on to his Passive Intellect through the mediation of the Acquired Intellect, and then to the faculty of representation. Thus he is, through the emanation from the Active Intellect to his Passive Intellect, a wise man and a philosopher and an accomplished thinker who employs an intellect of divine quality, and through the emanation from the Active Intellect to his faculty of representation a visionary prophet: who warns of things to come and tells of particular things which exist at present.

11. This man holds the most perfect rank of humanity and has reached the highest degree of felicity. His soul is united as it were with the Active Intellect, in the way stated by us. He is the man who knows every action by which felicity can be reached. This is the first condition for being a ruler. Moreover, he should be a good orator and able to rouse [other people's] imagination by well chosen words. He should be able to lead people well along the right path to felicity and to the actions by which felicity is reached. He should, in addition, be of tough physique, in order to shoulder the tasks of war.

This is the sovereign over whom no other human being has any sovereignty whatsoever; he is the Imām; he is the first sovereign of the excellent city, he is the sovereign of the excellent nation, and the sovereign of the universal state.

12. But this state can only be reached by a man in whom twelve natural qualities are found together, with which he is endowed by birth. (1) One of them is that he should have limbs and organs which are free from deficiency and strong, and that they will make him fit for the actions which depend on them; when he intends to perform an action with one of them, he accomplishes it with ease. (2) He should by nature be good at understanding and perceiving everything said to him, and grasp it in his mind according to what the speaker intends and what the thing itself demands. (3) He should be good at retaining what he comes to know and see and hear and apprehend in general, and forget almost nothing. (4) He should be well provided with ready intelligence and very bright; when he sees the slightest indication of a thing, he should grasp it in the way indicated. (5) He should have a fine diction, his tongue enabling him to explain to perfection all that is in the recess of his mind. (6) He should be fond of learning and acquiring knowledge, be devoted to it and grasp things eas-

ily, without finding the effort painful, nor feeling discomfort about the toil which it entails. (7) He should by nature be fond of truth and truthful men and hate falsehood and liars. (8) He should by nature not crave for food and drink and sexual intercourse, and have a natural aversion to gambling and hatred of the pleasures which these pursuits provide. (9) He should be proud of spirit and fond of honour, his soul being by his (?) nature above everything ugly and base, and rising naturally to the most lofty things. (10) Dirham and dīnār and the other worldly pursuits should be of little amount in his view. (11) He should by nature be fond of justice and of just people, and hate oppression and injustice and those who practice them, giving himself and others their due, and urging people to act justly and showing pity to those who are oppressed by injustice; he should lend his support to what he considers to be beautiful and noble and just; he should not be reluctant to give in nor should he be stubborn and obstinate if he is asked to do justice; but he should be reluctant to give in if he is asked to do injustice and evil altogether. (12) He should be strong in setting his mind firmly upon the thing which, in his view, ought to be done, and daringly and bravely carry it out without fear and weak-mindedness.

13. Now it is difficult to find all these qualities united in one man, and, therefore, men endowed with this nature will be found one at a time only, such men being altogether very rare. Therefore if there exists such a man in the excellent city who, after reaching maturity, fulfils the six aforementioned conditions—or five of them if one excludes the gift of vi-

sionary prophecy through the faculty of representation—he will be the sovereign. Now when it happens that, at a given time, no such man is to be found but there was previously an unbroken succession of sovereigns of this kind, the laws and the customs which were introduced will be adopted and eventually firmly established.

The next sovereign, who is the successor of the first sovereigns, will be someone in whom those [twelve] qualities are found together from the time of his birth and his early youth and who will, after reaching his maturity, be distinguished by the following six qualities: (1) He will be a philosopher. (2) He will know and remember the laws and customs (and rules of conduct) with which the first sovereigns had governed the city, conforming in all his actions to all their actions. (3) He will excel in deducing a new law by analogy where no law of his predecessors has been recorded, following for his deductions the principles laid down by the first Imāms. (4) He will be good at deliberating and be powerful in his deductions to meet new situations for which the first sovereigns could not have laid down any law; when doing this he will have in mind the good of the city. (5) He will be good at guiding the people by his speech to fulfil the laws of the first sovereigns as well as those laws which he will have deduced in conformity with their principles after their time. (6) He should be of tough physique in order to shoulder the tasks of war, mastering the serving as well as the ruling military art.

14. When one single man who fulfils all these conditions cannot be found but there are two, one of whom

is a philosopher and the other fulfils the remaining conditions, the two of them will be the sovereigns of this city.

But when all these six qualities exist separately in different men, philosophy in one man and the second quality in another man and so on, and when these men are all in agreement, they should all together be the excellent sovereigns.

But when it happens, at a given time, that philosophy has no share in the government, though every other condition may be present in it, the excellent city will remain without a king, the ruler actually in charge of this city will not be a king, and the city will be on the verge of destruction; and if it happens that no philosopher can be found who will be attached to the actual ruler of the city, then, after a certain interval, this city will undoubtedly perish.

Futo No Yasumaro

The *Kojiki,* or *Records of Ancient Matters,* filled as it is with inconsistencies and anomalies, is a document that is next to impossible for us today to disentangle, let alone comprehend. But it is of great historical importance because it is the earliest attempt made by the Japanese to give a written account of their beginnings, including the birth of the islands themselves and the descent of the imperial rulers. It would be gratuitous to suggest, as its author Yasumaro presumably believed, that the episodes he describes constitute authentic history, for they obviously are an amalgam of mythology and fantasy. Yet they provide us with valuable insights not only into ways of early thinking but also, in the special case of Japan, into a set of beliefs that has persisted in the national consciousness for millennia.

The history of the composition of the *Kojiki* is worthy of note. In the seventh century, as Yasumaro explains in his preface, the Emperor Temmu decided, probably following the precedent of China, to produce an accurate history of early Japan and the imperial line. So he appointed a young man of exceptional memory to carry out the project. But the emperor died before the task was completed and it was not renewed until the following century under the Empress Gemmyo, who commissioned Yasumaro to put the *Records* in writing, an undertaking he completed in a few months.

The selection that follows details the generation and activities of the innumerable gods who preceded human occupation of Japan, as well as of the origin of the Japanese islands themselves. Passages have been chosen in an attempt to provide a maximum amount of coherence to an often-unintelligible sequence of events. Many of the gods named are of relatively minor significance except for the fact that they indicate that the early Japanese were prepared to deify almost everything. Of particular significance is the description near the end of the generation of the early leaders of Japan, who culminated in the imperial line, from gods descended from heaven. The myth of the divine descent of the emperors persisted throughout Japanese history until 1946 when Emperor Hirohito, bowing to pressure from the American army of occupation, acknowledged in an official proclamation to his people that he was not really a divine descendant of the sun goddess but only an ordinary human being.

It should be noted that the *Kojiki* is of relatively late origin historically. As the first written records of early Japanese "history," thus an important symbol of the beginnings of that civilization, it appeared around a thousand years after the classics of ancient Chinese civilization.

The Kojiki or Records of Ancient Matters

PREFACE

• • •

The Heavenly Sovereign [Emperor Temmu] commanded, saying "I hear that the chronicles of the emperors and likewise the original words in the possession of the various families deviate from exact truth, and are most amplified by empty falsehoods. If at the present time these imperfections be not amended, ere many years shall have elapsed, the purport of this, the great basis of the country, the grand foundation of the monarchy, will be destroyed. So now I desire to have the chronicles of the emperors selected and recorded, and the old words examined and ascertained, falsehoods being erased and truth determined, in order to transmit the latter to after ages." At that time there was a retainer whose surname was Hiyeda and his personal name Are. He was twenty-eight years old, and of so intelligent a disposition that he could repeat with his mouth whatever met his eyes, and record in his heart whatever struck his ears. Forthwith Are was commanded to learn by heart the genealogies of the emperors, and likewise the words of former ages. Nevertheless, time elapsed and the age changed, and the thing was not yet carried out.

Prostrate I consider how Her Majesty the Empress [Gemmyo], having obtained Unity, illumines the empire. . . . Regretting the errors in the old words, and wishing to correct the misstatements in the former chronicles, She, on the eighteenth day of the ninth moon of the fourth year of Wado [A.D. 711], commanded me Yasumaro to select and record the old words learnt by heart by Hiyeda no Are according to the Imperial Decree, and dutifully to lift them up to Her.

In reverent obedience to the contents of the Decree, I have made a careful choice. . . . Altogether the things recorded commence with the separation of Heaven and Earth, and conclude with the august reign at Woharida [in 628, when Empress Sui-ko died]. . . . Altogether I have written three volumes, which I reverently and respectfully present. I Yasumaro, with true trembling and true fear, bow my head, bow my head.

Reverently presented by the Court

Trans Basil Hall Chamberlain

Noble Futo no Yasumaro, an Officer of the Upper Division of the First Class of the Fifth Rank and of the Fifth Order of Merit, on the 28th day of the first moon of the fifth year of Wa-do [March 10, 712].

SECTION I. THE BEGINNING OF HEAVEN AND EARTH*

The names of the Deities** that were born in the Plain of High Heaven when the Heaven and Earth began were the Deity Master-of-the-August-Centre-of-Heaven, next the High-August-Producing-Wondrous-Deity, next the Divine-Producing-Wondrous-Deity. These three Deities were all Deities born alone, and hid their persons [i.e., died]. The names of the Deities that were born next from a thing that sprouted up like unto a reed-shoot when the earth, young and like unto floating oil, drifted about medusa-like, were the Pleasant-Reed-Shoot-Prince-Elder-Deity, next the Heavenly-Eternally-Standing-Deity. These two Deities were likewise born alone, and hid their persons.

SECTION II. THE SEVEN DIVINE GENERATIONS

The names of the Deities that were born next were the Earthly-Eternally-

---

*Section titles have been added by the translator.

**The Japanese word *kami*, here and later translated as "deity" or "god," actually has a broader meaning; it can refer to anything superior, particularly to a superior being.

Standing-Deity, next the Luxuriant-Integrating-Master Deity. These two Deities were likewise Deities born alone, and hid their persons. The names of the Deities that were born next were the Deity Mud-Earth-Lord, next his younger sister the Deity Mud-Earth-Lady, next the Germ-Integrating-Deity, next his younger sister the Life-Integrating-Deity, next the Deity Elder-of-the-Great-Place, next his younger sister the Deity Elder-Lady-of-the-Great-Place, next the Deity Perfect-Exterior, next his younger sister the Deity Oh-Awful-Lady, next the Deity the Male-Who-Invites [also named Izanagi], next his younger sister the Deity the Female-Who-Invites [also named Izanami]. From the Earthly-Eternally-Standing-Deity down to the deity the Female-Who-Invites [Izanami] in the previous list are what are termed the Seven Divine Generations.

SECTION III. THE ISLAND OF ONOGORO

Hereupon all the Heavenly Deities commanded the two Deities His Augustness Izanagi and Her Augustness Izanami, ordering them to "make, consolidate, and give birth to this drifting land [Japan]." Granting to them a heavenly jewelled spear, they thus deigned to charge them. So the two Deities, standing upon the Floating Bridge of Heaven, pushed down the jewelled spear and stirred with it, whereupon when they had stirred the brine till it went curdle-curdle, and drew the spear up, the brine that dripped down from the end of the spear was piled up and became an island. This is the Island of Onogoro [a Japanese islet].

SECTION IV. COURTSHIP OF THE DEITIES THE MALE-WHO-INVITES AND THE FEMALE-WHO-INVITES

Having descended from Heaven onto this island, they saw to the erection of a heavenly august pillar, they saw to the erection of a hall of eight fathoms. [They then produced a child.] This child they placed in a boat of reeds, and let it float away. Next they gave birth to the Island of Aha [another islet]. . . .

SECTION V. BIRTH OF THE EIGHT GREAT ISLANDS

Hereupon the two Deities took counsel, saying: "The children to whom we have now given birth are not good. It will be best to announce this in the august place of the Heavenly Deities." They ascended forthwith to Heaven and inquired of Their Augustnesses the Heavenly Deities. Then the Heavenly Deities commanded and found out by grand divination, and ordered them, saying: "They were not good because the woman spoke first. Descend back again and amend your words." So thereupon descending back, they again went round the heavenly august pillar as before. Thereupon his Augustness Izanagi spoke first: "Ah! what a fair and lovely maiden!" Afterwards his younger sister Her Augustness Izanami spoke: "Ah! what a fair and lovely youth!" [They gave birth to another child.] Next they gave birth to the Island of Futa-na in Iyo. This island has one body and four faces, and each face has a name. So the Land of Iyo is called Lovely-Princess, the Land of Sanuki is called Prince-Good-Boiled-Rice, the Land

of Aha is called the Princess-of-Great-Food, the Land of Tosa is called Brave-Good-Youth. Next they gave birth to the Islands of Mitsu-go near Oki, another name for which islands is Heavenly-Great-Heart-Youth. Next they gave birth to the island of Tsukushi. This island likewise has one body and four faces, and each face has a name. So the Land of Tsukushi is called White-Sun-Youth, the Land of Toyo is called Luxuriant-Sun-Youth, the Land of Hi is called Brave-Sun-Confronting-Luxuriant-Wondrous-Lord-Youth, the Land of Kumaso is called Brave-Sun-Youth. Next they gave birth to the Island of Iki, another name for which is Heaven's-One-Pillar. Next they gave birth to the Island of Tsu, another name for which is Heavenly-Hand-net-Good-Princess. Next they gave birth to the Island of Sado. Next they gave birth to Great-Yamato-the-Luxuriant-Island-of-the-Dragon-Fly, another name for which is Heavenly-August-Sky-Luxuriant-Dragon-Fly-Lord-Youth. The name of "Land-of-the-Eight-Great-Islands" therefore originated in these eight islands having been born first. [They then completed giving birth to the islands of Japan.]

SECTION VI. BIRTH OF THE VARIOUS DEITIES

When they had finished giving birth to countries, they began afresh giving birth to Deities. [There follows a long list of deities to whom Izanagi and Izanami give birth, and who in turn give birth to further deities, and so on. Many of these deities have names descriptive of natural phenomena like rocks, wind, sea, autumn, trees, mountains, and moors.]

SECTION VII. RETIREMENT OF HER AUGUSTNESS THE PRINCESS-WHO-INVITES

Through giving birth to this child her august private parts were burnt, and she [Izanami] sickened and lay down. . . . So the Deity Izanami, through giving birth to the Deity-of-Fire, at length divinely retired [died]. The total number of islands given birth to jointly by the two Deities Izanagi and Izanami was fourteen, and of Deities thirty-five.

So then His Augustness Izanagi said: "Oh! Thine Augustness my lovely younger sister! Oh! that I should have exchanged thee for this single child!" And as he crept round her august pillow, and as he crept round her august feet and wept, there was born from his august tears the Deity that dwells at Konomoto near Unewo on Mount Kagu, and whose name is the Crying-Weeping-Female-Deity. So he buried the divinely retired Deity Izanami on Mount Hiba at the boundary of the Land of Idzumo and the Land of Hahaki.

• • •

SECTION IX. THE LAND OF HADES

Thereupon His Augustness Izanagi, wishing to meet and see his younger sister Her Augustness Izanami, followed after her to the Land of Hades. So when from the palace she raised the door and came out to meet him, His Augustness Izanagi spoke, saying: "Thine Augustness my lovely younger sister! the lands that I and thou made are not yet finished making, so come back." Then Her Augustness Izanami answered, saying: "Lamentable indeed that thou camest not sooner! I have eaten of the furnace of Hades. Nevertheless, as I reverence the entry here of Thine Augustness my lovely elder brother, I wish to return. Moreover I will discuss it particularly with the Deities of Hades. Look not at me!" Having thus spoken, she went back inside the palace; and as she tarried there very long, he could not wait. So having taken and broken off one of the end-teeth of the multitudinous and close-toothed comb stuck in the august left bunch of his hair, he lit one light and went in and looked. Maggots were swarming, and she was rotting, and in her head dwelt the Great-Thunder, in her breast dwelt the Fire-Thunder, in her belly dwelt the Black-Thunder, in her private parts dwelt the Cleaving-Thunder, in her left hand dwelt the Young-Thunder, in her right hand dwelt the Earth-Thunder, in her left foot dwelt the Rumbling-Thunder, in her right foot dwelt the Couchant-Thunder—altogether eight Thunder-Deities had been born and dwelt there. Hereupon His Augustness Izanagi, overawed at the sight, fled back, whereupon his younger sister Her Augustness Izanami said: "Thou hast put me to shame," and at once sent the Ugly-Female-of-Hades to pursue him. So His Augustness Izanagi took his black august head-dress and cast it down, and it instantly turned into grapes. While she picked them up and ate them, he fled on; but as she still pursued him, he took and broke the multitudinous and close-toothed comb in the right bunch of his hair and cast it down, and it instantly turned into bamboo-sprouts. While she pulled them up and ate them, he fled on. Again later his younger sister sent the eight Thunder-Deities with a thousand and five hundred warriors of Hades to pursue him. So he, drawing the ten-grasp sabre that was augustly girded on him, fled forward brandishing it in his back hand; and as they still pursued, he took, on reaching the base of the Even Pass of Hades, three peaches that were growing at its base, and waited and smote his pursuers therewith, so that they all fled back. Then His Augustness Izanagi announced to the peaches: "Like as ye have helped me, so much ye help all living people in the Central Land of Reed-Plains [Japan] when they shall fall into troublous circumstances and be harassed!"—and he gave to the peaches the designation of Their Augustnesses Great-Divine-Fruit. Last of all his younger sister Her Augustness Izanami came out herself in pursuit. So he drew a thousand-draught rock, and with it blocked up the Even Pass of Hades, and placed the rock in the middle; and they stood opposite to one another and exchanged leave-takings; and Her Augustness Izanami said: "My lovely elder brother, thine Augustness! If thou do like this, I will in one day strangle to death a thousand of the folks of thy land." Then His Augustness Izanagi replied: "My lovely younger sister, Thine Augustness! If *thou* do this *I* will in one day set up a thousand and five hundred parturition-houses. In this manner each day a thousand people would surely die, and each day a thousand and five hundred people would surely be born." So Her Augustness Izanami is called the Great-Deity-of-Hades. Again it is said that, owing to her having pursued and reached her elder brother, she is called the Road-Reaching-Great-Deity. Again the rock with which he blocked up the Pass of Hades is called the Great-Deity-of-the-Road-Turning-back, and again it is called the Blocking-Great-Deity-of-the-Door-of-Hades. . . .

SECTION X. THE PURIFICATION OF THE AUGUST PERSON

Therefore the Great Deity Izanagi said: "Nay! hideous! I have come to a hideous and polluted land, I have! So I will perform the purification of my august person." So he went out to a plain covered with bushclover at a small river mouth near Tachibana in Himuka [probably on Honshu] in the island of Tsukushi and purified and cleansed himself. [Izanagi removes his clothing and begins to bathe; as by-products of these activities he creates a sizeable number of diverse deities, of which only the last three are significant.] The name of the Deity that was born as he thereupon washed his left august eye was the Heaven-Shining-Great-August-Deity. The name of the Deity that was next born as he washed his right august eye was His Augustness Moon-Night-Possessor. The name of the Deity that was next born as he washed his august nose was His Brave-Swift-Impetuous-Male-Augustness (or Susanoo). . . .

SECTION XI. INVESTITURE OF THE THREE DEITIES THE ILLUSTRIOUS AUGUST CHILDREN

At this time His Augustness Izanagi greatly rejoiced, saying: "I, begetting child after child, have at my final begetting gotten three illustrious children," with which words, at once jinglingly taking off and shaking the jewel-string forming his august necklace, he bestowed it on the Heaven-Shining-Great-August-Deity, saying: "Do Thine Augustness rule the Plain-of-High-Heaven." With this charge he bestowed it on her. Now the name of this august necklace was the August-Store-house-Shelf-Deity. Next he said to His Augustness Moon-Night-Possessor: "Do Thine Augustness rule the Dominion of the Night." Thus he charged him. Next he said to Susanoo: "Do Thine Augustness rule the Sea-Plain."

SECTION XII. THE CRYING AND WEEPING OF HIS IMPETUOUS-MALE-AUGUSTNESS

So while the other two Deities each assumed his and her rule according to the command with which their father had deigned to charge them, Susanoo did not assume the rule of the dominion with which he had been charged, but cried and wept till his eight-grasp beard reached to the pit of his stomach. The fashion of his weeping was such as by his weeping to wither the green mountains into withered mountains and by his weeping to dry up all the rivers and seas. For this reason the sound of bad Deities was like unto the flies in the fifth moon as they all swarmed, and in all things every portent of woe arose. So the Great August Deity Izanagi said to Susanoo: "How is it that, instead of ruling the land with which I charged thee, thou dost wail and weep?" He replied, saying: "I wail because I wish to depart to my deceased mother's land, to the Nether Distant Land [Hades]." Then the Great August Deity Izanagi was very angry and said: "If that be so, thou shalt not dwell in this land," and forthwith expelled him with a divine expulsion. . . .

SECTION XIII. THE AUGUST OATH

So thereupon Susanoo said: "If that be so, I will take leave of the Heaven-Shining-Great-August-Deity, and depart." With these words he forthwith went up to Heaven, whereupon all the mountains and rivers shook, and every land and country quaked. So the Heaven-Shining-Great-August Deity, alarmed at the noise, said: "The reason of the the ascent hither of His Augustness my elder brother is surely no good intent. It is only that he wishes to wrest my land from me." And she forthwith, unbinding her august hair, twisted it into august bunches, and both into the left and into the right august bunch, as likewise into her august head-dress and likewise on to her left and her right august arm, she twisted an augustly complete string of curved jewels eight feet long, of five hundred jewels, and, slinging on her back a quiver holding a thousand arrows, and adding thereto a quiver holding five hundred arrows, she likewise took and slung at her side a mighty and high-sounding elbow-pad, and brandished and stuck her bow upright so that the top shook, and she stamped her feet into the hard ground up to her opposing thighs, kicking away the earth like rotten snow, and stood valiantly like unto a mighty man, and waiting, asked: "Wherefore ascendest thou hither?" Then Susanoo replied, saying: "I have no evil intent. It is only that when the Great-August-Deity our father spoke, deigning to inquire the cause of my wailing and weeping, I said: 'I wail because I wish to go to my deceased mother's land,' whereupon the Great-August-Deity said: 'Thou shalt not dwell in this land,' and deigned to expel me with a divine expulsion. It is therefore solely with the thought of taking leave of thee and departing, that I have ascended hither. I have no strange intentions. [The two deities then engage in a contest of producing children, the sun goddess begetting five male deities and Susanoo begetting three female deities.]

SECTION XV. THE AUGUST RAVAGES OF HIS IMPETUOUS-MALE-AUGUSTNESS

Then Susanoo said to the Heaven-Shining-Great-August-Deity: "Owing to the sincerity of my intentions I have, in begetting children, gotten delicate females. Judging from this, I have undoubtedly gained the victory." With these words, and impetuous with victory, he broke down the divisions of the ricefields laid out by the Heaven-Shining-Great-August-Deity, filled up the ditches, and moreover strewed excrements in the palace where she partook of the great food. So, though he did thus, the Heaven-Shining-Great-August-Deity upbraided him not, but said: "What looks like excrements must be something that His Augustness mine elder brother has vomited through drunkenness. Again, as to his breaking down the divisions of the rice-fields and filling up the ditches, it must be because he grudges the land they occupy that His Augustness mine elder brother acts thus." But notwithstanding these apologetic words, he still continued his evil acts, and was more and more violent. As the Heaven-Shining-Great-August-Deity sat in her awful [sacred] weaving-hall seeing to the weaving of the august garments of the Deities, he broke a hole in the top of the weaving-hall, and through it let fall a heavenly piebald horse which he had flayed. . . .

SECTION XVI. THE DOOR OF THE HEAVENLY ROCK DWELLING

So thereupon the Heaven-Shining-Great-August-Deity, terrified at the sight, closed behind her the door of the Heavenly Rock-Dwelling, made it fast, and retired. Then the whole Plain of High Heaven was obscured and all the Central Land of Reed-Plains [Japan] darkened. Owing to this, eternal night prevailed. Hereupon the voices of the myriad Deities were like unto the flies in the fifth moon as they swarm and a myriad portents of woe arose. Therefore did the eight hundred myriad Deities assemble in a divine assembly in the bed of the Tranquil River of Heaven, and bid the Deity Thought-Includer, child of the High-August-Producing-Wondrous-Deity, think of a plan, assembling the long-singing birds of eternal night and making them sing, taking the hard rocks of Heaven from the river-bed of the Tranquil River of Heaven, and taking the iron from the Heavenly Metal-Mountains, calling in the smith Ama-tsu-ma-ra, charging Her Augustness I-shi-ko-ri-do-me to make a mirror, and charging His Augustness Jewel-Ancestor to make an augustly complete string of curved jewels eight feet long, of five hundred jewels, and summoning His Augustness Heavenly-Beckoning-Ancestor-Lord and His Augustness Grand-Jewel, and causing them to pull out with a complete pulling the shoulder-blade of a true stag from the Heavenly Mount Kagu, and take cherry-bark from the Heavenly Mount Kagu, and perform divination, and pulling up by pulling its roots a true *Cleyera japonica* with five hundred branches from the Heavenly Mount Kagu, and taking and putting upon its upper branches the augustly complete string of curved jewels eight feet long, of five hundred jewels, and taking and tying to the middle branches the mirror eight feet long, and taking and hanging upon its lower branches the white pacificatory offerings and the blue pacificatory offerings, His Augustness Grand-Jewel taking these divers things and holding them together with the grand august offerings, and His Augustness Heavenly-Beckoning-Ancestor-Lord prayerfully reciting grand liturgies, and the Heavenly-Hand-Strength-Male-Deity standing hidden beside the door, and Her Augustness Heavenly-Alarming-Female hanging round her the heavenly clubmoss from the Heavenly Mount Kagu as a sash, and making the heavenly spindle-tree her head-dress, and binding the leaves of the bamboo-grass of the Heavenly Mount Kagu in a posy for her hands, laying a sounding-board before the door of the Heavenly Rock-Dwelling, and stamping till she made it resound and doing as if possessed by a Deity, and pulling out the nipples of her breasts, pushing down her skirt-string to her private parts. Then the Plain of High Heaven shook, and the eight hundred myriad Deities laughed together. Hereupon the Heaven-Shining-Great-August-Deity was amazed, and, slightly opening the door of the Heavenly Rock-Dwelling, spoke thus from the inside: "Methought that owing to my retirement the Plain of

Heaven would be dark, and likewise the Central Land of Reed-Plains would all be dark: how then is it that the Heavenly-Alarming-Female makes merry, and that likewise the eight hundred myriad Deities all laugh?" Then the Heavenly-Alarming-Female spoke, saying: "We rejoice and are glad because there is a Deity more illustrious than Thine Augustness." While she was thus speaking, His Augustness Heavenly-Beckoning-Ancestor-Lord and His Augustness Grand-Jewel pushed forward the mirror and respectfully showed it to the Heaven-Shining-Great-August-Deity, whereupon the Heaven-Shining-Great-August-Deity, more and more astonished, gradually came forth from the door and gazed upon it, whereupon the Heavenly-Hand-Strength-Male-Deity, who was standing hidden, took her august hand and drew her out, and then His Augustness Grand-Jewel drew the bottom-tied rope along at her august back, and spoke, saying: "Thou must not go back further in than this!" So when the Heaven-Shining-Great-August-Deity had come forth, both the Plain of High Heaven and the Central-Land-of-Reed-Plains of course again became light.

• • •

SECTION XXXIII. THE AUGUST DESCENT FROM HEAVEN OF HIS AUGUSTNESS THE AUGUST GRANDCHILD

Then the Heaven-Shining-Great-August-Deity and the High-Integrating-Deity commanded and charged the Heir Apparent His Augustness Truly-Conqueror-I-Conquer-Swift-Heavenly-Great-Great-Ears saying: "The Brave-Awful-Possessing-Male-Deity says that he has now finished pacifying the Central Land of Reed-Plains. So do thou, in accordance with our gracious charge, descend to and dwell in and rule over it." Then the Heir Apparent His Augustness Truly-Conqueror-I-Conquer-Conquering-Swift-Heavenly-Great-Great-Ears replied, saying: "While I have been getting ready to descend, there has been born to me a child whose name is His Augustness Heaven-Plenty-Earth-Plenty-Heaven's-Sun-Height-Prince-Rice-ear-Ruddy-Plenty. This child should be sent down." Therefore, in accordance with these words, they laid their command on His Augustness Prince-Rice-ear-Ruddy-Plenty, deigning to charge him with these words: "This Luxuriant Reed-Plain-Land-of-Fresh-Rice-ears [Japan] is the land over which thou shalt rule." So he replied: "I will descend from Heaven according to your commands."

Then ... they sent him down from Heaven. Thereupon they joined to him the eight-feet-long curved jewels and mirror that had allured the Heaven-Shining-Great-August-Deity from the Rock-Dwelling and also the Herb-Quelling-Great-Sword, and likewise the Deity Thought-Includer, the Hand-Strength-Male-Deity, and the Deity Heavenly-Rock-Door-Opener of Eternal Night, and charged him thus: "Regard this mirror exactly as if it were our august spirit, and reverence it as if reverencing us." Next did they say: "Let the Deity Thought-Includer take in hand our affairs, and carry on the government." These two Deities are worshipped at the temple of Isuzu [at Ise]. The next, the Deity of Luxuriant-Food, is the Deity dwelling in the outer temple of Watarahi. The next, the Deity Heavenly-Rock-Door-Opener, another name for whom is the Wondrous-Rock-True-Gate-Deity, and another name for whom is the Luxuriant-Rock-True-Gate-Deity—this Deity is the Deity of the August Gate [of the Imperial Palace]. The next, the Deity Hand-Strength-Male dwells in Sanagata. Now His Augustness the Heavenly-Beckoning-Ancestor-Lord is the ancestor of the Nakatomi Chieftains, His Augustness Grand Jewel is the ancestor of the Imibe Headmen, Her Augustness the Heavenly-Alarming-Female is the ancestress of the Duchesses of Saru, Her Augustness I-shi-ko-ri-do-me is the ancestress of the Mirror-Making Chieftains, His Augustness-Jewel-Ancestor is the ancestor of the Jewel-Ancestor Chieftains.

Einhard

Although we refer today to the period in European history extending roughly from A.D. 500 to 1000 as the Dark Ages, we make one exception to that general negative appraisal, speaking of the period of Charlemagne as the Carolingian Renaissance. During a brief interlude, learning and culture flourished in the West, but soon after Charlemagne's death twilight again descended for another two hundred years.

Charlemagne (c. 742–814) was a remarkable man. Although only semi-literate himself, he was a patron of learning, as well as of the arts. He made his capital at Aachen (Aix-la-Chapelle) a cultural center by establishing a palace school there to train both the clergy and the sons of the nobles of his court. He appointed, as director of the school, the English teacher and scholar, Alcuin of York, who was probably the outstanding intellectual of his time. He also brought together a number of other scholars from around Europe, among them Einhard.

Einhard (c. 770–844) was born in what is now southern Germany, of a wealthy family. After studying at the Abbey of Fulda, he went to Aachen as a student of Alcuin in the palace school. He remained in Aachen for nearly forty years, becoming a close friend and advisor of Charlemagne. An individual of many talents, Einhard not only continued the tradition of his mentor, Alcuin, as a teacher but also engaged in diplomatic missions for his lord. In addition he employed his skills as an architect to design the royal palace at Aachen, much of which still stands. But his major contribution to history was his biography of Charlemagne. Even after the death of the emperor in 814, Einhard remained in Aachen, continuing his position as advisor to the next monarch, Louis the Pious. It was during these years that he wrote his famous biography. He finally left the royal household in 830 and retired to a rural location in southern Germany where he founded an abbey.

Einhard's is not a disinterested biography, for the author's admiration for Charlemagne is evident throughout. Still it gives us an informative, if brief, description of the emperor and his times. Einhard used the classical biographer, Suetonius, for his literary model, copying his style and even re-producing the language of his *Life of Augustus*, but applying it to his own subject. The selection that follows reproduces his complete *Life of Charlemagne*.

The Life of Charlemagne

PROLOGUE

After I had made up my mind to describe the life and habits and, above all, the deeds of my lord and patron, the illustrious and deservedly famous King Charles, I set about doing so as succinctly as possible. I have tried not to omit anything that has come to my notice, and at the same time not to be long-winded and offend those discerning readers who object to the very idea of a modern history. But I also wanted to keep my new work from displeasing those who disapprove even of the masterpieces of the wisest and most learned authors of antiquity. To be sure, I am fully aware that there are many men of letters who do not regard contemporary matters so far beneath their notice as to treat them with contempt and consider them fit only to sink into silence and oblivion. On the contrary, the enthusiasm for things past leads some writers to recount the famous deeds of other men as best they can, and in this way they hope to insure that their own names will be remembered by posterity.

Be this as it may, none of these possible objections can prevent me from writing on the subject, since I am convinced that no one can de-scribe these events better than I can. For I was there when they took place and I know them as an eyewitness, so to speak. Furthermore, I am not entirely sure if they will be recorded by anyone else. And so I thought it would be better to write down what I had to say even at the risk of duplicating what others might write, rather than to allow the illustrious life of the greatest king of the age and his famous deeds, unmatched by his contemporaries, to disappear forever into forgetfulness.

Besides, there was another reason, important enough in itself, I think, to make me compose this book: namely, that Charles educated me and gave me his lifelong friendship and that of his children from the time I came to the court. In this way he attached me to his person and made me so devoted to him in life and death that I might well be called ungrateful if I were to forget everything he did for me and never say a word about his great and magnificent generosity, I, who owe him so much; indeed, that would mean allowing his life to remain unremembered and unpraised, as though he had never lived! To be sure, my abilities, feeble and inadequate as they are—nonexistent even—are inca-

Einhard, *The Life of Charlemagne*, trans. E. S. Firchow and E. H. Zeydel (Coral Gables: University of Miami Press, 1972). Used by permission of University of Miami Press.

pable of portraying his life as it really ought to be portrayed. Even the eloquence of a Cicero would not have been up to that.

Here, then, is the book containing the life story of a truly great man. You will marvel at his deeds, and probably also at the presumption of a barbarous Frank for imagining that he could write tastefully and elegantly in Latin. For I am not much versed in the Roman tongue. Then, too, you will perhaps be amazed at my temerity in ignoring the words of Cicero when, speaking of Latin writers, he said in the first book of his *Tusculan Disputations* that "whoever puts his thoughts in writing and can not arrange and state them clearly, and delight the reader with a pleasant style, makes a complete mockery of the writer's craft." This remark of the famous orator might have kept me from writing if I had not already made up my mind to brave the judgment of the world and take a chance with my feeble talents. I thought this would be better than to allow the memory of so great a man to perish out of petty concern for my own reputation.

majordomos, and their word was law. The king had no choice but to sit on the throne with flowing hair and full beard, content with his title and the semblance of sovereignty. He would listen to messengers coming from all around and, as they left, give them replies as though they were his own, but in reality, they had been dictated to him or even forced on him.

Except for the empty title of king and an intermittent allowance which the prefect of the palace gave or did not give him at his pleasure, the king owned nothing but a single estate, and that was not a very lucrative one. He lived on it and had a few servants there performing the most necessary duties and making a show of obsequiousness. Wherever he had to go, he went like a farmer in a cart drawn by a span of oxen with a carter driving them. That is how he went to the palace and how he went to the meetings of his people, which took place yearly for the good of the realm. And in the same way he returned home. But the administration of the state and all internal and external business was carried out by the prefect of the palace.

1. THE MEROVINGIANS

The family of the Merovingians from which the Franks customarily chose their kings is believed to have ruled until the time of King Hilderich. Hilderich was deposed, tonsured, and sent to a monastery by the command of the Roman Pope Stephen. Although the royal line apparently ended only with him, it had long before ceased to matter and possessed no more except the empty title of king. The real wealth and power of the kingdom were in the hands of the prefects of the palace, the so-called

2. CHARLES' ANCESTORS

When Hilderich was deposed, the office of majordomo was already hereditarily held by Pepin, the father of King Charles. For Pepin's father, Charles [Charles Martel—*Ed.*], had in his time crushed the rebels who were trying to take over all of Franconia. He had also defeated the Saracens so badly in two great battles, when they attempted to occupy Gaul, that they had to return to Spain. One of these battles had taken place in Aquitaine near Poitiers [in 732—*Ed.*], the other on the Berre River not far from Narbonne. This same Charles had in turn received the office of majordomo from his father Pepin and had administered it extremely well. It was customary for the people to bestow such an honor only on men of noble birth and great wealth.

When Pepin, the father of King Charles, held this office, bequeathed by his grandfather and father to him and to his brother Carloman, the two of them shared it quite amicably for several years, nominally under King Hilderich. But then for some unknown reason Carloman abandoned the burdensome government of the temporal kingdom—possibly because he longed for a more contemplative life—and went into retirement in Rome. There, giving up his worldly garb, he became a monk and built a monastery on Mt. Soracte near the church of St. Sylvester. For a number of years he enjoyed his longed-for seclusion, along with a few monks who had accompanied him. But when a great many noble Franks came on pilgrimages to Rome to fulfill vows and insisted on paying homage to their former lord, it was impossible for him to get any peace, which he cherished more than anything else, and he decided to move elsewhere. When he saw that the crowds of intruders were interfering with his resolve to be alone, he left the mountain and went away to the province of Samnium, to the monastery of St. Benedict on Monte Cassino, where he spent the rest of his life in prayer.

3. CHARLES BECOMES KING

Pepin, no longer majordomo but king by authority of the Roman pontiff, ruled alone over the Franks for

fifteen years or more. For nine unbroken years he fought against Waifar, duke of Aquitaine, and then, at the end of the war, he died of dropsy in Paris. His sons Charles and Carloman survived him, and on them, by the will of Providence, the succession devolved. In solemn assembly the Franks appointed them kings on condition that they share the realm equally, Charles ruling the part which had belonged to their father Pepin, Carloman the part formerly controlled by his uncle Carloman. Both accepted these conditions and each one took over that section of the divided kingdom which he had received according to the agreement.

But peace between the two brothers was maintained only with the greatest difficulty since many of Carloman's followers plotted to break up the partnership. A few even tried to provoke a war with their intrigues. The outcome, however, showed that there was more imagined than real danger. When Carloman died, his wife and sons fled to Italy with the most important members of their court. Without any apparent reason she spurned her brother-in-law and placed herself and her children under the protection of Desiderius, king of the Lombards. Carloman had succumbed to an illness after ruling jointly for two years, and at his death Charles was unanimously proclaimed king of the Franks.

4. PLAN OF THIS WORK

Because nothing has been recorded in writing about Charles' birth,[1] in-

---

[1] [The conjectural date of Charlemagne's birth is April 2, 742.—Ed.]

fancy, or even boyhood, and because no survivor has been found who claims to know of these matters, I consider it foolish to write about them. So I have decided to skip what we know nothing about and proceed to recount and describe Charles' exploits, habits, and other facts of his life. First I want to tell of his deeds at home and abroad, then describe his habits and interests, his rulership and finally his death, omitting nothing that is worth mentioning or necessary to know.

5. WAR IN AQUITAINE

Of all the wars Charles waged, the first was the Aquitainian campaign, begun but not finished by his father. Charles believed that it would soon be over. He asked his brother, who was still living at the time, to help him. But although his brother disappointed him and failed to provide the promised support, Charles completed the undertaking with great vigor. He was unwilling to give up what he had begun or to abandon a task once taken on until he had carried out his plans and brought them to a happy conclusion by force of perseverance and steadfastness. He even compelled Hunold, who after Waifar's death had tried to seize Aquitaine and revive a war that was almost finished, to leave the country and flee to the land of the Basques. But Charles gave him no respite. He crossed the Garonne River, built Fort Fronsac, and through diplomatic channels let the Basque Duke Lupus know that he had better return the fugitive speedily or he would come and get Hunold by force. Lupus thought better of it and not only handed over Hunold but also submitted himself and the province he ruled to the jurisdiction of Charles.

6. WAR WITH THE LOMBARDS

When the affairs of Aquitaine had been settled and the war ended, and after his brother had died, Charles undertook a campaign against the Lombards at the request and pleading of Bishop Hadrian of Rome. His father had once before fought the Lombards, that time in response to the entreaties of Pope Stephen. Pepin had done so under great difficulties, for certain nobles with whom he usually consulted had opposed his wishes so strongly that they openly declared they would desert the king and go home. Nevertheless, arms were taken up against King Aistulf at that time and the war brought to a speedy end. But although the reasons for this conflict seem to have been similar and indeed the same in both Charles' and Pepin's case, the difficulties of seeing it through and settling it varied in each instance. Pepin, after a few days' siege at Pavia, forced Aistulf to give hostages and to return to the Romans the cities and fortresses he had taken. He also made Aistulf swear a sacred oath that he would not try to regain what he had surrendered. Charles, on the other hand, pursued the war more single-mindedly and did not rest until he had forced King Desiderius to surrender unconditionally after weakening him in a lengthy siege. He also ordered Desiderius' son Adalgis, who was the favorite of his people, to leave the kingdom and Italy and to restore everything he had taken from the Romans. Charles then prevented Rotgaud, the duke of Friuli, from starting a revolt After that he subjected all of Italy to his rule and made his son Pepin king of the conquered Italian territories.

At this point I should describe how difficult it was for Charles to cross the Alps on the way to Italy and how the Franks toiled when crossing the trackless mountain ridges, the rocky cliffs, and the sharp peaks reaching to the sky. But I have decided to describe in this work Charles' way of life rather than the outcome of the wars he waged. Suffice it to say that the end of the campaign resulted in the subjugation of Italy, the deportation of Desiderius into permanent exile, the expulsion of his son Adalgis from Italy, and the restoration of the possessions taken by the Lombard kings to Pope Hadrian of Rome.

7. WAR WITH THE SAXONS

Then the Saxon war—which had merely been interrupted—was taken up again. The Franks have never been involved in any struggle that was more prolonged, more bitter, or more laborious. For the Saxons—like almost all of the nations inhabiting Germania—are savage by nature, given to the cult of demons, and hostile to our religion. They do not find it dishonorable to violate or break divine or human laws. Hardly a day passed without incidents threatening the peace. The border between our land and theirs runs almost entirely through plains, with the exception of a few areas where large forests or mountain ridges provide the territories with natural boundaries. Thus, murder, robbery, and arson never ceased on both sides. Eventually the Franks became so enraged that it no longer seemed enough to retaliate

and so they decided to wage open war. Accordingly, war was declared and fought by both parties with great ferocity. It continued for thirty-three years and cost the Saxons far more than the Franks. To be sure, it could have been concluded sooner if the treachery of the Saxons had allowed it. For it is difficult to say how many times they surrendered to the king and promised to do what they were ordered, how often and without delay they furnished hostages that were demanded, and how often they received legates. Many times they were so badly defeated and weakened that they vowed to give up their cult of demons and indicated their willingness to submit to the Christian faith. But just as they were often ready to do this, just as often were they in a hurry to break their promises. Thus, I cannot say with certainty which of these courses of action they more truthfully favored. It is a fact, however, that after the beginning of the war against the Saxons hardly a year passed without some vacillation on their part. And yet the king in his high purpose and unswerving constancy both in success and failure was not to be frustrated by their fickleness, nor could he be made to abandon what he had begun. He never allowed any of them who perpetrated such perfidy to go unpunished. In these instances he either led an army personally or sent one with his counts to avenge the crimes and mete out proper punishment. After he had defeated all of those who had been offering resistance, he subjected them to his power. Then he took ten thousand Saxons who lived on both banks of the Elbe river, with their wives and children, and resettled them in various contingents here and there throughout Gaul and Germania. And so the war which had dragged on for so many years was concluded under the conditions which the king imposed and the Saxons accepted. The conditions were that they give up the cult of demons, abandon the religious practices of their ancestors, adopt the sacraments of the Christian faith and religion, and become a single nation with the Franks.

8. WAR WITH THE SAXONS (continued)

Although this struggle had gone on for many years, the king himself fought the enemy not more than twice during the period, and this within a single month with only a few days intervening: once at the mountain Osning, in a place called Detmold, and once at the river Hase. The enemies were so routed and defeated in these two battles that they subsequently never dared to provoke the king again or to resist him when he approached, unless they were protected by fortifications. In these fights many noblemen and leaders in highest positions were killed, both among the Franks and Saxons. Finally, the strife ended in the thirty-third year. But meanwhile so many other great wars had been declared against the Franks in various parts of the world and were taken up under the king's guidance that anyone considering the matter might justifiably wonder whether Charles' endurance in time of trouble or his good fortune is more to be admired. The Saxon war had begun two years before the Italian, and, although it was carried on without interruption, none of the other pressing duties were set aside nor other equally difficult struggles dropped for its sake.

For the king surpassed everyone in his time in prudence and nobility of mind, and he turned down nothing that had to be undertaken or carried out. He did not shy at the difficulties or fear the dangers involved because he had learned to accept and endure everything in accordance with its nature. Neither in adversity did he yield nor was he misled by good fortune when it beckoned deceptively during times of great success.

9. EXPEDITION TO SPAIN

While Charles was engaged in the strenuous and almost incessant struggle with the Saxons and after he had built fortifications at strategic points along the frontier, he decided to invade Spain with as large an army as he could raise. He crossed the Pyrenees successfully and accepted the surrender of all the towns and castles on his way. Finally, he turned back with his forces safe and intact, but when recrossing the mountains he was made to feel the treachery of the Basques. In a densely wooded area well suited for ambush the Basques had prepared to attack the army from the top of the highest mountain. As the troops were proceeding in a long column through the narrow mountain passes, the Basques descended on the baggage train and the protecting rear guard and forced them into the valley. In the ensuing battle the Basques slaughtered them to a man. They seized the baggage and, under cover of the growing darkness, quickly scattered in all directions. In this encounter the Basques had the advantage of light weapons and a favorable terrain; the Franks on the other hand were hampered by their heavy equipment and the unevenness of the battle ground. Ekkehard, the royal steward, Anshelm, the count of the Palace, and Roland the Margrave of Brittany, as well as many others were killed in the engagement.[2] Unfortunately, the incident could not be avenged since the enemies disappeared without a trace after the attack and there were no signs where they might be found.

10. SUBMISSION OF THE BRETONS AND BENEVENTIANS

Charles also conquered the Bretons, who lived in a certain remote part of Gaul along the west coast and were not subject to him. He sent an expedition against them, which forced them to give hostages and made them promise to do what was expected of them.

Then he entered Italy with an army and, marching through Rome, went as far as Capua, a city in Campania. There he set up a camp and threatened to take up arms against the Beneventians unless they surrendered. Aregis, the duke of Benevento, prevented this by sending his sons Rumold and Grimold with a large sum of money asking the king to accept them as hostages. He promised that he and his people would do as Charles demanded, on the condition that he would not be forced to appear before the king in person. Charles was more concerned about the good of the people than about the duke's stubbornness, and so he accepted the hostages and agreed that, in view of the large gift

of money, the duke should not be compelled to come. He kept one of the two sons of Aregis, not yet of age, as a hostage and sent the older one back to his father. Charles also dispatched legates to receive oaths of loyalty from the Beneventians and from Aregis himself. After that he returned to Rome, spent several days there in worship at the holy places, and finally went back to Gaul.

11. TASSILO AND THE WAR WITH THE BENEVENTIANS

All at once a war broke out in Bavaria which was, however, swiftly concluded. It was caused by the pride and folly of Duke Tassilo. At the urging of his wife, who was a daughter of King Desiderius and who imagined that she could avenge her father's exile through her husband, he made an alliance with the Huns, the neighbors of the Bavarians to the east. According to its terms, Tassilo not only refused to do the king's bidding but also tried his best to challenge him to war. The dauntless king could not tolerate this outrageous insolence. He therefore collected his troops from all over and personally marched to Bavaria with a large army. He reached the river Lech, which separates the Bavarians from the Alemanni, and established his camp there. Before invading the province, however, he decided to find out about the plans of the duke by sending messengers to him. Tassilo realized that there was no point for him or his people to act stubbornly, and so he presented himself to the king to ask for forgiveness. He furnished the hostages that were demanded, among them also his son Theodo, and swore an oath that he would

---

[2][The Battle of Roncesvalles (778), described in the *Song of Roland.—Ed.*]

never again be persuaded by anyone to be disobedient to Charles. Thus a speedy end was made to the war which at first had threatened to become one of major proportions. Tassilo, however, was later summoned to the court and not permitted to return. His province was from that time on ruled not by one duke but by several counts.

12. WAR WITH THE SLAVS

After these problems had been solved arms were taken up against the Slavs, who were known to us as Wiltzes but who call themselves Welatabi in their own language. The Saxons fought as auxiliaries in this war, together with other peoples who followed the standards of the king. To be sure, their loyalty was more perfunctory than real. The conflict was caused by the Wiltzes, who were constantly invading and harassing the Abodrites—long-time allies of the Franks—and could not be intimidated by warnings.

A gulf of undetermined length stretches from the western Ocean toward the East, nowhere exceeding a hundred miles across, though narrower at many points [the Baltic Sea—Ed.]. Numerous nations live around its shores. The Danes, for instance, and the Swedes, whom we call Norsemen, occupy the northern shore and all the islands along it. The southern shore, on the other hand, is inhabited by Slavs, Estes, and various other nationalities. Among these are the Wiltzes whom Charles was attacking now. In a single campaign led by himself, he crushed and conquered them so effectively that they never again dared to refuse his order.

13. WAR WITH THE HUNS

Next to the Saxon the war which now followed was the most important of them all: it was directed against the Avars or Huns. Charles undertook it with greater energy and far better equipment than any other before. He made one expedition himself to Pannonia—the Huns were occupying this province at that time—and the execution of the rest of the campaign he assigned to his son Pepin and to his provincial prefects, counts, and representatives. Although the war was carried on most vigorously, it ended only in the eighth year. The deserted palace of the Khan as well as the way in which Pannonia was divested of all its population so that not even a trace of human habitation now remains, testify to the many battles fought and the great amount of blood shed there. The entire Hunnish nobility perished during these struggles and their glory vanished. All the money and treasures they had collected over many years were taken away. There is in memory of man no war ever fought against the Franks in which they became richer and accumulated greater wealth. Indeed, although up to that time the Huns had almost seemed to be paupers, so much gold and silver were found in their palace, and so much precious loot captured in the battles, that one can say with good reason: the Franks justly took away from the Huns what the latter had previously unjustly acquired from other peoples.

Only two leaders of the Franks perished in this campaign. Duke Eric of Friuli was killed through the treachery of the townspeople in the seaport town of Tarsatica in Liburnia. Gerold, the prefect of Bavaria, was slain by an unidentified person in Pannonia when he was about to join the attack against the Huns and was marshaling his lines on horseback. He died together with two others who accompanied him while he was exhorting his soldiers one by one to muster their courage for the battle. Otherwise the conflict was practically bloodless and its outcome highly advantageous for the Franks, although because of its magnitude, it lasted for a long time.

14. WAR WITH THE DANES

At long last the Saxon war, too, came to a proper conclusion befitting its long duration. The following wars in Bohemia and Linonia were bound to be brief. Under the leadership of the young King Charles they were quickly settled. Charles' last campaign was directed against those Norsemen who are called Danes. They first were engaged in piracy; later they invaded and devastated the coasts of Gaul and Germania with a rather large fleet. Godofrid, their king, was so filled with vain ambition that he saw himself as the future master over all of Germania. Already he regarded Frisia and Saxony as his own provinces and had subjugated his neighbors, the Abodrites, forcing them to pay tribute. Furthermore, he bragged that in a short time he would be coming with a very large force to the king's court at Aachen. However empty his boasts were, some people thought that he was about to do something of this kind. But he was prevented by sudden death from carrying out his plans. He was assassinated by his own guard, and this ended his life and the war he had begun.

15. CONQUEST

These were the wars which the mighty King Charles planned so carefully and executed so brilliantly in various parts of the world during his reign of forty-seven years. As a result the kingdom of the Franks, which was already great and powerful when Charles inherited it from his father Pepin, was almost doubled in size. Formerly, the Frankish territory had encompassed only that part of Gaul lying between the Rhine and the Loire, the ocean and the Balearic Sea, as well as that part of Germania inhabited by the so-called East Franconians and bordering on Saxony and the Danube, the Rhine and the Saale—a river separating the Thuringians from the Sorbs—and, finally, the land of the Alemanni and Bavarians.

Through the wars described above Charles conquered first Aquitaine, then Gascony and the entire Pyrenees region as far south as the Ebro River. This river originates in Navarre and flows through the most fertile plains of Spain, emptying into the Balearic Sea beneath the walls of the city of Tortosa. Charles also added to his territory all of Italy from Aosta to Lower Calabria, where the border runs between the Beneventians and the Greeks—an area extending over more than a thousand miles. Furthermore, he incorporated Saxony—no small part of Germania and considered equal in length and twice the width of Franconia—and both Upper and Lower Pannonia, as well as Dacia on the other side of the Danube, Istria, Liburnia, and Dalmatia. Only the coastal towns of the latter countries he left to the emperor of Constantinople out of friendship and in consideration of a treaty he had made with him. Finally, Charles subjugated and forced to pay tribute all of the barbarian and savage nations who inhabit Germania between the Rhine and the Vistula rivers, the ocean and the Danube. They speak almost the same language but have very different customs and habits. The most important of these tribes are the Wiltzes, Sorbs, Abodrites, and Bohemians. With these he was forced to fight, but others, by far the greater number, surrendered without a struggle.

16. FOREIGN RELATIONS

Charles also increased the glory of his empire by establishing friendly relations with many kings and peoples. An example is his close friendship with King Alfons of Galicia and Asturias, who always insisted on calling himself Charles' vassal when sending him letters or ambassadors. Charles also secured the favor of the Scottish kings by his great generosity, so that they always referred to him as their master and called themselves his subjects and servants. To this day there exist letters sent by them which clearly express these feelings.

With King Harun of Persia, who ruled almost all of the Orient except India, he was on such friendly terms that Harun preferred Charles' goodwill to the friendship of all other kings and potentates on earth and considered Charles alone worthy of his respect and homage. At one time the king of the Franks sent messengers with offerings to the most Holy Sepulcher, the site of the Resurrection of our Lord and Savior. When they appeared before Harun to relay their master's wishes, the king not only permitted them to carry out their mission but also gave Charles

the jurisdiction over their holy and blessed place. On their return Harun sent along his own messengers with precious gifts, garments, spices, and other riches of the Orient. A few years earlier Charles had asked him for an elephant and Harun had sent him the only one he owned.

The three emperors of Constantinople, Nicephorus, Michael, and Leo, all sought Charles' friendship and alliance and sent numerous legations to his court. Only when Charles assumed the title of emperor did they begin to distrust him out of fear that he would seize their lands. To allay these fears and make sure that there would be no occasion for further trouble, Charles at once concluded a firm treaty with them. But the Greeks and the Romans remained suspicious of Frankish power. Hence a Greek proverb: "Have a Frank as a friend, but not as a neighbor."

17. PUBLIC WORKS

No matter how much time and effort Charles spent on planning and carrying out campaigns to enlarge his realm and subjugate foreign nations, he still was able to begin work on a number of public projects designed to help and beautify his kingdom. Some of them he actually managed to complete. The Basilica of the Holy Mother of God in Aachen, a triumph of the arts in construction, is quite rightly considered among the most remarkable of these. So, too, the bridge spanning the Rhine at Mainz, which is a full five hundred paces long, since the river is that wide at this point [2250 feet—*Ed.*]. The bridge was destroyed by fire and was not rebuilt because Charles died a year later. He had intended to replace the wooden structure with one of stone. He also began building two magnificent palaces, one near the city of Mainz close to his estate at Ingelheim, the other in Nymwegen on the Waal River, which flows south of the island of the Batavians. But his chief concern was for the churches. When he discovered one in any part of his kingdom that was old and ready to collapse he charged the responsible bishops and priests with restoring it. And he made sure that his instructions were carried out by having his agents check up on them.

He also set up a navy to withstand the attacks of the Norsemen and had the necessary ships built on the rivers which flow from Gaul and Germania into the North Sea. Since the Norsemen were continuously invading and devastating the Gallic and Germanic coasts, he placed guards and fortifications in all harbors and large estuaries where ships could enter. In this way he prevented the enemy from landing and looting. He did the same in the south along the shores of Narbonensis, Septimania, and Italy as far south as Rome to ward off the Moors who had just begun to take up piracy. As a consequence Italy was hardly touched during his reign except for the Etruscan town of Civita Vecchia, which was treacherously captured and plundered by the Moors. Gaul and Germania were likewise spared except for a few Frisian islands along the Germanic coast which were laid waste by Norsemen.

18. PRIVATE LIFE

This is how Charles enlarged and defended his empire and at the same time made it beautiful. My subject from this point on will be his intellec-

tual abilities and his extraordinary steadfastness both in success and in adversity; and, further, whatever else concerns his private and domestic life.

After the death of his father, Charles ruled the kingdom together with his brother. Everyone was surprised that he bore the latter's animosity and envy with so much patience that he could never be provoked to anger by him. At his mother's request he married a daughter of the Lombard king Desiderius but repudiated her for unknown reasons after one year. Then he married Hildegard, who came from a very noble Swabian family. With her he had three sons, Charles, Pepin, and Louis, and as many daughters, Rotrud, Bertha, and Gisela. He had three more daughters, Theoderada, Hiltrud, and Rotheid, two of them with his [third] wife Fastrada, who came from Eastern Franconia and was therefore Germanic, the third by a concubine whose name I cannot recall at the moment. When Fastrada died he took Liutgard to wife, who was from Alemannia and with whom he had no children. After her death he had four concubines: Madelgard, who bore him a daughter by the name of Rothild; Gerswinda from Saxony, with whom he had another daughter called Adeltrud; Regnia, who gave him two sons, Drogo and Hugo; and Adelind, who had Theoderic.

His mother Berthrada spent her old age in great honor in his house. He always treated her with the greatest respect; only when he divorced the daughter of King Desiderius, whom he had married to please her, was there any disagreement between them. Berthrada died soon after Hildegard, but she had lived long enough to see three grandsons and three granddaughters in the house of her son. Charles buried her with highest honors in the church of St. Denis, where his father had been laid to rest.

Like his mother, he treated his only sister Gisela, who had entered a convent as a young girl, with the greatest affection. She died a few years before he did in the convent where she had spent most of her life.

19. PRIVATE LIFE (continued)

For the education of his children Charles made the following provisions: his sons as well as his daughters were to be instructed first in those liberal arts in which he took most interest himself. As soon as the boys were old enough they had to learn how to ride, hunt, and handle weapons in Frankish style. The girls had to get used to carding wool and to the distaff and the spindle. To prevent their becoming bored and lazy he gave orders for them to be taught to engage in these and all other virtuous activities. Of his children, only two sons and one daughter died before him: Charles, who was the oldest; Pepin, whom he had made king of Italy; and his oldest daughter Rotrud, who had been engaged to marry the emperor Constantine of Greece. Pepin was survived by one son, called Bernhard, and five daughters: Adelheid, Atula, Guntrada, Bertheid, and Theoderada. How much Charles cared for his grandchildren was proved after their father's death: he made Bernhard Pepin's successor and raised the five girls together with his own daughters. When his two sons and daughter died, Charles reacted to their deaths with much less equanimity than might

have been expected of so strong-minded a man. Because of his deep-seated devotion to them he broke down in tears. Also, when he was told of the death of the Roman Pope Hadrian, who was one of his best friends, he wept as much as if he had lost a brother or a favorite son. For Charles was by nature a man who had a great gift for friendship, who made friends easily and never wavered in his loyalty to them. Those whom he loved could rely on him absolutely.

He supervised the upbringing of his sons and daughters very carefully. When he was at home he never ate his meals without them and when he went away, he always took them along. At such times his sons rode by his side and his daughters followed close behind, protected by a bodyguard of hand-picked men. Although the girls were very beautiful and he loved them dearly, it was odd that he did not permit any of them to get married either to a man of his own nation or to a foreigner. Rather, he kept all of them with him until his death, saying that he could not live without their company. And on account of this, he had to suffer a number of unpleasant experiences, however lucky he was in every other respect. But he never let on that he had heard of any suspicions regarding their chastity or any rumors about them.

20. CONSPIRACIES AGAINST CHARLES

By one of the concubines he had a son whom I have not mentioned along with the others. His name was Pepin and he had a handsome face but was hunchbacked. While his father was wintering in Bavaria during the war against the Huns, Pepin pretended to be ill and became involved with some Frankish nobles in a plot against his father. He had been lured into it by empty promises that they would make him king. But the scheme was discovered and the traitors punished. Pepin was tonsured and allowed, on his own free will, to enter the monastery of Pruem, where he spent the rest of his life as a monk.

But even before this there had been a great conspiracy in Germania against Charles. All of the guilty ones were exiled; some of them only after being blinded, but the others were not harmed physically. Only three were killed because they had drawn their swords and tried to resist being taken prisoners. After they had slaughtered a number of men, they were killed themselves since there was no other way to subdue them. It was generally felt that Queen Fastrada's cruelty was responsible for these uprisings. And in both cases the reason they were aimed at Charles was because he apparently acquiesced in his wife's cruelty and seemed to have lost a good deal of his usual kindness and easy disposition. But for the rest, he was deeply loved and respected by everyone at home and abroad during all of his life, and no one ever accused him of being unnecessarily harsh.

21. TREATMENT OF FOREIGNERS

Charles liked foreigners and made every effort to see that they were well received. Often there were so many of them in his palace and kingdom that they were quite rightly considered a nuisance. But, magnanimous as he was, he was never bothered by such annoyances. For he felt that he would be rewarded for his troubles if they praised his generosity and gave him a good reputation.

22. PERSONAL APPEARANCE

Charles had a big and powerful body and was tall but well-proportioned. That his height was seven times the length of his own feet is well known. He had a round head, his eyes were unusually large and lively, his nose a little longer than average, his gray hair attractive, and his face cheerful and friendly. Whether he was standing or sitting his appearance was always impressive and dignified. His neck was somewhat short and thick and his stomach protruded a little, but this was rendered inconspicuous by the good proportion of the rest of his body. He walked firmly and his carriage was manly, yet his voice, though clear, was not as strong as one might have expected from someone his size. His health was always excellent except during the last four years of his life, when he frequently suffered from attacks of fever. And at the end he also limped with one foot. All the same, he continued to rely on his own judgment more than on that of his physicians, whom he almost hated because they ordered him to give up his customary roast meat and eat only boiled meat instead.

According to Frankish custom, he rode and hunted a great deal. There is probably no nation on earth that can match the Franks in these skills. Charles was also fond of the steam of natural hot springs. He swam a great deal and did it so well that no one could compete with him. This was why he built the palace in Aachen and spent there the last years of his life without interruption until he died. He invited not only his sons but also his nobles and friends, sometimes even his retinue and bodyguard, to bathe with him, so that frequently there would be more than a hundred people in the baths.

23. DRESS

He wore the national dress of the Franks. The trunk of his body was covered with a linen shirt, his thighs with linen pants. Over these he put a tunic trimmed at the border with silk. The legs from the knee downward were wound with leggings, fastened around the calves with laces, and on his feet he wore boots. In winter he protected his shoulders and chest with a vest made of otter skins or marten fur, and over that he wrapped a blue cloak. He always carried a sword strapped to his side, and the hilt and belt thereof were made either of gold or silver. Only on special holidays or when ambassadors from foreign nations were to be received did he sometimes carry a jewel-studded saber. He disliked foreign clothes no matter how beautiful they were, and would never allow himself to be dressed in them. Only in Rome was he seen on two occasions in a long tunic, chlamys, and Roman shoes: the first time at the entreaty of Pope Hadrian and the second by request of his successor Leo. On high festival days he wore a suit of golden cloth and boots ornamented with jewels. His cloak was fastened by a golden brooch, and on his head he carried a diadem of gold, embellished with gems. On the other days, however, his dress was not much different from that of the common people.

24. HABITS

Charles was a moderate eater and drinker, especially the latter, because he abominated drunkenness in any man, particularly in himself and in his associates. But he could not easily abstain from eating and often complained that fasting was bad for his health. He rarely gave banquets and then only on special feast days for large numbers of guests. His daily dinner consisted of four courses, besides the roast which the hunters used to bring in on spits and which he loved more than any other food. During the meal he either listened to music or to someone reading aloud. Stories and the deeds of the old heroes were recited to him. He also enjoyed the books of St. Augustine, especially *The City of God.*

He was so temperate in drinking wine or other beverages that he rarely drank more than three times during a meal. After his midday meal in the summer he would eat some fruit and take another drink, then remove his clothes and shoes, just as he did at night, and rest for two to three hours. His sleep at night would usually be interrupted four or five times, and as soon as he awoke, he got up. While he was being dressed and having his shoes put on, he would invite his friends to come into the room. If the count of the palace told him of some dispute which could not be settled without his decision, he ordered the litigants brought before him at once and, just as though he were sitting in a court of justice, would hear the case and pronounce judgment. At the same time he would give instructions on what had to be transacted that day, or what his ministers were to be charged with doing.

25. STUDIES

Charles was a gifted speaker. He spoke fluently and expressed whatever he had to say with great clarity. Not only was he proficient in his mother tongue but he also took trouble to learn foreign languages. He spoke Latin as well as his own language, but Greek he understood better than he could speak it. At times he was so eloquent that he almost seemed verbose. He was zealous in his cultivation of the liberal arts, and respected and honored highly those who taught them. He learned grammar from the Deacon Peter of Pisa, who was then already an old man. Another deacon, Albinus, surnamed Alcuin,[3] a man of Saxon origin who came from Britain and was the greatest scholar of his time, taught him the other subjects. Under his direction, the king spent a great deal of time and effort studying rhetoric, logic, and especially astronomy. He learned how to calculate and with great diligence and curiosity investigated the course of the stars. He also tried his hand at writing and to this end always kept writing tablets and notebooks under his pillow in bed in order to practice during spare moments. But since he had only started relatively late in life, he never became very accomplished in this art.

---

[3][Alcuin of York (735–804).—*Ed.*]

26. PIETY

The king practiced the Christian religion, in which he had been raised since childhood, with the greatest piety and devotion. That is why he built the beautiful basilica in Aachen and decorated it with gold and silver, candelabras, lattices, and portals of solid bronze. Since he was unable to get the columns and marble for the structure from anywhere else, he had them brought from Rome and Ravenna.

As long as his health permitted, the king attended church regularly in the morning and evening and took part in the late-night hours and morning mass. He was especially concerned that everything done in church should be carried out with the greatest possible dignity. Often he admonished the sacristans to see to it that nothing unseemly or unclean was brought into the church or left there. He gave many sacred vessels of gold and silver and so many priestly vestments that when services were held not even the doorkeepers—the humblest in ecclesiastical rank—had to perform their duties in everyday clothes.

Charles also worked very hard at improving the quality of liturgical reading and chanting of the psalms. He himself was well versed in both, although he would never read in public or sing, except in a low voice and together with the congregation.

27. GENEROSITY

Charles was especially interested in helping the poor, and his generosity was of the kind for which the Greeks use the word *eleemosyna* (alms). But his charity was not limited to his own country and kingdom, for wherever he heard of Christians living in poverty, he would send them money out of compassion for their wretched lot, even overseas, to Syria and Egypt, as well as to Africa, Jerusalem, Alexandria, and Carthage. This was also the chief reason why he cultivated friendships with kings across the seas, so that the Christians living in need under their jurisdiction would receive some aid and succor.

Of all sacred and hallowed places, he loved the Cathedral of the Holy Apostle Peter in Rome most of all. He endowed its treasure room with great quantities of gold, silver, and precious stones. He sent its pontiffs many, indeed innumerable, gifts. During his entire reign nothing seemed more important to him than to exert himself to restore the city of Rome to its old splendor and to have the Cathedral of St. Peter not only secured and defended but, through his generosity, adorned and enriched beyond all other churches. Although he favored this church so much, he only visited it four times during his reign of forty-seven years, there to fulfill his vows and offer his prayers.

28. CHARLES BECOMES EMPEROR

But there were also other reasons for Charles' last visit to Rome. The Romans had forced Pope Leo, on whom they had inflicted various injuries, like tearing out his eyes and cutting out his tongue, to beg for the king's assistance. Charles therefore went to Rome to put order into the confused situation and reestablish the status of the Church. This took the whole winter. It was on this occasion that he accepted the titles of Emperor and Augustus, which at first

he disliked so much that he said he would never have entered the church even on this highest of holy days[4] if he had beforehand realized the intentions of the Pope. Still, he bore with astonishing patience the envy his imperial title aroused in the indignant Eastern Roman emperors. He overcame their stubborn opposition with magnanimity—of which he unquestionably had far more than they did—and sent frequent embassies to them, always calling them his brothers in his letters.

29. REFORMS

After Charles had accepted the imperial title he noticed that there were many flaws in the legal code of his people, for the Franks have two separate sets of laws differing markedly in many details. He planned to fill in the gaps, to reconcile discrepancies, and to correct what was wrongly and improperly stated. But he was unable to get very much done, except for making a very few additions and even those incomplete. Even so, he did order all the unwritten laws of the nations under his rule collected and written down. He also had the same done for the very old heathen songs which tell of the deeds and wars of former kings, so that they might be preserved for posterity. In addition, he began a grammar of his native language.

Charles gave Frankish names to the months. Before that the Franks had used partly Latin, partly barbarian names for them. He also invited appropriate designations for the

---

[4][Charlemagne was crowned Emperor on Christmas day, 800.—*Ed.*]

twelve winds for which there had previously been barely four words. As for the months, he called January uuintarmanoth, February hornung, March lenzinmanoth, April ostarmanoth, May uuinnemanoth, June brachmanoth, July heuuimanoth, August aranmanoth, September uuitumanoth, October uuindumemanoth, November herbistmanoth, and December heilagmanoth. To the winds he gave the following names: the east wind (subsolanus) he called ostroniuuint, the southeaster (eurus) ostsundroni, the south-southeaster (euroauster) sundostroni, the south wind (auster) sundroni, the south-southwester (austroafricus) sunduuestroni, the southwester (africus) uuestsundroni, the west wind (zephyrus) uuestroni, the northwester (chorus) uuestnordroni, the north-northwester (circius) norduuestroni, the north wind (septentrio) nordroni, the northeaster (aquilo) nordostroni, and the north-northeaster (vulturnus) ostnordroni.

30. CORONATION OF LOUIS AND CHARLES' DEATH

At the end of his life, when he was already beset by illness and old age, Charles summoned Louis, the king of Aquitaine and Hildegard's only surviving son, to his presence. He invited all of the Frankish nobles to a solemn assembly, in which with their consent he appointed Louis coregent over the entire realm and heir to the imperial title. He crowned his son himself by placing the diadem on his head and ordering that he be addressed Emperor and Augustus. His decision was received by all those present with great acclaim since it seemed to be divinely inspired for the good of the kingdom. It in-

creased his reputation as a ruler and instilled considerable respect among foreign nations. After Charles had sent his son back to Aquitaine, he started out as usual for the hunt paying no heed to his advanced age. Thus occupied, he spent what was left of the autumn not far from Aachen and returned to the palace at approximately the beginning of November. While he was wintering there he was attacked by a high fever during the month of January and had to retire to bed. As he always did when he had a temperature, he began to diet in the belief that he could cure or at least alleviate his illness by abstaining from food. In addition to the fever he developed a pain in his side, which the Greeks call pleurisy, but he kept fasting and did not take any sustenance except for an occasional drink. On the seventh day after he had taken to bed he received the Holy Communion and died on 28 January between eight and nine o'clock in the morning. Charles was then in the seventy-second year of his life and in the forty-seventh year of his reign.

31. BURIAL

His body was washed and prepared for burial in the usual way, then brought to the basilica and buried amid the great lamentations of the entire population. At first there was uncertainty about where he should be laid to rest because he had never given any instructions on this point during his lifetime. Finally everyone agreed that there could be no more appropriate place than the basilica which he had built at his own expense in this city out of love for God and our Lord Jesus Christ and in honor of the Holy and Immaculate Virgin. He was interred there on the same day he died. Above his grave a gilded arch was raised with his image and an inscription reading as follows: "In this tomb lies the body of Charles, the great Christian Emperor, who gloriously increased the kingdom of the Franks and ruled successfully for forty-seven years. He died in his seventies in the seventh year of the indiction, on January 28th in the year of our Lord 814."

32. OMENS OF DEATH

There were many omens indicating the approach of his death, so that not only others but even himself took note of the forewarnings. During the last three years of his life there were frequent eclipses of the sun and moon, and black spots were seen on the face of the sun for seven days. On Ascension Day the portico between the cathedral and the palace which he had built with immense effort suddenly came crashing down in complete ruin. The wooden bridge across the Rhine at Mainz, which had taken ten years of hard work to build and which was so cleverly constructed that it seemed as if it would last forever, this bridge accidentally caught fire and burnt to ashes in three hours, so that not a single plank remained except what was under water. During his last campaign in Saxony against Godofrid, the king of the Danes, Charles all at once saw a ball of brilliant fire falling from the sky and flashing from right to left through the clear atmosphere. He had just left his camp before sunrise to start out on the march. While everybody was looking and wondering what his sign meant, his horse

fell headfirst and threw him to the ground so violently that the clasp on his cloak broke and his sword belt burst. The attendants who were near him and rushed to his aid helped him up without his weapons and cloak. The lance which he had been holding tightly in his hand was thrown a distance of more than twenty feet.

In addition to all this there were numerous earth tremors in his palace in Aachen, and in the houses which Charles visited the wooden beams in the ceilings creaked constantly. Furthermore, lightning had struck the basilica in which he was later to be buried and the golden ball which decorated the gable was destroyed and hurled onto the roof of the bishop's house next to the church. In the same basilica there was an inscription written in red ochre naming its builder and running along the edge of the circular space which surrounds the interior part of the building between the upper and lower arches. Its last words read: "Karolus Princeps." Several people noticed that during the last year of his life, only a few months before he died, the letters of the word "Princeps" had become so blurred that they could hardly be deciphered.

But Charles took no notice of these omens; in any case he acted as if they had nothing whatever to do with him.

33. LAST WILL

Charles had decided to draw up a will in which he wanted to make his daughters and illegitimate children heirs to some part of his estate. Since he started too late, however, he was unable to complete it. Nevertheless, three years before his death he made a division of his treasures, money, clothing, and other movable property in the presence of his friends and attendants. He called on them to bear witness that the apportionment which he had planned should be executed faithfully after his death. He had a brief statement prepared summarizing what he wanted done with the property he had divided. This document reads as follows: "In the name of the Almighty Lord God, the Father, the Son, and the Holy Ghost. Here is a description of the division which was made by the most glorious and pious Lord Charles, Emperor and Augustus, in the eight hundred and eleventh year after the incarnation of our Lord Jesus Christ, during the forty-third year of his reign over the Franks, in the thirty-sixth year of his rule over Italy, in the eleventh year of his imperial sovereignty, and in the fourth indiction. After much pious and prudent deliberation and with the help of God, he has decided to distribute the valuables and money which on this day are on deposit in his treasury. In doing so he wished above all to ensure that in his case the distribution of alms, which among Christians is traditionally made from their own personal belongings, would be carried out in an orderly and reasonable fashion. He also wanted to be certain that his heirs should understand quite clearly and definitely what was to be theirs, so that they could divide up the inheritance properly without any litigation or dispute. Such being his intention and purpose, he first divided all his tangible and movable possessions, consisting of gold and of silver, precious stones and royal vestments, deposited in his treasury on the stipulated day into three main parts. One part he left intact; the other two he subdivided into twenty-one smaller portions, the reason for this being that, as is well known, there are twenty-two capital cities in his realm. One of these portions shall be given for charitable purposes to each of the cities by his heirs and friends. The archbishop responsible for the diocese shall receive the portion and divide it with his suffragans in such a manner that one-third is kept for his church and two-thirds is given to the suffragans. These twenty-one portions into which two-thirds of his property were subdivided to correspond to the number of capital cities in the kingdom have been carefully separated and set aside in individual coffers on which the names of the cities of destination are written. The cities to which these alms and gifts are to be given are as follows: Rome, Ravenna, Milan, Cividale del Friuli, Grado, Cologne, Mainz, Salzburg, Trier, Sens, Besançon, Lyons, Rouen, Rheims, Arles, Vienne, Moûtiersen-Tarantaise, Embrun, Bordeaux, Tours, and Bourges.

"The third main part which is to be preserved intact shall be dealt with in the following manner: while both of the above-mentioned parts are to be divided in the way stated and are to be kept under seal, the third part is to be used for the defrayment of the daily expenses by the owner and will constitute property of which he cannot be deprived by any sworn obligation whatsoever. This provision shall remain in force for as long as he lives or for as long as he judges that he has need of it. After his death or voluntary withdrawal from the secular world the said part is to be divided into four shares. One of these shall be added to the above-mentioned twenty-one portions; the second share is to go to his sons and daughters and their sons and daughters and shall be distributed in a just and equitable way; the third shall be devoted to the poor in the customary Christian manner; the fourth is to be similarly parceled out in form of a pension, in the name of Christian charity, among the male and female servants of the Palace.

"To this third main part of his fortune, which like the rest consists of gold and silver, he desires that there be added all vessels and utensils made of bronze, iron, and other metal, together with his weapons, clothes, and other movable property, whether valuable or not, and for whatever use intended, such as curtains, coverlets, tapestries, woolens, leather goods, pack saddles, and whatever else might be found that day in the treasury or in his wardrobe. In this way the shares of the third part will be enlarged and the alms distributed among a greater number of people.

"Further, he has given orders that the chapel, that is to say the furnishings which he has donated and collected, or inherited from his father, be kept intact and not be subject to any kind of division. Should there, however, be any vessels, books, or other objects of which it is certainly known that they were not given to the chapel by him, then any person desiring them may buy them, provided a fair price is paid. In the same way he decreed that the large collection of books in his library may be bought by persons who want them and will pay a just price for them. The proceeds shall go to the poor.

"Among his other treasures and valuables there are known to be three silver tables and one of un-

usual size and weight made of gold. He has stipulated and decreed that one of them, square in shape and decorated with a plan of the city of Constantinople, be sent to Rome to the Cathedral of the Holy Apostle Peter along with the other gifts thereto intended. The second table, round in shape and engraved with a picture of the city of Rome, shall be given to the bishopric of the church of Ravenna. The third, far superior to the others, both in beauty of craftsmanship and in weight, consists of three concentric circles on which a map of the entire world is skillfully traced in great detail. This table together with the golden one, called the fourth, shall be added to the third main part of his fortune, which he has allotted to his heirs and to those who are to receive alms.

"These arrangements and stipulations were done in the presence of the following bishops, abbots, and counts who were able to attend on that day, and whose names are herein recorded:

Bishops

Hildebald	John
Richolf	Theodolf
Arno	Jesse
Wolfar	Heito
Bernoin	Waltgaud
Laidrad	

Abbots

Fridugis	Angilbert
Adalung	Irmino

Counts

Walach	Unruoch
Meginher	Burchard
Otolf	Meginhard
Stephan	Hatto

Counts

Richwin	Bero
Edo	Hildegern
Ercanger	Hroccolf."
Gerold	

After Charles' death, his son Louis, who succeeded him by divine ordination, examined this document and had its provisions carried out as speedily as possible and with the utmost scrupulousness.

Church and State

Throughout the Middle Ages in Europe the church and the temporal rulers waged a running battle for political supremacy. For a time, the church seemed assured of victory. It reached the height of its power during the pontificate of Innocent III (1198–1216), who succeeded in forcing King John to surrender England to him, to be held by John in the future as a fief from the papacy. The final victory, however, went to the secular powers, who gradually effected a separation between political authority and spiritual authority, reserving the former for themselves and permitting the church to exercise the latter.

The documents that follow reflect the church's position at two different phases during this long struggle. The first document is concerned with a dispute between the Holy Roman Emperor, Henry IV, and Pope Gregory VII, a dispute that led to Henry's famous winter pilgrimage to Canossa to seek absolution from the pope. The document is actually a letter,

written in 1081, from Gregory to the bishop of Metz, who had sought papal aid in combating the emperor. It is important because it contains Gregory's view of the position of the church relative to the state, as well as the main arguments on which that position rested.

The second document, the papal bull *Unam Sanctam*, was written over two hundred years later (1302), during a controversy between Pope Boniface VIII and King Philip the Fair of France. Philip replied to the bull, which flatly asserts the political supremacy of the church, by having the pope seized. Although Boniface was soon released, he died almost immediately afterward. Philip again took the initiative and managed to convert the papacy into an adjunct of the French throne. This episode marked the turning point in the political fortunes of the church, for the popes were never able to regain the ascendancy over the secular monarchs that the papacy had enjoyed under Pope Innocent III.

The Second Letter of Gregory VII to Hermann, Bishop of Metz, March 15, 1081

GREGORY, BISHOP, servant of the servants of God, to Our well-beloved brother in Christ, Hermann, Bishop of Metz, health and the Apostolic Benediction.

We know your desire to employ yourself, and to confront dangers, in the defence of truth, and We see in your good-will, the action of Divine Providence. The ineffable grace of God and His marvellous bounty never permit His chosen ones to lapse into complete error, nor do they allow them to be altogether conquered and enslaved by sin. After the salutary trials of persecution, and the anxieties which they have experienced, the elect come forth stronger than before. Fear makes cowards shamelessly rival one another in flight; in like manner, those inspired by manly courage, strive to be in the front rank and to obtain the palm of valour and bravery. If We address this language to your charity, it is because you too wish to be in the front rank in the Christian army; that is, amongst those who, you know well, are closest to, and most worthy of, the God who gives the Victory.

You ask Us to come to your aid by Our writings and to refute the insanity of those, who maintain with their guilty tongues, that the Holy Apostolic See has not the right to excommunicate King Henry, that despiser of the Christian law, that destroyer of Churches, and of the Empire, that abettor and accomplice of heretics, and that it had not power to absolve from the oath of fidelity, which had been sworn to him. It does not seem very necessary for Us to do this, for this power is established by many authentic texts of Holy Scripture. We cannot indeed believe, that those who, for their own damnation, and with unblushing impudence oppose and fight against truth can, in their ignorance or madness, have had the audacity to use these texts as their justification. There would not, however, be anything astonishing in that, for it is the custom of the wicked to seek protection for their vices, and to defend their accomplices; it matters little to them if they ruin themselves by their lies.

To quote one proof from among many. Who does not know that saying of Our Lord and Savior Jesus Christ, in the Gospel

Thou art Peter, and upon this rock I will build my church; and the gates of hell shall not prevail against it. I will give to you the keys of the Kingdom of Heaven, and whatsoever you shall bind on earth, shall be bound also in heaven, and whatsoever you shall loose upon earth, shall be loosed also in heaven. [Matthew XVI:18, 19]

Are kings an exception? Do they not form part of the flock confided to St. Peter by the Son of God? Then, We ask, who will dare to claim that he

Trans. A. H. Mathew

has nothing to do with the power of St. Peter, that the universal power of binding and loosing given to St. Peter, has no reference to him? No one would act in this manner, but that unhappy man, who, unwilling to bear the yoke of the Lord, would submit to that of the devil and renounce his right to belong to the fold of Christ. By this proud denial of the power divinely granted to St. Peter, he would obtain liberty, a sad liberty indeed, for the more he denied the power, the more heavily would his eternal damnation weigh upon him, on the day of judgment.

• • •

The blessed Pope Gregory, writing to a certain senator abbot, asserts that kings, who allow themselves to violate the decrees of the Apostolic See, ought to be deprived of their dignities. *If,* he writes,

any king, priest, judge, or any secular, knowing the present decree, dares to offend against it, let him lose his power and dignity, and let him declare himself guilty before God of the iniquity he has committed. If he does not restore what he has unjustly stolen, and do penance in proportion to his fault, let him be deprived of the most holy Body and Blood of our Lord and Redeemer Jesus Christ; and may the vengeance of the eternal judgment fall upon him.

If blessed Gregory, who was the meekest of the doctors, decreed that kings, who violated the statutes, which he gave to a hospital, should not only be deposed, but excommunicated and damned for ever, who would dare to reproach us for having deposed and excommunicated Henry, the despiser of the apostolic judgments, the fierce enemy of Mother Church, the infamous despoiler and merciless scourge of the whole kingdom, and of the churches? Who, but one, who is still more unworthy than he, would dare to cast reproach upon us? We read in a letter of the blessed Peter, concerning the ordination of Clement:

If any one is a friend to those whom he (Clement) does not speak, through that very fact, he belongs to those who wish to destroy the Church of God; in the body he seems to be with us; but his spirit and his heart are against us.

Such an enemy is to be dreaded more than one whose enmity is open, and apparent to all; for the former works evil under cover of false friendship and causes disunion and destruction in the Church. Remark this well, dearly beloved, the blessed Peter judges him, whose conduct is condemned by the Pope, in so severe a manner, that he even goes so far as to condemn those, who are bound to him by friendship, and even those who hold converse with him.

It is, therefore, impossible for a dignity which owes its origin to men of the world, and even to those ignorant of God, not to be in subjection to that dignity, which the Providence of the all-powerful God instituted, to bring honour to Him, and which, in His mercy, He has granted to the whole world. If the Son of this all-powerful God is undoubtedly God and Man, He is also the High Priest, the chief of all priests, and He is now seated at the right hand of the Father, where He intercedes for us without ceasing. The Son of God despised the earthly kingdoms, of which the sons of this world are so proud; it was of His own accord that He chose and embraced the priesthood of the Cross. Every one knows that the first kings and the first dukes, were men ignorant of God, who, influenced by blind cupidity, and intolerable presumption, aided, moreover, by the Demon-prince of this world, strove by the help of robbery, lies, and homicide, and almost every vice, to have dominion over their equals, that is, over other men. When these kings and dukes sought afterwards to draw the priests of the Lord into their ways, to whom can one more fitly compare them than to him who is the head of all the sons of pride, to him who tried to tempt the Sovereign of Pontiffs Himself, the Chief of Priests, the Son of the Most High, by showing Him all the kingdoms of the world and saying to Him, *I will give you all this if you fall down at my feet and adore me.* Who can doubt that the priests of Christ are the fathers and masters of kings; that they are the princes of all the faithful? Is it not an act of utter madness, when the son tries to rule the father, the disciple the master; when he wishes to reduce him to submission by imposing on him iniquitous conditions, though he knows well that this father and master has the power of binding and loosing on earth, as well as in heaven?

• • •

Moreover, on his death-bed, every Christian king who wishes to escape hell, to pass from darkness to light, to appear at the judgment-seat of God, after having received absolution for his faults, humbly implores the ministry of the priest. But who is there, I do not say, priest, but even layman, who has ever begged the help of an earthly king, when at the point of death, and filled with anxiety for the salvation of his soul? What king or emperor can, by right of his office, give holy baptism to a Christ-

ian, deliver him from the power of the devil, give him entrance among the children of God, or anoint him with the holy chrism? Who, among them, can consecrate the Body and Blood of the Lord, in other words, perform that greatest act of the Christian religion? Has the power of binding and absolving in heaven and on earth been given to any one of them? In all these things, the superiority of the sacerdotal dignity is evident. If no one among them has the power to ordain a cleric of Holy Church, still less have they the right of deposing him for any fault. In ecclesiastical orders, the authority which deposes ought to be superior to that which ordains. Bishops can consecrate other bishops, but they cannot depose them, without the authority of the Apostolic See. Very little discernment is therefore necessary to understand the superiority of the priesthood over the royal state. If, in all that concerns their sins, kings are amenable to priests, much more must they be so, to the Roman Pontiff.

On closer examination, the title of king is much better suited to good Christians than to bad princes. The former seek the glory of God, and know how to govern themselves; the latter, preoccupied with their own interests, and not with the interests of God, are enemies to themselves and tyrants to others. The former are part of the Body of Jesus Christ; the latter of the body of the devil. The first-mentioned govern themselves, that they may reign eternally with the Supreme Emperor; the power of the second is exercised in such a way, that they will be lost for ever, with the prince of darkness, the king of all the sons of pride.

It is not surprising if bad bishops make common cause with an impious king; they receive their honours from that king in an unlawful way, hence they both love and dread him at the same time. By their consent to perform simoniacal ordinations, they, as it were, sell God at a low price. The elect are indissolubly united to their head; the reprobate, in like manner clings tenaciously round him who is the author of evil, especially when the matter at stake is to resist the good. To argue with them is of little avail, rather weep over their sad fate, that the all-powerful God may deliver them from the snares of Satan, and that He may in the end open their eyes to the truth.

• • •

What emperor or king ever restored the dead to life, cured lepers or gave sight to the blind? We have the Emperor Constantine, of pious memory, the Emperors Theodosius, Honorius, Charles and Louis, who loved justice, spread the Christian religion, and defended the Church; the Church praises and venerates them, yet she does not say that they had, to a striking extent, the gift of miracles. What altars or basilicas are there dedicated to a king or to an emperor; has the church ever allowed Mass to be celebrated in honour of any one of them? Kings and princes, so proud of being above other men, in this life, ought to fear all the more, lest they should be condemned to eternal fire in the life hereafter. Thus it is written: *The mighty shall be mightily tormented.* They will have to render an account of each subject under their sway. If it is no small labour for any ordinary mortal, filled with the spirit of religion, to save one single soul, that is, his own; how great is not the responsibility of princes who have the

charge of thousands of souls! Holy Church punishes severely the sinner who has committed homicide; what then will happen to those who have caused death to thousands of persons for the sake of the glory of this world? It sometimes happens that, after having been the cause of death to many, they utter with their lips a *mea culpa*; but in the depths of their hearts, they rejoice at the extension of their glory and power. They are very far from wishing that they had left their great deeds undone; the fact of having sent their fellow-creatures to Tartarus, fills them with no compunction. Their repentance is worthless in the sight of God, it is not inspired by true contrition of heart, as they do not wish to give up what they have acquired by conquest, and at the cost of so much human blood. They have reason to fear; they ought often to recall to their minds what we have already said, that a very small number of saints is to be found amongst the multitude of kings who have succeeded one another, on the different thrones of the earth, since the beginning of the world. On the other hand, in one single line of Pontiffs, as for instance, the Roman Pontiffs from the time of St. Peter, more than a hundred are distinguished for eminent sanctity. What reason is there for this, unless, as has already been said, it is that kings of the earth and princes, fascinated by a vain desire of glory, subordinate their spiritual interests to the temporal interests of themselves and their kingdoms. Truly godly pontiffs, on the contrary, allow no earthly matters to come between them and the cause of God. The first-mentioned are remorseless in avenging personal affronts; but, when the offence is committed against God, they seem to lack energy to punish the offenders; the second easily forget the wrongs done to themselves, but with difficulty pardon the injuries done to God. The former, engrossed in the things of this world, set little value on spiritual things; the latter, having their thoughts constantly directed towards heaven, feel nothing but contempt for all that is of this earth.

• • •

In the name of the Omnipotent God, and through the authority of blessed Peter, prince of apostles, **We** grant you, brother Hermann, permission to fulfil the Episcopal duties in all the bishoprics of the kingdom of Lorraine in which the Bishops have been excommunicated, for having held intercourse with Henry, formerly called king. This permission will hold good so long as these Bishops remain excommunicated—that is, until they have been absolved, either by Us or by Our lawful successor.

The Bull *Unam Sanctam* of Boniface VIII

That there is one Holy Catholic and Apostolic Church we are impelled by our faith to believe and to hold—this we do firmly believe and openly confess—and outside of this there is neither salvation or remission of sins, as the bridegroom proclaims in Canticles, "My dove, my undefiled is but one; she is the only one of her mother; she is the choice one of her that bare her." The Church represents one mystic body and of this body Christ is the head; of Christ, indeed, God is the head. In it is one Lord, and one faith, and one baptism. In the time of the flood, there was one ark of Noah, prefiguring the one Church, finished in one cubit, having one Noah as steersman and commander. Outside of this, all things upon the face of the earth were, as we read, destroyed. This Church we venerate and this alone, the Lord saying through his prophets, "Deliver my soul, O God, from the sword; my darling from the power of the dog." He prays thus for his soul, that is for Himself, as head, and also for the body, which He calls one, namely, the Church on account of the unity of the bridegroom, of the faith, of the sacraments, and of the charity of the Church. It is that seamless coat of the Lord, which was not rent, but fell by lot. Therefore, in this one and only Church, there is one body and one head—not two heads as if it were a monster—namely, Christ and Christ's Vicar, Peter and Peter's successor, for the Lord said to Peter himself, "Feed my sheep": *my* sheep, he said, using a general term and not designating

"The Bull *Unam Sanctam* of Boniface VIII," in *Translations and Reprints from the Original Sources of European History*, Vol. III, No. 6 (Philadelphia: The Department of History of the University of Pennsylvania, 1912). Courtesy of the Department of History of the University of Pennsylvania.

these or those sheep, so that we must believe that all the sheep were committed to him. If, then, the Greeks, or others, shall say that they were not entrusted to Peter and his successors, they must perforce admit that they are not of Christ's sheep, as the Lord says in John, "there is one fold, and one shepherd."

In this Church and in its power are two swords, to wit, a spiritual and a temporal, and this we are taught by the words of the Gospel, for when the Apostles said, "Behold, here are two swords" (in the Church, namely, since the Apostles were speaking), the Lord did not reply that it was too many, but enough. And surely he who claims that the temporal sword is not in the power of Peter has but ill understood the word of our Lord when he said, "Put up the sword in its scabbard." Both, therefore, the spiritual and material swords, are in the power of the Church, the latter indeed to be used for the Church, the former by the Church, the one by the priest, the other by the hand of kings and soldiers, but by the will and sufferance of the priest. It is fitting, moreover, that one sword should be under the other, and the temporal authority subject to the spiritual power. For when the Apostle said "there is no power but of God and the powers that are of God are ordained," they would not be ordained unless one sword were under the other, and one, as inferior, was brought back by the other to the highest place. For, according to the Holy Dionysius, the law of divinity is to lead the lowest through the intermediate to the highest. Therefore, according to the law of the universe, things are not reduced to order directly, and upon the same footing, but the lowest through the interme-

diate and the inferior through the superior. It behooves us, therefore, the more freely to confess that the spiritual power excels in dignity and nobility any form whatsoever of earthly power, as spiritual interests exceed the temporal in importance. All this we see fairly from the giving of tithes, from the benediction and sanctification, from the recognition of this power and the control of the same things. For the truth bearing witness, it is for the spiritual power to establish the earthly power and judge it, if it be not good. Thus, in the case of the Church and the power of the Church, the prophecy of Jeremiah is fulfilled: "See, I have this day set thee over the nations and over the kingdoms"—and so forth. Therefore, if the earthly power shall err, it shall be judged by the spiritual power; if the lesser spiritual power err, it shall be judged by the higher. But if the supreme power err, it can be judged by God alone and not by man, the apostles bearing witness saying, the spiritual man judges all things but he himself is judged by no one. Hence this power, although given to man and exercised by man, is not human, but rather divine power, given by the divine lips to Peter, and founded on a rock for Him and his successors in Him whom he confessed, the Lord saying to Peter himself, "Whatsoever thou shalt bind," etc. Whoever, therefore, shall resist this power, ordained by God, resists the ordination of God, unless there should be two beginnings, as the Manichaean imagines. But this we judge to be false and heretical, since, by the testimony of Moses, not in the *beginnings*, but in the *beginning*, God created the heaven and the earth. We, moreover, proclaim, declare, and pronounce that it is altogether necessary to salvation for every human being to be subject to the Roman Pontiff.

Given at the Lateran the twelfth day before the Kalends of December, in our eighth year, as a perpetual memorial of this matter.

The Common People

One of the most difficult tasks for the historian, particularly of times long past, is to get information about the lives of common people. This is especially true of a generally unlettered society, such as medieval Europe; people who do not read or write tell few lasting tales. Nevertheless, information can be gained indirectly, mainly through records and documents whose authors belonged to the lettered classes. The two selections that follow are illustrative of these. The first gives some insight into rural life, the second into life in a town. Both are from medieval France.

The *Capitulare de Villis* is a set of instructions issued on behalf of the ruling monarch, in this case probably Louis the Pious, king of Aquitaine (in southwestern France), in the latter part of the eighth century. In it the writer instructs the stewards on a great variety of details concerning the care of the royal lands, the people who work on them, and their produce. From the details of these instructions it is possible to learn a good deal about the daily lives of people of that time, both peasants and nobility. The general impression one gains from reading the selection is that King Louis kept full and careful control over all the agricultural and related activities occurring on his domains; whether this was in fact true we have, of course, no way of knowing.

In the *Charter of the Liberties of Lorris* we turn to medieval town life. Lorris was (and still is) a small town in north-central France, not far from Orleans. The charter reproduced was granted to the inhabitants of Lorris by King Louis VII of France in 1155. It is, perhaps, of interest to note that most of the items concerning both the privileges and the obligations of the inhabitants of the town concerned economic matters, particularly taxes and fees that could be levied against them. The charter is historically important because it became a model for similar charters granted to many other towns in later years.

Capitulare de Villis

We wish that our estates which we have instituted to serve our needs discharge their services to us entirely and to no other men.

Our people shall be well taken care of and reduced to poverty by no one.

Our stewards shall not presume to put our people to their own service, either to force them to work, to cut wood, or to do any other task for them. And they shall accept no gifts from them, either horse, ox, cow, pig, sheep, little pig, lamb, or anything else excepting bottles of wine or other beverage, garden produce, fruits, chickens, and eggs.

If any of our people does injury to us either by stealing or by some other offense he shall make good the damage and for the remainder of the legal satisfaction he shall be punished by whipping, with the exception of homicide and arson cases which are punishable by fines. The stewards, for injuries of our people to other men, shall endeavor to secure justice according to the law. Instead of paying fines our people, as we have said, shall be whipped. Freemen who live in our domains or estates shall make good the injuries they do according to their law and the fines which they have incurred shall be paid for our use either in cattle or in equivalent value.

When our stewards ought to see that our work is done—the sowing, plowing, harvesting, cutting of hay, or gathering of grapes—let each one at the proper season and in each and every place organize and oversee what is to be done that it may be done well. If a steward shall not be in his district or can not be in some place let him choose a good substitute from our people or another in high repute to direct our affairs that they may be successfully accomplished. And he shall diligently see to it that a trustworthy man is delegated to take care of this work.

We wish our stewards to give a tithe of all our products to the churches on our domains and that the tithe not be given to the churches of another except to those entitled to it by ancient usage. And our churches shall not have clerics other than our own, that is, of our people or our palace.

Each steward shall perform his services fully, just as it has been prescribed, and if the necessity should arise that more must be done then he shall determine whether he should increase the service or the day-work.

Our stewards shall take care of our vines in their district and cultivate them well. And they shall put the wine in good vessels and carefully see to it that none is lost. And other required wine which is not from our vines they shall buy for provisioning the royal estates. And when they have bought more than is needed for this provisioning they shall inform us that we can let them know what is to be done with it. For they shall put

"Capitulare de Villis," in *Introduction to Contemporary Civilization in the West,* 3rd ed., eds. Contemporary Civilization Staff of Columbia College (1960, Columbia University Press, New York). Used by permission of the publisher.

the product of our vines to our use. The wine which those persons on our estates pay as rent shall be put in our cellars.

We wish that each steward in his district have measures of the *modius, sextarius,* the *situla* of eight *sextarii,* and the *corbus,* the same as we have in our palace.

Our mayors, foresters, stablemen, cellarers, deans, toll-collectors, and other officers shall do the regular and fixed labor and pay the due of pigs for their holdings and fulfill well their offices in return for the manual labor remitted them. And if any mayor holds a benefice he shall send his representative so that the manual labor and other services will be performed for him.

No steward shall take lodging for his own need or for his dogs from our people or from those in the forests.

No steward shall maintain at the expense of anyone else our hostages placed on our estates.

The stewards shall take good care of the stallions and not allow them to remain in one pasture too long lest they damage it. And if there should be any unsound or too old or about to die they shall inform us in good time before the season for putting them with the mares.

They shall take good care of our mares and separate them from the colts at the right time. And when the fillies increase in number they shall also be separated to form a new herd.

Our stewards shall have our foals sent to the palace in the winter at the Feast of Saint Martin.

We wish that our stewards fully perform in the manner established for them whatever we or the queen or our officers, the seneschal or the butler, in our name or that of the queen command. If anyone shall not do this through negligence he shall abstain from drink from the time that it is made known to him until he comes into our presence or that of the queen and seeks pardon from us. And if the steward is with the army, on guard duty, or on a mission or otherwise engaged and he commands his assistants to do something and they fail to do it, then they shall come afoot to the palace and abstain from food and drink until they have given their reasons for not doing it. Then they shall receive their sentence, a whipping or whatever we or the queen deem appropriate.

Each steward shall have as many men taking care of the bees for our use as he has estates in his district.

At our mills the stewards shall have hens and geese according to the nature of the mill or as many more as is possible.

In our barns on the chief estates they shall have at least 100 chickens and 30 geese and on our lesser estates at least 50 chickens and 12 geese.

Each steward shall have the produce [of the fowl] brought always in abundance to the manor every year and besides shall inspect it three or four or more times.

Each steward shall have fishponds on our estates where they were before and if it is possible to enlarge them, he shall do so. Where there were none before and it is now possible to have them let them be constructed.

Those who hold vines from us shall have no less than three or four circles of grapes for our use.

On each of our estates the stewards shall have cow-barns, pig-sties, sheepfolds, and stables for goats, as many as possible, and never be without them. And they shall further have for performing their services cows furnished by our serfs so that our barns and teams are not in the least diminished by the services of work on our demesne. And when they are charged with furnishing food they shall have lame but healthy oxens and cows, and horses that are not mangy, and other healthy animals. They shall not on that account strip, as we have said, the cow-barns or the plough-beasts.

Each steward shall be responsible that whatever ought to be supplied for our table is all good and excellent and prepared carefully and cleanly. And each steward shall have grain for two meals for each day of the service that he is charged with supplying our table. Similarly the other provisions shall be good in all respects, the flour as well as the meat.

The stewards shall make known on the first of September whether or not there is pasturage for the hogs.

The mayors shall not have more land in their administration than they can get about and oversee in one day.

Our houses shall constantly have fire and watch service that they may be safe. And when royal envoys or legates are coming to or leaving the palace, in no wise shall they exercise the right of bed and board in our manor houses except by our special order or that of the queen. But the count in his district or those persons who have been accustomed of old to caring for envoys and legates shall continue to do so as before. And pack-horses and other necessary things shall be provided in the customary fashion that they may come to the palace or depart in a fashion befitting them.

We wish that every year in Lent on Palm Sunday, which is called Hosanna Sunday, our stewards carefully render according to our instructions the money arising from the products of our land after we know for the particular year what our income is.

Each steward shall see to it that anyone of our people who have cases to plead shall not of necessity have to come to us so that he will not lose through negligence days on which he ought to be working. And if one of our serfs has some rights to claim outside our lands, his master shall do all that he can to secure justice for him. In case the serf shall not be able to get justice his master shall not permit him to exhaust himself in his efforts but shall see to it that the matter is made known to us by himself or by his representative.

Of those things that our stewards ought to provide for our needs, we wish them to put aside all the products due us from them, and what must be placed in the wagons for the army, taking it from the homes as well as from the herdsmen, and that they know how much they have reserved for this purpose.

They shall set aside each year what they ought to give as food and maintenance to the workers entitled to it and to the women working in the women's quarters and shall give it fully at the right time and make known to us what they have done with it and where they got it.

Each steward shall see to it that he always has the very best seed by purchase or otherwise.

After the above things have been set aside and after the sowing and other works have been done, all that remains of all the products shall be preserved until we give word to what extent they shall be sold or stored according to our order.

At all times it is to be seen to with diligence that whatever is worked upon or made with hands such as lard, smoked meat, salted meat, newly salted meat, wine, vinegar, mulberry wine, cooked wine, fermentations, mustard, cheese, butter, malt, beer, honey, wax, and flour shall be prepared or made with the greatest cleanliness.

We wish that fat be made of the fat sheep and pigs. Moreover the steward shall have in each estate not less than two fattened oxen either there to be made into fat or to be sent to us.

Our woods and forests shall be well taken care of and where there shall be a place for a clearing let it be cleared. Our stewards shall not allow the fields to become woods and where there ought to be woods they shall not allow anyone to cut too much or damage them. And they shall look carefully after our wild beasts in the forests and also take care of the goshawks and sparrowhawks reserved for our use. They shall collect diligently our tax for the use of our forests and if our stewards or our mayors or their men put their pigs for fattening in our forests they shall be the first to pay the tenth of them to give a good example so that thereafter the other men will pay the tenth in full.

The stewards shall keep our fields and cultivated lands in good shape and care for the meadows at the right time.

They shall always have sufficient fat geese and chickens for our use when they ought to provide it or send it to us.

We wish that the stewards collect the chickens and the eggs which the lesser officials and the holders of *mansi* pay each year and when they are not needed that they have them sold.

Each steward shall always have on our estates for the sake of adornment unusual birds, peacocks, pheasants, ducks, pigeons, partridges, and turtledoves.

The buildings on our estates and the fences which enclose them shall be well taken care of and the stables and kitchens, bake-houses and presses shall be carefully ordered so that the workers in our service can perform their duties fittingly and very cleanly.

Each manor shall have in the store-room counterpanes, bolsters, pillows, bedclothes, table and bench covers, vessels of brass, lead, iron, and wood, andirons, chains, pothooks, adzes, axes, augurs, knives, and all sorts of tools so that it will not be necessary to seek them elsewhere or to borrow them. And the stewards shall be responsible that the iron instruments sent to the army are in good condition and when they are returned that they are put back into the store-room.

For our women's work-shops the stewards shall provide the materials at the right time as it has been established, that is, flax, wool, woad, vermilion dye, madder, wool-combs, teasels, soap, grease, vessels, and the other lesser things which are necessary there.

Of the minor foods two-thirds shall be sent for our service each year, vegetables as well as fish, cheese, butter, honey, mustard, vinegar, millet, panic, dried and fresh herbs, radishes, and turnips; similarly wax, soap, and other lesser things. Whatever is left shall be made known to us in an inventory as we have said above. The stewards shall by no means neglect to do this as they have up to now because we wish to check by the two-thirds sent to us what that third is which remains.

Each steward shall have good workmen in his district—iron-workers, goldsmiths, silversmiths, leather-workers, turners, carpenters, shield-makers, fishermen, fowlers or falconers, soap-makers, brewers who know how to make beer, cider, perry or any other beverage fit to drink, bakers who can make bread for our needs, net-makers who are skilled in making nets for hunting as well as fishing or for taking birds, and other workmen whose listing would be a lengthy matter.

They shall take good care of our walled game preserves which the people call parks and always repair them in time and on no account delay so that it becomes necessary to rebuild them. They shall do the same for all the buildings.

Our hunters and falconers and other servitors who attend us zealously in the palace shall receive assistance on our estates in carrying out what we or the queen have ordered by our letters when we send them on any of our affairs, or when the seneschal or butler instructs them to do anything on our authority.

The wine-presses on our estates shall be well taken care of. The stewards shall see to it that no one presumes to press our grapes with his feet but that all is done cleanly and honestly.

The women's quarters, that is, their houses, heated rooms, and sitting-rooms, shall be well ordered and have good fences around them and strong gates that our work may be done well.

Each steward shall see to it that there are as many horses in one stable

as ought to be there and as many attendants as should be with them. And those stablemen who are free and hold benefices in that district shall live off their benefices. Similarly if they are men of the domain who hold *mansi* they shall live off them. Those who do not have such shall receive maintenance from the demesne.

Each steward shall see to it that in no manner wicked men conceal our seed under the ground or do otherwise with the result that our harvests are smaller. And likewise, concerning other misdeeds, they shall watch them so that they can do no harm.

We wish that our stewards render justice to our *coloni* and serfs and to the *coloni* living on our estates, to the different men fully and entirely such as they are due.

Each steward shall see to it that our men in their districts in no way become robbers or evil-doers.

Each steward shall see to it that our people work well at their tasks and do not go wandering off to markets.

We wish that whatever our stewards have sent, supplied, or set aside for our use they shall record in an inventory; whatever they have dispensed in another; and what is left they shall also make known to us in an inventory.

Each steward shall hold frequent audiences in his district, administer justice, and see to it that our peoples live uprightly.

If any of our serfs wishes to say anything to us about our affairs over and above his steward, the steward shall not obstruct the means of his coming to us. If the steward knows that his assistants wish to come to the palace to speak against him then he shall make known to the palace the arguments against them so that their denunciations in our ears may not engender disgust. Accordingly we wish to know whether they come from necessity or without sufficient cause.

When our pups are committed to the stewards to be raised, the steward shall feed them at his own expense or entrust them to his assistants, that is to the mayors and deans or to the cellarers, who shall feed them well at their own expense unless it happens that by our order or that of the queen they are to be fed on our estate at our expense. In that case the steward shall send a man for this work who will feed them well. And he shall set aside what is to be fed them so that it will not be necessary for him to go to the kennels every day.

Each steward when he should give service shall send every day three *librae* of wax and eight *sextaria* of soap; besides this he shall do his best to send six *librae* of wax wherever we shall be with our attendants on the Feast of Saint Andrew; he should do likewise at Mid-Lent.

On no account shall mayors be selected from the powerful men but from those of middling estate who are trustworthy.

Each steward when he should give service shall have his malt brought to the palace and at the same time have the master brewers come who are to make good beer there.

That we may know what and how much of everything we have, each steward every year at Christmas shall report those of our revenues which they hold, everything differentiated clearly and orderly. That is, an accounting of the land cultivated with the oxen which our ploughmen drive and that which is cultivated by the holders of *mansi* who owe us labor-service; of the payments of pigs, the taxes, the income from judgments and fines and from the beasts taken in our forests without our permission and from the other compositions; an accounting of the mills, forests, fields, bridges, and ships; of the free men and the hundred-men who owe service for parts of our domain; of the markets, vineyards, and of those who pay us wine; of the hay, firewood, torches, planks, and other lumber; of the income from the wasteland; of the vegetables, millet, panic, wool, flax, and hemp; of the fruit of the trees, of the big and little nuts, of the graftings of various trees, of the gardens, turnips, fish-ponds, hides, skins and horns; of the honey, wax, fat, tallow, and soap; of the mulberry wine, cooked wine, mead, and vinegar; of the beer, new and old wine, new and old grain, chickens and eggs, and geese; of the fishermen, smiths, shield-makers and leather-workers; of the troughs, boxes, and cases; of the turners and saddlers; of the forges and mines, that is iron, lead, and other mines; of those paying taxes; and of the colts and fillies.

Of all the above mentioned things nothing that we require shall seem hard to our stewards for we wish the stewards to require them from their assistants in the same fashion without any hardship. And all things which any man shall have in his house or on his estate our stewards ought also to have on our estates.

Our carts which accompany the army, that is, the war-carts, shall be well-constructed, and their coverings be good, with hides on top and so sewn together that if the necessity of swimming waters should arise they can cross rivers without any water getting to the provisions inside and in this fashion our things may, as we said, get across without damage. And we wish that flour for our use be put in each cart, that is 12 *modii*, and that they put in those in which wine is sent 12 *modii* of our measure. In each cart let them have a shield, a lance, a quiver, and a bow.

The fish in our fish-ponds shall be sold and others put in their place so that they may always have fish in them. However, when we are not coming to our estates they shall be sold and our stewards shall dispose of them to our advantage.

The stewards shall report to us the number of male and female goats and their horns and skins; and they shall bring to us annually newly salted cuts of fat goats.

The stewards shall inform us about any vacant *mansi* or any newly acquired serfs if they have any in their district for whom they have no place.

We wish that each steward always have ready good barrels bound with iron which they can send to the army or to the palace and that the stewards do not make containers of leather.

The stewards at all times shall report to us how many wolves each has taken and shall send the skins to us. And in the month of May they shall hunt down and destroy the whelps with poison, traps, pits, and dogs.

We wish that the stewards have all sorts of plants in the garden, namely, lilies, roses, fenugreek, costmary, sage, rue, southernwood, cucumbers, pumpkins, squash, kidney-beans, cumin, rosemary, caraway, chick-peas, squill, gladiolus, dragonarum, anise, colosynth, heliotrope, spicknel, seseli, lettuce, fennel-flower, rocket, garden cress, burdock, pennyroyal, horse-parsley, parsley, celery, lovage, juniper, dill, sweet-fennel, endive, dittany, mustard, savory, water-mint, garden mint, applemint, tansy, catnip, centaury, garden-poppy, beets, hazelwort, marshmallows, tree-hibiscus, mallows, carrots, parsnip, gardenorach, amaranth, kohlrabi, cabbages, onions, chives, leeks, radishes, shallots, cibols, garlic, madder, teasel, garden beans, Moorish peas, coriander, chervil, capers, clary. And the gardener shall have house-leek growing on his house.

As for trees, we wish that they have various kinds of apple, pear, and plum trees, sorb, medlar, chestnut, peach trees of different kinds, quince, filbert, almond, mulberry, laurel, pine, fig, walnut, and cherry trees of various kinds.

Names of apple trees: *gozmaringa, geroldinga, crevedella, spirauca,* sweet ones and sour ones, and all the kind that keep, as well as those which are eaten when picked and those that are forced.

They shall have three or four kinds of pears which will keep, sweet ones, cooking, and late pears.

Charter of the Liberties of Lorris

1. Let whoever shall have a house in the parish of Lorris pay a quitrent of six deniers only for his house, and each acre of land which he shall have in this parish; and if he make such an acquisition, let that be the quit-rent of his house.

2. Let no inhabitant of the parish of Lorris pay a duty of entry nor any tax for his food, and let him not pay any duty of measurement for the corn which his labor, or that of the animals which he may have shall procure him, and let him pay no duty for the wine which he shall get from his vines.

3. Let none of them go on a [military] expedition on foot or horseback, whence he cannot return home the same day if he desire to do so.

4. Let none of them pay toll to Étampes or Orleans, or to Milly, which is in Gâtinais, or to Melun.

5. Let no one who has property in the parish of Lorris lose any of it for any misdeed whatsoever, unless the said misdeed be committed against us or any of our guests.

6. Let no one going to the fairs or markets of Lorris, or in returning, be stopped or inconvenienced unless he shall have committed some misdeed that same day; and let no one on a fair or market day at Lorris, seize the bail given by his security; unless the bail be given the same day.

7. Let forfeitures of sixty sous be reduced to five, that of five sous to twelve deniers, and the provost's fee in cases of plaint, to four deniers.

8. Let no man of Lorris be forced to go out of it to plead before the lord king.

9. Let no one, neither us nor any other, take any tax, offering, or exaction from the men of Lorris.

10. Let no one sell wine at Lorris with public notice, except the king, who shall sell his wine in his cellar with that notice.

11. We will have at Lorris, for our service and that of the queen, a credit of a full fortnight, in the articles of provisions; and if any inhabitant have received a gage from the lord king, he shall not be bound to keep it more than eight days, unless he please.

12. If any have had a quarrel with another, but without breaking a closed house, and if it be accommodated without plaint brought before the provost, no fine shall be due, on this account, to us or to our provost; and if there has been a plaint they can still come to an agreement when they shall have paid the fine. And if any one bear plaint against another, and there has been no fine awarded against either one to the other, they shall not, on that account, owe anything to us or our provost.

13. If any one owe an oath to another, let the latter have permission to remit it.

14. If any men of Lorris have rashly given their pledge of a duel, and if with the consent of the provost they accommodate it before the pledges have been given, let each pay

Trans. W. Hazlitt.

two sous and a half; and if the pledges have been given, let each pay seven sous and a half; and if the duel has been between men having the right of fighting in the list, then let the hostages of the conquered pay one hundred and twelve sous.

15. Let no man of Lorris do forced work for us, unless it be twice a year to take our wine to Orleans, and nowhere else; and those only shall do this work who shall have horses and carts, and they shall be informed of it beforehand; and they shall receive no lodging from us. The laborers also shall bring wood for our kitchen.

16. No one shall be detained in prison if he can furnish bail for his appearance in court.

17. Whoever desires to sell his property may do so; and having received the price, he may leave the town, free and unmolested, if he please so to do, unless he has committed any misdeed in the town.

18. Whoever shall have remained a year and a day in the parish of Lorris without any claim having pursued him thither, and without the right having been interdicted him, whether by us or our provost, he shall remain there free and tranquil.

19. No one shall plead against another unless it be to recover, and ensure the observance of, what is his due.

20. When the men of Lorris shall go to Orleans with merchandise, they shall pay, upon leaving the town, one denier for their cart, when they go not for the sake of the fair; and when they go for the sake of the fair and the market, they shall pay, upon leaving Orleans, four deniers for each cart, and on entering, two deniers.

21. At marriages in Lorris, the public crier shall have no fee, nor he who keeps watch.

22. No cultivator of the parish of Lorris, cultivating his land with the plow, shall give, in the time of harvest more than one hermine [six bushels] of rye to all the serjeants of Lorris.

23. If any knight or serjeant find, in our forests, horses or other animals belonging to the men of Lorris, he must not take them to any other than to the provost of Lorris; and if any animal of the parish of Lorris be put to flight by bulls, or assailed by flies, have entered our forest, or leaped our banks, the owner of the animal shall owe no fine to the provost, if he can swear that the animal has entered in spite of his keeper. But if the animal entered with the knowledge of his keeper, the owner shall pay twelve deniers, and as much for each animal, if there be more than one.

24. There shall be at Lorris no duty paid for using the oven.

25. There shall be at Lorris no watch rate.

26. All men of Lorris who shall take salt or wine to Orleans, shall pay only one denier for each cart.

27. No men of Lorris shall owe any fine to the provost of Étampes, nor to the provost of Pithiviers nor to any in Gâtinais.

28. None among them shall pay the entry dues in Ferrières, nor in Château-Landon, nor in Puiseaux, nor in Nibelle.

29. Let the men of Lorris take the dead wood in the forest for their own use.

30. Whosoever, in the market of Lorris, shall have bought or sold anything, and shall have forgotten to pay the duty, may pay it within eight days

without being troubled, if he can swear that he did not withhold the right wittingly.

31. No man of Lorris having a house or a vineyard, or a meadow, or a field, or any buildings in the domain of St. Benedict, shall be under the jurisdiction of the abbot of St. Benedict or his serjeant, unless it be with regard to the quitrent in kind, to which he is bound; and, in that case, he shall not go out of Lorris to be judged.

32. If any of the men of Lorris be accused of anything, and the accuser cannot prove it by witness, he shall clear himself by a single oath from the assertion of his accuser.

33. No man of this parish shall pay any duty because of what he shall buy or sell for his use on the territory of the precincts, nor for what he shall buy on Wednesday at the market.

34. These customs are granted to the men of Lorris, and they are common to the men who inhabit Courpalais, Chanteloup, and the bailiwick of Harpard.

35. We order that whenever the provost shall be changed in the town, he shall swear faithfully to observe these customs; and the same shall be done by new serjeants when they shall be instituted.

Given at Orleans in the year of our Lord 1155.

Ssu-ma Kwang

Ancestor worship has formed a part of the religious traditions of many societies but none more so than that of China, where it has persisted from earliest times down to the twentieth century. From written records that survive from the Shang dynasty of the second millennium B.C. it would seem that the practice was at first confined to the nobility, perhaps because this class was the only one that possessed ancestors worthy of note. But the practice gradually spread so that later people at all levels of society engaged in it. It was "officially" sanctioned in the fifth century B.C. by Confucius who, in his treatise *The Doctrine of the Mean*, said:

To gather in the same places where our fathers before us have gathered; to perform the same ceremonies which they before us have performed; to play the same music which they before us have played; to pay respect to those whom they have honored; to love those who were dear to them—in fact, to serve those now dead as if they were living, and now departed as if they were still with us; this is the highest achievement of true filial piety.

Ancestor worship is actually an aspect of a larger, and very important feature of Chinese society—the family. For the Chinese the family has always been the center of life and family ties much stronger than in most other societies. Also, the family is a larger entity than elsewhere, for included in it, as an integral part of it, are departed ancestors. Living families have regularly sought the advice of ancestors before undertaking new enterprises, as well as approval for their conduct. When family finances permitted, special shrines were built where elaborate ceremonials were conducted and offerings made to the ancestors.

Early in Chinese history rules governing the ritual to be followed in ceremonies honoring ancestors were developed. With the passage of time and changes in society these ritualistic rules also changed. By the Sung dynasty (960–1279) the standard ritual was fully elaborated. It is laid out in detail in the following selection from the works of Ssu-ma Kwang (1019–1056) who was a distinguished historian and statesman, as well as the author of guides prescribing the proper procedures to be followed on a variety of social and ceremonial occasions.

Ancestral Rites

All ancestor worship should be conducted in the second month of a season [the first month being reserved for imperial ceremonies].

First, the master of the household, his younger brothers, sons, and grandsons, dressed in their formal attire, attend to the divination of an auspicious day for the ceremony. This is done outside of the Image Hall. The master of the household stands facing west, and all the others file behind him in one line, ordered according to their ranks in the family, from north to south. A table is set in front of the master on which are placed incense burners, incense boxes, and milfoil stalks. The master inserts his official tablet in his girdle, lights the incense, and addresses the diviner as follows:

"I would like to present a yearly offering to my ancestors on such-and-such a day. Please determine whether it is an auspicious day."

Then he steps back and hands the milfoil stalks to the diviner, who then performs the divination, facing west. If the proposed date turns out to be inauspicious, then the master of the household names another. When finally an auspicious day is found, all present enter the Image Hall. The master now stands facing north, with his sons and grandsons in file behind him as before, except that now they are ordered according to their ranks from west to east.

The master inserts the official tablet in his girdle, advances to light the incense, then returns to his former position. The deliverer of prayers now comes out from the left of the master, turns to face east, inserts his official tablet in his girdle, takes out the written prayer from his breast pocket, and kneels down to read: "Your filial grandson, officially entitled such-and-such, will on such-and-such a day offer the yearly sacrifice to his departed grandparents. This is to report to you that the date has been found auspicious and that the offering will be made." He then puts the prayer sheet away in his pocket, takes out his official tablet, and rises. After he has returned to his former position, the master of the household bows to the memorial tablets of the ancestors, and everyone exits.

Three days before the date set for the ceremony, the master of the household leads all the male members of the family (above ten years of age) to the outer quarters of the house to observe abstinence, while the women do so in the inner quarters. Thus, although there is wine-drinking, there is no disorder. Meat-eating is allowed, but strong-smelling foods such as onion, leek, and garlic are prohibited. During this period the family members do not attend funerals, nor do they listen to music. All inauspicious and unclean matters are avoided, so that

Trans. Clara Yu.

Reprinted with the permission of The Free Press, a Division of Macmillan, Inc. from *Chinese Civilization and Society: A Sourcebook* by Patricia Buckley Ebrey. Copyright © 1981 by The Free Press.

everyone can concentrate on the memory of the departed ancestors.

On the day before the ceremony, the master organizes all the male members of the family and the assistants to dust and sweep the place where the sacrifice will be held, to wash and clean the utensils and containers, and to arrange the furniture. The places for the departed ancestors are so arranged that each husband and wife are side by side, arranged according to proper ranking from west to east, and all facing south. The mistress of the house supervises the women of the household in cleaning the cooking utensils and preparing the food, which should include five kinds of vegetables and five kinds of fruits and not more than fifteen dishes of the following sorts: red stew, roast meat, fried meat, ribs, boiled white meat, dried meat, ground meat, special meats other than pork or lamb, foods made of flour. (If the family is poor, or if certain items cannot be obtained at a particular location or time, then merely include several items from each category, that is, vegetable, fruit, meat, flour-foods, and rice-foods.)

The assistants prepare a basin with a stand for washing hands and set it on the southeastern side of the eastern steps. To the north of the stand is set a rack of towels for drying hands. (These are for the relatives.) Then, on the east side of the eastern steps another basin and some towels are set; these, however, are without a stand or a rack. (These are for the assistants.)

On the day of the ceremony, all members of the family rise early and put on formal attire. The master and the mistress lead the assistants to the hall for the ceremony. In front of every seat, on the south side of the table, the assistants place vegetables and fruits, and on the north side, wine cups, spoons, chopsticks, teacups and saucers, and sauce bowls. Next they put a bottle of water and a bottle of wine on a table above the eastern steps. To its east is placed a table with a decanter, wine cups, knives, and towels on it. An incense table is placed in the center of the hall, with an incense burner and an incense box on it. An ash bowl is set on the east side, and a burner, a water bottle, an incense ash ladle, and a pair of tongs are set on the west side. Water is poured into the washing basins.

In the morning, when the cook reports that all the foods have been prepared, the master and mistress go to the Image Hall together. Two assistants carry the memorial tablets in a bamboo basket, and, with the master taking the lead and the mistress following him, all the members of the family form two rows, the men on the left-hand side and the women on the right-hand side. In this order they proceed to the hall of the ceremony. The basket is then placed at the top of the western steps, to the west of the burner.

The master and mistress now wash their hands and carry the memorial tablets to the seats: those of the male ancestors first, those of the female ones next. Afterwards, the master leads all the men in the family to form one line, from west to east according to their ranks, below the eastern steps, all facing north. The mistress, likewise, leads all the women in the same order, from east to west, below the western steps, also facing north. The assistants to the ceremony form another line, from west to east, behind the men. When all have taken their proper positions, they bow together to greet the spirits of the ancestors.

The master than ascends the eastern steps and goes to the south of the incense table. He puts his official tablet in his girdle and lights the incense. Then he bows and returns to his former position. The deliverer of prayers and the assistants to the ceremony now wash and dry their hands. One assistant ascends the steps, opens the wine bottle, wipes the mouth of the bottle, and pours the wine into the decanter. Then he takes the wine cup, fills it with wine from the decanter, and makes a libation toward the west.

The cook and servants have by now put the foods for offering on a table placed on the east side of the washing basin and towel rack. The men now wash their hands. Then, following the example of the master, they put down their official tablets and hold up bowls of meat—the master ascends from the eastern steps, all the others from the western steps— and place them in front of the memorial tablets of the ancestors, to the north of the vegetables and fruits. Afterwards, they take up their official tablets and return to their former positions. Now the women wash and dry their hands. Led by the mistress, they first carry the foods made of flour, ascend the western steps, and set them down to the north of the meats. Then they carry the foods made of rice, ascend the western steps, and set them down to the north of the foods made of flour. Afterwards they descend and return to their former positions.

The master now ascends the eastern steps, goes to the wine table, and turns to face west. An assistant takes the wine cup of the great-grandfather in his left hand and that of the great-grandmother in his right hand; another assistant, in the same manner, holds the cups of the grandparents and a third holds the cups of the parents. The three assistants now go to the master, who, after putting his official tablet away in his girdle, pours wine into the cups. With these cups in their hands, the assistants walk slowly back to the tables to set them down in their former positions. The master takes out his official tablet again, approaches the seats of his great-grandparents, facing north. One assistant now takes the wine cup of the great-grandfather and stands on the left side of the master; another holds the cup of the great-grandmother and stands on the right side of the master. The master, putting away his official tablet, kneels and receives the cup of the great-grandfather, offers a libation, and returns the cup to the assistant, who puts it back where it was. The master then takes out his official tablet, prostrates himself on the floor, then rises and steps back a little.

The deliverer of prayers steps out from the left of the master, turns to face east, puts away his official tablet, takes out the written prayer, kneels down and reads:

On such-and-such a day, of such-and-such a month, of such-and-such a year, your filial great-grandson, officially titled as such-and-such, presents the soft-haired sacrifice (for lamb; if a pig is offered, then he should say "hard-haired" sacrifice) and good wine in the yearly offering to his great-grandfather, officially titled such-and-such, and great-grandmother (give honorary title here). O that you enjoy the food!

He then rolls up the prayer sheet and puts it back into his pocket. Then he takes out his official tablet and rises. The master bows to the memorial tablets.

Next they proceed with the same ceremony at the seats of the grandparents and those of the parents, except that the prayer is slightly modified, so that for the grandparents it reads: "Your filial grandson presents the yearly offerings . . .," and for the parents, "Your filial son . . .", etc.

When this first round of offerings is completed, the deliverer of prayers and the master descend and return to their former positions. Now the second round of offering begins. (This is usually performed by the mistress herself or some close relative.) The offerer washes her hands if she has not done so already, ascends through the western steps, pours the wine and offers libations, just as the master has done. The only difference is that there is no reading of prayers.

When this second round of offerings is completed, the master ascends the eastern steps, takes off his official tablet, holds the decanter, and fills all the wine cups. Then he takes up his official tablet again and steps back to stand on the southeast side of the incense table, facing north. The mistress ascends the western steps, places spoons in the bowls of millet, and straightens the chopsticks. The handles of the spoons should point to the west. She now goes to stand on the southwest side of the incense table and faces north. The master bows twice at the memorial tablets and the mistress bows four times.

One assistant now removes the tea leaves and another ladles soup for the ancestors, both starting from the western end. When this is done they leave, and the deliverer of prayers closes the door for the ancestors to dine in private. The master now should stand on the east side of the closed door, facing west, with all

male members of the family in a file behind him; the mistress stands on the west side of the closed door and faces east, with all female members of the family in a file behind her. In this manner all persons wait for the duration of a meal. Then the deliverer of prayers ascends and approaches the door, facing north. He coughs three times to warn the ancestors before opening the door.

The assistants now go to the north of the table with the water, and the master comes in to take his position, facing west. The deliverer of prayers ascends the western steps and approaches the seat of the great-grandfather. He puts his official tablet in his girdle and raises the wine cup, slowly walks to the right of the master, turns to face south, and offers the cup to the master, who, after putting his official tablet away in the girdle, kneels down to receive the cup and to sip the wine.

An assistant then hands a container over to the deliverer of prayers, who uses a spoon to take a few grains of millet from the bowl of each ancestor and puts them in the container. He then carries the container and walks up to the left of the master, turns to face north, and offers the master this blessing: "Your grandfather commands me to confer many blessings on you, the filial grandson, enabling you to receive prosperity from Heaven, your fields to produce abundantly, and you to live a long life."

The master places the wine cup in front of him, takes up his official tablet, prostrates himself on the floor, rises, and bows. Then he puts his official tablet away in his girdle and kneels to receive the millet. He tastes a little of it, then puts the rest in his left sleeve. An assistant is standing on his right side, and the master gives the container of the millet to him. The master then folds the edge of his left sleeve over his fingers, takes up the wine cup, and drinks from it. Another assistant is standing on his right side, to whom the master gives the cup. On the left side of the master another assistant is holding a plate. He now puts the plate on the floor, and the master lets the millet fall from his sleeve into the plate, which is then carried out. The master takes up his official tablet, prostrates himself, rises, and goes to stand at the top of the eastern steps, facing west. After the master receives the blessed millet, the deliverer of prayers holds up his official tablet and steps back to the top of the western steps, facing east. When the master has taken his position at the top of the eastern steps, the deliverer of prayers announces the completion of the ceremony. Then he descends and takes his former position. All present bow to the memorial tablets, except for the master, for he has received the blessing. Afterwards, the master descends and bows with everyone else to bid the ancestors farewell.

The ceremony having been completed, the master and mistress ascend to take down the memorial tablets and put them back into the bamboo basket, the tablets of the female ancestors being taken down first, then those of the male ancestors. Two assistants carry the basket to the Image Hall, followed by everyone in the family in the same manner as when the tablets were brought out.

At this point the mistress returns to supervise the removal of the offerings. The wine that remains in the cups, together with that in the decanter, is poured into a pot and sealed. This is the "blessed wine."

The assistants bring the offered foods back to the kitchen, where they are removed from the special containers into ordinary bowls and plates, and the special containers are carefully washed and put away under the supervision of the mistress. A small portion is taken from each item of the offered foods, and put into food boxes, which are sealed together with some "blessed wine," and dispatched, with a letter, to relatives and friends who are ardent observers of rites and rituals. This activity the master supervises. (The food sample is precious because it is left by the ancestors' spirits; it does not have to be rich in itself.)

The assistants now help set up the feast. The men and women are seated separately: the master and all the other male members of the family in the main hall, the mistress and the other female members of the family in the inner quarters. Tables and chairs are set; fruits, vegetables, sauces, wine cups, spoons, chopsticks, and knives are all placed in their proper places. Then wine is poured into decanters, and the hot foods that were offered to the spirits are warmed up.

First, the master of the household takes his seat, and all the other male members of the family offer their good wishes to him. They should stand according to their ranks in the family, just as during the preceding ceremony, and for both men and women the right side ranks higher than the left side. The eldest among them (either a younger brother of the master or his eldest son) stands a trifle ahead of everyone else. An assistant holds the wine decanter and stands on his right. Another assistant holds the wine cup and stands on his left. This eldest of the males then sticks his official tablet in his girdle, kneels, and takes the decanter in his right hand and the wine cup in his left. He then pours the wine and offers good wishes: "Now that the memorial ceremonies have been completed, our ancestors have been offered good food. We wish that you will receive all the five blessings, protect our lineage, and benefit our family."

The assistant who was holding the decanter then steps back, and the one who was holding the cup presents the wine to the master of the household. The eldest male prostrates himself, rises, and returns to his former position. Then he bows to the master together with all the other males. The master then orders the assistant to bring the decanter and the cup of the eldest male member. He pours wine into the cup himself, declaring, "Now that the offerings to our ancestors are successfully accomplished, we celebrate the good fortune of the five blessings bestowed on us; I hereby share them with all of you."

The assistant then hands the cup to the eldest male who, after putting away his official tablet in his girdle, kneels down to receive the wine. After he drinks the wine, he gives the cup back to the assistant, prostrates himself, then rises. The master then orders the assistant to pour wine for everyone. When this is done, all the males again prostrate themselves, and they are then ordered to be seated by the master.

Meanwhile, in the inner quarters, all the female members of the family salute the mistress and are in turn offered wine by her; the procedure is the same as that for the male members, except that it is all performed

from a standing position with no kneeling or prostrating. When the round of drinking is over, the assistants bring in the meats. Afterwards, the women come to the main hall to offer their congratulations to the master, who then offers wine to the eldest female member (either a younger sister of his or the eldest daughter), who receives it without kneeling down. But all other procedures are the same as performed by the males. Then the men come to the inner quarters to offer their good wishes to the mistress, where the procedure is exactly as the one in the main hall.

Next the assistants bring in the foods made of flour, and all the assistants offer their good wishes to the master and mistress, in the same way that the female members saluted the mistress, but they are not offered wine.

Then the foods made of rice are brought in. After this, wine is liberally drunk, and wine games are played, and the offered food consumed. The number of rounds of wine-drinking is decided by the master. When the offered food and wine are used up, other food and wine is brought in. When the feast is over, the leftovers are given to the servants. The master distributes them to the servants of the outer quarters, and the mistress to the servants of the inner quarters, reaching down even to the lowliest in rank, so that the foods are entirely consumed on that day.

Whenever ancestor worship is performed, sincerity in one's love and respect for one's ancestors are what is most significant. Thus, those who are ill should only do as much as they can, but the young and strong should naturally follow the ceremonies closely.

Marco Polo

Early in the thirteenth century a powerful Mongolian chieftain, Chinghis Kaan (or Genghis Khan), mounted an attack against northern China and its ruling Chin dynasty. This marked the beginning of a long process that led eventually to the occupation of China by the Mongolians, a process that was completed only toward the end of the century when the grandson of Chinghis, Cublay Kaan (or Kublai Khan), finally broke the resistance of the Sung dynasty, which had dominated southern China, and proclaimed the Yuan dynasty, which then ruled China for the next hundred years.

The center of Chinese civilization in the Yuan period became the city of Cambaluc (now Beijing), where the emperor had his winter palace. To this imperial city came merchants from all parts of the civilized world, to trade goods and merchandise. Among the thousands of traders to arrive about the year 1275 were two brothers from Venice, Maffeo and Nicolo Polo. Accompanying them was Nicolo's son Marco, who was then a teenager. Marco Polo was to remain in China for nearly a quarter of a century. During this time he entered the Chinese bureaucracy, later performing a number of tasks for the emperor that led him to travel extensively throughout China and thus become well acquainted with the land and its people.

The Book of Ser Marco Polo, which is an account of his travels, paints a vivid picture of Chinese civilization in the thirteenth century, a civilization significantly more advanced than that of Europe. The origin of the book is an interesting story. When he finally returned home in 1295 Polo became involved in a war between the Venetians and the Genoese. He was captured in battle and thrown into prison. While incarcerated he passed the time telling stories of his travels and adventures to his cellmate, who in turn transcribed them. The selection that follows gives a description of the person of Cublay Kaan, his palace and court, the city of Cambaluc, and something of the imperial machinery for the rule of China.

The Book of Ser Marco Polo

BOOK II

I. Of Cublay Kaan, the Great Kaan now Reigning, and of his Great Puissance

Now am I come to that part of our Book in which I shall tell you of the great and wonderful magnificence of the Great Kaan now reigning, by name Cublay Kaan; Kaan being a title which signifyeth "The Great Lord of Lords," or Emperor. And of a surety he hath good right to such a title, for all men know for a certain truth that he is the most potent man, as regards forces and lands and treasure, that existeth in the world, or ever hath existed from the time of our first father Adam until this day. All this I will make clear to you for truth, in this book of ours, so that every one shall be fain to acknowledge that he is the greatest Lord that is now in the world, or ever hath been.

• • •

VIII. Concerning the Person of the Great Kaan

The personal appearance of the Great Kaan, Lord of Lords, whose name is Cublay, is such as I shall now tell you. He is of a good stature, neither tall nor short, but of a middle height. He has a becoming amount of flesh, and is very shapely in all his limbs. His complexion is white and red, the eyes black and fine, the nose well formed and well set on. He has four wives, whom he retains permanently as his legitimate consorts; and

the eldest of his sons by those four wives ought by rights to be emperor;—I mean when the father dies. Those four ladies are called empresses, but each is distinguished also by her proper name. And each of them has a special court of her own, very grand and ample; no one of them having fewer than 300 fair and charming damsels. They have also many pages and eunuchs, and a number of other attendants of both sexes; so that each of these ladies has not less than 10,000 persons attached to her court.

When the Emperor desires the society of one of these four consorts, he will sometimes send for the lady to his apartment and sometimes visit her at her own. He has also a great number of concubines, and I will tell you how he obtains them.

You must know that there is a tribe of Tartars called Ungrat, who are noted for their beauty. Now every year an hundred of the most beautiful maidens of this tribe are sent to the Great Kaan, who commits them to the charge of certain elderly ladies dwelling in his palace. And these old ladies make the girls sleep with them, in order to ascertain if they have sweet breath and do not snore, and are sound in all their limbs. Then such of them as are of approved beauty, and are good and sound in all respects, are appointed to attend on the Emperor by turns. Thus six of these damsels take their turn for three days and nights, and wait on him when he is in his chamber and

Trans. Henry Yule.

when he is in his bed, to serve him in any way, and to be entirely at his orders. At the end of the three days and nights they are relieved by other six. And so throughout the year, there are reliefs of maidens by six and six, changing every three days and nights.

IX. Concerning the Great Kaan's Sons

The Emperor hath, by those four wives of his, twenty-two male children; the eldest of whom was called Chinkin for the love of the good Chinghis Kaan, the first Lord of the Tartars. And this Chinkin, as the eldest son of the Kaan, was to have reigned after his father's death; but, as it came to pass, he died. He left a son behind him, however, whose name is Temur, and he is to be the Great Kaan and Emperor after the death of his grandfather, as is but right; he being the child of the Great Kaan's eldest son. And this Temur is an able and brave man, as he hath already proven on many occasions.

The Great Kaan hath also twenty-five other sons by his concubines; and these are good and valiant soldiers, and each of them is a great chief. I tell you moreover that of his children by his four lawful wives there are seven who are kings of vast realms or provinces, and govern them well; being all able and gallant men, as might by expected. . . .

X. Concerning the Palace of the Great Kaan

You must know that for three months of the year, to wit December, January, and February, the Great Kaan resides in the capital city of Cathay [China], which is called Cam-

baluc [now Beijing], and which is at the northeastern extremity of the country. In that city stands his great palace and now I will tell you what it is like.

It is enclosed all round by a great wall forming a square, each side of which is a mile in length; that is to say, the whole compass thereof is four miles. This you may depend on; it is also very thick, and a good ten paces in height, whitewashed and loop-holed all round. At each angle of the wall there is a very fine and rich palace in which the war-harness of the Emperor is kept, such as bows and quivers, saddles and bridles, and bowstrings, and everything needful for an army. Also midway between every two of these corner palaces there is another of the like; so that taking the whole compass of the enclosure you find eight vast palaces stored with the Great Lord's harness of war. And you must understand that each palace .is assigned to only one kind of article; thus one is stored with bows, a second with saddles, a third with bridles, and so on in succession right round.

The great wall has five gates on its southern face, the middle one being the great gate which is never opened on any occasion except when the Great Kaan himself goes forth or enters. Close on either side of this great gate is a smaller one by which all other people pass; and then towards each angle is another great gate, also open to people in general; so that on that side there are five gates in all.

Inside of this wall there is a second, enclosing a space that is somewhat greater in length than in breadth. This enclosure also has eight palaces corresponding to those of the outer wall, and stored like them with the Lord's harness of war.

This wall also hath five gates on the southern face, corresponding to those in the outer wall, and hath one gate on each of the other faces, as the outer wall hath also. In the middle of the second enclosure is the Lord's great palace, and I will tell you what it is like.

You must know that it is the greatest palace that ever was. Towards the north it is in contact with the outer wall, while towards the south there is a vacant space which the barons and the soldiers are constantly traversing. The palace itself hath no upper story, but is all on the ground floor, only the basement is raised some ten palms above the surrounding soil and this elevation is retained by a wall of marble raised to the level of the pavement, two paces in width and projecting beyond the base of the palace so as to form a kind of terrace-walk, by which people can pass round the building, and which is exposed to view, while on the outer edge of the wall there is a very fine pillared balustrade; and up to this the people are allowed to come. The roof is very lofty, and the walls of the palace are all covered with gold and silver. They are also adorned with representations of dragons sculptured and gilt, beasts and birds, knights and idols, and sundry other subjects. And on the ceiling too you see nothing but gold and silver and painting. On each of the four sides there is a great marble staircase leading to the top of the marble wall, and forming the approach to the palace.

The hall of the palace is so large that it could easily dine 6000 people; and it is quite a marvel to see how many rooms there are besides. The building is altogether so vast, so rich, and so beautiful, that no man on earth could design anything superior to it. The outside of the roof also is all colored with vermilion and yellow and green and blue and other hues, which are fixed with a varnish so fine and exquisite that they shine like crystal, and lend a resplendent luster to the palace as seen for a great way round. This roof is made too with such strength and solidity that it is fit to last for ever.

On the interior side of the palace are large buildings with halls and chambers, where the Emperor's private property is placed, such as his treasures of gold, silver, gems, pearls, and gold plate, and in which reside the ladies and concubines. There he occupies himself at his own convenience, and no one else has access.

Between the two walls of the enclosure which I have described, there are fine parks and beautiful trees bearing a variety of fruits. There are beasts also of sundry kinds, such as white stags and fallow deer, gazelles and roebucks, and fine squirrels of various sorts, with numbers also of the animal that gives the musk, and all manner of other beautiful creatures, insomuch that the whole place is full of them, and no spot remains void except where there is traffic of people going and coming. The parks are covered with abundant grass; and the roads through them being all paved and raised two cubits above the surface, they never become muddy, nor does the rain lodge on them, but flows off into the meadows, quickening the soil and producing that abundance of herbage.

From that corner of the enclosure which is towards the northwest there extends a fine lake, containing foison of fish of different kinds which the Emperor hath caused to be put in there, so that whenever he desires any he can have them at his pleasure.

A river enters this lake and issues from it, but there is a grating of iron or brass put up so that the fish cannot escape in that way.

Moreover on the north side of the palace, about a bow-shot off, there is a hill which has been made by art from the earth dug out of the lake; it is a good hundred paces in height and a mile in compass. This hill is entirely covered with trees that never lose their leaves, but remain ever green. And I assure you that wherever a beautiful tree may exist, and the Emperor gets news of it, he sends for it and has it transported bodily with all its roots and the earth attached to them, and planted on that hill of his. No matter how big the tree may be, he gets it carried by his elephants; and in this way he has got together the most beautiful collection of trees in all the world. And he has also caused the whole hill to be covered with the ore of azure, which is very green. And thus not only are the trees all green, but the hill itself is all green likewise; and there is nothing to be seen on it that is not green; and hence it is called the Green Mount; and in good sooth 'tis named well.

On the top of the hill again there is a fine big palace which is all green inside and out; and thus the hill, and the trees, and the palace form together a charming spectacle; and it is marvellous to see their uniformity of color. Everybody who sees them is delighted. And the Great Kaan had caused this beautiful prospect to be formed for the comfort and solace and delectation of his heart.

You must know that beside the palace (that we have been describing), *i.e.* the great palace, the Emperor has caused another to be built just like his own in every respect, and this he hath done for his son when he shall reign and be Emperor after him. Hence it is made just in the same fashion and of the same size, so that everything can be carried on in the same manner after his own death. It stands on the other side of the lake from the Great Kaan's palace, and there is a bridge crossing the water from one to the other. The Prince in question holds now a Seal of Empire, but not with such complete authority as the Great Kaan, who remains supreme as long as he lives.

Now I am going to tell you of the chief city of Cathay, in which these palaces stand, and why it was built, and how.

XI. Concerning the City of Cambaluc

Now there was on that spot in old times a great and noble city called Cambaluc, which is as much as to say in our tongue "The city of the Emperor." But the Great Kaan was informed by his astrologers that this city would prove rebellious and raise great disorders against his imperial authority. So he caused the present city to be built close beside the old one, with only a river between them. And he caused the people of the old city to be removed to the new town that he had founded, and this is called Taidu. However, he allowed a portion of the people which he did not suspect to remain in the old city because the new one could not hold the whole of them, big as it is.

As regards the size of this new city you must know that it has a compass of 24 miles, for each side of it hath a length of 6 miles, and it is four-square. And it is all walled round with walls of earth which have a thickness of full ten paces at bottom and a height of more than 10 paces; but they are not so thick at top for they diminish in thickness as they rise so that at top they are only about 3 paces thick. And they are provided throughout with loop-holed battlements which are all whitewashed.

There are 12 gates and over each gate there is a great and handsome palace, so that there are on each side of the square three gates and five palaces for (I ought to mention) there is at each angle also a great and handsome palace. In those palaces are vast halls in which are kept the arms of the city garrison.

The streets are so straight and wide that you can see right along them from end to end and from one gate to the other. And up and down the city there are beautiful palaces and many great and fine hostelries and fine houses in great numbers. All the plots of ground on which the houses of the city are built are four-square and laid out with straight lines, all the plots being occupied by great and spacious palaces with courts and gardens of proportionate size. All these plots were assigned to different heads of families. Each square plot is encompassed by handsome streets for traffic and thus the whole city is arranged in squares just like a chess board and disposed in a manner so perfect and masterly that it is impossible to give a description that should do it justice.

Moreover, in the middle of the city there is a great clock—that is to say, a bell—which is struck at night. And after it has struck three times no one must go out in the city, unless it be for the needs of a woman in labor, or

of the sick. And those who go about on such errands are bound to carry lanterns with them. Moreover, the established guard at each gate of the city is 1000 armed men, not that you are to imagine the guard is kept up for fear of any attack, but only as a guard of honor for the sovereign, who resides there, and to prevent thieves from doing mischief in the town.

• • •

XIII. The Fashion of the Great Kaan's Table at his High Feasts

And when the Great Kaan sits at table on any great court occasion, it is in this fashion. His table is elevated a good deal above the others, and he sits at the north end of the hall, looking towards the south, with his chief wife besides him on the left. On his right sit his sons and his nephews, and other kinsmen of the blood imperial, but lower, so that their heads are on a level with the Emperor's feet. And then the other barons sit at other tables lower still. So also with the women; for all the wives of the Lord's sons, and of his nephews and other kinsmen, sit at the lower table to his right; and below them again the ladies of the other barons and knights, each in the place assigned by the Lord's orders. The tables are so disposed that the Emperor can see the whole of them from end to end, many as they are. Further, you are not to suppose that everybody sits at table; on the contrary, the greater part of the soldiers and their officers sit at their meal in the hall on the carpets. Outside the hall will be found more than 40,000 people; for there is a great concourse of folk bringing presents to the Lord, or come from foreign countries with curiosities.

In a certain part of the hall near where the Great Kaan holds his table, there is set a large and very beautiful piece of workmanship in the form of a square coffer, or buffet, about three paces each way, exquisitely wrought with figures of animals, finely carved and gilt. The middle is hollow, and in it stands a great vessel of pure gold, holding as much as an ordinary butt; and at each corner of the great vessel is one of smaller size of the capacity of a firkin, and from the former the wine or beverage flavored with fine and costly spices is drawn off into the latter. And on the buffet aforesaid are set all the Lord's drinking vessels, among which are certain pitchers of the finest gold, which are called verniques, and are big enough to hold drink for eight or ten persons. And one of these is put between every two persons, besides a couple of golden cups with handles, so that every man helps himself from the pitcher that stands between him and his neighbor. And the ladies are supplied in the same way. The value of these pitchers and cups is something immense; in fact, the Great Kaan has such a quantity of this kind of plate, and of gold and silver in other shapes, as no one ever before saw or heard tell of, or could believe.

There are certain barons specially deputed to see that foreigners who do not know the customs of the court are provided with places suited to their rank and these barons are continually moving to and fro in the hall, looking to the wants of the guests at table and causing the servants to supply them promptly with wine, milk, meat, or whatever they lack. At every door of the hall (or, indeed, wherever the Emperor may be) there stand a couple of big men like giants, one on each side, armed with staves. Their business is to see that no one steps upon the threshold in entering, and if this does happen they strip the offender of his clothes and he must pay a forfeit to have them back again, or in lieu of taking his clothes they give him a certain number of blows. If they are foreigners ignorant of the order, then there are barons appointed to introduce them and explain it to them. They think, in fact, that it brings bad luck if any one touches the threshold. Howbeit, they are not expected to stick at this in going forth again, for at that time some are like to be the worse for liquor and incapable of looking to their steps.

And you must know that those who wait upon the Great Kaan with his dishes and his drink are some of the great barons. They have the mouth and nose muffled with fine napkins of silk and gold, so that no breath nor odor from their persons should taint the dish or the goblet presented to the Lord. And when the Emperor is going to drink, all the musical instruments, of which he has vast store of every kind, begin to play. And when he takes the cup all the barons and the rest of the company drop on their knees and make the deepest obeisance before him, and then the Emperor doth drink. But each time that he does so the whole ceremony is repeated.

I will say nought about the dishes, as you may easily conceive that there is a great plenty of every possible kind. But you should know that in every case where a baron or knight dines at those tables, their wives also dine there with the other ladies. And when all have dined and the tables have been removed, then come in a great number of players and jugglers, adepts at all sorts of wonderful feats, and perform before the Emperor and the rest of the company, creating great diversion and mirth, so that everybody is full of laughter and enjoyment. And when the performance is over, the company breaks up and every one goes to his quarters.

XIV. Concerning the Great Feast Held by the Grand Kaan Every Year on his Birthday

You must know that the Tartars keep high festival yearly on their birthdays. And the Great Kaan was born on the 28th day of the September moon, so on that day is held the greatest feast of the year at the Kaan's court, always excepting that which he holds on New Year's Day, of which I shall tell you afterwards. Now, on his birthday the Great Kaan dresses in the best of his robes, all wrought with beaten gold; and full 12,000 barons and knights on that day come forth dressed in robes of the same color and precisely like those of the Great Kaan, except that they are not so costly, but still they are all of the same color as his and are also of silk and gold. Every man so clothed has also a girdle of gold and this as well as the dress is given him by the sovereign. And I will aver that there are some of these decked with so many pearls and precious stones that a single suit shall be worth full 10,000 golden bezants.

And of such raiment there are several sets. For you must know that the Great Kaan thirteen times in the year presents to his barons and knights such suits of raiment as I am speaking of. And on each occasion they wear the same color that he does, a

different color being assigned to each festival. Hence you may see what a huge business it is and that there is no prince in the world but he alone who could keep up such customs as these.

On his birthday also all the Tartars in the world and all the countries and governments that owe allegiance to the Kaan offer him great presents according to their several ability and as prescription or orders have fixed the amount. And many other persons also come with great presents to the Kaan, in order to beg for some employment from him. And the Great Kaan has chosen twelve barons on whom is laid the charge of assigning to each of these supplicants a suitable answer.

On this day likewise all the idolaters, all the Saracens, and all the Christians and other descriptions of people make great and solemn devotions with much chanting and lighting of lamps and burning of incense, each to the God whom he doth worship, praying that he would save the Emperor and grant him long life and health and happiness.

And thus, as I have related, is celebrated the joyous feast of the Kaan's birthday.

Now I will tell you of another festival which the Kaan holds at the New Year and which is called the White Feast.

XV. Of the Great Festival which the Kaan Holds on New Year's Day.

The beginning of their New Year is the month of February, and on that occasion the Great Kaan and all his subjects made such a Feast as I now shall describe.

It is the custom that on this occasion the Kaan and all his subjects should be clothed entirely in white so that day everybody is in white, men and women, great and small. And this is done in order that they may thrive all through the year for they deem that white clothing is lucky. On that day also all the people of all the provinces and governments and kingdoms and countries that owe allegiance to the Kaan bring him great presents of gold and silver, and pearls and gems, and rich textures of divers kinds. And this they do that the Emperor throughout the year may have abundance of treasure and enjoyment without care. And the people also make presents to each other of white things and embrace and kiss and make merry and wish each other happiness and good luck for the coming year. On that day, I can assure you, among the customary presents there shall be offered to the Kaan from various quarters more than 100,000 white horses, beautiful animals, and richly caparisoned. And you must know 'tis their custom in offering presents to the Great Kaan (at least when the province making the present is able to do so), to present nine times nine articles. For instance, if a province sends horses, it sends nine times nine or 81 horses; of gold, nine times nine pieces of gold, and so with stuffs or whatever else the present may consist of.

On that day also the whole of the Kaan's elephants, amounting fully to 5000 in number, are exhibited, all covered with rich and gay housings of inlaid cloth representing beasts and birds, while each of them carries on his back two splendid coffers, all of these being filled with the Emperor's plate and other costly furniture required for the court on the occasion of the White Feast. And these are followed by a vast number of camels which are likewise covered with rich housings and laden with things needful for the Feast. All these are paraded before the Emperor and it makes the finest sight in the world.

Moreover, on the morning of the Feast, before the tables are set, all the kings and all the dukes, marquesses, counts, barons, knights, and astrologers, and philosophers, and leeches, and falconers, and other officials of sundry kinds from all the places round about present themselves in the Great Hall before the Emperor, while those who can find no room to enter stand outside in such a position that the Emperor can see them all well. And the whole company is marshalled in this wise. First are the Kaan's sons, and his nephews, and the other princes of the blood imperial; next to them all kings; then dukes, and then all others in succession according to the degree of each. And when they are all seated, each in his proper place, then a great prelate rises and says with a loud voice: "Bow and adore!" And as soon as he has said this the company bow down until their foreheads touch the earth in adoration towards the Emperor as if he were a god. And this adoration they repeat four times, and then go to a highly decorated altar on which is a vermilion tablet with the name of the Grand Kaan inscribed thereon, and a beautiful censer of gold. So they incense the tablet and the altar with great reverence and then return each man to his seat.

When all have performed this then the presents are offered, of which I have spoken as being so rich and costly. And after all have been offered and been seen by the Emperor the tables are set and all take their places at them with perfect order as I have already told you. And after dinner the jugglers come in and amuse the court as you have heard before and when that is over every man goes to his quarters.

• • •

XXII. Concerning the City of Cambaluc and its Great Traffic and Population

You must know that the city of Cambaluc hath such a multitude of houses, and such a vast population inside the walls and outside, that it seems quite past all possibility. There is a suburb outside each of the gates, which are twelve in number; and these suburbs are so great that they contain more people than the city itself for the suburb of one gate spreads in width till it meets the suburb of the next, while they extend in length some three or four miles. In those suburbs lodge the foreign merchants and travellers, of whom there are always great numbers who have come to bring presents to the Emperor, or to sell articles at court, or because the city affords so good a mart to attract traders. There are in each of the suburbs, to a distance of a mile from the city, numerous fine hostelries for the lodgement of merchants from different parts of the world, and a special hostelry is assigned to each description of people, as if we should say there is one for the Lombards, another for the Germans, and a third for the Frenchmen. And thus there are as many good houses outside of the city as inside, without counting those that belong to the great lords and barons, which are very numerous.

You must know that it is forbidden to bury any dead body inside the city.

If the body be that of an idolater it is carried out beyond the city and suburbs to a remote place assigned for the purpose, to be burnt. And if it be of one belonging to a religion the custom of which is to bury, such as the Christian, the Saracen, or what not, it is also carried out beyond the suburbs to a distant place assigned for the purpose. And thus the city is preserved in a better and more healthy state.

Moreover, no public woman resides inside the city, but all such abide outside in the suburbs. And 'tis wonderful what a vast number of these there are for the foreigners; it is a certain fact that there are more than 20,000 of them living by prostitution. And that so many can live in this way will show you how vast is the population.

Guards patrol the city every night in parties of 30 or 40, looking out for any persons who may be abroad at unseasonable hours, *i.e* after the great bell hath stricken thrice. If they find any such person he is immediately taken to prison, and examined next morning by the proper officers. If these find him guilty of any misdemeanor they order him a proportionate beating with the stick. Under this punishment people sometimes die; but they adopt it in order to eschew bloodshed; for their *Bacsis* say that it is an evil thing to shed man's blood.

To this city also are brought articles of greater cost and rarity, and in greater abundance of all kinds, than to any other city in the world. For people of every description, and from every region, bring things including all the costly wares of India, as well as the fine and precious goods of Cathay itself with its provinces, some for the sovereign, some for the court, some for the city which is so great, some for the crowds of barons and knights, some for the great hosts of the Emperor which are quartered round about; and thus between court and city the quantity brought in is endless.

As a sample, I tell you, no day in the year passes that there do not enter the city 1000 cart loads of silk alone, from which are made quantities of cloth of silk and gold, and of other goods. And this is not to be wondered at; for in all the countries round about there is no flax, so that everything has to be made of silk. It is true, indeed, that in some parts of the country there is cotton and hemp, but not sufficient for their wants. This, however, is not of much consequence, because silk is so abundant and cheap, and is a more valuable substance than either flax or cotton.

Round about this great city of Cambaluc there are some 200 other cities at various distances, from which traders come to sell their goods and buy others for their lords; and all find means to make their sales and purchases, so that the traffic of the city is passing great.

• • •

XXIV. How the Great Kaan Causeth the Bark of Trees, Made into Something like Paper, to Pass for Money over all His Country

Now that I have told you in detail of the splendor of the city of the Emperor's, I shall proceed to tell you of the mint which he hath in the same city, in which he hath his money coined and struck, as I shall relate to you. And in doing so I shall make manifest to you how it is that the Great Lord may well be able to ac-complish even much more than I have told you, or am going to tell you, in this Book. For, tell it how I might, you never would be satisfied that I was keeping within truth and reason.

The Emperor's mint then is in this same city of Cambaluc and the way it is wrought is such that you might say he hath the secret of alchemy in perfection, and you would be right. For he makes his money after this fashion.

He makes them take of the bark of a certain tree, in fact of the mulberry tree, the leaves of which are the food of the silkworms,—these trees being so numerous that whole districts are full of them. What they take is a certain fine white bast or skin which lies between the wood of the tree and the thick outer bark, and this they make into something resembling sheets of paper, but black. When these sheets have been prepared they are cut up into pieces of different sizes. The smallest of these sizes is worth a half tornesel; the next, a little larger, one tornesel; one, a little larger still, is worth half a silver groat of Venice; another a whole groat; others yet two groats, five groats, and ten groats. There is also a kind worth one bezant of gold, and others of three bezants, and so up to ten. All these pieces of paper are issued with as much solemnity and authority as if they were of pure gold or silver; and on every piece a variety of officials, whose duty it is, have to write their names, and to put their seals. And when all is prepared duly, the chief officer deputed by the Kaan smears the seal entrusted to him with vermilion, and impresses it on the paper, so that the form of the seal remains printed upon it in red; the money is then authentic. Any one forging it would be punished with death. And the Kaan causes every year to be made such a vast quantity of this money, which costs him nothing, that it must equal in amount all the treasure in the world.

With these pieces of paper, made as I have described, he causes all payments on his own account to be made; and he makes them to pass current universally over all his kingdoms and provinces and territories, and whithersoever his power and sovereignty extends. And nobody, however important he may think himself, dares to refuse them on pain of death. And indeed everybody takes them readily, for wheresoever a person may go throughout the Great Kaan's dominions he shall find these pieces of paper current, and shall be able to transact all sales and purchases of goods by means of them just as well as if they were coins of pure gold. And all the while they are so light that ten bezants' worth does not weigh one golden bezant.

• • •

XXVI. How the Kaan's Posts and Runners are Sped through Many Lands and Provinces

Now you must know that from this city of Cambaluc proceed many roads and highways leading to a variety of provinces, one to one province, another to another; and each road receives the name of the province to which it leads; and it is a very sensible plan. And the messengers of the Emperor in travelling from Cambaluc, be the road whichsoever they will, find at every twenty-five miles of the journey a station which they call *Yamb*, or, as we should say, the "Horse-Post-House." And at each of those stations used by the messengers, there is a large and handsome building for them to put up at, in which they find all the rooms furnished with fine beds and all other necessary articles in rich silk, and where they are provided with everything they can want. If even a king were to arrive at one of these, he would find himself well lodged.

At some of these stations, moreover, there shall be posted some four hundred horses standing ready for the use of the messengers; at others there shall be two hundred, according to the requirements, and to what the Emperor has established in each case. At every twenty-five miles, as I said, or anyhow at every thirty miles, you find one of these stations, on all the principal highways leading to the different provincial governments; and the same is the case throughout all the chief provinces subject to the Great Kaan. Even when the messengers have to pass through a roadless tract where neither house nor hostel exists, still there the station-houses have been established just the same, excepting that the intervals are somewhat greater and the day's journey is fixed at thirty-five to forty-five miles, instead of twenty-five to thirty. But they are provided with horses and all the other necessaries just like those we have described, so that the Emperor's messengers, come they from what region they may, find everything ready for them.

And in sooth this is a thing done on the greatest scale of magnificence that ever was seen. Never had emperor, king, or lord such wealth as this manifests. For it is a fact that on all these posts taken together there are more than 300,000 horses kept up, specially for the use of the messengers. And the great buildings that

I have mentioned are more than 10,000 in number, all richly furnished, as I told you. The thing is on a scale so wonderful and costly that it is hard to bring oneself to describe it.

But now I will tell you another thing that I had forgotten, but which ought to be told while I am on this subject. You must know that by the Great Kaan's orders there has been established between those post-houses, at every interval of three miles, a little fort with some forty houses round about it, in which dwell the people who act as the Emperor's foot-runners. Every one of those runners wears a great wide belt, set all over with bells, so that as they run the three miles from post to post their bells are heard jingling a long way off. And thus on reaching the post the runner finds another man similarly equipt, and all ready to take his place, who instantly takes over whatsoever he has in charge, and with it receives a slip of paper from the clerk, who is always at hand for the purpose; and so the new man sets off and runs his three miles. At the next station he finds his relief ready in like manner; and so the post proceeds, with a change at every three miles. And in this way the Emperor, who has an immense number of these runners, receives despatches with news from places ten day's journey off in one day and night; or, if need be, news from a hundred days off in ten days and nights; and that is no small matter. In fact in the fruit season many a fine fruit shall be gathered one morning in Cambaluc and the evening of the next day it shall reach the Great Kaan in Chandu, a distance of ten days' journey. The clerk at each of the posts notes the time of each courier's ar-

rival and departure; and there are often other officers whose business it is to make monthly visitations of all the posts, and to punish those runners who have been slack in their work. The Emperor exempts these men from all tribute, and pays them besides.

Moreover, there are also at those stations other men equipt similarly with girdles hung with bells, who are employed for expresses when there is a call for great haste in sending despatches to any governor of a province, or to give news when any baron has revolted, or in other such emergencies; and these men travel a good two hundred or two hundred and fifty miles in the day and as much in the night. I'll tell you how it stands. They take a horse from those at the station which are standing ready saddled, all fresh and in wind, and mount and go at full speed, as hard as they can ride in fact. And when those at the next post hear the bells they get ready another horse and a man equipt in the same way, and he takes over the letter or whatever it be, and is off full-speed to the third station, where again a fresh horse is found all ready, and so the despatch speeds along from post to post, always at full gallop, with regular change of horses. And the speed at which they go is marvellous.

• • •

XXVIII. How the Great Kaan Causes Trees to be Planted by the Highways

The Emperor moreover hath taken order that all the highways travelled by his messengers and the people generally should be planted with rows of great trees a few paces apart; and thus these trees are visible a long way off, and no one can miss the way by day or night. Even the roads through uninhabited tracts are thus planted, and it is the greatest possible solace to travellers. And this is done on all the ways, where it can be of service. The Great Kaan plants these trees all the more readily, because his astrologers and diviners tell him that he who plants trees lives long.

But where the ground is so sandy and desert that trees will not grow, he causes other landmarks, pillars or stones, to be set up to show the way.

XXIX. Concerning the Rice Wine Drunk by the People of Cathay

Most of the people of Cathay drink wine of the kind that I shall now describe. It is a liquor which they brew of rice with a quantity of excellent spice, in such fashion that it makes better drink than any other kind of wine; it is not only good, but clear and pleasing to the eye. And being very hot stuff, it makes one drunk sooner than any other wine.

XXX. Concerning the Black Stones that are Dug in Cathay and are Burnt for Fuel

It is a fact that all over the country of Cathay there is a kind of black stones existing in beds in the mountains, which they dig out and burn like firewood. If you supply the fire with them at night, and see that they are well kindled, you will find them still alight in the morning; and they make such capital fuel that no other is used throughout the country. It is true that they have plenty of wood also, but they do not burn it, because those stones burn better and cost less.

Moreover with that vast number of people, and the number of hot baths that they maintain—for every one has such a bath at least three times a week, and in winter if possible every day, while every nobleman and man of wealth has a private bath for his own use—the wood would not suffice for the purpose.

XXXI. How the Great Kaan Causes Stores of Corn to be Made, to Help His People Withal in Time of Dearth

You must know that when the Emperor sees that corn is cheap and abundant, he buys up large quantities, and has it stored in all his provinces in great granaries, where it is so well looked after that it will keep for three or four years.

And this applies, let me tell you, to all kinds of corn, whether wheat, barley, millet, rice, panic, or what not, and when there is any scarcity of a particular kind of corn, he causes that to be issued. And if the price of the corn is at one bezant the measure, he lets them have it at a bezant for four measures, or at whatever price will produce general cheapness; and every one can have food in this way. And by this providence of the Emperor's, his people can never suffer from dearth. He does the same over his whole Empire; causing these supplies to be stored everywhere, according to calculation of the wants and necessities of the people.

XXXII. On the Charity of the Emperor to the Poor

I have told you how the Great Kaan provides for the distribution of necessaries to his people in time of dearth, by making store in time of cheapness. Now I will tell you of his alms and great charity to the poor of his city of Cambaluc.

You see he causes selection to be made of a number of families in the city which are in a state of indigence, and of such families some may consist of six in the house, sone of eight, some of ten, more or fewer in each as it may hap, but the whole number being very great. And each family he causes annually to be supplied with wheat and other corn sufficient for the whole year. And this he never fails to do every year. Moreover, all those who choose to go to the daily dole at the court receive a great loaf apiece, hot from the baking, and nobody is denied; for so the Lord hath ordered. And so some 30,000 people go for it every day from year's end to year's end. Now this is a great goodness in the Emperor to take pity of his poor people thus. And they benefit so much by it that they worship him as he were God.

He also provides the poor with clothes. For he lays a tithe upon all wool, silk, hemp, and the like from which clothing can be made and he has these woven and laid up in a building set apart for the purpose and as all artisans are bound to give a day's labor weekly, in this way the Kaan has these stuffs made into clothing for those poor families, suitable for summer or winter, according to the time of year. He also provides the clothing for his troops and has woolens woven for them in every city, the material for which is furnished by the tithe aforesaid. You should know that the Tartars, before they were converted to the religion of the idolaters, never practised almsgiving. Indeed, when any poor man begged of them they would tell him, "Go with God's curse, for if he loved you as he loves me he would have provided for you." But the sages of the idolaters told the Great Kaan that it was a good work to provide for the poor and that his idols would be greatly pleased if he did so. And since then he has taken to do so for the poor so much as you have heard.

XXXIII. Concerning the Astrologers in the City of Cambaluc

There are in the city of Cambaluc, what with Christians, Saracens, and Cathayans, some five thousand astrologers and soothsayers, whom the Great Kaan provides with annual maintenance and clothing, just as he provides the poor of whom we have spoken, and they are in the constant exercise of their art in this city.

They have a kind of astrolabe on which are inscribed the planetary signs, the hours and critical points of the whole year. And every year these Christian, Saracen, and Cathayan astrologers, each sect apart, investigate by means of this astrolabe the course and character of the whole year, according to the indications of each of its Moons, in order to discover by the natural course and disposition of the planets and the other circumstances of the heavens what shall be the nature of the weather, and what peculiarities shall be produced by each Moon of the year as, for example, under which Moon there shall be thunderstorms and tempests, under which there shall be disease, murrain, wars, disorder, and treasons, and so on, according to the indications of each, but always adding that it lies with God to do less or more according to his pleasure. And they write down the results of their examination in certain little pamphlets for the year, which are called *Tacuin*, and these are sold for a groat to all who desire to know what is coming. Those of the astrologers, of course, whose predictions are found to be most exact are held to be the greatest adepts in their art and get the greater fame.

And if any one have some great matter in hand, or proposing to make a long journey for traffic or other business, desires to know what will be the upshot, he goes to one of these astrologers and says: "Turn up your books and see what is the present aspect of the heavens for I am going away on such and such a business." Then the astrologer will reply that the applicant must also tell the year, month, and hour of his birth, and when he has got that information he will see how the horoscope of his nativity combines with the indications of the time when the question is put, and then he predicts the result, good or bad, according to the aspect of the heavens.

You must know, too, that the Tartars reckon their years by twelves, the sign of the first year being the Lion, of the second the Ox, of the third the Dragon, of the fourth the Dog, and so forth up to the twelfth, so that when one is asked the year of his birth he answers that it was in the year of the Lion (let us say), on such a day or night, at such an hour, and such a moment. And the father of a child always takes care to write these particulars down in a book. When the twelve yearly symbols have been gone through then they come back to the first and go through

with them again in the same succession.

XXXIV. Concerning the Religion of the Cathayans, Their Views as to the Soul, and Their Customs

As we have said before, these people are idolaters and, as regards their gods, each has a tablet fixed high up on the wall of his chamber on which is inscribed a name which represents the most high and heavenly God, and before this they pay daily worship, offering incense from a thurible, raising their hands aloft and gnashing their teeth three times, praying him to grant them health of mind and body, but of him they ask nought else. And below on the ground there is a figure which they call *Natigai*, which is the god of things terrestrial. To him they give a wife and children and they worship him in the same manner, with incense and gnashing of teeth and lifting up of hands, and of him they ask seasonable weather and the fruits of the earth, children, and so forth.

Their view of the immortality of the soul is after this fashion. They believe that as soon as a man dies his soul enters into another body, going from a good to a better, or from a bad to a worse, according as he hath conducted himself well or ill. That is to say, a poor man, if he have passed through life good and sober, shall be born again of a gentlewoman, and shall be a gentleman, and on a second occasion shall be born of a princess and shall be a prince, and so on, always rising, til he be absorbed into the Deity. But if he have borne himself ill he who was the son of a gentleman shall be reborn as the son of a boor, and from a boor shall become a dog, always going down lower and lower.[1]

The people have an ornate style of speech; they salute each other with a cheerful countenance and with great politeness; they behave like gentlemen, and eat with great propriety. They show great respect to their parents and should there be any son who offends his parents or fails to minister to their necessities there is a public office which has no other charge but that of punishing unnatural children, who are proved to have acted with ingratitude towards their parents.

Criminals of sundry kinds who have been imprisoned are released at a time fixed by the Great Kaan (which occurs every three years), but on leaving prison they are branded on one cheek that they may be recognized.

The Great Kaan hath prohibited all gambling and sharping, things more prevalent there than in any other part of the world. In doing this

---

[1] [Buddhism had penetrated China more than a thousand years before.— *Ed.*]

he said: "I have conquered you by force of arms and all that you have is mine; if, therefore, you gamble away your property it is in fact my property that you are gambling away." Not that he took anything from them however.

I must not omit to tell you of the orderly way in which the Kaan's barons and others conduct themselves in coming to his presence. In the first place, within a half mile of the place where he is, out of reverence for his exalted majesty, everybody preserves a mien of the greatest meekness and quiet, so that no noise of shrill voices or loud talk shall be heard. And every one of the chiefs and nobles carries always with him a handsome little vessel to spit in while he remains in the Hall of Audience—for no one dares spit on the floor of the hall—and when he hath spitten he covers it up and puts it aside. So also they all have certain handsome buskins of white leather, which they carry with them, and, when summoned by the sovereign, on arriving at the entrance to the hall they put on these white buskins, and give their others in charge to the servants, in order that they may not foul the fine carpets of silk and gold and divers colors.

Magna Carta

What was Magna Carta? Historically it has come to be regarded as a document that guarantees the legal rights of free men, thus as a foundation for a democratic social order. This conclusion is based on Article 39, which states that a free man will not be prosecuted, except through lawful means and the judgment of his peers. But this Article, however important, is only one of sixty-three of which the Great Charter is composed. The others say little about such fundamental human rights but rather are devoted mainly to feudal liberties and obligations in thirteenth-century England. A recognition of this fact should help us to focus our attention on the central significance of the document, at least as it was conceived by those who were responsible for its writing.

Magna Carta was the consequence of a dispute that had been developing over a period of years between the monarchs and the barons of England. From the time of the Norman conquest in 1066 succeeding English kings had embarked on a practice of consolidating administration and, as a result, power around the throne.

Such a policy, of course, worked to the disadvantage of the barons who, in their reaction against these royal encroachments, claimed that they constituted violations of the feudal contract. Thus Magna Carta reveals much about feudal society, and the customary and legal relationships between individuals and classes, as these existed in the England of that time.

The dispute between king and barons intensified after the accession of King John to the throne in 1199. Much of the blame for this development lay with John himself, for he succeeded in making himself unpopular with almost every segment of his population. He alienated many of the clergy by his quarrels with Pope Innocent III; he discouraged the military class by his armed incursions into France, which led to defeat; he enraged the London merchants by imposing an ever-increasing tax burden on them; and he kept infringing on the feudal rights and privileges of the baronial class. In all of this he displayed himself as an insensitive autocrat.

The selection that follows contains about half of the Magna Carta; from it one can get a good grasp of the charter's general nature. Although it may appear from the flavor of the language employed that John is graciously granting royal favors to his subjects, it must be remembered that these concessions were forced from him by his rebellious barons.

Magna Carta

John, by the grace of God, King of England, Lord of Ireland, Duke of Normandy and Aquitaine, and Count of Anjou: To the Archbishops, Bishops, Abbots, Earls, Barons, Justiciaries, Foresters, Sheriffs, Reeves, Ministers, and all Bailiffs and others, his faithful subjects, Greeting. Know ye that in the presence of God, and for the health of Our soul, and the souls of Our ancestors and heirs, to the honor of God, and the exaltation of Holy Church, and amendment of Our kingdom, by the advice of Our reverend Fathers, Stephen, Archbishop of Canterbury, Primate of all England, and Cardinal of the Holy Roman Church; Henry, Archbishop of Dublin; William of London, Peter of Winchester, Jocelin of Bath and Glastonbury, Hugh of Lincoln, Walter of Worcester, William of Coventry, and Benedict of Rochester, Bishops; Master Pandulph, the Pope's subdeacon and familiar; Brother Aymeric, Master of the Knights of the Temple in England; and the noble persons, William Marshal, Earl of Pembroke: William, Earl of Salisbury; William, Earl of Warren; William, Earl of Arundel; Alan de Galloway, Constable of Scotland; Warin FitzGerald, Peter Fitz-Herbert, Hubert de Burgh, Seneschal of Poitou, Hugh de Neville, Matthew Fitz-Herbert, Thomas Basset, Alan Basset, Philip Daubeny, Robert de Roppelay, John Marshal, John Fitz-Hugh, and others, Our liegemen:

1. We have, in the first place, granted to God, and by this Our present Charter confirmed for Us and Our heirs forever—That the English Church shall be free and enjoy her rights in their integrity and her liberties untouched. And that We will this so to be observed appears from the fact that We of Our own free will, before the outbreak of the dissensions between Us and Our barons, granted, confirmed, and procured to be confirmed by Pope Innocent III the freedom of elections, which is considered most important and necessary to the English Church, which Charter We will both keep Ourself and will it to be kept with good faith by Our heirs forever. We have also granted to all the free men of Our kingdom, for Us and Our heirs forever, all the liberties underwritten, to have and to hold to them and their heirs of Us and Our heirs.

2. If any of Our earls, barons, or others who hold of Us in chief by knight's service shall die, and at the time of his death his heir shall be of full age and owe a relief [a form of

Magna Carta, trans. A. E. Dick Howard (Charlottesville: The University Press of Virginia, 1964). Courtesy of the Rector and Visitors of the University of Virginia.

tax], he shall have his inheritance by ancient relief; to wit, the heir or heirs of an earl of an entire earl's barony, £100; the heir or heirs of a baron of an entire barony, ;£100; the heir or heirs of a knight of an entire knight's fee, 100s. at the most; and he that owes less shall give less, according to the ancient custom of fees.

3. If, however, any such heir shall be under age and in ward, he shall, when he comes of age, have his inheritance without relief or fine.

4. The guardian of the land of any heir thus under age shall take therefrom only reasonable issues, customs, and services, without destruction or waste of men or property; and if We shall have committed the wardship of any such land to the sheriff or any other person answerable to Us for the issues thereof, and he commit destruction or waste, We will take an amends from him, and the land shall be committed to two lawful and discreet men of that fee, who shall be answerable for the issues to Us or to whomsoever We shall have assigned them. And if We shall give or sell the wardship of any such land to anyone, and he commit destruction or waste upon it, he shall lose the wardship, which shall be committed to two lawful and discreet men of that fee, who shall, in like manner, be answerable unto Us as has been aforesaid.

5. The guardian, so long as he shall have the custody of the land, shall keep up and maintain the houses, parks, fishponds, pools, mills, and other things pertaining thereto, out of the issues of the same, and shall restore the whole to the heir when he comes of age, stocked with ploughs and tillage, according as the season may require and the issues of the land can reasonably bear.

6. Heirs shall be married without loss of station, and the marriage shall be made known to the heir's nearest of kin before it be contracted.

7. A widow, after the death of her husband, shall immediately and without difficulty have her marriage portion and inheritance. She shall not give anything for her marriage portion, dower, or inheritance which she and her husband held on the day of his death, and she may remain in her husband's house for forty days after his death, within which time her dower shall be assigned to her.

8. No widow shall be compelled to marry so long as she has a mind to live without a husband, provided, however, that she give security that she will not marry without Our assent, if she holds of Us, or that of the lord of whom she holds, if she holds of another.

9. Neither We nor Our bailiffs shall seize any land or rent for any debt so long as the debtor's chattels are sufficient to discharge the same; nor shall the debtor's sureties be distrained so long as the debtor is able to pay the debt. If the debtor fails to pay, not having the means to pay, then the sureties shall answer the debt, and, if they desire, they shall hold the debtor's lands and rents until they have received satisfaction of the debt which they have paid for him, unless the debtor can show that he has discharged his obligation to them.

10. If anyone who has borrowed from the Jews any sum of money, great or small, dies before the debt has been paid, the heir shall pay no interest on the debt so long as he remains under age, of whomsoever he may hold. If the debt shall fall into Our hands, We will take only the principal sum named in the bond.

• • •

12. No scutage [a payment in place of a personal service — *Ed.*] or aid shall be imposed in Our kingdom unless by common counsel thereof, except to ransom Our person, make Our eldest son a knight, and once to marry Our eldest daughter, and for these only a reasonable aid shall be levied. So shall it be with regard to aids from the City of London.

13. The City of London shall have all her ancient liberties and free customs, both by land and water. Moreover, We will and grant that all other cities, boroughs, towns, and ports shall have all their liberties and free customs.

14. For obtaining the common counsel of the kingdom concerning the assessment of aids (other than in the three cases aforesaid) or of scutage, We will cause to be summoned, severally by Our letters, the archbishops, bishops, abbots, earls, and great barons. We will also cause to be summoned, generally, by Our sheriffs and bailiffs, all those who hold lands directly to Us, to meet on a fixed day, but with at least forty days' notice, and at a fixed place. In all letters of such summons We will explain the cause thereof. The summons being thus made, the business shall proceed on the day appointed, according to the advice of those who shall be present, even though not all the persons summoned have come.

15. We will not in the future grant permission to any man to levy an aid upon his free men, except to ransom his person, make his eldest son a knight, and once to marry his eldest daughter, and on each of these occasions only a reasonable aid shall be levied.

16. No man shall be compelled to perform more service for a knight's fee or other free tenement than is due therefrom.

17. Common Pleas shall not follow Our Court, but shall be held in some certain place.

• • •

20. A free man shall be amerced [fined] for a small fault only according to the measure thereof, and for a great crime according to its magnitude, saving his position; and in like manner a merchant saving his trade, and a villein [serf] saving his tillage, if they should fall under Our mercy. None of these amercements shall be imposed except by the oath of honest men of the neighborhood.

21. Earls and barons shall be amerced only by their peers, and only in proportion to the measure of the offense.

22. No amercement shall be imposed upon a clerk's [clergyman's] lay property, except after the manner of the other persons aforesaid, and without regard to the value of his ecclesiastical benefice.

• • •

28. No constable or other of Our bailiffs shall take corn or other chattels of any man without immediate payment, unless the seller voluntarily consents to postponement of payment.

29. No constable shall compel any knight to give money in lieu of castle-guard when the knight is willing to perform it in person or (if reasonable cause prevents him from performing it himself) by some other fit man. Further, if We lead or send him into military service, he shall be quit of castle-guard for the time he shall remain in service by Our command.

30. No sheriff or other of Our bailiffs, or any other man, shall take the horses or carts of any free man for carriage without the owner's consent.

• • •

31. Neither We nor Our bailiffs will take another man's wood for Our castles or for any other purpose without the owner's consent.

35. There shall be one measure of wine throughout Our kingdom, and one of ale, and one measure of corn, to wit, the London quarter, and one breadth of dyed cloth, russets, and haberjets, to wit, two ells within the selvages. As with measures so shall it also be with weights.

• • •

38. In the future no bailiff shall upon his own unsupported accusation put any man to trial without producing credible witnesses to the truth of the accusation.

39. No free man shall be taken, imprisoned, disseised [dispossessed], outlawed, banished, or in any way destroyed, nor will We proceed against him or prosecute him, except by the lawful judgment of his peers and by the law of the land.

40. To no one will We sell, to none will We deny or delay, right or justice.

41. All merchants shall have safe conduct to go and come out of and into England, and to stay in and travel through England by land and water for purposes of buying and selling, free of illegal tolls, in accordance with ancient and just customs, except, in time of war, such merchants as are of a country at war with Us. If any such be found in Our dominion at the outbreak of war, they shall be attached, without injury to their persons or goods, until it be known to Us or Our Chief Justiciary how Our merchants are being treated in the country at war with Us, and if Our merchants be safe there, then theirs shall be safe with Us.

42. In the future it shall be lawful (except for a short period in time of war, for the common benefit of the realm) for anyone to leave and return to our kingdom safely and securely by land and water, saving his fealty to Us. Excepted are those who have been imprisoned or outlawed according to the law of the land, people of the country at war with Us, and merchants, who shall be dealt with as aforesaid.

• • •

52. If anyone has been disseised or deprived by Us, without the legal judgment of his peers, of lands, castles, liberties, or rights, We will immediately restore the same, and if any dispute shall arise thereupon, the matter shall be decided by judgment of the twenty-five barons mentioned below in the clause for securing the peace. With regard to all those things, however, of which any man was disseised or deprived, without the legal judgment of his peers, by King Henry Our Father or Our Brother King Richard, and which remain in Our hands or are held by others under Our warranty, We shall have respite during the term commonly allowed to the Crusaders, except as to those matters on which a plea had arisen, or an inquisition had been taken by Our command, prior to Our taking the Cross. Immediately after Our return from Our pilgrimmage, or if by chance We should remain behind from it, We will at once do full justice.

• • •

54. No one shall be arrested or imprisoned upon a woman's appeal for the death of any person other than her husband.

55. All fines unjustly and unlawfully given to Us, and all amercements levied unjustly and against the law of the land, shall be entirely re-

mitted or the matter settled by judgment of the twenty-five barons of whom mention is made below in the clause for securing the peace, or the majority of them, together with the aforesaid Stephen, Archbishop of Canterbury, if he himself can be present, and any others whom he may wish to bring with him for the purpose; if he cannot be present, the business shall nevertheless proceed without him. If any one or more of the said twenty-five barons be interested in a suit of this kind, he or they shall be set aside, as to this particular judgment, and another or others, elected and sworn by the rest of said barons for this occasion only, be substituted in his or their stead.

* * *

60. All the customs and liberties aforesaid, which We have granted to be enjoyed, as far as in Us lies, by Our people throughout Our kingdom, let all Our subjects, whether clerks or laymen, observe, as far as in them lies, toward their dependents.

61. Whereas We, for the honor of God and the amendment of Our realm, and in order the better to allay the discord arisen between Us and Our barons, have granted all these things aforesaid, We, willing that they be forever enjoyed wholly and in lasting strength, do give and grant to Our subjects the following security, to wit, that the barons shall elect any twenty-five barons of the kingdom at will, who shall, with their utmost power, keep, hold, and cause to be kept the peace and liberties which We have granted unto them and by this Our present Charter have confirmed, so that if We, Our Justiciary, bailiffs, or any of Our ministers offend in any respect against any man, or shall transgress any of these articles of peace or security, and the

offense be brought before four of the said twenty-five barons, these four barons shall come before Us, or Our Chief Justiciary if We are out of the kingdom, declaring the offense, and shall demand speedy amends for the same. If We, or, in case of Our being out of the kingdom, Our Chief Justiciary fail to afford redress within the space of forty days from the time the case was brought before Us or, in the event of Our having been out of the kingdom, Our Chief Justiciary, the aforesaid four barons shall refer the matter to the rest of the twenty-five barons, who, together with the commonalty of the whole country, shall distrain and distress Us to the utmost of their power, to wit, by capture of Our castles, lands, and possessions and by all other possible means, until compensation be made according to their decision, saving Our person and that of Our Queen and children; as soon as redress has been had, they shall return to their former allegiance. Anyone in the kingdom may take oath that, for the accomplishment of all the aforesaid matters, he will obey the orders of the said twenty-five barons and distress Us to the utmost of his power; and We give public and free leave to everyone wishing to take such oath to do so, and to none will we deny the same. Moreover, all such of Our subjects who shall not of their own free will and accord agree to swear to the said twenty-five barons, to distrain and distress Us together with them, We will compel to do so by Our command in the manner aforesaid. If any one of the twenty-five barons shall die or leave the country or be in any way hindered from executing the said office, the rest of the said twenty-five barons shall choose another in his stead, at their discretion, who shall be sworn in like manner as the others. In all cases which are referred to the said twenty-five barons to execute, and in which a difference shall arise among them, supposing them all to be present, or in which not all who have been summoned are willing or able to appear, the verdict of the majority shall be considered as firm and binding as if the whole number should have been of one mind. The aforesaid twenty-five shall swear to keep faithfully all the aforesaid articles and, to the best of their power, to cause them to be kept by others. We will not procure, either by Ourself or any other, anything from any man whereby any of these concessions or liberties may be revoked or abated. If any such procurement be made, let it be null and void; it shall never be made use of either by Us or by any other.

62. We have also wholly remitted and pardoned all ill-will, wrath, and malice which has arisen between Us and Our subjects, both clergy and laymen, during the disputes, to and with all men. Morover, We have fully remitted and, as far as in Us lies, wholly pardoned to and with all,

clergy and laymen, all trespasses made in consequence of the said disputes from Easter in the sixteenth year of Our reign till the restoration of peace. Over and above this, We have caused to be made in their behalf letters patent by testimony of Stephen, Archbishop of Canterbury, Henry, Archbishop of Dublin, the Bishops above-mentioned, and Master Pandulph, for the security and concessions aforesaid.

63. Wherefore We will, and firmly charge, that the English Church shall be free, and that all men in Our kingdom shall have and hold all the aforesaid liberties, rights, and concessions, well and peaceably, freely, quietly, fully, and wholly, to them and their heirs, of Us and Our heirs, in all things and places forever, as is aforesaid. It is moreover sworn, as well on Our part as on the part of the barons, that all these matters aforesaid shall be kept in good faith and without deceit. Witness the above-named and many others. Given by Our hand in the meadow which is called Runnymede, between Windsor and Staines, on the fifteenth day of June in the seventeenth year of Our reign.

St. Thomas Aquinas

St. Thomas Aquinas (1225–1274), the leading philosopher and theologian of medieval scholasticism, was one of the greatest synthesizers in European thought. The task he undertook was to reconcile the philosophy of Aristotle, rediscovered by European scholars through their contacts with the Muslims in Spain and elsewhere, with Christian theology. During a relatively short lifetime, he succeeded in combining these two disparate elements into a single system capable in principle of explaining everything in the universe that people could know. Questions have been raised about the logical consistency of the Thomistic synthesis, but, whether successful or not, it still stands as a substantial intellectual achievement.

Beyond their general historical importance, the writings of Thomas have a special significance in the history of Catholicism. Although Thomas was opposed during his lifetime by various religious leaders because of his heavy reliance on the pagan Aristotle, and although his writings were even condemned at several theological centers in the years immediately after his death, within a century his system was generally accepted as the basis for orthodox Roman Catholic philosophy. The authoritativeness of Thomistic doctrine was formally recognized by the church in 1879 in the encyclical *Aeterni Patris* of Pope Leo XIII, which ordered all Catholic schools to teach Thomas's position as the true philosophy. Leo's order was reiterated in 1923 by Pius X, who wrote, "The following canon of the church's code should be held as a sacred command: In the study of rational philosophy and theology and in the instruction of students the professor should follow entirely the method, doctrine and principles of the Angelic Doctor [Thomas], and hold them religiously."

Of noble Italian lineage, Thomas decided early in life to become a Dominican monk, much to the displeasure of his family. As a student, he was nicknamed "the dumb ox" because of his quietness and ponderous bulk. Later, as a teacher at the University of Paris, he was so popular that it was difficult to find a hall large enough to accommodate the students who flocked to his lectures.

The selection that follows illustrates Thomas's attempt to establish the consonance between the philosophers' quest for truth based on reason and the Christians' acceptance of divine truth based on revelation. It is clear from the nature of his argument that, however much we should rely on reason, in the final analysis revelation is the arbiter of truth.

Summa Contra Gentiles

CHAPTER III

In What Way It Is Possible to Make Known the Divine Truth

Since, however, not every truth is to be made known in the same way,

and it is the part of an educated man to seek for conviction in each subject, only so far as the nature of the subject allows,

as the Philosopher[1] most rightly observes as quoted by Boethius, it is necessary to show first of all in what way it is possible to make known the aforesaid truth.

Now in those things which we hold about God there is truth in two ways. For certain things that are true about God wholly surpass the capability of human reason, for instance that God is three and one: while there are certain things to which even natural reason can attain, for instance that God is, that God is one, and others like these, which even the philosophers proved demonstratively of God, being guided by the light of natural reason.

That certain divine truths wholly surpass the capability of human reason, is most clearly evident. For since the principle of all the knowledge which the reason acquires about a thing, is the understanding of that thing's essence, because according to the Philosopher's teaching the principle of a demonstration is *what a thing is*, it follows that our knowledge about a thing will be in proportion to our understanding of its essence. Wherefore, if the human intellect comprehends the essence of a particular thing, for instance a stone or a triangle, no truth about that thing will surpass the capability of human reason. But this does not happen to us in relation to God, because the human intellect is incapable by its natural power of attaining to the comprehension of His essence: since our intellect's knowledge, according to the mode of the present life, originates from the senses: so that things which are not objects of sense cannot be comprehended by the human intellect, except in so far as knowledge of them is

---

[1] [Aristotle—*Ed.*]

The "Summa Contra Gentiles" of St. Thomas Aquinas, trans. Fathers of the English Dominican Province (New York: Benziger Brothers, Inc., 1924). Courtesy of Benziger Publishing Co.

gathered from sensibles. Now sensibles cannot lead our intellect to see in them what God is, because they are effects unequal to the power of their cause. And yet our intellect is led by sensibles to the divine knowledge so as to know about God that He is, and other such truths, which need to be ascribed to the first principle. Accordingly some divine truths are attainable by human reason, while others altogether surpass the power of human reason.

Again. The same is easy to see from the degrees of intellects. For if one of two men perceives a thing with his intellect with greater subtlety, the one whose intellect is of a higher degree understands many things which the other is altogether unable to grasp; as instanced in a yokel who is utterly incapable of grasping the subtleties of philosophy. Now the angelic intellect surpasses the human intellect more than the intellect of the cleverest philosopher surpasses that of the most uncultured. For an angel knows God through a more excellent effect than does man, for as much as the angel's essence, through which he is led to know God by natural knowledge, is more excellent than sensible things, even than the soul itself, by which the human intellect mounts to the knowledge of God. And the divine intellect surpasses the angelic intellect much more than the angelic surpasses the human. For the divine intellect by its capacity equals the divine essence, wherefore God perfectly understands of Himself what He is, and He knows all the things that can be understood about Him: whereas the angel knows not what God is by his natural knowledge, because the angel's essence, by which

he is led to the knowledge of God, is an effect unequal to the power of its cause. Consequently an angel is unable by his natural knowledge to grasp all that God understands about Himself: nor again is human reason capable of grasping all that an angel understands by his natural power. Accordingly just as a man would show himself to be a most insane fool if he declared the assertions of a philosopher to be false because he was unable to understand them, so, and much more, a man would be exceedingly foolish, were he to suspect of falsehood the things revealed by God through the ministry of His angels, because they cannot be the object of reason's investigations.

Furthermore. The same is made abundantly clear by the deficiency which every day we experience in our knowledge of things. For we are ignorant of many of the properties of sensible things, and in many cases we are unable to discover the nature of those properties which we perceive by our senses. Much less therefore is human reason capable of investigating all the truths about the most sublime existence.

With this the saying of the Philosopher is in accord where he says that *our intellect in relation to those primary things which are most evident in nature is like the eye of a bat in relation to the sun.*

To this truth Holy Writ also bears witness. For it is written (Job xi. 7): *Peradventure thou wilt comprehend the steps of God and wilt find out the Almighty perfectly?* and (xxxvi. 26) *Behold God is great, exceeding our knowledge,* and (I Cor. xiii. 9): *We know in part.*

Therefore all that is said about God, though it cannot be investigated by reason, must not be forthwith rejected as false, as the Manicheans and many unbelievers have thought.

CHAPTER IV

That the Truth about Divine Things Which Is Attainable by Reason Is Fittingly Proposd to Man as an Object of Belief

While then the truth of the intelligible things of God is twofold, one to which the inquiry of reason can attain, the other which surpasses the whole range of human reason, both are fittingly proposed by God to man as an object of belief. We must first show this with regard to that truth which is attainable by the inquiry of reason, lest it appears to some, that since it can be attained by reason, it was useless to make it an object of faith by supernatural inspiration. Now three disadvantages would result if this truth were left solely to the inquiry of reason. One is that few men would have knowledge of God: because very many are hindered from gathering the fruit of diligent inquiry, which is the discovery of truth, for three reasons. Some indeed on account of an indisposition of temperament, by reason of which many are naturally indisposed to knowledge: so that no efforts of theirs would enable them to reach to the attainment of the highest degree of human knowledge, which consists in knowing God. Some are hindered by the needs of household affairs. For there must needs be among men some that devote themselves to the conduct of temporal affairs, who would be unable to devote so much time to the leisure of contemplative research as to reach the summit of human inquiry, namely the knowledge of God. And some are hindered by laziness. For in order to acquire the knowledge of God in those things which reason is able to investigate, it is necessary to have a previous knowledge of many things: since almost the entire consideration of philosophy is directed to the knowledge of God: for which reason metaphysics, which is about divine things, is the last of the parts of philosophy to be studied. Wherefore it is not possible to arrive at the inquiry about the aforesaid truth except after a most laborious study: and few are willing to take upon themselves this labour for the love of a knowledge, the natural desire for which has nevertheless been instilled into the mind of man by God.

The second disadvantage is that those who would arrive at the discovery of the aforesaid truth would scarcely succeed in doing so after a long time. First, because this truth is so profound, that it is only after long practice that the human intellect is enabled to grasp it by means of reason. Secondly, because many things are required beforehand, as stated above. Thirdly, because at the time of youth, the mind, when tossed about by the various movements of the passions, is not fit for the knowledge of so sublime a truth, whereas *calm gives prudence and knowledge*, as stated in 7 *Phys.* Hence mankind would remain in the deepest darkness of ignorance, if the path of reason were the only available way to the knowledge of God: because the knowledge of God which especially makes men perfect and good, would be acquired only by the few, and by these only after a long time.

The third disadvantage is that

much falsehood is mingled with the investigations of human reason, on account of the weakness of our intellect in forming its judgments, and by reason of the admixture of phantasms. Consequently many would remain in doubt about those things even which are most truly demonstrated, through ignoring the force of the demonstration: especially when they perceive that different things are taught by the various men who are called wise. Moreover among the many demonstrated truths, there is sometimes a mixture of falsehood that is not demonstrated, but assumed for some probable or sophistical reason which at times is mistaken for a demonstration. Therefore it was necessary that definite certainty and pure truth about divine things should be offered to man by the way of faith.

Accordingly the divine clemency has made this salutary commandment, that even some things which reason is able to investigate must be held by faith: so that all may share in the knowledge of God easily, and without doubt or error.

Hence it is written (Eph. iv. 17, 18): That *henceforth you walk not as also the Gentiles walk in the vanity of their mind, having their understanding darkened*; and (Isa. liv. 13): *All thy children shall be taught of the Lord.*

CHAPTER V

That Those Things Which Cannot Be Investigated by Reason Are Fittingly Proposed to Man as an Object of Faith

It may appear to some that those things which cannot be investigated by reason ought not to be proposed to man as an object of faith: because

divine wisdom provides for each thing according to the mode of its nature. We must therefore prove that it is necessary also for those things which surpass reason to be proposed by God to man as an object of faith.

For no man tends to do a thing by his desire and endeavour unless it be previously known to him. Wherefore since man is directed by divine providence to a higher good than human frailty can attain in the present life, as we shall show in the sequel, it was necessary for his mind to be bidden to something higher than those things to which our reason can reach in the present life, so that he might learn to aspire, and by his endeavors to tend to something surpassing the whole state of the present life. And this is especially competent to the Christian religion, which alone promises goods spiritual and eternal: for which reason it proposes many things surpassing the thought of man: whereas the old law which contained promises of temporal things, proposed few things that are above human inquiry. It was with this motive that the philosophers, in order to wean men from sensible pleasures to virtue, took care to show that there are other goods of greater account than those which appeal to the senses, the taste of which things affords much greater delight to those who devote themselves to active or contemplative virtues.

Again it is necessary for this truth to be proposed to man as an object of faith in order that he may have truer knowledge of God. For then alone do we know God truly, when we believe that He is far above all that man can possibly think of God, because the divine essence surpasses man's natural knowledge, as stated above. Hence by the fact that certain things about God are proposed to man, which surpass his reason, he is strengthened in his opinion that God is far above what he is able to think.

There results also another advantage from this, namely, the checking of presumption which is the mother of error. For some there are who presume so far on their wits that they think themselves capable of measuring the whole nature of things by their intellect, in that they esteem all things true which they see, and false which they see not. Accordingly, in order that man's mind might be freed from this presumption, and seek the truth humbly, it was necessary that certain things far surpassing his intellect should be proposed to man by God.

Yet another advantage is made apparent by the words of the Philosopher (10 *Ethic.*). For when a certain Simonides maintained that man should neglect the knowledge of God, and apply his mind to human affairs, and declared that *a man ought to relish human things, and a mortal, mortal things*: the Philosopher contradicted him, saying that *a man ought to devote himself to immortal and divine things as much as he can.* Hence he says (11 *De Anima.*) that though it is but little that we perceive of higher substances, yet that little is more loved and desired than all the knowledge we have of lower substances. He says also (2 *De Coelo et Mundo*) that when questions about the heavenly bodies can be answered by a short and probable solution, it happens that the hearer is very much rejoiced. All this shows that however imperfect the knowledge of the highest things may be, it bestows very great perfection on the soul: and

consequently, although human reason is unable to grasp fully things that are above reason, it nevertheless acquires much perfection, if at least it hold things, in any way whatever, by faith.

Wherefore it is written (Eccles. iii. 25): *Many things are shown to thee above the understanding of men,* and (I Cor. ii. 10, 11): *The things . . . that are of God no man knoweth, but the Spirit of God: but to us God hath revealed them by His Spirit.*

CHAPTER VI

That It Is Not a Mark of Levity to Assent to the Things That Are of Faith, Although They Are Above Reason

Now those who believe this truth, *of which reason affords a proof,* believe not lightly, as though *following foolish fables* (2 Pet. i. 16). For divine Wisdom Himself, Who knows all things most fully, designed to reveal to man *the secrets of God's wisdom:* and by suitable arguments proves His presence, and the truth of His doctrine and inspiration, by performing works surpassing the capability of the whole of nature, namely, the wondrous healing of the sick, the raising of the dead to life, a marvellous control over the heavenly bodies, and what excites yet more wonder, the inspiration of human minds, so that unlettered and simple persons are filled with the Holy Ghost, and in one instant are endowed with the most sublime wisdom and eloquence. And after considering these arguments, convinced by the strength of the proof, and not by the force of arms, nor by the promise of delights, but— and this is the greatest marvel of all—

amidst the tyranny of persecutions, a countless crowd of not only simple but also of the wisest men, embraced the Christian faith, which inculcates things surpassing all human understanding, curbs the pleasures of the flesh, and teaches contempt of all worldly things. That the minds of mortal beings should assent to such things, is both the greatest of miracles, and the evident work of divine inspiration, seeing that they despise visible things and desire only those that are invisible. And that this happened not suddenly nor by chance, but by the disposition of God, is shown by the fact that God foretold that He would do so by the manifold oracles of the prophets, whose books we hold in veneration as bearing witness to our faith. This particular kind of proof is alluded to in the words of Heb. ii, 3, 4: *Which*, namely the salvation of mankind, *having begun to be declared by the Lord, was confirmed with us by them that heard Him, God also bearing witness by signs and wonders, and divers . . . distributions of the Holy Ghost.*

Now such a wondrous conversion of the world to the Christian faith is a most indubitable proof that such signs did take place, so that there is no need to repeat them, seeing that there is evidence of them in their result. For it would be the most wondrous sign of all if without any wondrous signs the world were persuaded by simple and lowly men to believe things so arduous, to accomplish things so difficult, and to hope for things so sublime. Although God ceases not even in our time to work miracles through His saints in confirmation of the faith.

On the other hand those who introduced the errors of the sects proceeded in contrary fashion, as instanced by Mohammed, who enticed people with the promise of carnal pleasures, to the desire of which the concupiscence of the flesh instigates. He also delivered commandments in keeping with his promises, by giving the reins to carnal pleasure, wherein it is easy for carnal men to obey: and the lessons of truth which he inculcated were only such as can be easily known to any man of average wisdom by his natural powers: yea, rather the truths which he taught were mingled by him with many fables and most false doctrines. Nor did he add any signs of supernatural agency, which alone are a fitting witness to divine inspiration, since a visible work that can be from God alone, proves the teacher of truth to be invisibly inspired: but he asserted that he was sent in the power of arms, a sign that is not lacking even to robbers and tyrants. Again, those who believed in him from the outset were not wise men practised in things divine and human, but beastlike men who dwelt in the wilds, utterly ignorant of all divine teaching; and it was by a multitude of such men and the force of arms that he impelled others to submit to his law.

Lastly, no divine oracles or prophets in a previous age bore witness to him; rather he did corrupt almost all the teaching of the Old and New Testaments by a narrative replete with fables, as one may see by a perusal of his law. Hence by a cunning device, he did not commit the reading of the Old and New Testament Books to his followers, lest he should thereby be convicted of falsehood. Thus it is evident that those who believe his words believe lightly.

CHAPTER VII

That the Truth of Reason Is Not in Opposition to the Truth of the Christian Faith

Now though the aforesaid truth of the Christian faith surpasses the ability of human reason, nevertheless those things which are naturally instilled in human reason cannot be opposed to this truth. For it is clear that those things which are implanted in reason by nature, are most true, so much so that it is impossible to think them to be false. Nor is it lawful to deem false that which is held by faith, since it is so evidently confirmed by God. Seeing then that the false alone is opposed to the true, as evidently appears if we examine their definitions, it is impossible for the aforesaid truth of faith to be contrary to those principles which reason knows naturally.

Again. The same thing which the disciple's mind receives from its teacher is contained in the knowledge of the teacher, unless he teach insincerely, which it were wicked to say of God. Now the knowledge of naturally known principles is instilled into us by God, since God Himself is the author of our nature. Therefore the divine Wisdom also contains these principles. Consequently whatever is contrary to these principles, is contrary to the divine Wisdom; wherefore it cannot be from God. Therefore those things which are received by faith from divine revelation cannot be contrary to our natural knowledge.

Moreover. Our intellect is stayed by contrary arguments, so that it cannot advance to the knowledge of truth. Wherefore if conflicting knowledges were instilled into us by God, our intellect would thereby be hindered from knowing the truth. And this cannot be ascribed to God.

Furthermore. Things that are natural are unchangeable so long as nature remains. Now contrary opinions alone cannot be together in the same subject. Therefore God does not instil into man any opinion or belief contrary to natural knowledge.

Hence the Apostle says (Rom. x. 8): *Thy word is nigh thee even in thy heart and in thy mouth. This is the word of faith which we preach.* Yet because it surpasses reason some look upon it as though it were contrary thereto; which is impossible.

This is confirmed also by the authority of Augustine who says *That which truth shall make known can nowise be in opposition to the holy books whether of the Old or of the New Testament.*

From this we may evidently conclude that whatever arguments are alleged against the teachings of faith, they do not rightly proceed from the first self-evident principles instilled by nature. Wherefore they lack the force of demonstration, and are either probable or sophistical arguments, and consequently it is possible to solve them.

Jean, Sire de Joinville

The Crusades were a phenomenon symbolic of medieval Christian faith. The idea of Crusades originated with Pope Urban II in 1095, and during the next two centuries thousands of European knights "took up the cross" (hence the word "Crusade") and headed for the Near East, their ostensible purpose being to liberate Jerusalem and other sites sacred to Christianity from the yoke of the Muslims (or Saracens), who had captured and occupied them. There was even a children's Crusade in 1212, consisting of several thousand youths (mostly under twelve years of age). None reached their goal, most of the children being sold into slavery along the way.

One of the later Crusades was organized and led by the warrior-king, Louis IX of France, in 1248. To mount his Crusade Louis built a city on the southern coast of France. This city, Aigues Mortes—with its encircling stone walls and giant towers, its chapel where the crusading knights prayed, and its equestrian statue of Louis in the town square—remains today as a living museum of the European Middle Ages.

Although the Crusaders finally failed in their primary, religious objective, they succeeded in other ways. Perhaps most important, they brought together two disparate cultures—that of Christian western Europe and that of the Muslim Middle East. This intermingling of cultures was to have substantial effects in the years to follow, particularly on the social and economic structure of the West.

The selection that follows is taken from an account of King Louis' first Crusade, which sailed to the island of Cyprus and then on to Damietta, on the Mediterranean coast of Egypt, written by one of its participants, Jean, Sire de Joinville (1224–1319). Following his victory at Damietta Louis moved up the Nile against Cairo but his army was defeated and he was captured and held for ransom. The selection is interesting not only for its vivid description of the Crusaders' travels and the battles they fought but as well for the glimpses it gives of feudal society and the knightly caste.

Memoirs

• • •
Joinville Leaves His Castle
• • •

I departed from Joinville on foot, barefoot, in my shirt—not to reenter the castle till my return; and thus I went to Blécourt, and Saint-Urbain, and to other places thereabouts where there are holy relics. And never while I went to Blécourt and Saint-Urbain would I turn my eyes towards Joinville for fear my heart should melt within me at the thought of the fair castle I was leaving behind, and my two children.

I and my companions ate that day at Fontaine-l'Archevêque before Donjeux; and the Abbot Adam of Saint-Urbain—whom God have in His grace!—gave a great quantity of fair jewels to myself and the nine knights I had with me. Thence we went to Auxonne, and thence again, with the baggage, which we had placed in boats, from Auxonne to Lyons down the river Saône; and along by the side of the boats were led the great warhorses.

At Lyons we embarked on the Rhône to go to Arles the White; and on the Rhône we found a castle called Roche-de-Glun, which the king had caused to be destroyed, because Roger, the lord of the castle, was accused of robbing pilgrims and merchants.

The Crusaders Embark, August 1248

In the month of August we entered into our ship at the Roche-de-Mar-seille. On the day that we entered into our ship, they opened the door of the ship and put therein all the horses we were to take overseas; and then they reclosed the door, and caulked it well, as when a cask is sunk in water, because, when the ship is on the high seas, all the said door is under water.

When the horses were in the ship, our master mariner called to his seamen, who stood at the prow, and said: "Are you ready?" and they answered, "Aye, sir—let the clerks and priests come forward!" As soon as these had come forward, he called to them, "Sing, for God's sake!" and they all, with one voice, chanted: *"Veni Creator Spiritus."*

Then he cried to his seamen "Unfurl the sails, for God's sake!" and they did so.

In a short space the wind filled our sails and had borne us out of sight of land, so that we saw naught save sky and water, and every day the wind carried us further from the land where we were born. And these things I tell you, that you may understand how foolhardy is that man who dares, having other's chattels in his possession, or being in mortal sin, to place himself in such peril, seeing that, when you lie down to sleep at night on shipboard, you lie down not knowing whether, in the morning, you may find yourself at the bottom of the sea.

At sea a singular marvel befell us; for we came across a mountain, quite round, before the coast of Barbary.

Trans. Frank T. Marzials.

We came across it about the hour of vespers, and sailed all night, and thought to have gone about fifty leagues; and, on the morrow, we found ourselves before the same mountain; and this same thing happened to us some two or three times. When the sailors saw this, they were all amazed, and told us we were in very great peril; for we were nigh unto the land of the Saracens of Barbary.

Then spake a certain right worthy priest, who was called the Dean of Maurupt; and he told us that never had any mischance occurred in his parish—whether lack of water, or overplus of rain, or any other mischance—but so soon as he had made three processions, on three Saturdays, God and His mother sent them deliverance. It was then a Saturday. We made the first procession round the two masts of the ship. I had myself carried in men's arms, because I was grievously sick. Never again did we see the mountain, and on the third Saturday we came to Cyprus.

• • •

Sojourn in Cyprus— Embassage from the Tartars— Joinville Takes Service with the King

When we came to Cyprus, the king was already there, and we found great quantities of the king's supplies; that is to say, the cellarage of the king, and his treasure, and his granaries. The king's cellarage was set in the middle of the fields, on the shore by the sea. There his people had stacked great barrels of wine, which they had been buying for two years before the king's arrival; and the barrels were stacked one upon the other in such sort that when you looked at them in front, the stacks seemed as if they were barns.

The wheat and the barley they had set up in heaps in the midst of the fields, and when you looked at them, it seemed as if they were mountains, for the rain, which had long been beating on the grain, had caused it to sprout, so that the outside looked like green grass. Now it happened that when they wished to take the grain into Egypt, they took away the upper crust with the green grass, and found the wheat and barley within as fresh as if newly threshed.

The king himself, as I heard tell in Syria, would very willingly have gone on to Egypt, without stopping, had it not been for his barons, who advised him to wait for such of his people as had not yet arrived.

While the king was sojourning in Cyprus, the great king of the Tartars sent envoys to him, with many good and gracious words. Among other things, he signified that he was ready to help the king to conquer the Holy Land, and to deliver Jerusalem from the hands of the Saracens.

The king received the envoys in very friendly fashion, and sent other envoys in return, who remained away two years. And the king, by his envoys, sent to the King of the Tartars a tent made like a chapel, very costly, for it was all of fair, fine scarlet cloth. The king, moreover, to see if he could draw the Tartars to our faith, caused images to be graven in the said chapel, representing the Annunciation of our Lady, and all the other points of the faith. And these things he sent by two brothers of the order of Preachers, who knew the Saracen language, and could show and teach the Tartars what they ought to believe.

The two brothers came back to the king at the time when the king's brothers were returning to France; and they found the king, who had left Acre, where his brothers had parted from him, and had come to Caesarea, which he was fortifying; nor was there at that time any truce or peace with the Saracens. How the king's envoys were received will I tell you, as they themselves told it to the king; and in what they reported you may hear much that is strange and marvellous; but I will not tell you of it now, because, in order to do so, I should have to interrupt matters already begun;—so to proceed.

I, who had not a thousand *livres* yearly in land, had undertaken, when I went oversea, to bear, beside my own charges, the charges of nine knights, and two knights-banneret; and so it happened, when I arrived in Cyprus, that I had no more left, my ship being paid for, than twelve score *livres tournois*; wherefore some of my knights apprised me that if I did not provide myself with moneys, they would leave me. But God, who never failed me yet, provided for me in such fashion that the king, who was at Nicosia, sent for me, and took me into his service, and placed eight hundred livres in my coffers; and thus I had more moneys than I required.

• • •

The Host Leaves Cyprus— 1249

As soon as we entered into the month of March, by the king's command the king, the barons, and the other pilgrims ordered that the ships should be re-laden with wine and provisions, so as to be ready to move when the king directed. And when the king saw that all had been duly ordered, the king and queen embarked on their ships on the Friday before Pentecost (21st May 1249), and the king told his barons to follow in their ships straight to Egypt. On the Saturday the king set sail and all the others besides, which was a fair thing to look upon, for it seemed as if all the sea, so far as the eye could reach, were covered by the canvas of the ships' sails; and the number of the ships, great and small, was reckoned at eighteen hundred.

The king anchored at the head of a hillock which is called the Point of Limassol, and all the other vessels anchored round about him. The king landed on the day of Pentecost. After we had heard mass a fierce and powerful wind, coming from the Egyptian side, arose in such sort that out of two thousand eight hundred knights, whom the king was taking into Egypt, there remained no more than seven hundred whom the wind had not separated from the king's company and carried away to Acre and other strange lands; nor did they afterwards return to the king for a long while.

The day after Pentecost the wind had fallen. The king and such of us as had, according to God's will remained with him, set sail forthwith, and met the Prince of Morea, and the Duke of Burgundy, who had been sojourning in Morea. On the Thursday after Pentecost the king arrived before Damietta, and we found there, arrayed on the seashore, all the power of the soldan—a host fair to look upon, for the soldan's arms are of gold, and when the sun struck upon them they were resplendent. The noises they made with their cymbals and horns was fearful to listen to.

The king summoned his barons to take counsel what they should do. Many advised that he should wait till his people returned, seeing that no more than a third part had remained with him; but to this he would by no means agree. The reason he gave was, that to delay would put the foe in good heart, and, paticularly, he said that there was no port before Damietta in which he could wait for his people, and that, therefore, any strong wind arising might drive the ships to other lands, like as the ships had been driven on the day after Pentecost.

Preparation for Disembarkation in Egypt

It was settled that the king should land on the Friday before Trinity and do battle with the Saracens, unless they refused to stand. The king ordered my Lord John of Beaumont to assign a galley to my Lord Everard of Brienne and to myself, so as that we might land, we and our knights, because the great ships could not get close up to the shore.

As God so willed, when I returned to my ship, I found a little ship that my Lady of Beyrout, who was cousin-german to my Lord of Montbéliard and to myself, had given me, and that carried eight of my horses.

When the Friday came I and my Lord Everard went, fully armed, to the king and asked for the galley; whereupon my Lord John of Beaumont told us that we should not have it. When our people saw that they would get no galley, they let themselves drop from the great ship into the ship's boat, pell-mell, and as best they could, so that the boat began to sink. The sailors saw that the boat was sinking, little by little, and they escaped into the big ship and left my knights in the boat. I asked the master how many more people there

were in the boat than the boat could hold. He told me twenty men-at-arms; and I asked him whether he could take our people to land if I relieved him of so many, and he said, "Yes." So I relieved him in such sort that in three journeys he took them to the ship that had carried my horses.

While I was conducting these people a knight belonging to my Lord Everard of Brienne, and whose name was Plonquet, thought to go down from the great ship into the boat; but the boat moved away, and he fell into the sea and was drowned.

When I came back to my ship I put into my little boat a squire whom I made a knight, and whose name was my Lord Hugh of Vaucouleurs, and two very valiant bachelors—of whom the one had the name my Lord Villain of Versey, and the other my Lord William of Dammartin—who were at bitter enmity the one against the other. Nor could any one make peace between them, because they had seized each other by the hair in Morea. And I made them forgive their grievances and embrace, for I swore to them on holy relics that we should not land in company of their enmity.

Then we set ourselves to get to land, and came alongside of the barge belonging to the king's great ship, there where the king himself was. And his people began to cry to us because we were going more quickly than they, that I should land by the ensign of St. Denis, which was being borne in another vessel before the king. But I heeded them not, and caused my people to land in front of a great body of Turks, at a place where there were full six thousand men on horseback.

So soon as these saw us land, they

came toward us, hotly spurring. We, when we saw them coming, fixed the points of our shields into the sand and the handles of our lances in the sand with the points set towards them. But when they were so near that they saw the lances about to enter their bellies, they turned about and fled.

The Crusaders Disembark in Front of the Saracens

My Lord Baldwin of Rheims, a right good man, who had come to land, requested me, by his squire, to wait for him; and I let him know I should do so willingly, for that a right good man such as he ought surely to be waited for in like case of need,—whereby I had his favour all the time that he lived. With him came to us a thousand knights; and you may be assured that, when I landed, I had neither squire, no knight, no varlet that I had brought with me from my own country, and yet God never left me without such as I needed.

At our left hand landed the Count of Jaffa, who was cousin-german to the Count of Montbéliard, and of the lineage of Joinville. It was he who landed in greatest pride, for his galley came all painted, within and without, with escutcheons of his arms, which arms are *or* with a cross of gules *patée*. He had at least three hundred rowers in his galley, and for each rower there was a targe, with the count's arms thereon, and to each targe was a pennon attached with his arms wrought in gold.

While he was coming it seemed as if his galley flew, so did the rowers urge it forward with their sweeps; and it seemed as if the lightning were falling from the skies at the sound that the pennants made, and the cymbals, and the drums, and the Saracenic horns that were in his galley. So soon as the galley had been driven into the sand as far up as they could drive it, both he and his knights leapt from the galley, well armed and well equipped, and came and arrayed themselves beside us.

I had forgotten to tell you that when the Count of Jaffa landed he immediately caused his tents and pavilions to be pitched; and so soon as the Saracens saw them pitched, they all came and gathered before us, and then came on again, spurring hotly, as if to run in upon us. But when they saw that we should not fly, they shortly turned and went back again.

On the right hand, at about a long-crossbow-shot's distance, landed the galley that bore the ensign of St. Denis. And there was a Saracen who, when they had landed, came and charged in around them, either because he could not hold in his horse, or because he thought the other Saracens would follow him; but he was hacked in pieces.

St. Louis Takes Possession of Damietta

When the king heard tell that the ensign of St. Denis was on shore he went across his ship with large steps; and maugre the legate who was with him would not leave from following the ensign, but leapt into the sea, which was up to his armpits. So he went, with his shield hung to his neck, and his helmet on his head, and his lance in his hand, till he came to his people who were on the shore. When he reached the land, and looked upon the Saracens, he asked what people they were, and they told him they were Saracens;

and he put his lance to his shoulder, and his shield before him, and would have run in upon the Saracens if the right worthy men who were about him would have suffered it.

The Saracens sent thrice to the soldan, by carrier-pigeons, to say that the king had landed, but never received any message in return, because the soldan's sickness was upon him. Wherefore they thought that the soldan was dead, and abandoned Damietta. The king sent a knight forward to know if it was sooth that Damietta was so abandoned. The knight returned to the king and said it was sooth and that he had been in the houses of the soldan. Then the king sent for the legate and all the prelates of the host, and all chanted with a loud voice, *Te Deum laudamus.* Afterwards the king mounted his horse, and we all likewise, and we went and encamped before Damietta.

Very unadvisedly did the Turks leave Damietta, in that they did not cut the bridge of boats, for that would have been a great hindrance to us; but they wrought us very much hurt in setting fire to the bazaar, where all the merchandise is collected, and everything that is sold by weight. The damage that followed from this was as great as if—which God forbid!—some one were, tomorrow, to set fire to the Petit-Pont in Paris.

Now let us declare that God Almighty was very gracious to us when he preserved us from death and peril on our disembarkation, seeing that we landed on foot and affronted our enemies who were mounted. Great grace did our Lord also show us when He delivered Damietta into our hands, for otherwise we could only have taken it by famine, and of this we may be fully assured, for it was by famine that King John had taken it in the days of our fathers (in 1219).

Mistake of St. Louis— Disorder among the Crusaders

Our Lord can say of us, as He said of the children of Israel—*et pro nihilo habuerunt terram desiderabilem.*[1] And what does He say afterwards? He says that they forgot God their Saviour. And so did we forget Him as I will shortly tell you.

But first I will tell you of the king who summoned his barons, the clerks, and the laymen, and asked them to help him decide how the booty taken in the city should be divided. The patriarch was the first to speak, and he spoke thus: "Sire, methinks it were well that you should keep the wheat, and the barley, and the rice, and whatever is needed to sustain life, so as to provision the city; and that you should have it cried throughout the host that all other goods are to be brought to the legate's quarters, under pain of excommunication." To this advice all the other barons assented. Now, as it fell out, all the goods brought to the legate's quarters did not amount in value to more than six thousand livres.

When this had been done, the king and the barons summoned John of Valery, the right worthy man, and spoke to him thus: "Sir of Valery," said the king, "we are agreed that the legate should hand over to you the six thousand livres, so that you may divide them as may

---

[1] "They despised the pleasant land."

seem best to you." "Sire," replied the right worthy man, "you do me much honour, and great thanks be yours! But, please God! that honour can I not accept, nor can I carry out your wish, for by doing so I should make null the good customs of the Holy Land, whereby, when the cities of the enemy are captured, the king takes a third of the goods found therein, and the pilgrims take two thirds. And this custom was well observed by King John when he took Damietta, and as old folks tell us, the same custom was observed by the kings of Jerusalem, who were before King John. If then it pleases you to hand over to me the two parts of the wheat, and the barley, and the rice, and the other provisions, then shall I willingly undertake to make division among the pilgrims."

The king did not decide to do this; so matters remained as they were; and many were ill-pleased that the king should set aside the good old customs.

The king's people, who ought, by liberal dealing, to have retained the merchants, made them pay, so it was said, the highest rents they could exact for the shops in which to sell their goods; and the rumour of this got abroad to foreign lands, so that many merchants forebore to come and bring supplies to the host.

The barons, who ought to have kept what was theirs so as to spend it in fitting time and place, took to giving great feasts, and an outrageous excess of meats. The common people took to consorting with lewd women; whereby it happened, after we returned from captivity, that the king discharged a great many of his people. And when I asked him why he had done this, he told me that those

whom he had discharged held their ill places of assemblage at a short stone's throw from his pavilion, and that at a time when the host was in greatest distress and misery.

The Saracens Attack the Camp—Death of Walter of Autrèche

Now let us go back to the matter in hand, and tell how, shortly after we had taken Damietta, all the horsemen of the soldan came before the camp, and attacked it from the land side. The king and all the horsemen armed themselves. I, being in full armour, went to speak to the king, and found him fully armed, sitting on a settle, and round him were the right worthy knights belonging to his own division, all in full armour. I asked if he desired that I and my people should issue from the camp, so that the Saracens should not fall upon our tents. When my Lord John of Beaumont heard my question, he cried to me in a very loud voice, and commanded me, in the king's name, not to leave my quarters till the king so ordered.

I have told you of the right worthy knights who were of the king's special following, for there were eight of them, all good knights who had won prizes for arms on the further or hither side of the seas, and such knights it was customary to call good knights. These are the names of the knights about the king:—my Lord Geoffry of Sargines, my Lord Matthew of Marly, my Lord Philip of Nanteuil, and my Lord Imbert of Beaujeu, Constable of France; but the last was not then present, he was outside the camp—he and the master of the crossbowmen, with most of the king's sergeants-at-arms—to guard the camp so that the Turks might not do any mischief thereto.

Now it happened that my Lord Walter Autrèche got himself armed at all points of his pavilion; and when he was mounted upon his horse, with a shield at his neck and his helmet on his head, he caused the flaps of his pavilion to be lifted, and struck spurs into his horse to ride against the Turks; and as he left his pavilion, all alone, all his men shouted with a loud voice, "Chatillon." But so it chanced that or ever he came up to the Turks he fell, and his horse flew over his body; and the horse went on, covered with his arms, to our enemies, because the Saracens were, for the most part, mounted on mares, for which reason the horse drew to the side of the Saracens.

And those who looked on told us that four Turks came by Lord Walter, who lay upon the ground, and as they went by, gave him great blows with their maces there where he lay. Then did the Constable of France and several of the king's sergeants deliver him, and they brought him back in their arms to his pavilion. When he came there he was speechless. Several of the surgeons and physicians of the host went to him, and because it did not seem to them that he was in danger of death, they had him blooded in both arms.

That night, very late, my Lord Aubert of Narcy proposed that we should go and see him, for as yet we had not seen him, and he was a man of great name and of great valour. We entered into his pavilion, and the chamberlain came to meet us, and asked us to move quietly, so as not to wake his master. We found him lying on coverlets of miniver, and went to him very softly, and found him dead. When this was told to the king, he replied that he would not willingly have a thousand such men acting contrary to his orders as this man had done.

Renewed Attacks on the Part of the Saracens—the King Decides to Await the Arrival of the Count of Poitiers

The Saracens entered every night into the camp on foot and killed our people there where they found them sleeping, whereby it chanced that they killed the sentinel of the lord of Courtenay, and left him lying on a table, and cut off his head, and took it away with them. And this they did because the soldan gave a besant of gold for every Christian man's head.

And we were at this disadvantage because the battalions guarded the camp, each one its night, on horseback; and when the Saracens wished to enter into the camp, they waited till the noise of the horses and of the battalions had passed, and then crept into the camp behind the horses, making their way out before it was day. So the king ordered that the battalion that had been used to keep guard on horseback should keep guard on foot, whereby all the camp was in safety, because of our men who kept guard, and were spread out in such wise that one man touched the other.

After this was done, the king decided not to leave Damietta until his brother, the Count of Poitiers, had arrived with the remaining forces of France. And so that the Saracens might not charge on their horses into the midst of the camp, the king caused all the camp to be enclosed with great earthworks, and on the earthworks were set crossbowmen to watch every night, and sergeants;

and such were set also at the entrance to the camp.

• • •

When the feast of St. Remigius had passed, and no news came of the Count of Poitiers—whereby the king and all those of the host were greatly troubled, for they feared lest some mischief had befallen him—then I reminded the legate how the Dean of Maurupt had caused us, when at sea, to go three times in procession, on three Saturdays, and how before the third Saturday we had arrived in Cyprus. The legate put faith in what I said, and caused three processions, on three separate Saturdays, to be proclaimed throughout the host.

The first procession started from the legate's quarters, and they went to the church of our Lady in the city, which church had been the mosque of the Saracens, but the legate had dedicated it to the honour of the Mother of God. The legate preached the sermon on two Saturdays. Thither came the king and the honourable men of the host, to whom the legate gave full indulgences.

Before the third Saturday came the Count of Poitiers; nor would it have been well if he had come before, for between the three Saturdays there had been so great a tempest in the sea before Damietta, that at least twelve score ships, great and small, had gone to pieces and been lost, and all the people therein drowned. If therefore the Count of Poitiers had come before, both he and his people would have utterly perished.

When the Count of Poitiers arrived, the king summoned all the barons of the host to decide what course he should hold, whether to Alexandria or to Babylon. Now the good Count Peter of Brittany, and the main part of the barons of the host, were agreed that the king should go and besiege Alexandria, because there was before that city a good harbour to which the ships could bring provisions for the host. But to this the Count of Artois was contrary, and said he would never agree that they should go anywhere except to Babylon, forasmuch as Babylon was the capital of Egypt; and if you wanted to kill the serpent, you must first crush its head. The king set aside the advice of his barons, and accepted the advice of his brother.

St. Catherine of Siena

It is relatively easy to analyze the structure of the medieval Christian church, to describe its long struggle for political supremacy with the secular rulers of western Europe, and even to grasp the main points of its theology. But what of the central fact that lay behind all of these things—the religious beliefs and practices of ordinary Christians during the Middle Ages? What did the religious life really mean to the average person? Obviously, we can never fully answer this question. Nevertheless, we do have numerous accounts written by or about individuals that describe in detail their inner lives of faith and devotion; people such as St. Francis of Assisi, St. Bonaventure, St. Catherine of Siena, and many others. In most of these accounts we can discern a strain of mysticism, a sincere belief in one's having had a direct, personal contact with the divine. Usually this meant a form of mystical communion, in which the person's soul experienced a direct union with God. An even stronger, physical connection was experienced by St. Francis: he had imprinted on his body the stigmata, or the wounds suffered by

Jesus on the cross. In the case of St. Catherine, she believed that in her mystical experiences, she had direct conversations with God. As Raymond of Capua, her religious superior, describes these experiences,

About two years before her death, such a clarity of Truth was revealed to her from Heaven that Catherine was constrained to spread it about by means of writing, asking her secretaries to stand ready to take down whatever came from her mouth as soon as they noticed that she had gone into ecstasy. Thus in a short time was composed a dialogue between a soul who asks the Lord four questions, and the Lord himself who replies to the soul.

The selection that follows contains excerpts from the beginning and end of this mystical dialogue between St. Catherine and God.

St. Catherine was born in Siena, in northern Italy, in 1347, the twenty-fourth of twenty-five children; she died in Rome in 1380 while on a mission for Pope Urban VI to try to heal schisms within the church. Although she was a mystic, she was also a tireless social worker, an able theologian, a political negotiator, and a religious administrator—in other words, a gifted woman of practical affairs. Her greatest mystical experience, her "mystical death," occurred in 1368, when for four hours she experienced mystical union with God while her body lay seemingly lifeless to those around her.

The Dialogue

PROLOGUE

In the Name of Christ Crucified and of Gentle Mary

A soul rises up, restless with tremendous desire for God's honor and the salvation of souls. She has for some time exercised herself in virtue and has become accustomed to dwelling in the cell of self-knowledge in order to know better God's goodness toward her, since upon knowledge follows love. And loving, she seeks to pursue truth and clothe herself in it.

But there is no way she can so savor and be enlightened by this truth as in continual humble prayer, grounded in the knowledge of herself and of God. For by such prayer the soul is united with God, following in the footsteps of Christ crucified, and through desire and affection and the union of love he makes of her another himself. So Christ seems to have meant when he said, "If you will love me and keep my word, I will show myself to you, and you will be one thing with me and I with you."[1] And we find similar words in other places from which we can see it is the truth that by love's affection the soul becomes another himself.

To make this clearer still, I remember having heard from a certain servant of God[2] that, when she was at prayer, lifted high in spirit, God would not hide from her mind's eye his love for his servants. No, he would reveal it, saying among other things, "Open your mind's eye and look within me, and you will see the dignity and beauty of my reasoning creature. But beyond the beauty I have given the soul by creating her in my image and likeness, look at those who are clothed in the wedding garment of charity, adorned with many true virtues: They are united with me through love. So I say, if you should ask me who they are, I would answer," said the gentle loving Word, "that they are another me; for they

---

[1] Cf. Jn. 14:21-23.

[2] Catherine refers to herself in the third person throughout *The Dialogue*. Almost imperceptibly at this point she changes from present to past tense, a perspective she maintains in the narrative passages throughout the rest of the work.

have lost and drowned their own will
and have clothed themselves and
united themselves and conformed
themselves with mine.''

It is true, then, that the soul is
united to God through love's affection.

Now this soul's will was to know
and follow truth more courageously.
So she addressed four petitions to
the most high and eternal Father,
holding up her desire for herself first
of all—for she knew that she could
be of no service to her neighbors in
teaching or example or prayer without first doing herself the service of
attaining and possessing virtue.

Her first petition, therefore, was
for herself. The second was for the
reform of holy Church. The third
was for the whole world in general,
and in particular for the peace of
Christians who are rebelling against
holy Church with great disrespect
and persecution. In her fourth petition she asked divine providence to
supply in general and in particular
for a certain case which had arisen.

This desire of hers was great and
continuous. But it grew even more
when First Truth [God—*Ed.*] showed
her the world's need and how storm-
tossed and offensive to God it is. And
she had on her mind, besides, a letter she had received from her spiritual father, a letter in which he
expressed pain and unbearable sad-
ness over the offense against God,
the damnation of souls, and persecutions against holy Church. All of this
stirred up the flame of her holy desire with grief for the offense but
with gladness in the hope by which
she waited for God to provide against
such great evils.

She found herself eager for the
next day's Mass—it would be Mary's
day[3]—because in communion the
soul seems more sweetly bound to
God and better knows his truth. For
then the soul is in God and God in
the soul just as the fish is in the sea
and the sea in the fish. So when
it was morning and time for Mass
she took her place with eager desire.
From her deep knowledge of herself, a holy justice gave birth to hatred and displeasure against herself,
ashamed as she was of her imperfec-
tion, which seemed to her to be the
cause of all the evils in the world. In
this knowledge and hatred and justice she washed away the stains of
guilt, which it seemed to her were,
and which indeed were, in her own
soul, saying, ''O eternal Father, I accuse myself before you, asking that
you punish my sins in this life. And
since I by my sins am the cause of the
sufferings my neighbors must endure, I beg you in mercy to punish
me for them.''

• • •

CONCLUSION
• • •

Now that soul had seen the truth and
the excellence of obedience with the
eye of her understanding, and had
known it by the light of most holy
faith; she had heard it with feeling
and tasted it with anguished longing
in her will as she gazed into the divine majesty. So she gave him thanks,
saying:

Thanks, thanks be to you, eternal
Father, that you have not despised
me, your handiwork, nor turned
your face from me, nor made light of
these desires of mine. You, Light,

---

[3]Saturday, the day traditionally dedicated to Mary.

have disregarded my darksomeness; you, Life, have not considered that I am death; nor you, Doctor, considered these grave weaknesses of mine. You, eternal Purity, have disregarded my wretched filthiness; you who are infinite have overlooked the fact that I am finite, and you, Wisdom, the fact that I am foolishness.

For all these and so many other endless evils and sins of mine, your wisdom, your kindness, your mercy, your infinite goodness have not despised me. No, in your light you have given me light. In your wisdom I have come to know the truth; in your mercy I have found your charity and affection for my neighbors. What has compelled you? Not my virtues, but only your charity.

Let this same love compel you to enlighten the eye of my understanding with the light of faith, so that I may know your truth, which you have revealed to me. Let my memory be great enough to hold your favors, and set my will ablaze in your charity's fire. Let that fire burst the seed of my body and bring forth blood; then with that blood, given for love of your blood, and with the key of obedience, let me unlock heaven's gate.

I heartily ask the same of you for every reasoning creature, all and each of them, and for the mystic body of holy Church. I acknowledge and do not deny that you loved me before I existed, and that you love me unspeakably much, as one gone mad over your creature.

O eternal Trinity! O Godhead! That Godhead, your divine nature, gave the price of your Son's blood its value. You, eternal Trinity, are a deep sea: The more I enter you, the more I discover, and the more I discover, the more I seek you. You are insatiable, you in whose depth the soul is sated yet remains always hungry for you, thirsty for you, eternal Trinity, longing to see you with the light in your light. Just as the deer longs for the fountain of living water, so does my soul long to escape from the prison of my darksome body and see you in truth. O how long will you hide your face from my eyes?

O eternal Trinity, fire and abyss of charity, dissolve this very day the cloud of my body! I am driven to desire, in the knowledge of yourself that you have given me in your truth, to leave behind the weight of this body of mine, and give my life for the glory and praise of your name. For by the light of understanding within your light I have tasted and seen your depth, eternal Trinity, and the beauty of your creation. Then, when I considered myself in you, I saw that I am your image. You have gifted me with power from yourself, eternal Father, and my understanding with your wisdom—such wisdom as is proper to your only-begotten Son; and the Holy Spirit, who proceeds from you and from your Son, has given me a will, and so I am able to love.

You, eternal Trinity, are the craftsman; and I your handiwork have come to know that you are in love with the beauty of what you have made, since you made of me a new creation in the blood of your Son.

O abyss! O eternal Godhead! O deep sea! What more could you have given me than the gift of your very self?

You are a fire always burning but never consuming; you are a fire consuming in your heat all the soul's selfish love; you are a fire lifting all chill and giving light. In your light you have made me know your truth: You are that light beyond all light who gives the mind's eye supernatural light in such fullness and perfection that you bring clarity even to the light of faith. In that faith I see that my soul has life, and in that light receives you who are Light.

In the light of faith I gain wisdom in the wisdom of the Word your Son, in the light of faith I am strong, constant, persevering; in the light of faith I have hope: It does not let me faint along the way. This light teaches me the way, and without this light I would be walking in the dark. This is why I asked you, eternal Father, to enlighten me with the light of most holy faith.

Truly this light is a sea, for it nourishes the soul in you, peaceful sea, eternal Trinity. Its water is not sluggish, so the soul is not afraid because she knows the truth. It distills, revealing hidden things, so that here, where the most abundant light of your faith abounds, the soul has, as it were, a guarantee of what she believes. This water is a mirror in which you, eternal Trinity, grant me knowledge; for when I look into this mirror, holding it in the hand of love, it shows me myself, as your creation, in you, and you in me through the union you have brought about of the Godhead with our humanity.

This light shows you to me, and in this light I know you, highest and infinite Good: Good above every good, joyous Good, Good beyond measure and understanding! Beauty above all beauty; Wisdom above all wisdom—indeed you are wisdom itself! You who are the angels' food are given to humans with burning love. You, gar-ment who covers all nakedness, pasture the starving within your sweetness, for you are sweet without trace of bitterness.

O eternal Trinity, when I received with the light of most holy faith your light that you gave me, I came to know therein the way of great perfection, made smooth for me by so many wonderful explanations. Thus I may serve you in the light, not in the dark; and I may be a mirror of a good and holy life; and I may rouse myself from my wretched life in which, always through my own fault, I have served you in darkness. I did not know your truth, and so I did not love it. Why did I not know you? Because I did not see you with the glorious light of most holy faith, since the cloud of selfish love darkened the eye of my understanding. Then with your light, eternal Trinity, you dispelled the darkness.

But who could reach to your height to thank you for so immeasurable a gift, for such generous favors, for the teaching of truth that you have given me? A special grace, this, beyond the common grace you give to other creatures. You willed to bend down to my need and that of others who might see themselves mirrored here.

You responded, Lord; you yourself have given and you yourself answered and satisfied me by flooding me with a gracious light, so that with that light I may return thanks to you. Clothe, clothe me with yourself, eternal Truth, so that I may run the course of this mortal life in true obedience and in the light of most holy faith. With that light I sense my soul once again becoming drunk! Thanks be to God! Amen.

D. T. Niane

Mali was, as it is today, a country in western Africa. During the Middle Ages it gained ascendency over a number of neighboring lands, thus creating the Mali Empire, which reached its height in the fourteenth century. This expansion of Mali's territory and power was accomplished in part by the great king and later emperor, Sundiata, who flourished in the early part of the thirteenth century. The epic, *Sundiata*, is an account of his life and exploits. Although for obvious reasons it gives a somewhat romanticized picture of this great leader, it also offers glimpses into life as it was really lived in the Africa of his time. Of special interest are descriptions of royal court life, religious beliefs and practices, agriculture and industry, politics, trade, and warfare.

It is possible in the selection that follows to include only an excerpt from the epic of *Sundiata*. Born the son of the king of Mali, on his father's death Sundiata was forced, with his mother, Sogolon, and his brother and sister, to flee the country at the age of ten through the machinations of another wife of the late king, who put her own son on the throne. For the next seven years Sundiata wandered around west Africa. But he had made a vow to return to Mali. In the meantime Soumaoro, the sorcerer-king of the land of Sosso, had gained great power, conquering Mali and destroying its capital city of Niani. Before he could return to Mali, therefore, Sundiata had to defeat Soumaoro. Befriended by the king of Mema, Sundiata developed into a great warrior. He gathered together an army and, after defeating a Sosso contingent under Soumaoro's son, Sosso Balla, at the stronghold of Tabon, Sundiata and his forces advanced to the plain of Krina, where Soumaoro lay in wait for him with his great army. The selection begins at this point. The following individuals need special mention: Sundiata (also referred to as Djata); his half-brother, Manding Bory; his half-sister, Nana Triban, who had learned the secret of Soumaoro's magical power while held captive in Sosso; Balla Fasséké, Sundiata's griot; and Fakoli, the nephew of Soumaoro, who had turned against his uncle after the latter stole his wife, Keleya, from him.

A special word needs to be added

about griots. These were highly trained specialists who were the historians of Africa; they memorized the past and repeated it orally generation after generation. But a griot was more than simply a narrator of past events. As the current author of *Sundiata*, D. T. Niane, who translated the epic from the words of a griot, puts it: "If today the griot is reduced to turning his musical art to account or even to working with his hands in order to live, it was not always so in ancient Africa. Formerly 'griots' were the counsellors of kings, they conserved the constitutions of kingdoms by memory work alone; each princely family had its griot appointed to preserve tradition. . . ."

Sundiata

THE BATTLE OF KRINA

Sundiata wanted to have done with Soumaoro before the rainy season, so he struck camp and marched on Krina where Soumaoro was encamped. The latter realized that the decisive battle had come. Sundiata deployed his men on the little hill that dominates the plain. The great battle was for the next day.

In the evening, to raise the men's spirits, Djata gave a great feast, for he was anxious that his men should wake up happy in the morning. Several oxen were slaughtered and that evening Balla Fasséké, in front of the whole army, called to mind the history of old Mali. He praised Sundiata, seated amidst his lieutenants, in this manner:

'Now I address myself to you, Maghan Sundiata, I speak to you king of Mali, to whom dethroned monarchs flock. The time foretold to you by the jinn is now coming. Sundiata, kingdoms and empires are in the likeness of man; like him they are born, they grow and disappear. Each sovereign embodies one moment of that life. Formerly, the kings of Ghana extended their kingdom over all the lands inhabited by the black man, but the circle has closed and the Cissés of Wagadou are nothing more than petty princes in a desolate land. Today, another kingdom looms up, powerful, the kingdom of Sosso. Humbled kings have borne their tribute to Sosso, Soumaoro's arrogance knows no more bounds and his cruelty is equal to his ambition. But will Soumaoro dominate the world? Are we, the griots of Mali, condemned to pass on to future generations the humiliations which the king of Sosso cares to inflict on our country? No, you may be glad, children of the "Bright Country," for the kingship of Sosso is but the growth of yesterday, whereas that of Mali dates from the time of Bilali. Each kingdom has its childhood, but Soumaoro wants to force the pace,

Niane, D. T., *Sundiata*, trans. G. D. Pickett (Harlow: Longman, 1965). Courtesy of Presence Africaine.

and so Sosso will collapse under him like a horse worn out beneath its rider.

'You, Maghan, you are Mali. It has had a long and difficult childhood like you. Sixteen kings have preceded you on the throne of Niani, sixteen kings have reigned with varying fortunes, but from being village chiefs the Keitas have become tribal chiefs and then kings. Sixteen generations have consolidated their power. You are the outgrowth of Mali just as the silk-cotton tree is the growth of the earth, born of deep and mighty roots. To face the tempest the tree must have long roots and gnarled branches. Maghan Sundiata, has not the tree grown?

'I would have you know, son of Sogolon, that there is not room for two kings around the same calabash of rice. When a new cock comes to the poultry run the old cock picks a quarrel with him and the docile hens wait to see if the new arrival asserts himself or yields. You have come to Mali. Very well, then, assert yourself. Strength makes a law of its own self and power allows no division.

• • •

'Griots are men of the spoken word, and by the spoken word we give life to the gestures of kings. But words are nothing but words; power lies in deeds. Be a man of action; do not answer me any more with your mouth, but tomorrow, on the plain of Krina, show me what you would have me recount to coming generations. Tomorrow allow me to sing the "Song of the Vultures" over the bodies of the thousands of Sossos whom your sword will have laid low before evening.'

It was on the eve of Krina. In this way Balla Fasséké reminded Sundiata of the history of Mali so that, in the

morning, he would show himself worthy of his ancestors.

At break of day, Fakoli came and woke up Sundiata to tell him that Soumaoro had begun to move his sofas out of Krina. The son of Sogolon appeared dressed like a hunter king. He wore tight-fitting, ochre-coloured trousers. He gave the order to draw up the sofas across the plain, and while his chiefs bustled about, Manding Bory and Nana Triban came into Djata's tent.

'Brother,' said Manding Bory, 'have you got the bow ready?'

'Yes,' replied Sundiata. 'Look.'

He unhooked his bow from the wall, along with the deadly arrow. It was not an iron arrow at all, but was made of wood and pointed with the spur of a white cock. The cock's spur was the Tana of Soumaoro, the secret which Nana Triban had managed to draw out of the king of Sosso.

'Brother,' said Nana Triban, 'Soumaoro now knows that I have fled from Sosso. Try to get near him for he will avoid you the whole battle long.'

These words of Nana Triban left Djata worried, but Balla Fasséké, who had just come into the tent, said to Sundiata that the soothsayer had seen the end of Soumaoro in a dream.

The sun had risen on the other side of the river and already lit the whole plain. Sundiata's troops deployed from the edge of the river across the plain, but Soumaoro's army was so big that other sofas remaining in Krina had ascended the ramparts to see the battle. Soumaoro was already distinguishable in the distance by his tall headdress, and the wings of his enormous army brushed the river on one side and the hills on the other. As at Negué-boria, Sundiata did not deploy all his forces. The bowmen of Wagadou and the Djallonkés stood at the rear ready to spill out on the left towards the hills as the battle spread. Fakoli Koroma and Kamandjan were in the front line with Sundiata and his cavalry.

With his powerful voice Sundiata cried 'An gnewa.' The order was repeated from tribe to tribe and the army started off. Soumaoro stood on the right with his cavalry.

Djata and his cavalry charged with great dash but they were stopped by the horsemen of Diaghan and a struggle to the death began. Tabon Wana and the archers of Wagadou stretched out their lines towards the hills and the battle spread over the entire plain, while an unrelenting sun climbed in the sky. The horses of Mema were extremely agile, and they reared forward with their fore hooves raised and swooped down on the horsemen of Diaghan, who rolled on the ground trampled under the horses' hooves. Presently the men of Diaghan gave ground and fell back towards the rear. The enemy centre was broken.

It was then that Manding Bory galloped up to announce to Sundiata that Soumaoro, having thrown in all his reserve, had swept down on Fakoli and his smiths. Obviously Soumaoro was bent on punishing his nephew. Already overwhelmed by the numbers, Fakoli's men were beginning to give ground. The battle was not yet won.

His eyes red with anger, Sundiata pulled his cavalry over to the left in the direction of the hills where Fakoli was valiantly enduring his uncle's blows. But wherever the son of the buffalo passed, death rejoiced.

Sundiata's presence restored the balance momentarily, but Soumaoro's sofas were too numerous all the same. Sogolon's son looked for Soumaoro and caught sight of him in the middle of the fray. Sundiata struck out right and left and the Sossos scrambled out of his way. The king of Sosso, who did not want Sundiata to get near him, retreated far behind his men, but Sundiata followed him with his eyes. He stopped and bent his bow. The arrow flew and grazed Soumaoro on the shoulder. The cock's spur no more than scratched him, but the effect was immediate and Soumaoro felt his powers leave him. His eyes met Sundiata's. Now trembling like a man in the grip of a fever, the vanquished Soumaoro looked up towards the sun. A great black bird flew over above the fray and he understood. It was a bird of misfortune.

'The bird of Krina,' he muttered.

THE PURSUIT OF SOUMAORO

The king of Sosso let out a great cry and, turning his horse's head, he took to flight. The Sossos saw the king and fled in their turn. It was a rout. Death hovered over the great plain and blood poured out of a thousand wounds. Who can tell how many Sossos perished at Krina? The rout was complete and Sundiata then dashed off in pursuit of Soumaoro. The sun was at the middle of its course. Fakoli had caught up with Sundiata and they both rode in pursuit of the fugitives. Soumaoro had a good start. Leaving the plain, the king of Sosso had dashed across the open bush followed by his son Balla and a few Sosso chiefs. When night fell Sundiata and Fakoli stopped at a hamlet. There they took a little food and rest. None of the inhabitants had seen Soumaoro. Sundiata and Fakoli started off in pursuit again as soon as they were joined by some horsemen of Mema. They galloped all night and at daybreak Djata learnt from some peasants that some horsemen had passed that way when it was still dark. The king of Sosso shunned all centres of population for he knew that the inhabitants, seeing him on the run, would no longer hesitate to lay hands on him in order to get into favour with the new master. Soumaoro was followed by none but his son Balla. After having changed his mount at daybreak, the king of Sosso was still galloping to the north.

With difficulty Sundiata found the trail of the fugitives. Fakoli was as resolute as Djata and he knew this country better. It was difficult to tell which of these two men harboured the greatest hatred towards Soumaoro. The one was avenging his humiliated country while the other was prompted by the love of a wife. At noon the horses of Sundiata and Fakoli were out of breath and the pursuers halted at Bankoumana. They took a little food and Djata learnt that Soumaoro was heading for Koulikoro. He had only given himself enough time to change horses. Sundiata and Fakoli set off again straight away. Fakoli said, 'I know a short cut to Koulikoro, but it is a difficult track and our horses will be tired.'

'Come on,' said Djata.

They tackled a difficult path scooped out by the rain in a gully. Cutting across country they now crossed the bush until, pointing a finger in front of him, Fakoli said, 'Look at the hills over there which herald Koulikoro. We have made up some time.'

'Good,' replied Djata simply.

However, the horses were fatigued, they went more slowly and painfully lifted their hooves from the ground. As there was no village in sight, Djata and Fakoli dismounted to let their mounts get their wind back. Fakoli, who had a small bag of millet in his saddle, fed them. The two men rested under a tree. Fakoli even said that Soumaoro, who had taken an easy but lengthy route, would not arrive at Koulikoro until nightfall. He was speaking like a man who had ridden over the whole country.

They continued on their way and soon climbed the hills. Arrived at the top, they saw two horsemen at the bottom of the valley going towards the mountain.

'There they are,' cried Djata.

Evening was coming on and the sun's rays were already kissing the summit of Koulikoro mountain. When Soumaoro and his son saw the two riders behind them, they broke off and began to climb the mountain. The king of Sosso and his son Balla seemed to have fresher horses. Djata and Fakoli redoubled their efforts.

The fugitives were within spear range when Djata shouted to them, 'Stop, stop.'

Like Djata, Fakoli wanted to take Soumaoro alive. Keleya's husband sheered off and outflanked Soumaoro on the right, making his horse jump. He was going to lay hands on his uncle but the latter escaped him by a sudden turn. Through his impetus Fakoli bumped into Balla and they both rolled on the ground. Fakoli got up and seized his cousin while Sundiata, throwing his spear with all his might, brought Soumaoro's horse tumbling down. The old king got up and the foot race began. Soumaoro was a sturdy old man and he climbed the mountain with great agility. Djata did not want either to wound him or kill him. He wanted to take him alive.

The sun had just disappeared completely. For a second time the king of Sosso escaped from Djata. Having reached the summit of Koulikoro, Soumaoro hurried down the slope followed by Djata. To the right he saw the gaping cave of Koulikoro and without hesitation he entered the black cavern. Sundiata stopped in front of the cave. At this moment arrived Fakoli who had just tied the hands of Sosso Balla, his cousin.

'There,' said Sundiata, 'he has gone into the cave.'

'But it is connected to the river,' said Fakoli.

The noise of horses' hooves was heard and it turned out to be a detachment of Mema horsemen. Straight away the son of Sogolon sent some of them towards the river and had all the mountain guarded. The darkness was complete. Sundiata went into the village of Koulikoro and waited there for the rest of his army.

THE DESTRUCTION OF SOSSO

The victory of Krina was dazzling. The remains of Soumaoro's army went to shut themselves up in Sosso. But the empire of Sosso was done for. From everywhere around kings sent their submission to Sundiata. The king of Guidimakhan sent a richly furnished embassy to Djata and at the same time gave his daughter in marriage to the victor. Embassies flocked to Koulikoro, but when Djata had been joined by all the army he marched on Sosso. Soumaoro's city, Sosso, the impregnable city, the city of smiths skilled in wielding the spear.

In the absence of the king and his son, Noumounkeba, a tribal chief, directed the defence of the city. He had quickly amassed all that he could find in the way of provisions from the surrounding countryside.

Sosso was a magnificent city. In the open plain her triple rampart with awe-inspiring towers reached into the sky. The city comprised a hundred and eighty-eight fortresses and the palace of Soumaoro loomed above the whole city like a gigantic tower. Sosso had but one gate; colossal and made of iron, the work of the sons of fire. Noumounkeba hoped to tie Sundiata down outside of Sosso, for he had enough provisions to hold out for a year.

The sun was beginning to set when Sogolon-Djata appeared before Sosso the Magnificent. From the top of a hill, Djata and his general staff gazed upon the fearsome city of the sorcerer-king. The army encamped in the plain opposite the great gate of the city and fires were lit in the camp. Djata resolved to take Sosso in the course of a morning. He fed his men a double ration and the tamtams beat all night to stir up the victors of Krina.

At daybreak the towers of the ramparts were black with sofas. Others were positioned on the ramparts themselves. They were the archers. The Mandingoes were masters in the art of storming a town. In the front line Sundiata placed the sofas of Mali, while those who held the ladders were in the second line protected by the shields of the spearmen. The main body of the army was to attack the city gate. When all was ready, Djata gave the order to attack. The drums resounded, the horns blared and like a tide the Mandingo front line moved off, giving mighty shouts.

With their shields raised above their heads the Mandingoes advanced up to the foot of the wall, then the Sossos began to rain large stones down on the assailants. From the rear, the bowmen of Wagadou shot arrows at the ramparts. The attack spread and the town was assaulted at all points. Sundiata had a murderous reserve; they were the bowmen whom the king of the Bobos had sent shortly before Krina. The archers of Bobo are the best in the world. On one knee the archers fired flaming arrows over the ramparts. Within the walls the thatched huts took fire and the smoke swirled up. The ladders stood against the curtain wall and the first Mandingo sofas were already at the top. Seized by panic through seeing the town on fire, the Sossos hesitated a moment. The huge tower surmounting the gate surrendered, for Fakoli's smiths had made themselves masters of it. They got into the city where the screams of women and children brought the Sossos' panic to a head. They opened the gates to the main body of the army.

Then began the massacre. Women and children in the midst of fleeing Sossos implored mercy of the victors. Djata and his cavalry were now in front of the awesome tower palace of Soumaoro. Noumounkeba, conscious that he was lost, came out to fight. With his sword held aloft he bore down on Djata, but the latter dodged him and, catching hold of the Sosso's braced arm, forced him to his knees whilst the sword dropped to the ground. He did not kill him but delivered him into the hands of Manding Bory.

Soumaoro's palace was now at Sundiata's mercy. While everywhere the Sossos were begging for quarter, Sundiata, preceded by Balla Fasséké, entered Soumaoro's tower. The griot knew every nook and cranny of the palace from his captivity and he led Sundiata to Soumaoro's magic chamber.

When Balla Fasséké opened the door to the room it was found to have changed its appearance since Soumaoro had been touched by the fatal arrow. The inmates of the chamber had lost their power. The snake in the pitcher was in the throes of death, the owls from the perch were flapping pitifully about on the ground. Everything was dying in the sorcerer's abode. It was all up with the power of Soumaoro. Sundiata had all Soumaoro's fetishes taken down and before the palace were gathered together all Soumaoro's wives, all princesses taken from their families by force. The prisoners, their hands tied behind their backs, were already herded together. Just as he had wished, Sundiata had taken Sosso in the course of a morning. When everything was outside of the town and all that there was to take had been taken out, Sundiata gave the order to complete its destruction. The last houses were set fire to and prisoners were employed in the razing of the walls. Thus, as Djata intended, Sosso was destroyed to its very foundations.

Yes, Sosso was razed to the ground. It has disappeared, the proud city of Soumaoro. A ghastly wilderness extends over the places where kings came and humbled themselves before the sorcerer king. All traces of the houses have vanished and of Soumaoro's seven-storey palace there remains nothing more. A field of desolation, Sosso is now a spot where guinea fowl and young partridges come to take their dust baths.

Many years have rolled by and

many times the moon has traversed the heaven since these places lost their inhabitants. The bourein, the tree of desolation, spreads out its thorny undergrowth and insolently grows in Soumaoro's capital. Sosso the Proud is nothing but a memory in the mouths of griots. The hyenas come to wail there at night, the hare and the hind come and feed on the site of the palace of Soumaoro, the king who wore robes of human skin.

Sosso vanished from the earth and it was Sundiata, the son of the buffalo, who gave these places over to solitude. After the destruction of Soumaoro's capital the world knew no other master but Sundiata.

• • •

THE MALI EMPIRE

Ka-ba was a small town founded by Niagalin M'Bali Faly, a hunter of Sibi, and by Sounoumba Traore, a fisherman. Ka-ba belonged to the king of Sibi and nowadays you can also find Keitas at Ka-ba, but the Keitas did not come there until after Sundiata's time. Ka-ba stands on the left bank of the Niger and it is through Ka-ba that the road to old Mali passes.

To the north of the town stretches a spacious clearing and it is there that the great assembly was to foregather. King Kamandjan had the whole clearing cleaned up and a great dais was got ready. Even before Djata's arrival the delegations from all the conquered peoples had made their way to Ka-ba. Huts were hastily built to house all these people. When all the armies had reunited, camps had to be set up in the big plain lying between the river and the town. On the appointed day the troops were drawn up on the vast square that had been prepared. As at

Sibi, each people was gathered round its king's pennant. Sundiata had put on robes such as are worn by a great Muslim king. Balla Fasséké, the high master of ceremonies, set the allies around Djata's great throne. Everything was in position. The sofas, forming a vast semicircle bristling with spears, stood motionless. The delegations of the various peoples had been planted at the foot of the dais. A complete silence reigned. On Sundiata's right, Balla Fasséké, holding his mighty spear, addressed the throng in this manner:

'Peace reigns today in the whole country; may it always be thus. . . .'

'Amen,' replied the crowd, then the herald continued:

'I speak to you, assembled peoples. To those of Mali I convey Maghan Sundiata's greeting; greetings to those of Do, greetings to those of Ghana, to those from Mema greetings, and to those of Fakoli's tribe. Greetings to the Bobo warriors and, finally, greetings to those of Sibi and Ka-ba. To all the peoples assembled, Djata gives greetings.

'May I be humbly forgiven if I have made any omission. I am nervous before so many people gathered together.

'Peoples, here we are, after years of hard trials, gathered around our saviour, the restorer of peace and order. From the east to the west, from the north to the south, everywhere his victorious arms have established peace. I convey to you the greetings of Soumaoro's vanquisher, Maghan Sundiata, king of Mali.

'But in order to respect tradition, I must first of all address myself to the host of us all, Kamandjan, king of Sibi; Djata greets you and gives you the floor.'

Kamandjan, who was sitting close by Sundiata, stood up and stepped down from the dais. He mounted his horse and brandished his sword, crying 'I salute you all, warriors of Mali, of Do, of Tabon, of Mema, of Wagadou, of Bobo, of Fakoli . . . ; warriors, peace has returned to our homes, may God long preserve it.'

'Amen,' replied the warriors and the crowd. The king of Sibi continued.

'In the world man suffers for a season, but never eternally. Here we are at the end of our trials. We are at peace. May God be praised. But we owe this peace to one man who, by his courage and his valiance, was able to lead our troops to victory.

'Which one of us, alone, would have dared face Soumaoro? Ay, we were all cowards. How many times did we pay him tribute? The insolent rogue thought that everything was permitted him. What family was not dishonoured by Soumaoro? He took our daughters and wives from us and we were more craven than women. He carried his insolence to the point of stealing the wife of his nephew Fakoli! We were prostrated and humiliated in front of our children. But it was in the midst of so many calamities that our destiny suddenly changed. A new sun arose in the east. After the battle of Tabon we felt ourselves to be men, we realized that Soumaoro was a human being and not an incarnation of the devil, for he was no longer invincible. A man came to us. He had heard our groans and came to our aid, like a father when he sees his son in tears. Here is that man. Maghan Sundiata, the man with two names foretold by the soothsayers.

'It is to you that I now address myself, son of Sogolon, you, the nephew of the valorous warriors of Do. Henceforth it is from you that I derive my kingdom for I acknowledge you my sovereign. My tribe and I place ourselves in your hands. I salute you, supreme chief, I salute you, Fama of Famas. I salute you, Mansa!'

The huzza that greeted these words was so loud that you could hear the echo repeat the tremendous clamour twelve times over. With a strong hand Kamandjan stuck his spear in the ground in front of the dais and said, 'Sundiata, here is my spear, it is yours.'

Then he climbed up to sit in his place. Thereafter, one by one, the twelve kings of the bright savanna country got up and proclaimed Sundiata 'Mansa' in their turn. Twelve royal spears were stuck in the ground in front of the dais. Sundiata had become emperor. The old tabala of Niani announced to the world that the lands of the savanna had provided themselves with one single king. When the imperial tabala had stopped reverberating, Balla Fasséké, the grand master of ceremonies, took the floor again following the crowd's ovation.

'Sundiata, Maghan Sundiata, king of Mali, in the name of the twelve kings of the "Bright Country", I salute you as "Mansa".'

The crowd shouted 'Wassa, Wassa. . . . Ayé.'

It was amid such joy that Balla Fasséké composed the great hymn 'Niama' which the griots still sing:

Niama, Niama, Niama,
You, you serve as a shelter for all,
All come to seek refuge under you.
And as for you, Niama,
Nothing serves you for shelter,
God alone protects you.

The festival began. The musicians of all the countries were there. Each people in turn came forward to the dais under Sundiata's impassive gaze. Then the war dances began. The sofas of all the countries had lined themselves up in six ranks amid a great clatter of bows and spears knocking together. The war chiefs were on horseback. The warriors faced the enormous dais and at a signal from Balla Fasséké, the musicians, massed on the right of the dais, struck up. The heavy war drums thundered, the bolons gave off muted notes while the griot's voice gave the throng the pitch for the 'Hymn to the Bow'. The spearmen, advancing like hyenas in the night, held their spears above their heads; the archers of Wagadou and Tabon, walking with a noiseless tread, seemed to be lying in ambush behind bushes. They rose suddenly to their feet and let fly their arrows at imaginary enemies. In front of the great dais the Kéakéa-Tigui, or war chiefs, made their horses perform dance steps under the eyes of the Mansa. The horses whinnied and reared, then, overmastered by the spurs, knelt, got up and cut little capers, or else scraped the ground with their hooves.

The rapturous people shouted the 'Hymn to the Bow' and clapped their hands. The sweating bodies of the warriors glistened in the sun while the exhausting rhythm of the tam-tams wrenched from them shrill cries. But presently they made way for the cavalry, beloved by Djata. The horsemen of Mema threw their swords in the air and caught them in flight, uttering mighty shouts. A smile of contentment took shape on Sundiata's lips, for he was happy to see his cavalry manoeuvre with so much skill.

• • •

THE RETURN TO NIANI

But it was time to return to his native Mali. Sundiata assembled his army in the plain and each people provided a contingent to accompany the Mansa to Niani. At Ka-ba all the peoples separated in friendship and in joy at their new-found peace.

Sundiata and his men had to cross the Niger in order to enter old Mali. One might have thought that all the dug-out canoes in the world had arranged to meet at the port of Ka-ba. It was the dry season and there was not much water in the river. The fishing tribe of Somono, to whom Djata had given the monopoly of the water, were bent on expressing their thanks to the son of Sogolon. They put all their dug-outs side by side across the Niger so that Sundiata's sofas could cross without wetting their feet.

When the whole army was on the other side of the river, Sundiata ordered great sacrifices. A hundred oxen and a hundred rams were sacrificed. It was thus that Sundiata thanked God on returning to Mali.

The villages of Mali gave Maghan Sundiata an unprecedented welcome. At normal times a traveller on foot can cover the distance from Ka-ba to Niani with only two halts, but Sogolon's son with his army took three days. The road to Mali from the river was flanked by a double human hedge. Flocking from every corner of Mali, all the inhabitants were resolved to see their saviour from close up. The women of Mali tried to create a sensation and they did not fail. At the entrance to each village they had carpeted the road with their multi-coloured pagnes so that Sundiata's horse would not so much as dirty its feet on entering their village. At the village exits the children, holding leafy branches in their hands, greeted Djata with cries of 'Wassa, Wassa, Ayé'.

Sundiata was leading the van. He had donned his costume of a hunter king—a plain smock, skin-tight trousers and his bow slung across his back. At his side Balla Fasséké was still wearing his festive garments gleaming with gold. Between Djata's general staff and the army Sosso Balla had been placed, amid his father's fetishes. But his hands were no longer tied. As at Ka-ba, abuse was everywhere heaped upon him and the prisoner did not dare look up at the hostile crowd. Some people, always ready to feel sympathy, were saying among themselves:

'How few things good fortune prizes!'

'Yes, the day you are fortunate is also the day when you are the most unfortunate, for in good fortune you cannot imagine what suffering is.'

The troops were marching along singing the 'Hymn to the Bow', which the crowd took up. New songs flew from mouth to mouth. Young women offered the soldiers cool water and cola nuts. And so the triumphal march across Mali ended outside Niani, Sundiata's city.

It was a ruined town which was beginning to be rebuilt by its inhabitants. A part of the ramparts had been destroyed and the charred walls still bore the marks of the fire. From the top of the hill Djata looked on Niani, which looked like a dead city. He saw the plain of Sounkarani, and he also saw the site of the young baobab tree. The survivors of the catastrophe were standing in rows on the Mali road. The children were waving branches, a few young women were singing, but the adults were mute.

'Rejoice,' said Balla Fasséké to Sundiata, 'for your part you will have the bliss of rebuilding Niani, the city of your fathers, but nevermore will anyone rebuild Sosso out of its ruins. Men will lose recollection of the very site of Soumaoro's city.'

With Sundiata peace and happiness entered Niani. Lovingly Sogolon's son had his native city rebuilt. He restored in the ancient style his father's old enclosure where he had grown up. People came from all the villages of Mali to settle in Niani. The walls had to be destroyed to enlarge the town, and new quarters were built for each kin group in the enormous army.

• • •

Djata's justice spared nobody. He followed the very word of God. He protected the weak against the strong and people would make journeys lasting several days to come and demand justice of him. Under his sun the upright man was rewarded and the wicked one punished.

In their new-found peace the villages knew prosperity again, for with Sundiata happiness had come into everyone's home. Vast fields of millet, rice, cotton, indigo and fonio surrounded the villages. Whoever worked always had something to live on. Each year long caravans carried the taxes in kind to Niani. You could go from village to village without fearing brigands. A thief would have his right hand chopped off and if he stole again he would be put to the sword.

New villages and new towns sprang up in Mali and elsewhere. 'Dyulas', or traders, became numerous and during the reign of Sundiata the world knew happiness.

There are some kings who are powerful through their military strength. Everybody trembles before them, but when they die nothing but ill is spoken of them. Others do neither good nor ill and when they die they are forgotten. Others are feared because they have power, but they know how to use it and they are loved because they love justice. Sundiata belonged to this group. He was feared, but loved as well. He was the father of Mali and gave the world peace. After him the world has not seen a greater conqueror, for he was the seventh and last conqueror. He had made the capital of an empire out of his father's village, and Niani became the navel of the earth.